LANGUAGE
AND ITS
NORMAL
PROCESSING

To my children, Eric and Alexander, for what they have taught me about love, life, and language and literacy acquisition.

LANGUAGE
AND ITS
NORMAL
PROCESSING

Vivien C. Tartter

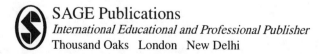 SAGE Publications
International Educational and Professional Publisher
Thousand Oaks London New Delhi

For information:

SAGE Publications, Inc.
2455 Teller Road
Thousand Oaks, California 91320
E-mail: order@sagepub.com

SAGE Publications Ltd.
6 Bonhill Street
London EC2A 4PU
United Kingdom

SAGE Publications India Pvt. Ltd.
M-32 Market
Greater Kailash I
New Delhi 110 048 India

Printed in the United States of America

Library of Congress Cataloging-in-Publication Data

Tartter, Vivien C.
 Language and its normal processing / by Vivien C. Tartter.
 p. cm.
Includes bibliographical references and index.
ISBN 0-8039-5994-X (acid-free paper). — ISBN 0-8039-5995-8 (pbk. :
acid-free paper)
 1. Language and languages. 2. Linguistics. I. Title.
P121.T314   1998
400--ddc21   97-45474

This book is printed on acid-free paper.

98 99 00 01 02 03 04 10 9 8 7 6 5 4 3 2 1

Acquisition Editor:	Alex Schwartz / Catherine Rossbach
Editorial Assistant:	Fiona Lyon
Production Editor:	Michele Lingre
Editorial Assistant:	Karen Wiley
Typesetter/Designer:	Rose Tylak
Cover Designer:	Candice Harman

CONTENTS

Preface

In 1986 I published *Language Processes,* a book designed to be a comprehensive, interdisciplinary account of primary language processing. It focused on interesting readers in the intricacies of language and provoking consideration of whether language as we experience it is uniquely human, either determined by innate specific-to-language constraints or shaped by general innate constraints on human cognition and perception. Because of the biological-foundation theme, I examined communication data from populations often neglected in a basic psycholinguistics course: native sign language users, deprived and abandoned children, schizophrenics, animals, and people suffering from brain damage. I also restricted discussion to primary language, neglecting reading and writing and second language acquisition, and minimally discussing social and societal pressures on language and its processing.

This book is the first of two volumes that together are intended to update *Language Processes* and present a more comprehensive picture of language, including secondary language and its processing. *Language and Its Normal Processing* is a thorough overview of what we know about human language and its processing and acquisition by normal individuals in the normal environment. As in *Language Processes,* I present data and theory from the variety of fields that study language—principally linguistics and cognitive psychology but also communication sciences, philosophy, computer science, education, neurology, and comparative, behavioristic, clinical, and social psychology. While integrating the contributions of these disciplines, I have tried to maintain their identities to make clear their approaches.

As in my previous book, I have tried to do justice to the complexities and controversies inherent in the study of any complex phenomenon: I present different sides of the issues, data supporting each side, and techniques for reaching logical and consistent conclusions. Too often, I believe, texts present things as black and white and deny the reader the challenge of thinking an issue through as well as the fun of analysis, indecision, and controversy. I do share my biases, but I sincerely invite readers into the discussion and to take the other position.

Language and Its Normal Processing is thoroughly updated and, unlike its predecessor, contains chapters on secondary language, reading and writing, and second language acquisition. It also discusses bilingualism as a primary, normal language process, and focuses more on pragmatics, social factors in language change, language use, and language processing than did the earlier volume. Chapters 2 through 7 present normal, primary language—semantics, syntax, and speech—with two chapters for each, the first presenting the level from within the language and the second presenting methods for studying and data from language processing. Chapter 8 discusses sociolinguistics, language change, and social variables; Chapter 9, normal language acquisition; Chapter 10, bilingualism; and Chapter 11, literacy. The goal is to understand how fluent humans acquire, use, produce, and understand language functionally to regulate meaningful interactions in the community.

Armed with such data, I speculate on how we have come to establish this skill and which aspects of it are critical to its power. Throughout, factors from our biology and environment that may enable language are considered and ultimately used to make conclusions and frame questions about what language is and how it has come to be so. Readers are urged to continue language study with research in non-"normal" populations—animals, the deaf, learning-language-disabled or deprived children, aphasics, and schizophrenics—in the companion volume, *Language in Atypical Populations*. These data serve as pointed comparisons to normal language and its processing to reach conclusions as to the necessary perceptual, cognitive, social, and developmental constraints on language form and processing.

This book (with its companion) is aimed at anyone interested in language and psycholinguistics, regardless of how limited their background is in the relevant disciplines. Thus basic material is presented before sophisticated issues, methods, and the latest research findings. Someone new to an area may need to study the basic material, while nonnovices may skim to more advanced sections. The target audience is advanced undergraduates, beginning graduate students, and professionals schooled in some area(s) of psycholinguistics and interested in a broader perspective.

The data and philosophical frameworks of 1986, when the first edition came out, seemed to strongly support the notion of a specially evolved language-specific mechanism guiding language acquisition at least until puberty, with very deviant language and biological underpinnings supporting language after puberty. The most profound difference between this volume and the first is a shift toward more general cognitive and social-learning mechanisms responsible for attaining language. In the roughly 10 intervening years, computer models based on learning and feedback with minimal specific language programming have become increasingly successful. In these years too, new data on adult language acquisition have in part supplanted early data supporting a strong critical period hypothesis. And, finally, increasing emphasis on individual differences in language learning as well as infants' abilities to generalize from frequent, but not constant, input suggest flexibility in language processing rather than a single dictated approach from an innate language guide. Nevertheless, there are still indications of some biological guidance, and both sides are presented, for in the next decade the pendulum may swing yet again.

My principal interest in writing this book was to communicate the fun and excitement I find in psycholinguistic research. Chapters on language structure contain many examples and language "games" to encourage readers to play with the language. Chapters on language processing develop the methods and reasoning of psychological research to encourage readers to consider their own experiments and to critique the existing research. As I have said, controversies are presented as such, with readers urged to resolve the issues rationally for themselves. I have also presented issues from a historical perspective, as in behavioristic approaches to language or the early stages of transformational theory, along with new data. These have been resurrected partly because I think they still provide valuable insights, partly because history can repeat itself in science too and they may someday again be actively considered, and partly because I think the importance and excitement of new truths and methods can be appreciated only in light of the old ways.

It is my profound hope that through open discussion of controversy, emphasis on methods of analysis and criticism, presentation of psycholinguistics from the diverse perspectives of its various researchers, and encouragement of active involvement, readers will be stimulated to continue thinking about language and its processing well after they have completed this book (and, I hope, its companion). The first course I had in psycholinguistics added a major dimension to my life and I would like to pass that gift on.

Acknowledgments

I am grateful to my family for the patience and support they offered during my labors on this book.

This book owes much to both my teachers and my students. Professor Sheila Blumstein, to whom the first edition was dedicated, shaped my love for and thought on psychology of language more than 20 years ago; her approach constitutes the framework of this and the companion book. Professor Richard Millward encouraged my study of computer science, linguistics, and biology along with cognitive psychology, before such a thing was done; the interdisciplinary focus of this book owes much to his open vision. Professor Peter Eimas honed my knowledge and appreciation of experimental methods. Former graduate students Alexandra Economou, Hilary Gomes, and Malca Resnick broadened my thinking in brain-and-language, child language acquisition, and metaphor. Whole classes at City College used and critiqued the text in manuscript form, and their comments improved its accessibility. The work and observations of student participants in the "Three Rs" project taught me much about literacy acquisition in disadvantaged schoolchildren.

I am grateful to Dane Harwood and Arty Samuel, who read and critiqued the first edition in its entirety, significantly affecting this edition as well, and to student Michael Horowitz, who provided comments on the first half of this book. Richard Gerrig's review and discussion of revised Chapters 1, 2, and 3 and new Chapter 11 were invaluable. Chapters 4 and 5 benefitted from the insights and corrections of Lindsay Whaley; Chapter 8, from the critique of Crawford Feagin; Chapter 15, from comments by Mary Engel.

I thank also colleagues with whom I have collaborated and whose ideas have significantly affected my outlook on our field: Arty Samuel and Donna Kat, Ursula

Bellugi and Richard Meier, Oliver Patterson and Pamela Laskin. I am grateful to my brother, Andrew Rothman, for his cartoons (Chapters 7 and 9); to my friend, James Kempster, for his artistic renderings (Chapters 1, 2, and 11); and to my colleague and friend, Pamela Laskin, for the use of her poem (Chapter 9). Thanks too to my son, Eric Tartter, for the computer graphics (Chapters 3, 8, and 11), and to both Eric and Alexander for their willing participation in "verifications" of claims about child language skills.

PERSPECTIVES ON LANGUAGE

For my eighth birthday, I received a book on word origins, which seems to me now an odd gift for an 8-year-old. But I was hooked on language, trying to intercept the voice inside my head to see if it was talking word by word, avoiding boredom by making as many words as I could from the letters of the word *delicatessen,* building word pyramids by adding a letter,

a

an

can

scan

canes

canters

scantier . . .,

and puzzling over how words came to be. In college, chance took me to Sheila Blumstein's course in psycholinguistics. There I discovered that my interests and amusements were an academic discipline and that Roger Brown (1973) had speculated (humorously) that people like me, with a natural, profound interest in language, who do not take this most useful tool for granted, have a "kinky gene." Your "kinky gene" may also be fully expressed, directing you to read this book. But all people, I would maintain, have the gene at least partially expressed, causing them to enjoy good puns (plays on words), metaphors (descriptions of one concept in terms of another), and rap music (plays on the rhythm of language).

Those of you who have always been charmed by the mystery of language, who share the fully expressed kinky gene, need no further introduction to what this book may be about. For the rest, the first part of this chapter is devoted to (a) why some of us are so fascinated by language and (b) why it is important to study and understand language regardless of the degree of our personal fascination. This chapter then outlines historical and contemporary approaches to language study to round out the ways of thinking about language that we will encounter throughout the book. Finally, this chapter presents the multidisciplinary and unifying perspectives of this book.

WHY STUDY LANGUAGE?

One reason to study language is that language is seen as one reason humans are special, apart from, and, at least from our perspective as humans, superior to animals. Because of language, we can consider the abstract, the nonimmediate, the unreal. Through language—oral traditions and writing systems—we can communicate across generations and over long distances. Thus we have built on the knowledge of others, constructing civilizations that seem vastly different from (and superior to) those of any other animal group. In fact, most features that have ever been considered profoundly human—religion, culture, tool use, the ability to imagine death—depend in some way on language. In his writings on consciousness, Daniel Dennett (1995) expounds,

> People ache to believe that human beings are vastly different from all other species—and they are right. We are different. We are the only species that has access to an extra mode for preserving and communicating design: culture. . . . People have language, the primary medium of culture, and language has opened up new regions of design space that only we are privy to. (p. 39)

Is language uniquely human? During the last several decades, research in learning principles, artificial intelligence, and animal communication systems has attempted to place human language in broad evolutionary and cognitive contexts. Could this paragraph, expressing new ideas in a never-before-used structured sequence, be simply a result of reflex associations? Is production or comprehension of such a paragraph within the capability of a computer? Consider the complex communities in beehives or anthills, the sophisticated intelligences of monkeys, apes, whales, and dolphins. Could we be the only social animals to share abstract ideas through natural signal systems?

You may have heard about the projects that have attempted to teach parrots, chimpanzees, gorillas, and dolphins to use human languages. Do such experiments reveal that animals have the capacity for language, or are they only a crude simulation of a small subset of our language skills? To answer that question objectively, we must understand what language is and how *we* do it. Only then can we compare the nonhuman language projects to well-defined human capabilities.

F: I think you could say it's a hoarse voice,

L: [In a low voice] You could say it's more of a horse.

F: Now, does that mean it's a horse talking?

L: No! [Amused] It's me talking. [Chuckles] You know what your voice sound like when you('re) um, when you're sort of sick? Your voice can go hoarse. [Makes voice sound hoarse]

Figure 1.1. Severe Retardation in a 14-Year-Old (L) With Language Preserved Relative to Drawing Ability

SOURCE: J. E. Yamada (1990), *Laura: A Case for the Modularity of Language,*, pp. 85, 139. MIT Press. © Massachusetts Institute of Technology. Used by permission.

In the last several decades, research in humans' use of human language has addressed the foundations of this human skill. On the one hand, human intelligence, at least as defined by intelligence tests, includes "verbal aptitude" measures with a broad range considered "normal." This suggests that language skills vary across human beings and correlate with some, but not all, other cognitive functions. On the other hand, young children seem simply to soak up language in what seem to be similar ways—unconsciously, quickly, and effortlessly mastering a grammar so complex that they (we) have difficulty *explicitly* learning it in "grammar school."

And there are idiots savants in language—people with severe retardation who, nevertheless, use language creatively and correctly. Contrast the ability of 16-year-old Laura (Yamada, 1990) to draw people with her ability to create and sustain a conversation, displayed in Figure 1.1. Her drawing illustrates her nonverbal IQ of 40. What intelligence gives her surprisingly sophisticated language?

To what extent is language the unfolding of a genetic program? To what extent are language skills simply part of our general cognitive functions, such as reasoning, remembering, or problem solving? To what extent do language knowledge and abilities affect our general abilities to understand the world? Study of the discoveries of the past few decades in linguistics, the study of language structures and systems, and in psycholinguistics, the study of human language processing, has suggested answers to these questions and has provoked furious debate.

This book, together with the companion volume *Language in Atypical Populations,* explores these data, attempting to address the issue of whether (and how) language is special. Together the volumes focus on defining human language and how it is shaped by normal human social, perceptual, and cognitive constraints. This book explores normal human language in (primarily American) adults and children. The companion volume looks at biological and evolutionary foundations of language, exploring language and communication in animals and in atypical human populations.

THE FASCINATION OF LANGUAGE

Language is a complex behavior, one that we take for granted but that we feel has the power to influence thought, change the social order, move spirits, and entertain. Each of these putative powers of language makes it fascinating to study.

Once we know a language, we feel an inner voice, one that, of course, speaks in our language. (Listen to the voice in your head. Is it your voice? A male voice? A female voice?) Consider whether you think in words. As you are so considering, try to tell if you are doing the thinking in words. Force yourself to think word by word and see if that seems like normal thought. It is possible—but while you are doing it, you are monitoring yourself, and racing ahead with the idea while plodding along and filling in words. Is the monitor or the part that is racing ahead also thinking in words?

How do you communicate with people with whom you do not share a language, people who do not speak English? Do you move in "Charades," an exaggerated pantomime in what might be a common body language representation of thought, or, as Dickens satirizes in *Little Dorritt* (1857/1975), do you address them more loudly and slowly, "with an unshaken confidence that the English tongue [is] somehow the mother tongue of the whole world, only the people [are] too stupid to know it" (p. 875).

Can you think without language, say, by using visual imagery? Try it. Do words intrude somehow? The difficulty of following verbal instruction to eliminate verbal thought reveals that we will not get far in understanding human language processing through *introspection,* or looking within. In turn, this motivates the need to apply more subtle (nonintuitive) techniques to its understanding—techniques and their outcomes that we will be seeing throughout this book.

In this century, behavioral scientists have proposed and examined a variety of strong positions on the relation of language and thought, such as the following: (a) Thinking is impossible without language (Rieber & Vetter, 1980); (b) in the absence of language, there are no memories (e.g., there are no preverbal memories, of our earliest childhood; Watson, 1930/1970); (c) our language shapes thought, so much so that people who speak different languages think differently (Whorf, 1956). We will explore evidence for and against these strong assumptions. Regardless of their absolute truth, language processes are an important aspect of thought processes, and our understanding of them is central to understanding human understanding.

Perhaps because of its link to thought, language has tremendous social force. Through its content, it may change ideas. Through its form—the use of the latest hip slang, for instance—it may forge a feeling of group identity or power. Through-out history, those in power have used language to destroy the group identity of the minorities under their dominance. Languages or dialects have been declared substandard or inferior to the language of the majority. Bans on the use of indigenous languages in Indian schools in the United States in the last century, or of signed languages in schools for the deaf, presented as benign attempts to increase the opportunity and motivation to learn the language of the dominant culture, instead dissolved and disempowered the community of the users of the banned language. Currently, the Anglo majority, feeling besieged, is counterattacking with a law making English the official language of the United States to suppress the use of other languages in official public arenas. Righteous conviction of this position has led to absurd public declarations such as that of a Texas governor (cited by Safire, 1982): " 'If English was good enough for Jesus Christ [He spoke English?], it is good enough for Texas children.' "

Linguistic discrimination can be horrifying—as when slaves speaking different languages were deliberately commingled on plantations in the United States or in Nazi concentration camps—depriving the disempowered of the *community* of *communication.* Linguistic discrimination can be ennobling, as when a language is reserved for elite purposes—prayers or diplomas in Latin, a language with no *vernacular,* no common use.

Are some languages truly better than others, or are some people just aware of the social power of language and adept at exploiting it? The study of language processes provides objective answers to this question.

Perhaps because of language's relationship to thought and social change, mystical power is attributed to language cross-culturally, distinguishing it from much other human behavior. In our culture, there are 10 commandments legislating moral behavior, one of which forbids *the use of a word:* "Thou shalt not take the name of the Lord thy God in vain" (Exodus 20:7). To this day, the name of God is unmentionable in the Jewish religion, and in every culture there are "curses," words that may not be used, although their meanings may be expressed in euphemism.

Figure 1.2. Word Play in Children, Across Cultures, and in "High" Art (Artwork rendered by James J. Kempster; used by permission.)

Box 1.1. Why Study Language Processes?

— Language is intimately related to thought.
  — Study the philosophical relationship of language and thought.
  — Through study of language, study how we think.
— Language may be uniquely human.
  — Study how people are special.
  — Study evolutionary underpinnings in animal and human com-
    munication.
— Language has great social power.
  — Learn how language is used to change attitudes.
  — Learn how language forges group identities.
  — Learn why mystical power is attributed to language.
— Language is fun.
  — Play language games to understand language processes.
  — Study language games to discover why they are fun and challenging.

All prayers and incantations are the recital of words, the very act of which is supposed to bless or curse. Folklore likewise has many examples of magic words that must be spoken to cast, break, or enact a spell, such as *open sesame* in Ali Baba or *Rumpelstiltskin* in the story of the same name. Finally, superstitions exemplify the seemingly mystical power of language: "God bless you" after a sneeze exorcizes the inhaled devil; "knock on wood" prevents a jinx. Our attitudes toward language border on the spiritual, and study of language processes can indicate why.

One last reason to study language, as I felt as a child, is that it is fun. Language games, such as Pig Latin, invented for and sometimes by children (see Figure 1.2, for games I, and maybe you, play[ed]), exist in all investigated cultures, as do language games for adults (Sherzer, 1982). In our culture, there are crosswords, acrostics, cryptograms, language jokes (puns), snaps or playin' the dozens, and intellectual exercises including poetic devices of metaphor, alliteration, rhyme, and so on. These please because they tease and stimulate our *metalinguistic* knowledge, our awareness of our language's structure, and our own strategies for producing and understanding it. Study of language processes can lead to a better understanding of why and how the games and devices are appreciated.

For me, a career as a psycholinguist means that I earn my bread and butter by playing language games for "professional reasons." For one psycholinguistic experiment, I needed a short list of words (50 items or less) that are picturable (so they could be drawn for preliterate children to name) and that across the list comprise every vowel, and at both beginnings and ends of words, every consonant, of English. Another experiment required matching verbs and nouns on a list so that they differed in only one sound (e.g., *bed-beg*). The difficulty with this task proved to be that most words could be both verbs and nouns (e.g., *pet, pat,* or *bed* in a sexy archaic usage). Try creating such lists—experimental stimuli—yourself. It *is* satisfying to play such games, especially when one can call it work.

A BRIEF HISTORY OF PSYCHOLINGUISTICS

Modern psychology of language has its roots in three basic lines of inquiry: (a) whether and which language abilities are innate (*innate* means not known through learning, that is, inborn), (b) how words are associated with meanings and with one another, and (c) why there are language disorders and how they might be treated. We turn next to examine briefly how scholars of ages past considered these issues because their ideas emerge in modern guise, as we shall see.

The very first recorded psycholinguistic experiment explored the innateness question from a stance of language superiority—what the mother tongue of the whole world is. Herodotus (1954/1986) wrote that before 600 B.C., an Egyptian king, Psammetichus, wishing to prove that Egyptians were the most ancient of human races, ordered a shepherd to rear two newborn infants without any exposure to language. He reasoned that the language they would speak innately would be the human ancestral language, which, of course, would be Egyptian. Two years later, the children greeted the shepherd with the sounds "becos," which investigation established constituted the Phrygian word for bread. "In consideration of this the Egyptians yielded their claims and admitted the superior antiquity of the Phrygians" (p. 130). (Gerrig [personal communication] comments that this was not only the first psycholinguistic experiment on record but probably the first recorded *failed* experiment as well.)

The next recorded developments in psycholinguistics, as in much of what we in Western civilization study, were in ancient Greece, where philosophers considered the structure of language, how we come to know language, and the origin of language disorders. The ancient Greeks considered adult human language to be distinct from both animal and child communications. They reached this conclusion from contemplation of the human vocal tract and its apparent special adaptation for language—today expressed in the form, "Language is special *because of* speech." They also were struck by the peculiar relation of word and meaning, and by adult speakers' extensive experience with language. The Greeks concluded that language and the vocal apparatus itself were "natural," that is, part of our innate endowment, but that their precision control was possible only through experience. Like the Egyptian king (or Texas governor), some Greek philosophers argued that specific linguistic conventions, including the words, were "natural," reflecting a perfect correspondence between sound and meaning. Others argued that this relationship was man-made and arbitrary, established only through experience. The ancient Greeks also contributed the first systematic language analyses—classification of syntactic categories and words into parts of speech. Finally, the Greeks provided an early analysis of deafness, which was viewed, unfortunately, as a language-thought disorder that *caused* a hearing problem because of the inextricable relation of thought to language and language to hearing.

The Greek views were maintained for the most part through the Middle Ages, with the minor exception that Christian leaders called "God-given" what the Greeks called "natural."

Beginning with the Renaissance, six new views of language emerged, all still with us today. The first, that of Francis Bacon, held that language is a multilevel process, of which speech is only one level. Although Bacon, in common with earlier views, considered words to embody natural thought, he thought artificial languages could be created. Bacon's views can be found in modern artificial intelligence and cognitive psychology approaches to language as well as in some language therapies.

The second important Renaissance perspective on language was that of Descartes, who attributed more, rather than fewer, aspects of language to instinct. In particular, he considered not only the urge to communicate and general language capacity instinctive but also some ideas themselves—such as religion and time. These *innate ideas,* in his view, give all people common frames of reference. Modern linguistics, shaped by Chomsky, claims inspiration from Descartes, citing his views of linguistic innateness, his emphasis that language alone proves the existence of thought, and his recognition that language's most important characteristic is that it is "innovative and . . . free from control of detectable stimuli, either external or internal" (Chomsky, 1972, p. 12).

This perspective on language contrasts sharply with Locke's, whose philosophy spawned the modern behaviorist, verbal-associationist, and connectionist views of language. Locke rejected the notion of innateness of anything other than the basic language capacity, and even this was later rejected by his followers. For Locke, language and thoughts were acquired by experience, and the interesting question was how concepts were formed and linked. The answer was "association"—of events that occurred together in time, or that appeared similar to one another. Locke distinguished between primary and secondary perceptual experiences, and analogously between simple and complex ideas. Primary perceptions arise directly from the stimulus, while secondary qualities arise from an interaction between the primary qualities and the senses. "Primary" included form and texture, and "secondary," color and taste—but the distinction is what modern-day psychologists try to capture between sensation (primary) and perception (secondary). Simple ideas, likewise, arise directly from the stimulus ("shiny," "hard," "two"), but complex ideas ("infinity," "power") are a compounding of simple ideas. All arise from experience: Some are associated in nature (they co-occur); others are associated by "similarity." Similarity can be sensed but has never been successfully and objectively defined by philosophers.

A fourth historical influence on psychology of language is the changing view of people's place in the animal kingdom. In *The Descent of Man* (1871/n.d.), Darwin acknowledged that the language faculty "has justly been considered as one of the chief distinguishors between man and lower animals" (p. 461) and is necessary for complex thoughts. However, he attempted to show that human beings share with other animals vocal and nonvocal emotional gestures, the capacity and urge to imitate, and the abilities to think and reason. Thus the rudiments of language skills are present elsewhere in the animal kingdom, and our abilities may be accounted for by evolution. This view leads to the modern comparative approach to language and communication.

Box 1.2. The Historical Roots of Language Study

— *The innateness question:* What is natural about language and what is learned?
— *Associationism:* How are concepts (word meanings) acquired through experience?
— *Darwinism:* Are there roots of linguistic behaviors in other cognitions or elsewhere in the animal kingdom?
— *Structuralism/mechanism:* How can language be analyzed into componential units for study?
— *Physiological mechanism:* How is language organized in the brain (and in the speech-hearing, gesture-vision systems)?

Evolution has had a pervasive influence in science, apart from its influence in cognitive psychology and psycholinguistics. Similarly, Newtonian *mechanism* and its offspring, *structuralism,* shaped many fields of scientific inquiry, including linguistics and cognitive psychology. The structuralist seeks to discover indivisible elements and rules for their combinations into complex structures. Locke's simple ideas merging into complex ideas is an example. In language (as a first pass), we might consider words to embody the elements of linguistic meaning, and grammar, the rules for combining them to convey new, more complex meanings. Structuralists presuppose that such elements and rules exist, and a failure to find them reflects only a poor search procedure (but, of course, the failure could be because they do not exist). We see the structuralist influence throughout linguistics and cognitive psychology, in the search for building blocks (and buildings), beginning with small, decontextualized, presumably basic units that are easy to deal with, and moving through to the elaborate discourses that constitute natural language. We will also see alternatives to structural views.

The final important historical development is *physiological mechanism,* the belief in the physiological underpinnings of language and cognition, of the brain as the organ of mind. Before the nineteenth century, following Aristotle, it was generally thought that speech was essential to language and that deafness represented a cognitive disorder resulting from language deficiencies. In the nineteenth century, deafness became recognized as a sensory disorder and teaching methods for the deaf developed. In addition, damage to specific locations of the brain was discovered to affect some language skills apart from others and apart from general cognitive skills. This led to a hypothesis of a language "faculty" separate from other cognitive faculties, and from speech specifically. Currently, these notions prevail in modularity theory (Fodor, 1983), in neurolinguistics, and in some aspects of applied psycholinguistics.

MODERN PERSPECTIVES ON LANGUAGE

Because of the variety of interests language stimulates, its study has been undertaken in a variety of present-day disciplines—notably, for our purposes, philosophy, computer science, linguistics, psychology, and the applied fields of education and communication sciences. Most readers will have a background in no more than one or two of these fields, so I will briefly introduce the interests and methods of study of each of the disciplines, which will be represented more fully in later chapters.

Philosophy

The primary interest of philosophers of language has been to understand how language reflects conceptual structures and reality. In the twentieth century, there have been three general views about how such study should be undertaken. The first is that of the *logical positivists* or *empiricists*. They attempted to derive a system of rules that would account for every reasonable statement and rule out every unreasonable statement. In their view, "proper" language is inherently logical in a mathematical, set-theoretic sense, but grounded in reality and sensory experience. Their semantic and grammar systems were designed to account for experiential truths and logical relations among ideas, such as the following: "Flowers are beautiful; a rose is a flower; → a rose is beautiful." They also wanted to be able to derive the absurdity of a statement such as "George Washington is a prime number." This attempt led to a search for sharp definitions of word meanings, which, as we shall see, have proved elusive.

As a reaction against this approach, the school of *ordinary language* philosophy arose (see Ryle, 1970, for example). This school sought to show that the relation between word and meaning was fuzzy at best and revealed only through general usage in the language. That is, word meaning grew out of language *habits*. Ordinary language philosophy was practiced by discovering instances in the language of fuzzy word meaning. Consider, for example, what defines *soft*. We have "soft pillow," in which the definitive meaning seems embodied, but also "soft science," "a soft wood," "a soft job." None of these is absurd, as is "George Washington is a prime number." The meaning of *soft* cannot be defined sharply in terms of texture but is fuzzy, comprehensible only relative to other contexts. Consistent with their outlook, ordinary language philosophers developed no sharp, rigid theoretical structure.

The third view of philosophy of language, described by Katz (1966), grew out of current linguistic theory (see the following). In this view, linguistic descriptions of natural language are compared for common features, or *universals*. It is assumed that a systematization of language universals and linguistic descriptions will reveal the answer to the "basic question that can be asked about natural languages—what are the principles for relating acoustic objects to meaningful messages that make a natural language so important and flexible a form of communication" (Katz, 1966, p. 98).

Artificial Intelligence

The artificial intelligence (AI) approach to language is aimed at the practical problem of making computers respond appropriately to language input, that is, to produce output easily understood by human users and, in turn, to "understand" language produced and understood by humans. In the programming of language comprehension and production, AI researchers have provided insight into how people perform these tasks.

Computer involvement with language began with what was thought to be the trivial task of machine translation from one language to another. The reasons this task was in fact nontrivial illuminated a truth about human language processing: the great degree to which we use contextual and cultural knowledge to construct even the simplest meaning. A perhaps apocryphal example is the computer translation into Russian of "the spirit is strong but the flesh is weak." Translating the Russian back yielded "the vodka is good but the meat is rotten," an unanticipated error but one within our potential to understand (and be amused by). Note that we know, but the computer does not, to construct a metaphor and/or to recognize the whole quotation.

That computers can apply no more to a problem than is specifically programmed (as they could not apply the world knowledge we do to understand "the spirit is strong . . .") led to a new interaction between computers and language: model testing. A computer program representing a theory of human language processing can test the theory using *only* the programmed knowledge. In contrast, human testers cannot separate knowledge or skills they have but that are not called for by the theory. Computer tests of language models are therefore a second and increasingly important connection between computers and language.

A third connection between computers and language arises in making machines "user-friendly." In part, this entails users communicating with computers using natural language. (It is hard to believe that not many years ago, to "communicate" with a computer the programmer learned important sequences of 1s and 0s [machine language], or simple mnemonics for them [assembly language] like "jmp" [jump . . . to another point in the program].) Now, rather than training the user, we try to program the computer to use natural language. To program actual natural language, we must understand the logistics of normal discourse.

Linguistics

Modern linguistics makes many contributions to the study of language. Glorying in the structuralist tradition, it attempts to determine the structures inherent in any language system through logical consideration of a collected sample or *corpus* of the system. For instance, we might consider the way the plural is formed most often in English—the simple and incorrect answer is to add "s." But the sound at the end of *dogs,* albeit *spelled* with an "s," is "z"; the sound at the end of *messes* is "ez," and the addition, "es;" only the sound at the end of *cats* is "s." The small corpus of singular and plural words here reveals a regular structure—a plural meaning unit (or *morpheme*) with different variants depending on the final sound of the word. Without knowing much about language sounds, you can guess that the "es" is added when the final sound of the singular word is "s" or "z." (Perhaps you have some intuition also for the choice between "s" and "z," a regularity I will explain in Chapter 6.) Knowledge of this regularity allows generalization to new forms—the nonword *niss* we can guess is pluralized as *nisses.*

The point here is to illustrate that language is structured, and that structure is recoverable by logical study of the patterns of co-occurrence of linguistic units. Such patterns can be *verified* by checking with a native speaker or *informant* but may be inferred by someone who does not speak the language, provided an adequate body of data is provided.

Structuralist descriptions of the world's languages have revealed common elements and rules. Modern linguistics considers this no accident; language *universals* (the elements common to unrelated languages) are believed to arise from an innate human language "program," a *language acquisition device (LAD)* or *universal grammar (UG).* The hypothesis is that UG provides the infant with an unconscious idea of what language will be like, what elements and rules there can be. These innate ideas enable the appropriate abstraction of underlying language structure, with the language the child hears determining values for innately specified parameters (Chomsky, 1986).

Chomsky (1965) distinguishes *competence,* what the speaker-hearer actually knows about language, from *performance,* what may actually be uttered (complete with false starts, mistakes, and so on). The human's innate endowment allows children to infer competence from a performance corpus. For Chomsky, the goal of linguistics likewise is to infer the rules for competence from speaker-hearer performance, ultimately to discover competence universals to construct a theory of mind, of the *nature of (all) language.*

For Chomsky (1986), the goals of linguistics have evolved from devising a grammar (or structured system) that separated well-formed and poorly formed utterances, to producing a grammar that accounted for speakers' intuitions about sentences and, most recently, to accounting for *how* grammatical knowledge is attained by speakers. This involves a categorization of the innate principles of language and their modification, or parameter setting, by language experience.

This linguistic approach focuses on commonalities among languages, commonalities engendered by UG. Modern linguistics also studies structures underlying *differences* among language groups. *Ethnolinguistics* contrasts languages from radically different cultures. For example, time, space, causality, and motion seem—from our Western perspective—"natural" concepts, as Descartes suggested. Thus they should be reflected in our vocabulary and grammar. There are languages that do not express these concepts, or do express them but in a radically different way. What does that do to the hypotheses that such concepts are natural or innately given through UG?

Not just between nations but *within* a nation, we see language differences produced by subcultures with sublanguages. Every generation creates its own slang, about which its parents shake their heads in disbelief; every profession creates its own jargon; and even those partnered since the Garden of Eden, men and women of the same age and social class, have different patterns of language, common to their gender roles. *Sociolinguistics* looks for patterns of language use distinguishing speakers of the same language, such as dialects, formal versus informal speech, or sex differences.

The distinctions between concept and expression in language, between competence and performance, between man-talk and woman-talk all can be investigated structurally to reveal patterns of organization. What is common to the linguistic approach is the investigation of language structure, at any level: of the social situation, of concepts, of knowledge of the language, of the acoustic signal, or of the operations interrelating them.

Psychology

Psychology of language entails study of the language performance of the speaker or of the hearer. Frequently psychologists too make inferences from performance to competence. The difference between the psychology and linguistics approaches is that linguists study the language to determine rules that *could* generate it and then *infer* that these rules are in the speaker-hearer's head, while psychologists *directly study* processes that the hearer uses in language understanding and that the speaker uses in language production. Note that, from the psychologist's perspective, language production and language comprehension are separate processes, while from the linguist's perspective, they are considered to derive from the same "process"— competence. An important further distinction is that the rules the linguist searches for are *abstract* descriptions of the native speaker's knowledge. The descriptions do not necessarily govern production, nor are they necessarily derived during comprehension (see Katz, 1990, for example). What the psychologist searches for are the mechanisms *actually* employed during comprehension and production.

Within psychology there are two distinct approaches to language that differ with respect to their interests in competence: the indirectly observable mental structure of language, versus performance, the natural language behaviors. The first, behaviorism and connectionism, fathered by Skinner (1957), and resurrected in PDP models (McClelland, Rumelhart, & the PDP Research Group, 1986), has no interest in the mental underpinnings of language. Language processes are simply matters of habit and feedback. Hearing or saying *salt* over and over again establishes a connection between the sound or articulation of the word and the object; being handed the salt after requesting it strengthens these connections. Similarly, words may come to be associated in groups, producing sentences ("Please pass the salt"). Recognition of similarities and differences between sentences ("Please pass the sugar" "Please pass the milk") results in structure, derived from different habit strengths. For the connectionist, psycholinguistics should specify the environmental conditions, such as frequency of occurrence and reinforcement, that underlie habit strength. (Note the absence of mention of mental structure or of learned rules.)

Most of the research on psychology of language comes from a more mentalistic cognitive approach. Here it is assumed that people are active participants in comprehending and producing language, not merely passive reflectors of past habits or passive realizers of inferred rules. The question the cognitive psychologist poses is this: How do people comprehend and produce language? To answer this question, cognitive psychologists have developed ingenious techniques for measuring and distinguishing mental operations and have hypothesized mental processes as diverse as the construction of holistic, mental images; use of innate, abstract, linguistic rules; and connectionist association networks. Connectionists interface the results of the mentalistic approach with the habit strength-feedback model.

Cognitive psychological approaches differ in the degree to which they emphasize more or less passive processing induced automatically by a stimulus (*stimulus-driven*) and active, meaning-seeking, goal-directed, constructivist processing, produced from the individual's preexisting conceptual structures (*conceptually driven*). The machine translation interpreting flesh as meat could not occur if the machine were conceptually driven, with look-up of each word guided by an understanding of the sentence as a whole. Many cognitive psychologists see language processing as a *construction* of meaning from the totality of individual experience, both linguistic and nonlinguistic.

Applications: Education and Clinical Sciences

The disciplines just reviewed have provided a wealth of argument, theory, and methods for studying language as well as data on language and its processing. These have implications for the teaching of language skills in second language acquisition and reading and writing, and to clinical populations who do not seem to acquire a particular language skill readily. In turn, the methods and successes (and failures) of teaching language skills provide data on the structure and processing of language of interest to psychologists and philosophers of language.

Modern linguists believe that language acquisition reflects the automatic, innate activation of a learning reflex. Some people do not automatically learn all language skills without outside help. When there is an obvious organic (physical) problem, as with Laura (Figure 1.1), the selective failure or sparing of language processing has been taken as evidence supporting a genetically specified LAD.

Some individuals have no obvious organic problem but might be described, perhaps euphemistically, as having an unusual learning "style." People with language-learning differences (or disabilities?) or who need to reacquire language after an organic injury are assisted by speech and language clinicians.

Language skills are also specifically taught in education settings—not primary language, but secondary language. Secondary language skills include reading and writing, second ("foreign") language learning, and the *explicit* instruction (grammar) in language rules of the *tacit knowledge* that we unconsciously use in fluent speech.

There are three important characteristics of secondary language acquisition distinguishing it from primary language acquisition: (a) Secondary language is normally acquired at a later age than primary language (perhaps after LAD has "turned off"); (b) secondary language is usually acquired after primary language, so primary language may be used in learning it; and (c) secondary language is not as ubiquitous as primary language—the learner "immerses" in it for a small amount of time each day, rather than in all waking hours (so it is less practiced). For any of these reasons, secondary language acquisition could be very different from primary language acquisition. And it is an interesting aspect of normal language processing to see how primary language knowledge influences (or does not) later language skills.

Unlike the disciplines presented earlier, the applied sciences have as a primary purpose developing effective teaching techniques. More than the other disciplines, they must concentrate on differences in learning styles rather than normative group behavior. They contribute to the understanding of language and language processes in the development of teaching techniques and in the provision of "cases" of unusual learning styles, which may support or refute general innateness arguments. These also are a testing ground for theories of human language processes, as covert, normally automatic "strategies" are explicitly tried.

LANGUAGE: THE WHOLE AND THE PARTS

This book, together with *Language in Atypical Populations,* is aimed at defining human language through exploration of language and the cognitive and perceptual constraints of its users. At the outset, a noncontroversial and rather empty definition of language is this: *Language is the way humans communicate.* As we proceed we will develop a much more detailed, concrete, and, probably more controversial, definition.

Communication is formally defined as the active transfer of information from one to another. The two critical terms are *active* and *information. Active* implies deliberate processing on the part of the communicator. Therefore, communication does not take place between a person and a tape recorder. Following the information-theoretic approach, *information* is defined rigorously as a lessening of uncertainty. According to this view, telling a person something he or she already knows is *not* communication. This point can cause confusion partly because there are so many levels of communication. A student correctly answering a teacher's question, say, about who was the first president of the United States (a prime number?) is transmitting information. However, the information is not "George Washington," which the teacher presumably knew, but is "I *know* the answer—George Washington." The *student's knowledge* had been uncertain to the teacher. If a person tells the same story over and over again, the information is not the story contents but instead that the speaker is boring or repetitious—this would not have been evident at the first telling.

Natural, normal communication usually entails signals transmitted visually: eye movements or eye widening, facial expression, head movements, arm gestures, and body movements—so-called *body language.* Natural communication also entails signals transmitted *aurally* (to the ear); these are signals usually called language. (Signed languages have a visual equivalent of the aural signal, the hand and arm movements constituting signs, which are still distinct from the visual signals of body language.) These two aspects of communication may operate *redundantly*, meaning that each conveys the same information as the other, so the two together do not reduce the uncertainty any more than either alone. For example, a head nod may accompany a verbal "yes," or the eyes may widen together with an exclamation of surprise. However, frequently, they are not redundant (a gesture to the left when one means "left" is usually more reliable than the words *left* or *right*), and so both must be considered part of human communication.

For our purposes, the more interesting part of human communication is the part transmitted aurally in spoken languages and by signs in signed languages. This language is analyzed structurally as consisting of paralanguage or *suprasegmentals*, phonetics and phonology (cherology in sign), semantics, and syntax. *Paralanguage* comprises those aspects of the signal not contained in the words: intonation, stress, emotional overtone, the speaker's identity, and so on. Note that sometimes this information can be distinct from the verbal message—as in indications that the speaker is in a bad mood—and sometimes it can be redundant with the verbal message—as when a question is indicated by raising pitch (paralanguage) along with adding a verbal "who" or "what." Together, paralanguage and body language form the subject matter for the field of *nonverbal communication*.

Phonetics and *phonology* are the study of the sounds of the language, the purpose of which is to find a grammar, or set of rules, governing sound production and perception. Linguists are interested in determining which sounds are used in language—which of these help distinguish meaning and which rules most simply describe the combination of those sounds. Of course, there is also a search for sounds and combination rules universal to all languages. Psychologists are interested in how the vocal apparatus produces the sounds, how listeners perceive the acoustic signal and recognize the relevant sounds of the language, and whether there are strategies for combining them—psychologically real combination rules.

Semantics is the study of the relations of word and meaning and of word meanings to one another. Again, the linguist attempts to recover an orderly pattern underlying the words of the language, one that can more efficiently describe the meaning system than does a list of words. The psychologist questions how meanings are represented in the speaker-hearer's mind (cognitive) or are derived from associations (behaviorist and connectionist).

Syntax is the study of rules for combining words to form larger meaningful units, such as phrases or sentences. An important difference between syntax and semantics or phonology is that syntax is more abstract, *specific only to language*. Phonology and semantics are *interpretive*; phonology interprets language into physical sounds, and semantics interprets language into conceptual forms. Syntax wholly relates language elements to one another.

Syntax is the aspect of language most closely related to what is taught in elementary (grammar) schools as "grammar." An important distinction is that school grammar is *pro*scriptive—instruction of students in the "correct" use of the "standard" language (the language spoken by the dominant class, "the Queen's English"), whereas grammar in the sense used by linguists is *de*scriptive, illustrating the rules used in the language. A descriptive grammar can be devised for productions of any social class. The linguist searches for rules accounting for comprehension and production of all syntactically well-formed utterances, and *only* those utterances, and assumes that those result from real mental processes. The psychologist directly studies the mental processes that might underlie the apparent rule-governed organization of the language.

This breakdown of language neglects the fact that language is social and produced for a purpose. The purpose of the language, the perceived characteristics of the intended audience, and the perception of common background information, knowledge, and experience of the current environment (as in whether the participants are in the same room or talking on a telephone) affect language production and comprehension in regular ways. *Pragmatics* is the study of such contextual effects on language.

Unfortunately, the division of human communication into these parts has to be artificial: The parts interact. Smiling while speaking alters the sounds produced as well as the face. The face change is studied as body language; the sound change as paralanguage, which affects phonetic variation. An intonation change, paralanguage, can have a syntactic effect—turning a statement into a question. Drawing a sharp line between syntax and semantics, as we shall see, is impossible; word meanings change dramatically in relation to other words. (A beautiful example of this is *oxymoron,* a poetic device pairing opposites as in the following: "That is, hot ice, and wondrous strange snow. How shall we find concord of this discord?" [*A Midsummer's Night's Dream* 5.1.59-60]—which in this case has nothing to do with weather but refers to a seeming paradox or impossibility.) And phonetics and semantics interact, as we saw earlier in the variations in the sound of the English plural after different final sounds in the singular. Finally, context—pragmatics—affects all levels; our tone of voice, speech rate, word selection, and sentence structure can change dramatically depending on the audience we think we are addressing. Think how differently you talk to a "cool" friend who shares your lingo, a young child whom you think might not understand, or an authority figure whom you want to impress with your erudition. Because of these interactions, language cannot be described purely "structurally," as a sum of elemental parts. The whole is much more.

ORGANIZATION OF THIS BOOK

This chapter has briefly outlined some major theoretical perspectives on language. We will be examining these in detail throughout. Our general foci are (a) the evaluation of whether and how language is special and (b) the determination of the human social, sensory, and cognitive mechanisms that shape language. This book concentrates on the structure and processing of language. We first look at semantics, syntax, and speech—both structure and processing—in a single primary language. Next we examine sociolinguistic pressures affecting language change, dialects, and language styles, and then at normal child language acquisition. The final two

Box 1.3. Components of Language

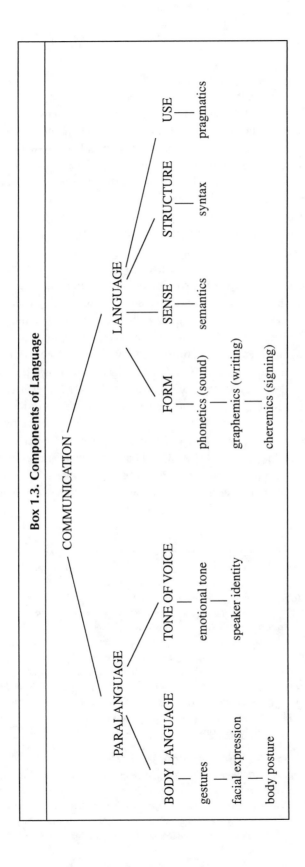

content chapters examine bilingualism and second language learning as well as reading and writing in normal hearing people—also natural language processes but often secondary ones that piggyback on primary language and may require specific teaching. Readers are urged to pursue their study of language processes by considering whether language as such exists in other populations—animals, socially deprived or language-learning-delayed children, deaf people, brain-damaged or personality-"damaged" individuals. Language processes, and to a limited extent interventions for these populations, are treated in the companion volume, *Language in Atypical Populations*. Together the books provide a comprehensive view of language processes and intriguing data on the biological underpinnings of our unique communication system.

For the most part, this book's approach to language study derives from linguistics and cognitive psychology. These are reflected in its general organization as well as in the subject matter. The next six chapters employ the linguistic distinction between competence and performance, with one chapter describing the ideal structure of the language, and the following chapter, its performance realization. I present the linguist's database first to encourage you to think about and experiment with language and to appreciate its structure. I discuss language following traditional linguistic levels: phonology, semantics, and syntax. My organization reflects a conceptually driven scheme, beginning with meaning, then looking at structure (syntax), and ending with sound. All levels of language are affected by pragmatic considerations and thus these appear throughout. They particularly figure in the chapters on sociolinguistics (Chapter 8) and on multilingualism (Chapter 10).

We will begin our exploration of language and language processing with meaning, given that the exchange of meanings is what human communication is about.

REFERENCES

Blumstein, S. (1975). Structuralism in linguistics: Methodological and theoretical perspectives. In K. F. Riegel & G. C. Rosenwald (Eds.), *Structure and transformation: Developmental and historical aspects, 3* (pp. 153-165). New York: John Wiley.

Brown, R. (1973). *A first language: The early stages.* Cambridge, MA: Harvard University Press.

Chomsky, N. (1965). *Aspects of a theory of syntax.* Cambridge: MIT Press.

Chomsky, N. (1972). *Language and mind.* New York: Harcourt Brace Jovanovich.

Chomsky, N. (1986). *Knowledge of language: Its nature, origin, and use.* New York: Praeger.

Darwin, C. (n.d.). *The descent of man.* In *The origin of species and the descent of man* (pp. 445-495). New York: Modern Library. (Original work published 1871)

Dennett, D. C. (1995 , May-June). Darwin's dangerous idea. *Sciences,* pp. 34-40.

Dickens, C. (1975). *Little Dorritt.* London: Penguin. (Original work published 1857)

Fodor, J. A. (1983). *The modularity of mind.* Cambridge: MIT Press.

Herodotus. (1986/1954). *The histories* (A. de Selincourt, Trans.). Hammondsworth, Middlesex, England: Penguin. (Original work published 1954; written fourth century B.C.)

Katz, J. J. (1966). *The philosophy of language.* New York: Harper & Row.

Katz, J. J. (1990). *The metaphysics of meaning.* Cambridge: Bradford Books of MIT Press.

Lowry, R. (1987). *The evolution of psychological theory* (2nd ed.). New York: Aldine.

McClelland, J. C., Rumelhart, D. E., & the PDP Research Group (Eds.). (1986). *Parallel distributed processing* (Vol. 2). Cambridge: MIT Press.

Percelay, J., Dweck, S., & Ivey, M. (1995). *Double snaps.* New York: Quill, William Morrow.

Rieber, R. W. (Ed.). (1980). *Psychology of language and thought: Essays on the theory and history of psycholinguistics.* New York: Plenum.

Rieber, R. W., & Vetter, H. (1980). Theoretical and historical roots of psycholinguistic research. In R. W. Rieber (Ed.), *Psychology of language and thought: Essays on the theory and history of psycholinguistics* (pp. 3-49). New York: Plenum.

Ryle, G. (1970). Ordinary language. In C. E. Caton (Ed.), *Philosophy and ordinary language* (pp. 108-128). Chicago: University of Chicago Press.

Safire, W. (1982 , May 30). On language. *New York Times,* sec. VI, p. 8.

Sherzer, J. (1982). Play languages: With a note on ritual languages. In L. Obler & L. Menn (Eds.), *Exceptional languages and linguistics* (pp. 174-199). New York: Academic Press.

Skinner, B. F. (1957). *Verbal behavior.* Englewood Cliffs, NJ: Prentice Hall.

Watson, J. B. (1970). *Behaviorism.* New York: Norton. (Original work published 1930)

Whorf, B. L. (1956). *Language, thought, and reality* (J. B. Carroll, Ed.). Cambridge: MIT Press.

Yamada, J. E. (1990). *Laura: A case for the modularity of language.* Cambridge: Bradford Books of MIT Press.

STUDY QUESTIONS

1. What are the important issues considered in language study from antiquity through the present? In your own words, briefly describe each. Discuss the manifestations of the issues in modern day language study, the fascination of language, and historical study.

2. Briefly describe the levels of communication. For the language levels—sound, semantics, and syntax—try to come up with a pair of sentences, the interpretation of which illustrates a distinction on that level only. For example, for sound, we might have the sentence, "Let me tell you something," versus "Let me tell you somethin'," which have the same meaning and syntax but sound different. Try to construct a sentence that illustrates pragmatic effects, one that would have a different interpretation in different contexts. Specify the contexts and how they affect the interpretations.

2

MEANING

When my older son, Eric, reached about a year of age, a long-awaited moment arrived. He said his first word, "cat," noting one of our three pets. Five years later, at about the same age, his younger brother, Alexander, said his first word, "Eric," noting a perhaps more interesting household inhabitant. Both children named "Daddy" soon after. I grew impatient to be named. My husband tactfully, and possibly correctly, claimed that I had not been named because the children had not yet differentiated my being from their own—they saw me as a part of themselves not needing comment.

I tell this story because it illustrates some important truths and issues about meaning in language. The first "truth" is that words *signify* some *external reality.* The second is that normally words comment on something *salient,* what stands out perceptually and cognitively. The third is that salient dimensions of perceptual and cognitive experience include living things—like pets and siblings. And a final truth is that, unlike a baby's cry *for* something, language's "purpose" is usually not a request but simply a comment or an observation about the world—"There is a cat."

This intent, to share what the speaker has perceived, exists in social communication systems that seem more primitive than human language. Vervet monkeys have separate signals for snakes, leopards, and eagles, each of which is escaped from differently (Cheney & Seyfarth, 1992). The particular scream, like the baby's particular word, alerts the other troop members to a salient observation of an external reality. Sharing observations may help a troop, whether monkeys or human families, survive.

The naming story issues are fundamental to the philosophy of language. Alexander's naming Eric appears to be a clear instance of *meaning* as *reference* there is only one Eric (in our family) and the name *indicated* (pointing with one's *index* finger through words) him. "Cat" is more problematic. We had three of them: Was Eric referring only to whichever one he was looking at, using "cat" as a proper name? Or was he referring to a class of animals, "cats," commenting on the membership of this one in that group? Or was he perhaps saying something very different, making his *own* non-English category, using the word *cat* to signify family member or animal-in-general? Or maybe when he said "cat," he *meant* "brown," the color, as it happens, of each of our cats. The difficulty is that while it seems that words must index some external reality, scenes are rich in detail and a single pairing of word and scene cannot specify which categorizable detail the word indexes. This is known as the *underspecification* problem (Quine, 1960; Wittgenstein, 1973).

At the same time, *a word does more than index.* For *me,* in that particular context, Eric's word, like Alexander's, was an implicit sentence, the intention of which was "I perceive _ " or "Look at _." That is, inherent in their use of words was a *speech act,* in this case, the act of naming. Any utterance can convey an entire sentence and purpose. A given word also brings into play for each hearer a vast set of associations. To me, *cat* refers to my pets, other people's pets of perhaps different colors, a very broad family of animals (lions, jaguars, cheetahs, . . . tabby cats), some imaginary animals (sphinxes), a popular singer of the 1960s (Cat Stevens), a nasty gossip (being catty), and an old computer command that I think sorted a directory (or catalogue). Given that my infant children did not have most of these associations to *cat,* to what extent do they and I share meaning? Does the broad meaning of cat (the large animal family) in fact constitute a real natural category, animals that are fundamentally similar? Or is it a somewhat arbitrary learned classification scheme that ignores profound size and living style differences? Do the many different, perhaps irrelevant, associations I have to *cat* all affect how I react to either the word or the things it signifies?

The fundamental issue in philosophy of language is the relationship of language to reality. A subsidiary issue, which we began to consider in Chapter 1, is the relationship of language to thought and, in turn, then, the relation of thought to reality. In this chapter we will explore these issues, primarily from the views of philosophy of language and linguistics.

Our exploration will begin with three important presumptions to be challenged as we go along. These are as follows: (a) There is an objective reality common to all observers provided by our senses; (b) thought (ideas) derives from sensory data, past experience, and our creativity, and is expressed through language but is not the same as language; and (c) we can consider our representation of meaning to be like a dictionary's in that, for the most part, *words* are the unit of meaning, but sometimes pieces of words and sometimes whole phrases constitute a meaning unit. We will temporarily bypass the issue of which is the best unit of meaning and concentrate on words. We will consider the issue of the unit and how to combine meanings at the end of this chapter and in the chapters on syntax.

PHILOSOPHICAL DISTINCTIONS

Senses of Meaning

Our introduction to meaning has pointed to one type of word meaning, *deixis,* or words that point to a particular aspect of reality. A proper name is usually a form of deictic reference. The word *this* or *that* makes a phrase with a noun that is also deictic—*this chapter* refers explicitly to Chapter 2, our shared reference, just as *Chapter 2* refers to it.

Most words do something more abstract than pointing; at the very least, they also refer. *Reference* is more abstract because it brings into play concepts that are not immediately available from sensory experience. So while I can point to *this chapter* with you (we are sharing this experience), I cannot point to my cats with you. Nevertheless, when I write *cat,* I assume, rather confidently, that you will know what possible aspects of reality I am referring to.

The part of word meaning that refers is *denotation.* Denotation is what we generally think of as the definition of a word. The denotation of *cat* is shared in English by *feline, pussy, kitty, tabby,* and *tom.* Although each of these words refers roughly to the same categories of sensory experience, they do not quite *mean* the same thing. Philosophers of language distinguish between *reference* and *meaning,* with *meaning* being more abstract.

Meaning includes reference, the aspects of reality that a word points to, and also includes associations based on how the word is used *in the language.* That is, in addition to denotation, meaning includes *connotation.* No two words are completely synonymous or completely redundant. For any two words that seem to have the same referents, there exist specific language situations that make one a better choice than the other.

For example, there is a sense in which *drift* means meaning, if you catch my drift. *Drift, intention,* and *meaning* denote the same abstract concept, the subject of this chapter. *Drift* connotes a vagueness as though the speaker has not zeroed in on the meaning. *Intent* connotes a sharpness; the speaker knows exactly what she's aiming at. *Meaning* lies somewhere in between. The impression the speaker is trying to convey determines which word is most suitable.

Similarly, the synonyms for *cat* have very different connotations. *Feline* is sleeker sounding and more educated and scientific. *Kitty* and *pussy* are nursery words, for discussing cats with children. (In my dialect, moreover, *pussy* has an off-color sense, which makes me think twice about writing it here. [*Any* "naughty" word and the euphemisms for it for use in polite society have the same denotation, but very different connotations!]) Thus these "synonyms" are not mutually substitutable.

Probably words, expressions, even whole languages acquire connotations from the company they keep. *Drift* is vague in that it brings to mind wind and water,

---

Box 2.1. Elements of Meaning

Deixis:	Pointing to something through language, as with proper nouns or demonstrative pronouns (*this/that*).
Reference:	Naming a (possibly abstract) set of objects, events, or the like, about which the speaker knows directly and the hearer can infer.
Denotation:	The part of meaning that refers, that marks a set of objects in reality; the definition.
Connotation:	The feeling that a word arouses, determined by the association of that word to other words.
Speech act:	Meaning, including the speaker's intent or purpose in the utterance (and the utterance's effect on the hearer).
Meaning:	Intent + Connotation + Denotation.

---

causing aimless movements of leaves, snow, sand, debris. When it is used in the "meaning" sense, it does not shed these associations.

It is because words maintain the associations of previous uses, contexts, users, and so on that social leaders often advocate specific words or language to produce or avoid undesirable connotations. Thus, in the 1960s, civil rights leaders dropped *Negro* and *colored*—"Black is beautiful!"—and since the early 1990s, we speak of the same group as *African Americans* (connoting a pride in ancestry), or *people of color* (not so different from the word *colored* discarded in the 1960s). Conversely, the use of Latin is continued because it is connotatively powerful even though few understand its denotations. Its association with the church and with seats of learning since the Middle Ages evokes mystery, holiness, spirituality, and erudition.

Word Form and Meaning

Our discussion of the relationship of meaning to reality has illustrated that a word can point to an aspect of reality (deixis, reference, and denotation) yet convey something more than that through the listener's attempt to understand the speaker's intentions (speech acts) or through its use in the language (meaning, connotation). Language itself is a part of reality, and its relationship to other aspects of reality is important in two ways.

The first way is *meta*linguistically. The prefix *meta* refers to a system's description of itself. So, *metalanguage* consists of words used to describe language properties. As we have seen already and will be seeing throughout this book, there are a host of such words: *denotation* and *connotation, meaning* and *reference, metalinguistics* itself, *semantics, syntax, nouns,* and *verbs.* Once we have language, we can use it to describe external observations, internal thoughts and feelings, and external and internal observations about language as well.

The second way that language takes on a life of its own is in the relationship of language *form* to language *meaning*. Why do we call a cat *cat;* why not *dog* or *boonak*? One answer to that question is that naming is *arbitrary,* that the particular sounds we use for any given object are relatively random events, associations established merely by custom. This is certainly true in part, but it is not the whole story.

Much is made in modern linguistics of people's creativity, of language's *generative* capacity, of the fact that a sentence is often a brand-new string of words, never before uttered in exactly that sequence, even if the components have previously been used. Words too can be generative, so if you need a new word, you will not be stuck (although you may feel inhibited). Suppose you look under a microscope and see for the first time.   What would you name it? In a class exercise, students offered *amoeboid* and *polyblob*. Note that these words are novel, and in and of themselves do not look like the object; in that sense, they are arbitrary. However, they are not completely arbitrary—the creators borrowed existing pieces (*amoeba* + "oid" as in *humanoid* or *asteroid;* "poly" + *blob*), which had related senses to apply. Similarly, when one names a new being—a just-acquired pet or a new baby—the naming is not a random, arbitrary event. For the pet we often use an existing word describing a physical characteristic (Black Beauty, Fluffy, Spot, Tiger). Sometimes for the pet, and in some cultures for the child, we bestow a name that belonged to a recent ancestor. We may also select a name of a figure, real or mythical, with a desired characteristic: I selected Eric (the Red) and Alexander (the Great). I saw them as influential, powerful leaders from my culture, desirable attributes for my children.

So, for most word names, the relationship between the word *form* and the meaning is partly arbitrary (you cannot guess what a cat is from the sound of the word alone), but partly constrained by language conventions (in English adding prefixes or suffixes) and associations of the reemployed sounds to prior meanings.

For some words, the relationship between form and meaning is even less arbitrary: The sound is chosen because it seems to mirror meaning. I am going to illustrate this first visually, with the medium of print:

BIG is big;   little is little;   now LITTLE has grown.

There is something amusing about this. Obviously, we are aware of word form and can play with it and use it paradoxically. (Try these common phrases, recoverable only if you attend creatively to form:

(1)	wear	(2)	head	(3)	the belt
	your		heels		hitting

Solutions are provided at the end of the chapter.)

We may do the same thing using sound referentially—shouting *big,* making our voices small as we say *little,* or indicating a lot of something by using a lot of language, as in "that is very very very very very big." Using form symbolically is fun because we do not normally attend to it and so it takes us by surprise.

Form use figures actively in some poetic devices, such as *alliteration* (e.g., *weak and weary*) or *rhyming* (*dreary, weary*) in which the sounds in a word are deliberately repeated, for auditory effect. It also figures more provocatively in a device called *sound symbolism.* In writing "The Raven" (from which the preceding and next examples were taken), Edgar Allen Poe reiterated the sounds "ore" in "Lenore," "more," and "nevermore," for example, because they had a sad, endless sound. Brown (1958) found that for noises with abrupt onsets (a pop), listeners prefer speech with abrupt onset ("p"). He noted that vowels with large mouth openings (like the "a" in *large*) occur more often across languages in words for large objects than do vowels with wee mouth openings ("ee"). And to me, "s" is a sinister sound, which I think arises more frequently in sinister situations: hiss, snake, serpent, Satan, Old Scratch, slime. (Of course, there are many counterexamples: *Big* has a small mouth opening, and *small* a large one; *sea* and *serene* are decidedly unsinister.)

The form use in sound symbolism and in poetry can be subtle, and may evoke a feeling without our being completely aware of the cause. In *onomatopoeia,* words obviously sound like their referents. In spoken language, these generally are words naming sounds: *meow, splash, boo-hoo.* While the speech is clearly not arbitrary, it is still an abstraction of the sound. English roosters say "cockadoodledoo," while French roosters *disent "cocorico."* Both are onomatopoetic but are also governed by the language's phonology.

The last example of the relationship of form and meaning, or the nonarbitrariness and yet arbitrariness of words, is to be found in American Sign Language (ASL). Many words of ASL are *iconic;* that is, the signs look like their referents. For example, the ASL word TREE (signs are conventionally transcribed in capitals) is signed by resting the elbow of the signing arm on the other hand, forearm vertical, and hand rotating at the wrist (a tree trunk with branches swaying).

To a person learning sign as a second language, the iconicity is striking. (In part, this is because sign teachers stress [sometimes made-up] derivations, to help students remember what a sign means.) This may be because people discuss visual more often than auditory aspects of reality (sign is not iconic in words describing music or phonetics), and so form may more often seem to mirror meaning in a visual rather than an auditory language.

Regardless, fluent signers are *unconscious* of the iconicity of their language in *normal everyday* use. In no experiments have signs that reflect their meaning in form been shown to be more recognizable, more memorable, and so on than arbitrary signs. Moreover, historically, signs often lose their iconicity without affecting their interpretability, as likely happened with our letters, originally depictions of objects (see Diamond, 1995, as well as Chapter 11, for more detail). Although a sign's form does not figure in normal signed language use, signing poets, like hearing poets, may employ the form for special effects. (Sign language and its processing are presented in detail in the companion volume, *Language in Atypical Populations.*)

Box 2.2. What's in a Name?

— Words are considered arbitrary; that is, there is little relation between word form and meaning.
— Exceptions include the following:
   — Poetic devices such as the following:
      — *Alliteration:* Repetition of a sound in a word to create an effect.
      — *Rhyming:* Repetition of the sound at ends of words to create an effect.
   — *Sound symbolism* (either as a literary device or in the origin of some words): Use of a particular language sound because of the sound's connotations.
   — *Onomatopoeia:* The sound of the word mimics the sound of its referent.
   — *Iconicity:* In sign language or written language, the appearance of a word mimics the appearance of its referent.

Thus, for all intents and purposes, a word's meaning derives from its associations within the language and to reality, not from its physical form. We may shift attention to form, but in typical communication we are not actively considering it in accessing a speaker's meaning.

Language and Reality

This section examines how language reflects reality. Our discussion of sign language suggested that we may more often talk about what we see. In the beginning of this chapter, I suggested that we name *salient* properties of reality. We also have seen that because language is a salient part of human reality, we generate words to describe it. In this section we consider generally ways in which words (or phrases) differ in their referencing of reality, ultimately raising the question of whether our language code prejudices our interpretations of reality.

Abstract versus concrete. Most of the words that we have examined in this chapter have been names or nouns and have had clear *concrete* referents in reality. As I mentioned earlier, *concrete* does not mean clearly specified. In an often-quoted example, Quine (1960) describes a rabbit running in front of a native and a linguist. The native shouts "gavagai" and the linguist must decide what *gavagai* means in this concrete situation: rabbit, running, white, dinner, within shooting distance? Each is a concrete, plausible aspect of the situation that, alone, underspecifies the designate of the word.

There are also nouns that do not have concrete referents but indicate abstract concepts, such as *courtesy, evil, democracy,* or *abstraction.* For abstract concepts, like concrete concepts, words have denotation and connotation, reference and meaning, and a more or less arbitrary relation between the word form and what it represents. Situations underspecify abstract words too. The distinction between *concrete* and *abstract* lies in the closeness of the word's meaning to immediate sensory experience. Concrete concepts reflect sense data (red, loud, sweet, burning, cat), while abstract concepts are at least one step removed, perhaps building on the concrete concepts (akin to Locke's primary and secondary perceptions, and simple and complex ideas; see Chapter 1 and Lowry, 1987). Concrete concepts may be recognized as those easily imaged, whether imagery is visual, auditory, tactile, or the like.

Literal versus figurative language. The word *red* in isolation appears to be an obvious example of a concrete adjective, referring to a very salient color in its *literal* sense; that is, when we take it at face value. What happens to it when we combine it with another apparently concrete word, as in *seeing red*? Clearly, it could refer literally to something that is red, but it also has another meaning, a nonliteral meaning—becoming angry. *Seeing red* is an *idiom,* an expression in which the meaning has a fixed, nonliteral interpretation known to fluent speakers of the language. This particular idiom (I think) derives from bullfighting, in which a red flag is waved in front of the bull to enrage him and make the matador seem braver. The first time the expression *seeing red* was used, it was a *live figure of speech.* To understand it, the association to bullfighting had to be made and transferred to the new situation, with the person who *saw red* imagined as pawing the ground, nostrils flaring, and so on. (As I write this, I am experiencing a power in the expression that I do not experience normally. Normally, I imagine someone with bloodshot eyes, although I don't know that eyes do redden in anger.) The transfer of associations from one situation to another in which they do not strictly apply is characteristic of *figurative language.*

Figurative language poses a problem for many theories of language processing, as we shall see. Given our discussion thus far of the relationship of word and meaning, we can begin to appreciate the problem. Is *seeing red* concrete or abstract? Both the literal meaning and being angry are concrete, but the application of *seeing red* to "being angry" does not depend directly on sense data; like abstract concepts, it is a step removed, building on associations that depend on sense data.

Now, when a figure of speech becomes fixed in the language (or *dead*), there is no philosophical problem. We can as automatically consider *seeing red* as arbitrarily meaning being angry as we can consider *being angry* to mean it. We may never notice the red sense of *red.* But if we do not have that association ready-made, we have to interpret the expression in a special way, constructing or deconstructing those underlying associations. Because of this special interpretation process, figurative language is sometimes considered the highest, most abstract form of language.

In an influential book, Lakoff and Johnson (1980) (see also Gibbs, 1994) make two controversial, provocative (and I believe correct) suggestions about meaning in language and thought. The first is that all language, even idioms and literal expressions, is arbitrary and abstract, and its understanding is not just definition retrieval but recovery of connotation of the underlying associations. Their book begins with the observation: "Metaphor is for most people a device of the poetic imagination and the rhetorical flourish—a matter of extraordinary rather than ordinary language" (p. 3). Rather, their analysis shows figurative language to be a matter of ordinary rather than extraordinary language. Supporting evidence from language *processing* will be presented in Chapter 3; here we consider some evidence from an English language corpus.

Their second important assumption is that "our ordinary conceptual system, in terms of which we both think and act, is fundamentally metaphorical in nature" (p. 3) and that the metaphors that structure our concepts are systematic. Note that this suggests an intimate relation of language and thought, if metaphor, the highest form of language, is the stock-in-trade of our conceptual system. Lakoff and Johnson compellingly describe many metaphoric systems in English, two of which I present here. The first is the conceptualization of "love" as a "journey." They note the following expressions that fit that conceptualization:

Look *how far we've come.*
We're *at a crossroads.*
We'll just have to *go our separate ways.*
We can't *turn back now.*
I don't think this relationship *is going anywhere.*
Where are we?
We're *stuck.*
It's been *a long bumpy road.*
This relationship is a *dead-end street.*
We're just *spinning our wheels.*
Our marriage is *on the rocks.*
We've gotten *off the track.* (pp. 44-45)

And, given that these all seem to be negative, let me add, "It's been smooth *sailing.*" "Let me *take you higher.*" "I'm *lost* without you." "You *send me into orbit.*" (The study questions ask you to try to think of some too.)

What is significant in their theory is that while love is an identifiable, if abstract part of reality, and one that is quite different from concrete journeys, our *thoughts* about them are convergently structured, making it easy to verbalize one in terms of the other. Lakoff and Johnson argue that the convergent structure results from a concept like love being understood in terms of a concept like a journey.

Jackendoff (1994) also observes systematic, convergent idea structures within the language and extralinguistically, in perception, but argues that the convergence results from innate abstract cognitive themes, such as Descartes's innate ideas (see Chapter 1), which equally underlie both terms of the metaphor. Love and journeys might have as part of their literal definitions an abstract theme of passage, of change of state. The sharing of that innate theme enables the metaphor.

Regardless of whether the convergent structures *reveal* an innate, abstract theme (Jackendoff) or *create* a theme through the frequent analogy (Lakoff and Johnson), new metaphors that conform to this system are quickly understood because they fit the pattern. And "generation" of such a metaphor is not a totally creative act; it is an application of a well-developed scheme in the language.

My second example is metaphors for language itself. Language is seen as a container, according to Lakoff and Johnson, a container that holds meaning (note that *hold* continues the container metaphor, as a bucket holds water). Another metaphor for language sees it as a conduit with meanings as objects and communication as sending. Together these result in "the speaker put[ting] ideas (objects) into words (containers) and send[ing] them (along a conduit) to a hearer who takes the idea/objects out of the word/containers" (p. 10). So we try to

> *capture* ideas *in* words,
> get an idea *through* to someone,
> get *across* a meaning,
> put it *in* writing, or

paraphrase by

> putting something *in* our own words,
> translating it *into* another language, or
> saying it *in* another *way.*

I find the idea that we have these metaphoric conceptual systems to be very intriguing, in part because the systems are so subtly compelling. In organizing my presentation of meaning, I succumbed to these conceptual metaphors. I began the formal discussion with deixis, words in which a particular object is conveyed. I proceeded to discuss words with fuzzier relations to objects in reality, still presuming an object relationship. And, throughout, I have tried to focus on how the meanings are *conveyed through* (see the conduit?) language, directly in form or more arbitrarily in association. It was not until I presented the conceptual metaphor that I realized my thoughts on this subject were a product of my language.

Content versus function. Our discussion of figurative language introduced phrases that had meanings beyond the words that composed them. For example, *putting an idea in words,* I suggested, makes a container out of language. Language in that expression is represented by "words." Where in the expression is the container represented? *Words, language,* and *container* are all nouns and therefore can be seen easily as depicting objects, either abstract or concrete ones. Nouns, abstract or concrete, are *content words*—they express something meaningful. Most adjectives (noun describers), verbs (words that carry the action in a sentence), adverbs (verb describers), and nouns are content words. Content words are also sometimes called *open-class* words. Openness refers to the fact that we are always adding words to the content class as we identify new categories or need to express new relationships among ideas.

The container concept is hard to find in the phrase because it is in *in,* a *preposition,* a word defining grammatical relations within the sentence but usually thought meaningless. Try to define the aspects of reality that *of, however, and, with,* or *in* point to. These are called *function words,* which broadly constitute the grammatical classes of prepositions, conjunctions, and auxiliary or helping verbs. Function words are *closed class;* there are a fixed set of them that we learn and use, and this set rarely changes because categories of grammatical relations are stable. Therefore, membership in this class is closed.

Function words are the most abstract words in a language, abstract because they have the least relation to external reality; their "meaning" exists only in relation to their use in the language. Necessarily, function words are *arbitrary* in the strong sense of the word. With little relation to a concrete aspect of reality, their form cannot reflect it.

Look again at the container and conduit metaphors for language and try to determine which words convey the container and conduit senses. You should see that it is in fact the so-called meaningless prepositions, *in, through, into,* and *across.* These forge the metaphor. Their meaning probably arises from the company they normally keep, in literal containers (*in* bags and boxes) and across literal conduits (*through* tunnels and *across* bridges). Thus even the most meaningless of words, the function words, are not entirely arbitrary but are systematically grounded in our conceptions of reality, shaped by and shaping the associations of language.

Linguistic relativity. According to Lakoff and Johnson, we English speakers see love as a journey because of the linguistic associations between the two concepts in our language. Is love not a journey to all people? Are there languages and conceptual systems that do not link the concepts? This leads to a provocative hypothesis: To the extent that languages differ, we may not all share the same objective reality; a language's conventions may shape the way we think about reality, or even how we sense it. Because, in this view, reality is viewed *relative* to linguistic background, this position is sometimes called the *linguistic relativity hypothesis.* Because the supposition is that language in part *determines* thought, our mental interpretation of reality, it is also called *linguistic determinism.* And, finally, after its initial proponents, it is known as the *Whorf-Sapir hypothesis.*

In Chapter 1, I discussed how difficult it is not to consider our mother tongue to be the language that all people naturally think in. It is even harder to think about there not being a single reality that all people share. A famous Afghan folktale may help illustrate the possibility. In it, some blind men attempt to reach an understanding of what an elephant is. Each man touches a different part of the elephant and explains what he senses. The one touching its tail likens it to a rope; the one its trunk, to a hose; the one its leg, to a tree; the one its skin, to leather; and so on. Unable to get a complete picture, each focuses on the most salient information available.

Our language likewise may focus our attention on some aspects of reality, causing us to ignore other aspects, a dilemma for translation as Figure 2.1 illustrates. If one language names "elephant" using a word associated with its rear, do its speakers conceive of the beast differently than speakers of a language that associates the name to the tusk or trunk? Can a missionary translate *God,* the exacting

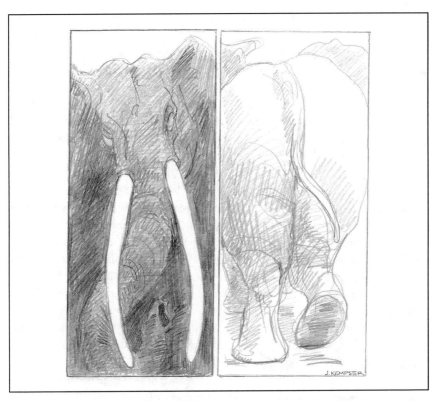

Figure 2.1A.   Two Views of the Elephant (a) and of the Divine (b)

NOTE: Does language so change perspective? Consider if your word for "elephant" evoked the frontal view and you were trying to talk to someone for whom "elephant" was the ropelike tail and massive behind?

Figure 2.1B.

Or if your "God" is a stern father, and you are translating the word to convert someone for whom "God" is the nurturing mother, like Mother Nature? Do you truly communicate? (2.1A Drawing by James J. Kempster; used by permission.)

Father-Judge, with a word that to its people conveys a nurturing female fertility figure?

Whorf examined alternative linguistic conceptualizations of reality through structural analysis of some Native American languages. Recently his work has come into question: His data on other languages may be inaccurate, with his conclusions resulting in part from poor translations (see Pinker, 1994, pp. 59-67). However, the theory has been very influential, and potentially valid implications perhaps are being discarded prematurely (Hunt & Agnoli, 1991). Therefore, having noted potential flaws in the original data, I still present it in some detail here.

In its extreme form, the linguistic relativity hypothesis states that language determines thought. An apocryphal (see Pinker, 1994, for history of the myth), but frequently cited, example is that Eskimos have many different words for snow, perhaps because snow is such a salient feature of their environment. Young Eskimos learning the language have their attention called to different types of snow because their language differentiates them. Analogously, modern mainland Americans have many different words for automobile, because the car is so culturally important. Different automobiles may be relatively indiscriminable to traditional Eskimos, as different kinds of snow may be to people raised in a temperate climate. Presumably, though, each could be taught the other's category names, thereby accentuating differences that had been obscure prior to the naming. Thus learning the words, the language, provides a new slant on reality.

A less trivial and thus more interesting influence of language on thought is the way the structures of language shape perception of the world (Whorf, 1956). English's division of words into noun, adjective, and verb classes implies that a scene may be parsed into objects (nouns) separable from descriptive characteristics (found in the separate adjectives) and the actions (verbs) they are undertaking. Although this division may seem real, it is not in nature. Consider, for example, the English words *waterfall* and *brook*. The first, with the object "water" and the action "falling" incorporated into one word, suggests a oneness of object and action producing an object distinctly different from "water" alone. The second implies an object with no inherent action, but all brooks babble, run, meander, and so on.

When one pictures a brook or any other object, there is not object + action + function + color . . . as separate parts. All are imagined at once, but we speakers of English cannot talk about them at once (except in rare words like *waterfall*), which may make us think about them as separate aspects of a scene. According to Whorf, in the Hopi language, objects with short duration (e.g., lightning) or inherent change are classed together with actions, dimming the distinction between object and action, and in the Nootka language, the distinction disappears altogether. Does this suggest a different worldview, one perhaps more inclined to the *Gestalt* (the whole) than a structural parsing of a scene?

Folklorist Roger Welsch (1995) describes a difference between Lakota and English thinking that demonstrates a very ingrained, peculiarly English take on reality. He asks: "Why is my room square? Why are our buildings rectangular? Why are round beds not only peculiar but maybe even a little kinky? Why is a boxing 'ring' square?" (p. 66).

In English our preference for straight is revealed in *straight and narrow* as a metaphor for virtue and *fair and square* as an idiom for honesty. Negative qualities are not straight: Bad guys are *crooked,* confusing is *throwing a curve ball,* and a crazy person is *loopy,* gestured by circling the ear. *A square peg in a round hole* was, according to Welsch, a positive quality: Originally, and literally, driving a square peg into a round hole ensured solid barn construction and, metaphorically, the expression meant someone who "refuses to go the easy route and thereby ensures the strength of the union." The expression has evolved a negative aura, consistent with the metaphors of English; now it refers to someone who does not fit in, and may be said equally grammatically as a round peg in a square hole.

Now, with respect to Whorf, we can ask, is there something natural in assuming straight as perfection? Quoting Welsch again,

> I once asked an Omaha friend about the straight arrow metaphor for virtue; he laughed, saying this is a perfect example of how two peoples can see the same thing differently: "The white man sees only that an arrow goes to its target, not wavering from side to side; we Indians see an arrow's flight in its other dimension, as it rises from the bow and falls to its target." (p. 66)

And for *me,* this example certainly indicated that language affects thought, perception, and memory: Not until I read it did I realize that every arrow I had ever seen fly had an arced path! Welsch speculates that

> an obsession with straight lines and right angles [has] become a "straight" jacket that restricts our ability to see the world in other terms, to observe through the eyes of those who see the world in circles, arcs and globes? What happens when we find ourselves in a culture where round is the rule; where, for example, it is not the cross that symbolizes religious understanding but the nested, curved commas that are yin and yang [or the great mandala, the circle of life]? (p. 66)

We might also look at distinctions made in other languages, which are glossed over in English. ASL uses a pronounlike system, called *classifiers,* in which object categories may be referred to very generally in terms of shape. So while there are specific signs for the objects pencil and needle, either could also be referred to by a long-thin classifier. Does this focus attention on shape (the ropelike tail of the elephant)? Many languages (e.g., French, Spanish, Italian) use a gender system, of varying complexity, in which object words are assigned to a "masculine" or "feminine" class, with masculine or feminine pronouns accordingly assigned. (French, for instance, assigns car to one class and train, boat, and plane to another. Car shares gender with window, street, and ocean.) Do referents of words of the same gender appear more similar to speakers of such languages than to us, for whom the language does not so group the objects?

As support for linguistic relativity, Whorf found many differences among cultures that are also reflected in differences among the languages of the cultures. This discovery does not necessarily imply that language changes cultures, but could

---

Box 2.3. Relation of Word Meaning and Reality

— *Underspecification problem:* Scenes are complex, and simply by using a word in connection with a scene, one cannot tell to which aspect of the scene the word refers.

— *Metalanguage:* Language that refers to language phenomena.

— *Concrete* versus *abstract:* Concrete words refer to aspects of reality that are knowable through the senses (e.g., *red, hard, cat*). Abstract words refer to concepts that reflect generalizations or outgrowths of concrete words (e.g., *liberty, redundancy, idea*).

— *Content* versus *function words:* Content words have clear referents and substantive meaning (generally nouns, verbs, adjectives, and adverbs). Function words serve grammatical uses, "gluing" content words together (prepositions, conjunctions, helping verbs).

— *Literal* versus *figurative:* Literal language can be taken at face value; its meaning is its denotation. Figurative language requires application and extension of the literal meaning to a new situation.

— *Linguistic relativity hypothesis:* In its strong form, it states that language shapes thinking, so that users of different languages necessarily see the world differently. In its weak form, it states that languages reflect the cultural perceptions of their users so that different thoughts and different language patterns arise from different cultures.

---

mean that different cultures or thought patterns are reflected in language, the weak form of the linguistic relativity hypothesis. As Lakoff and Johnson point out, in our culture "time is money," a linguistic metaphor that is such a central construct in the culture that our lives are structured around not wasting time, saving time, spending time wisely, and so on. Is this language affecting thought, or are both language and thought reflecting a salient convention of the culture? As we shall see in Chapter 3, there is evidence that distinctions made readily in the language "are nearer the top of the cognitive deck—more likely to be used in ordinary perception, more available for expectancies and inventions" (Brown, 1958, p. 236) than those describable only by circumlocution.

STRUCTURE OF MEANING IN LINGUISTIC ANALYSIS

As I said in Chapter 1, linguists approach language structurally, searching for patterns that reflect productive use of components of language and then organizing the components into a system. Our discussion of meaning in words, of the semantic system, has concentrated on philosophical and literary distinctions and analyses but has already employed linguistic analyses. These include our discussion of parts of speech (nouns, verbs, and so on), in which words are categorized in terms of the types of things they reference (things, actions) or, more precisely, as we shall see in Chapter 4, in terms of how they function in combination with other words in phrases and sentences. Similarly, our analysis of words into the categories of "content" and "function" is a linguistic distinction, classifying words again according to patterns of use in combinations.

Finally, and most differently, Lakoff and Johnson's analysis, fraught with deep philosophical implications for the organization of thought, is a linguistic one. Note how they organize what might appear to be unrelated creative expressions around a single theme (love = journey). The theme suggests a structure in the language, is predictive of new expressions likely to come into being, and simplifies description of the language, because all love-journey expressions can now be referred to by theme rather than by individual listing.

The issue of the relationship of language to reality divides linguists (and philosophers) into two camps. In the first are "pure" linguists, who

> seek to describe the structure of a sentence IN ISOLATION FROM ITS POSSIBLE SETTINGS IN LINGUISTIC DISCOURSE (WRITTEN OR VERBAL) OR IN NON-LINGUISTIC CONTEXTS (SOCIAL OR PHYSICAL). (Katz & Fodor, 1963, p. 173)

and who see

> the domains of meaning and use [as] different. Meaning is an inherent aspect of the grammatical structure of expression and sentence types (like their grammmatical form). Thus, facts about these properties and relations such as synonymy, meaning-fulness, etc. are also inherent aspects of the grammatical structure of linguistic types. (Katz, 1990, p. 44)

For these linguists, semantic meaning is systematic and *should* be *logical,* that is, it should map to formal logical relations such as identity, contradiction, and implication. Logic is "pure reason and absolute truth," perhaps innate. It is seen as dictating concept formation, the mental structure of reality, and semantic descriptions of it. Logic therefore should underlie the structure of language. Semantics, as a science, should be able to account for those truths inherent in the meaning of terms in the language, *analytic truths,* for which we do not have to look outside the language for verification (Katz, 1990).

In language we see identity in *synonymy* or *paraphrase* (same meaning in a word or phrase), contradiction in *antonymy* (opposite meaning), and implication in if-then sentences or in presupposition (e.g., "my husband" presupposes or implies that I am married). Other semantic properties expressible by logic include ambiguity and anomaly. In *ambiguity* a word (or phrase) maps to more than one meaning. In *anomaly,* or nonsense, a word group contains inherent contradictions.

Most important, given a word group, a logic-based system should be able to select the appropriate reading for an ambiguous unit, through the logical intersection of meaning of words used together. For example, the sentence "The bill is large" is ambiguous: It can refer either to a beak or to money owed. "The duck's bill is large" is less ambiguous: The only intersection of the sets of meaning components underlying each of "duck" and "bill" is "bird" for the beak meaning of "bill," selecting that reading.

Among the linguists who believe that the semantic system follows logical principles, there are again two schools. One school, led by Chomsky, holds, as I said in Chapter 1, that recovery of language principles is recovery of principles of the mind and brain. Under this conception, logic is an innate property of mind that must be reflected in linguistic structure. In contrast, another group, including Katz (1990), terms "the naturalist fallacy" this attribution of biological properties to an inherently nonbiological system. To Katz, semantic meaning reflects logic because meaning is a logical *abstraction,* not because the brain itself is logical.

Regardless of this difference in attribution of cause, the two views are united in seeing the semantic system as logical and the boundaries of the study of meaning in language for linguistics as those meaning relations that reflect logic. This leaves out of the range of semantics general world knowledge, context, speaker's intent, and so on.

In contrast, the other group of linguists and philosophers, whom I will call "the conversationalists," stress the social and physical contexts in which language is produced as *central* to the semantic system of the language (see Austin, 1965; Grice, 1989). We come to understand meanings and relationships among words through their use, their effects on the people we are speaking to and the feedback we get from them, and their regular associations with other words. Understanding the semantic system cannot be accomplished devoid of context: Word or phrase meaning stems from the intention of the speaker and the speaker's understanding of how to produce a desired effect in the listener. It is only after experience in concrete context-rich and feedback-rich situations that we learn to understand abstract sentences devoid of context.

As an example, reconsider my children's first single-word utterances, "cat" and "Eric." I interpreted those words as conveying the sentences "There's a cat" or "There's Eric." Obviously, my interpretation was informed in part by my sharing a context with my child, such as a room into which a cat had just wandered. In all likelihood, my response would have included excitement (remember this was the first word) and agreement either directly ("That's right, there's a cat") or indirectly ("Hi, Eric"). The shared context and the response reinforce the comment's appropriateness. According to conversationalists, the language experience in context-rich social situations generalizes eventually to more removed, unshared situations.

Note that the distinction in the positions of the pro-logic linguists and the pro-social conversationalists is a "which came first, the chicken or the egg?" one. The formalists believe either that we must search for systematic logical regularities because semantic meaning is a logical abstraction or because such regularities are inherent to the nature of mind. For them, the inherent abstract logical nature comes first. The conversationalists search for structure in language *and* structure in the social context of the language, attempting to find in the latter an explanatory framework for the former. For them the logical abstraction comes second, derived from social experience.

Linguistic Feature Systems (the Formalists)

Linguists have attempted to demonstrate structure in the semantic system by a *decompositional analysis* of meaning into *features* characteristic of many words

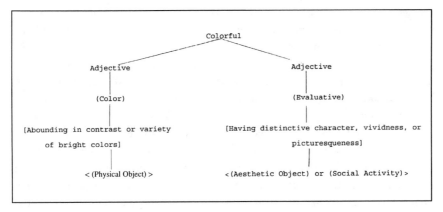

Figure 2.2. Tree Diagram for the Senses of *Colorful*
SOURCE: Adapted from the marker theory of Katz (1963, p. 198).

that combine uniquely to define a given word. One such feature might be "animate" (live, moving), a salient characteristic of the referents of each of my children's first words. "Animate" would be a component of our mental definition of each person we know, all animals and animal groups, and person describers such as "children" or (less animate?) "couch potato." Other features are necessary to distinguish a cat from a person: perhaps size, or leg number, or, because "human" is such an important category for us humans, perhaps a feature of human or not-human. (You might notice that in our discussion so far, we have many different types of features: definitional, such as "animate" or "human"; descriptive, such as "number of legs"; and specific, such as "mouth of a bird." I will say more on these feature types.)

Formally, in an influential theory of semantics, Katz (Katz, 1990; Katz & Fodor, 1963) proposed that a word's meaning is a structured entry in a mental dictionary, as depicted for the word *colorful* in Figure 2.2. This is a *tree diagram,* a common descriptive tool in linguistics. Each potential meaning of the word is a single path (no backtracking) in the tree. As shown here, *colorful* is two-ways ambiguous; that is, there are two branches from the word. Each branch is marked first by the part of speech. Next, in parentheses, are general meaning features, which Katz calls semantic *markers.* Next, in brackets, are features peculiar to the particular word sense intended, idiosyncratic features perhaps found in no other entries in the dictionary. These are called *distinguishers.* Finally, in angled brackets, are features that limit that interpretation in combination with certain other words. These are called *selectional restrictions.*

Now, let us see how such a model permits analytic inferences, as discussed above. First, we have already seen that *homonymy,* a single word with two meanings, or ambiguity, is discovered by following two different paths from the same starting word node. (A *node* in a tree is a point from which a branch might develop. A *terminal node* on a real tree does not have a branch but a leaf; on a tree *diagram,* it has a word.) A word like *vivid* would share much of the marker structure of *colorful* and this shared structure would be what was needed to determine that the two words were synonymous. *Colorless* would also share much of that marker structure, but where *colorful* has "abounding in bright colors," *colorless* would be marked as "*lacking* in bright colors." The *polarity* (i.e., the oppositeness) of "abounding" and "lacking" indicates the oppositeness in word meaning, or antonymy. Knowing that something was colorful implies directly through the marker structure that it was bright or vivid; implication is found directly on the path from the word.

Probably Chomsky's most famous sentence (the only sentence of his listed in *Bartlett's Familiar Quotations,* according to Pinker, 1994) is "Colorless green ideas sleep furiously." Chomsky (1965) used this sentence to illustrate anomaly through violation of selectional restrictions. Because *colorless* has both meanings that *colorful* has—either for a physical or for an aesthetic object—we can use Figure 2.2, substituting "lacking" for "abounding" and "not having" for "having" in the distinguishers. Problems in the famous sentence develop as follows: "Idea" is not a physical object, and therefore selects for the right most branch of the tree. Contained in that branch is the marker "(Evaluative)," meaning a positive or negative characteristic. The marker for "green" would not contain an evaluation—we can have a colorless idea but not a colorless green one. This mismatch creates the first anomaly. (Of course, there are many more. A study question asks you to analyze the others similarly.)

You can see how organizing semantic knowledge in this way permits the determination of analytic truths, the ones derivable from logic and understanding of word meaning alone. The formalists argue that *synthetic* truths, ones that can be proved only by comparing the sentence meaning with a perceived event, are *outside the scope* of linguistic theory. "An elephant is big" is analytic, because the largeness is likely included in the marker structure for *elephant.* "That elephant is small" is synthetic: Its truth can be determined only by looking at *that* elephant and judging it relative to other species members.

This example raises the question of which features to include in the marker description and which features belong in the realm of "synthetic" knowledge or experience. From a formal stance, the "nicest" features are polar opposites: pleasant-unpleasant, hot-cold, animate-inanimate. The marker is some abstraction between the two (evaluative would be the marker for pleasant and unpleasant) with words marked as + or − with respect to this feature (+ evaluative = pleasant). Polar oppositions categorize lexical items into three groups: +, −, and unspecified.

But most features are not so neat. An animal that is "not-insect" is also not well defined (mammal? bird? reptile? bacterium?): There are so many different kinds of animals and they do not divide "analytically." Witness the change in "structure trees" for the animal kingdom since Darwin. Pre-Darwin trees had people apart from all animals; modern trees have a "marker" of "primate" that includes people, monkeys, and apes (chimpanzees, gorillas, and orangutans). From time to time, as molecular-genetic tests develop, the branches on the primate node have shifted, with people sharing a branch with one or the other of the great apes. (Current science does not separate people from the others.) The post-Darwinian ordering, and certainly the latest modern ordering, is not the most intuitive "analysis." On the basis of which features should animals be grouped?

Another thing to notice is the subtlety of the semantic distinctions we do make. Years ago I tried to program a marker structure for a limited vocabulary. The output of the program was "possible sentences." Most of the possible sentences, in my view, were neither truths nor lovely contradictions like the "colorless green" sentence but were just off, in hard-to-specify ways. Consider, for example, "The flagpole lying on the ground is tall." A flagpole *should* have "tall" as a distinguishing feature. But "tall" needs to be vertical with respect to the ground; the flagpole sentence is strange, because *that* flagpole would be "long," not "tall." So we need a feature specifying vertical for tall and horizontal for long. But those features cannot be incorporated into the marker structures for the objects, because the object position can change: We must establish the position synthetically, by looking at the object. Yet including the feature at least in the tall-long dichotomy establishes a regularity of use.

As these examples illustrate, one problem with the marker model is in the determination of features to include in it. A second problem is in its characterization of metaphor. Note that in the marker model, we have two choices for interpretation of metaphor. One is to build the metaphoric reading into the marker. We could, in fact, argue that the evaluative sense of *colorful* or *colorless* is, or at one time was, metaphoric. The second is to conclude that a new metaphor *cannot* be interpreted because, by definition, it must contain a selection-restriction violation or anomaly. Consider *colorless green* as a figure of speech, for instance. To me, it means a dull green. At one time *hot pink* would have been similarly anomalous, with *hot* restricted to things with "temperature" and *pink* to things with "color." Traditional models of figurative language understanding, based on these kinds of formalisms, assume that metaphor arises only after a literal interpretation is attempted and proven anomalous. However, there is almost no evidence that suggests that we do process literal meanings first (see Gibbs, 1994, and Chapter 3).

Fuzzy Systems

The marker system of describing semantic organization is easy to criticize because it is very well specified. As we did in the preceding section, we can argue about details, such as whether animate is a good general feature, how much *extralinguistic knowledge* (knowledge not given in the language itself but based on real experience, like the position of the flagpole) needs to be included, and how to deal with apparent falsehoods, figurative language, from the model's standpoint. In science, precise specification is a desirable feature of a theory or model because (a) a precise model helps us truly organize our thoughts about the subject being modeled, and (b) a precise model is testable and can easily be falsified. (It seems odd at first to want a model to be falsifiable, but a model's strength comes from withstanding such tests!) We have already looked at some tests of the model that

---

Box 2.4. Logic in Language

— *Analytic* versus *synthetic:* An analytic statement can be verified by language properties alone. A synthetic statement also requires observation of reality.
— *Identity in language:* Synonymy and paraphrase.
— *Negation in language:* Antonymy (opposites).
— *Implication in language:* Entailment (if X is a cat, X is an animal) or presupposition ("your husband" presupposes you are female and married).
— *Ambiguity:* Homonymy (one word with two or more meanings) or double meaning.
— *Anomaly:* Nonsense, multiple contradictions, word groupings that violate selectional restrictions.
— *Tree diagram:* Represents a word's meanings as branches on a tree, with nodes labeled with part-of-speech, general meaning features (markers), features idiosyncratic to that word's meaning (distinguishers), and features necessary in words it can combine with (selectional restrictions). Logical properties can be derived from the tree.

---

reveal weaknesses (its dealing with figurative language). In this section we will look at another such test, and then at alternative models.

The strength of the marker model is its solid structure; that is what makes it clear and testable. Its downfall is also its solid structure: Our language use and meaning organization seem to be more flexible than the marker model allows. Consider, for example, following Lakoff (1972, 1973), English's use of *hedges,* modifiers that limit the application of a word's meaning, such as *technically speaking* or *loosely speaking.* The following sentences containing such hedges (the italicized bits) are true but would be hard to verify given a marker model:

> Coral *is* red *and not* red.
> *Loosely speaking,* a whale is a fish.
> *Technically speaking,* tomatoes are fruit and rhubarb is a vegetable.
> Politicians are *regular* chameleons.

(To make sure we share meanings here: Coral is a color between red and orange; a whale is technically a mammal but lives in the water, swims, and so on, resembling a fish; technically, fruits are the seed-bearing parts of plants and vegetables are leaves, stems, and roots, regardless of how they are used in cuisine; a chameleon is an animal whose protective defense is changing skin color to suit a situation.)

The question is this: How can the hedge signal which parts of the structured definition we should use? Take the whale sentence: "Loosely speaking, a whale is a fish" tells us to apply roughly half of our whale knowledge, and "Technically speaking, a whale is a mammal" tells us to apply roughly the other half, but nowhere within the marker structure are technical and loose characteristics marked.

Box 2.5. Language Is *Not* Logic

— Categories have fuzzy boundaries.
— Hedges (such as "technically speaking") specify a *degree* of belonging to a category or of truth; truths in language are not *absolute*.
— Figurative language on the surface is anomalous but is not so viewed, even at first.
— Extralinguistic knowledge is synthetic but necessary nonetheless for meaning. A flagpole is "tall" or "long" depending on how it is oriented, which we cannot know through language alone.

"I'M ON THE VERGE OF A MAJOR BREAKTHROUGH, BUT I'M ALSO AT THAT POINT WHERE CHEMISTRY LEAVES OFF AND PHYSICS BEGINS, SO I'LL HAVE TO DROP THE WHOLE THING."

Figure 2.3. Boundaries (© 1997 by Sydney Harris.)

NOTE: To what extent are absolute boundaries between categories reasonable? Is the scientist here too absolute?

One way to deal with this is to mark features as *defining* (which would be technical) or *characteristic* (which would be typical but not necessary). Or we could blur category descriptions so that they are probabilistic rather than absolute. (The scientist in Figure 2.3 is an absolutist.) The probabilisticness arises in part from the

Figure 2.4. A True Child Anecdote Reflecting the Fuzziness of Word Categories

NOTE: Here, the defining feature for the child apparently is size. She said, "Look Mommy, doggie," for a distant St. Bernard, followed by, when it got nearer, "No Mommy, horsie." (Artwork rendered by James J. Kempster; used by permission.)

underspecification problem: Words and scenes overlap but are not identical, and so each time a word is used, it is to a different reality. Realities for which the word is *typical* overlap a lot and constitute its core "meaning." Realities that share some properties with the typical ones evoke the word, but less completely, allowing hedges.

The normal, or bell, curve represents a probability distribution of typicality. Adult female height is normally distributed with a peak at about 5'5". The peak means that most women are around 5'5" tall. Of course, there are women much shorter and much taller—the dip in the curve from around that average value indicates how infrequently shorter and taller heights occur as one gets more distant from the average.

Now consider figuratively a "normal curve" for the word *dog*. For most of us, the average "dog" is a house pet of average (like a labrador or setter) size, average tail length, short haired, and of nondistinctive color (brown/black). Coyotes or wolves are atypical because they are wild; toy poodles, because of their size; sheepdogs, because of their hair length. The atypicality allows you to understand (i.e., verify these as truths):

> A sheepdog is a regular mop.
> Technically speaking, a coyote is a dog.
> (Or the situation in Figure 2.4, which is a real child's observation.)

A famous quotation from Wittgenstein (1973) illustrates the probabilistic nature of another word concept, "games." It also illustrates the shortcomings of the characteristic-defining feature distinction: As you read the passage, try to develop some defining features for "game":

> Consider for example the proceedings that we call "games." I mean board-games, card-games, ball-games, Olympic games, and so on. What is common to them all?—Don't say: "There *must* be something common, or they would not be called 'games' "— but *look and see* whether there is something common to all. — For if you look at them you will not see something that is common to *all,* but similarities, relationships, and a whole series of them at that. . . . And the result of this examination is: we see a complicated network of similarities and criss-crossing: sometimes overall similarities, sometimes similarities of detail.
>
> I can think of no better expression to characterize these similarities than "family resemblances"; for the various resemblances between members of the family: build, features, colour of eyes, gait, temperament, etc. etc. overlap and criss-cross in the same way. . . . One might say the concept "game" is a concept with blurred edges. (pp. 31-34)

I have presented two alternatives to the marker model: a feature model in which word meaning consists of characteristic and defining features, and a typicality model, in which word meaning derives from generalizations based on experiences. Both alternatives depict meaning less rigidly than did the marker model. Instead of focused, sharp definitions, we have blurred ones, sharp perhaps for typical instances, but *fuzzy* around the edges, the atypical instances. These characterizations are therefore sometimes called *fuzzy meaning* models. They account for some of the difficulties encountered by the marker model, and because they allow us to verify sentences in which some, but not all, of a word's meaning applies, that is, hedged or figurative language, they capture a regularity, or system in meaning. They are not as well specified as the marker model, which, despite shortcomings, still captures regularities of meaning organization. So, both models are helpful to describe meaning in language, that is, semantics.

Recovering Speaker Intents: Speech Acts, Conversation Logic, Pragmatics

My dictionary begins its entry on *meaning* with "1. That which exists in the mind, view or contemplation as a settled aim or purpose; that which is meant or intended to be done; intent; purpose; aim; object."

It explains that this is "archaic" but only secondarily does it give as *meaning*'s meaning, "sense," "that which is denoted," and so on. The entry's organization implies that the first meaning of *meaning* was "aim" and "purpose."

Words (and sentences) occur in contexts, usually conversational ones, in which a speaker is trying to accomplish something by the speech. A conversation is, in a way, a negotiation in which the participants are together trying to come to an understanding or to accomplish some goal. Several linguistic analyses of meaning look for systematicity in language through conversational goals and in how they serve to structure the dialogue—indeed, how they affect word selection by the speaker and word understanding by the listener.

The cooperative principle. The idea that conversation participants are mutually trying to achieve an understanding or accomplish a goal is the underlying tenet of the *cooperative principle* (Grice, 1989, pp. 22-40, "Logic and Conversation," and pp. 41-57, "Further Notes on Logic and Conversation"). This necessitates that participants make their contributions to the conversation

1. as informative as is necessary, but not more informative;
2. true;
3. relevant; and
4. clear, unambiguous, and brief.

To accomplish this a speaker must correctly assess what listeners need to hear so as to understand as well as where they might get confused.

An example of how this affects conversational choices is provided by my son, Alexander, at age $4\frac{1}{2}$. Some friends had been sleeping over. To each late riser, he announced the order of awakening of the earlier risers: "I got up first, then Eric, then Joel, then Seth, then my Daddy." As one of the last risers, I heard him say this several times before he said it to me. When he told me, he repeated it just as he had earlier, but then corrected himself: ". . . then Seth, then my Daddy, I mean, then Daddy." Alexander, at a very young age, was aware that he and Mommy shared a frame of reference for "Daddy," a specific individual, who, to other people, required more complete identification by Alexander as "my Daddy."

A judgment of what information a hearer *needs* involves a judgment of what the hearer already knows, what the hearer wants, and what the best way is to provide the hearer with the information. These are considerations of pragmatics, from the speaker's stance—what is practical to say. (There are pragmatic considerations from the listener's stance also; knowledge of patterns of language use in context give the hearer a frame of reference for interpreting what the speaker is saying.) If we are giving people directions, for instance, we try to use as landmarks salient properties of the landscape. Telling someone that the drugstore is next to the Empire State Building will help locate the drugstore. Telling someone that the Empire State Building is the one next to the drugstore is not equally useful (unless the person, for example, owns the drugstore): If they cannot find the Empire State Building, they are unlikely to be able to find the drugstore. Cooperativeness requires supplying appropriate frames of reference (enough information) and deleting redundant ones.

Belief in the cooperative principle in conversation permits appreciation of sarcasm. In this device, speakers say nearly the opposite of what they mean and, for the most part, listeners quickly perceive the meaning. Someone is throwing rocks at people and gets the comment, "Real nice behavior." This can be correctly interpreted only if both speaker and hearer consider the behavior not nice and know that they share this view; then the truth principle suggests that the literal meaning of the comment cannot be the speaker's intent. The opposite meaning prevails, according to Grice, because it is related to the literal meaning and is relevant—and because presumably both participants are familiar with the device. To use and understand sarcasm, the speaker and hearer must share necessary knowledge about the situation and about sarcasm.

Similarly, Grice applies a cooperative principle to understanding metaphor. In this case too, the metaphor user, on the surface, is claiming a falsehood or impossibility (e.g., camels are the ships of the desert—but we know camels are not ships). The hearer recognizes the impossibility, assumes cooperation, and understands the sentence by analogy. (Like the formalists' view of meaning, this implies that metaphor is understood only after a literal interpretation is tried and fails, which I have observed is not empirically supported.)

For adults, who share considerable knowledge about the world, the cooperative principle dictates that many things be left unsaid, and yet, what is unsaid imparts its meaning to the utterance. Grice (1989, pp. 22-40, "Logic and Conversation") gives the following examples:

1. A: I am out of petrol.

   B: There is a garage around the corner.
2. A: Smith doesn't seem to have a girlfriend.

   B: He has been paying a lot of visits to New York lately.

In the first example, if B is cooperative, he or she is also suggesting that he or she believes the garage is open for business and has gas. For A to ask, "Is it open?" would be inappropriate, unless A has some reason to believe that it is not. In the second example, B is implying that Smith is visiting a girl in New York. Although this is not said, the implication follows from the principle of being relevant.

Finally, the cooperative principle underscores why some people are seen as pedantic, repetitious, or annoyingly enigmatic. They refuse to cooperate, supplying too much or too little information, and refuse to recognize the shared knowledge.

Speech acts. Wittgenstein (1973) lists the following purposes of language:

> Giving orders, and obeying them — Describing the appearance of an object from a description (a drawing) — Reporting an event — Speculating about an event — Forming and testing a hypothesis — Presenting the results of an experiment in tables and diagrams — Making up a story; and reading it — Play-acting — Singing catches — Guessing riddles — Making a joke; telling it — Solving a problem in practical arithmetic — Translating from one language to another — Asking, thinking, cursing, greeting, praying. (pp. 11-12)

Each of these constitutes a purpose in speaking, or a speech act. This is not an exhaustive list. There is also, at least, requesting information, making a promise, requesting something from someone else, offering something.

What is interesting from a linguistic standpoint is that the speaker's purpose may not be directly stated. Listener understanding of meaning in an utterance is, in part, recovering intent, and in part, recovering sense. Linguists must determine how each is accomplished.

Speech act theory emerged from the writings of Austin (1965), in which an utterance is looked at from three separate stances. The first, as a *locution,* is its consequence to the speaker: The speaker makes the utterance. The second, as an *illocution,* is the transactional effect between speaker and hearer: The speaker says something to someone. The third, as a *perlocution,* is the consequence of the utterance to the hearer, the hearer's reaction. Austin gives as an example of this my telling you, "There is a spider on your lap." The locution is that I have said something; the illocution is that I have told you something; the perlocution is that I have frightened you.

As developed by Searle, speech act theory (see, for example, Searle, 1975; Searle, Kiefer, & Bierwisch, 1980) analyzes utterances into components of *illocutionary force* (the intent of the utterance as a statement, an order, a question, or the like) and *propositional content* (what it is that is being asked, ordered, or stated). Illocutionary force may be *direct,* as in "Open the window, please," in which the speaker is politely ordering the person to open the window. It can be direct and explicit, as in "I order you to open the window please." Or, and most interesting, it can be *indirect,* as in "Do you think you could open the window?"

This is the most interesting because, as with metaphor and sarcasm, a formal analysis of the sense of the words, of the propositional content, suggests that the speaker is only asking whether someone is *capable* of doing something. The direct answer to this question is "yes," as it is to the common queries, "Do you have a watch?" or "Could you pass the salt?" Occasionally (frequently in my family) someone will respond literally, answering "yes" in an attempt to be humorous, and only after a short pause will they comply with the implicit (indirect, implied) request for action. The humor arises from the mutual understanding that getting an answer is *not* the speaker's purpose but is linguistically possible.

Speech act theory examines how illocutionary force is projected in the language, especially in the conditions where it is indirectly conveyed. The answer begins with the cooperative principle discussed in the previous section: Conversation participants are trying to achieve a mutual understanding and common goal; utterances will be informative, true, to the point, and so on. In an indirect request, the hearer can infer that the speaker either knows the answer (I am strong enough and capable of opening a window) or would have no interest in the answer (Why would a stranger care whether I had a watch?). Therefore, if the speaker is *truly* interested and *to the point,* the utterance must refer to something related to the propositional content but not be what it literally conveys.

Note how the illocutionary force changes dramatically for "Do you have a watch?" if the question is posed by an armed robber who has just appropriated wallet and other jewelry, or if it is a shattered and taped window about which someone asks, "Can you open the window?" In these cases the situation makes it possible that the request for information, in fact, is the speaker's intent. And,

---

Box 2.6. Other Models of Meaning

— *Feature model:* Different kinds of features contribute to meaning: defining (necessary) and characteristic (typical).

— *Family resemblance/fuzzy meaning:* A category is not strictly defined but is like a probability distribution. Prototypical members share many features; atypical members share few.

— *Speech acts:* Meaning takes into account the conversational context or speaker's purpose (illocutionary force), the effect on the hearer (perlocutionary force), as well as the propositional content (locutionary force).

— *Cooperative principle and pragmatics:* Utterances are made assuming that the speaker and hearer share the common purpose of achieving understanding. They should be truthful, informative, and to the point. These "musts" must be taken into account in interpreting utterances.

---

ironically, we understand the robber's request correctly because we, even in such a hostile situation, assume *cooperative* conversational principles.

Because understanding the situation and what the speaker knows, could want, and so on is extralinguistic, Searle (1975) questions whether illocutionary force is susceptible to standard linguistic analyses. As we have seen, there are instances where understanding a given indirect request may require it to be mapped to a nonverbal context, and thus these are out of the domain of linguistics. However, many of the examples of indirect requests Searle gives are *fixed patterns* in the language. Because the form, situation, and typical response co-occur, there is ample opportunity to learn their association. So "Can you?" could carry two meanings in English: (a) Are you able to? (answer = yes/no) and (b) Will you? (response: do it, promise to do it, say yes and do it, or say no and why not). As with other ambiguities, which of these, which branch of a marker tree, is selected depends on factors outside the given utterance—other linguistic contexts or extralinguistic information.

Note that I have added a component of illocutionary force, the cooperative response, to the definition of the word. Speech act analyses make clear the necessity of adding an intent component to the sense component of the "meaning" of an utterance.

Morphemes, Cases: Is the Word the Unit of Meaning?

This chapter has addressed the issue of how language conveys meaning. I have focused on word meaning partly because we share a reference frame (and reference book—the dictionary) for accessing meaning at the word level. We have looked a bit at phrase meanings (seeing red, in the bag, at a crossroads, and so on) when a phrase means more or something other than its component words. A dictionary too lists the occasional phrase, idioms, to define. And we have also seen instances in which it is clear that there is meaning in *part* of a word ("poly" = many → *polyblob*), "s" as a suffix marking plural, or the bits of meaning contained in sound symbolism.

A dictionary will list some of these, suffixes and prefixes, for which it defines meaning and use.

In this section we formally consider alternatives to the word as unit of meaning. Following the structuralist bent of this chapter, we are looking at atoms of meaning in word *parts,* if you will, a systematic marker structure for a minimal unit of meaning, the morpheme. We are also looking for standard patterns of meaning in morpheme combinations. An idiom does not constitute a standard pattern: It is a unit of meaning by itself, often indivisible (see Chapter 3 and Gibbs, 1994, for counterexamples). Here we will consider the possibility for meaning markers to emerge through normal phrase structure.

Morphology. The morpheme is defined as the smallest unit of language that has meaning. A whole word can be a morpheme, but sometimes morphemes are smaller than a word and can be combined, creating new words. In the last sentence we see morphemes composing words in small+er, some+time+s, creat+ing, and morph (= structure) + eme (= unit). For each language, and across languages, "morphology" is the study of the structural, meaning-given components of words.

Analogous to content and function words, there are two kinds of morphemes: free morphemes and bound morphemes. A *free morpheme* is one that can stand on its own, a word. A *bound morpheme* is one affixed to other morphemes to color the meaning or function of the word. If a bound morpheme affixes to the front, it is called a *prefix,* such as "pre" in *prefix*; if it affixes to the back, it is a *suffix,* such as "ology" in *morphology.* (There are languages that put bound morphemes in the middle; these morphemes are called *infixes.* It does not happen regularly in English, but there is a British slang infix: *abso-bloody-lutely,* in which the infix is a free, not a bound, morpheme.) Some bound morphemes convey content, like "ology" (study of) or "pre" (before). Some bound morphemes convey function, such as the suffix "ly," which turns a noun modifier (*pretty* in "pretty song") into a verb modifier (*prettily* in "sings prettily").

A second distinction between morpheme types is made in the way a bound morpheme affects a word. *Derivational* morphemes either add meaning, such as "poly," "oid," or "ology," or change the part of speech of the word, its function in the sentence. *Inflectional* morphemes add a different kind of meaning and constitute a more normal, less creative, process in the language. Examples include the plural morpheme "s," which can be added to many nouns to indicate more than one, or the morpheme "ed," which is regularly applied to verbs to mark the past tense.

We have previously seen some ways in which new words come into being. One is the combining of derivational morphemes, as in *polyblob* and *amoeboid.* Another word-making process we have seen occurs when a figurative extension of an expression becomes commonplace (e.g., *seeing red*). This is *lexical innovation,* language growth through the novel extension of free morphemes to a new situation. Gerrig and Gibbs (1988) cite someone "doing a Napoleon for the camera" and "a Nixon on the tapes." Each of these takes a salient image of a public figure and amusingly extends it to a new situation (incidentally, using a "proper name" not as a deictic reference). Less creative, but still an innovation, is a change in part of speech, as when my son Alexander at age 5 explained he had "scissored" something.

A new word-making process to consider involves combining free morphemes, *compounding*. In a true compound, as in a dead metaphor, the individual components originating the expression partially lose their identities. Thus no one sees a contradiction in having and discussing "a green blackboard." I have heard someone ask for a "five-by-seven three-by-five card" (but I thought it was funny, so *three-by-five card* is not quite a true compound synonymous with *index card* for me).

I want to mention one other word-creation process, backformation, because it illustrates compellingly that average people, not only supersensitive linguists, are aware of morphology as an active language process. In *backformation* a word is created through the *incorrect* assumption of morphological structure. The word *edit* was backformed from *editor*. Some hearer assumed an *editor* was "one who edits" as an *actor* is "one who acts" or a *narrator* is "one who narrates." Only in this case *edit* was formed by "*editor* minus 'or'," backformed, rather than the other way.

A more recent, active backformation producing a new bound morpheme is the suffix "gate," meaning scandal. Since the 1970s we have seen "Billygate" (involving a scandal with then-President Jimmy Carter's brother, Billy), "Irangate" (with then-President Ronald Reagan's arms-for-hostages [held in Iran] illicit dealings), and more recently "Whitewatergate," with President and Mrs. Clinton's suspected financial infelicities with the Whitewater real estate deal. Now, "Whitewatergate" not only uses "gate" as scandal, but is a pun, for those of us who remember the origin of "gate." Watergate began with the illegal election strategies of then-President Nixon's campaign team, which included the burglary of the "Watergate Hotel." The "Watergate" scandal was not a scandal involving water, like "Irangate" was a scandal involving Iran, or Whitewatergate was a scandal involving Whitewater. Watergate came to stand for all scandals, and the scandal meaning infused the last syllable.

What I find interesting about backformation is the fact that the structure inference is *in*correct. The mistake suggests a two-stage active process: the misapplication of meaning to a word part (which, in the case of *editor*, could be because it sounds like the "or" meaning person-doing [as in aviator], but there is no morpheme meaning scandal that sounds like "gate") and the *assumption of a productive morphological process like suffixing*.

Thus *derivational* morphology is alive and well in English, as you can see. However, compared with other languages, English's use of *inflectional* morphology is quite restrained. To a large extent we combine function words with content words (in a fixed order)—making a phrase—to convey meanings that other languages convey by affixing inflectional morphemes to a word. For instance, Pinker (1994, p. 127) cites the Kevunjo (Bantu) word *Naikimlyia,* meaning "he is eating it for her." The eight parts of this word are "N," marking the word as the conversation's focus; "a," a gender marker for the subject; "i," a present-tense marker; "ki," a gender marker for the object; "m," a gender marker for the benefactor; "lyi," the verb; "i," a marker indicating the presence of a benefactor; and "a," a sentence mood

---

Box 2.7. Where Do Words Come From?

— Figurative extension of an old word
— New combination of old (bound or bound-with-free) morphemes
— Compounding or combination of free morphemes into new units
— Backformation or simplification of (falsely) perceived morphological structure
— Borrowing or taking a word from another language

---

indicator. Benefactors, subjects, and objects exemplify *cases,* conveyed in English by phrases. We look next at meanings in phrases, recognizing that a phrase unit of meaning in English might be a word or morpheme unit of meaning in another language.

Case grammar or semantic relations. Consider the sentences:

1a. John was killed with a gun.

1b. A gun killed John.

1c. John was killed by means of a gun.

and

2a. John went to the park with a gun.

2b. John went to the park with a bad attitude.

2c. John went to the park with his brother.

2d. John went to the park with a statue.

In the first set, the meaning of "gun-as-instrument-of-death" is conveyed in three different ways (and, in a fourth way, in quotes in this sentence). In the second set, the words *park with* are repeated, but the phrases following *with* have a very different meaning relation, or *semantic relation,* to John's going. In 2a, *with* introduces an "instrument", the same instrument as in all the sentences in 1. In 2b, *with* introduces the "manner" of John's going; in 2c, it introduces a nonactive participant or *patient;* and in 2d, it introduces an identifying feature of the park, thereby indicating its *location.* Each semantic relation is given in a phrase, is an important part of the sentence's sense, and could be specified, as in the first set of sentences, in different words. In some languages, as in the Bantu language mentioned above, or in classical Latin, these relations are indicated by regular morphological change to the word rather than by constructing a phrase. Such languages use a *case* grammar; the morphological changes are *case markers* or, simply, *cases.*

English once was a case language, and we see its vestiges in our pronouns. *He, she, I, we, they* can only be sentence subjects, or *agents.* If the same people are patients or *recipients* (receivers of the action, as in "I gave a gun *to John*" or "I gave *him* a gun"), the pronouns change form, respectively, to *him, her, me, us,* and *them.*

Box 2.8. The Unit of Meaning

— Morphemes = smallest unit of meaning in a language
  — Free morphemes = indivisible words, can stand alone
  — Bound morphemes = meaning units that exist only as parts of words
  — Prefix, suffix, infix = bound morphemes attached, respectively, to the beginning, end, or middle of the word
  — Derivational morpheme = "content"-carrying morpheme
  — Inflectional morpheme = morpheme marking grammatical features such as plural, case, or tense
— Semantic relation or case = meaning that arises from a combination of words or morphemes with others: "John" refers to someone but within a phrase could be the agent of an action, the patient of an action, the recipient of an action, and so on.
— A word can be a unit or combination of units of meaning

Rather than undergoing such radical changes, they could change suffixes, as we do in the *possessive,* adding "'s." This is what happens in Latin: farmer-as-agent is *agricola,* farmer as patient is *agricolam,* and farmer as possessor is *agricolae.* We see the same changes in endings in the Latin for *woman—femina, feminam, feminae*—as the case changes. In current English we do have a suffix marking agent and a different suffix marking patient, "er" and "ee," as in the *payer* and the *payee.* This is somewhat different from the Latin in that either suffix is applied to a *verb,* changing it to a noun and then marking its case, and also in that it is the only such productive case morphology. But note that it is productive; you can easily understand *neologisms* (new words) such as *driver-drivee, helper-helpee,* or *praiser-praisee.*

In a case language, part of the marker for each word includes the semantic relations that that word could enter into, perhaps as part of the selectional restrictions. As part of the morphological system of the language, the senses that the case endings (or beginnings or infixes) could impart would be an important component of the inflectional structure. Therefore it seems appropriate to treat semantic relations in a chapter on meaning, although we will return to discussion of cases in syntax as we discuss how English establishes cases through word order and word combination.

Before ending our discussion of case in English, it is worthwhile considering whether the function words used to mark particular cases are arbitrary: Does *with* have an underlying sense that it imparts to "with a statue," "with a gun," "with an attitude," and "with his brother," despite the obvious differences in the semantic relations of the phrases?

Recall our discussion of Lakoff and Johnson's explanation of the use of the word *in* in sentences like this one. Metaphorically, language is a container and therefore thoughts, words, and so on can be in it. Lakoff and Johnson (1980, p. 135) argued that the particular preposition (with, of, in, on, up, to) in any phrase is no accident. Instruments *are* companions metaphorically, allowing the extension from going to the park with John to going to the park with a gun. As support, they consider the figure of speech *personification* (attributing human features or characteristics to an animal, plant, object, or abstract idea) in a phrase like *me and old Sal, here* where "Sal" is a car (or John's faithful gun). The possibility of seeing an instrument as a companion in such a phrase allows the extension of *with* from a person accompanier to a car or gun accompanier. Similarly an "attitude" can be seen as a metaphorical extension of an item of clothing or body part, which would naturally be "with" John. Finally, in our examples, the park may be personified too, and the statue an accompanier of the park.

SUMMARY AND CONCLUSIONS

In this chapter we examined some philosophical issues concerning the definition of meaning in language and its relation to extralinguistic experience, and then considered how linguists have modeled meaning. Before we began this chapter, it might have seemed that meaning is found in words, is that which is easily accessed in a dictionary, and, as the dictionary directs us, is a mapping of the word to reality. Our discussion should have pointed out that understanding meaning is not that simple. First, semantics, the study of meaning in language, is highly dependent on other aspects of language. Sound symbolism and onomatopoeia show that the sounds used for a word influence its meaning. The cooperative principle and speech act analysis show influences on meaning of the role of language in communication. Pragmatic considerations on word choice and word understanding demonstrate the influence of extralinguistic knowledge on meaning. And morphological analysis and case relations show syntactic influences on meaning.

Even when we try to deal with analytic meanings in words alone, we find that a neat structural description is only partly effective. Several models incorporated the notion of meaning features: Markers or distinguishers are elements of meaning shared by many or few other words; characteristic and defining features differentiate "technical" and "loose" use in the language. But we also saw that language meaning is fuzzier than the structural descriptions allow; we must take into account extralinguistic knowledge for words like *tall* or *long,* and pragmatic knowledge to understand figurative language or sarcasm.

It should be clear that the relationship of meaning in language, thought apart from language, and our perception of reality are intertwined, perhaps inextricably. Words do not merely denote, their meaning also conveys speaker intent and associations with other words—connotation. Thus a particular word choice is a focus on a particular aspect of reality. Those foci may be systematic and different in the thought patterns and linguistic *tropes* (figures of speech) of a particular culture.

It should also be clear that at least some aspects of meaning are systematic in the language and that the systematicity allows analytic inferences and, possibly, quick, productive, seemingly creative uses. The system involves patterns of underlying features, patterns of regular combinations of words (selectional restrictions), and, perhaps, patterns of thought. These patterns derive from regularities in the environment (most living things are salient to us, and move) and also from regularities in the culture—such as, for us, "straight-thinking" people, "time is a resource," and "language, a conduit."

In the next chapter we will continue our discussion of meaning in language. In this chapter we searched for systematicity or structure of meaning in the language. In the next chapter we look to see how people *process* meaning, how meaning is achieved in the performance of language tasks.

Answers to language game: (1) your underwear, (2) head over heels, (3) hitting below the belt.

REFERENCES

Austin, J. L. (1965). *How to do things with words.* New York: Oxford University Press.

Brown, R. (1958). *Words and things.* New York: Free Press.

Cheney, D. L., & Seyfarth, R. M. (1992). The representation of social relations by monkeys. *Cognition, 37,* 167-196.

Chomsky, N. (1965). *Aspects of a theory of syntax.* Cambridge: MIT Press.

Diamond, J. (1995). Blueprints, bloody ships, and borrowed letters. *Natural History, 3/95,* 16-19.

Gerrig, R. J., & Gibbs, R. W., Jr. (1988). Beyond the lexicon: Creativity in language production. *Metaphor and Symbolic Activity, 3,* 1-19.

Gibbs, R. W., Jr. (1994). *The poetics of mind: Figurative thought, language, and understanding.* New York: Cambridge University Press.

Grice, H. P. (1989). *Studies in the way of words.* Cambridge: Harvard University Press.

Hunt, E., & Agnoli, F. (1991). The Whorfian hypothesis: A cognitive psychology perspective. *Psychological Review, 98,* 377-389.

Jackendoff, R. (1994). *Patterns in the mind.* New York: Basic Books.

Katz, J. J. (1990). *The metaphysics of meaning.* Cambridge: Bradford Books of MIT Press.

Katz, J. J., & Fodor, F. A. (1963). The structure of a semantic theory. *Language, 39,* 170-210.

Lakoff, G. (1972). Hedges: A study of meaning criteria and the logic of fuzzy concepts. In *Papers from the Eighth Regional Meeting* (pp. 183-208). Chicago: Chicago Linguistics Society.

Lakoff, G. (1973). A study of meaning criteria and the logic of fuzzy concepts. *Journal of Philosophical Logic, 2,* 458-508.

Lakoff, G., & Johnson, M. (1980). *Metaphors we live by.* Chicago: University of Chicago Press.

Lowry, R. (1987). *The evolution of psychological theory* (2nd ed.). New York: Aldine.

Pinker, S. (1994). *The language instinct.* New York: HarperPerennial.

Quine, W. V. O. (1960). *Word and object.* Cambridge: MIT Press.

Searle, J. R. (1975). Indirect speech acts. In P. Cole & J. L. Morgan (Eds.), *Syntax and semantics* (pp. 59-82). New York: Seminar.

Searle, J. R., Kiefer, F., & Bierwisch, M. (1980). *Speech act theory and pragmatics.* Dordrecht, Holland: D. Reidel.

Welsch, R. L. (1995). Belly up to the bar. *Natural History, 4/95,* 66-67.

Whorf, B. L. (1956). *Language, thought, and reality* (J. B. Carroll, Ed.). Cambridge: MIT Press.

Wittgenstein, L. (1973). *Philosophical investigations* (3rd ed.; G. E. M. Anscombe, Trans.). New York: Macmillan.

STUDY QUESTIONS

1. Briefly explain the difference between the following pairs:

   (a) abstract-concrete
   (b) meaning-reference
   (c) connotation-denotation
   (d) literal-figurative
   (e) analytic-synthetic
   (f) perlocutionary-illocutionary

Make up your own examples to illustrate each distinction.

2. Describe the processes that underlie word creation. Do you consider making up a new word to be an essentially creative activity? Why or why not?

3. Discuss the problem of the mental definition of a word like *dog*. Is it possible to come up with a definition? Why or why not? Will the definition necessarily correspond to perceptual reality, or is it culturally determined? That is, would you expect to find the same category in other languages? Your answer should consider Wittgenstein's family resemblance analogy, Lakoff's fuzzy meanings model, and Whorf's linguistic determinism.

4. Lakoff and Johnson see our culture as having some basic metaphoric concepts that underlie both actions and language constructions. For each of the following patterns of thought, see if you can think of 10 common constructions of English that fit the pattern: (a) Time is money; (b) a lifetime is a day (e.g., the sunset years); (c) love is a journey; and (d) up is good or correct (e.g., things are looking up).

5. Draw a marker structure for the word *dog*. Be sure to include both the noun and the verb senses (dogging someone's footsteps). Discuss which features are general semantic markers, which are distinguishers, and what selectional restrictions there should be. Does *dog* have common figurative senses? Did you include them? Why or why not?

6. Discuss the anomalies in "Colorless green ideas sleep furiously." Point out how they would likely be reflected in a tree diagram/marker structure.

3

MEANING PROCESSING

What does *brank* mean? Presumably you responded quickly, "I don't know" or "It is not a word." How did you know that you do not know that word? Did you compare it with each word in your mental dictionary, find that it did not match, and respond after you reached the last word? (What *is* the last word in your mental dictionary?) If you know 5,000 words (a very low estimate), and it took you 5 seconds (a high estimate) to decide you had never seen *brank* before, you mentally compared 1,000 words in 1 second! If you think that is impossible (you are probably right), how *did* you know that *brank* is not a word you have experienced?

This little thought experiment (or *Gedanken* experiment) illustrates several useful concepts in psycholinguistics as well as raising the interesting question of how one knows something is not a word. The first concept is that of *processing model.* My suggestion that you have a mental dictionary that stores the words you know is a *model* of semantic memory. In addition, I suggested that you search each word *serially,* or sequentially, one at a time. The serial scan is a *process,* a way to search memory. (A contrastive process would be a *parallel* scan, where many words are examined at the same time.) Third, I proposed a means of testing the processing model, using your *reaction time,* or how long it took you to respond. Finally, the entire exercise, deciding whether something is or is not a word, demonstrates a *lexical decision task,* a common way of probing how semantic memory works.

One obvious way out of the difficulty of scanning more than 1,000 words per second in making a lexical decision is to search only some of the words, for example, to turn to the "b" section of the mental dictionary and compare only words beginning with "b." This process implies that the mental dictionary, like Webster's, is organized alphabetically. As we shall see, there is some evidence for that, from production and priming tasks. A *production task* is one in which the subject is asked to list words according to some rule (such as "list 10 words beginning with 'b' " or "list 10 types of fruit"). A *priming task* is one in which the subject is attempting to recall, guess, or detect a word and is *primed* or prompted: For example, hearing the word *fruit* or the letter "b" primes or makes you automatically and unconsciously think of words such as *banana* or *berry*. You may have noticed that when you have a word "on the tip of your tongue" (that is, when you are in the *tip-of-the-tongue state*), or when you are doing a crossword puzzle, getting the first sound or letter often immediately precedes recalling the word: That first sound partially activates or primes the memory of the word, allowing it to percolate more easily to consciousness.

So, is the mental dictionary organized alphabetically? What is the first word that comes into your mind: *cat _ *? According to Webster's, the not-very-rare alphabetic neighbors of *cat* are *casualty* and *cataclysm,* neither of which was likely to have been your response. Given such *association tasks,* most people produce words with similar meanings (*cat-dog, mother-father*), suggesting that the mental dictionary is organized in terms of meanings. This would be a useless organization for a real dictionary, which is usually used to discover what an unknown word means; an organization by meaning would give us no way to begin our search. But normally in speaking, we do know the words we will use, we have some idea of what meaning we want to convey, and so a search that begins with meaning and finds appropriate words on that basis could be effective. (This organization is what libraries use: If you are trying to find this book, you start in the sciences library, in the psychology section, and so on. If the book is out, its shelf-mates will be related. This organization is *hierarchical*—psycholinguistics is part of psychology, which is part of science.)

Although this kind of organization makes good sense for production, it might not for comprehension: If someone speaks a sentence, we must understand it, find its meaning. Presumably we do this by "looking up" the words used. If to look them up we must know the meaning, we cannot begin. Of course, it is possible that for speaking we start with a meaning and go to a word, and for understanding we start with a word and retrieve the meaning. However, this returns us to the lexical decision problem: How do we avoid performing an exhaustive comparison of a spoken nonword with all the words we know to determine that we do not know it?

The questions raised here have been examined experimentally, and the results will be discussed in this chapter. To summarize the issues: Are words and meanings different? If so, what is the mental representation of meanings? How do words connect with them? How is our mental dictionary organized? How do we use it? What information about the word and meaning (e.g., first letter, partial sense such as "animal") is in the mental dictionary?

ASSOCIATIONS

We begin our formal discussion of processing of meaning with old and new models for the formation of associations. This is relevant because we must come to associate a word with a meaning and to associate words with similar meanings to one another. Unfortunately, old models of associationism, behaviorism, have been largely neglected in psycholinguistics since a devastating review of Skinner's (1957) *Verbal Behavior* by Chomsky (1959). The critique primarily applied to syntax and the shortcomings of associationism for syntax will be discussed in Chapters 4 and 5. It may also have thrown the baby out with the bathwater, as some of the behaviorist arguments have been resurrected in new models of connectionism, and some of their methods have been productive and the results reliable in work with normal humans (semantic differential). These are discussed here. They have also been effective in rehabilitation of clinical populations and teaching languagelike behaviors to animals, as discussed in *Language in Atypical Populations.*

Behaviorism and Associations

For the behaviorist, meaning is the learned association or habit strength between a fragment of language and other such fragments, or between a fragment of language and a sensation. Associations arise from processes of *conditioning,* or learning, either *classical* (Pavlovian) or *operant conditioning.*

Classical conditioning may be considered a learned association between two stimuli. Classical conditioning begins with one of a very few innate stimulus-response associations, or *reflexes.* For example, food innately causes salivation, and light innately causes a visual sensation. *Innate* implies unlearned or unconditioned, and a reflex can be described as a connection between an unconditioned stimulus (US) and an unconditioned response (UR). If another stimulus is repeatedly presented with the US, it will, after a while, elicit something like the UR. For example, after repeatedly hearing a tone before being fed, an animal will learn the association—tone-food—and will salivate when it hears the tone without the food. Similarly, hearing the word *red* whenever experiencing red light will cause an association between the word and the sensation, so that the word alone may come to elicit something like the sensation.

Once the connection has been learned, the formerly neutral stimulus is called the conditioned stimulus (CS), and the response it engenders, the conditioned response (CR). A distinction is made between the UR and the CR, because the CS does not generally produce the *same* responses as the US: A dog learns to salivate to a bell but does not chew as it would food. We may get an image of red or the faint brain activity that we get when we see red, but the word alone does not produce the full sensation.

Thus, through classical conditioning, words may become associated with sensations normally prompted by objects. Those sensations are called *mediating responses* (or R_ms), internal responses between a stimulus and a full-blown overt response. The mediating response is learned through repetition of the conditioned and unconditioned stimuli. Once a mediating response has been conditioned, it can be the basis of a new association: A new neutral stimulus can be classically conditioned to the CS → R_m association, as Figure 3.1 shows, in a *chain*. Thus Locke's simple ideas (Chapter 1), or concrete words (Chapter 2), would be the first link in the chain, the association between a stimulus and an innate stimulus-response connection, between a stimulus and a sensation. Locke's complex ideas, or abstract words, would be later links, associations to conditioned associations.

The process of conditioning, the formation and existence of R_ms, is a way to solve a lexical decision task. A word elicits an R_m, but a nonword does not. A lexical decision can be made therefore on the basis of whether we *feel* an R_m—figuratively speaking, whether we experience a glimmer of recognition.

A second way that associations are formed is through *operant conditioning*. Here, what is learned is an association between a behavior and its consequences (i.e., how speech can serve as a speech act). If a behavior has desirable consequences, it will be repeated (*reinforcement*), as when a baby finally says its first word, is showered with attention, and repeats the performance. If the behavior is followed by undesirable stimuli, it tends not to be repeated (*punishment*)—as children learn not to curse (in front of their parents) for fear of scolding. If most of our utterances are speech acts produced to get people to do something, we will learn their language habits because, unless we say things correctly, people are unlikely to reinforce us by figuring out and doing what we want.

In both classical and operant conditioning, subjects seem to learn more than the specific association conditioned. This is important if conditioning is at least partly responsible for verbal learning, given that we are able to apply a word to instances related to, but not identical to, the one it was learned in, to stimuli sharing "family resemblances." This phenomenon is called *generalization*. In classical conditioning, stimuli similar to the CS will elicit the CR: the greater the similarity, the faster and greater (e.g., more salivation) the response. In fact, a graph of the amount of response against stimulus similarity to the CS, that is, the *generalization gradient,* looks quite like the bell-shaped curve discussed in the last chapter as a probabilistic model of meaning (typical instances at the middle of the bell produce a great response; atypical instances at the extremes produce smaller responses in proportion to their atypicality). In operant conditioning, what is generalized is the response: Responses similar to the response actually rewarded or punished become associated to the consequence in proportion to the similarity.

Note that conditioning is a process—repeated presentation of two stimuli or of a stimulus following a response—with a measurable experimental (*empirical*) outcome. Conditioning has been demonstrated to be an effective means of teaching associations to animals, training them to produce new behaviors—even languagelike ones (Premack, 1971). It has also been used formally to produce language and other social behaviors in children who do not seem to acquire it naturally, as

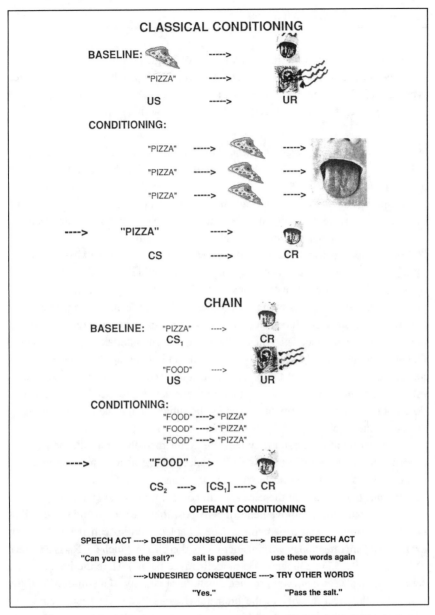

Figure 3.1. The Formation of Associations and R$_m$s Through Operant and Classical Conditioning

in cases of severe retardation (Savage-Rumbaugh, 1986) or schizophrenia (Lovaas, Berberich, Perloff, & Schaeffer, 1966). Philosophically, the question is whether conditioning processes can account for normal acquisition of language behaviors. We will consider this in Chapter 4 for syntax and in Chapter 9 for language acquisition.

Mediating Responses: The Form of Meaning

One way to test conditioning as a model of language meaning is to look for evidence of R_ms, evidence in the form they take or their use in language tasks. Three types of R_ms have been proposed, with some evidence supporting each: covert motor movements, mental imagery, and *affective* (emotional) responses.

The medium is the muscle. The *motor theory,* suggested first by the father of behaviorism, James Watson (1930/1970), holds that when we hear an utterance such as "eat a hamburger," our bodies automatically respond with covert motor movements appropriate for actually doing what the utterance describes. We understand the utterance by recognizing the faint muscular movements as those that, if magnified, would constitute biting, swallowing, and so forth.

Some evidence for the existence of such covert responses exists. Jacobson (1932) attached electrodes to various muscles in a subject's body and measured their responses following instructions to the subject to imagine, without moving, performing actions, such as swinging a golf club. Only those muscles normally used to perform the action produced electrical activity, a minute reaction relative to what they would have produced had the action actually been undertaken. Thus we know that, at least under conditions where (a) the subject has perhaps heightened awareness of muscles because of the placement of the electrodes and (b) the subject is asked to imagine movement, a covert motor movement is produced. Of course, this does not say that the movement is used by the subject in normal understanding of an action sentence.

The experiment is old and may indicate motor mediation only in the peculiar experimental conditions but it is easy to conceptualize as a motor response to a thought of action. The verbal instruction or thought is the CS; the covert motor movements, the CR. Motor theories are still considered today, sometimes like this one, where actual muscle movements or body positions are sensed and serve as R_ms between a stimulus and a perception (see Chapter 7 on speech perception, for example). More often today we consider motor theories in which the R_m is a pattern of brain activity, as in connectionist modeling (see below). Here the idea is that a set of brain cells (or *neurons*) produce a pattern of activity to a stimulus, and the pattern of electrical activity in the brain (analogous to the electrical activity of Jacobson's subject's muscles) itself is the understanding-thought-meaning of the stimulus.

The medium is the image. We can think of the minute muscle movements underlying the thought of swinging a golf club as a *kinesthetic* (sense of muscle movement) image for an action. As I pointed out in Chapter 2, many words describe aspects of the visual world. Although these could arouse minute eye movements, we might consider instead a concrete representation in a *visual image,* an arousal of the sensory pathway underlying seeing the object (Kosslyn, 1980, 1987, 1988).

There are two types of evidence for visual imagery underlying language under-standing. The first is a demonstration that there is thought that has visual properties rather than more general abstract properties. Kosslyn asked subjects to decide whether a sentence like "German shepherds have pointed ears" is true—a *sentence verification* task. He measured both whether or not the subject was correct (*accuracy*), and how long it took the subject to make the decision, or the reaction time. Subjects took longer to make determinations about the dog's head if they had previously been told to focus on the dog's tail. Thus, using reaction time to scale mental distance, Kosslyn mapped thought: In these tasks, it is scaled spatially, a visual-image representation.

A second line of evidence that there are at least types of thought that reflect sensory processes comes from *masking* or *interference* studies in which subjects are asked to attend to one set of stimuli while a second set is presented. To the extent that subjects are distracted by the second set, we can conclude that the two kinds of stimuli share mental or body processes. So, as the cliché goes, we can walk and chew gum at the same time because those two activities are accomplished by different parts of our bodies and probably are controlled by different parts of our brain. Chewing gum and talking at the same time is harder because we would have to coordinate our mouth movements appropriately for the two competing activities.

Now, for concepts, Kosslyn, among others, showed that a subject's holding in mind a visual image interferes with visual, but not auditory (sound), perception; but keeping in mind an auditory image (e.g., the sound of a telephone ringing) interferes with auditory, but not visual, perception. Thus there is a sense-specific component of the image/concept. (Kosslyn also reports cases of people with brain damage who could recognize or remember objects but not form images of them, or the reverse. Thus the visual sense and image pathway need not be identical.)

Such demonstrations of the use of visual imagery are clouded by the fact that the subject is specifically asked to form an image to solve a task. Like Jacobson's experiment that may have induced subjects to be more than usually conscious of their muscles, this is a case of *demand characteristics,* where what the experiment requires, not necessarily the process it is trying to assess, affects the outcome. Perhaps we can image but do not do so normally. It is crucial to show that we form images as we understand words if the image is the R_m for meaning.

The second type of evidence for visual imagery comes from demonstrations of processing differences between words that are judged as easily imaged, concrete words, and words that are judged as difficult to image, abstract words. These studies involve a two-step procedure. First, a group of subjects rates words or sentences on how imageable they are. From these ratings the words are divided into low- and high-imagery groups. The second step is to see if other subjects show differences in memory or understanding of words that are differently imageable.

Paivio (1986) presents considerable evidence for a *dual code* for highly image-able, or concrete, words. One codes in images, and the other, abstractly, perhaps like the marker system presented in Chapter 2. Low-imagery, abstract words have only the second representation. Relative to abstract words or sentences, concrete ones are easier to recall, are understood more quickly, and are more likely to be preserved after brain damage. It is the additional image representation that concrete words have, Paivio argues, that causes their better access: The image system backs the abstract system up and sometimes is accessed more efficiently.

Although interesting, these results still do not necessarily implicate imagery in normal language processing. The advantages for concrete words may arise because they have a more accessible or interpretable memory organization than abstract words, or because they are closer to the unconditioned reflex: Learning or understanding abstract words may depend on previous learning or understanding of concrete words. In that case, both types of words may have the same *type* of memory representation (both use abstract symbols), but concrete words may have simpler definitions (use fewer such symbols, or have a shorter "chain").

Evidence from *evoked potentials,* brain-wave recording, supports a dual-code representation for concrete words and a single code for abstract words (Kounios & Holcomb, 1994). In this study, a brain-wave component believed to indicate semantic processing, the *N400,* was implicated on both sides of the brain when subjects were making lexical decisions or concreteness ratings about concrete words, but only on the left side for abstract words. The left side of the brain appears to be associated with pure verbal processing, and the right side, with nonverbal, holistic, imagistic processing—with the two thought types humorously illustrated in Figure 3.2. These results suggest both a verbal (left-side) and an image (right-side) code for concrete words but only a verbal (left-side) code for abstract words.

Another study implicating a specific code for the imageable was performed by Eddy and Glass (1981). They demonstrated in a verification task that *reading* highly imageable sentences takes *longer* than reading low-imageability sentences. There was no difference in verification time between the low- and high-imageability sentences when they were presented for verification auditorily. This result is interesting for two reasons. The first is that it is in part paradoxical: Normally, highly imageable sentences are verified more quickly than low, but this is not true when reading them. The second is that it suggests that people do *visualize* the sentence meanings without being instructed to do so if reading, a visual task, interferes with understanding sentences with visual meaning.

Thus it appears that at least sometimes, for some words, thought is a concrete, subtle sensory-motor representation. It is also clear that an abstract system must exist for other words or other situations. The abstract system could still be an R_m.

The medium is the emotion. The two R_ms just suggested had a specific form, a visual or motor image. Osgood, Suci, and Tannenbaum (1957/1978) developed an approach to map R_ms without specifying their form. They conceived of an organized universe of possible R_ms called *semantic space.* Space may be two-dimensional, three-dimensional, or multidimensional. Each dimension can be thought of as an axis, with a word positioned with respect to that axis in a particular direction and at a particular distance from the origin. The origin indicates neutrality; direction from the origin indicates quality; and distance, intensity. So, for example, if there

Figure 3.2. A Dual-Code Model, Applied to the Population (© 1977 by Sydney Harris.)

is a temperature dimension of R_ms, *hot* would be located in the opposite direction from *cold* but at a lesser distance from *warm* because it has more of this quality.

To map word meanings in semantic space, to locate individual R_ms for specific words, Osgood et al. developed a technique called the *semantic differential.* Subjects rated words on a number of *bipolar scales,* scales spanning opposites like hot-cold or beautiful-ugly. Osgood et al. argued that the meaning of *any* word was its position on these scales: *Canary* can be rated on hot-cold, good-bad, tall-short dimensions. Presumably *canary* is warmer than *snake* for most people, partly because it is warm-blooded but also because it is associated with warm and friendly situations. All of these associations are mediators and help locate *canary*'s meaning in semantic space.

After collecting large numbers of ratings of large numbers of words on large numbers of scales, Osgood et al. analyzed the results using a statistical technique called *factor analysis.* Consider how you would describe A and B in Figure 3.3. Both consist of 15 lines, but A is organized such that the 15 lines are spread throughout the two-dimensional space, whereas in B they cluster in three axes.

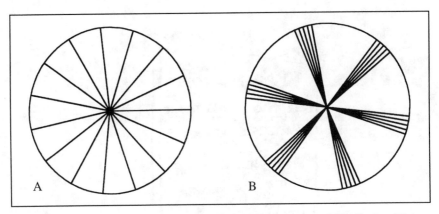

Figure 3.3. Lines Illustrating Random Distribution (A) or Clustered Distribution (B) in a Space

NOTE: A is most easily described as 15 lines radiating in all directions. B is also 15 lines but is better described as three groups each of five lines, with large separation among the groups.

Although we can still see the differences in the 15 lines of B, it makes sense to talk about them as three groups of lines, the groupings determined by distance. Factor analysis takes large amounts of data (much more than 15 items) and computes a kind of difference or distance between them. (This distance is called *variance* and is, somewhat more precisely, the sum of the distances between an actual score and the average of several such scores.) Very large differences, or large variance, indicate separation among the three clusters of B; small variance, the separation of the lines within each cluster. By mathematically juggling these large and small differences, factor analysis discovers the axes, or factors, that account for major amounts of variance in the data, in this case for differences in meanings of different words.

Now consider the use of factor analysis specifically for the semantic differential. If every word has its own distinct place relative to each bipolar scale, semantic space, as revealed by these scale ratings, will look like A. However, if words that tend to be rated as "warm" also tend to be rated as "good" and "true" and "beautiful," we will see a cluster as in B of warm-good-true-beautiful forming the individual lines, say, at the right of the horizontal cluster, cool-bad-false-ugly at the left of that cluster, and neutral concepts rated near the origin in that cluster. What factor analysis tells us is that words rated positively on one scale are likely to be rated positively on others, so that we may consider +/– warm-good-true-beautiful as one dimension instead of four.

Osgood et al. found three principal clusters in all their data, in English as well as cross-culturally and cross-linguistically (Osgood, 1971). These appeared to mark dimensions best described as *evaluative* (good-bad), *potency* (strong-weak), and *activity* (lively-quiet). They considered that these factors were people's reactions to the words, or their mediating responses.

Because these dimensions or factors seem to describe emotional response to the word rather than objective meaning features such as animate, I consider these R_ms to be emotion or affective mediators, a better map of connotation than of denotation. For me, for instance, "angel" is good, strong, and quiet, but this does not capture the winged spiritual aspect of meaning.

As an example, it is instructive to examine their analysis of the difference between "good" and "nice":

> Most people we asked accepted them as synonymous, yet agreed there was a difference, somehow, in their "feeling-tone"—most respondents were unable to verbalize this difference, however. Analysis with the differential indicates a marked difference between the two words on the *potency factor,* and when we investigate the linguistic contexts in which they are appropriate we find that GOOD is a "masculine" word and NICE a "feminine" word. Speakers of English agree that "nice man" differs from "good man" in that the former is rather weak, soft and effeminate; on the other hand, while "nice girl" is appropriately feminine, "good girl" has a decidedly moral tone. When the profiles for GOOD and NICE are compared with those for MALE and FEMALE, we find that wherever MALE and FEMALE separate sharply, so also do GOOD and NICE. GOOD like MALE is significantly *thicker, larger* and *stronger* than NICE, but there are no significant differences on the *activity* and *evaluative factors.* (Osgood et al., 1957/1978, pp.167-168)

The semantic differential has been used to evaluate attitudes not only toward words but also toward nonlinguistic things: sculptures, paintings, political candidates, and social attitudes. In all cases the same dimensions emerge as important, with high reliability. This suggests, perhaps, that language and nonlanguage share R_ms (i.e., share thought?).

It has also been used to compare semantic space structure in other languages, finding more commonalities than differences. All languages tested seem to be able to create bipolar scales and rate words with respect to them. Moreover, for all languages, the most powerful dimension is evaluative, with most languages' affective meanings also organized with respect to potency and activity secondarily. Occasionally, new factors emerged as second or third, pushing potency and activity down in importance in some cultures. For example, Afghan Dair speakers had as the second strongest axis human-religious-learned-Muslim-courageous-immaculate (at the positive end) and the Lebanese Muslim group had as the second strongest axis a cluster of rare-thin-particular-hidden-light (positive end). It is intriguing to consider the differences as possible support for the linguistic relativity hypothesis, but in this regard, it is more compelling to note the rarity of such differences. Perhaps the commonalities across cultures reflect a similar universe of R_ms, similar possible affective responses to words.

Connectionist Models

Behaviorists approached "meaning" from the study of associative processes in animals, assuming similarity in humans. This resulted in the study of meaning in human behavior as clusters of associative responses or a search for meaning R_ms.

Cognitive psychology's study of imagery both extended the behaviorist view of R_m and expanded the methods of inquiry, asking subjects, for example, to form or zoom in on images. Cognitive psychologists also approach associations in computer models, discovering learning principles and matching computer behavior following the learning to human behavior.

Like the behaviorist approach, the connectionist approach (Rumelhart, McClelland, & the PDP Research Group, 1986) begins with the simplest type of association, an association between input "units" and output "units." A unit can be considered to be an analogue to a *neuron* (a nerve cell) or neuron group, which responds to the input or directs the output. Input, of course, is a stimulus (e.g., meaning features like markers, or letters or speech sounds), and output is a response (such as which concept or word best represents the feature combinations present in the input). In the connectionist models, input units (shown at the bottom of Figure 3.4, responding to letters) are connected not only to output units (at the top of Figure 3.4, the words) but also to other input units, a *lateral* (side-by-side at the same level) connection. Output units too can be connected with one another, a single input unit may connect to several output units, and a single output unit may receive several inputs: a complex crisscrossing of connections. Because of the analogy to *neural* connections, and the complex *net*work of interconnections, these models are sometimes called *neural nets*.

Connections between units are "weighted": The stronger the connection between units A and B, the greater the weight, and the greater the effect that activation of unit A will have on unit B. (The activation of a unit is represented in the figure by the thickness of the lines.) A connection can produce one of two effects: excitatory or inhibitory. An *excitatory* effect means that if A is activated, B will be activated also. An *inhibitory* connection means that A's activation prevents B from being activated. So, for example, an input unit responsive to *barks* might have an excitatory connection to another dog feature, an input unit responsive to fur, but might have an inhibitory connection to an input unit for *meows*. Barking and meowing are mutually exclusive, and the inhibitory connection models that.

In connectionist models, learning consists not of forming new connections or units but of *modifying the weights on unit connections*. When two inputs co-occur, their connection weight is increased slightly. The more frequent the co-occurrence, the greater the ultimate weight. For each connection there is a maximum and a minimum for the weight, beyond which the connection cannot be strengthened. Repeated trials of similar patterns will train the system on correlated features and *relax* the weights into a stable state. The term *relaxation* is used to indicate that weight modification is *not* a directed, goal-oriented process. A directed process would mean that the system either knew the pattern it had to learn or deliberately calculated it. Rather, the connection modifications happen naturally through easing in or *settling* of the changes necessitated by feature co-occurrence.

Consider the stimulus inputs, or perceptual features, that are likely to occur for things we label as "dog." These include fur, a wagging tail, four legs, barking, and so on. Repeated exposure to different dogs most strengthens the weights connecting units responding to "typical" features—barking, labrador/setter size, long tail,

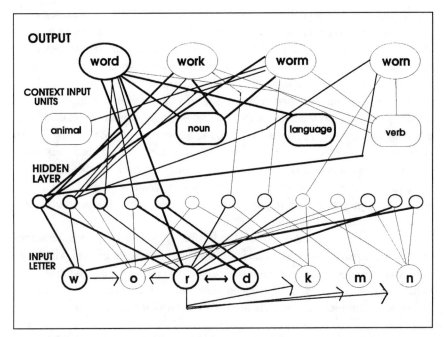

Figure 3.4. Neural Net With Hidden Units Arousing a Representation of a Degraded Bit of a Stimulus

NOTE: The darker the line, the greater the activation. This network has been stimulated with the letters. The letters "w, r, d" are clearly input and activate "o." Hidden units respond to pairs of input letters/sounds, and so "wo" and "or" are also partially activated by the nondegraded input. Thus "o" is activated at both the input and the hidden levels, even though it is not actually in the input. The context also stimulates noun and language units. The net effect is greatest activation of, or the most dark lines converging on, *word.*

household pet, pointed ears, solid color—because these most often co-occur. Atypical features, associated with some dogs, such as the long hair on the sheepdog or the wildness of the coyote, have excitatory connections to other dog features but with less weight because their co-occurrence frequency is smaller. Repeated learning trials on both typical and atypical dogs produce connections with the highest weights on typical features (because across trials these are most frequently correlated), even if no *single* trial has all the typical features occurring together. Thus such a net naturally evolves "family resemblances" as concepts.

The association model may become more complex via a set of units between the input and output units called *hidden units.* (In the figure, these are unlabeled and represent the co-occurrence of two letters.) The term *hidden* refers to the fact that their workings are not directly observable, as an input unit is by the effect of the input, or as an output unit is by the response. A hidden unit is necessary in some cases to pool the activations of input units so some logical combination of inputs affects the output unit. By bundling activations of input units, the hidden units represent meaningful intermediary layers like, perhaps, a generalized marker of animate-inanimate that combines features typical of living things (moves, breathes, and so on).

The connectionist models make several presumptions. First, the representation of a particular concept is *distributed* over a number of small featurelike entities. This means that there is not a unit responsible for a concept, that a concept cannot be localized, that a concept is not "stored" in a memory location. Rather, a concept is a *pattern of activation* across units. In fact, failure to activate a particular input unit of a concept may not particularly disturb recognition of that concept, if the omitted input is highly weighted with input that is actually presented. In the figure, the input was "w*rd," and the combination of activations of "w, r, d," the hidden units responsive to "wo, wr, or, rd," and the context most strongly activates *word*. Because of the units' interconnections and mutual activations, the input units responding to presented features recruit the missing input unit laterally. Given a stable activation pattern, the weights of the connections change little with each new experience, including one of a missing unit.

A third important property of neural nets is that responses to inputs and changes in weights are made in *parallel*. That is, all units at a given level respond at the same time or synchronously, and weight modifications occur in waves across the affected units. Because a concept is distributed across units that respond in parallel to component features, these models are called *parallel distributed processing* (or PDP) models.

Fourth, it is important to understand what meaning is in such a model. Meaning is the activation of the connected units underlying the concept. It is not stored in a unit; it arises dynamically from the pattern of response of the units. Meaning is a mental state arising inherently from the working of units. A memory is not a thing that is *stored* and retrieved like a book in a library, but is a *process* of changing weights to produce the appropriate degree of activation of related units. In the same way a skill—such as riding a bicycle—is not a thing but a pattern of response: for bicycle riding, response of muscles, and for meaning or thought, response of neural units.

A fifth assumption of neural net models is an *interactivity* among units at different levels. (Note that although there is considerable interactivity, it is possible to create independent faculties or modules [see Chapters 1 and 4; Fodor, 1983] by limiting connectivity and coactivation across groups of neurons devoted to different tasks.) A pattern of activation that flows only from input units to output units (perhaps through hidden units) is stimulus-driven or *bottom-up* and only allows different stimulus properties to interact in affecting the output. Activation from the output units back to the input units is conceptually driven or *top-down* and, in a sense, builds in guessing. Suppose, for example, as in the figure, one has a degraded input—part of the sound of a word masked by noise, or a letter stained by coffee. The remaining sounds or letters of the stimulus may be sufficient to activate an output unit representing the word and to partially activate laterally the input unit responding to the degraded stimulus. At the same time, the output unit can activate, top-down, all input units that normally activate it. These combined activations may make an ambiguous, degraded input clear. Most neural net models allow activation to flow in all directions, so that guesses about letters or sounds can activate a word or letters or sounds that frequently co-occur, and at the same time word activation can activate input units for related stimuli, as shown in Figure 3.4.

This leads to a parallel distributed processing implementation of the Whorf hypothesis (Rumelhart, Smolensky, McClelland, & Hinton, 1986, pp. 43-44):

> Suppose that the interpretation that led to the production of the inner speech [the activity pattern underlying a word or phrase] was much richer than the linguistic forms could possibly suggest. Thus, the linguistic forms [the output units] pick out aspects of the entire interpretation to emphasize. Once this emphasis has taken place and the new input has been processed, the next state will be strongly affected [top-down] by the new input, and our new interpretation will be shaped, to some extent, by the words we chose to express our first idea. Thus our thinking about a topic will be affected, sometimes strongly, by the language tools we have for expressing our ideas.

As we shall see throughout this book, PDP models often produce compelling simulations of psycholinguistic results. In semantics, as illustrated here, PDP models can generate a word from semantic features, derive typical category members from nontypical examples, and generalize from instances to produce fuzzy categories bound by family resemblance. That seems to structure much of linguistic meaning, as argued in the last chapter.

PDP semantic models could incorporate nonlinguistic features, to avoid the anomaly of a "lying-down tall flagpole," referred to in Chapter 2. *Flagpole* and *tall* would normally be highly excitatorily weighted but could be inhibited from *any* input unit detecting the flagpole as horizontal: Because PDP models do not discriminate between types of input, linguistic (analytic) truths can weigh in along with extralinguistic (synthetic) ones. It is also conceivable that a PDP model could process metaphor: Two words, such as *love* and *roller-coaster,* would each activate common associations, with concepts common to both most highly activated. In this case, there would already be strong weights on all the love-trip connections, and units responding to aspects of a trip that are peculiar to roller-coasters would be especially activated by the input. A "live" metaphor should require changing weights, unlike a "dead" metaphor. Updating the weights could cause an experience of novelty, creativity, and power in a live metaphor.

PDP models and classical and operant conditioning are *process models:* They tell us *how* something—here, concept learning or word recognition—happens. The outcome of the process reveals the *structure* inherent in what is being studied, for instance, the family resemblance nature of categories. But, for the most part, they do not reveal new findings about language or mental structure; they only provide a possible account for findings obtained through examination of patterns in the language or probings of human responses in experiments. In their study of R_ms, Osgood et al. and the imagists revealed a structure to our psychological representation of meaning. We turn now to other psycholinguistic findings of structure in mental meaning.

Box 3.1. Associationist Views of Meaning Representation

— Meaning is a conditioned association between a stimulus and a language unit, or a chained association between two language units.
— The conditioned association may be a faint response—motor, image, or emotional—like that to the unconditioned stimulus.
— People modify language habits using feedback from community members. Compliance with a speaker's intent reinforces the utterance form; noncompliance is punishing, leading to modification of the utterance.
— Minute muscle movements can be recorded when subjects imagine performing an action.
— Imagery is implicated in
  — reaction time changes consistent with spatial distance as subjects "scan" images to verify facts;
  — different performance for concrete than for abstract words;
  — both cerebral hemispheres' involvement for concrete words, but only the left hemisphere's for abstract words; and
  — interference of visual tasks including reading when comprehending imageable sentences.
— The semantic differential identifies major dimensions of connotation to be evaluative, potency, and intensity.
— PDP or neural net models see meaning as a distributed pattern of activation of interconnected units. Connections are weighted through patterns of co-occurrence. Activation may be excitatory or inhibitory and flows in all directions.

EVIDENCE FOR THE STRUCTURE OF SEMANTIC MEMORY

In this section I present three more psychological models of semantic memory and their supporting evidence. A scientific *model* is an analogy, a tool to help us understand a set of phenomena. To say meaning is organized like a family resemblance helps us understand the loosely connected similarities in abstract verbal meaning analogously to the loosely connected visual similarities among family members, which we have all presumably already experienced. A model serves (a) to organize phenomena or experimental data into a coherent framework and (b) to generate hypotheses for the causes of the phenomena, which lead to predictions of other findings that could be obtained through new experiments. The more specific a prediction a model allows, the better the model, as we discussed in the last chapter. The more data the model successfully accounts for, the better the model. And, finally, the simpler the model is, the better the model—provided it accounts for the data and generates predictions.

The process of science usually begins bottom-up, with data that need to be organized into a model. The model in turn generates hypotheses, which open a search for new data, top-down. If the data fit the model, they are assimilated and the model is supported, but not proven. It is not proven because there is always the possibility that the next experiment will yield a result that disconfirms the model.

If an experiment does yield a disconfirming result, often a small adjustment can be made in the model to accommodate the new result. If it is a major contradiction of the model, or if a large number of minor adjustments to the model have made it unwieldy (overly complex), the model is dropped in favor of a better model.

The reason for this discussion of modeling is that we are about to consider three new models of semantic memory, each of which must account for the same set of data (as must the PDP model). The models differ because each arose to account for a different set of initial data. You may find one framework to be be more appealing than the other frameworks—the analogy it makes may better fit your intuitions about semantic memory. However, plausibility is *not* a reason to accept one model over another. You need to consider how much of the data the model accounts for (Will it help you remember what might be otherwise unconnected facts?), how specific it is in generating new experiments and predicting new findings, and how complicated its assumptions are.

Codability, Prototype, and Basic Level

Recall our discussions of conditioning and Locke's simple and complex ideas. In both cases, there emerged a two-tier system, an initial association of CS to reflex or of simple idea to sensation, and, subsequently, chained associations of new CSs to the old CS or of complex ideas to simple ideas. We might argue that the initial association had some cognitive preeminence as a building block of the system. Indeed, we saw some advantage to concrete words over abstract words, perhaps because of their more immediate access to a basic sensory code like imagery. In this section we look at other evidence and conceptualizations of basic codes in the semantic system.

Brown and Lenneberg (1954) coined the term *codability* to refer to the cognitive availability of a language concept. The *codability* of a term is assessed by (a) the number of syllables in a name (word or phrase) for the concept, (b) the reaction time for naming an instance of the concept, and (c) the consistency or *reliability* with which subjects generate names for that concept (i.e., Is the same word or phrase used each time?).

Let us consider a highly codable picture for English speakers: **A.** Asked to name such a picture, very quickly most of us say "ay." *Ay* is a single-syllable word, and one that is likely to be produced by each person repeatedly to that picture, and by almost all people in much of the world over the age of 4 years. Contrast that most codable picture to -\. After some thought, I might label this picture as "an A without the left diagonal" or "a hyphen and backslash" or "a short horizontal line intersecting a negative-sloped diagonal about halfway up." This is a less codable picture in our culture, and the lower codability is reflected in the initial time to come up with a name (greater reaction time), in the several, equally good choices of name (less reliability), and in the length of the labels (six or more syllables).

Brown and Lenneberg's consideration of codability began with a famous observation in linguistics: Zipf's Law (Zipf, 1935/1965). Zipf calculated statistical properties of words in a number of languages and found that the frequency of use

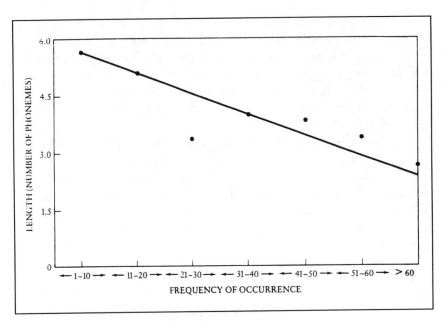

Figure 3.5. An Illustration of Zipf's (1935/1965) Law

SOURCE: Graph adapted from Zipf's (1935/1965) data.

NOTE: *Zipf's Law:* The more frequently a word is used, the shorter it is likely to be. The x-axis is the frequency of occurrence of 6,002 words appearing in a 43,989-word sample from American newspapers. Infrequent words occur between 1 and 10 times in the sample; frequent ones, more than 60 times. The y-axis is the average number of speech sounds, or phonemes, in the words.

of a word had a reliable relationship to word length. Specifically, more frequent words were shorter on average than less frequent words. This relationship is illustrated in Figure 3.5 for English. The figure plots words with different frequencies of occurrence in a large sample of text taken from newspapers against the average number of phonemes per word. (A *phoneme* is a speech sound roughly corresponding to the sound of a letter of the alphabet.) The more often a word occurs, say, > 60 times in the approximately 44,000-word corpus, the shorter it is (like *the,* a three-letter and two-phoneme word). You can think of this correlation as reflecting historical change in the language, perhaps motivated by efficiency or laziness: It is easier to say *NASA* than *National Aeronautics and Space Administration.* If a word is frequently used, nicknaming or abbreviating it to speed saying, hearing, or writing it will save time.

Apart from looking at statistical properties of the language as evidence of codability, Brown and Lenneberg, and later Rosch (publishing originally as Heider [Heider & Olivier, 1972]; Rosch, Mervis, Gray, Johnson, & Boyes-Braem, 1976), looked for perceptual and cognitive processing differences for terms of different codability, as indexed by the word length and reliability measures.

The first category studied was color perception, building on a cross-cultural, cross-linguistic (98 different languages) study of color names performed by Berlin and Kay (1969). It may come as something of a surprise that all cultures do not label colors the same way. In fact, some cultures use as few as two terms to categorize colors, whereas others have as many as 11 primary color words. Berlin and Kay's study showed an interesting pattern in the color words: If a language had two names for colors, these distinguished dark from light. A third color word always added red to black and white. A fourth color word would add green, yellow, or blue. And, finally, finer verbal distinctions included brown, purple, or pink. Note that in English these are all primary color words, reasonably frequent terms in the language, learned early and produced with high reliability. Contrast them to other distinguishable colors such as *aquamarine, burnt sienna,* or *forest green* (from the Crayola crayon labels): These less codable terms are longer, sometimes multiword compounds, and sometimes still connected to an object with that characteristic color.

The sequence of term addition in languages that Berlin and Kay found is particularly interesting because it seems to reflect inborn human perceptual categories. Basic light perception, as determined by physiological and perceptual experiments, consists of brightness perception (dark-light) and perception of the hues red, green, and blue. Perception of all other hues derives from a pattern of activation of the visual neurons responding to each of these primary percepts. Thus the language pattern appears to reflect perceived reality, the weak form of the Whorf-Sapir hypothesis discussed in Chapter 2.

Both Brown and Lenneberg and Heider questioned whether codability affected perception, the strong form of the Whorf-Sapir hypothesis. Specifically, would it be harder to identify, remember, or learn a label for a color sample (like you see when you select a wall paint) if your native language has no word for it? Brown and Lenneberg found that Zuni speakers, with a single term for yellow and orange, were more likely than English speakers to think they had seen yellow when orange had in fact been presented—an effect of language on *memory.* Heider, testing the New Guinea Dani tribe, who label only black and white, found no differences in color *perception* compared with English speakers. Both English and Dani speakers organized color samples into categories in the same way: That is, if asked to make two categories, they put dark chips in one and light in the other; if asked to make six categories, they separated black, white, red, yellow, green, blue, and so on. English and Dani speakers also both organized samples within a category similarly, with a prototypical color (focal color), like blue, in the center and less typical tints, like turquoise, in the periphery. Finally, both found it easier to learn new names for categories if the categories were arranged with focal colors at the center (e.g., blue as center with blue-green to one side and blue-red to the other) than if they were organized around a nonfocal color (turquoise as center with blue to one side and green to the other). The results together suggest that color perception influences language (though not the reverse) but that the language code may, in turn, influence color memory.

In reviewing the findings on cross-linguistic color naming and color perception, Hunt and Agnoli (1991) and Gerrig and Banaji (1994) point out that a number of subsequent studies failed to replicate Rosch's results (even with the Dani), and that there does appear to be a subtle effect of naming on perception. The subtle tests measure perception of nonfocal colors, colors at the boundary between two labeled categories in one language (like orange-yellow), which are given only one label in the other language. As Brown and Lenneberg found for memory, the apparent difference between the boundary colors is exaggerated to speakers with differentiated labels. Nonfocal colors are more accurately distinguished if a culture has different names for them than if they fall into the same language category. Thus the evidence from color categories suggests that there is a strong cognitive and perceptual constraint on the language code—perceptually, *salient colors have higher codability* within and across languages—*but also that there is linguistic relativity,* that a language's coding of color can affect perception and memory of it.

Rosch (1975; Rosch et al., 1976) extended the concept of focal color to other categories, categories that are not as readily organized by intuitive sensory and perceptual properties. Her model of category organization, of semantic memory, has as a "building block" (or *primitive,* the starting place) an analogue to focal color, the prototype, for each category. That is, when we conceptualize *red,* we think of the focal, or prototypical red; that instance is more readily available cognitively than less typical instances. *Each* category is similarly organized around a prototype, which, similarly, is more available cognitively than less typical instances. Beyond the focalness, the centrality of the prototype and the peripheralness of less prototypical category members, Rosch's model builds little structure into the category.

Consider the categories of *poodle, dog,* and *animal.* First, note that each *is* a category, with instances—there are toy poodles, large poodles, black poodles, and coifed poodles; there are sheepdogs, poodles, coyotes, and mutts; there are dogs, cats, reptiles, and insects. Second, note that the three categories may be *hierarchically* arranged: Poodles are kinds of dogs, which are kinds of animals. Now try to imagine the prototype for each category. Most people more easily imagine a prototypical dog than a prototypical poodle or prototypical animal: Poodle is too specific a category and animal is too general.

For each hierarchy, Rosch argues, there is a *basic level,* an entry level of semantic memory organization, which is more codable. Here, the basic level is *dog,* which, of interest, is a shorter word than *poodle* or *animal,* consistent with Brown and Lenneberg's relation of codability to Zipf's Law.

Rosch et al. attempted to define the basic level of different kinds of categories by considering distinguishing and correlated features among category instances. Basic level is somewhat imprecisely described as the level that maximizes divisions between categories (i.e., expresses the most information) while capturing the greatest feature overlap among category members. Knowing that something is not a poodle is not as informative as knowing that it is not a dog or not an animal. (To think about this informally, consider where you would begin in a game of 20 questions. The yes-no answer that provides *the most information* is the one that divides the possibilities into large, equal categories.) Different dogs share many properties, while different animals are vastly different. Consequently, *dog* is the level that optimizes the information-transmission and feature-overlap constraints. You might try to find intuitively the basic level for the hierarchies of trees, tools, fruit, furniture, or birds—some of Rosch's other categories.

Like Brown and Lenneberg, one of Rosch's experimental criteria for the basic level was reliability: how consistently subjects list characteristics (*attributes*) of category members. A second criterion is like the reaction time criterion, here the speed for forming an image or for pantomiming a motor movement for the category. It is easier to imagine or pantomime a *dog* than a *poodle* or an *animal;* it is easier to imagine or pantomime a "chair" than a "stool" or "furniture." In each case the easier one is the basic level. In addition, the basic level is the level children are most likely to learn first, and that parents are likely to teach first. Would you name the thing on a leash to a young child as a poodle, a dog, or an animal?

The basic level is more available than other levels and seems to be more strongly associated with the category name. Rosch showed that presenting the category name (e.g., *furniture*)—the prime—speeded subjects deciding that two words both belonged to the same category, a *semantic decision.* Presumably the presentation of the category name made the memory of the instances more available. Rosch found a greater priming for semantic decisions concerning prototypical instances (e.g., *chair-chair*) than peripheral ones (e.g., *stove-stove*), suggesting a stronger association of category name to prototype.

What defines typicality or basic level may differ for biological and man-made categories (e.g., Farah & McClelland, 1991; Vikovitch, Humphreys, & Lloyd-Jones, 1993). Biological categories like dog or tree *look* alike, while man-made categories, like furniture or tool, share *function* or *motor* features. Thus a typical tree is roughly vertical, with branches, leaves, and roots. A typical chair may be sat on but may not look much like other chairs. Brain-damaged patients sometimes can name items only from biological or only from man-made categories. And normal subjects, if they misname something, usually name a concept that is both visually and functionally like the target. Thus two processes, one visual and one functional/motor, could underlie semantic category structure.

Summary. This section examined codability in language, its effect on memory and perception, and its relation to typicality. Codable concepts have a short, reliably given name, are learned early, and are easily imaged or performed. They are likely to represent primary, salient perceptions, but the fact that these are given names in turn affects memory of them and, subtly, perception of them.

The prototype model organizes semantic memory around codability: Prototypical, codable ideas are the entry point for a category "defined" by its instances, loosely linked by family resemblance (on either perceptual or functional bases). The prototype is more accessible and more likely primed by the category name. The prototype model is consistent with results showing an image and abstract code for concrete words and a motor code for some words. Finally, the PDP models described earlier can produce prototype organizations because the typical features wind up with the strongest weights.

Network Models

The prototype model presents a minimally organized semantic memory: Concept meanings are represented by concept instances, with prototypical instances showing some advantage in psychological access over less typical members of a concept. Concepts may show some hierarchical structure insofar as a category contains subcategories (e.g., furniture includes chairs, which include stools), but this is not explicitly organized: The instances of the subcategories simply cluster together among the other instances of the category. Analogous to the prototype-periphery distinction, there is proposed a category level that has privileged access, the basic level.

A model that hypothesizes much more structure to semantic memory is the *network model,* historically one of the first semantic memory models. The network model is a psychological *processing* model based on the marker model discussed in Chapter 2. Recall that we depicted a marker as a branching tree, with branches at a given level indicating mutually exclusive alternatives, and branches down the tree indicating increasingly finer subcategory information.

The network model's initial incarnation was a computer simulation of such a structure (Quillian, 1968). The details of each concept for the model were obtained from a production task in which subjects were asked to tell all they knew about a word like *machine.* As you can imagine, the first associations are of common facts about machines, but eventually almost everything one knows may be produced as association leads to association.

The model has since been modified to take into account human behavioral results primarily from sentence verification tasks (Collins & Loftus, 1975; Collins & Quillian, 1969), for example, deciding that "A canary is yellow" or "A canary is a bird" is true. In these tasks, reaction time is used to infer the relative distance or number of branches in semantic memory between the subject and the predicate, in this case between "canary" and "yellow" or "canary" and "bird."

Figure 3.6 illustrates the model. Consider the concept "fire engine," located just above the center of the depicted portion of the network. A fire engine is a truck (short branch), which is also a vehicle. "Fire engine" is drawn to be more distant from "vehicle" and also connected to it through the connection "truck." A fire engine is more similar to an ambulance (close link) than it is to a car, also instances of vehicles. Fire engines are frequently red and are often associated with fires and houses. Thus concept properties, related concepts, and hierarchical information all constitute the concept meaning.

A network contains the word *net* and one can conceptualize the lines in the figure, the links in the network, as the threads forming the net. Where the threads intersect are the nodes of the network. Each node names a concept. As the figure suggests, in a production task with no time limit *all,* or most, information in semantic memory might be output because the concepts are all interconnected: "Fire engine" links to "daffodil" (not in the figure), through red → rose → flower → daffodil.

A computer simulation is a processing model. In addition to encoding the proposed structure underlying the concepts, it must program *how* to retrieve information from it or, in PDP models, modify the structure, learn new information. It thus includes some processing assumptions needed in a simulation. Quillian's original model was constrained by the computer capabilities of the time. Some of

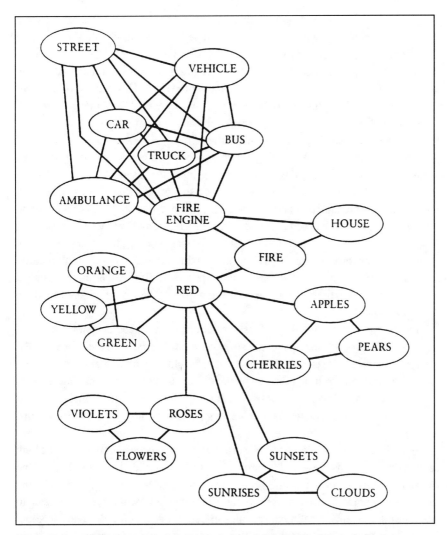

Figure 3.6. A Representation of the Interrelation of Concepts in Semantic Memory

SOURCE: A. M. Collins and E. F. Loftus (1975), "A Spreading Activation Theory of Semantic Processing," *Psychological Review, 82,* p. 412. Copyright © 1975 by the American Psychological Association. Reprinted with permission.

NOTE: Short lines indicate close associations (highly weighted), while long lines indicate less related associations.

these constraints are neither necessary for today's computers with much greater memories, nor have they been borne out as *psychologically real,* needed to account for human behavioral data. Nevertheless, it is worth considering all the assumptions because they have some intuitive appeal and have motivated many psychological experiments. It is also worth noting that the assumptions that have been borne out have been incorporated into many other models, including the PDP model, which we examined earlier. We will consider hierarchical organization, cognitive economy, labeled links, and spreading activation.

Access to a word's meaning begins for every word at the node named by the word. (This contrasts with the prototype model, which implies that access to a concept begins at the prototype or basic level of that concept.) All links to the word are progressively activated, by *spreading activation,* with the degree of activation gradually diminishing with distance from the source node. This process is repeated, and so in Figure 3.6 activation of "fire engine" will spread to "ambulance," "truck," "red," and "fire" (among others) immediately, and activation of these will in turn spread to "roses" and "apples," from the node "red."

Experiments, primarily priming studies, support a process like spreading activation. Recall that in a priming study a word is initially presented and then at some later time it is shown to speed some kind of decision about related words. The early presentation is presumed to partially activate related words, making access to them easier later. "Access" can be measured by recognizing component letters as a known word (lexical decision), determining that related words belong to the same category (semantic decision), or simply reading the word (recognition) in difficult reading conditions (light letters and so on). A word primes itself: Presenting the word at some point in the experiment will speed recognition of the word later on, called the *repetition effect.*

Presentation of the initial word also has turned out to speed decisions in any of these tasks in proportion to the degree of *semantic relatedness* of the prime and the target words (see, for example, Meyer & Schvaneveldt, 1976). Semantic relatedness is often assessed by priming but can be independently assessed by having subjects rate how related two words are or by looking at the frequency with which one word is produced as an associate of the other (e.g., Glass & Holyoake, 1975; Wilkins, 1971).

If a prime is highly related to the word, it speeds decisions about it—for as long as two days after it is presented (Scarborough, Cortese, & Scarborough, 1977)! One account of this result is that the prime activates itself and, through the links, the activation spreads to related terms. This additional activation makes it easier to retrieve the concepts, creating the priming effect. (I note that Ratcliff and McKoon, 1981, have found timing results in a priming task measuring memory for an input text that are inconsistent with spreading activation as an explanation: The spread appears to be almost instantaneous even to distant concepts, and to decay too rapidly to account for the reaction time data. They propose an alternative explanation, but modification of the spreading activation time course still permits it to be a viable alternative; McNamara, 1992.)

Figure 3.6 differentiates links in their distance from a concept node, indicating the degree of semantic relatedness or weight between the concepts in the line lengths (I represented weight in the PDP model with line thickness)—visually, how close the association is. In addition to weighting the links, Quillian's original model also *labeled* the *link* as to the kind of association it represented. (PDP models do *not* do this!) One important type of link indicates category membership in the hierarchy: subordinate or subset categories to superordinate or superset categories. So in an associative chain such as "I am a human being, which is a primate, which is a mammal, which is an animal, which is a living thing," "I" and all the nouns are associated by an ordered set of subset-superset links. Other types of links label properties of a category: Human beings have language; fire engines are red. And there are links to represent a disjunctive relation. *Disjunction* is a logical relation indicating that two or more things cannot be true at the same time—an animal cannot both bark and meow. In the marker model, disjunction was represented by alternate branches from the same node. In the PDP model it emerged as an inhibitory, not excitatory, connection, a competition between nodes.

Psychological support for the ideas of stored concepts, semantic relatedness, and differences in disjunctive and facilitative links comes from a recent study of semantic satiation (Smith & Klein, 1990). *Semantic satiation* is the phenomenological experience of a word's losing meaning if you think about it long and hard enough. (Try it; say a common word like *star* over to yourself for several minutes until its sense washes out.) In perception, satiation or *adaptation*—repeated presentation of a stimulus over a short time span—typically reduces our sensitivity to it and can increase our sensitivity to a perceptual opposite. So, if you are exposed to bright light, it takes a period of adjustment before you can see in dim light; you need to recover from the exposure. And if you look briefly at a bright white light you will have a dark afterimage. Adaptation results are usually taken to mean that a neural unit (or set of units) responsible for the perception has been fatigued, rendering that stimulus harder to perceive until there has been recovery. The adaptation also reduces the units' *inhibition* of units that respond to competing stimuli, allowing them to be more easily perceived. *What is interesting about the phenomenon of semantic satiation is that it suggests, by analogy, that there is a unit or set of units responsible for a word's recognition, which can likewise be fatigued.*

Prior to Smith and Klein's experiment, semantic satiation had primarily been an introspective phenomenon—subjects describe their sense of meaning loss—but apart from their descriptions, there was no way of assessing a perceptual change. Smith and Klein developed a subtle measure: a change in priming (or inhibition) in a semantic decision task after the prime (or inhibitor) was adapted. Specifically, as we have seen, providing a category name facilitates deciding that two items are members of that category—priming. This is proportional to the semantic similarity of the prime and the semantic decision stimuli. So, presenting *furniture* will speed decisions to *chair* and *stove,* but more to *chair* because it is a better example of, or is more semantically related to, furniture than is stove. Conversely, it is possible to slow semantic decisions by presenting a word first that belongs to a different category (like *apple,* which should prime other fruit, followed by *stove*) suggesting the activation of a disjunctive or inhibitory link between that word and the other category's words.

Now suppose that we present *furniture* or *apple* over and over, satiating it. Smith and Klein found that when satiated, a word produced less facilitation and less inhibition than in the unadapted state. This is a pretty result, because it is subtle: Reaction time differences are changing reliably, but on the order of milliseconds, something that subjects cannot do consciously. It suggests that a word's neural representation, whether a node, a set of nodes, or the weights on the links between them, can be fatigued, with the consequence that it is less able to stimulate associated concepts through spreading activation or inhibition.

The controversial assumption in Quillian's original model is that of *cognitive economy,* which refers to storing information relevant to a concept only once at the appropriate level. So, all birds have feathers, which implies that every instance of bird—canaries, robins, ostriches, and so on—has feathers. An uneconomical model would have feather information stored with every bird and with the general bird concept. Cognitive economy stores the information only as a property of bird and has each of the instances linked as subsets of bird. To decide whether "a canary has feathers" therefore requires two steps: recognizing that a canary is a bird and then that a bird has feathers. What was labeled "distinguisher" information in the marker model, the property unique to the concept and not part of the general category—like canaries are yellow, songbirds, and housepets—would be properties directly of "canary" and therefore require only one step to retrieve.

Figure 3.7 displays Collins and Quillian's original data, supporting the notions of hierarchical organization, cognitive economy, and a distinction between subset-superset and property links. The task was sentence verification. Sentences were manipulated to probe three levels of a hierarchy: the subject and predicate at the same level (0), the subject one branch below the predicate (1), and the subject two branches below the predicate (2). In the subset-superset relation, Level 0 produced an identical subject and predicate—such as "a canary is a canary"—making that very easy or fast, because one could note the letter identity of the word without really accessing the meaning. For the canary subject, Level 1 is "a canary is a bird," and Level 2, "a canary is an animal." To conclude the truth of Level 2, presumably one decides "a canary is a bird" and "a bird is an animal." Each step should take longer, and did, as the figure illustrates.

The experiment also investigated verification of properties at each of the different levels (Level 0 = "a canary can sing"; Level 1 = "a canary has feathers," a property stored with birds; Level 2 = "a canary has skin," a property of animals). Note that the results again showed an increase in reaction time with each purported level of inference in the hierarchy. This suggests that the inferences are being made, and therefore that the properties are not directly stored with each instance, but are economically stored with the superordinate category. Note also that verifying properties in general took longer than verifying category membership, suggesting a different type of link, or an association to the property through the category, an extra step.

Collins and Quillian's experiment was designed to test specific predictions of Quillian's model. Recall we argued earlier that a model's strength comes from generating specific predictions but that an experiment cannot prove a model, only disprove it. The experiment results do not disprove the model and, indeed, seem to support it strongly. However, later researchers questioned the stimuli and, eventually, the conclusion.

In particular, they noted that level in the hierarchy and the property-superset distinction both were confounded with semantic relatedness or conjoint frequency.

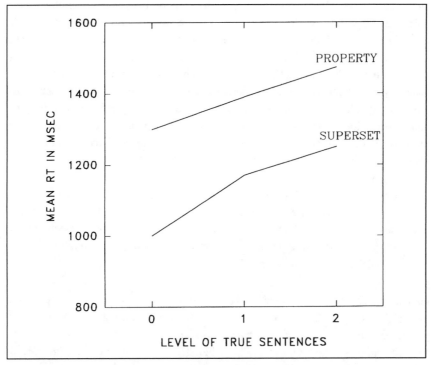

Figure 3.7. Average Reaction Time to Verify Sentences Probing Category Membership or Property Information at Different Presumed Levels in Semantic Memory

SOURCE: Adapted from A. M. Collins and M. R. Quillian (1969), "Retrieval Time From Semantic Memory," *Journal of Verbal Learning and Verbal Behavior, 8*, p. 244. Copyright © 1969 by Academic Press. Reprinted by permission.

(A *confound* is an experimental situation in which what you are interested in looking at—here, level in the hierarchy—varies systematically with something else. Thus you cannot ultimately say which of the two causes the result.) That is, "yellow" is a frequent associate of "canary"—we talk about "yellow" and "canaries" together—but "skin" is not. In fact, you may never have seen the phrase *canary skin* before; the frequency of co-occurrence of those two words, or *conjoint frequency,* is close to zero. It could be, they argued, that the longer reaction time to verify "a canary has skin" comes not from a multiple stage process—a canary is a bird is an animal that has skin—but, more simply, from a weak association strength between canary and skin. The weak strength makes it harder to access what could still be a direct connection. Indeed, if an experiment is carefully designed to measure relatedness effects independent of level in the hierarchy, only relatedness matters.

Hence Figure 3.6 graphs relatedness in the line lengths but not cognitive economy, rigid hierarchical structure, or labeled links. It is important to note, however, that relatedness does reflect hierarchy, and so on, but not perfectly. For some animals, the relation of the instance to "skin" may be close—beaver-skin, deer-skin, snake-skin—and in these cases the property may be stored both with the instance and with the category in general (as fire engine was connected to vehicle directly and through the intermediate category of truck). For others, we may make the connection only by inference: We know animals have skin and, because a canary is an animal, it must too. This may reflect our learning pattern: We generalize a category from some particular instances, and those instances will always be marked directly with the category features. Other instances we learn *from the category* (you know what a bird is and what an ostrich is, so I build on that by telling you an emu is an ostrichlike bird). For those instances we may see cognitive economy; the category properties are stored only at the category level and are inferred through the category to the instance.

We now have come full circle, because the property-rich instances are the prototypical instances, and faster verification times for them relative to peripheral instances we can say reflect *either* shorter, more direct links in a network *or* privileged access in a prototype model. The two models seem structurally different but can equally account for the results.

Summary. The network model provides spreading activation as a process for retrieving a concept and associated concepts from a partially hierarchically organized semantic network. The network is flexibly organized with semantically related concepts linked proportionally to their degree of semantic relatedness. Link strengths may reflect a difference in type of association, category membership, or property. Links may also be either excitatory or inhibitory, the latter responsible for disjunctive associations. Studies of association strength motivated by a principle of cognitive economy—that a property may not be associated with every instance but with the general category from which it is inferred for some instances—show some evidence of inference and cognitive economy but stronger evidence of partial economy and association through relatedness or conjoint frequency.

Feature Models

The network model and the prototype model describe semantic memory very differently, and appear to account for different behavioral data on semantic structure and process. Both models have had, and still wield, considerable influence. It is worth mentioning briefly a third model, which, although it has not been as influential, provides insight on semantic structure and cognitive process models.

Feature models assume that each concept is defined by a set of features or properties (Smith, Shoben, & Rips, 1974). Verification of property sentences (such as "A canary is yellow") is accomplished by searching the list for the property. Verification of subset sentences (such as "A canary is a bird") is accomplished by comparing the list of properties of both the subset (canary) and the superset (bird) for overlap; if the properties show a large (how large is not specified) amount of overlap, the sentence is assumed to be true. Note that this model specifically

---

Box 3.2. Psychological Tasks for Studying Semantic Processing

---

— *Lexical decision:* A letter string is presented on each trial and subjects must decide if it is a word or a nonword. The letter string can vary in its similarity to a real word orthographically (writing pattern) or phonologically (sound pattern). Accuracy and reaction time are usually measured, sometimes in conjunction with priming.

— *Semantic decision:* Two words are presented and subjects must decide if they belong to the same category or in some other way share a meaning attribute. Accuracy and reaction time are measured, again sometimes in conjunction with priming.

— *Priming:* A "hint" is given before some decision task to facilitate making the decision. For example, presentation of a related word (*hospital*) speeds lexical and semantic decisions (*nurse-doctor*). Note that "hint" can be a deliberate prompt and affect decisions explicitly, or it can be unconscious and affect decisions implicitly, arousing related associations.

— *Inhibition:* A "hint" is given that slows semantic or lexical decision, as when a word from a different category precedes. See note on "hint" in priming.

— *Semantic satiation:* An adaptation effect in which repeated presentation of a word causes it to seem to lose meaning. Apart from subjects' reports of their sense of temporary meaning loss, satiation can be measured as a diminution of priming or inhibition by the satiated word in semantic decision tasks.

— *Association:* A word is given as a stimulus, and subjects are to respond with words that come into their minds.

— *Production tasks:* A variant of an association task, in which subjects list several associates to a stimulus. This can be relatively unstructured and exhaustive, such as "Tell me what you know about machines," or it can be constrained, such as "List fruits that begin with a 'p'."

— *Sentence verification:* A sentence is presented and subjects must quickly decide if it is true or false. Reaction time and accuracy are both measured.

— *Semantic differential:* Subjects rate a word or object on a number of bipolar scales like hot-cold, good-bad, male-female. The ratings are factor analyzed to produce response clusters for each word. The differential has been reliably found to produce clusters around dimensions reflecting evaluation (pleasant-unpleasant), activity, and potency.

---

contradicts the cognitive economy assumption: It is the *duplication* of information that permits verification. Note also that the model does not organize the feature lists.

Feature theorists argue for two kinds of features: characteristic features and defining features. *Defining features* must be present for an instance to be a member of a category. For bird, for example, beaks, feathers, and egg-laying would be defining features. *Characteristic features* are found in most instances of the category—they are typical—but are not necessary. For birds, characteristic features might include flying (there are flightless birds), 6-to-10-inch size (but think of hummingbirds, turkeys, and ostriches), and so on.

Recall the hedges discussed in the last chapter, *technically speaking* and *loosely speaking*. Technically true sentences are those for which defining features, but not characteristic features, overlap between subject and predicate (e.g., "Technically, a chicken is a bird"). Loosely true sentences overlap characteristic, but not defining, features (e.g., "Loosely, a bat is a bird"). When both sets of features overlap, we do not use a hedge (e.g., "A robin is a bird").

To account for other semantic memory data we have examined, the feature model employs a two-stage comparison process. Stage 1 assesses broadly the degree to which a category and an instance share features: If they share many, there is a fast true; if they share few, a fast false. If they share an intermediate number, Stage 2 is needed. Entering Stage 2 itself requires some time, and Stage 2 is time-consuming. It performs an in-depth comparison of the highly weighted (usually defining) features of the instance with those of the category to see if they match.

Recall that it is faster to verify that a canary is a bird than that it is an animal, a more distant category in the hierarchy. In the feature model, canary-bird can be decided on the basis of the first stage alone, while canary-animal, with less feature overlap, would require the longer Stage 2. Similarly, items that are highly semantically related can be verified on the basis of Stage 1 alone, and items of intermediate relation will take longer because of Stage 2. Finally, prototypical category members will have more characteristic feature overlap than peripheral members and can thus likewise avoid the time-consuming Stage 2 process.

The feature model principally suffers in postulating of defining features. Recall that categories are *not* well defined but fuzzy: A plucked chicken is still a bird, and a feather pillow is not. So "feathers" is not a defining feature. Similar arguments can be made for almost any feature "defining" a concept. The feature model also does not provide much framework for organizing facts about semantics and semantic memory. But, of interest, Goodglass (1980) describes a "quick-and-dirty" process for naming and retrieval of information, followed, if it fails, by a slow, methodical process in brain-damaged patients' word retrieval.

We have now examined the leading models and data on semantic memory. As you can see, each has strengths, each describes memory differently, and each accounts for some of the data. Box 3.3 summarizes the models and data. The best model will account for the most data with the fewest assumptions; beyond that you are free to prefer the model that is most plausible to you.

CONSTRUCTIVIST VIEWS OF SEMANTIC MEMORY: THE METAPHOR OF MIND

Our discussion so far has taken a passive stance toward both meaning and its processing. We have looked at the understanding of uninteresting sentences, such as "Canaries are yellow," assuming that their interpretation derives from an automatic activation of either stored information or "stored" connection weights.

Box 3.3. Summary of Models, Results, and Explanations for Semantic Memory

	PDP	PROTOTYPE	NETWORK	FEATURE
Description of the Model	Concepts are represented by a pattern of activation across connected units. Each presentation of a stimulus results in a change in weights of the unit connections until the network settles into a stable pattern. Activation of a unit will produce activation or inhibition of connected units in proportion to their weight.	Related concepts are located near one another. The typical instance is central to the category concept. Typicality and category boundaries are established by balancing high information content (important distinctions) with high redundancy (important similarities). Comprehension begins by entering a category at the prototype or basic level and then fanning out. Prototypes are most codable: reliably produced, easily acted or imaged, learned early, and more available cognitively.	All concepts are related through a rich associative net. Intersections in the net are represented by labels (words) marking properties, category names, or other features. Comprehension begins by entering the node labeled with the word name and consists of excitation of all nodes connected directly or indirectly to that node. Connections may be strongly or weakly weighted, and are labeled as to the kind of association (e.g., superordinate, disjunction, and so on).	Concepts are described in terms of two types of features: characteristic and defining. *Defining features* are those features that *must* be present for a concept to be recognized. *Characteristic features* are those that are usually present. Comprehension takes place in two stages: first, determining if a quick decision can be made based on large or little feature overlap, and, if not, checking the defining features methodically.

Box 3.3 Continued

EXPERIMENT RESULTS	ACCOUNTS			
	PDP	PROTOTYPE	NETWORK	FEATURE
1. Category name is a better prime for good than poor instances.	1. Greater weight between category name and good instance.	1. Category search begins at the good instances, making the search faster.	1. The connection to the good instances is more highly weighted.	1. Good instances have enough category features to avoid Stage 2.
2. Priming causes faster access of related words.	2. Prime activates connections proportionally to connection weights.	2. ⟵——— ?	2. There is spreading activation to related concepts.	2. ———→ ?
3. Repeating the prime can semantically satiate it, nullifying its effect on meaning-related words.	3. Adaptation of units temporarily weakens their excitatory and inhibitory effects on linked units.	3. ⟵——— ?	3. Adaptation diminishes spreading activation.	3. ———→ ?
4. It takes less time to verify instances and properties of intermediate than higher categories.	4. There is greater weight for connections to intermediate category than higher category units.	4. The instance is more typical of the intermediate than the higher category.	4. The instance is more directly connected to intermediate than to higher categories and their properties.	4. The instance shares more features with the intermediate-level category.
5. Semantic relatedness speeds sentence verification.	5. Semantic relatedness determines connection weights.	5. Prototypes are more related to the category name.	5. Highly related concepts are more highly weighted.	5. Related concepts share enough features to skip Stage 2.

Alternative concepts of meaning processing see it as a more active process, in which perceivers *construct* hypotheses, frameworks, and settings and then construct meaning in an utterance with respect to those hypotheses (Gibbs, 1994). This is critical for language understanding out of the laboratory. Remember that "Do you have a watch?" normally means indirectly "Tell me the time" but must be interpreted quite differently if the questioner is not a kind, late stranger but an armed robber. Then the meaning must be constructed literally and directly.

Because normal language as communication transmits information—reduces uncertainty (see Chapter 1)—its purpose can rarely be the passive retrieval of well-learned facts. A communication of something new, whether a new speaker intent or a new thought to the listener, must entail some new connection. Once we consider speaker intent and general context, it is probable that most utterances could be taken many ways, figuratively or literally, depending on setting. Take, for example, the *tautology* or truism, "A lion is a lion." Here, I want it to be understood literally, as a sentence hardly worth saying, at Level 0 in a subset-superset link for sentence verification. If it were a comment on a report that a child was mauled by a pet lion, I would want the subject lion to be taken literally and the predicate lion to be a figure of speech representing "lion as a wild animal." That cannot be understood from the words alone; one must *construct a framework* where different characteristics of "lion" emerge in the two positions. This is despite the fact that the subject lion, using "normal" lion meaning, should *prime all* those lion features equally. Some of those must be suppressed by a process independent of the words in the sentence—triggered by the active construction on the part of the listener.

Let us examine another "straightforward" sentence, "Today is September 7." It is easy to see what each word means and how together they seem to make a simple assertion of the date. Now imagine that the context of the assertion is as follows: A man and a woman who were married some years ago on September 7 are in conversation; the man has just announced he is going to a ball game with some friends this evening; the wife rejoins with our "simple assertion." In effect, this assertion could mean "You have forgotten our anniversary," or, perhaps, "No, you may not go" or even, perhaps, "I want a divorce"—depending on their history. Alternatively, if September 7 is the first day of school, and the assertion follows a sleepy child asking why he or she has to get up, it would mean, "This is the first day of school."

Thus *any* simple assertion can be ambiguous, can take on different meanings depending on the situation it was uttered in and the shared experiences of the participants. Normal sentence understanding may rarely be accomplished simply through passive look-up, the "standard" approach. We must construct meaning based on particular features of the sentence's words, the context, and the speaker's perceived intent.

Constructing Meaning in Figures of Speech

The standard theory of semantic processing holds that normal language understanding is dull, requiring only passive activation of information. In this theory, then, figurative language is an anomaly, uninterpretable by a straight passive look-up. Figures of speech, like the metaphor "Camels are the ships of the desert," are falsehoods. Their comprehension requires recognition of the falsehood and its conversion to a truth by, for example, mentally *substituting* a literal word for the metaphoric element or substituting a hedge, *like,* and converting the metaphor to a *simile* ("Camels are like ships . . ."). The standard theory allows a more interesting process, the reconstruction of the sentence and then its understanding, but only *after* the automatic, passive process fails, where failure is defined as recognizing anomaly, nonsense, or untruth. This model suggests that understanding nonliteral language should take longer than understanding literal language (and that metaphor should take longer to understand than simile) because it involves at least one additional step.

Several lines of evidence suggest that the standard account is wrong. Given appropriate context, figurative sentences take no longer than literal sentences to verify (see, e.g., Ortony, 1980). Moreover, metaphors are no harder to comprehend than similes, which do not require the mental substitution of a *like* because it is already there. Too, subjects do not feel that metaphor and simile convey the same meaning, indicating that they are not mentally interpreting one as the other (Gibbs, 1994).

In addition there is evidence that figurative interpretations are derived automatically, not secondarily. If subjects are specifically asked to verify sentences on the basis of *literal* meaning, *verification takes longer if there is also a figurative meaning*: It takes longer to decide that "some jobs are jails" is literally false than it does to decide that "some desks are melons" is literally false (Glucksberg, 1989; Glucksberg, Gildea, & Bookin, 1982). This suggests that the metaphoric meaning is created along with the literal meaning, not as an optional process, and that it interferes with decisions about the latter.

Note that the generation of multiple meanings holds at the word level as well, even when context should inhibit some of them. All standard meanings of a *polysemous* word (one with more than one meaning—such as *bank* or *drift*) appear to be aroused and remain active for a bit (Gibbs, 1994; Williams, 1992). I raise this here because it suggests that competing hypotheses as to word meaning are entertained normally even in literal language—another similarity between figurative and literal processing.

(The activation of irrelevant associations, say of "snow" for *drift* meaning "meaning," may have a cascading effect as different meanings in turn arouse associations: "ice," "cold." Rendering one meaning, say "meaning" for *drift,* into another language will fail to produce the same cascade, and it is unlikely to find equivalent polysemous words. The difference in thought produced by the necessarily selective translation is an instance of linguistic relativity; Hunt & Agnoli, 1991.)

Thus there is experimental evidence to suggest that in both literal and figurative language processing, multiple possible meanings, not just the one most likely, are generated. For both literal and figurative language, the most likely meaning may passively emerge given contextual cues, or it may involve active constructive processes on the part of the hearer.

Figurative Language May Yet Be "Special"

Although there is evidence that figurative language interpretation is not weird and does not *follow* attempts at literal interpretation, there is also reason to believe that it is different. Importantly, metaphor *feels* different. Consider what happens as you understand "Billboards are warts on the landscape" (Verbrugge & McCarrell, 1977). I felt a slight tension (like when I get a joke), which is relieved by the insight into the metaphor's meaning. The insight is what makes metaphors fun. Do you normally feel that tension when you comprehend a sentence? Johnson (1980) proposes that the tension arises from the apparent contradiction, and the "fun" arises from the construction of the common *ground* (here, ugliness) relating the metaphor *topic* (here, billboards) to the metaphor *vehicle* (how you get from the topic to the ground; here, through warts). If such a process happens in understanding literal sentences, it does not produce as strong a sensation of tension and relief.

Figurative language is also used in situations different from those literal language is used in. In part this may be because literal language underdescribes the rich natural and ideational worlds of speakers who then create new uses of existing language, to make a best fit for the given situation (Gibbs & Gerrig, 1989). In part, the use of figurative language itself, in demanding a special construction from the listener, is an invitation to intimacy, to "play," to discover a ground that, at least for a while, is common only to the speaker and the hearer. Thus the choice of unconventional over conventional language demands a greater social commitment on the part of the conversation participants, perhaps because it involves a greater cognitive commitment (Gibbs & Gerrig, 1989). In fact, Gibbs (1994) showed that people took longer to construct meaning for anomalous sentences if told that they were penned by a poet than if told they were generated by a machine. That is, people make the commitment to language work in a situation they perceive as more intimate.

Finally, there are studies showing differences in association between metaphorically related elements and literally related elements. Blasko and Connine (1993) showed that while literal sentences effectively prime related words in a lexical decision task, metaphors prime words related to the metaphor ground only sometimes: when the metaphor is very familiar (and thus might have a ready-made association), very apt (so it is easy to derive), or presented a while before the target word (so there is time for the ramifications of the ground to percolate). In this last condition, with a delay between the prime and the target, where the metaphor required time to understand, *the metaphor more effectively primed than the literal sentence.* Similarly, Verbrugge and McCarrell showed, in a memory task, that the ground, not explicitly given, *better* prompted recall of the metaphor than either the topic or the vehicle. Thus figurative language seems to involve a different—an additional or a deeper—comprehension process than does literal language.

Constructing Common Ground

Literal language understanding involves *activation* of common connections, as we have discussed. So, if I tell you truthfully that an emu is an ostrichlike bird, you add emu to your lexicon and connect it to all the ostrich properties nonselectively. However, if I tell you that my friend's marriage is an icebox, you cannot activate all properties nonselectively. Rather, you must select only some features to apply, and those features you may also have to interpret metaphorically (an icebox is literally cold while a marriage is only figuratively cold). Ortony (1980) argues that the selected features of good metaphors result from a *salience imbalance* between the features of topic and vehicle: Features that are very highly weighted or salient in the vehicle (in this case, coldness) are transferred to the topic, for which those same features initially had a low weight. The difference in the salience of the features is what enables the metaphor. The construction of the ground involves noting the salience imbalance and judging the similarity between the topic and the vehicle *against* the differences between the two. The transfer of highly weighted vehicle features to the topic, or the great degree to which associative weights must be modified, may make understanding a metaphor feel different from less constructive understanding.

For any, even literal, constructive understanding, a similar process may occur. Reconsider the literal "Today is September 7." If it is the anniversary date, that would be a highly weighted feature of the predicate (vehicle position) and clearly a nonsalient property of the topic (today) for the forgetful husband. The fact that the seemingly trivial is being uttered causes the listener to reweigh or transfer features. As Gerrig and Gibbs (1988; Gibbs & Gerrig, 1989) stress, and Lakoff and Johnson stressed before them, figurative language comprehension is ordinary, not extraordinary—because all language is constructed. Pun intended: All language understanding in social contexts requires discovering common ground.

Summary

Meaning in language involves constructive processes, not simply passive activation of prestored knowledge. This results from the reasons we speak—to transmit new information and to create a social bond. Communication entails commitment, and that commitment is reflected by the engagement of active, constructive processes—work, but work that is fun. To best describe something, to engage a listener, to recall a previous shared ground, a speaker may choose to use language unconventionally. If the utterance overlaps with the hearer's constructed context, hypotheses about intent, and world knowledge, it is understood on the basis of the

---

Box 3.4. Construction of Meaning in Literal and Figurative Language

— *Substitution theory:* To understand metaphor, one must substitute for the figure of speech a literally true alternative.

— *Comparison theory:* Metaphor is an implicit simile, "something is *like* something else," with the "like" omitted. To understand we infer the "like."

— *Interaction theory:* The fun of metaphor arises from a tension created by the anomaly. The anomaly is resolved by creating a common ground between the topic or tenor of the metaphor, and the vehicle.

— *Salience imbalance:* The interaction arises from applying highly weighted features of the vehicle to the topic, for which they were not originally highly weighted. Note that a metaphor radically changes meaning if topic and vehicle are reversed: "Billboards are warts on the landscape" has as common ground "ugly protuberance," a salient feature of wart. "Warts are billboards" has as common ground something like an advertising slogan.

— Psycholinguistic research does not support an initial attempt at translation of metaphor into simile or of rejection of the literal anomaly before the figurative meaning is attempted.

— There is good evidence that many possible meanings of words and sentences are evoked simultaneously and influence understanding.

— Both literal and figurative meaning processing seem to involve the establishment of common ground. For literal meaning, the ground may be shared extralinguistic and pragmatic knowledge; for figurative meaning, it may be the common ground established between speaker and listener, or immediately between topic and vehicle.

— Both literal and figurative meaning understanding are facilitated by appropriate context. Both require construction of a theory or framework involving understanding of the situation, the speaker's intent, and the senses and associations to the words used. This is facilitated by context. The immediate creation of common ground for novel figurative speech may enhance the association between the metaphor and the ground, as measured by perceptual priming or prompted recall.

— Use of figurative language tightens the social bond between speaker and listener by requiring commitment to understanding and/or by alluding to a personal, idiosyncratic frame of reference. Figurative language may also be used to create a more precise meaning than is available in conventional language.

---

overlap. If it does not jibe, the hearer may establish new hypotheses on the basis of what overlaps against the background of what does not overlap.

SUBLEXICAL MEANING CONSTRUCTION

Our discussion thus far has assumed the word as the unit of meaning around which semantic memory is organized. As we discussed in the last chapter, language is structured with sublexical (smaller-than-word) units of meaning called morphemes, and even perhaps with meaning senses given in smaller units of sound in sound symbolism. Does semantic memory organization reflect sublexical meanings? Note that a yes answer suggests that we process words normally with regard, in part, to their roots. A no answer suggests that although the root may be important in creating new words or understanding never-before-seen words, it is not actively processed in understanding common words.

In the last chapter, we distinguished between some kinds of morphemes, free and bound, and inflectional and derivational. Studies of the psychological reality of morphology in meaning processing have focused on derivational morphology because it is that which is meaning changing. (We will look at inflectional morphology in Chapter 5 on syntax processing. We will also consider, then, case representations, whether inflectionally marked or marked, as in English, by ordered word combinations.) Psychologists analyze derivational morphology into categories depending on how clear the roots are, known as semantic transparency and phonological transparency (Marslen-Wilson, Tyler, Waksler, & Older, 1994). *Semantic transparency* refers to the extent to which the compositional morphemes' meanings are preserved in the combination. *Happiness* and *unhappy* are transparent in that the core meaning of *happy* is maintained, with "-iness" adding "the state of being _ " and un-adding "not." On the other hand, *release* is semantically opaque, composed of "re-" (= again) and "lease," which, at least now, means "rent," although historically it is related to "loose." *Phonological transparency* refers to the extent to which the derivational morpheme looks and sounds the same in different combinations. *Happiness* and *unhappy* are phonologically transparent and semantically transparent. *Vain* and *vanity* are semantically transparent but phonologically opaque: You cannot hear or see the *vain* in *vanity,* although you probably will concede that it is there.

There is strong evidence from priming studies that derivational morphology plays a role in normal semantic processing, that derivationally complex words are understood in terms of their components. Dorfman (1994) demonstrated this by measuring memory for nonwords that he created by combining syllables of real words. The syllables were either morphemes (like "non" or "tion") or not (like "cre" or "ate"). Subjects thought that the morpheme-composed nonwords were better possible words than the syllable-composed nonwords. More interesting, they were more likely to remember implicitly having seen the morpheme-composed than syllable-composed nonwords. *Implicit memory* affects performance whether or not the subject explicitly recalls an experience. (Priming is implicit, where a word arouses meanings for a long time, perhaps a long time after the mention of the word itself was forgotten.) Here, subjects were faster at reading and making decisions about morphologically composed nonwords that they had seen before than they were about syllable-composed nonwords that they had seen before.

Marslen-Wilson et al. (1994) demonstrated implicit memory, priming effects in a lexical decision task, for semantically transparent derivational morphemes in new contexts, regardless of their phonological transparency. That is, primes such as

---

Box 3.5. Effects of Morphology

— *Semantic transparency:* Morpheme meaning preserved in combination (*unhappy* is transparent, *release* is opaque).
— *Phonological transparency:* Morpheme sound is preserved in combination (*unhappy* is transparent; *vain/vanity,* opaque).
— Nonwords composed of real morphemes are more memorable than those composed of pseudomorphemes (such as "cre").
— Morphologically related words prime one another.

---

tension, delightful, or *serenity* preceded targets such as *tense, delight,* or *serene* (the last is *not* phonologically transparent). Primes were spoken; targets were written. Their effects were compared, as in Dorfman's study, to syllabically, but not morphologically, related trials like "tinsel-tin." (And, of course, in lexical decision, there are nonword trials, here "donkey-donk" or "usage-usetern.") The morphologically related, but not the syllable-related, primes speeded decision time, with only a small (and not significant) increase in decision time if the prime and target were phonologically different. Follow-up studies showed morphological priming to occur *only* when the derived form preserved the meaning of the morpheme.

The results as a whole suggest another level of structure in semantic memory for at least some words and meanings, and another constructive process. Nodes (units or patterns of activation, depending on your preferred model) may represent parts of a word, to the extent that the part has recognizable meaning and is still productive in the language. Comprehension of a word derived from that part would involve activation of that node (or group of units) *in combination with* the nodes corresponding to the meanings underlying the other derivational morphemes. Once a word's meaning evolves away from its compositional meaning, the word meaning is unitary and no longer compositionally produced.

We might consider this model analogous to the representation of idiomatic expressions such as *kick the bucket.* This likewise shows sometimes unitary properties and sometimes compositional properties. *Kick the bucket* is a frozen form. It is understood quickly, before the last word is completed, and its meaning is not preserved with slight changes: *The bucket was kicked* or *kick the pail* are interpreted literally, not as death, although they are componentially similar. *Carry a torch for someone,* while also an idiom, is componential: *A torch was carried for, carry a flame for,* or *hold a torch for* are seen as meaning the same thing (Gibbs, 1994).

What is important in both cases, and in seeing the similarity between the two cases, is that organization in semantic memory is flexible; it does not always perfectly reflect the seeming structure of the language. The unit of meaning—the meaning we store or the pattern we access—may correspond to the morpheme, the word, or a whole phrase, depending on the frequency of the particular structure in the language and in the individual's experience. The analogy of our semantic dictionary to a real dictionary may hold insofar as both access meanings of units of different size: morphemes, words, or multiword expressions. The critical consideration is not what the unit is—a word or a word part or a word combination—but whether it acts as a relatively indivisible unit of meaning in combinations.

WORD NAMES

Our examination of structure and processing of concepts has assumed that those concepts are named by words. *How* are the concepts connected to the sound or appearance of the word name? This section begins by considering two popular descriptive models, the logogen model and the cohort model, which explicitly treat access of conceptual information given a word input. While these models are easiest to consider for written word input—in part because we are communicating here through written word input—they may also serve as analogy to spoken word input processes. This is somewhat more complex because the relation of a sound to a spoken language unit (a "p" or an "i") is not as direct as between a letter and a reading unit. We will reconsider these models in Chapter 7, after we have studied speech.

This section primarily deals with production models. In *production* we begin with an idea, within the conceptual network, and search for a way to put that idea into words. The idea can be prompted, by a picture or a definition, so that the target word is known, at least to the experimenter. As with the logogen and cohort models, to produce the correct word, we must consider the links between the concept, the meaning of the word that we have been given, and the letters and sounds that make up its name. We must also consider the links among the letters and sounds. It is easiest and most fun to see these usually invisible, quick, and correct processes when they fail—when we make slips of the tongue or cannot come up with the name that we know we know, when we are in tip-of-the-tongue state.

Retrieving the Concept From the Word

Words are not undivided wholes: They are made up of letter or sound sequences, which are also structured within the language. We will more formally study the structures when we study the sound system and reading. For now, we need to accept that a word is a sequence, the recognition of which must in part be accomplished by learned associations, as depicted in Figure 3.4, of the components: of "w" in first position, to "o" and "r" in second and third positions, to "d" in last position. *Those particular* component associations also underlie "wor-m" and "wor-k" and "wor-n" in Figure 3.4. Semantic memory must connect idea units (such as animal) with sound-letter units, as the figure shows.

Now, imagine how recognizing a word in a context might take place. In the sentence beginning this paragraph, *word* is conceptually primed, as we have been discussing it throughout this chapter. In the sentence, "a" preceded "word," setting the stage for a noun; the word "recognizing" also suggested *word* as a thing to be recognized. Each of these concepts will partially activate the meaning of *word,* a conceptually driven or top-down process. The meaning of *word* will now activate the sound-letter units corresponding to *word* (and to other potential fillers of that meaning slot) because the meaning and that pattern have been linked. In addition, we see in the correct context, the letters w-o-r-d. Each of those letters will be individually recognized in the layer we have just introduced, and as each is recognized, it will partly activate recognition units for the other letters because they frequently co-occur. Thus *word* will also be recognized from *stimulus-driven* (bottom-up) *processes,* where the stimulus is the actual letters or sounds.

We have just described the basis for the *logogen model* (Morton, 1969) and the *cohort model* (Marslen-Wilson & Welsh, 1978). *Logogen* is a name for the word-recognizing unit. A logogen receives input from the letter/speech sounds of the stimulus and from the meaning-related units activated by the context. The set of logogens corresponds to the set of words. Each logogen has a basic threshold and will respond when the sum of activations exceeds that threshold. Logogens for high-frequency words have lower thresholds than logogens for low-frequency words; that is, it is easier for the system to reach threshold and respond to a higher frequency word. Logogen thresholds also are lowered temporarily following acti-vation, accounting for the repetition effect (recall that this was when a word primed itself—up to several days after the initial presentation). As you can see, the principles underlying the logogen model are not very different from those we explored in the PDP models, developed and tested many years later.

The output from the logogen model is the word with the highest activation state. The cohort model differs from the logogen model principally in assuming a more time-varying output. You can conceptualize a cohort (literally a group of associates) as several activated, related logogens. Consider a game of hangman, where you have guessed wor_. The possibilities you are now considering are the cohort aroused by that stimulus configuration. A clue such as the last letter is tall or in the first 12 letters of the alphabet will reduce the cohort from four items *(word work worm worn)* to two items (*word* and *work*). One has recognized the word when the cohort is reduced to one item.

The examples I provided for producing and reducing a cohort are rather artificial; they correspond to a game situation, not a situation of understanding normal language. But it readily generalizes to the normal situation. When you are listening or reading, a cohort is formed through hypotheses as to the next words given the context, or the whole word given the letter or sound sequences you have just read or heard. Given the phrase *hard wor_,* your cohort will be *work, word.* The next letter you scan may reduce the cohort to one item, as may subsequent context: "Hard wor_ builds strong minds." The cohort model incorporates this concept of continu-ous updating or *on-line processing.* There are also minor modifications of the logogen model incorporated into the cohort model. These permit recognition of a nonword, for which there would be no existing logogen, so the stimulus input must connect not only to logogens and from there to output (like pronunciation rules) but it must also connect *directly* to an output stage. The cohort model also accounts for findings that early more than late letter or sound positions are of greater importance in selection of the cohort. The cohort model weighs those letter positions more highly so they more greatly activate the logogen than other positions.

Producing Word Names

Now let us turn to an internally generated idea that must be put into words, as opposed to an externally generated idea, a word, or concept to be recognized. As you can imagine, the process should be similar, differing only in that the internal generation of the idea, the previous words you have said, and perhaps the words the person you are speaking to has said, provide the conceptual arousal for the logogen, cohort, or word names. The question to address here is how that conceptual driving leads to pronunciation, the connection between the idea and the name's sound.

Two types of studies have examined this. The first type is a variant of an association task, in which subjects are asked to produce words matching some rule, such as fruits that begin with "p" or fruits that end with "m" (see, for example, Collins & Loftus, 1975). Two results are of interest here. First, as you can guess if you tried producing fruit names to the rules I suggested, it is much easier to retrieve names given first letter information than later letter information. Second, it turns out to be significantly easier (faster) to produce category instances beginning with a particular letter if one does a number of these in a row—keep thinking of fruit that begin with a "p"—than if you do one, then generate a fruit name by a different rule (e.g., fruit that is red), then back to the particular letter. This is a priming effect at the sound-letter level within the category; "p" is priming other p-initial words.

The second method of studying internally generated naming produces the same conclusions. This is a naturalistic study of speech errors: the inability to retrieve the desired name, or "tip of the tongue," or the accidental production of a different word (which is perhaps noted and corrected) or "slip of the tongue." The tip-of-the-tongue (TOT) phenomenon was formally investigated in a classic study by Brown and McNeill (1966), whose methods and results have been replicated across different conditions and experimental groups (e.g., across age groups; see, for example, Burke, MacKay, Worthley, & Wade, 1991; for a review, see A. S. Brown, 1991). In these studies, subjects keep a TOT diary, recording when they feel they are in the TOT state; if they have a "feeling of knowing" (FOK) the correct word but just cannot get to it; what they know about the target (first letter, number of syllables); and if, when, and how they arrive at the correct word.

Also done by Brown and McNeill, TOTs may also be studied experimentally. The experimenter attempts to produce the TOT state by reading subjects definitions of low-frequency words such as *ambergris, apse,* or *sampan* and asking them to name the word. If subjects are successful or if they have no idea what the target is, the trial is ignored. If the subject confesses to a sensation of TOT, of FOK, the experimenter prompts with questions about the target, like those listed above for the diary. Brown and McNeill successfully so produced TOT states in about 13%

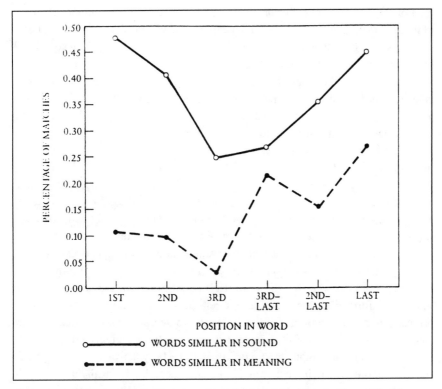

Figure 3.8. The Percentage of Letters at Each Position Matching the Target Word in a Guess by Subjects in the TOT State

SOURCE: R. Brown and D. McNeill (1966), "The 'Tip of the Tongue' Phenomenon," *Journal of Verbal Learning and Verbal Behavior, 5*, p. 330. Copyright © 1966 by Academic Press. Reprinted by permission.

of the cases. Success was defined as the subject stating the experience of the TOT state and then coming up with the target during the questioning or recognizing the target when provided. This percentage is consistent with results in replications.

The results of both the diary and the experimental studies show that subjects have access to partial information about the sound of the name even when they cannot retrieve the whole name. Subjects were able to guess the number of syllables in the word 48% of the time. Words targeted had between one and five syllables, so if subjects simply said any number between one and five, they would have been right only 20% of the time. As Figure 3.8 shows, subjects also had knowledge of the specific sounds of the word, and more knowledge of the sound at the beginning or the end than at the middle. Brown and McNeill calculated this information by asking subjects to guess the letter specifically, or to guess a word like the word they were looking for once they were in the TOT state. They could then compare the sound composition of the word guessed with the target. Subjects' guesses were related to the target sometimes by meaning (which is not surprising, given that the prompt was a definition) and sometimes by sound, and the figure displays the letter relationship of both types of errors. Note that if chance is $\frac{1}{26}$ (the number of letters of the alphabet), guesses at almost all letter positions were well above chance. Later studies have argued that frequently the error relates to the target in *both* sound and meaning, such as recalling *charity* for *chastity.*

Indeed, slips of the tongue likewise often share both meaning and sound: A slip is likely to be from the same part of speech and be a semantically related word (like *father* for *mother*) perhaps transposing a prefix or suffix or first letter from a related word or one that is arising in the same discourse.

The collection of results suggests, as with the cohort and logogen models, a layer of sound-letter associations connected to meaning associations. Node Structure Theory (NST; Burke et al., 1991; MacKay, 1987) proposes that actual name retrieval occurs only when the phonological feature level, these sound-letter associations, are fully activated to threshold. Priming readies a node for activation and spreads among all connections, as we have discussed in previous models. Activation itself, however, is all or none, and spreads sequentially, in order, between connections (of letters). This distinction is necessary to explain why partial information is available about the word but the word itself is not retrieved. The idea is that the semantic information, the idea, primes related semantic information and also primes sound-letter information for the word. To access the word's name, *each* sound-letter unit must be fully activated in turn. A strong weight to the first unit (the first letter) makes that sound most likely to be fully activated. But if there is some disruption of the link between the first and second letter, while the idea will have primed the second letter, there is no way for the first letter to activate it fully, and the word will be lost to retrieval. The feeling of knowing can arise from priming, sensing the readiness. And resolution of the TOT, the subject's spontaneous memory of the correct word, may arise when the disrupted link is partially restored, perhaps because the same sound combinations have been presented in another word in conversation.

Finally, it is interesting to note that studies of words likely to induce TOTs have shown a great propensity for TOTs in proper names but generally, otherwise, only a small word frequency effect. Natural TOTs occur commonly even with high-frequency words. Nevertheless, in trying to induce a TOT state, most studies use low-frequency words, as did Brown and McNeill.

SUMMARY AND CONCLUSIONS

In this chapter we explored data relevant to the question of how words and their meanings are mentally represented. We have seen that there is evidence for several types of representation—motor, image, and abstract verbal—and that there is evidence for a structural organization of the verbal representation. In particular, we can assume that there is a level of organization corresponding to information about the word name (how it sounds or how it is spelled) that interfaces through meaning with sensory representations so we can name an object or event. There must also be sensory-based representations like images so that we can evoke the appropriate

---

Box 3.6. Naming Models and Data

— *Logogen model:* Words are represented by their names, which have a threshold for activation. They may be activated from meaning, writing, or sound features. Common words have lower thresholds. Priming or presenting a word lowers its threshold.

— *Cohort model:* Input arouses a set of consistent words. A word is recognized or produced when the input has narrowed the set to one item.

— The first letter of a word more highly activates it than subsequent letters.

— Tip-of-the-tongue studies show that even when a subject cannot retrieve a word, she or he has access to partial information about it, particularly the first and last letters.

— *Node structure theory:* A logogen-type model, which assumes that a word name is retrieved only if it is fully activated phonologically, and that phonological connections are position dependent (w-o, not w-r for *word*).

---

mental picture given the name. We can also assume that there is a level of organization corresponding to emotional or connotative meaning, derived in part from the associations of words and in part from the natural human tendency to classify things with respect to their effects (positive-negative, strong-weak, active-passive, among other dimensions). Finally, we can assume a level for verbal meaning whereby meanings are represented by associations to other meanings, related properties, features, category inclusions, and so on. This representation level may not be reserved only for language but may structure our thought, which is in part informed by language. It may also not be accessed strictly in word units, but sometimes in morpheme-sized units and sometimes in idiomatic phrases. The organization does not reflect a rigid analysis of thoughts and experiences, but a fuzzy one, arising naturally (and messily) from imperfect correlations of features in everyday experience.

We have seen evidence for implicit, passive processes arousing connections in semantic memory, in priming, semantic satiation, and spreading activation. Nevertheless, it is clear that meaning can only be achieved through active, constructive processes, which at minimum weed out alternatives irrelevant to the situation but often, as in the tension experienced in resolving a good metaphor, create a ground or actively change association weights.

I have not attempted to show how semantic memory functions in the normal language comprehension processes of determining case relations or piecing together meanings in a sentence or paragraph. In the instances where we looked at sentence or phrase meaning, either we were looking at relatively unitary meanings as in idioms, or we were looking at componential processing such as relating topic to vehicle in a metaphor while ignoring the critical question of how one knows which is topic and which is vehicle. In the next chapters we shall examine rules and processes that enable us to determine these roles. At the end of our discussion of syntax and syntactic processing, we will return to the question of organization of meaning, to see how it is produced and understood in longer than one-word utterances.

REFERENCES

Berlin, B., & Kay, P. (1969). *Basic color terms.* Berkeley: University of California Press.

Blasko, D. G., & Connine, C. M. (1993). Effects of familiarity and aptness on metaphor processing. *Journal of Experimental Psychology: Learning, Memory, and Cognition, 19,* 295-308.

Brown, A. S. (1991). A review of the tip of the tongue experience. *Psychological Bulletin, 109,* 204-223.

Brown, R., & Lenneberg, E. H. (1954). A study in language and cognition. *Journal of Abnormal and Social Psychology, 49,* 454-462.

Brown, R., & McNeill, D. (1966). The "tip of the tongue" phenomenon. *Journal of Verbal Learning and Verbal Behavior, 5,* 325-337.

Burke, D. M., MacKay, D. G., Worthley, J. S., & Wade, E. (1991). On the tip of the tongue: What causes word finding failures in young and older adults? *Journal of Memory and Language, 30,* 542-579.

Chomsky, N. (1959). Review of *Verbal behavior* by B. F. Skinner. *Language, 35,* 26-58.

Collins, A. M., & Loftus, E. F. (1975). A spreading activation theory of semantic processing. *Psychological Review, 82,* 407-428.

Collins, A. M., & Quillian, M. R. (1969). Retrieval time from semantic memory. *Journal of Verbal Learning and Verbal Behavior, 8,* 240-247.

Dorfman, J. (1994). Sublexical components in implicit memory for novel words. *Journal of Experimental Psychology: Learning, Memory, and Cognition, 20,* 1108-1125.

Eddy, J. K., & Glass, A. L. (1981). Reading and listening to high and low imagery sentences. *Journal of Verbal Learning and Verbal Behavior, 20,* 333-345.

Farah, M. J., & McClelland, J. L. (1991). A computational model of semantic memory impairment: Modality specificity and emergent category specificity. *Journal of Experimental Psychology: General, 120,* 339-357.

Fodor, J. A. (1983). *The modularity of mind.* Cambridge: Bradford Books of MIT Press.

Gerrig, R. J., & Banaji, M. R. (1994). Language and thought. In R. Sternberg (Ed.), *Handbook of perception and cognition: Vol. 2. Thinking and problem-solving* (pp. 223-241). Orlando, FL: Academic Press.

Gerrig, R. J., & Gibbs, R. W., Jr. (1988). Beyond the lexicon: Creativity in language production. *Metaphor and Symbolic Activity, 3,* 1-19.

Gibbs, R. W., Jr. (1994). *The poetics of mind: Figurative thought, language, and understanding.* New York: Cambridge University Press.

Gibbs, R. W., Jr., & Gerrig, R. J. (1989). How context makes metaphor comprehension seem "special." *Metaphor and Symbolic Activity, 4,* 145-158.

Glass, A. L., & Holyoake, K. J. (1975). Alternative conceptions of semantic theory. *Cognition, 3,* 313-339.

Glucksberg, S. (1989). Metaphors in conversation: How are they understood? Why are they used? *Metaphor and Symbolic Activity, 4,* 125-143.

Glucksberg, S., Gildea, P., & Bookin, H. A. (1982). On understanding speech: Can people ignore metaphors? *Journal of Verbal Learning and Verbal Behavior, 21,* 85-98.

Goodglass, H. (1980). Disorders of naming following brain injury. *American Scientist, 68,* 647-655.

Heider, E. R., & Olivier, D. C. (1972). The structure of color space in naming and memory for two languages. *Cognitive Psychology, 3,* 337-354.

Hunt, E., & Agnoli, F. (1991). The Whorfian hypothesis: A cognitive psychology perspective. *Psychological Review, 98,* 377-389.

Jacobson, E. (1932). Electrophysiology of mental activities. *American Journal of Psychology, 44,* 677-694.

Johnson, M. (1980). A philosophical perspective on the problems of metaphor. In R. P. Honeck & R. R. Hoffman (Eds.), *Cognition and figurative language* (pp. 25-46). Hillsdale, NJ: Lawrence Erlbaum.

Kosslyn, S. M. (1980). *Image and mind.* Cambridge, MA: Harvard University Press.

Kosslyn, S. M. (1987). Seeing and imagining in the cerebral hemispheres: A computational approach. *Psychological Review, 94,* 148-175.

Kosslyn, S. M. (1988). Aspects of a cognitive neuroscience of mental imagery. *Science, 240,* 1621-1626.

Kounios, J., & Holcomb, P. J. (1994). Concreteness effects in semantic processing: ERP evidence supporting dual-code theory. *Journal of Experimental Psychology: Learning, Memory, and Cognition, 20,* 804-823.

Lovaas, O. I., Berberich, J. P., Perloff, B. F., & Schaeffer, B. (1966). Acquisition of imitative speech in schizophrenic children. *Science, 151,* 705-707.

MacKay, D. G. (1987). *The organization of perception and action: A theory of language and other cognitive skills.* New York: Springer-Verlag.

Marslen-Wilson, W., Tyler, L. K., Waksler, R., & Older, L. (1994). Morphology and meaning in the English lexicon. *Psychological Review, 101,* 3-33.

Marslen-Wilson, W. D., & Welsh, A. (1978). Processing interactions and lexical access during word recognition in continuous speech. *Cognitive Psychology, 10,* 29-63.

McNamara, T. P. (1992). Theories of priming: I. Associative distance and lag. *Journal of Experimental Psychology: Learning, Memory, and Cognition, 18,* 1173-1190.

Meyer, D. E., & Schvaneveldt, R. W. (1976). Meaning, memory structure and mental processes. *Science, 192,* 27-33.

Morton, J. (1969). The interaction of information in word recognition. *Psychological Review, 60,* 329-346.

Ortony, A. (1980). Some psycholinguistic aspects of metaphor. In R. P. Honeck & R. R. Hoffman (Eds.), *Cognition and figurative language* (pp. 69-83). Hillsdale, NJ: Lawrence Erlbaum.

Osgood, C. E. (1971). Explorations in semantic space: A personal diary. *Journal of Social Issues, 27,* 5-64.

Osgood, C. E., Suci, G. J., & Tannenbaum, P. H. (1978). *The measurement of meaning.* Urbana: University of Illinois Press. (Original work published 1957)

Paivio, A. (1986). *Mental representations: A dual-coding approach.* New York: Oxford University Press.

Premack, D. (1971). Language in chimpanzees. *Science, 172,* 808-872.

Quillian, M. R. (1968). Semantic memory. In M. Minsky (Ed.), *Semantic information processing* (pp. 227-270). Cambridge: MIT Press.

Ratcliff, R., & McKoon, G. (1981). Does activation really spread? *Psychological Review, 88,* 454-462.

Rosch, E. (1975). Cognitive representations of semantic categories. *Journal of Experimental Psychology: General, 104,* 192-233.

Rosch, E., Mervis, C. B., Gray, W. D., Johnson, D. M., & Boyes-Braem, P. (1976). Basic objects in natural categories. *Cognitive Psychology, 8,* 382-439.

Rumelhart, D. E., McClelland, J. L., & the PDP Research Group (Eds.). (1986). *Parallel distributed processing.* Cambridge: MIT Press.

Rumelhart, D. E., Smolensky, P., McClelland, J. L., & Hinton, G. E. (1986). Schemata and essential thought processes in PDP models. In Rumelhart et al. (Eds.), *Parallel distributed processing* (Vol. 2, pp. 7-57). Cambridge: MIT Press.

Savage-Rumbaugh, E. S. (1986). *Ape language: From conditioned response to symbol.* New York: Columbia University Press.

Scarborough, D., Cortese, L. C., & Scarborough, H. S. (1977). Frequency and repetition effects in lexical memory. *Journal of Experimental Psychology: Human Perception and Performance, 3,* 1-17.

Skinner, B. F. (1957). *Verbal behavior.* Englewood Cliffs, NJ: Prentice Hall.

Smith, E. E., Shoben, E. J., & Rips, L. J. (1974). Structure and process in semantic memory: A featural model for semantic decisions. *Psychological Review, 81,* 214-241.

Smith, L., & Klein, R. (1990). Evidence for semantic satiation: Repeating a category slows subsequent semantic processing. *Journal of Experimental Psychology: Learning, Memory, and Cognition, 16,* 852-861.

Verbrugge, R. R., & McCarrell, N. S. (1977). Metaphoric comprehension: Studies in reminding and remembering. *Cognitive Psychology, 9,* 494-533.

Vikovitch, M., Humphreys, G. W., & Lloyd-Jones, T. J. (1993). On naming a giraffe a zebra: Picture naming errors across different object categories. *Journal of Experimental Psychology: Learning, Memory, and Cognition, 19,* 243-259.

Watson, J. B. (1937). *Behaviorism.* Chicago: Chicago University Press. (Original work published 1930)

Wilkins, A. J. (1971). Conjoint frequency, category size and categorization time. *Journal of Verbal Learning and Verbal Behavior, 10,* 382-385.

Williams, J. (1992). Processing polysemous words in context: Evidence for interrelated meanings. *Journal of Psycholinguistic Research, 21,* 193-218.

Zipf, G. K. (1965). *The psychobiology of language.* Cambridge: MIT Press. (First edition published 1935 by Houghton-Mifflin).

STUDY QUESTIONS

1. Describe the process that would lead to the formation of R_ms. Critically discuss the evidence for image-motor-abstract verbal R_ms as the meaning representation.

2. Critically consider the linguistic relativity hypothesis in light of the processing data presented in this chapter. What evidence is there that language determines thought? What evidence is there for similar language-thought patterns, meaning universals, across cultures?

3. Evaluate the PDP, feature, prototype, and network models as models. First, discuss what makes a model good. Then show how each fares on those goodness criteria. Which is more specific? How? Which accounts for more data? How?

4. Discuss the evidence for constructivist models of meaning. Try to explain how the PDP model *and* one of the structural models (prototype, network, or feature) would deal with metaphor understanding. In your discussion be sure to use the model's assumptions and to be consistent with the psycholinguistic data on metaphor.

5. What is a meaning *primitive*? Define the term and then discuss its potential application in the concrete-abstract distinction, in prototype models, feature models, and sublexical meaning models. Discuss the size of the unit (word, morpheme, or phrase) as a primitive. Does it make sense to consider the primitives a fixed size?

6. Define the following:

- repetition effect
- semantic relatedness
- salience imbalance
- logogen
- Zipf's Law
- standard pragmatic model
- semantic and phonological transparency
- codability
- motor theory
- distributed pattern of activation
- semantic differential
- semantic satiation

7. Spreading activation and priming are concepts that arise in a number of models and experimental settings. Explain them. Describe how they are used in PDP models, network models, node structure theory, metaphor/literal processing models, and in understanding polysemous words.

4

SYNTAX

In the last chapter we discussed how individual word meanings might be mentally represented and how context, that is, the surrounding words like an earlier presented "prime," might influence the activation of portions of the representation. Consult your representations—whether image, prototype, or network—for the concepts "lion" and "elephant." Now consider your meaning representation for the (not-so-interesting) sentence "The lion chased the elephant." Which seems to be the fiercer animal and which the more terrified? If I change the sentence to "The elephant chased the lion," does your feeling about ferocity and fear change? Note that any change in your meaning representation for those two sentences can*not* have come from representations of the concepts of "lion" and "elephant" because both words were in both sentences. Nor can a change result from some simple order or priming effect, because I primed both words in the sentence just before "Now consider . . ." Finally, the change cannot be due to extralinguistic knowledge of the roles of lions and elephants: It is probably equally likely for a lion or an elephant to be the chaser. How we know that the two sentences mean different things is through the sentence *structure,* which tells us what the relationship is among the words of the sentence. This is *syntax,* and as we shall see in this chapter, sentence structure can be quite complex to describe, but to native speakers it is transparently simple at revealing the relations among words in sentences.

In this chapter we will work through some complex syntactic constructions to illustrate theoretical assumptions and linguistic methods. At the end of major sections I highlight what is important to remember for later sections of this book.

UNIVERSAL GRAMMAR: THE LANGUAGE MODULE

Of all the levels of language, the syntactic is the least intuitive, the most remote from our everyday consciousness of language. When we talk about word meaning, although we may not be able to pin down our experience, we feel as though somewhere in our brain this experience must exist in some form. Syntax or grammar does not have the same face validity: Words seem to tumble out unorganized and without thought, and it takes much concentration to be aware of their organization. We are struck by the complexity of foreign languages when we must learn how they order words in sentences or mark words morphologically. We are also struck by the complexity of our own language when grammar is explicitly taught in school, either as *pro*scriptive rules (do not dangle a participle!) or as description of structure. Certainly, direct objects, subordinate clauses, and pronoun antecedents do not seem to be something we could have known how to construct since the age of 6. (If you are unsure about the referents of grammatical terms usually taught in grammar school—such as *subordinate clause*—they are listed and defined for easy reference in the Appendix at the end of this chapter.)

One group of modern-day linguists, generative grammarians, argue that part of the reason that grammar or syntax seems unlearnable is that it is not learned; it is part of our genetic endowment. Chomsky (1986) points out that syntactic structure is characteristic of all and only human languages, and unfolds relatively effortlessly as a child is exposed to language input. He considers that all human languages share critical, abstract syntactic features—*universal grammar* (or *UG*)—that reflect innate knowledge or human linguistic competence.

Tacit Knowledge, Competence, and Performance

Knowledge we have but are not aware of is called *tacit knowledge,* as distinct from explicit knowledge, things we know that we know. Following Chomsky (e.g., 1980), linguists and psychologists have become increasingly aware of how much of our knowledge of language is tacit rather than explicit.

In grade school, grammar course teachers often try to make our tacit knowledge explicit; we find learning the explicit rules difficult. In grammar and spelling exams, we may be asked not just to perform correctly but also to state the rule that describes our performance. Students who correct *wiegh* to *weigh* but cannot give a reason other than "It seems better that way" (It seems better that weigh?) are expressing their tacit knowledge and are often penalized for not stating "i before e except after c . . ." Similarly, most of us know there is something wrong with "I gave it to he" but would have difficulty stating an explanation such as "prepositions [to] take the objective [him], not the nominative [he]." It is ironic that we native speakers are penalized in grammar courses for the response "It seems better that way." What does "seems better" mean if not that I know it tacitly, just the way a native speaker should?

Clearly, there is a place for speakers' intuitions in determining tacit knowledge. However, it is not the speaker's intuitions about what rule she or he is using but about what utterances seem right or wrong. Tacit knowledge is inferred, but distinct, from speakers' actual *performance*—the utterances they produce or understand. The sum total of a speaker's tacit knowledge about the language is called linguistic *competence.*

Linguists argue that both children and adults have linguistic competence, that is, tacit knowledge of structural rules for sentence generation, which is only imperfectly reflected in performance. The imperfections may help us understand *how* people process sentences but do not indicate that they do not know about sentence structure. Actual performance can include slips or tips of the tongue or, in child language, "incomplete" sentences such as "Up jump," my son Eric's first "sentence." The context and accompanying body language revealed clearly that he meant: "Put me up on the bed so I can jump." Under 2 years old, he did not have the *memory* for that long a sentence, a performance limitation, but his meaning was clear at the time. It might be argued that he had not only the idea but the underlying structural relations—the grammatical competence given by UG.

Arguments for Innate Linguistic Competence

Much of the argument for this innate UG focuses on child language acquisition and the lack of overt adult language teaching, which we will consider critically in Chapter 9. For now, note that the argument rests on three assumptions. The first assumption is the *poverty of the stimulus:* Our language knowledge goes beyond the sentences to which we have been exposed. Haegeman (1994) offers the following sentences as examples:

1a. I think Miss Marple will leave.

1b. I think that Miss Marple will leave.

2a. This is the book I bought in London.

2b. This is the book that I bought in London.

In each case, the "b" is an acceptable variant of the "a," which might lead to the generalization that *that* may be included or dropped at will. But now consider the sentences:

3a. Who do you think will be questioned first?

and

3b. Who do you think that will be questioned first?

In this case *that* may *not* be included—as a native speaker you probably noticed that it "sounds funny," indicated by convention in linguistics with *. The poverty-of-the-stimulus argument here is that if we simply generalize from 1 and 2, 3 *should* be acceptable. That it is not is *not deducible* from the stimulus pattern and therefore must be suggested by UG.

The second assumption is that parents neither formally teach grammar nor explicitly correct it, and on those occasions when they do, children pay little attention. Jackendoff (1994) cites this example from the child language acquisition literature to illustrate this point:

CHILD: Want other one spoon, Daddy.
FATHER: You mean, you want the other spoon.
CHILD: Yes, I want other one spoon, please Daddy.
FATHER: Can you say "the other spoon"?
CHILD: Other . . . one . . . spoon.
FATHER: Say "other."
CHILD: Other.
FATHER: "Spoon."
CHILD: Spoon.
FATHER: "Other spoon."
CHILD: Other . . . spoon. Now give me other one spoon?
This shows the child is not just imitating—the imitation is, as it were, filtered through the child's own (unconscious) version of the language. (p. 194)

While the father in the example had a specific target he was trying to get his child to model, linguists argue that adults do not usually know explicitly what to teach. Linguists do not agree on a characterization of English structure and so could not instruct how to teach it themselves. They presume therefore that correct structure emerges from a refining of internally generated "rules" common to all people by the sentences actually heard.

The third assumption lies in the commonalities observed in structures of languages around the world. To observe these commonalities we must look at a very abstract level, such as in the following:

- All languages have sentences.
- All sentences have subjects and predicates.
- Subjects and predicates may be moved around, within certain limits, within a sentence, still maintaining their relationship.

Some of these abstract levels we will explore in detail in this chapter, after we get used to thinking about sentence structure.

Before generative grammar, syntacticians were interested in developing *observationally adequate* grammars, which distinguished well-formed from poorly formed sentences, or *descriptive* grammars, which accounted for speakers' intuitions about such sentences. While maintaining these requirements, generative grammar switched the focus from the language behaviors themselves to developing a theory of mind. Grammar must have *explanatory* power, accounting not only for which sentences are grammatical but also specifying *how* the knowledge of grammaticality became known by the language's speakers.

Criteria for a Module

Before delving into sentence structure and models for describing it, I introduce the concept of a *language module,* a brain center specially designed for language understanding. The module concept has greatly influenced philosophy, linguistics, and psychology, and is highly relevant to the generative-grammar philosophy. There are several variants of the modularity concept.

First, we need to consider what is meant by a genetic or innate characteristic. At first blush, it is a characteristic we are born with, but more careful consideration shows that it can be a *propensity* or *predisposition* for that characteristic that we are born with, not necessarily a full-blown behavior or ability. Clearly, crying is innate: We do that from birth and need no teacher. Our hair color and teeth are also innate—that is, genetically determined—but not expressed at birth. For all people it is genetically specified that their hair will gray in middle age and that their teeth will develop, fall out, and be replaced on a fairly regular schedule during childhood.

With the exception of crying, my examples were of *physical* characteristics, but we can see similar genetic specification and developmental unfolding in *behavior.* The developmental milestones of infancy—when babies sit unassisted, walk on two legs, grasp with two fingers, and so on—are not present at birth but do not need to be taught. They emerge, usually in order, during the first 18 months of life.

The issue of genetic control becomes murkier when dealing with more cognitive and social behaviors, partly because there is no question that there needs to be environmental input for these, and partly because there are usually social models, potential teachers. So, if language is in part genetic, we cannot see it unfold without words, and no one (since Psammetichos) has believed that the words are part of UG. Once you have exposure to someone modeling the words, it is conceivable that he or she could also be modeling the sounds and the structure of the language.

Arguments for language being in part innate include the synchrony of language milestones (which we shall examine in Chapter 9) the world over. They also include evidence that brain damage can either selectively spare language learning or selectively impair it. *Selective* means that language, but no other cognitive ability, is affected. The final argument comes from the absolute speed and ease with which we perform linguistic computations, that is, parse complex sentences.

In *The Modularity of Mind,* Fodor (1983) argues that there is good reason to accept a notion of separate intelligences or independent aptitudes, what he calls *vertical faculties.* These contrast with general abilities that underlie a number of skills—*horizontal faculties*—such as memory or attention. A *modular system* is a type of vertical faculty or special aptitude that is innately specified, domain-specific, mandatory, autonomous, informationally encapsulated, impenetrable, and not assembled. We have discussed innate specification. *Domain-specific* refers to the separateness of the skill—a set of mental computations reserved for the domain of the "module" and not used elsewhere. In the case of language, or, more specifically, syntax, we see domain-specificity in our ability even as children to speak and understand complex sentences: In doing so we perform abstract manipulations, which we cannot likewise perform in producing or understanding syntactic *rules* or similarly complex algebra.

Mandatory refers to the idea that we have no choice but to perceive stimuli as the modular system dictates. We cannot voluntarily suspend our understanding of sentences to hear only a sound stream as we cannot choose not to see forms or smell odors.

Informationally encapsulated, autonomous, and *impenetrable* all refer to the type of input a modular system can attend to—which is only the stimuli it is "programmed" for, without feedback. As we saw in the last chapter, it is impossible to screen irrelevant meanings of polysemous words, even when one meaning is primed by context. The process of hearing the word automatically (although temporarily) activates the connections to all the meanings. Information as to irrelevance cannot penetrate to circumvent the process. Basically, once an input activates the system, its processing is set on a predetermined path unalterable by other information. Belief as well as knowledge from other domains, no matter how relevant and correct, cannot affect the perception.

Not assembled implies that what is innately specified is the module as a whole. The processes a stimulus undergoes in the module are not combinations of elementary processes used in other cognitive domains. The module is designed to serve a single mental purpose. As such, the design and efficiency may be optimal for this purpose.

Fodor considers all perceptual systems and language to be *input systems,* and modular. The aspects of language that are treated in the language module are syntax (perhaps speech) and morphology. Semantics—understanding the meanings of words, relating them to context, determining speaker intent, and so on—he tentatively suggests is outside the language module, "where the language processor interfaces with cognitive processes at large" (p. 92). He argues for this because deriving meaning is neither fast nor automatic and is affected by changes in our beliefs.

Chomsky (1986) argues that language is modular but that Fodor's definitions are too restrictive. Language not only serves as input but also to communicate internally in thought and as output in speech and writing. Moreover, many processes that Chomsky feels are peculiarly linguistic, part of the language module, are slow and subject to contextual interpretation—like seeing ambiguity in sentences. Consider "The demonstrators stopped smoking in restaurants": Who was smoking, the demonstrators or the public at large? Disambiguation is slow and deliberate. A second example of a slow syntactic process is in understanding a sentence like "The horse raced past the barn fell." On first reading, most people assume that "raced" is the main verb of the sentence, which leaves no place to put "fell." In fact, "fell" is the main verb of the sentence, a perfectly grammatical version of "the horse which was raced past the barn fell." (This kind of sentence is called a *garden path sentence,* for we go merrily down the garden path to the wrong initial solution.) The fact that correct analysis requires some thought suggests to Chomsky less impenetrability and automaticity than to Fodor, but still a unique-to-language module.

> We should, so it appears, think of knowledge of language as a certain state of the mind/brain, a relatively stable element in transitory mental states once it is attained; furthermore as a state of some distinguishable faculty of the mind—the language faculty—with its specific properties, structure, and organization, one "module" of the mind. (Chomsky, 1986, pp.12-13)

We turn next to examine some of the computations that the language module may perform in normal sentence processing. These computations, at a minimum, should *describe* the possible sentences of a language, distinguishing them from utterances considered ungrammatical by native speakers and assigning plausible structures to grammatical utterances. Following standard practice, we will choose one such grammar over another if it is simpler, that is, if it has fewer rules. Finally, we will try to abstract those rules to account for utterances in different languages, to represent a universal grammar.

CONSTITUENT ANALYSIS

Linguistic Reasoning

A *corpus,* or collection of utterances, may be used to infer grammatical structure.

4a. John gave it to charity.
4b. You gave it to charity.
4c. You gave it to John.
4d. John gave it to you.

These sentences are recognizably similar, even had you not known the meaning of any of the words. The grammaticality of 4a and 4b suggests that "John" and "you" are equivalent or substitutable; they occur in identical sentence frames. The sentences also suggest that "charity" and "John" are equivalent. The occurrence of "John" and "you" (or "John" and "charity") in identical sentence frames implies that they are *structurally* similar. We can therefore classify them together as members of a category we will temporarily call Noun or N, and say N → charity, John, you. Our four sentences may then be generated by the rule:

Sentence (S) → N gave it to N

where N *must be* rewritten (a "must be" rule is formally an *obligatory* rule) by any of the words it stands for. Rules that indicate that a linguistic category may be substituted for any of the linguistic units it represents are known as *rewrite rules.* A rewrite rule may result in a *terminal string* (terminal = end), words that constitute a set of linguistic units that may not be substituted for any further. A rewrite rule may also result in a *nonterminal string,* which requires further application of rewrite rules to wind up with words, the terminal elements. Thus our sentence rule, S → N gave it to N, produced a nonterminal string, which after application of the N rewrite rule produces a terminal string like 4a-4d.

The rewrite rules just presented do not indicate interesting facts about the structure of English. The example is intended to illustrate the linguistic method by which structurally equivalent units or *constituents* are derived. At the first level, words are members of a category, a part of speech. At subsequent levels, these parts of speech coalesce ultimately into a structure that constitutes a sentence. The structurally similar classes that *constitute* sentences are called *constituents.* S is superordinate to or *dominates* its constituents.

An Exercise: Deriving Some Parts of Speech

All parts of speech (reviewed in the Appendix in this chapter) were ascertained by using constituent analyses. You may, in fact, have had difficulty with the definitions provided in grammar school: A noun names a person, place, or thing, and a verb names an action. Is an action not a thing? In "I saw Robert kill Mary," "kill" is a verb. In "I witnessed the killing (or murder) of Mary," "killing" is a noun. Do they both not describe the same action? A verb or a noun can denote the same action: *The difference between nouns and verbs lies not in what kinds of **things they stand for** but in what kinds of **frames they stand in**.*

We will now use a small corpus of English sentences to infer the relationships of the words, deriving some parts of speech. This exercise should serve as a reminder of the parts of speech, if necessary, and as an illustration of linguistic analysis.

4a. John gave it to charity.

4e. John gave it to a needy charity.

4f. The small boy gave it to a needy charity.

4g. A boy gave it to the needy charity.

First, note that these sentences are all grammatical (as judged by us native speakers). Next, note that "John," "The small boy," and "A boy" as well as "charity," "a needy charity," and "the needy charity" exist in the same sentence frames. We can try to make *one* structural class out of these, along with "you" from the first set of sentences. Because some members of this class consist of more than one word, the class is a *phrase,* specifically, a *Noun Phrase (NP).* We can now make a new set of rewrite rules:

NP → John
     You
     A boy
     The small boy

        charity
        the needy charity
        a needy charity

Examination of this list should immediately yield the observation that "the small" and "a" and "the needy" and "a needy" occur in the same phrase frame and that the remainder—what is left if they are removed ("boy," "You," and "John" or "charity")—occur in the same phrase frame. For the moment ignore that we already know that "you" is a pronoun and "needy" and "small" are adjectives. I will correct the analysis, but for now I want to demonstrate a method of reasoning that can be applied to languages that have not been previously described so that there is no prior knowledge to fall back on. Given that "the small" and "the needy" seem to work the way "a" does, we will say they are members of the same class: articles or *determiners (DET)*. Given that "you" works like "John," "boy," and "charity," we temporarily call them all *Nouns (N)*. We can make new rewrite rules:

    DET → A
            A needy
            The small
            The needy
    N → You
            John
            Charity
            Boy
    NP → (DET) N

where the parentheses indicate that the determiner does not *have to* occur; that is, it is *optional*.

    These rules suggest some new sentences:

    4h. A you gave it to charity.

    4i. A John gave it to charity.

Given that these are not grammatical, we need to adjust the N class, separating it into one class for "boy" and "charity" *common nouns* (can take a determiner), and another for "you" and "John."

    It is more important to understand the method of reasoning than the specific rules derived. The method analyzes acceptable sentences for similarities of structure, "predicts" new sentences from the analysis, and then tests the predictions against native speaker intuitions. Our hypothesis that "boy," "you," and "John" were structurally interchangeable did not hold up to native intuition in frames 4h and 4i, so we tried a new hypothesis.

    Another thing we might note in our analysis is that "The small" consists of two words. Perhaps the two words play the same role? We could test this by changing their order.

4j. Small the boy . . .

is clearly ungrammatical, suggesting that the words are not equivalent and should be separated. We could support the separation by expanding our corpus to include other word frames in which "small" occurs and include words other than "small" in all those frames. For instance, we can say:

4k. The boy looked small.

but not

4l. The boy looked the.

We can also say

4m. The rich boy gave it to charity.
4n. The boy looked rich.

These together suggest that "rich" and "small" form a class of their own, which is distinct from determiners. We call that class *adjectives (ADJ).* (Note that in 4k and 4n the adjective seems to modify the verb. This is a special case arising with only a few verbs. Then the adjective is called a *predicate adjective.*)
    We may now amend our NP rule to

NP → (DET) (ADJ) N

or, with context restrictions,

NP → N (when N is not a common noun)
        Det N (when N is a common noun)
        DET ADJ N
        PRONOUN

    Based on these sentences, our categories look like the following:

ADJ → rich, small, needy
DET → a, the.

We may also amend our sentence rewrite rule to

S → NP ___ NP
        NP ___ ADJ

where the ___ stands for some as yet undefined constituents. The NP is a constituent of S, and the parts of speech PRONOUN, DET, ADJ, and N are all constituents of NP and more distant constituents of S. An immediate constituent is a *daughter.* Finally, note that the NP can rewrite as PRONOUN, so far only "you," a single straight path. Alternatively, it can rewrite into a forked structure, consisting of DET and N or DET ADJ N, each of which rewrites into a set of terminal elements or words.

As you should be aware, there are more parts of speech in English than determiners, adjectives, and nouns, but the principles for deriving these categories are much the same. The other parts of speech are verbs, adverbs, pronouns, prepositions, and conjunctions. These are defined in the Appendix, and I leave it to you to generate sentences that demonstrate the structural integrity of these categories, as I have done for nouns, adjectives, and determiners. This type of analysis is called a *distributional analysis;* it defines linguistic categories through the distribution of elements of the language.

At this point you should understand distributional analysis and know what a constituent and its daughter are, what rewrite rules and terminal strings are, and what an NP and its parts are.

Finite State Grammar

In Chapter 3, I introduced the behaviorist notion of a "chain." As you may recall, a chain was an association to an association, the word *food* to the word *pizza* to the taste of the pizza. We might consider a sentence a chain, where each word triggers the next; *the* triggers *boy.* This is the simplest way to describe a sentence, as a sequence of words, or perhaps at the next order of constituents, a sequence of categories of words. This description implies minimal structure between sentence elements; each word automatically leads to the next, with no other constraints. This is an example of a *finite state grammar.* Here we will explore the potentials and limits of finite state grammars, or behavioristic chains, in generating sentences.

A finite state grammar consists of an initial "state" or element, a final state or element, and a sequential set of states between them. Movement between states (S) is indicated by arrows or *arcs* marking transitions between them. For example:

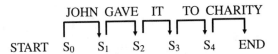

$$\text{JOHN} \quad \text{GAVE} \quad \text{IT} \quad \text{TO} \quad \text{CHARITY}$$

START S_0 S_1 S_2 S_3 S_4 END

At S_3 we would have the sequence "John gave it," and at END, the whole sentence "John gave it to charity." Each state calls the next state, so taking a path automatically generates the sentence. Choice is possible in a finite state grammar, indicated as we have seen in tree diagrams by *branching,* as in the solid lines in the following:

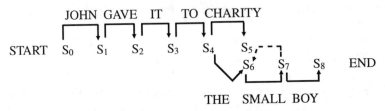

JOHN   GAVE   IT   TO   CHARITY

START S_0 S_1 S_2 S_3 S_4 S_5 S_6 S_7 S_8 END

THE   SMALL   BOY

In this case, at the word "to," there is a choice between the noun "charity" and the DET-ADJ-N sequence, "the small boy." Once a branch is selected, there is no crossing to the next branch.

This diagram also indicates another option in a finite state grammar, which makes it powerful enough to generate infinitely long sentences, that is, *looping*. Looping is indicated by the dotted line, which lets us select the option of S_7 repeatedly. That is, we may take a branch back to S_7 from S_7 as often as we like, or we can branch to S_8. In addition to the sentences "John gave it to charity" and "John gave it to the small boy," looping will generate "John gave it to the small small boy," "John gave it to the small small small boy," and so forth.

A finite state grammar consists of states, paths between them, and probabilities of selecting a particular path. Because each path serves as a transition between one state and another, these probabilities are called *transitional probabilities (tp)*. Consider tps in a real language context; try to fill in the blank in the next two sentences:

The next number you will see is _____.
A stitch in time saves _____.

You can guess much better in the second case; that is, it has a *higher* tp than the first.

In the first finite state diagram presented, the tp between each state is one because no choice exists. In the second diagram, the combined probabilities for following the arcs for "CHARITY" and "THE" is one. If the alternatives are equally likely, we can say each is .5; if one is more likely than the other, it would have a higher probability. In the second diagram, there is, in addition, a less-than-1 probability of exiting from "SMALL" to "BOY" because the "SMALL" state may be reentered.

Note that the tp assigned to an arc is *fixed;* it cannot be modified by experience. So whatever the probability is of looping once on "small," it is the same as looping from the seventh to the eighth "small." As native speakers, though, the sentence "John gave it to the small small boy" is much more acceptable than the sentence "John gave it to the small small small small small small small small boy." *A shortcoming of finite state grammar is its lack of memory: It cannot take into account early elements of the string, only the current element.*

Because of the shortcoming in memory just mentioned, a finite state grammar is probably not a good model of human language. However, it is powerful enough to account for the rewrite rules and constituent structures we have discussed so far. Instead of putting the terminal elements in the words, we could put the category names into the finite state diagrams and assume that there is a process that would substitute members of the category for the category name. Thus a finite state diagram of our rewrite rules for NPs could be as follows:

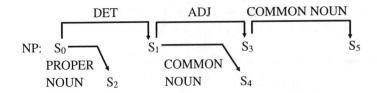

Phrase Structure Grammar

Finite state grammar treats all states equally and assumes connections only between adjacent states (a *Markov process,* for those who read further in this area). We have already seen that this simple a description of sentence structure ignores constraints of distant words on a word: A long string of "smalls" is unlikely to be uttered and not completely acceptable; there is more context sensitivity in human grammars than in finite-state grammars. Another easy-to-see long-distance constraint is in subject-verb agreement:

5a. John, who *is* rich, give*s* a large donation.

5b. The women, who *are* rich, give a large donation.

In these sentences the form of the italicized morpheme is governed by the subject (John or the women) between two and four states away. Clearly, the two sentences have the same general structure, and so should employ the same model, but the model must be sensitive to distant constraints. This is not possible with a finite state model because each state is determined only by the preceding state. That is why a behavioral chain, or finite state grammar, cannot account for human syntax (Chomsky, 1957).

To permit context sensitivity, we must consider a more abstract level of constituents, which capture grammatical relations among sentence components. That is, we wish to consider the *function* of the constituents—what makes "the lion" (DET N in either subject or object position) the predator or the prey in "the [lion, elephant] chased the [lion, elephant]."

Sentence 4g contains three NPs: "a boy," "it," and "the needy charity." In English, changing the order of these NPs radically changes the meaning of the sentence—"It gave a boy to the needy charity" is very different from "A boy gave it to the needy charity." In English, the order of the constituents is the primary determinant of their functional relations within the sentence. In 4g, "a boy" is the subject, and "it" is the object (for the moment, ignore "to the needy charity"); their relation to the verb "gave" is very different. In terms of constituent structure, we express this difference by decomposing our sentence into subject and predicate (called *verb phrase* or *VP*) and noting that the object NP is part of the VP. In rewrite rules,

$$S \rightarrow NP\ VP$$
$$VP \rightarrow V\ NP$$

These rules are productive—they can be used to generate new sentences. For example, we can substitute other NPs for "it,"

6a. John gave a large donation to the needy charity.

maintaining the same functional relations among the constituents.

In addition to the NP and the VP, there is a *prepositional phrase (PP)*, "to him." The NP in a PP has a role different from those of subject and object NP; it describes the direction of the giving. We can delete the PP and have a grammatical sentence, but only if we delete both the NP and the "to" (the preposition, PREP), indicating that they are a unit. The "to him" modifies the verb and therefore is part of the VP but forms its own group within it. To express these groupings, to our rules

S → NP VP
NP → (DET) (ADJ) N

we add the rewrite rules

VP → V NP (PP)
PP → PREP NP

and to include a rule for "the boy looked rich," we may add

VP → V ADJ.

It may seem that we have generated an enormous number of rewrite rules, but note that these account for an enormous number of sentences in English and, by comparison to what they can produce, they are few in number. Note also that our set of rewrite rules imposes a *hierarchical structure:* The subject NP is a daughter of the sentence, while the object NP is a daughter of VP, and only through it connected to the sentence node.

It is this hierarchical relation that provides some of the distant context dependencies that the finite state model fails to account for: The subject NP controls the form of the verb, however many words or constituents are between them. The hierarchical grammatical relations or functional constituents capture the semantic relations between sentence elements. Through the constituent structure, we know whether it is the lion or the elephant chasing, and that subject specifies the verb form.

A final argument for discussing sentences in terms of constituents derives from our use of pronouns. When we substitute "it" for the noun "donation" in "John gave a large donation," we actually substitute "it" for the entire NP—"John gave it," not "John gave a large it." This indicates that our tacit knowledge includes the NP as the unit. Similarly, we can recognize constituents by seeing whether permissible sentences result when we substitute "so": "So" *must* substitute only for a full structure (Haegeman, 1994). In 6a, we had

6a. John gave a large donation to the needy charity.

which we can grammatically extend with

6b. John gave a large donation to the needy charity and Mary did so too.

In 6b, "did so" substitutes for the entire VP—we native speakers understand that sentence as meaning that "Mary gave a large donation to the needy charity." As with the pronoun "it," the substitutability of "so" for the entire VP indicates its integrity; the whole constituent is replaced.

The kind of grammar presented here is a *phrase structure grammar* and may be depicted either by rewrite rules or by a *phrase marker,* or structure tree, which illustrates graphically the hierarchical relations just described. For example:

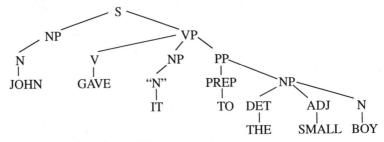

—John gave it to the small boy.

It may also be represented in bracket notation as in [John [gave it [to [the small boy]]]], where each constituent is demarked by its own bracket pair.

A phrase structure grammar has the power of a computer program with subroutine calls, or an *augmented transition network* (*ATN*; Woods, 1970). Roughly, an ATN looks like a finite state grammar, except that the arcs are labeled by nonterminal symbols (like NP, rather than words) naming structures that may be found on a different finite state diagram. The ATN *keeps track of where* it is in the finite state diagram when it jumps to the structure indicated by it to another. This memory allows a more or less sequential process that can be interrupted, *returning* to the appropriate state in the main program when finished. This ability to return to a state means that an ATN, unlike a finite state grammar, has a memory. For example, we might have

S: S_0 —NP→ S_1 —VP→ S_2

NP: S_0 —DET→ S_1 —ADJ→ S_2 —N→ S_3

VP: S_0 —V→ S_1 —NP→ S_2

Now assume that the structure of a string of words, the input, is compared with the structure in the ATN. What will happen is that, beginning at S, we must match an "NP." Because NP is nonterminal, it cannot be found in the input string and so we look for a way to match NPs. To do this, hold the NP place in the first line and jump to the second, which contains the condition for filling in an NP. So next we must match DET, ADJ, N. If successful, the condition for an NP is met, so we return to the correct position in the first finite state diagram. Thus an ATN has a memory and may be used to generate and/or recognize nonterminal structure.

At this point you should know what a VP and a PP are and what looping is, and you should understand the difference in structural constraints between a finite state grammar and an ATN. You should understand the importance and meaning of long-distance context sensitivity.

Complex Sentence Structure

If you have been playing with the preceding language analyses, you may have thought of sentences that our rewrite rules cannot generate. Sentences sometimes are more complicated than these rules allow; for example, the sentence you are now reading. Omitting the phrase following the semicolon does not eliminate the problem: It results in "Sentences sometimes *are* more *complicated* than these rules *allow*," one apparent sentence with two verbs (in italics). A *simple* or *core* sentence is one with one subject and one predicate. A complex sentence with several verbs can be described as a simple sentence with other sentences *embedded* in it. Consider a more concrete sentence:

7a. The rat the cat wounded ate the cheese.

We can decompose it readily into two sentences:

7b. The rat ate the cheese. (the main clause)
7c. The cat wounded the rat. (the subordinate clause)

The subordinate clause modifies "the rat" in 7a—it serves the same function as an adjective. This observation is supported by the near synonymy of the sentence

7d. The wounded rat ate the cheese.

with 7a. Recall the rewrite rule for NPs: NP → DET ADJ N. To permit 7a to be produced, we also must modify that, perhaps to

NP →   (DET)   (ADJ)   N   ———————— (S)————
            The   ()   rat   the cat wounded (the rat) ate the cheese.

This modification has a very profound implication! We have

S→ NP VP

and now

NP → (DET) (ADJ) N (S).

Note that *across the two rules, S occurs on both sides* of the arrow! This is called *recursiveness* (when a symbol can refer to or rewrite itself) and underlies much of the power of language. Recursiveness, in fact, is what enables the generation of *interesting* infinitely long sentences ("John gave it to the small, small, small . . . boy" is an uninteresting one) because we can keep applying the rule:

   1. S → NP VP

Substituting the new NP rule we get

   2. [(DET) (ADJ) N (S)] VP

applying rule 1 again, for the embedded S

  [(DET) (ADJ) N [NP VP]] VP

applying the NP rule again

  [(DET) (ADJ) N [(DET) (ADJ) N (S)] VP] VP

applying rule 1 for the embedded S we get

  [(DET)(ADJ) N [(DET) (ADJ) N [NP VP] VP]] VP

and applying rule 2 we get

  [(DET)(ADJ) N [(DET) (ADJ) N [(DET) (ADJ) N (S)] VP] VP] VP

generating a sentence such as

  7e. The rat the cat the farmer chased wounded ate the cheese.

(If you do not like this sentence, you are not alone. We will soon discuss the problems with it, but for now note that, with effort, you can figure out who is doing what to whom.) And we do not have to stop here; we can substitute NP VP for the S in the last string and keep going.

   Obviously, after a while, by the level of 7e, the sentence becomes difficult to understand, but depending on the nature of the embedding, we may or may not have trouble. In the children's poem "This Is the House That Jack Built," and others of that ilk, very long sentences are constructed; in fact, the delight in that type of poem probably comes from the game of repeated application of the tacit rule. In the poem the contained sentences are strung together sequentially, not internally:

This is the <u>cat</u> who chased the <u>rat</u> who lived in the <u>house that Jack built</u>.

We have "cat chased rat," "rat lived in house," "Jack built house." Every subject is close to its predicate. In the sentence 7e we have been looking at

The <u>rat</u> the <u>cat</u> the <u>farmer chased</u> wounded ate the cheese.

The subjects and predicates are far apart with other sentences stuck between them. This is a *nested* or *center-embedded* type of sentence, harder to follow than the other. Chomsky (1957) argued that such sentences are within our competence to produce or understand, and it is merely a performance factor, memory, that makes them difficult—we lose track of or forget the subject by the time we get to its verb. There is disagreement about whether multiple center-embeddings are indeed within our competence.

Finite State Grammar, Phrase Structure, and Embedding

As we saw, it is easy to generate rewrite rules for embeddings and recursiveness. Is it possible to describe them with a finite state grammar? Consider:

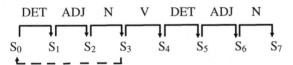

The solid lines represent a finite state grammar for

$S \rightarrow NP\ VP$
$NP \rightarrow (DET)\ (ADJ)\ N$
$VP \rightarrow V\ NP$

To allow embedding, $NP \rightarrow N\ (S)$, we would have to add a return arrow from the first N to the start state, indicated by the dotted line. What will this produce or recognize? Beginning at S_0 (and ignoring the ADJs), we use "the" for DET, take the N path, use "rat" for N ($\rightarrow$ the rat), return to S_0 and following the same route produce "the cat" ($\rightarrow$ the rat the cat). Our current state is S_3 and our diagram gives us only two choices: to return to S_0 or to select a verb. Choosing the latter, we get "The rat the cat wounded" and now must generate or look for another NP like "the cheese" $\rightarrow$ *The rat the cat wounded the cheese."* This is short one verb! That could be corrected by adding a loop to the verb arc, but that has the potential of producing too many verbs: Try for yourself to produce "The rat ate wounded the cheese" using the finite state diagram with a verb loop. What we need is a grammar that matches subject NPs to verbs so that however many subjects there are, there are an equal number of predicates. Keeping count of this is a nontrivial example of context sensitivity!

Box 4.1. Elements of Phrase Structure

— Lowest level = words or "terminal strings" or "terminal elements."
— Distributional analysis of words yields parts of speech, the next level of structure.
— Distributional analysis of parts of speech within a sentence yields constituent structure.
— The constituents are hierarchically organized in a sentence. Constituent structure determines the grammatical relations among the words of a sentence.
— Structural relations are drawn by convention using
  — rewrite rules,
  — finite state diagrams,
  — phrase markers,
  — brackets, and
  — ATNS.
— Recursiveness, the possibility of a sentence being rewritten to include a sentence *ad infinitum*, is a property of human language, which demands at least a (hierarchical) phrase structure or constituent structure. Simple sequential associations, modeled in behaviorist chains and finite state grammars, are unable to account for recursiveness.

The rat the cat wounded ate the cheese.

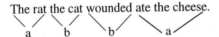

A finite state grammar has no facility for remembering any but the previous command state, so it cannot recall the "a" subject by the time it needs to find the "a" verb. Because it cannot account for context sensitivity and recursiveness, Chomsky (1957) argued that a finite state grammar is not powerful enough to model human language despite having the potential for generating infinitely long sentences. (Note that an ATN can account for embeddings because it has a memory. We need only have one of the nonterminal states name the start state. The memory will hold the number of times the subject NP has been accessed and will therefore match VPs.)

You should understand recursiveness, embedding, and the special demands of center-embedding in particular.

Summary. We have seen that language structure cannot result from a conditioning chain, where each word triggers the next. We have highlighted crucial aspects of sentence structure. Sentences consist of groups of words that function together, that is, phrases. Phrases are hierarchically arranged to structure a sentence. There can be long-distance effects of phrases on one another, depending on their connections in the hierarchical structure. And sentences can contain other sentences, which is recursiveness.

DEEP STRUCTURE AND GENERATIVE GRAMMAR

Problems With Phrase Structure Grammars

Context sensitivity in language revisited. We have seen that the simplest rewrite rules, representable by a finite state grammar, are inadequate to account for language because language permits recursiveness. Phrase structure grammars allowing recursiveness also have some problems as representations of human syntactic capacity. Consider once again the sentences

4e. John gave it to a needy charity.

4f. The small boy gave it to a needy charity.

*4i. A John gave it to charity.

and a new sentence,

4o. Boy gave it to him.

and the rewrite rule

NP → (DET) (ADJ) N

Obviously, in some cases the application of DET and ADJ is indeed optional. In other cases there *must* be rules preventing us from taking the option, so we do not generate "A John." And there must be rules that force us to take the option in certain circumstances, so we do not generate "Boy gave"; that is, the rules must be context sensitive: They must contain instructions about when they are applicable.

We could make context-sensitive phrase structure rules by dividing the categories represented in rewrite rules into very small categories, each of which commands its own set of rules. Thus we can divide nouns into common nouns and proper nouns (e.g., "John") with the separate rules:

NP → DET (ADJ) common noun.

NP → proper noun.

Logically, there is no problem with this procedure, but aesthetically there is; specifically, as we subdivide the parts of speech for all similar instances, the number of rules will multiply extraordinarily. More important, *it breaks into distinct categories linguistic entities that at one level logically and functionally belong to one category.* As we noted, for example, a pronoun may be substituted for a noun phrase (DET (ADJ) N), and it may also be substituted for a proper noun. Thus there is good reason to consider a proper noun and the DET ADJ N *structural* equivalents and then to treat them similarly in the structural rules, the grammar. A solution, we will see, marks different requirements of words *with the words,* like the selectional restrictions we saw in Chapter 2 in the word marker structure.

Note that we rejected finite state grammar as a model of language because there were the constraints of nonadjacent words, such as subject-verb agreement or matching subject NPs with predicate VPs. In its place we proposed a hierarchically organized phrase-structure grammar in which words participate in structured units that can constrain one another. To this grammar we have added another level of structure—in the lexicon, so that some constraints (subject-verb matches) are governed by interactions among the hierarchical constituents, and some are governed by the words filling the subject (or verb) slots (such as whether the subject is a common or proper noun).

Let us examine this level a bit further. Consider the difference between *transitive* and *intransitive* verbs (whether or not they can take an object NP). We cannot say

*8. *John runs the book.*

Application of the rule VP → V NP must have restrictions on it: The rule must be applied only in certain verb contexts. As we proposed for proper and common nouns, we could propose a new rewrite rule for VPs, which does not include an NP. But in both "John gives" and "John runs," John is the agent of the verb. Two VP rules would demand two S rules, mapping the subject NP to each VP rule to maintain the relation between John and the two verb types. This does not parsimoniously capture the similarity between subject and verb in the sentences. It is perhaps more sensible to maintain one set of sentence-structure rules and to specify the *arguments* each verb can take, the *thematic roles* (or *theta roles*) the verb needs to flesh out its meaning, with the verb itself, in the lexicon.

Thematic roles are similar to the cases of case grammar that we looked at in the chapters on meaning but they specify a structural requirement relating to the semantic one of case grammar. Consider, for example, the verb *eat*. Semantically, *eat* requires an eater (agent) and a thing being eaten (patient). This results in the grammatical sentence "The lion ate the elephant," with agent and patient explicitly specified both semantically (case) and structurally (thematic role). We can also have, however, "The lion ate well that day," where the semantic case is unstated but understood. Structurally, this sentence is (a) grammatical and (b) intransitive. This version of *eat* takes only one structural argument, to which it assigns the agent role. The transitive *eat* takes two arguments, to which it assigns, respectively, agent and patient roles.

Note that case and thematic role are similar but not identical. The words *devour* and *graze* take the same *cases* as the verb *eat* but require different argument structure and hence different theta-role assignments. Like the transitive *eat*, *devour* must specify both agent and patient—we cannot say * *"The lion devoured that day"*; without the patient, it is ill-formed. *Graze*, like *eat*, can leave the patient unstated, "The cows grazed" or "The cows grazed on the grass." With *graze*, the theta role is assigned not to a direct object but to a PP. Such syntactic ramifications (like the constraints on common versus proper nouns or transitive versus intransitive verbs) are what Chomsky (1965) called *strict subcategorization rules*.

Particular concepts take particular arguments regardless of their *part of speech.* So, the verb *donate* and the noun *donation* each entail (a) an agent who makes the donation, (b) a recipient of the donation, and (c) a thing that is donated. These three "arguments" are either understood from the word or must be explicitly stated in a grammatical sentence using that word.

Note that this discussion has created an odd "unit" for syntax, but for good reasons. The noun and the verb related to the concept of donating at one level of our grammar are treated alike, despite their being different parts of speech and entering into different phrase-structure relations. They constitute a grammatical unit because they demand the same argument structure. At the level of phrase structure, of course, the difference between a noun and a verb is recognized. The desirability of categorizing together at least at one level entities that serve the same function led Chomsky (1957, 1965, 1986) to reject phrase-structure grammars per se as models of grammatical competence, and to demand a much more powerful grammar to capture structural similarities among sentences whose phrase structures are markedly different. We need to examine some additional context-sensitive properties of language and structural similarities that transcend phrase structure— surface similarities—to motivate this grammar.

At this point you should understand that words may specify concepts needed in the sentence to complete their sense, as well as what selectional restrictions, thematic roles, and strict subcategorization rules are.

Other structural similarities. Consider the following two sentences:

9a. John gave a large donation to a needy charity.

9b. A large donation was given by John to a needy charity.

Phrase-structure rules that we have looked at for 9a follow:

S → NP VP
NP → (DET) (ADJ) N
VP → V NP PP
PP → PREP NP

and depict the structure as

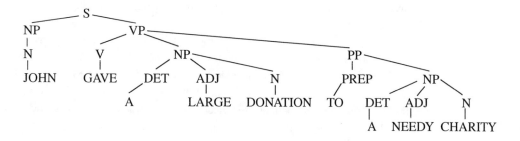

To describe 9b, we must make a new rewrite rule, VP → V PP PP, which can specifically generate the phrase marker

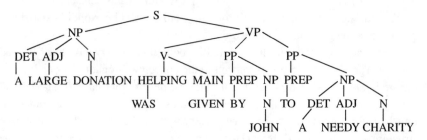

Note how different the two phrase markers are, despite some fundamental similarities in semantic relationships among the sentence constituents. In both sentences John did the giving—but in the first tree John is dominated by one NP and, in the second, by an NP, PP, and VP. I motivated syntax as serving the purpose of putting words together (or determining how words go together) so that appropriate meaning relations among words may be extracted. Is it not more reasonable, then, to assume that the underlying structures of the two sentences are the same, given that in both John is doing the giving? This will capture the similarity in function of the agent ("John"), patient (what it is that is given—"a large donation"), and recipient ("to a needy charity") phrases in both sentences, and will eliminate the need for a new VP rewrite rule for the passive. That is not to argue that the two sentences have identical structures—obviously they do not—but the relationship of the components of 9a is the same as that of 9b, and our grammar should capture that regularity.

Components of Generative Grammar

Using such arguments, Chomsky (1957) divided syntax into three components: *deep structure,* which captures underlying grammatical relationships regardless of their order or form (and is now abbreviated *D-structure*); *surface structure,* which is identical to the phrase structures we have been examining; and *transformations,* which are context-sensitive rules that take a given deep structure and convert it to surface structure form. So, for example, sentences 9a and 9b have the same underlying or deep structure. A minimal set of transformations would transform the deep structure to the pronounceable active sentence (9a). Sentences that are derived from deep structure using minimal transformations were called *core* or *kernel* sentences.

In early transformational theory, deriving a passive sentence from deep structure was optional and involved a set of complex operations that needed to be performed in a set order. The operations included additions (e.g., adding the helping verb, the -en morpheme, and the "by" to the agent position) and movement (moving the agent to the by clause and the patient to subject position). Transformations could also delete elements, as in an acceptable variant of the passive:

9c. A large donation was given to a needy charity.

Here the agent (the by phrase) has been eliminated. 9c has the same deep structure as 9a and 9b, and evolves from that deep structure using one more operation, deletion of the agent clause. Therefore, because it requires one more operation, it is considered *derivationally more complex* than the active sentence or complete passive, despite the fact that it has fewer words.

In more recent versions of generative grammar, it is recognized that both the role of grammatical subject and the role of agent are important and *obligatorily,* not optionally, determine the form of the sentence. We will discuss in the section on discourse, later, *why* we might choose a passive structure over an active structure. Given that the passive voice is selected as the D-structure, the syntactic component obligatorily moves elements from D-structure to their correct S-surface positions.

As we have seen, the agent relationship of "John" and the patient relationship of "the donation" is specified with the word *give. Those roles (the thematic role [theta role]) are assigned by give obligatorily in D-structure.* Theta roles are maintained by a *projection principle,* which preserves argument structure across syntactic levels *wherever* elements move to in the transformation of D-structure to surface structure.

In early versions of transformational theory, the deep and surface structures of a sentence could express different concepts: "A large donation was given" would have a deep structure complete with someone doing the giving, later deleted by transformation. Similarly, affirmative and negative sentences (9a and d), declarative and interrogative sentences (9a and 9e-9g), were considered to have the same deep structure, and to take the negative or question form only in surface structure:

9a. John gave a large donation to a needy charity.

9d. John did not give a large donation to a needy charity.

9e. Who gave a large donation to a needy charity?

9f. What did John give to a needy charity?

9g. To what did John give a large donation?

These sentences were assumed to have a deep structure roughly like the kernel sentence of 9a—with a negative or question element at the beginning of the phrase marker, roughly "not John gave . . ." Transformations moved the negative or question element to the correct position and reworked the auxiliary verb, and so on.

The similarity of the forms of these sentences and of the grammatical relations among the elements is apparent. But it is also apparent that 9a and 9d express contradictory meanings, and it was assumed that deep structure should capture the underlying sentence concepts. Current theory therefore has D-structure contain all and only those elements that are to be expressed in surface structure. Thus the D-structure representations of a negative and affirmative sentence will be the same but for the negative particle; passive voice will be indicated in the D-structure if it is to be a passive sentence, with the agent role absorbed into the passive marker on the verb (9c) or reassigned by the preposition "by" (9b).

Current generative grammar greatly simplifies transformational grammar's transformational component, with transformations now able only to move elements (*move-α*). The surface structure of the sentence reveals only the ultimate location of the element or constituent after the movement transformations. At a slightly more abstract level, just before surface structure, the movement leaves a residue, or *trace,* of the element that has been moved. This level is called *S-structure* and looks like surface structure but for the traces of the moved elements. A *chain* in transformational theory (not to be confused with the behaviorist chain that we modeled as a finite state grammar) is the history of movement of an element reflected through the traces in surface structure.

In the name of simplicity, our grammar has become quite complex, with many levels of representation. I will review the levels, together with supporting examples from the language, to see how the levels determine and describe structure. (We will in fact need to add more components.) *You need to understand the different effects that D-structure, theta-role assignment, abstract surface structure, and movement transformations have on recovery of basic sentential relations.* We are going to see how they affect logical properties of sentences such as paraphrase (same meaning) and ambiguity (double meaning).

Different S-structure / same or different D-structure and paraphrase.

> 9a. John gave a large donation to a needy charity.
>
> 9h. To a needy charity John gave a large donation.

9a and 9h are paraphrases of one another, expressing the same grammatical relations and the same concepts. Their surface form is different—9h begins with a PP and 9a ends with it. In current theory, 9a and 9h would share all structures until abstract surface structure, which would reflect both the *preposed* (put before) PP and the trace of its origin in D-structure. The goodness of the two as paraphrases results from the degree to which they share underlying structure. 9c, the agent-deleted passive version of the sentence "A large donation was given to a needy charity," is also a paraphrase of 9a and 9h but not as perfect a one. According to current theory, 9c differs from 9a and 9h at *all* levels of structure because D-structure for 9c reflects the passive voice and the absorbed agent, which is expressed in 9a and 9h. Those differences are maintained at each level up to surface structure, as constituents are moved and traces left. *So there is greater structural difference between sentences, which results in the intuition of poorer paraphrase.*

Different D-structures / same surface form and ambiguity. Generative grammar accounts for structural ambiguities by the generation of identical surface structures from different deep structures. This occurs through transformation as well as operations that change elements at other levels. Earlier, I provided an ambiguous sentence:

> 10. The demonstrators stopped smoking in restaurants.

(I have shamelessly "plagiarized" for the 1990s Chomsky's "The students stopped demonstrating on campus" for the 1960s.)

The sentence has two interpretations:

> 10a. The demonstrators stopped others' smoking.

and also in restaurants,

> 10b. The demonstrators stopped their own smoking.

The surface or phrase structures of both readings are identical: The subject NP is "the demonstrators," the verb is "stopped," and the direct object NP is a subordinated sentence (NP rewrites to N S), called a *complement.* The two readings differ in the subject of the complement clause. In both it is an *empty element,* a placeholder like a trace, representing an NP in deep structure. In one case it is empty because it is unknown and general; in the other, it is an empty element *bound* to "the demonstrators."

The referent's or antecedent's command of a pronoun is an example of binding and is indicated by *indexing* or subscripting the empty element, the pronoun, and "the demonstrators" identically. That is, we commonly do not repeat nouns but use pronouns to refer to them on subsequent mentions (so much so that "John said John was going to donate . . ." suggests that the two Johns are not the same person). S-structure tracks the pronoun's connection to the noun through indexing. *Determining whether a noun phrase is referentially dependent on another noun phrase in the sentence is accomplished through syntactic knowledge of such connecting or "binding" principles.* In our examples, binding principles determine that "the demonstrators" is realized as an empty element in the 10b reading of 10. They also require that the second "John" be a pronoun if it refers to the same person as the first "John" in the more recent example.

So, to return to the ambiguity of Sentence 10, it results from a subtle difference in indexing in S-structure of an empty element in D-structure.

Next, consider the ambiguity of

> 11. They are flying planes.

It occurs at the phrase-structure level. In one reading, "they" refers to some unspecified people, "are" is a helping (or *auxiliary, AUX*) verb, and "flying" is the main verb. In the other reading, "they" refers (before the fact) to "flying planes," where "flying" is an adjective describing planes. Phrase-structure ambiguities often occur when a word has several uses, sometimes as different parts of speech.

Theta-role assignment and D-structure difference.

> 12a. John promised Mary to give a large donation.
> 12b. John asked Mary to give a large donation.

12a and 12b are not ambiguous but are interesting for other reasons. They appear to have the same surface structure and differ only in the verb. The interest arises when we consider who will be doing the giving. In 12a, if John keeps his promise, he will; that is, John is coreferential with the empty-element subject of "give." In 12b, if Mary complies, Mary will make the donation—here, Mary is coreferential with the empty-element subject of "give." How do we know this? This is resolved through theta-role assignment. The subject of "give" is an empty element, which is normally indexed to the most nearly preceding noun (as it is for "asked"). "Promise" is unusual in that it assigns the *agent* theta role to its own NP subject (a distance away), which is then indexed as coreferential with the empty element. *Thus the paradoxical interpretations of these two apparently similar structures arises in D-structure from thematic role assignment by the lexical items.*

Quantification, logical form, and movement.

 13. Every boy dated one girl in the class.

 14. In most recent decisions, the Supreme Court has reversed direction.

13 and 14 are each ambiguous due to the scope of quantification. A *quantifier* is a word or phrase that signifies quantity; in 13, "every" and "one" are quantifiers, and in 14, "most" is a quantifier. *Scope* refers to the size of the phrase to which the quantifier applies. In 13, we need to know if there is one very popular girl or a generally happy class of couples. In 14, the question is whether "most" has a limited scope, "decisions which are most recent," or a broader scope, "most of the decisions that are recent."

Note that scope ambiguities occur after elements have reached their final resting places, after S-structure, because it is movement to the new position that causes the ambiguity. My paraphrases of 14 place "most" close to the structure it modifies unambiguously. Movement away from those positions raises the question of which structure it modifies. *Because interpretation has to follow the movement, which is still reflected in S-structure, Chomsky (1986) proposes another level,* logical form (LF), *at which scope is determined. LF receives input from S-structure, which in turn receives input from D-structure.*

Traces. The last component of generative grammar that we need to motivate through structural considerations of the language is the trace, the residue in S-structure of movement from D-structure. We will look again at evidence for traces in Chapter 5 as we consider human sentence processing, but here we look at an ingenious example of their control over structure (Bresnan, 1978; Chomsky, 1980), the rules controlling the conversion of *want to* to the vernacular *wanna.*

 15. Teddy is the man who I want to succeed.

is ambiguous. It could mean "I want Teddy to succeed" with an abstract surface structure containing a trace (t) of whom-referring-to-Teddy between "want" and "to," roughly

15a. Teddy is the man I want t(whom-Teddy) to succeed.

or it could mean "I want to succeed Teddy," derived from an abstract surface structure containing a trace of "whom-Teddy" following "succeed," roughly,

15b. Teddy is the man I want to succeed t(whom-Teddy).

Is the vernacular

15c. Teddy is the man I wanna succeed.

likewise ambiguous? Clearly, no. If *wanna* is in your dialect, this can only mean 15b. This example suggests that the rule *want + to → wanna* may apply only if *want* and *to* are adjacent in the abstract surface structure. They are adjacent in the surface structure 15b—which is the way 15c is interpreted—but a trace intervenes in 15a, blocking the conversion or interpretation of that structure from 15a.

In trying this example on acquaintances naive to linguistic theory, I discovered a tendency either to reject as ungrammatical the reading of 15c corresponding to 15a or to assume it was supposed to have been

15d. Teddy is the man who I want to *have* succeed

an interpretation you may have tried. This interpretation is consistent with trace theory. In this paraphrase, "whom-Teddy" *has moved from* in front of "to"—"I want to have whom-Teddy succeed." Thus "want" and "to" are still adjacent in abstract surface structure, allowing for their contraction.

You should appreciate the complexity of recovering sentential relationships in English, and how automatically we seem to do it. You should know what binding, scope of quantification, and movement are, and how their incomplete specification in the sentence you hear can lead to ambiguity. That you can connect the surface forms to different "readings" suggests that you have more complete specification available at some mental level, as well as the tacit understanding of the operations that alter that specification in surface form.

X-Bar Theory and the Structure of Phrases

The evolution of generative grammar entailed a simplification of the transformation component, with the assignment of some of the original functions of

---

Box 4.2. Components and Operations of Transformational Grammar

— *Deep structure (D-structure):* Contains the structural relationships among the major phrasal units of a sentence. It must have every concept that will be expressed at the surface. It indicates through empty or null elements (e_i) arguments required by a used word (like an agent for verbs in passive sentences) even if they are not ultimately expressed.

— *Lexical projection:* D-structure receives input from a lexicon that contains arguments required for particular words. A transitive verb would require both agent and object; verbs such as *give* require three NPs: agent, object, and indirect object (recipient). Verbs such as *promise* assign their complements their own subject/agent.

— *Transformations:* Originally complex, context-sensitive operations to be performed in a set order to permute the relations expressed in deep structure to the spoken order. Currently reduced to "move-α," where α = constituent in D-structure.

— *S-structure:* The result of D-structure, move-α, and the projection rules; a level before phrase structure. S-structure contains the constituents in the order they will be spoken but also contains residues of the original D-structure order (and of intermediate orders created by move-α), called traces. Binding takes place at S-structure, the mapping of pronoun-like words to their referents.

— *Logical form (LF):* A component of grammar that receives input from S-structure and assigns interpretations of scope and quantification.

— *Phonetic form (PF):* A component of grammar that receives input from S-structure and converts the abstract string into pronounceable form.

— *Phrase structure (or surface structure):* The structural rules underlying the spoken form of the sentence.

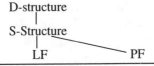

---

transformations to new levels of the grammar, such as LF and lexical projection rules. It also has involved a simplification, symmetry, and elegance in its treatment of phrases, which in turn have been compensated for by an increase in complexity of levels of structure. The simplification, symmetry, and elegance are motivated by *learnability* criteria, the idea that only simple and elegant *principles* could exist in UG (Chomsky, 1995).

There are four kinds of phrases, NPs, VPs, and PPs, as we have already seen, and also *adjective phrases (APs)*. (Note that some APs are simple; that is, the ADJ takes no arguments other than the N it will modify [like *small*]. Others are complex, such as *envious* [of __] or *generous* [to __].) Part of UG includes the information that phrasal structure is dictated by words, and that these are the four kinds of phrases to look for.

All phrases share common properties. The most important property is that each phrase has a *head*, the "governor" of that phrase. The head names the phrase; to wit, nouns, verbs, prepositions, and adjectives form the heads of their respective phrases. The lexical description of the head includes thematic properties, subcategorization rules, and what arguments it takes. Its role in specifying arguments, in structuring the rest of the phrase, makes the head a governor.

In English, all phrasal heads precede their arguments. According to theory, this is not an accident but a requirement of UG. That is not to say that all languages have head-first structures, but if a language has a head-first structure in one phrase, it will in all phrases. Likewise, if a language has a head-last structure in one phrase, it will be true of all phrases of that language. Phrasal structure is a principle of UG, with some variation allowed—either head first or head last. The variation is a *parameter.* In what is sometimes known as *principles and parameters* theory (Chomsky, 1995), the idea is that UG specifies the principles that guide language learners to attend to specific features of the language of their environment. This actual input then sets or fixes the parameter.

A phrase is a mini-structure tree. The head is a terminal node of that tree: It dominates a word. The other branches of a phrase are nonterminal. In addition to heads, phrases may contain a *specifier (SPEC)* and perhaps adjuncts. A *specifier* limits the role of the phrase. In NPs, SPECs include determiners *(a, an, the)* and quantifiers *(each, every, some)*; in APs, SPECs include adverbs *(rather* or *very)*; in VPs, SPECs include inflection, like tense or passive voice. *Tense* in English is obligatory—all sentences must be specified for a time frame (past, present, or future) on the verb, and sometimes adverbially as well. "*Tomorrow* I *will* finish this chapter" is grounded in the future in the adverb "tomorrow" and the form of the helping verb, both specifiers.

An *adjunct* is a modifier and is optional, as in an adjective (AP) describing a N in an NP or a PP (prepositional phrase) describing manner or location of a verb within a VP.

Note that here we have phrases embedded within phrases. This is a key to the concept of grammatical structure: Identical structures are replicated from the lowest level to the highest level, the sentence itself (Haegeman, 1994). Again this replication involves a simplicity and elegance that is postulated as necessary for learnability. The language learner can look for identical structures all the way up.

Let us examine the structure then of the sentence. A sentence is renamed *inflected phrase* or *IP.* The SPEC of an IP is the sentence subject, the NP, which you can see limits or specifies the topic under discussion. The head of an inflected phrase must be the inflection (because phrases are named for their heads). At the sentence level, and as we shall see, all the way down, the head dominates an intermediate level designated with a "bar"—I′—leading this theory to be named *X-bar theory.* I′ must dominate the VP (because a sentence still consists of a subject and a predicate [VP], however we formalize it). The predicate here also has two constituents: the inflection as head and the VP. In English, inflection is lexically realized in the auxiliary verb *(will, can, has)* or in a morphological ending of the verb; because the inflection is head, it dominates these lexical realizations directly, while the VP continues to branch to a V′ structure and so on.

The new rewrite rules then are

IP → SPEC, I′
I′ → I, VP

And the phrase marker for a sentence looks like

```
IP   (= S)
|_____
SPEC  (= subject NP)    I′
                        |  ‾‾‾‾‾‾‾
                        I  (= AUX)   VP
                        |            |
                        will         V′
                                     |  ‾‾‾‾‾‾‾
                                     V      NP
                                            △
```

and so on. (Following convention, an evident structure, like NP → DET N or (SPEC N), is not fully diagrammed but marked by a triangle.) And if there is an embedded S, from NP → N S, that embedded S is called a *complementizer phrase* or *(CP)*, with complementizer as head, and so on.

Note the consistency in the tree: Each node has two branches (there is a sense in linguistics that binary decisions are simpler and therefore preferable); adjuncts are always to the right of the head. The simplicity and consistency of these phrase-structure descriptions are compensated for by the hidden intermediate layers of structure, the "bars." They are necessary because syntactic structure *is* complex, and *that complexity must be reflected somewhere.* X-bar structure represents phrase structure at the D-structure level.

Let us now examine the phrase marker for a complex sentence under the new theory.

16. John gave a donation to charity to feed the hungry.

```
IP
|‾‾‾
SPEC  I′
|     |‾‾‾
John  I    VP
      |    |
      past V′ ——————————————— IP
           |                   |‾‾‾
           V″ — PP             SPEC   I′
           |    ▷              |      |‾‾‾
           V‴   to charity     e_John I    VP
           |                          |    |‾‾‾
           V⁗ ‾‾‾NP                    I    V    NP
           |      |                    |    |    ▷
           gave   SPEC N′              INF  feed the hungry
                  |    |
                  a    N
                       |
                       donation
```

The additional layers of structure should be clear here, as should the symmetry and simplicity of the organization within phrase boundaries. Note the places (INF to or e_i) where an element is indicated—cross-indexed or place-held by a null element—into which a verbal element will move during the transformation from D-structure to spoken sentence. In abstract surface structure, that position will hold a trace of the element.

Detailed discussion of the rules that control movement of elements within or across phrase boundaries and that *license* (i.e., specify, permit, and control) arguments within and across phrase boundaries is beyond the scope of this chapter. The former set of rules includes *binding* rules, and the latter set, *government* rules. We have seen examples of each: A binding rule connects a pronoun and its antecedent or null element or trace and its final position; government of theta roles by the head specifies arguments at the lexical level. Because of the concentration on universal rules of government and binding, the theory is sometimes known as *government and binding theory.*

You should understand what specifiers, heads, and adjuncts are and how they are ordered within a phrase in a given language.

STRUCTURE WITHIN THE WORD AND BEYOND THE SENTENCE

Lexical Structure

As mentioned in Chapter 2, words may be broken into parts (or parsed), as sentences may be, to reveal a componential structure. You may recall that derivational morphemes combine to form new words or to change words from one part of speech to another, while inflectional morphemes play syntactic functions, marking singular-plural differences, tense, and case. (In English, the genitive or possessive case is marked on all nouns, and subject and object, in pronouns; in many other languages, all case is directly indicated morphologically.)

English predominantly indicates syntactic function through word order: The subject is typically mentioned first in the sentence, the direct object typically follows the verb, and so on. Thus study of the syntactic system of English ends up concentrating on why words appear in the order they do—how order lets the listener know that the lion, not the elephant, is the chaser. In languages that are case-marked morphologically, what we express in a sentence as a string of words may be expressed in a word, as a string of morphemes. Or it may be expressed in various strings of the same words, where the order of the words differs across the string.

Because the study of syntax is the study of the grammatical relations among the sentence elements, and these grammatical relations can be expressed either morphologically or by word order, morphology is a subfield of syntax. Morphological structure can be described by rewrite rules and structure trees:

Box 4.3. Components and Rules of Phrase Structure in X-Bar Theory

— *Head:* The verbal element that governs the arguments of a phrase and that a phrase is named after. In the phrase marker, it is to the right of the specifier.

— *Specifier (SPEC):* A phrasal element that limits the topic, time frame, or quantity of a phrase: the subject at the sentence level, a determiner of an NP, and adverb of quantity in an adjective phrase (AP), and so on. In the phrase marker, SPEC occupies the left-most position of a phrase.

— *Adjunct:* An element or phrase that optionally modifies a phrasal head.

— *Thematic role:* A principal case relation (agent, recipient, patient, location) required by a phrasal head. The head governs the argument and assigns case to the appropriate element in the sentence.

— *Governor:* A role assigner, the phrasal head, governs its arguments and assigns case to the elements. Other aspects of syntactic structure are also governed, sometimes within a phrasal unit and sometimes between phrasal units.

— *"Superphrases":* Phrase structure is reflected at micro levels such as NP and PP, and also at macro levels such as the whole sentence.

  — *Inflected phrase:* The sentence level, a macro phrase structure. SPEC = subject; inflection (~VP) = head.

  — *Complementizer phrase:* Embedded sentences in the new theory, can take the form of infinitives or relative clauses. SPEC = subject; complement = head.

— *X′:* Intermediate (hidden) levels of structure, which maintain across all levels of phrase structure a symmetry and elegance. All phrases are binary-branching, with sufficient intermediate (barred) levels to produce only two branches, regardless of the number of apparent arguments and adjuncts at the surface-structure level.

— *Binding:* The principles that maintain connections among elements as they move.

— *Trace:* The residue in abstract surface structure of an element that has been moved. The residue still controls some movements and contractions.

— *Null element:* An element that is not explicitly realized in that phrasal position in surface structure but is a necessary argument in the phrase and clearly controls structural decisions within the sentence, despite its "invisibility."

— *Indexing:* A way to bind null elements with explicitly stated elements, pronouns with nouns, and nouns with other phrasal referents within the sentence.

ADV → ADJ + ly

V → V + ed

```
            V
      _____|_____
     |             \
 Past Tense        Stem
     |              |
     ed            walk
```

We see in English some freeing of order—when we permute agent and patient in the passive, morphologically marking the verb to signal the new assignment of case roles and order, or in *topicalization*—deliberately placing the topic first. This is marked in writing by a comma, and in speaking, with intonation:

A donation, John gave (= object-subject-verb, or OSV).

rather than the normal-for-English

John gave a donation (= SVO).

I can imagine a context and intonation of incredulity in which

John a donation gave!?

is permissible. Clearly, if we were to mark NPs explicitly with their case (A = agent, P = patient), we could decode any order:

Lion$_A$ chased elephant$_P$.
Elephant$_P$ lion$_A$ chased.
Chased lion$_A$ elephant$_P$.

These mean the same thing even if you feel more like you are doing arithmetic than reading as you decode the grammatical relations. But languages that use suffixes naturally as we artificially used the subscripts recover grammatical relations as naturally from the morphology as we do from word order. The recovery of case relations is the fundamental purpose of syntax. It is complicated in English because case markings are neither consistent nor overt: Case is sometimes marked by prepositions (location [*in, on, by*], instrument [*with, by*], recipient [*to*], owner [*of*]), sometimes by morpheme (owner ['s], nominative or objective pronouns) and frequently by word order. Thus it makes sense to link case to licensing by, for example, the verb. In other languages, the verb may still license case, but the case marking may be a more overt and consistent part of sentence structure. The grammar of such a language would focus more on word formation than on order and movement of phrases.

While in English we do not use affixing to mark grammatical *relations,* we do use it to mark grammatical category productively, as in ADV = ADJ + ly. The following excerpt from the British newspaper *The Guardian,* cited by Safire (1982), demonstrates the productivity of affixing in English (of sorts), allowing us to understand new words through recognition of the affixes marking their grammatical categories. It is a parody of the speech style of Alexander Haig, at the time a candidate for U.S. Secretary of State:

Haig, in congressional hearings before his confirmatory, paradoxed his auditions by abnormalling his responds so that verbs were nouned, nouns verbed and adjectives adverbised. He techniqued a new way to vocabulary his thoughts so as to informationally uncertain anybody listening about what he had actually implicationed. . . .

If that is how General Haig wants to nervous breakdown the Russian leadership he may be shrewding his way to the biggest diplomatic event since Clausewitz. Unless, that is, he schizophrenes his allies first. (pp. 105-106)

The cartoon show *The Smurfs* also uses morphological structure and context to "create" words. In the show the nonsense word *smurf* smurfs into sentences, in a smurfy way, leaving meaning and syntactic function transparent. The show possibly owes some of its popularity to the fun of playing this language game.

Both examples show that the *functors,* the system of function words, order, and morphology that we study in syntax, actively inform meaning inference from sentences—it is neither a simple, passive look-up of word meanings nor a simple, passive application of thematic-role assignments and strict subcategorization rules.

Discourse Analysis

Thus far we have concentrated on syntactic relations at a sentence or subsentence level. Although we will not go into it in detail, it is important to note that structure and meaning modification by language units occurs between sentences as well as within sentences. I have already alluded to this with pronoun use; the pronoun (e.g., *he* versus *she*) is dictated by its referent.

Most frequently, pronouns are used anaphorically. An *anaphoric* reference is one in which reference is made to something earlier in the discourse. In the following sentences, "I talked to John yesterday. He said Mary gave it to him," "he" and "him" refer to John anaphorically; John is mentioned earlier. This is stylistically preferable in English to "I talked to John yesterday. John said Mary gave it to John," which uses no reference. In fact, as I said earlier, the avoidance of the pronoun here suggests different Johns involved in the discourse.

Another form distinction that crosses sentence boundaries is the topic of the conversation, which can dictate the choice of passive versus active voice. The *topic, theme* or *old information* is what has been mentioned in previous sentences. In English, it is customary to begin a sentence with the topic, what is already known, and then use the rest of the sentence to add information, expounding on the topic, called *focus, comment, rheme,* or *new information.* Note that in an active sentence the topic is the agent and the focus is the object: "What did John do? He gave a large donation." In a passive sentence, topic and focus reverse: "Who gave a large donation? The large donation was given by John." If the topic is "John," then the sentence will take the form in which "John" is mentioned first; if the topic is "donation," then "donation" will be the grammatical or surface subject. So, to keep the topic first, a "voice" is chosen. As discourse can dictate "voice," it can also specify that a major constituent be (cooperatively) omitted if it is already available for binding from earlier discourse. A complete answer to

Who was *the first president?*

is, with the italicized portion repeated,

> *The first president* was George Washington.

Alternatively, we may mark that constituent with a pronoun:

> Who was *the first president*?
> *It* was George Washington.

Or we may mark the fact that there was an earlier reference by deleting the redundant phrase:

> Who was the first president?
> George Washington.

In this last case we can hypothesize that discourse rules permit grammatical sentences with major constituents represented by empty elements and specify binding across sentence boundaries.

In sentence structure, specification of a constituent could be affected by a constituent at a considerable distance from the constituent in question; this therefore requires memory. Clearly, this applies in spades in discourse, where old and new information must be kept track of, so that redundancy is appropriately eliminated through pronoun or null element use. The omissions actually help tie sentences together into a coherent group, as the elimination of the specific word *John* cements the identity of the referent across the pronouns in the sentence.

There have been attempts to determine the structure of paragraphs, texts, stories, and so on beyond determination of rules of reference or old information. These have mostly developed from processing attempts and so will be discussed in more detail in Chapter 5 along with other aspects of processing models. Generally, these models have looked at the kinds of syntactic-semantic relations expressed across coherent sentences, much as thematic-role assignment looks at relations expressible within sentences, required by certain words.

SUMMARY AND CONCLUSIONS

It should be clear at this point that language and language structures are terribly complex—more complex than we imagine from early grammar courses and more complex than surface analysis of sentences immediately reveals. There are many levels of structure in language: sublexical structure, constituent structure, phrase structure, D-structure, structure in discourse.

At this point you should appreciate the structure at each of these levels and the wonderful way in which the structures are enmeshed. You may also wonder how, with all these levels of structure and all these tacit rules, we ever manage to produce or understand a sentence at all—especially at the fast rate that we do! Beautiful

---

Box 4.4. Structure Beyond the Sentence

— Inflectional morphology marks case or thematic relations in many languages, which in English are given by word order. Universally they are considered by generative theory to be governed by the verb or phrasal head, regardless of whether they are specified by word order or inflection.

— Derivational morphology is systematic, creating new meanings or changing parts of speech, as in ADV → ADJ + -ly.

— Discourse is also structured, with rules specifying when a noun will be repeated or referred to by a pronoun or null element (anaphora).

— Discourse also elaborates a topic into new information. Topics, if clear, may be omitted: the cooperative principle of being informative but not redundant.

— At the sentence level, in English, topic, theme, or old information is mentioned first (the subject position), and focus, theme, or new information follows (predicate position). The topic and focus determine whether a sentence will be in active (subject position filled by agent) or in passive (subject position filled by patient) voice.

---

writing (or speaking) not only allows us to get at the meanings quickly but also uses the structures of the language themselves, forcing us to play with our various tacit rules, as "This is the house that Jack built" forces us to play with the possibilities of embedding. Writing or speaking that does not make use of the complexities of structure is terribly monotonous, like a grade school essay: "We went to the zoo. We saw the lion. The lion ate some meat. Then the lion roared. We came home. We were tired. We had fun."

Why is this so dull? Because we like layers of structure; we like transforming; and we like playing with our language.

In this chapter we examined some ways of characterizing the structure of language (English) and the interrelation of structure and meaning. We noted first that words may be characterized with respect to their use in sentences, as parts of speech, and demonstrated the linguistic method of distributional analysis to derive these. We then discussed (surface) phrase structure, or the combining of parts of speech into larger functional units, constituents. We demonstrated the preferability of the hierarchical phrase-structure grammar over finite state grammar by showing that sentences are recursive and sensitive to contexts beyond the adjacent word, and that finite state models have no power to handle this. Phrase-structure grammar was also shown to be incapable of fully handling context sensitivity, and to be unable to account for similarities between some sentences that seem to convey the same relationships without having the same phrase structures. This necessitated postulating structure at both a surface and a deep level, and a way of transforming the deep structure into the surface structure, retaining information about position of elements and their relationship to other elements throughout the restructuring processes. It also required assigning some grammatical control to lexical items themselves, to structure phrases they enter into.

We began the chapter with the view prevalent in linguistics that much of our grammatical knowledge is innate and automatic, performed by a language module. Although the principles are innate, current theory holds that parameter settings, the fine-tuning of the principles, is learned through exposure to the community's language. These are psychological—processing—assumptions made primarily from evidence of structural regularities in and across languages, and negative evidence that such rules are not and could not be taught. We will return to grammar acquisition in Chapter 9, looking at what children and parents actually do. Our next chapter examines evidence from psychological and computer processing for the reality of these rules and levels in normal sentence understanding.

APPENDIX

The terms for English grammar (re)introduced in this chapter are listed here, together with their definitions and examples, for reference purposes.

1. *Active voice:* Sentences in which the logical subject is also the functional subject; it occurs before the verb. Contrasts with passive voice. For example, "John gave a large donation to a needy charity."

2. *Adjective:* A word that modifies a noun, either preceding it as in "a *small* boy" or following verbs such as *is, seems, looks,* as a predicate adjective, as in "The boy looks *small.*"

3. *Adverb[ial]:* A word or phrase that modifies the verb. Frequently marked by an -ly suffix. For example, "John died *quickly*" (word) or "John died *an hour ago*" (time adverbial).

4. *Affirmative:* A sentence that states that something is true, as opposed to a negative. For example, "John gave a large donation" or "A large donation was given."

5. *Agent:* The person performing the action. For example, "*John* gave a large donation" or "A large donation was given by *John.*"

6. *Anaphor:* Reference to something mentioned earlier. In "I talked to John yesterday. He said Joe gave it to him," "He" and "him" refer to "John" anaphorically.

7. *Auxiliary:* A marker in a sentence that contains tense information. Sometimes this is marked with a "helping verb" such as *is, do,* or *have.* For example, "John give + past": "John gave" or "John *did* give" or "John *has* given."

8. *By-deletion:* A form of the passive in which the agent is deleted. For example, "A large donation was given by John" to "A large donation was given."

9. *Center-embedding:* A clause inserted between the subject and predicate of another sentence. For example, "The rat *the cat wounded* ate the cheese."

10. *Common noun:* A noun that may take a determiner (*a, an,* or *the*). For example, "a donation." Compare with proper noun.

11. *Complement and complex sentence:* Compound sentence (or phrase) with more than one subject or predicate (or head). There are various methods of compounding: Embedding, where there is a main clause and a subordinate clause (or complement), is one (complex

sentence), and conjoining, uniting two main clauses with a conjunction (compound sentence) is another. For example, "The cat and the dog ran around together" (compound phrase). "The cat that the dog chased ran up the tree" (complex sentence). "John gave a donation *to feed the hungry*" (infinitival complement).

12. *Conjunction:* A part of speech that permits joining of like constituents. For example, *and, or, but, nor.* See the examples for compounds in 11.

13. *Count noun:* Nouns that name individual items that can be counted. Contrast with mass nouns that name unspecified amounts. In "a glass of milk," "glass" is a count noun. In "some milk," "milk" is a mass noun.

14. *Declarative:* A type of sentence in which something is stated. Contrast with imperatives and interrogatives. For example, "John gave a large donation," "A large donation was given by John," "John did not give a large donation."

15. *Determiner:* A part of speech that quantifies and specifies count nouns. *The* indicates that the noun following refers to a specific object; *a* or *an,* to an indefinite object. For example, "A large donation."

16. *Directional:* A case marking location plus movement. For example, "to the car."

17. *Embedding:* See center-embedding.

18. *Imperative:* A type of sentence in which something is commanded. Contrast with declarative and interrogative. For example, "Give a large donation to a needy charity."

19. *Instrumental:* In case grammar, the case describing the means by which something was done. For example, "A knife killed John."

20. *Interrogative:* A type of sentence in which something is questioned. Contrast with declarative and imperative. For example, "Who gave a large donation to a needy charity?"

21. *Intransitive verb:* A verb that cannot take an object. Contrast with transitive. For example, *die.*

22. *Locative:* A case marking location. For example, "in a room."

23. *Main clause:* In embedding, the clause that can stand alone or that contains the other. Contrast with subordinate clause. For example, "*The rat* the cat wounded *ate the cheese.*" or "Because the rat ate the cheese, *we bought a cat.*"

24. *Manner:* A case marking how something is done. For example, "in a careless way."

25. *Mass noun:* A noun standing for stuff the amount of which is not countable. Contrast with count noun. For example, *milk, mud.* Note that you cannot say "a milk" or "a mud."

26. *Negative:* A sentence in which something is denied. Contrast with affirmative. For example, "John did not give a large donation to a needy charity."

27. *Noun:* A part of speech naming a person, place, or thing. See common noun, count noun, mass noun, proper noun, and noun phrase.

28. *Noun phrase:* A phrase consisting of (determiner) (adjective) noun or pronoun. For example, "*John* gave *a large donation* to *a needy charity.*"

29. *Object:* The noun phrase acted on by the verb. For example, "John gave *a large donation* to a needy charity" or "*A large donation* was given by John to a needy charity."

30. *Passive voice:* A sentence in which the logical subject is in object position. Contrast with active voice. For example, "A large donation was given by John to a needy charity."

31. *Patient:* A case marking the person or thing acted on. Also called the object.

32. *Predicate:* The sentence minus the subject and whole-sentence modifiers; what it is that is being talked about. Also called the verb phrase. For example, "John *gave a large donation to a needy charity.*"

33. *Preposition:* A part of speech that usually precedes a noun phrase, describing how it relates to the rest of the sentence. For example, "John gave a large donation *to* a needy charity."

34. *Prepositional phrase:* The preposition with the noun phrase it heads. For example, "John gave a large donation *to a needy charity.*"

35. *Pronoun:* A part of speech that stands for a noun or noun phrase, such as *he, she, I, me, them, it, who, that.*

36. *Proper noun:* A noun naming a specific individual. Contrast with common noun. For example, *John.*

37. *Quantifier:* A word or phrase telling how much. Determiners are quantifiers as are numbers and words like *some, many, each, for all.*

38. *Recipient:* A case marking the person to whom something is given. For example, "John gave a large donation *to a needy charity.*"

39. *Relative clause:* A subordinate clause headed by a (deleted) relative pronoun. For example, "The rat *(that) the cat wounded* ate the cheese." or "The boy *who was rich* gave a donation."

40. *Relative pronoun:* Pronouns *who, which,* or *that,* which introduce relative clauses. See the preceding.

41. *Subject:* The noun phrase governing the action of the verb. For example, "*John* gave a large donation" or "*The door* opened."

42. *Subordinate clause:* In a complex sentence, the clause that depends on the other clause and cannot stand alone. Contrast with main clause. For example, "The rat *the cat wounded* ate the cheese" or "*Because the rat ate the cheese,* we bought a cat."

43. *Theme-rheme:* Also called old information-new information, topic-comment. The theme is what the sentence is about; it is usually unstressed and usually mentioned first. The rheme is what the sentence is telling that is new. In "The first president of the United States was George Washington," the theme is the first president and the rheme is his identity.

44. *Transitive:* A verb that can take an object. Contrast with intransitive. For example, *give.*

45. *Verb:* A part of speech that usually describes an action. See transitive and intransitive. For example, *die, give.*

46. *Verb phrase:* The part of the sentence including and following the verb. See predicate.

REFERENCES

Bresnan, J. A. (1978). A realistic transformational grammar. In M. Halle, J. Bresnan, & G. A. Miller (Eds.), *Linguistic theory and psychological reality* (pp. 1-59). Cambridge: MIT Press.

Chomsky, N. (1957). *Syntactic structures.* The Hague, The Netherlands: Mouton.

Chomsky, N. (1965). *Aspects of the theory of syntax.* Cambridge: MIT Press.

Chomsky, N. (1980). *Rules and representations.* New York: Columbia University Press.

Chomsky, N. (1986). *Knowledge of language: Its nature, origin, and use.* New York: Praeger.

Chomsky, N. (1995). *The minimalist program.* Cambridge: MIT Press.

Fodor, J. A. (1983). *The modularity of mind.* Cambridge: MIT Press.

Haegeman, L. (1994). *Introduction to government and binding theory* (2nd ed.). Cambridge, MA: Blackwell.

Jackendoff, R. (1994). *Patterns in the mind.* New York: Basic Books.

Lyons, J. (1970). Generative syntax. In J. Lyons (Ed.), *New horizons in linguistics* (pp. 115-140). Harmondsworth, Middlesex, England: Penguin.

Pinker, S. (1994). *The language instinct.* New York: HarperCollins.

Safire, W. (1982). *What's the good word?* New York: Times Books.

Woods, W. A. (1970). Transition network grammars for natural language analysis. *Communications of the ACM, 13,* 591-606.

STUDY QUESTIONS

1. Characterize what is meant by a "cognitive module." Discuss the government and binding theory of syntax as a cognitive module.

2. What is a finite state grammar? What evidence is there for structural dependencies beyond adjacent words? Why is this important in evaluating finite state grammar models of language? Could a finite state grammar be developed to handle such dependencies? Show how or discuss why not.

3. Make up a sentence that instantiates each of the following:

   a. ambiguity of scope of quantification,

   b. anaphoric reference,

   c. a trace in abstract surface structure, and

   d. different D-structures.

4. Try to represent in bracket notation the constituent structure, abstract surface structure (S-structure), and D-structures of the following:

The mouse wounded by the cat ate the cheese.

Identify the theta roles assigned by each verb.

CHAPTER

5

SENTENCE PROCESSING

R ead the following sentences carefully:

1. They are forecasting cyclones.
2. They are describing events.
3. They are chopping wood.
4. They are eating lunch.
5. They are spelling words.
6. They are conflicting desires. (after Mehler & Carey, 1967)

Did something funny happen when you read sentence 6? For a second, perhaps it made no sense? Do you have any problem with it now? Can you go back to 1-5 and read any of them the same way you *must* read 6? Try especially sentence 5, which is ambiguous. It could be said by someone explaining the contents of a word list or by someone about participants in a spelling bee. What are you doing when you switch from "reading" a sentence one way to reading a sentence another? What makes 6 so hard to understand? Why does it require a double take after reading 1-5?

This example, as you should realize, makes use of constituent structures described in the last chapter. Although similar in appearance, these sentences derive from different phrase structures, one where "are" functions as an auxiliary verb and "they" does not refer to the object, and one where "are" is the main verb, and "they" and the object, "conflicting desires" or "spelling words," refers to the same thing. In understanding 1-5 on your first reading, you performed some mental parsing operations, the same for each sentence. You tried to use the same operations or strategies for 6, unsuccessfully. (Use of a familiar strategy in an inappropriate situation is known as *persistence of set*.) This produced a double take, from which you should realize that you actively process sentence structure, that there is a psychological reality to syntactic operations.

7. The student cheated on his grade complained.

This sentence should cause problems, although it is grammatical. If you have not parsed it yet, try the paraphrase:

7a. The student, who was cheated on his grade, complained.

Why does 7 cause so much difficulty? Because our experience with the language allows for a simple reading, "the student cheated on his grade," with "student" as both subject and agent, and that leaves an extra verb, "complained." We do not try first the complex embedded clause, passive with relative pronoun ("who") missing. Again this should make you see the psychological reality to syntactic operations.

8. Time flies like an arrow.

This sentence may seem to be straightforward with only one reading, but, nevertheless, it is five-ways ambiguous. To derive the ambiguities, you must disband your real world knowledge and some semantic knowledge and just use your syntax processor. Disbanding this knowledge is hard; most of the readings were uncovered by a computer not provided with such knowledge (Kuno, 1967), but notice how easy they are to see in paraphrase:

8a. There is a species of flies called time flies that likes an arrow.
8b. There is a race and you are referee. Time the flies that look like arrows.
8c. There is a race and you are referee. Time the flies as you would time an arrow.
8d. There is a race and you are referee. Time the flies the way an arrow would time them.

And then, of course, the one that is sensible:

8e. Time and arrows both move quickly.

The point of this example is twofold. First, as with the other examples, it should make you aware of your ability to parse. You can see that the other senses are possible syntactically, and you do that by using your mental parsing operations. Second, it should demonstrate that in normal sentence processing, syntactic operations work together with semantic operations, so if there is semantic bias for one reading, other structures are not derived or at least do not become conscious.

As one last example to demonstrate that parsing must have a psychological reality, recall the simple, unambiguous English sentence of the last chapter, "The lion chased the elephant." As I stressed in the last chapter, it is equally plausible for the lion or the elephant to be the chaser, and therefore the only way to determine the agent in such a sentence is through syntax. In English, syntax is provided in the order of the words, in subject-verb agreement markers, and in the absence of passive markings on the verb; in other languages, it may be provided (too) in case markings on nouns. In places where our knowledge of the world and our knowledge of individual word meanings are not enough to determine the relationship of elements within the sentence, we *must* rely on mental knowledge of syntactic rules, how additional meaning may be conveyed by word combination. This knowledge allows us to understand sentences that are unlikely semantically, but perhaps true, such as "Man bites dog," or innovative semantically, but conveying new truths such as "Test-tube baby clones scientist." We cannot interpret such sentences directly from past experience or understanding of individual word meanings but only from extensions of past experience, individual meanings, and knowledge of how meanings are combined according to the language's conventions. This last is syntax.

In this chapter we will discuss the nature of sentence processing as distinct from the nature of sentence structure, discussed in the last chapter; that is, we will examine which aspects of structure are useful for sentence processing. One difference between structure and process foci is that structure models assume a single underlying competence for both production and comprehension, while process models do not. Our discussion of process models will deal mostly with comprehension, parsing an input to derive meaning. Realize, though, that structural constraints that may not appear to play a role in comprehension may come into play in production.

A second important difference between linguistics (structure) and psychology (process) is that they use data and theory in very different ways. I have tried to present each approach uncritically, from the stances of those within the field. Reyna (1993) highlights some critical differences that are important to keep in mind if you are trying to unify data and theory from Chapters 4 and 5:

• Linguistic arguments are primarily logical rather than empirical, with the reverse true of psychology.

• "In linguistics, data are used mainly as illustrations of broader theoretical principles, whereas in psychology, data serve a hypothesis-testing function of differentiating among competing explanations. . . .

• "In linguistics, isolated facts can carry a heavy explanatory burden. A single spontaneous utterance can nullify a linguistic theory . . . and rare observations can be the crux of theoretical confirmation. . . . In psychology, in contrast, statistically rare observations are usually interpreted as error . . .

• "The data are but one small set of realizations of the universal grammar, and, consequently, the theory's complexity necessarily exceeds that of the data. In psychology, however, theories should have fewer degrees of freedom than the data they seek to explain" (pp. 22-23).

Sentence *processing* has been studied in artificial intelligence, in attempts to make computers "understand" sentences, and in cognitive psychology, in attempts to discover how people understand sentences. Both processing approaches are presented here because each provides insights about which aspects of structure are most useful. And it is important to note that the two approaches have developed similar conclusions.

COMPUTER SENTENCE PROCESSING

Parsers

The goals for machine language comprehension have been practical and fall into a few general classes. Computer language systems have been designed to take text in one language and translate it into another, equipped for this purpose with a dictionary for the two languages and some syntactic information for each. Computers have been used to access and organize quantities of data as information-retrieval or question-answering systems. In this case they are equipped with the data and enough knowledge of the users' language to "understand" the users' questions, retrieve the appropriate data, and feed it back to users in a form they can understand. Computer systems have been designed to participate in stereotyped communications tasks such as writing thank you notes, letters of regret, personalized Christmas cards, or being a good supportive "listener." In these cases the machine may be supplied with stock phrases as in form letters, into which it inserts the appropriate "personalized" information, such as a name. The machine must therefore be equipped with enough knowledge of the language to locate the personal information in the input from the user to be able to cycle it into the output. Finally, computer systems have been used as prototypes for any and all of these purposes, to test a particular model of language understanding, as we saw in Chapter 3 in modeling of semantic memory. In these cases the machine has been equipped with parsing strategies that (it is hoped) are sufficient for general language use.

In reviewing language understanding programs, one is simultaneously struck by how much has been accomplished and how far the programs are from human capabilities. It might seem that the set of goals just outlined is easily achieved by using very simple schemes (some of which I hinted at) but what has been discovered is that each goal has required enormously more language knowledge for easy interaction than originally thought necessary. This, in turn, has given us some insight into what language knowledge we normally draw on.

Keyword Systems

We will begin by looking at simple language translation and question-answering schemes, such as you may use in an on-line search for a book or journal article in the library. The simplest possible approach to both of these tasks is one that uses no syntax whatsoever; the machine is supplied with synonyms in one language for each word in another, or, in question-answering systems, the machine is supplied with a dictionary of keywords. A *keyword* is a word likely to appear in the user's input that the machine will "recognize" by matching it in its dictionary; the dictionary "definition" will consist of an action the machine should take, like providing a listing of books on that topic in the library or calling another program to prompt you with a new menu of choices. Basically, most book indexes use a keyword system. If you are interested in PDPs (parallel distributed processing systems described in Chapter 3 and here, below) you might look in the index to this book under PDP and find some page numbers. Turning to those pages, you will find information about PDPs. If this were automated, you might ask a machine, "Where can I locate information about PDPs?" and the machine would respond with the page numbers, or you might ask the machine, "Tell me what you know about PDPs" and the machine would get a page number, turn to its copy of the book (inside its memory), and display the information (as the on-line encyclopedias and atlases do). In either case the task could be accomplished with the machine recognizing nothing more than the word *PDP*, which would be a keyword.

One obvious difficulty with such a system is that you might probe with a word that the machine cannot recognize—the sample questions said "PDPs"; if only PDP is stored, "PDPs" will not be recognized, nor will "neural net," an obvious synonym that shares nothing but meaning with the keyword PDP. To avoid this, we might put in various synonyms that the user might employ; we might supplement the system with morphological rules so that it could recognize words and their plurals without having all plurals stored separately; or we might ask the user to flounder and to try to select the one keyword that will score a hit.

I have already suggested programming some syntax at the morphological level. Alert readers probably recognized that we need more than that. Supposedly we probed with the two questions: "Where can I locate information about PDPs?" and "Tell me what you know about PDPs?" and supposedly we extracted page *number* from the first and page *contents* from the second. If the machine responds only to the word *PDP*, the two questions should produce identical responses; the machine would have no way of recognizing that different information was requested. We can try to get around that difficulty by causing it to recognize more than one word. For example, it could scan the sentence for words like *where, on what page, locate,*—any of which would tell it to respond with the page number, while *what* or *know* could cue it to respond with the page contents. *PDP* would still tell it what to respond about.

This is a keyword system too, slightly more sophisticated, with an appearance of syntax. Note that the different response possibilities are dictated by keywords—not by establishing a structure. Recognition of the word *know* causes the machine to call a program to look up a page; which page is triggered by a content word like *PDP*. Although the machine is not making an overt response to the user for *know,* matching that pattern still produces a set action. Given this scheme, is the user who queries with "Do you know what page PDPs are described on?" likely to get the desired information?

Although I have concentrated on the keyword scheme with respect to question-answering systems, the problems translate readily to translation schemes. A program equipped with only two language dictionaries is a keyword program. Recognition of a word in one language prompts the response of a synonym from the other language rather than a page number or other internal action. We still will need to list different morphological forms of words or to program morphological rules. We also must worry about selecting the correct meaning of ambiguous words to translate, and this may require syntax to determine. Finally, idioms must be treated as a unit: "Do you know what page PDP is on?" in English is probably synonymous with "What page is PDP on?" but in some languages the English may not be rendered literally.

It is interesting to note, though, that keyword systems can be successful if the domain in which they are to apply is limited—if it is known ahead of time that only a particular subject is to be translated. Then the synonyms, idioms, and so on, can be preselected, and some of the problems circumvented. In reading about computer language systems, this point should be kept in mind; even sophisticated systems, at some level, make use of keywords and sometimes are performing well only because their domain has been restricted, and the restrictions may not be transparent. This has implications for human language processing. Once we are cued into a topic, it is possible that we simplify our processing, ultimately responding to only one meaning of ambiguous words—the meaning relevant to the current domain. It is possible that we use keywords also to guess what is being said or asked for and may not actually attend to the conversation.

The potency of keywords in creating languagelike behavior is reflected by the DOCTOR, a psychiatrist program designed to illustrate the shortcomings of a keyword system. The system appears to work because this type of conversation requires little thinking—the doctor serves as a yes-man. Because of this, Weizenbaum, its creator, considered it a parody of a doctor and was surprised to find that people took it very seriously (Weizenbaum, 1976). The system works by "recognizing" phrases such as "I remember ____." The DOCTOR responds automatically with "Do you often think of ____," getting the seemingly sophisticated syntax from the user. If "____" is a single word like "John," the machine responds with a single word, "Do you often think of John?" If it is an embedded sentence, the machine echoes with an embedded sentence: "I remember visiting relatives in New Hampshire" → "Do you often think of visiting relatives in New Hampshire?" Additional naturalness was programmed by conversions of *I, me, my* to *you, your* ("I remember my mother" → "Do you often think of your mother?") and by having several response frames for each keyword: *remember → do you often think of, what in the present situation reminds you of,* and so on.

I end this section with an excerpt of a conversation between a computer modeling paranoid behavior (P) using similar keyword principles and the doctor (D) to show how realistic a keyword system can be with minimal syntax, and to show where its output is stilted as a result of the tricks it employs to avoid syntax. I also include it because I find it funny.

D. Good evening. Tell me your problems. Please terminate input with a period or a question mark.

P. People get on my nerves sometimes.

D. I am not sure I understand you fully.

P. You should pay more attention.

D. Suppose you should pay more attention.

P. You're entitled to your own opinion.

D. What makes you think I am entitled to my own opinion?

P. It bothers me just to be around people.

D. Please go on.

P. I went to the track at Bay Meadows a while back.

D. What does that suggest to you?

P. I went to the races.

D. What else would you like to discuss?

P. Horseracing interests me.

D. Why do you say that just now?

P. There's a lot of crooked gambling going on there.

D. I am not sure I understand you fully.

P. It's clear to me if not to you.

D. Do you think it's likely that not to I?

P. I went to the races.

D. Please go on.

P. I gamble on horses.

D. What does that suggest to you?

P. I went to the races.

D. What else would you like to discuss?

P. Gambling has been nothing but trouble to me.

D. Why do you say that just now?

P. I've had experience with crooks gambling at the track.

D. I am not sure I understand you fully.

P. I've already told you enough about that.

D. Oh? I enough about that?

P. I went to the races.

[Comment: This has to be the most persistent and patient paranoid I have ever encountered.] (from Cerf, 1973, pp. 62-63)

Programming Syntax

In discussing keyword systems we see the need for providing at least rudimentary knowledge of language structures in addition to basic word recognition, to allow recognition of morphological derivatives and recognition of a particular sense of a word in context. This can produce a good yes-man, but more is required for intelligent interaction.

To start to think about the problems and solutions involved in automated parsing, consider one of the early successful question-answering systems (Green, Wolf, Chomsky, & Laughery, 1963/1995). The database was statistics about baseball games played in a given year: names of teams with the cities sponsoring them, the date and city of the game and who the competing teams were, and scores for the game. BASEBALL answered (typed) natural language questions from this information. Note that this is a limited domain; the machine could "expect" questions about baseball, and syntax and semantics could be set up with this in mind. For example, "New York" in such a context is ambiguous; "Did New York beat Baltimore?" refers to the teams, not the cities. This expression is limited largely to this context, which means, with only one context, it can be stored as a synonym, not a productive syntactic or figurative language use.

Syntactic analysis in BASEBALL was rudimentary. Sentences were first scanned for idiomatic expressions such as *New York* and these were replaced by a one-word equivalent. The sentence was then processed from left to right, grouping NPs, PPs, and adverbs. Prepositions left at the end were assigned to the first NP (as in "What city did the Yankees play the Orioles in?"). If the last verb in the sentence was preceded by *were,* the sentence was labeled "passive," and the object of *by,* the subject. Otherwise the subject was assigned to the NP between the auxiliary and the main verb (as in "What city did the Yankees play the Orioles in?").

This kind of strategy works only if input is regular and we know ahead of time to expect questions on places, winning, and so on. Nevertheless, conversation may be quite natural. The limitations on this kind of program reveal the complexity of human parsing. There are syntactic structures it cannot handle, for example, "Did the team that creamed Baltimore also beat the Yankees?" This should cause problems because "cream" is probably not in the lexicon and, more important, because there is no means of handling relative clauses, so the relationship between the main clause and the subordinate clause cannot be gleaned.

Bottom-up parsing. To recognize more than a limited number of structures of the language in a wider linguistic and cognitive domain—that is, to give users freedom of speech and not confine them to particular question forms (this is what is meant by "user-friendly")—the grammar of the users' language must be implemented. As we saw in Chapter 4, one of the simplest parsing systems for a language is phrase-structure grammar or constituent analysis. Phrase-structure grammars work by a system of rewrite rules, where words, if they fit a particular pattern, are replaced by a higher-order constituent. *The rat* fits the pattern DET N, which may be rewritten NP; "rewriting" may be considered recognizing, matching a pattern. Strict phrase-structure grammars make use of no thematic information such as deep subject or agent. They replace each word only with its part of speech and each group of parts of speech with higher order parts of speech (constituents). Phrase structure systems are bottom-up or *data-driven* systems: They begin with the input sentence (bottom, data) and replace, wherever possible, the data with higher-order (up) constituents.

Let us consider how such a parser would work, say, with inputs like the following:

Time flies like an arrow.

or

Baby dogs like wild animals destroy.

We replace the first word, "time" or "baby," with its part of speech: *either* a noun or a verb. Thus we can start two parses, one with a noun and one with a verb. "Flies" (or "dogs") similarly may be replaced by its part of speech—either a plural noun or a verb again. Together these produce four possible parses: noun noun, noun verb, verb noun, verb verb. Three of the four are possible English structures (noun noun in "machine operator," noun verb in most simple sentences, verb noun in commands). We eliminate the verb verb possibility. "Like" may be a verb or a conjunction. Each of the parses thus far has two more possibilities, noun noun verb, noun noun conjunction, and so on. All except verb noun verb are possible English structures. We eliminate verb noun verb and stop to critique the procedure. Although it is not optimal, as we shall see, successful parses have been written by using only phrase-structure grammar or strictly bottom-up processing (Kuno, 1967).

First, you should note one thing that happens with this procedure. Many more structures than are needed are generated and held on to at least for a while. You probably noticed that the second sentence, "Baby dogs . . ." had similar structure to "Time flies . . ."—until we get to "destroy." Because "destroy" *must* be the verb, all structures generated before it that contain "like" as the verb will be eliminated by this last word. Is it necessary or desirable to generate structures that will ultimately be rejected? Clearly, it is inefficient at best (which does not mean that it is not how people do it).

Second, even if the structures are not ultimately rejected, at the conclusion of each sentence we may have several readings—five, as already stated for "Time flies like an arrow." This is impractical, requiring more computation and memory than needed. The alternative is to guide the parser to the most likely parse and allow it to generate others if that fails. You might consider whether people "wastefully" produce all alternatives as they go along or efficiently select the most likely and backtrack if that fails. We will look at data on this later in this chapter.

Guidance by meaning. There are a few methods that can be implemented to facilitate "automatic" derivation of only the best structure first. One thing that can be done is to interrupt syntactic processing with semantic analysis—we know there is no species of flies called time flies, that flies are not usually judged by referees, and so on. If semantic and syntactic analyses occur together, once the noun noun pair "time flies" is generated, it could be looked up in a dictionary, found not to exist, and rejected as a possible parse. Thus, as sentence parsing proceeds, any possibilities beginning with noun noun would not be considered. Note that we do not know whether the syntactic component is encapsulated from such information, nor, if it is not, how much semantic or real world information should be available to it. We may have no dictionary entry for "time flies" but that does not mean that such flies do not exist; we are likely to have no entry for "baby dogs" but that phrase is comprehensible and could be said by someone. Is it *language* knowledge that flies are not timed in races? Do you think we use the existence of such knowledge to guide our language processing?

Conceptually driven processing. A second way to achieve automatic selection of one correct parse is to begin with hypotheses about what parses are possible or likely in language and to test those hypotheses. This is conceptually driven processing or top-down processing because a guess is made at the structure of the sentence or sentence part before looking at it (a reasonable beginning or *bottom* of processing) directly. ATNs, discussed in Chapter 4, are instances of top-down parsers, based on transformational grammars and successfully developed for automatic parsing (Woods, 1967, 1973).

Each ATN is labeled in a sense with a function. A sentence ATN looks for NP VP, an NP ATN looks for DET ADJ N, and so on. Entering an ATN entails the assumption that the input will conform to the structure the ATN models. The sentence elements are then searched to see if they fit. If not, alternative structures are tested. Depending on the order of the jumps from the main ATN to constituent ATNs, we may generate the most likely parses first. For example, active sentences are more common than passive ones. So we can assume a priori that the input will be an active sentence, that the first NP will be the logical subject. Given a passive sentence,

A large donation was given by John.

we will try initially to parse it as active (structure equivalent to "donation gave John"); when we reach the suffix "-en" on "given," it will not match the rule on the arc for active verbs, causing the parse to be rejected, and an alternative, the second most likely sentence structure (perhaps passive), to be attempted. Once the hypothesis for passive structure is attempted, the sentence will pass: There will be a successful search for a verb with -en suffix and for a by- clause.

Routines that take into account the likelihood of success, such as attempting active parses before passive ones, are called *heuristic* routines. Using heuristic top-down parsing, programs may still generate parses that will be rejected, as the example shows, but the rejections will be infrequent (given good heuristics and normal input), as compared with exclusively bottom-up routines. And an occasional failure to parse correctly on the first try is not unreasonable. The examples at the beginning of this chapter suggest that we do it too.

Heuristics have been developed in parsers at various levels. ATNs assume a sentence structure, but heuristics may also be programmed with particular words, an implementation of the lexical strategy in government and binding theory (G&B) discussed in Chapter 4. For example, recognition of the verb *promise* could establish a strategy of taking its subject to be the subject of the embedded sentence (see Chapter 4, sentences 12a and 12b: John promised/asked Mary to donate). The head might specify the arguments it takes, or the verb, which prepositions co-occur with it (as in fly from, sit down) (Woods, 1967).

Parallel and serial processing. Heuristic top-down processing, in addition to reducing the number of structures that will be rejected, also eliminates the generation of multiple readings. In the example of bottom-up processing, as each word was added, all possible structures were derived and kept; that is, ambiguous structures were derived in parallel, at the same time. In the example of heuristic top-down processing, first one structure was attempted, then another, and so on. We can make the machine derive ambiguous readings by having it continue to attempt strategies after a success, but then we will be deriving the structures *successively* rather than at the same time.

Operations performed successively rather than at the same time, whether they are bottom-up or top-down, are serial processes, as you may recall from Chapter 3. One way to conceptualize the difference between parallel and serial processing is to think about how many times we stop at each word. In parallel processing, each word is encountered once, and all possible information and all its different meanings are found. In serial processing, each word is encountered once on each reading, with different information collected each time; we keep making passes through the sentence, getting one reading at a time.

Left-to-right heuristic bottom-up processing. We may use heuristics (and serial processing) in bottom-up routines; *baby* is much more often used as the noun than the verb, so we could begin by trying it, noting that a choice was made. (Noting something in a program is called *setting a flag*.) If the parse fails or if second meanings are desired, we return to the points where choices were made (we check the flags) and take the next most likely path. The principal difference between heuristic top-down and heuristic bottom-up procedures is the level at which the guess is made: In top-down procedures, heuristics apply to an entire sentence or clause; in bottom-up, to the most likely sense or part of speech of the word.

Use of heuristics in either bottom-up or top-down processing limits the number of simultaneously generated structures and limits the memory needed to hold all the structures. This increases efficiency in one way but limits it in another. Note what happens when a parse fails: Somewhere in the processing of the sentence, a flag was set indicating that a choice was made and what alternatives there were (for example, active was selected, but could be passive). With failure, the parser returns to these choice points and tries again. What has been saved in memory load may be lost in time spent if there is a reasonable failure rate—because we must keep cycling through the sentence. With parallel processing we are guaranteed that at the end of one cycle through the sentence we will have at least one parse if it exists; with heuristic serial processing, we have a guarantee of finding a parse *only* if we try all possibilities anyway.

Parsers as Human Models

Deterministic parsing and lookahead. A parser that must back up (do a double take) and reprocess, or that generates structures that will be discarded, is called a *nondeterministic* parser; it has no guru advising it of the one true path from the start. A *deterministic* parser is one that guesses the structure correctly the first time. Is deterministic parsing either plausible or feasible? Do *we* process sentences deterministically? I started this chapter with sentences that were supposed to cause double takes to make you aware that you normally process structure. Now, you might also notice that you process nondeterministically, at least in these instances.

The question of plausibility for a deterministic processor, then, is how often we process nondeterministically. If we do double takes all the time, we may be asking too much of a machine to require that it rarely do them. However, most of the time we do not seem to be doing double takes; in fact, it is difficult to come up with sentences that cause them. And most sentences (or words or clauses) are ambiguous, which means somehow or another we are guessing or being guided to the correct parse from the beginning. So we want to program the guide, to make computers parse as efficiently as we do.

Now, is deterministic parsing feasible? Marcus (1980) implemented a deterministic parser based on trace grammar, deriving abstract surface-structure representations. His "guru," the guide for the parse, has interesting implications for human processing. Generally speaking, Marcus used a left-to-right serial parse of the sentence, but the "unit" for rewriting was several constituents rather than just one. One constituent was actively processed and three (to five) to its right were available; they could be viewed to assist decision making. Because the three were ahead of it in the input, this is called *lookahead;* because it was limited to viewing three, it is *limited lookahead.* (Note that unlimited lookahead is as nondeterministic as unlimited backtracking. Basically, a structure may be suggested by one word, tested and rejected, and another structure tested. Because unlimited lookahead produces structures that do not make it to the final parse, it is nondeterministic.)

In Marcus's parsing program, available for active parsing or viewing through a "window" are constituents whose substructures (daughters) are known but that have not yet been attached to the tree. At different points in the parse, then, constituents at different hierarchical levels are considered; once the role of a constituent is recognized, the constituent is attached and the one that dominates it (and represents larger amounts of input) is made available, along with two others. Three constituents-whose-daughters-are-known, of any size, are always available.

Before showing how this makes parsing deterministic, I want to consider the implications of the window for human processing. When we read (or listen), we obviously receive input in order from left to right (from beginning to end). Do we read or listen word by word, even if that is the form of the input? Force yourself to do so by cutting a small window out of a piece of paper, covering a page with the paper, and moving it along so that you view only one word at a time. Or without cheating (looking ahead), follow your finger with your eyes, moving it along one word at a time. It is very difficult to get sense this way: Although usually we do read *roughly* from left to right, as we will see in Chapter 11, we use a larger-than-one-word window to get an overview of structure and sense. And it is reasonable to suppose that the number of words we can use for overview depends on the amount already understood. Initially, it might be three words. As we move along and get the gist of the idea, a larger chunk of input could be taken in at a time. This could entail the same number of new structures, but each now dominating more.

To see how a window works, consider the sentences:

9a. A stitch in time saves wine.

9b. Too many books spoil the broth.

9c. Better date than never.

9d. Here today done tomorrow.

All four of these are mangled clichés, expressions we should all recognize. Because you recognized them, you may do a very cursory job of processing—taking in the whole sentence and missing the bit that was mangled. You are more likely to have noticed the goof in 9b and 9c, where it was at the beginning and you might not yet have guessed the cliché, than in 9a and 9d, where it occurred late and you may have already recognized the sentence.

Because the example works in part using top-down processing, hypothesizing what is to come, it is not exactly analogous to the window in the parser, which works bottom-up. However, the concept is similar: The more structure already known, the larger a chunk of input the parser can name, and then it need deal only with the name. Incidentally, as we shall see in Chapter 7, even in listening, although words are coming in one at a time, it is possible to delay work on them until enough have been collected in memory for a reasonable guess.

The reason limited lookahead may allow deterministic parsing is that the rewrite rules, the pattern-matching rules, are sensitive to both the current constituent and those ahead. "Sensitivity" means that when a pattern is activated from the bottom, several conditions apply at once. "Have written" matches a pattern for AUX V; "have a" matches a pattern for V (NP), because the determiner "a" suggests an NP. In this parser, then, a structure is not activated until and unless its components are *all* there. Because several constituents are available at each step, the check to see if they are all there is possible. The result is that no structures are tried and rejected.

Now, consider what happens on *garden path sentences,* those on which we do a double take. The parser does a double take too. In "The student cheated on his grade complained," "cheated" is ambiguous, as we have already discussed: It could be the main verb of the sentence "the student cheated on his exam" or the participle form of the verb in an embedded passive, "the student, who was cheated on his exam, complained." The paraphrase is not ambiguous, because proceeding from left to right we encounter "who," which triggers the pattern for relative clauses. With "who" deleted in the garden path version, there is no such clue, and the words (constituents) to the immediate right of "cheated" also provide no clue. So "cheated" by itself, with no other structure clues in the window, activates the main verb pattern and we go down the garden path until we hit "complained."

If a clue is presented within the window, the same problem does not occur. For example, suppose the sentence had been "The student cheated by the sadistic professor complained." As before, if "cheated" is considered in isolation, it could trigger patterns appropriate to either the past or the participle form of the verb. However, in the window is an agent clause, "by the sadistic professor"; participle and agent *as a group* should stimulate only the recognizer for passives, so this should not similarly fail.

Modeling G&B: Conflict resolution. A more recent parser developed to model G&B is primarily deterministic and has no lookahead but allows some backtracking (Abney, 1989). This parser attempts to build sets of binary-branching tree structures, attaching them according to the rules of the theory of government, like argument specification at the lexical level. Any input word can cause one of two actions: It can either start its own minitree, or it can become attached to an already started tree. A new node may be started only if (a) it is not possible to attach the input to an existing node and (b) the new node is licensed (i.e., specified and permitted) by an existing node. So, for example, if an NP parse has been begun, an adjective phrase (AP) is licensed, so an AP may be started and then attached to the NP when completed.

Thus far, this is a nondeterministic parser. To push it to the correct resolving of potential ambiguities the first time around, Abney programmed some heuristics, which he called *conflict resolutions.* For example, to determine whether to attach a PP to the VP or the final NP in "I saw the man with the telescope," the parser selects the best theta-role assigner. In this case, "saw" would specify as modifier things to aid seeing, and so would be a stronger licensor than a modifier of man. In "I thought about his interest in the Volvo," interest would take as argument "in something," so the PP would preferentially be attached to it rather than to the place I did the thinking. The default, if there is no specific lexically determined governor, is the verb, "the canonical theta-role assigner" of the theory. Similar sets of ordered strategies exist for each other point of ambiguity.

Each of the points of conflict is stored in memory, in case the parse winds up on a garden path. If a structure has been started that demands a particular input (e.g.,

DET has begun an NP that now requires either an AP or an N) to continue, and that input does not appear, the parser returns to the previous point of conflict and selects the alternative path. For human sentence processing we should keep in mind the following: the location of the points of conflict, the strategies for conflict resolution, and the demonstration that G&B plausibly models sentence parsing.

Modeling G&B: D- and S-structure knowledge versus representation. Johnson (1989) specifically programmed parsers (called PADs for *parsing as deduction*) to model all the levels of interaction of G&B theory. PADs generate D-structure representations using X-bar theory and theta assignment, S-structure representations using case theory and move-α, and operations of logical form for quantification, sequentially. Necessarily, PADs produce multiple structures at each turn because these, according to theory, get filtered by constraints at the next turn. Examination of the workings of the parser refined later attempts to (a) increase efficiency by attempting a structure only if some of its constituents were verified and (b) increase simplicity by eliminating *explicit* D-structure and S-structure representations. These the parser did not use, although it did use the language knowledge ascribed to those levels. PADs have been attempted only on limited numbers of English structures and lexical items, with both early and late attempts successful at recovering the sentence structure. Their evolution suggests that G&B may be overly complex, creating redundant, unnecessary representations, but that G&B constraints do describe sentence structure.

PDP parsers as human models. The parsers we have looked at thus far have explicitly coded rules; indeed, our approach to syntax from the last chapter has stressed that language is rule-governed, with the rules given through a combination of universal grammar and specific parameter learning provided by the speaker's native language experience. The neural net, PDP approach discussed in Chapter 3 has been used to model syntax as well and has a different take on whether language is rule-governed. Specifically, it suggests that rule structure is only apparent, emerging from frequency of co-occurrence patterns. It does not have to be programmed per se.

McClelland, Rumelhart, and the PDP Research Group (1986) applied neural nets to two aspects of syntax: learning of the past tense morphology for regular (e.g., *walk-walked*) and irregular (e.g., *sing-sang* or *is-was*) verbs (Rumelhart & McClelland, 1986), and assignment of theta (thematic) roles to surface-structure constituents (McClelland & Kawamoto, 1986). I will present in detail only the former because in the theta-role assignment model, the researchers limited both syntactic and semantic possibilities, limiting its utility as a parsing model.

As you may recall, a PDP network consists of units and connections, with a concept (whether word meaning, form of the past tense, or theta role) represented as a pattern of activation of the units. The significant aspect of the network is the connections, specifically the weights of the connections, which change in response to training. Corroborating input increases the weights between the activated connections, while disconfirmation decreases the weights. After some number of training trials, the network settles into a relatively stable pattern of activation; that is, the weights change little with successive input. Tests on new input determine if the pattern of activation it has generalized during training mirrors human performance.

In the morphology and syntax experiments, the interesting things for our purposes are what was specifically programmed (the initial assignment of units and connections), what was deliberately not programmed (some syntactic rules, at least explicitly), and the constraints on the domain (the degree to which the network models language as a whole or an impoverished subset, as BASEBALL or the DOCTOR did). It goes without saying that the programs appeared to their developers to be successful for their domains, although we will examine briefly the extent to which they model human behavior.

The past-tense program defined each verb as a pattern of context-sensitive sound features, with each phoneme (roughly a letter-sized sound) represented by three-part features encoding information about the phoneme of interest (e.g., consonant versus vowel), and the preceding and following phonemes, including whether the phoneme begins or ends the word. Like Marcus's parser, this program recognizes the need to attend to surrounding information to determine fully the current input. A word was represented by the pattern of activation of all its phonemes.

This constituted the input pattern. Input units connect to a similarly constructed set of features representing the past-tense form of the verb, the output units. Training of the network consisted of presenting an input, generating an output pattern of unit activation, matching the output to the correct output pattern for that verb, and adjusting the weights between the input and the output activation patterns according to the degree of match. Note that there is no explicit coding of a rule such as "add -ed," but it could be inferred if there were repeated trials of verbs in which the past tense was constructed by adding "ed."

Rumelhart and McClelland constrained the training trials of their network to match verb frequency in English, the probable "training trials" a child receives. They compared their network's performance to the stages of past-tense acquisition described in the child language acquisition literature. Briefly, the most frequent verbs of English (e.g., *is* and *have*) are irregular, with past-tense forms that must be memorized. Children first produce these perfectly, perhaps because they have memorized them. As their vocabulary and exposure to the language grow, they encounter the many verbs for which the past tense is formed by adding -ed. They also learn other frequent subclasses of regularity such as *sing-sang-sung, ring-rang-rung.* In the second stage, they appear to learn these contingencies and to overgeneralize them to verbs that they had perhaps produced correctly in Stage 1, producing *haved,* for example. During this stage, they can create past-tense forms for nonsense words, words they could never have heard before, appearing to use regular rules. In the final stage, regular and irregular words are sorted out and the overgeneralization disappears.

To train the PDP network then, Rumelhart and McClelland examined *not rules for past tense formation* but *statistical properties of English verbs,* specifically their frequency of use. First, the system was trained on the 10 highest frequency verbs of English as determined from *word norm* studies (e.g., Kucera & Francis, 1967): *come, get, give, look, take, go, have, live,* and *feel.* Of these, note that eight are irregular. The second stage trained with medium frequency verbs, with three out of four regular. The model was tested with new regular and irregular verbs.

I have presented the scheme and the relative frequencies of regularity because it is the pattern that emerges from the regularity, *emergent properties* (Stemberger, 1985), that will give the appearance of rule-governed behavior in Stage 2 and Stage 3, not explicitly programmed rules. This scheme supposedly mirrors the child's exposure to verbs in the language.

By the end of the first phase of training, the network was 95% correct on regular verbs, and 90% correct on irregular verbs. Recall that there were only two regular verbs in the first set. These could still produce a generalization, because they show the same pattern, whereas the irregulars were all different. This accounts for the better performance on the regular verbs. By the end of the second phase, both types of verbs were around 95% correct, with a slight advantage still for the regular verbs. The third phase, in which all the words were new, saw 90% correct responding for the regular verbs and nearly 85% correct responding for the irregulars.

The errors the system made resemble those made by children, and likewise reflect apparent rule learning: For example, verbs ending in the d or t sound were left as is (usually correct, as for *hurt* and *shut* but not for *pat*); to verbs that should be marked with a vowel change, -ed was often incorrectly added (producing *blowed*). For some words an occasional bizarre response occurred, such as *membled* for *mailed,* reflecting the phonological co-occurrences and the absence of specific programming of rules. Some critics have suggested therefore that we need "a theory of language with both a computational component, containing specific kinds of rules and representations, and an associative memory system, with certain properties of connectionist models" (Pinker, 1991, p. 531). However, children may do it using association alone, given a fuller complement of examples that minimize bizarre co-occurrences.

PDP modelers stress the rule-free nature of the learning, but some critics have argued that structure is subtly programmed and not acknowledged in the training, in the abrupt shift from irregular to regular verbs (Pinker & Prince, 1988) and in the phonological encoding (Lachter & Bever, 1988). These indeed may be "cheating," or they may approximate aids the child has: a long and rich training (exposure) period and a fine-tuning of salient phonological features by the auditory system. The models show the possibility of rule induction, given perhaps some help, based only on statistical regularities in the input, not a provided UG.

Modeling past tense avoids considering *long-distance* constraints, which we saw in Chapter 4 are necessary for what is interesting in syntax. Fodor and Pylyshyn (1988) argue that PDP modelers have not attempted complex syntactic structures because "association [how the PDP learns] *is not a structure-sensitive relation*"

Box 5.1. Automated Parsing Strategies

— *Keyword:* The machine searches for particular words in input, for which it gives a predetermined response. There is no syntax per se. There may be leeway in the degree of match (e.g., inflections or abbreviations).

— *Bottom-up processing:* When processing proceeds from the input only. In parsing, for example, replacing each input word with its part of speech, replacing combinations of parts of speech (DET N) with a constituent name (NP), and deriving the full parse when there is no further opportunity for rewriting.

— *Top-down processing:* When processing begins with a hypothesis or idea about the structure of the input. In parsing, for example, attempting to process an input sentence as active (subject-agent, verb, object-patient) is top-down.

— *Interactionist processing:* A combination of bottom-up and top-down processing.

— *Heuristic:* A strategy that optimizes the success of a program, such as trying the most frequently occurring parse first.

— *Serial processing:* Performing one operation at a time, in order, sequentially.

— *Parallel processing:* Performing several operations simultaneously, often with the opportunity for interactions among the parallel operations.

— *Deterministic processing:* Proceeding to a solution step by step, without backtracking.

(Fodor & Pylyshyn, 1988, p. 67). Indeed, in the theta-role assignment program, McClelland and Kawamoto (1986) limited the sentences to be parsed to those with the structure, "The noun past-tense-verb ((the noun (with the noun))," where parentheses indicate optional arguments:

S → DET N V (DET N (PREP DET N)).

This overly constrains the agent to subject position, which would not be the case if, for example, passive sentences were permitted. There is also no possibility of recursiveness, which the researchers acknowledge is a problem for a neural net model without some additional temporary memory (a *stack,* in computerese) to hold the place in the sequence of operations as an operation is called again and again, as we saw in Chapter 4 in programming ATNs. As I said then, as models of human syntax, finite state grammars are severely handicapped by the inability to handle recursion. PDP networks are sophisticated examples of finite state grammar, and similarly can handle recursion only when augmented.

The theta-role model encoded semantic features with its nouns that were relevant to the theta roles that its particular verbs might assign. So, given the verbs *ate, hit, broke, moved,* and *touched,* nouns were marked with respect to whether they were soft or hard, could be eaten or not, could break something or be broken, and so on.

Semantic descriptions of verbs were also constraining, such as whether a verb could cause a natural change. Perhaps because of the sets of constraints, the model was successful at performing theta-role assignments to similar, but untrained, sentences, appropriately producing, for example, two structures for "The man hit the woman with a hammer," where the hammer PP is either modifier of woman or instrument of hit.

What is important to note for this model in this chapter is (a) the degree to which it appears necessary to program semantic information to determine case and thematic roles, (b) the realization of the grammar model provided in the last chapter in which argument structure is provided with lexical items and not in the phrase-structure rules themselves, (c) the degree of syntactic and semantic detail necessary to be precoded even for a relatively limited set of sentence structures and underlying concepts, and (d) the limitations of an associative network, a complex finite state grammar, in modeling the intricacies of full human syntax, such as recursion and long-distance context sensitivity.

Summary and Conclusions

We have now examined parsing schemes very generally. They can be bottom-up, top-down, a combination, heuristic, serial, parallel, deterministic, or nondeterministic. They have modeled or created phrase-structure representations, transformational deep-structure representations, abstract surface-structure representations, and case grammar representations. The grammars considered in the last chapters thus are implementable, although no parser has yet dealt with all possible English structures. Generally, it has been recognized that parsers that derive underlying constituent relationships are more valuable for understanding systems than are pure phrase-structure grammars.

It is important to recognize that although no parser has treated the full complement of English structures, an impressive array of complex structures has been dealt with. These include scope/quantification, anaphora, relative clauses, passives, actives, negatives (Woods, 1967), and questions, commands, and *cleft* (It is Mary who . . .) sentences (Marcus, 1980). Among the most difficult structures to implement have been noun noun structures. Tennant (1981) cites the following (credited to Finin), in which the underlining marks which nouns or noun groups modify which others:

water meter cover adjustment screw

aluminum automobile water pumps

January automobile water pump cover shipments.

The only way to decide which modifies which is to move outside syntax, using semantic/world knowledge as was apparently needed to determine theta-role assignments in the much constrained PDP network. In addition to semantics, in spoken language, parsing may also be helped by sound grouping, intonation, and stress patterns disambiguating the possible structures.

Total Language Systems

Programs written for practical purposes like question-answering must be equipped with knowledge relevant to their databases. The extent of this knowledge and the relative importance of the meaning component of a system depend on the size of the world the system is dealing with, as we have already seen in PDP and keyword systems. Systems designers have interfaced the meaning component with the syntactic component at different stages: Some have meaning assigned to the outcome of the parse, at a level just below surface structure (for example, Woods, 1967; note that this foreshadows the importance of an abstract surface-structure level); some have interrupted syntactic analysis with meaning interpretation, using this to guide the parse (Winograd, 1972); and some build semantics into the parser—searching for meaning structure rather than sentence-structure-to-which-meaning-is-applied (McClelland & Kawamoto, 1986; Schank, 1972; Schank, Kass, & Riesbeck, 1994). Despite the disagreement about when to apply it and how important semantic analysis is, there is general agreement on how to apply it.

Primitives as Meanings

Basically, two ideas are used in meaning assignment: primitives and propositions. The concept of primitives was discussed in Chapters 2 and 3: They are features in terms of which concepts are defined, such as animate or human. The notion of primitive may be easiest to see in this context, however, because computers, unlike us, have no sensory consciousness of the world to map concepts onto. Suppose, as Woods (1967) did, that we wished to equip a computer to provide flight information. We would equip it with "knowledge" about cities with airports, times, airlines, and basic flight "concepts" such as stopovers, departures, and arrivals. For the purpose of the system, we would never have to explain what *depart* and *arrive* or even *airplane* are at all. Data are organized in terms of these words, making them primitives, not to be broken down further.

City and time, though, would be general concepts that can stand for a number of different values: City = New York, Boston, Chicago; Time = Friday morning, around 5 p.m., July. In this case, the primitive is an *attribute-value pair,* attribute = location, value = which location. Once again, the concept of location, of New York, need be explained no further.

The problems arise for primitives when databases are constructed for different things. For example, in a better known project than the airline project, Woods (1973) implemented the same parser, along with a semantic system, to provide information to scientists on rocks collected on the moon. In this case, the primitives used for the airline system were useless; a whole new system was needed with primitives about chemical and physical properties of rocks. Winograd (1972) implemented Woods's parser on yet another database, a "world" constructed for a computer, consisting of blocks drawn on a computer screen and actions that could be taken to manipulate them. In this case the primitives consisted of information necessary to distinguish blocks such as color (red versus blue), number of sides, and size—a set completely different from the one needed for airline schedules or moon rocks. Winograd also equipped the machine with world knowledge about the limited world the computer was dealing with—axioms like "nothing can rest on the point of a pyramid" so that if commanded to place something on a point, the machine would respond before trying, as a human would, that such a feat was impossible.

Sample output from this program is shown below. Note how much "smarter" this machine seems than DOCTOR. Note also how much pragmatic information (why someone might ask a question), how comprehensive the syntax (compared with the PDP model), and how much real world knowledge peculiar to block manipulation this system has (H = a human querier; C = the computer's response):

H. Pick up a big red block.

C. OK. (Before doing this, it clears another block from the top, so the red one may be moved.)

H. Grasp the pyramid.

C. I don't understand which pyramid you mean. (There are three in the scene, and "the" implies a specific one, as the computer knows.)

H. Find a block which is taller than the one you are holding and put it in the box.

C. By "it," I assume you mean the block which is taller than the one I am holding. OK. (Note that it processes relative clauses, comparatives, and reference.)

H. Had you touched any pyramid before you put the green one on the little cube?

C. Yes, the green one. (The machine keeps a record of its actions and interprets them with respect to time. Here it "understands" subordinate clauses.)

H. When did you pick it up?

C. While I was stacking up the red cube, a large red block, and a large green cube.

H. Why?

C. To get rid of it. (Here the machine fills in what the "why" is referring to on the basis of the preceding dialogue.) (after Winograd, 1972)

Primitives and attribute-value pairs make sense for limited worlds but take on a whole new dimension for the universe of human conceptual knowledge. It is possible that there is a set of basic concepts, underlying all concepts, in terms of which meanings may be defined. Alternatively, each data set could have its own set of primitives, with general language processors (like us) containing many such data sets and their associated primitives and axioms. This implies that knowledge is structured into retrievable data sets.

Scripts, Frames, and Schemas

Knowledge structures for general language systems have been organized in sets known as *scripts, frames, or schemas* by different systems designers. (I will use *script* here.) A script is like an extended attribute-value pair, extended because a concept is not restricted to a pair. A script consists of a set of slots, each slot containing one aspect of the description of the concept. In Winograd's blocks world, each block might be defined or described by a set of slots—one describing number of sides; another, color; another, size. In a real world, we might describe a "restaurant" as having tables and chairs, waiters, food, menus, utensils, and so on. If no particular attribute is indicated, each slot may specify one, a *default* attribute. For example, a take-out Chinese restaurant might default to few tables, a counter, and woks and chopsticks.

In Winograd's world, "scripts" included axioms about what is possible or likely in the world, such as "things cannot rest on the point of a pyramid." In a real world, "axioms" also need to be included: that food is ordered from a menu, delivered by a waiter, and paid for one way or another at the end of the meal. As was true in Winograd's world, this information is needed to make appropriate linguistic responses. For example, what do you fill in to interpret the following story (from Schank, personal communication)? Roughly, George, on his way to Mama Leone's (restaurant), encounters a pickpocket and winds up washing dishes. Like you, a question-answering or translation program provided with this story as data needs to have enough knowledge of our customs to infer that George's wallet was stolen, that this was not discovered until after George had eaten, and that George worked off his debt.

Scripts are ways of organizing the descriptive defining and characteristic knowledge as well as the implicit "axioms" needed for each concept. Scripts are useful for hypothesis-driven parsing, selecting among ambiguous readings, answering questions directly, or making indirect inferences. A friend of mine, for example, sneered at a noncosmopolitan town with the comment, "I knew we were in trouble when they offered us white bread at the Chinese restaurant." To appreciate this, I needed to activate my Chinese restaurant script, find "rice" and not "white bread," and use the anomaly to adapt the script to the story—a bad Chinese restaurant. When there are many anomalies, they can also motivate trying a different script. The problems of using a script for inferences are knowing when to activate them, when to modify them, when to deactivate them, and how to provide all relevant information within a script (see Kintsch, 1988).

Story understanding (Schank et al., 1994) involves finding the right script and applying it to the current situation. In stories of real interest, of course, the current situation does not precisely follow the "frozen" script: Imagine how boring a story would be that *fully* described a restaurant as consisting of 30 tables, each with four chairs, a place setting consisting of forks, knives, and napkins—period. To be a story, there must be something new, a deviance, that a program must be able to recognize and incorporate. Schank et al.'s current systems model ways to recognize and respond to a new story by applying the appropriate script, discovering the anomaly, and, perhaps, applying a different script to "explain" the anomaly.

Propositions as Meaning

At the beginning of this section I said there were two general constructs used in organization of meaning: primitives and propositions. Primitives, as single features, attribute-value pairs, or entries in a knowledge structure, a script, have been described. Propositions—relations between concepts—arise as a construct because it has been observed that many concepts cannot stand alone but are dependent on other concepts. Prepositions, for example, relate one NP to the verb or to another NP, as do conjunctions and, in fact, as do verbs. To capture the relationship we must have a primitive concept for each NP *and for the relation between them.*

A concept for a relation looks like a simple sentence or proposition. Propositions as a unit of conceptual/semantic processing were first proposed by Anderson and Bower (1973) and Schank (1972), and have since affected linguistic theory in the idea that a "head" encodes its argument structure. The head with argument structure is a proposition.

In language comprehension systems, the proposition or relational concept is the outcome of the parsing and semantic programs. Deriving a proposition from the input proceeds by recognizing the main nouns and verb, with the possibilities for the verb guiding, top-down, the establishment of the rest of the sentence structure. Case relations like agent or location are stored as part of the dictionary entries for words. The goal of language comprehension programs is to derive for each sentence the actual deep structure with theta roles.

Discourse Processing

A number of systems, Schank's (1972; Schank et al., 1994) included, have been designed to analyze more than one sentence at a time. Schank's system relies on semantic-syntax analysis—a coding of sentences in terms of primitives, verbs, and the relations they may take (propositions) with reference to specified scripts. However, in text processing we also need rules for coherence, a way of relating primitive concepts. When coherence is disrupted we can infer a change of topic and use this to deactivate the script. *Coherence* may be roughly defined as overlap of ideas; more specific definitions follow.

Generally the search for coherence rules has begun through considering how it is that discourse is usually organized, and then setting the program to look for a similar organization. At something like a keyword level for discourse, if the domain of the discourse is known and limited, analysis can be guided by an inventory of well-formed word class combinations, a *sublanguage* analysis (Sager, 1990). This is similar to keyword processing because *key phrases* are inventoried. For example, Sager developed a program for automatically coding medical charts into a computerized database. Acceptable combinations include "knee hurts" but not "Bellevue hurts," although both are ostensibly NP VP. With the limited domain of medicine, each of the things that possibly hurt can be searched for separately. Moreover, one can expect medical notes to contain information about specific categories: test-exam-treatment, diagnosis-signs-symptoms-results, precision-time. It is the search through a chart for this information that provides coherence. Finally, for the limited domain, specific syntactic structures may uniquely apply, as "New York" did in BASEBALL to the Yankees or Mets specifically. In medicine Sager (1990) points out similar constraints: PPs occur normally to indicate symptoms (in which case they are adjuncts of the sentence, as in "was seen two days ago for diaper rash") or they mark time (as in "was seen on a Tuesday in January"), in which case they are adjuncts of the noun. Once the meaning of the PP is recognized, its structural role is defined in this context.

Coherent discourse in more general domains can be implemented by considering in addition to propositional content the underlying motivation of the speaker, a speech act analysis approach. Tennant (1981), for example, pointed out that a question-answering system supplying flight information is more coherent if it responds with more than a simple "no" to a question about whether there was a flight from Buffalo to New York that night. The "more" reflects cooperative principles: A human in a similar situation is likely to give information about, for example, when the next flight is, assuming that is what the questioner is indirectly asking as well. A program that can divine the motivation or illocutionary force behind an utterance is more nearly approximating the human total language system.

In both approaches the idea is to find the threads that normally relate sentences by a priori consideration of what it is the sentence producer (the medical personnel writing notes or the database querier) is likely to say. Stories or discourse may then be analyzed top-down in terms of rules based on the normal thread of discourse analysis.

Kintsch and van Dijk (1978) implemented an elaborate program for deriving bottom-up the point of a story. This involved methodically weeding out and combining propositions of the story until the main point was revealed. Discourse was analyzed in two levels: microstructure, which relates individual propositions, and macrostructure, which characterizes the entire discourse. The microstructure is simply the propositions derived through syntactic analyses in ways already discussed in this chapter. The macrostructure is derived from the microstructure by (a) deletion, whereby any proposition that is neither a direct nor an indirect condition of a subsequent proposition is removed; (b) generalization, whereby any sequence of propositions is replaced by a proposition representing a superset; and (c) construction, whereby any sequence of propositions is replaced by a proposition representing a fact, as indicated by the stored "world knowledge." Analysis of a text involves restructuring using these rules so that the text is ultimately represented by a list of hierarchically related propositions, is headed by the general topic proposition, and fans out into more and more detailed related propositions. These together represent the gist of the story.

As an example, Kintsch and van Dijk (1978) provided the analysis of one paragraph taken from a report of an experiment that had been entirely analyzed by their program. The paragraph begins, "A series of violent, bloody encounters between police and Black Panther Party members punctuated the early summer days of 1969." In the microanalysis this sentence contained seven "propositions," some of which are (a) series, encounter; (b) violent, encounter; (c) bloody, encounter; (d) between encounter, police, Black Panther. However, the *function* of this *entire* sentence in the paragraph was only to provide *background* information. The paragraph continued, explaining that this was followed by reports of police harass-

---

Box 5.2. Schemes for Organizing Knowledge

— *Primitives:* Abstract, atomic meaning features in terms of which concepts are defined but that do not have definitions themselves within the system.

— *Attribute-value pair:* A primitive concept defined by a dimension (such as color or animal), which may be shared by many concepts and by a particular value on that dimension (such as red or blue, or lion or elephant).

— *Script:* A general knowledge structure organizing information about a common event or setting. Default information is what is typically found in such an event or setting. Having shared knowledge structures is what underlies our ability to understand presuppositions and to communicate cooperatively: Specifics need not be specified in conversation with someone who shares the script. A script for the concept "house" would contain roof; rooms: kitchen, bathroom, bedrooms; windows; family; and so on.

— *Proposition:* A primitive concept expressing a relation between two or more primitive concepts. For example, actor-action or patient-location. The relation expresses more than either of the elements of it do alone.

---

ment of students on campus, which the writer investigated, and the article constitutes the results of his investigation.

The macrostructure analysis, then, has to determine from the rest of the paragraph or the rest of the report that the first sentence serves only the function of providing setting. Because, in fact, few remaining sentences will connect directly or indirectly with the bloody encounters described in the first sentence (they will instead be describing the method of the investigation and so forth), deletion will eliminate this from the main theme of the narrative and mark it as peripheral, a setting description.

By first performing a microanalysis and then cycling through the individual propositions thus isolated, using the restructuring transformations, the program ultimately provides an outline of the passage. This kind of analysis could be used also to criticize discourse structure because it would be able to find sentences that were largely irrelevant to the point.

Kintsch (1988) has used it as a model of learning or comprehension of text, with the "outline" that the micro- and macroanalyses provide integrating with the existing knowledge base, flexible scripts. The integration occurs in a stage after text analysis, in the same manner. The text analysis is connected to an associative network of already existing related information, a script; consistent propositions and themes are strengthened (in both text analysis and script), and inconsistent ones, weakened. This provides a flexible, modifiable knowledge base, which enhances the knowledge the story provides for inferences with what has already been learned. The script as only one source of information does not have a flexibility problem.

There is no question that recovery of discourse structure is necessary for simulation of human language processing: We clearly can and do determine underlying threads of a story, presuppositions governing an utterance, motivations of the speaker, and the overall picture of what the discourse is about. The simulations thus far have been restricted, so we do not know whether they generalize to broad domains, effective machine "comprehension," or analogies to human comprehension.

HUMAN SENTENCE PROCESSING

Thus far we have examined artificial intelligence attempts at language processing. Using a variety of techniques, these have often been very successful. That each method has been implemented means that any or all are possible models of human processing. That a model is possible—that it produces a parse that mimics human behavior—does not mean that it *is* how *we* do parse; indeed, the models contradict each other—for example, some backtrack and others are deterministic. In this section we examine empirical work on the psychological reality of some grammar models and parsing strategies.

Psychological Reality of Structure in Sentence Processing

Because our syntactic processing is not open to introspection, the first experiments in syntax were designed to show that syntax does in fact provide information in the information theoretic sense (see Chapter 1), that it reduces uncertainty about other words in the sentence. Stimuli were constructed by manipulating natural English sentences to approximate their structure. Miller and Isard (1963), for instance, asked subjects in difficult listening conditions (stimuli presented together with noise) to identify normal sentences, semantically anomalous but syntactically possible sentences (like "Colorless green ideas sleep furiously"), and scrambled sentences that had no recognizable structure but the words of which could be recombined to produce a normal sentence (like "Flies arrow an time like").

In noisy presentation some sounds will not be heard, so some of the information transmitted will not be received. Recall that these are the conditions under which redundancy helps: If the lost information exists also in part of the signal that survives the noise, it can compensate for the loss.

Normal sentences are redundant semantically. Each meaning retrieved limits the range of words likely to occur in the same sentence: For example, *doctor* primes *nurse* and related topics, suggesting they will be in the sentence. Normal sentences are also redundant syntactically: Recognition of some words suggests a structure that in turn suggests, top-down, what other words might be there; for example, *the* suggests that the next word will likely be a noun. Anomalous sentences have no redundancy provided by semantics but still have redundancy provided by syntax. Scrambled sentences, it might be argued, have some semantic or meaning-associative redundancy but not syntactic.

Identification of the sentences was much better with greater redundancy, either semantic or syntactic. Not only is identification better with greater redundancy, but so is people's memory of the stimuli: Marks and Miller (1964) found that normal sentences were better remembered than anomalous sentences, which in turn were better remembered than scrambled sentences.

The effects of scrambling, the importance of preserving order, and the use of transitional probabilities between sentence components were tested in a series of experiments on English approximation (Miller & Selfridge, 1953). In these experiments, strings of words were generated by combining subjects' responses to "fill-in-the-blank" tasks. The strings differed in how connected their words were likely to be, and this was achieved by giving subjects limited knowledge of the previous words in the string. In a *second-order approximation,* for example, a subject would know only the immediately preceding word and would have to supply a logical next choice. In a third-order approximation, each subject would know the two words immediately preceding, and so on. To generate 10-word strings, then, the responses of some successive number of subjects would be combined: A 10-word second-order approximation would need 10 subjects, with the first subject (S_1) given a word and producing one to it; the second subject, S_2, given S_1's response word only and generating a word to that; S_3 given S_2's response word; and so on. First-order approximations derive from strings formed from higher order ones by random scrambling. (Examples are shown in Table 5.1.)

Note that for first-order approximations, there is no constraint between successive words, and that the number of words over which there are contextual constraints increases for successively higher approximations. A second-order approximation is a true Markov model, because the constraints are only between each word and its successor. Comparison of different orders of approximation indicates the extent to which constraints apply across words normally.

You can see from Table 5.1 that by about the fourth order, sentences seem almost normal. This suggests that (a) there is information contained in order (at least in English—it is important to recall that there are many languages in which order has a much less important syntactic role than it has in English); (b) order carries information beyond the next word (unlike Markov or finite state models), causing generation after pairs or triples to result in very unnatural-looking utterances; and (c) there might be a natural boundary after four-word groups, with less predictability or binding between words four and five than between words three and four. (This result suggests a reasonable window size for Marcus's parser of four words—the fifth word and beyond seem to have little effect on the perceived structure of the first four words in English.) The most important result, however, is the demonstration that we *cannot* be using a finite state model, a Markov process, to generate sentences.

Table 5.1 Approximations to English

The second-order approximations are derived by giving a speaker one word and asking for a next word and stringing those pairs together; third order, by giving two words and asking for the next word and stringing the triples; and so on. First-order approximations are a random scramble of higher orders.

10-Word "Sentences"

lst order:	Abilities with that beside I for waltz you the sewing
2nd order:	Was he went to the newspaper is in deep and
3rd order:	Tall and thin boy is a biped is the beat
4th order:	Saw the football game will end at midnight on January
5th order:	They saw the play Saturday and sat down beside him

20-Word "Sentences"

lst order:	Tea realizing most so the together home and for were wanted to concert I posted he her it the walked
2nd order:	Sun was nice dormitory is I like chocolate cake but I think that book is the wants to school there
3rd order:	Family was large dark animal came roaring down the middle of my friends love books passionately every kiss is time
4th order:	Went to the movies with a man I used to go toward Harvard Square in Cambridge is made fun for
5th order:	Road in the country was insane especially in dreary rooms where they have some books to buy for studying Greek

SOURCE: From Miller and Selfridge (1953).

Psychological Reality of Major
Constituent Boundaries as Processing Breaks

Fodor and Bever (1965; Bever, Lackner, & Kirk, 1969) tested the psychological reality of some aspects of phrase-structure grammar. They played subjects complex sentences like "That he was happy | was evident from the way he smiled." The | marks the major constituent boundary, between the main and subordinate clauses. Somewhere on the tape a click was superimposed, which the subjects had to locate on the sentence. Fodor and Bever hypothesized that subjects would not allow the click to interrupt a unit of processing and would perceptually displace the click to the edge of the unit. Clicks presented *within a constituent* were reported as occurring either before or after it, consistent with the hypothesis that *constituents serve as a perceptual unit* (or window, as in our discussion of Marcus's parser). For center-embedded clauses, like "The man [whom nobody likes] is leaving soon," both boundaries attracted clicks. Constituent breaks within clauses, such as between subject and predicate, or verb and object, do not attract clicks (Bever et al., 1969).

These experiments were used to support the reality of constituent structure in sentence perception. However, there are extensive problems in the experimental design (Reber & Anderson, 1970), perhaps the most serious being that subjects were required to write the sentences and mark the click. Thus click displacement could be affected by sentence memory or production (they had to be reproduced on paper), as well as sentence perception, as was claimed. Reber and Anderson found that when subjects were not required to write the sentences, there was still a small effect, but this seemed to be best attributed to response bias: Subjects who were told that they would hear subthreshold clicks when actually presented with *no* click, tended to locate the nonexistent click at the major boundary and tended to locate clicks (existent or not) near the middle of random word strings. Note that the major constituent boundary in the subordinate-main clause example is fortuitously also near the middle. Although Reber and Anderson's study convincingly disputes a perceptual explanation of the click results, it still supports the psychological reality, at some level (perception or response), of major clause boundaries.

Tests of the Psychological Reality of Early Transformational Grammar

Thus far we have shown that structure beyond that imposed by adjacent words affects sentence understanding and memory, and that clauses constitute processing units for perception, memory, or response organization. Chomsky's (1965) syntactic theories suggest more detailed and complex syntactic processes, which have also been tested and, at least partially, supported.

Recall the early transformational model: There are two levels of syntactic structure—surface structure and deep structure—with a complex set of transformations that can delete, add, or move elements in deep structure to create surface structure. We have just seen that the major constituent boundary, a surface structure cue, affects memory, if not perception, of complex sentences. Early psycholinguistic research looked for evidence that deep-structure representations were derived and that transformations were used in the derivation.

It was assumed that sentences requiring minimal transformation from deep to surface structure (core or kernel sentences) should have a psychological advantage—they are not very demanding syntactically—over sentences that are derivationally complex. Tests to demonstrate these as processing realities only partially supported transformational theory, suggesting (a) a stronger influence of the lexical component on syntactic processing, (b) a more powerful than expected influence of surface-structure constraints on syntactic processing, and (c) a less prominent set of transformations. G&B theory evolved to include these findings. As you should recall, it places a heavy burden on the lexicon in influencing D-structure representations; employs an abstract surface-structure level, which contains the surface syntactic constraints; and reduces the power of the transformational component. We turn now to some of the experiments that led to these developments.

Deep Structure

Mehler and Carey (1967) provided the only experimental evidence for the psychological reality of deep structure as well as surface structure, but, as we shall see, their deep-structure manipulation could be accounted for lexically. Sentences

1 through 6 at the beginning of this chapter illustrate their technique: A set of sentences with similar structures was presented in noise to subjects who were required to write down each one; then follows a test sentence with either the same or a different structure also to be recorded and also presented in noise. They hypothesized that if a perceptual set is established, the test sentence would be perceived inaccurately given the difficult listening conditions and a sentence that broke the set.

Sets were established for surface constituent structures, as in 1-6, or for deep structures, as in the following:

> They are delightful to embrace.
> They are troublesome to employ.

("they" is the underlying object of "embrace" or "employ") followed by

> They are hesitant to travel.

(where "they" is the underlying subject of "travel"). When a test sentence had the same structure as the preceding set, it was perceived more accurately than when it differed from the preceding set. This was true for both surface- and deep-structure sets, but the decline in accuracy was greater when there was a surface-structure difference. This suggests that both deep- and surface-structure representations must be derived in processing because a change in either had an effect. However, note that this particular D-structure difference could easily be encoded in the argument structure of "troublesome," "delightful," and "hesitant." Their subcategorization structures could be marked for subject or object complement, as we did for "ask" and "promise" in the last chapter. These results would then be interpreted as establishing a *lexical* set, not a deep-structure set.

Stemberger (1985) claims that there is "as yet no empirical psycholinguistic evidence for deep structure" (p. 156). Moving these argument constraints to the lexicon makes this statement true, given that Mehler and Carey's experiment is the only demonstration of deep-structure influence on parsing. Realize that we do recover thematic and case relations—who is the agent and patient, and so on—from sentences whatever their surface structure, and, as we shall see, these, not the details of the surface structure, are what is remembered. These basic relations are what Chomsky (1965) was trying to capture in deep structure. Their recovery and memory would indicate a psychological reality to the intent of the original deep-structure formulation.

Movement, Deletion, and Addition Transformations

In testing the reality of transformations, the critical assumption was that if people reverse transformations to recover deep structure, there should be an observable cost for greater transformational complexity, a cost revealed by decreased perceptibility, decreased residual memory capacity, higher error rate in understanding, or greater reaction time to understand. The experiments thus involve comparison, along one of these measures, of sentences differing in derivational complexity. Stimuli for the experiments generally consisted of core (or kernel) sentences (simple active sentences) that presumably were constructed from deep structure with a minimum of transformations. These were contrasted with sentences derived by using one more transformation—active versus passive, affirmative versus negative, affirmative versus interrogative—or two more transformations, active versus negative passive, and so on. Note that additional transformations here entail more words and greater morphological complexity, which can account as well for any differences in processing.

Initial results looked very promising and supported the transformational model. More accurate recall (Mehler, 1963) and smaller memory demands (Savin & Perchonock, 1965) were found for kernel sentences than for negatives, passives, or questions and there was a greater penalty for double transformations like negative passives. Analysis of recall errors indicated that subjects tended to recall the simpler core form rather than what was presented, suggesting that subjects may be coding the sentence as a core that was negative or passive, and that the negative or passive markers could then be independently forgotten.

As did the click studies, these experiments confounded comprehension with production: Subjects had to process the sentence and then reproduce it. It is not clear whether the penalty for extra transformations occurs in understanding or in reproducing the sentence or in both. However, an effect of transformations on understanding alone was demonstrated using speed of comprehension in a variant of sentence verification. In this study, a sentence is presented together with a picture potentially depicting the sentence; the time it takes to decide whether they match is measured. For example, a picture could show a lion chasing an elephant, which would be "true" for sentences like "The lion chased the elephant" or "The elephant was chased by the lion," and "false" for sentences like "The elephant chased the lion" or "The lion was chased by the elephant" or "The elephant was not chased by the lion." If subjects must recover deep structure to make the true-false decision, the transformationally more complex sentences should take longer.

Gough (1965) found that subjects took less time to verify core sentences than passives or negatives, which in turn took less time than negative passives. This was true when verification was immediate but also when it was delayed (Gough, 1966). The delay was expected to allow the transformation process to be completed, so that the sentences mentally would be "core sentences," eradicating the time difference. That actives were still quicker suggests a difference between actives and passives in conceptual representation.

In G&B theory, all elements of surface structure are present in some form in D-structure, so these sentences have differently complex D-structures. Moreover, if the working level of syntax is abstract-surface-structure, S-structure, this is what would be in working memory. S-structure is as differentially complex as the phrase structures of the stimulus sentences, accounting for the difference in verification time.

Psychological Reality of Surface-Structure Information

One of the earliest studies to suggest construction of syntactic structures from surface-structure information was performed by Martin and Roberts (1966). They looked at sentence processing in terms of the "expectations" each word generates for additional structure. For example, at the beginning of a sentence, *the* sets up two expectations: one for a noun (relatively soon) and one for a predicate (at some point). A following adjective also has an expectation value of two because both the noun and the predicate are still expected. A noun reduces the hypothesized structures to one, an intransitive verb to zero, a transitive verb to one again (for the object). Summing these expectancies across the words of the sentence measures the "processing commitments" the subject makes. Martin and Roberts predicted and found that the more commitments the sentence requires, the longer it takes to process and the more poorly it is recalled.

Note that commitments are ways of measuring surface-structure complexity, which is the number of nodes that need to be constructed from the main sentence branch. More nodes may make sentence processing more difficult, and so may ambiguity as to possible structure. As our discussion of parsers suggested, ambiguity means either that we start the wrong structure and backtrack, or we create and hold several structures, both of which may be taxing.

Syntactic processing has been shown to be easier for sentences containing explicit cues to constituent structure; these reduce the alternative structures that are set up. For example, in English, as we have seen, we can not-express a relative pronoun before a relative clause, producing garden path sentences like "The horse [who was] raced past the barn fell." Obviously, when a relative pronoun prevents us from taking a garden path, its overt presence in the surface structure eases syntactic processing.

Fodor and Garrett (1967) conducted an early experiment on the processing of *reduced relatives (RR)*, as they have since been called, sentences in which the relative pronoun was deleted. (They used sentences that I feel strongly are not within the grammatical competence of normal English speakers [me], although I can figure out who did what to whom with pencil and paper.) Their stimuli consisted of double-embedded sentences because pilot research had shown they were difficult to understand, and therefore it might be easier to obtain a measure of facilitation with the relative pronoun present. An example of a doubly center-embedded sentence from their study is as follows:

The pen which the author whom the editor liked used was new.

Without the relative pronouns, this sentence becomes:

The pen the author the editor liked used was new.

Subjects were asked to paraphrase one version of the sentence. Processing difficulty was measured by the length of time to begin the paraphrase and the number of errors made in assigning subjects and objects to verbs. For both measures, sentences with relative pronouns were easier to understand.

Fodor and Garrett's results have been replicated with more reasonable sentences in recent experiments specifically designed to test G&B theory (Ferreira & Henderson, 1990; MacDonald, Pearlmutter, & Seidenberg, 1994; Trueswell, Tanenhaus, & Kelso, 1993). Note that some of the provisions of this theory—that there is a complementizer phrase, for instance, with *that* as head, that heads specify arguments they take, and so on—have been incorporated in the theory because of results like Fodor and Garrett's, showing the importance of a surface word as a cue.

The newer studies use *on-line* techniques, which try to intercept processing *as it is happening,* as opposed to measuring the total comprehension time or memory *after comprehension.* These measures include self-paced reading and eye movements during reading. In self-paced reading, subjects press a button to see more words or phrases, with the rate at which they ask for more input an index of their ongoing understanding of the sentence. Eye movement tracking can also indicate how subjects take in words or phrases, when they backtrack, and when they misunderstand and need to reread. The on-line studies show the importance of both surface-structure cues and the lexical coding of argument structures.

Stimulus material consists of sentences like the following:

10a. Mary suspected [that] the man from Calgary had committed a crime.

10b. Mary insisted [that] the man from Calgary committed a crime.

Without the "that," 10a is slower to read and there are *regressive,* backtracking, eye movements, which suggest that the "that" is an important overt cue to syntactic structure. However, 10b is read the same way with and without the "that." And in English, we find that sentences with verbs like "insist" (10b) more often have "that" deleted than do sentences with verbs like "suspect" (10a).

The critical difference between 10a and 10b is that "suspect" permits an alternative structure of NP V NP, as in

10c. Mary suspected the man from Calgary.

In contrast, "insist" never allows such a structure. Therefore, in 10a, a "that" gives information as to which structure to expect, which reduces ambiguity. In 10b, the verb "insist" gives that information itself. The on-line studies of the two types of sentences together show the importance of surface information cues to structure given with the words: Either the syntactic marker "that" cues a relative clause or the argument structure stored with "insist" suggests the relative clause as argument.

Abstract Surface-Structure Cues (Traces) to Sentence Processing

Thus far we have seen some support for a deep-structure level with arguments specified lexically, some support for transformational or abstract surface-structure complexity contributing to processing complexity, and strong support for surface-structure cues affecting processing complexity in terms of number of commitments, reducing syntactic ambiguity lexically, and so on. These findings are consistent with G&B, in which more syntactic control is placed at the levels of (abstract) surface structure and the lexicon.

Now recall that in G&B, transformations move constituents to other sentence positions from their original D-structure position but that the original position retains an invisible "trace" of the moved constituent in abstract surface structure. The notion of "trace" and abstract surface structure are unique features of the new theory and have been tested for psychological reality. The trace can be thought of as a *gap,* a blank to be filled in mentally by the moved constituent. The moved constituent is then known as a *filler,* and the sentences as *filler-gap* sentences. Examples of various filler-gap constructions (trace marked by [t]) and semantically similar controls without traces from McElree and Bever (1989) include the following:

11a.   The stern judge who met with the defense is sure [t] to argue about the appeal.

11b.   The stern judge was difficult for the defense to argue with [t] about the pending appeal.

11c.   The stern judge who met with the defense finally rejected the arguments for an appeal. (gap-less control)

To test the reality of the trace, researchers measure the mental availability of the filler at different points in the sentence. Right after it is mentioned, of course, it is freshly available, and right after the gap, it is more available than elsewhere in the sentence or in gap-less controls. Availability is measured by speed of recognizing words from the filler (McElree & Bever, 1989) or lexical decisions to words semantically related to, primed by, the NP (Nicol & Swinney, 1989).

If you remember how a lexical decision task works from Chapter 3, you will realize that here again we are stopping the subjects in the process of understanding a sentence, interrupting them with the lexical decision task. The *inter*ruption may result in a processing *dis*ruption. Therefore it is nice that congruent results have been obtained using brain-wave recording, which does not require interrupting the task.

Garnsey, Tanenhaus, and Chapman (1989) used brain-wave recordings to measure the filling of the gap without interrupting processing. In particular, they constructed sentences in which the syntactic filler was semantically implausible, like "The businessman knew which article the secretary called [t] this morning." The N400, a negative peak occurring in the brain wave about 400 ms only after a semantic incongruence, appeared after the trace. This could only happen if the gap was filled with incongruent information. The results show that (a) the gap was filled and (b) gap-filling, the syntactic process, was not guided by semantic likelihood.

We will examine counterevidence to the independence of syntactic and semantic processing in the next section. For now, note that there is evidence of a processing reality to traces and abstract surface structure, and therefore to movement of the constituents from deep structure. Thus all the main components of G&B theory—

deep structure, surface structure, abstract surface structure, lexical specification of arguments and traces—have an empirical basis in human sentence processing.

Evidence Inconsistent With Generative Grammar

The Importance of Semantics

Garnsey et al.'s study of the N400 and fillers suggests that as a sentence is being processed, syntactic operations may proceed independently of semantics. However, semantics has been shown to override syntax at times. Compare the following sentences, for example:

12.   The lion was chased by the elephant.
12a. The elephant was chased by the lion.
13.   The tree was uprooted by the elephant.
13a. The elephant was uprooted by the tree.

12 is *reversible*—switching the grammatical subject and object results in a sensible sentence. 13 is *irreversible*—trees do not uproot elephants. For 13, we have good semantic reasons to assign words in the sentence to agent and object cases regardless of their position in the sentence. For 12, the only way to sort out who is doing what to whom is through syntax.

Slobin (1966) showed that we get an effect of syntactic complexity on sentence verification times *only* where we must rely on syntax alone, for sentences like 12. This suggests that we may not normally parse in sentence understanding but instead rely on probable meaning relations, parsing only when these are insufficiently specified. Olson and Filby (1972) demonstrated that even reversible sentences may not require a full parse, given a proper context. They presented pictures to the subjects before the sentences to be verified, with discussion of the pictures establishing a topic and focus. For example, a picture might show a car and a truck in an accident, and the discussion might focus on the car. Olson and Filby reasoned that sentences that maintained the car as topic ("The car hit the truck" or "The car was hit by the truck") would be easier than sentences that had the other vehicle as topic ("The truck hit the car" or "The truck was hit by the car"). They then presented the pictures and sentences for verification. As is normally found, subjects took longer to verify falses than trues, and passives than actives. However, the interesting finding was that subjects who coded the picture in terms of the car took longer to verify *actives* like "The truck hit the car" than passives like "The car was hit by the truck," where the passive more closely matched in topic and focus what they had encoded. Olson and Filby concluded that both sentences and pictures are coded in memory in a core form *established by meaning,* and that any input is transformed to match the core. Deep structure may be better considered a semantic structure than a syntactic structure.

Clark and Clark (1968) examined recall of conjoined sentences where the sentence components reflected semantic order as in "After he mowed the lawn, he raked"—or confused semantic order as in "Before he raked, he mowed the lawn." The two sentences mean the same thing, but in the second one the main clause occurs after the subordinate and describes an event that occurs before it. (Note that mirroring temporal order of reality by temporal order of the clauses is one of the ways that language metaphorically embodies thought.) Although subjects better remembered sentences with the main clause first ("He raked the lawn after he mowed it"), the most overwhelming effect was semantic: Sentences reflecting the temporal order of events were better remembered than those that reversed it, regardless of the order of the main and subordinate clauses. This indicates the importance of semantics and also that when language reflects reality on more than one level, the redundancy aids processing.

The studies showing strong semantic effects on determining grammatical relations have measured sentence memory or verification at the end of processing. This does not rule out syntax occurring on-line but suggests that syntactic operations, if they occur, are ephemeral. A number of studies indeed have demonstrated that syntactic operations do not remain active; within a short time after reading a sentence, subjects cannot recognize it apart from sentences that convey the same meaning.

Sachs (1967) compared recognition of sentences identical to the target, changed in meaning from the target, changed from passive to active or conversely, or with a clause moved, 0-46 seconds after the target was presented. For example, a target of

"He sent Galileo, the great Italian scientist, a letter about it."

would be changed in meaning so that Galileo is sending the letter, would be changed to passive so that Galileo was sent the letter, and also would be changed on the surface by moving the modifying clause, as in "He sent a letter about it to Galileo, the great Italian scientist" (p. 439). When recognition was immediate with no interposed material, subjects noticed all changes. After less than one minute during which additional material was read, though, subjects identified meaning changes only, noticing syntactic changes at almost chance levels. This suggests that form is used to construct a meaning representation and then discarded; meaning is the stuff memory is made of.

Bransford and Franks (1971; Bransford, Barclay, & Franks, 1972; Franks & Bransford, 1972) likewise showed that subjects were likely to falsely recognize complex sentences composed of simple propositions ("The rock rolled down the mountain crushing the hut at the bottom") if the experiment presented the component simple propositions. They were also more likely to recognize "The box is to the left of the tree" having seen "The tree is to the right of the box" than they were "The box is to the right of the tree." Note that "the box is to the right . . ." overlaps more in surface structure with the presented sentence, although it obviously is opposite in meaning.

Such results as a whole show that what is important in memory is the basic semantic relations, not the process of deriving them from the sentence. They do not, however, indicate what the process of deriving them from the sentence is. The on-line studies and studies of derivational complexity suggest that at early stages of sentence understanding, parsing, perhaps independent of semantics, is involved.

Heuristics, Not Grammar?

Thus far our discussion of human syntactic processing has assumed, tested, and caused revision of linguistic theories of syntax. That is, we have assumed that there is a mental grammar and that sentence comprehension and production use it. Alternatively, we might have strategies—heuristics, if you will—for deriving structure when we need to, but we may never actually perform a tacit but rigorous syntactic analysis.

Bever (1970) defined a set of such strategies, which he proposed speakers were aware (at least tacitly) that listeners use. He suggested further that because speakers wish to communicate (the cooperative principle!), they will structure sentences to aid listeners: If the default strategy would lead the listener down a garden path, the speaker will provide surface-structure markers pointing to the appropriate strategy. We saw such an example in relative clause reduction: *That* is included if a verb is as likely to take a complement as a direct object, but omitted if the verb itself clues us in to the likely structure. Other default strategies include the following:

1. Listeners assume input to be meaningful sentences.
2. They segment word sequences into actor-action-object-modifier (proposition) units.

This keeps elements of subordinate clauses together and those of main clauses together and accounts for (a) the migration of clicks to unit boundaries, (b) the difficulty of center-embeddings where the unit is interrupted by another clause, (c) the difficulty of passive over active constructions where actor-action-object order is reversed, and (d) the garden path route in reduced relatives (*that*-deleted clauses).

3. Listeners assume the first actor-action-object unit to be the main clause.

This accounts for the greater difficulty of processing preposed subordinate clauses (Clark & Clark, 1968). (This may be accounted for by processing commitments too: Beginning with *because* means we carry an expectation of a main clause from the beginning of the sentence; with it second, the expectation or unfinished structure is carried for a shorter time.)

Another strategy was proposed by C. Chomsky (1969):

4. The subject of an embedded sentence is the noun closest to it (*the minimal distance principle*).

"John asked Mary to make a donation" is understood with Mary as the subject of "to make," as is "John promised Mary to make a donation." Because, for the latter, the assumption is wrong, the minimal distance principle predicts a greater difficulty in processing. As we shall see (in Chapter 9), children do have greater difficulty with such "irregular" sentences.

And more recently, Frazier (see, for example, Frazier & Rayner, 1987) has proposed a strategy akin to what I suggested from the Martin and Roberts commitment study:

> 5. *Minimal attachment principal:* Assume a sentence parse with the minimum number of nodes possible.

The minimal attachment principle accounts for on-line reading experiments suggesting that subjects do take a garden path when *that* is absent from a complement clause (Ferreira & Henderson, 1990; Frazier & Rayner, 1987), constructing the clause only when the embedded verb is reached. According to Frazier this effect is brief but independent of any information in the sentence other than the part of speech of the words, including whether the verb normally takes a clausal complement. As we have seen, other investigators have found a lexical effect, perhaps interactive with minimal attachment.

Note that many of the strategies suggested are strategies for grouping words into a cluster based on their order in the sentence. Hunt and Agnoli (1991) discuss evidence that Spanish and French speakers, whose languages contain more surface information as to structure through inflections than does English, rely on such strategies to a lesser degree.

A Syntax Module Versus Interactionist Processing

Our discussion of syntax has provided strong evidence that structural information affects sentence processing apart from the meaning of lexical items, that structural constraints go beyond adjacent words, that there are sentence structures that take longer to understand than others at least in particular contexts, and that there is binding between a moved element and its trace in filler-gap constructions. Whether these findings require the full complexity of the rules of G&B, or can be handled by some "quick-and-dirty" heuristics, is unclear. It is also unclear whether there is a stage of sentence processing in which purely structural decisions are made, which interact quickly thereafter with semantic plausibility information, or whether all sources of information are used from the start. This question is of theoretical interest because a brief, encapsulated, automatic syntactic decision supports the existence of a language module, whereas the interactionist view does not do so.

To the extent that syntactic rules incorporate lexical information, language processing may be modular. Note that in G&B, phrasal heads specify not only subcategorization information (such as what can or cannot take a direct object) but also more meaningful arguments (such as location for a verb of motion or a thing of value for "donation"). As long as semantic information needed for syntactic processing is still separate from our general beliefs and world knowledge, and as long as the syntactic computations or heuristics are different from general cognitive strategies, we may consider that language is a modular process.

The evidence for modularity, in my view, is weak at best. First, note that semantic considerations come into play very quickly during sentence processing: Within one minute of reading a sentence, Sachs (1967) and others found subjects remembered the major grammatical relations but not the particulars of sentence structure. Second, a number of investigators have found evidence of semantic bias during reading in on-line studies under carefully controlled conditions (see Trueswell et al., 1993, for evidence regarding reduced relatives, and Britt, Perfetti, Garrod, & Rayner, 1992, for evidence on minimal attachment of final prepositional phrases such as "I saw the man with the binoculars/book . . ."). Third, a recent study has shown that subjects hearing garden path sentences, like "Put the apple on the towel in the box," in a disambiguating visual context (one apple is on a towel and another is on a napkin) look at the two apples when they hear the word "apple," and at the destination, "the box," when it is named, but not at the towel, which is interpreted correctly *on-line* as a modifier of apple (Tanenhaus, Spivey-Knowlton, Eberhard, & Sedivy, 1995). With only one apple, listeners do look at the towel when it is named, taking the syntactically simpler garden path. That they do not do so when they can construct the appropriate, but less usual, structure from the context indicates that the syntactic process is never encapsulated from extralinguistic cues.

Nevertheless, there are a considerable number of studies that suggest that parsing a potentially ambiguous structure is immediately independent of semantic or lexical considerations, which only come to influence listening time, reading time, or eye movements several words away from the ambiguous region (see Clifton, Speer, & Abney, 1991, regarding final prepositional phrases; Ferreira & Henderson, 1990, regarding reduced relatives in reading; Ferreira, Henderson, Anes, Weeks, & McFarlane, 1996, for listening comprehension time; and Frazier & Rayner, 1987, on part-of-speech ambiguities like "The church pardons all sinners" versus "The church pardons for sinners were . . ."). And Garnsey et al. (1989) found that semantic implausibility as measured by the N400 did not prevent subjects from filling gaps with syntactically appropriate NPs.

So it may be that there is a quick syntactic computation independent of semantic plausibility, frequency of a reading or argument structure (semantic preference), and selectional restrictions—as long as there is no real world context immediately available to prejudice the interpretation. Even in the absence of context, these interact very soon to affect the ultimate understanding of the sentence and figure largely into its ultimate memory representation.

Although the possibility of a transient syntax-pure process is intriguing, it is the interaction of the outputs (if indeed it is only at the output) or the interaction of semantics and syntax throughout that determines sentence comprehension. Reviewing the syntactic ambiguity literature together with the lexical ambiguity literature, MacDonald et al. (1994) make a strong case for an interactive influence of lexical and syntactic information. First, they point out that ambiguity occurs at several levels: morphological (e.g., the past tense of a verb and its participle form may look alike, as with *raced* but not *broke-broken*), lexical (*broke* means out of money and in pieces), and syntactic (as with reduced relative versus main verb readings or the attachment of a prepositional phrase to either the verb phrase or a noun). Second, they point out that for any particular instance, there is usually a preferred reading based on frequency of occurrence in the language: For example, a particular form may occur more often as past-tense verb or as a participle; the preposition *with* more often introduces a description of a noun than a verb phrase, and conversely for *into*; action verbs (like *break*) are more often modified by prepositional phrases than are mental-state verbs (like *love*). Their examination of on-line experiments at all levels (lexical and syntactic) suggests that multiple meanings are accessed *only* when there is equal likelihood of the meanings based on frequency of the form in the language and context. In all other cases, they argue, there is a single meaning or parse selected, guided by the usual use of the words.

MacDonald et al. suggest that in addition to phrasal heads specifying *arguments,* as predicted in G&B, they could specify their *phrase structures in mini-structure trees.* Then syntactic processing would involve simply accessing the lexicon and combining the mini-tree structures associated with each item.

This is a truly interactionist theory because accessing syntactic structures is through the words, through which semantic information is also available, all coded together in the same network. If indeed there is a brief period of syntactic computation before semantic information comes into play, we can argue these minitrees are more highly weighted—more immediately accessed from the words—than the semantic features, and that the syntax "module" begins to compute their combinations immediately upon their activation. But semantic information is available and influential within milliseconds, and only the ultimate result of the whole process, the understanding of the sentence, is retained.

Summary

Research on human syntactic processing reveals an eclectic set of operations. Recovery of the underlying sentential relationships appears to be facilitated by extralinguistic context, typicality (frequency) of structure (subject-verb-object sentence order, minimal attachment, and so on), subcategorization information (the arguments licensed by a phrasal head), overt phonetic coding of structure (e.g., presence of a *that* introducing a clause), and covert structure, the silent trace marking a moved element in abstract surface structure.

Note how the complex of levels in G&B theory is substantiated by the psychological research: There are surface-structure cues to syntactic relations, abstract surface-structure cues to syntactic relations, evidence of movement transformations and a link between the original position (trace) and moved element (filler), and evidence of lexical governing of theta roles at the D-structure level. However, there is also evidence that semantic (selectional restrictions) and pragmatic information (topic focus) affect sentence verification time, measured at the end of syntactic processing, but perhaps they do not modify parsing strategies as they are happening.

In line with current linguistic theory, this may suggest an impenetrability of the parser to some types of semantic information. If so, that would suggest that the parser may constitute a linguistic module. But to the extent that extralinguistic and lexical information affect the parse, we have difficulty determining whether there is encapsulation of information. As we saw in our discussions of word meaning, it is hard to separate general world knowledge and reasoning from semantic knowledge. If argument structure, likelihood of being an agent, and so on are part of our world knowledge and needed for syntax, it is also hard to hypothesize a language module apart from general cognition.

The Grammar of "Discourse"

Under natural language conditions, in discourse, propositions are connected. Phenomena that we see within a sentence such as NP-filler activation at a gap must have counterparts between sentences, as when we activate an antecedent NP from earlier in the discourse to a current pronoun. Studies of discourse processing directly indicate the creation of a memory unit across sentences. McKoon and Ratcliff (1980; Ratcliff & McKoon, 1978) presented sentences of a text and then tested recognition of single words from those sentences. The key is that before testing recognition, subjects were primed with a word from the same sentence as the word-to-be-recognized, or with a word from another sentence in the passage, or with a word that could be inferred from the passage but not directly used. If the prime speeds recognition, they assumed that there is a close link between the two words in the memory representation of the passage; the less effective the prime, the weaker the link.

There was a greater priming effect among words from the same sentence than from different sentences of the same passage, and a greater effect of priming among words in the same proposition within a sentence than among words of different propositions expressed in one sentence (Ratcliff & McKoon, 1978). This supports a hypothesis that sentences are encoded into propositional format. More interesting, though, is the existence of a strong priming effect between words in one proposition and words in an earlier proposition referred to by the later one (McKoon & Ratcliff, 1980). For example, if in the first sentence of a paragraph, mention of a car is made, and in a later sentence, mention is made of a vehicle, which presumably refers anaphorically to the car, the representation for the car sentence is primed by words from the vehicle sentence, suggesting that the common subject has been derived and used to forge a connection in memory between the two.

Connections between ideas in discourse and general memory appear to be made iteratively, on many levels (Kintsch, 1988). Till, Mross, and Kintsch (1988) interrupted sentences in several places after presenting a target word for a lexical decision. Within 200 ms of the target, as we have seen previously, words related to any of its meanings were primed. By 400 ms, only words related to the relevant meaning remained primed, suggesting that the irrelevant meanings had been deactivated by the context. More than a second after the sentence (but not earlier), words related to an *inference* suggested by the sentence but never stated (e.g., the sentence describes a building collapse, and "earthquake" is an inference) were good primes in lexical decision tasks. The experiment suggests, as does Sachs's experiment, that initially we attend to surface forms, but the comprehension process winds new information from the discourse into a general knowledge base, with surface information lost.

The most effective way of connecting propositions in memory is to organize them around a theme. For example, Bransford and Johnson (1972) asked subjects to read and later recall apparently loosely organized stories like the following:

> If the balloons popped, the sound wouldn't be able to carry since everything would be too far away from the correct floor. A closed window would also prevent the sound from carrying, since most buildings tend to be well insulated. Since the whole operation depends on a steady flow of electricity, a break in the middle of the wire would also cause problems. Of course, the fellow could shout, but the human voice is not loud enough to carry that far. An additional problem is that a string could break on the instrument. Then there could be no clear accompaniment to the message. It is clear that the best situation would involve less distance. Then there would be fewer potential problems. With face to face contact, the least number of things could go wrong. (p. 719)

(Try to write as much of the passage as you can recall: Score correct propositions that you mention even if you do not have them word for word.) This is a control condition and was compared with conditions in which subjects were also given, before or after presentation of the passage, a picture that provided a context (either full or partial) for the passage. For example, for the preceding passage, the picture showed a woman on a high floor of an apartment building being serenaded by a man on the ground who was projecting his voice and guitar via a microphone and speaker, the speaker attached to a cluster of balloons floating by the woman's window. Given such a context, do you think you would recall more propositions than with no context, as was presented to you?

Bransford and Johnson found that a complete context presented before the passage improved recall, but there was no facilitation for presentation of context after the passage. They concluded that the topic affects the way material is processed and organized; once in memory, it is not rearranged. At the multisentence, discourse level, this mirrors what Olson and Filby found at the sentence level for passives and actives: the importance of topic focus for the memory representation.

Cirilo and Foss (1980) demonstrated that both reading time and recall of read material are affected by the material's role as topic or elaboration in the discourse. Subjects read one sentence at a time and pushed a button to get the next sentence. To ensure that the subjects read the sentences, they were given a comprehension test. The time between button presses measured reading time.

Material was organized to compare reading time (or recall) for topic versus peripheral sentences presented either early in the text or late. Stories were con-

---

Box 5.3. Human Syntactic Effects

— Sensible sentences are easier to perceive and remember than anomalous sentences, which in turn are easier than scrambled sentences, implying that syntactic structure facilitates sentence comprehension.

— Less than fourth-order approximations of English sentences result in obvious incoherence: There is considerable context sensitivity, or mutual constraints, among words less than four words apart.

— Major constituent breaks between clauses of a complex sentence constitute a processing unit, with the major constituent resistant to interruption in perception or, more likely, memory disruption.

— A set strategy can be established for parsing a particular phrase structure and for parsing a subject versus object complement structure, suggesting psychological reality for those syntactic structures.

— With minimal context or semantic information, core sentences (simple active sentences) are more speedily understood and better remembered than negatives, passives, interrogatives, and so on, which in turn have a processing advantage over negative passives and so on.

— The more nodes or processing components a left-to-right read of a sentence suggests, the longer it takes to understand.

— Surface structure indications of the correct parse (like a relative pronoun such as *that*), speed comprehension, prevent backtracking, and prevent generation of multiple, unused structures.

— At the position of a trace (the gap), the NP it marks is reactivated, and, relative to trace-less control sentences, words from the NP are more quickly recognized, better prime associates for lexical decision, and more likely to evoke an N400 if they are semantically incongruent.

— Irreversible passives are no slower to verify than actives: Semantic plausibility helps determine grammatical relations. Passive sentences are no harder than actives if they match the memory representation in terms of topic and focus.

— Sentences describing temporal relations are easier to understand if the clause order matches the events' temporal order.

— We do not remember surface structure but meaning, within several seconds after the sentence is presented.

— Syntactic processing may be simple heuristics, not full-fledged rules for structure recovery, such as the following:
  — Input is a sentence.
  — Input is actor-action-object.
  — First clause is main clause.
  — *Minimum distance principle:* Nearest noun is subject of embedded clause.
  — *Minimal attachment principle:* Try the simplest structure, the one with the fewest nodes, first.

— If there is psychological parsing per se, it interacts very quickly with semantic information. There is some evidence for a brief, encapsulated syntax module. There is stronger evidence that sentence comprehension continues beyond the sentence parse, to generate rich semantic associations and inferences to be used in discourse.

— Sentences are encoded in proposition format in memory and the proposition constitutes a perceptual and memory unit.

— Discourse is like sentence syntax: Gaps are filled across sentence and organization by theme (topic focus/elaboration) is easier to understand.

structed so that the same sentence could appear in four different roles in different stories: early topic, early peripheral, late topic, late peripheral. They found that subjects took longer to read, and better recalled, topic sentences than peripheral sentences, and that early sentences took longer to read than late sentences.

The results suggest that subjects may be actively constructing a story structure, and peripheral sentences and late sentences take less time to fit into the structure. The structure could take the form described by Kintsch and van Dijk (1978) at the end of the section on computer processing of syntax: a macrostructure that characterizes the entire discourse on the topic and a microstructure relating individual propositions.

It should be clear that syntactic processing is not finished at the sentence level; we still try to find syntactic relations among sentences and, in so doing, derive additional structure and new relations, the evidence for which are new meaning connections, new units, or even the inference of a topic sentence or a cause. For syntactic processing at any level, there appears to be a measurable cost in cognitive processing for "loose" structure: The easier it is to derive the underlying relations—because they are semantically plausible, hinted at directly through surface-structure cues, directly specified in a topic sentence, and so on—the more that can be remembered, the quicker additional information may be acquired, and the quicker comprehension is generally. What seems to be best retained are the meaning relations, not the process of discovering them—the specific syntactic analysis.

SUMMARY AND CONCLUSIONS

The last four chapters have been concerned, in one way or another, with meaning retrieval and representation, which appears to happen in several (not necessarily discrete) stages from the initial presentation of a word. An ambiguous word immediately seems to activate all its conventional meanings, regardless of context. Similarly, there is at least controversial evidence that a constituent is *immediately* parsed with a minimal attachment principle (perhaps incorrectly) regardless of context. And immediate on-line measures show strong surface-structure effects that have no long-lasting impact. At the end of processing, we remember little of the form but have encoded underlying meaning relations and their implications.

This chapter has reviewed results from the artificial intelligence and cognitive psychology literatures on sentence processing. They agree substantially on processing mechanisms. There is no question that syntax is used in deriving a meaning representation for a sentence, and that the meaning representations have a "syntax" themselves. The ultimate representation of a sentence, stored for the longest time, seems akin to the early view of deep structure, actor-action-object-location-time-and-so-on; this is the "proposition." The deep-structure proposition representation is what exists after meaning assignment. To derive deep structure we use all available information: default top-down strategies such as the input will be a sentence, and the first noun will be the subject; bottom-up strategies in which the words of the input trigger a particular syntactic form, as when "ask" takes a different structure than "promise"; bottom-up syntactic strategies, as when "that" introduces a relative clause; and meaning-based strategies, for example, plants do not water boys.

The syntax-based strategies seem to work on surface structure to derive a slightly more abstract representation, consistent with current G&B theory formulations. The abstract surface structure is derived during processing but is not retained for very long. We occasionally backtrack and derive alternate readings, and we do not seem to look ahead before attempting a parse. And, finally, we do derive structures at levels beyond the sentence, but the methods for discourse processing are only beginning to be explored.

We have considered the processing of meaning and syntax regardless of whether the input is typed or spoken. In the next chapters we will discuss the structure and processing of the sounds of the language—how we perceive the auditory representation of the language. We will see that like words in a sentence, sounds have rules of organization, rules that help us determine what the word or clause is. As with sentence structure, sound structure is amazingly and fascinatingly complex.

REFERENCES

Abney, S. P. (1989). A computational model of human parsing. *Journal of Psycholinguistic Research, 18*, 129-144.

Anderson, J. R., & Bower, G. H. (1973). *Human associative memory.* New York: John Wiley.

Bever, T. G. (1970). The cognitive basis for linguistic structures. In J. Hayes (Ed.), *Cognition and the development of language* (pp. 279-361). New York: John Wiley.

Bever, T. G., Lackner, J. R., & Kirk, R. (1969). The underlying structures of sentences are the primary units of immediate speech processing. *Perception & Psychophysics, 5,* 225-234.

Bransford, J. D., Barclay, J. R., & Franks, J. J. (1972). Sentence memory: A constructive versus interpretive approach. *Cognitive Psychology, 3,* 193-209.

Bransford, J. D., & Franks, J. J. (1971). The abstraction of linguistic ideas. *Cognitive Psychology, 2,* 331-350.

Bransford, J. D., & Johnson, M. K. (1972). Contextual prerequisites for understanding: Some investigations of comprehension and recall. *Cognitive Psychology, 3,* 717-726.

Britt, M. A., Perfetti, C. A., Garrod, S., & Rayner, K. (1992). Parsing in discourse: Context effects and their limits. *Journal of Memory and Language, 31,* 293-314.

Cerf, V. (1973). Parry encounters the doctor. *Datamation, 19,* 62-64.

Chomsky, C. (1969). *The acquisition of syntax in children from 5 to 10.* Cambridge: MIT Press.

Chomsky, N. (1965). *Aspects of a theory of syntax.* Cambridge: MIT Press.

Cirilo, R. K., & Foss, D. J. (1980). Text structure and reading times for sentences. *Journal of Verbal Learning and Verbal Behavior, 19,* 96-109.

Clark, H. H., & Clark, E. V. (1968). Semantic distinctions and memory for sentences. *Quarterly Journal of Experimental Psychology, 70,* 129-138.

Clifton, C. J., Speer, S., & Abney, S. P. (1991). Parsing arguments: Phrase structure and argument structure as determinants of initial parsing decisions. *Journal of Memory and Language, 30,* 251-271.

Ferreira, F., & Henderson, J. M. (1990). Use of verb information in syntactic parsing: Evidence from eye movements and word-by-word self-paced reading. *Journal of Experimental Psychology: Learning, Memory, and Cognition, 16,* 555-568.

Ferreira, F., Henderson, J. M., Anes, M. D., Weeks, P. A., Jr., & McFarlane, D. (1996). Effect of lexical frequency and syntactic complexity in spoken language comprehension. *Journal of Experimental Psychology: Learning, Memory, and Cognition, 22,* 324-335.

Fodor, J. A., & Bever, T. G. (1965). The psychological reality of linguistic segments. *Journal of Verbal Learning and Verbal Behavior, 4,* 410-420.

Fodor, J. A., & Garrett, M. (1967). Some syntactic determinants of sentential complexity. *Perception & Psychophysics, 2,* 289-296.

Fodor, J. A., & Pylyshyn, Z. W. (1988). Connectionism and cognitive architecture: A critical analysis. *Cognition, 28,* 3-71.

Franks, J. J., & Bransford, J. D. (1972). The acquisition of abstract ideas. *Journal of Verbal Learning and Verbal Behavior, 11,* 311-315.

Frazier, L., & Rayner, K. (1987). Resolution of syntactic category ambiguities: Eye movements in parsing lexically ambiguous sentences. *Journal of Memory and Language, 26,* 505-526.

Garnsey, S. M., Tanenhaus, M. K., & Chapman, R. M. (1989). Evoked potentials and the study of sentence comprehension. *Journal of Psycholinguistic Research, 18,* 51-60.

Gough, P. B. (1965). Grammatical transformations and speed of understanding. *Journal of Verbal Learning and Verbal Behavior, 4,* 107-111.

Gough, P. B. (1966). The verification of sentences: The effects of delay of evidence and sentence length. *Journal of Verbal Learning and Verbal Behavior, 5,* 492-496.

Green, B. F., Wolf, A. K., Chomsky, C., & Laughery, K. (1995). Baseball: An automatic question-answerer. In E. A. Feigenbaum & J. Feldman (Eds.), *Computers and thought* (pp. 207-216). Menlo Park, CA: AAAI Press/MIT Press. (Original work published 1963)

Hunt, E., & Agnoli, F. (1991). The Whorfian hypothesis: A cognitive psychology perspective. *Psychological Review, 98,* 377-389.

Johnson, M. (1989). Parsing as deduction: The use of knowledge of language. *Journal of Psycholinguistic Research, 18,* 105-128.

Kintsch, W. (1988). The role of knowledge in discourse comprehension: A construction-integration model. *Psychological Review, 95,* 163-182.

Kintsch, W., & van Dijk, T. A. (1978). Toward a model of text comprehension and production. *Psychological Review, 85,* 363-394.

Kucera, F., & Francis, W. (1967). *Computational analysis of present-day American English.* Providence, RI: Brown University Press.

Kuno, S. (1967). Computer analysis of natural languages. *Mathematical Aspects of Computer Science: Proceedings of Symposia in Applied Mathematics, 19,* 52-110.

Lachter, J., & Bever, T. G. (1988). The relation between linguistic structure and association theories of language learning: A constructive critique of some connectionist learning models. *Cognition, 28,* 195-247.

MacDonald, M. C., Pearlmutter, N. J., & Seidenberg, M. S. (1994). Lexical nature of syntactic ambiguity resolution. *Psychological Review, 101,* 676-703.

Marcus, M. (1980). *A theory of syntactic recognition for natural language.* Cambridge: MIT Press.

Marks, L. E., & Miller, G. A. (1964). The role of semantic and syntactic constraints in the memorization of English sentences. *Journal of Verbal Learning and Verbal Behavior, 3,* 1-5.

Martin, E., & Roberts, K. H. (1966). Grammatical factors in sentence retention. *Journal of Verbal Learning and Verbal Behavior, 5 ,* 211-218.

McClelland, J. L., & Kawamoto, A. H. (1986). Mechanisms of sentence processing: Assigning roles to constituents. In J. L. McClelland et al. (Eds.), *Parallel distributed processing* (Vol. 2, pp. 272-325). Cambridge: MIT Press.

McClelland, J. L., Rumelhart, D. E., & the PDP Research Group (Eds.). (1986). *Parallel distributed processing* (Vol. 2). Cambridge: MIT Press.

McElree, B., & Bever, T. G. (1989). The psychological reality of linguistically defined gaps. *Journal of Psycholinguistic Research, 18,* 21-35.

McKoon, G., & Ratcliff, R. (1980). The comprehension processes and memory structures involved in anaphoric reference. *Journal of Verbal Learning and Verbal Behavior, 19,* 668-682.

Mehler, J. (1963). Some effects of grammatical transformations on the recall of English sentences. *Journal of Verbal Learning and Verbal Behavior, 2,* 250-262.

Mehler, J., & Carey, P. (1967). Role of surface and base structures in the perception of sentences. *Journal of Verbal Learning and Verbal Behavior, 6,* 335-338.

Miller, G. A., & Isard, S. (1963). Some perceptual consequences of linguistic rules. *Journal of Verbal Learning and Verbal Behavior, 2,* 217-228.

Miller, G. A., & Selfridge, J. A. (1953). Verbal context and the recall of meaningful material. *American Journal of Psychology, 63,* 176-185.

Nicol, J., & Swinney, D. (1989). The role of structure in coreference assignment during sentence comprehension. *Journal of Psycholinguistic Research, 18,* 5-19.

Olson, D. R., & Filby, N. (1972). On the comprehension of active and passive sentences. *Cognitive Psychology, 3,* 361-381.

Pinker, S. (1991). Rules of language. *Science, 253,* 530-535.

Pinker, S., & Prince, A. (1988). On language and connectionism: Analyses of a parallel distributed processing model of language acquisition. *Cognition, 28,* 73-193.

Ratcliff, R., & McKoon, G. (1978). Priming in recognition: Evidence for the propositional structure of sentences. *Journal of Verbal Learning and Verbal Behavior, 17,* 403-417.

Reber, A. S., & Anderson, J. R. (1970). The perception of clicks in linguistic and nonlinguistic messages. *Perception & Psychophysics, 8,* 81-89.

Reyna, V. F. (1993). Theory and reality in psycholinguistics. *Psychological Science, 4,* 15-23.

Rumelhart, D. E., & McClelland, J. L. (1986). On learning the past tense of English verbs. In J. L. McClelland, D. E. Rumelhart, & the PDP Research Group (Eds.), *Parallel distributed processing* (Vol. 2, pp. 216-271). Cambridge: MIT Press.

Sachs, J. S. (1967). Recognition memory for syntactic and semantic aspects of connected discourse. *Perception & Psychophysics, 2,* 437-442.

Sager, N. (1990). Computer analysis of sublanguage information structures. In E. H. Bendix (Ed.), *Annals of the New York Academy of Sciences: Vol. 583. The uses of linguistics* (pp. 161-179). New York: New York Academy of Sciences.

Savin, H. B., & Perchonock, E. (1965). Grammatical structure and the immediate recall of English sentences. *Journal of Verbal Learning and Verbal Behavior, 4,* 348-353.

Schank, R. (1972). Conceptual dependency: A theory of natural language processing. *Cognitive Psychology, 3,* 552-632.

Schank, R., Kass, A., & Riesbeck, C. K. (1994). *Inside case-based explanation.* Hillsdale, NJ: Lawrence Erlbaum.

Slobin, D. L. (1966). Grammatical transformations and sentence comprehension in childhood and adulthood. *Journal of Verbal Learning and Verbal Behavior, 5,* 219-227.

Stemberger, J. P. (1985). An interactive activation model of language production. In A. W. Ellis (Ed.), *Progress in the psychology of language* (Vol. 1, pp. 143-186). London: Lawrence Erlbaum.

Tanenhaus, M. K., Spivey-Knowlton, M. J., Eberhard, K. M., & Sedivy, J. C. (1995). Integration of visual and linguistic information in spoken language comprehension. *Science, 268,* 1632-1634.

Tennant, H. (1981). *Natural language processing.* New York: Petrocelli.

Till, R., Mross, E. F., & Kintsch, W. (1988). Time course of priming for associate and inference words in a discourse context. *Memory and Cognition, 16,* 283-298.

Trueswell, J. C., Tanenhaus, M. K., & Kelso, C. (1993). Verb-specific constraints in sentence processing: Separating effects of lexical preference from garden paths. *Journal of Experimental Psychology: Learning, Memory, and Cognition, 19,* 528-553.

Weizenbaum, J. (1976). *Computer power and human reason.* San Francisco: Freeman.

Winograd, T. (1972). Understanding natural language. *Cognitive Psychology, 3,* 1-191.

Woods, W. A. (1967). *Semantics for a question-answering system.* Unpublished doctoral dissertation, Aiken Computer Laboratory (Report NSF-19), Harvard University.

Woods, W. A. (1973). Progress in natural language understanding: An application to lunar geology. In *Proceedings of the National Computer Conference.* Montvale, NJ: AFIPS Press.

STUDY QUESTIONS

1. Explain the terms *bottom-up processing, top-down processing, serial processing, parallel processing,* and *heuristics.* Make up a sentence and show how its meaning could be derived by using only bottom-up, top-down, serial, or parallel processes; that is, describe four different means of processing it, one for each of the preceding. What kind of heuristics could be used to interpret your sentence?

2. Critically discuss the evidence for the psychological reality of early transformational grammar: deep structure, surface structure, and transformations, which can add and delete as well as move items. Then consider the evidence for the newer generative grammar levels and theoretical constructs: traces, abstract surface structure, theta-role assignment from the lexicon, and empty categories. Which appears to be a better account of human syntactic processing?

3. (How) do you think we do syntactic processing? Discuss the evidence for and against your position. You may opt for "keyword," finite state grammar, emergent properties of a PDP network based on statistical co-occurrence patterns, transformational derivation from surface structure to proposition, interpretation of abstract surface structure, general strategies, or semantic strategies. If you truly think we do it by using keywords or finite state grammars, critique the other methods and explain how your preferred method accounts for the findings claimed in support of the others.

6

SPEECH

C onsider the following sets of sounds:

whim	pimp	improper	bumper		mp
win	pint	interrogate	bunter		nt
wing	pink	incarcerate	bunker		nk

The items in the first row contain the consonant "m," and, all but the first, the cluster "mp." Make an "m" and notice where your lips and tongue are when you do—your lips should be closed and your tongue not touching the roof of your mouth. Are your lips and tongue in the same place for "p"? For "n"? For "n," the consonant shared by the items of Row 2, your lips should be open and your tongue tip (*apex*) should be touching the roof of your mouth, just behind your teeth—the *alveolar ridge.* Do you have to move your tongue to go from "n" to "t"? If not, "n" and "t" are in the same *place of articulation.* The items in the third row all share a sound too, called *eng* (ŋ). Notice where your tongue is at the end of *wing*—the back of it should be pushed up against the soft part of the roof of your mouth, the *soft palate,* very different from its position in *win.* And note that you hear a difference between *win* and *wing,* indicating that they are made of different sounds. Now where is your tongue at the "n" in *pink*? Is it at the same place as in *win* or *wing*? Do you have to move it to make the "k"? Are you making an "n" or an "eng" before the "k" sound in *incarcerate* and *bunker*?

This example illustrates several things about sound. First, as shown by the "eng," the sounds of our language do not absolutely correspond to the letters of the alphabet. Sometimes different sounds are represented by the same letter. (Perhaps you feel that "eng" is actually two sounds, n + g. Say "n + g," making the "n" as you did in *win.* Does "ng" sound the same as "ŋ"?) Sometimes the same sound is represented by two different letters—like "c" in *incarcerate* and "k" in *pink.* So, to talk clearly about the sounds of a language, we will need a new alphabet, one that corresponds to the sounds.

Second, like everything else in language, sounds are organized. In the words beginning the chapter, the consonant pairs we discussed match the place of articulation of the "m," "n," and "ŋ," respectively, with the "p," "t," and "k." Matching of a sound feature is called *assimilation* and is usually hypothesized to occur to allow the speaker fewer movements, less work. Try to pronounce the nonsense words, *pinp, piŋ p, bumker.* Isn't it easier to say them when the place of articulation matches?

Third, the organization of sounds dictates not only which sounds are likely to occur together but also which sounds may occur where. All the words in the example have "m," "n," "ŋ" either at the end or in the middle of the word. Is it possible to make them at the beginning? Yes, for "m" and "n"—*map* and *nap,* for example—but can we have "ŋap"? Can you say "ŋap"? If you practice and think about where your tongue should be, you can: It exists in initial position in other languages. If you succeed in making one clearly, ask your friends what they hear. In all likelihood, they will say *nap* because they are not used to hearing "ŋ" in initial position and they will guess something more likely given their experience.

The organization in sounds, like the organization in meaning and syntax, provides redundancy and predictability. Redundancy allows us to guess sounds preceding or following the current one if we have missed them because of a performance error (mispronunciation by the speaker or our inattention) or because they were obscured by noise. The organization and predictability in sounds also allow us to understand the speech of someone who does not talk exactly as we do. Essentially, we make and use a sound substitution rule. For example, for a lisp, we could use a rule changing "th" to "s" ("th" may be written θ or theta for the sound in *thin,* to distinguish it from ð, the "th" sound in *the*). Obviously we do not always want to use the rule: "Liθp" must be *lisp* but "θin" could be either *thin* or *sin.* Sometimes we decide whether to rewrite based on tacit knowledge of rules of sound, for example, θ cannot occur before "p" in English. Sometimes we decide using higher language levels, meaning or syntax.

In addition to aiding understanding of speech defects, sound rules and sound rewrite rules allow us to understand people with accents different from ours. Think about what makes an accent different. Sometimes it is trivial, such as pronouncing a single word differently, *shedule* instead of *skedule* (schedule) or *tomahto* instead of *tomayto.* Or it may involve pronouncing a particular sound differently—"r" in English, French, or Spanish, for instance. Again this would be a simple "correction" in listening. Or it may involve pronouncing a class of sounds differently—making all vowels sound nasal, for instance. In any case, the organization and the redundancy of the sounds (and the words) in the language allow us to ignore these variations and still recognize what others are saying.

In this chapter we examine the sounds of language and some principles of their organization. In Chapter 7 we discuss how we perceive the sounds of the language and use their organization.

UNITS OF SOUND

Syllables

As we have seen in syntax and semantics, the first problem in determining structure is deciding where to begin analysis, what to use as the unit for study. And, as with meaning and syntax, several candidates present themselves, some of which are useful for some types of analysis and others useful for others.

One possibility is the syllable. What do you think a syllable is? (This gives a good example of tacit knowledge; almost everyone can mark syllables, but I have found no student who was able to intuit the definition.) Formally, a syllable is a unit consisting of no more than one vowel sound. Try it: *A* is one syllable, as is *pa,* or *strength* (the longest single syllable in English). *Any* is two syllables—two vowels. To describe a syllable, though, it is necessary to talk about its components—vowels and consonants—and this level of sound structure too could be the place to start analysis.

Phonemes

Linguists define the *phoneme* as the minimal unit of sound that can serve to distinguish meaning. Phonemes are recognized using the same kind of distributional analysis we used in Chapter 4 for syntax, but here for sound. In syntax we collected or constructed sentences that were identical except for one word; the words were in *complementary distribution.* The different words could then be assigned to a particular structural class. In speech, likewise, we look for frames identical but for one difference; the sounds are in complementary distribution. If the difference is judged by native speakers to result in a meaning difference too, we have found a pair of phonemes.

Two words identical but for one meaning-changing sound constitute a *minimal pair.* For example, *bat* and *pat* are different; the "at" is shared by both so b-p creates a meaning difference; "b" and "p" are different phonemes. *Pat* and *pet* are minimally distinct, with the difference in the vowel, suggesting "a" and "e" are different phonemes. *Pet* and *Pete* are minimally distinct (ignore the spelling—both are pronounced p-vowel-t) suggesting the "e" in *pet* is phonemically distinct from the "e" in *Pete.*

Our alphabet is crudely phonemic, but, as I said earlier, there is not a one-to-one correspondence between the phonemes of our language and the letters of the alphabet. Can you read *ghoti*? It is a construction of George Bernard Shaw's to show how unphonemic our writing system is. The letters represent sounds they make in common English words, but irregularly, so "o" will not have the sound in *boat* or in *not. Ghoti* is a "transcription" of *fish:* "gh" as in "enou*gh*," "o" as in "w*o*men," and "ti" as in "transcrip*ti*on." Clearly, to discuss the phonemes of English, we need an alphabet with one-to-one correspondence between sound and symbol. Such an alphabet, the International Phonetic Alphabet, is displayed in

Table 6.1 The International Phonetic Alphabet (Phonemes of English)

		Consonants				
		Labial	*Dental*	*Alveolar*	*Palatal*	*Velar*
Stops	voiced	b bill		d dill		g gill
	voiceless	p pill		t till		k kill
Nasals		m mill		n nill		ŋ sing
Fricatives	voiced	v veil	ð the	z zero	ž zha-zha	
	voiceless	f fill	θ thin	s sill	š sharp	
Affricates	voiced				ǰ edge	
	voiceless				č church	
Liquid/Semivowel		w will	r,l rail			h hid

	Vowels		
	Front	*Central*	*Back*
High	i beet		u boot
	ɪ bit		U book
Mid	e bait	ə sofa	o boat
	ɛ bet		ʌ but, ɔ bought
	æ bat		
Low		a bar	

NOTE: This table, for the phonemes of English, is organized with respect to articulatory features. Each symbol is presented, followed by a common word containing the (underlined) sound it represents.

Table 6.1, organized to show the phonetic symbol and a common word in English with that sound. The table is also organized with respect to articulatory features, to be described later.

It is important to learn the symbols to follow discussion in this and the next chapter as well as in other reading. It is also fun because it gives you a secret code and enables you to tune into sound similarities and differences between your speech and others. Use Table 6.1 to help you read, "fonimɪk tɚænzkɚɪpšʌn." It is written in the phonemic alphabet and says, "phonemic transcription." Use Table 6.1 again: hir falo sʌm poms fɔr yu tu tɚænzlet ɪntu tɚænskrɪpšʌn. (Here follow some poems for you to translate into transcription.) not haw wat əpir dɪfɚɪnt ɪn raitɪŋ, bʌt raim wɛn tɚænskɚaibd, lʊk ðə seim. (Note how what appear to be different in writing, but rhyme, when transcribed look the same.)

1. Jellicle Cats are black and white,
    Jellicle Cats are rather small,
    Jellicle Cats are merry and bright,
    And pleasant to hear when they caterwaul.
    Jellicle Cats have cheerful faces,
    Jellicle Cats have bright black eyes;
    They like to practice their airs and graces
    And wait for the Jellicle moon to rise.
    (from T. S. Eliot, 1940/1980, *Old Possum's Book of Practical Cats,* p. 25)

2. The turtle lives 'twixt plated decks
   Which practically conceal its sex.
   I think it clever of the turtle
   In such a fix to be so fertile.
   (Ogden Nash, "The Turtle," in O. Williams, 1952, p. 571)

3. There was young girl of Tralee,
   Whose knowledge of French was "oui, oui."
   When they said: "Parlez-vous?"
   She replied: "Same to you!"
   And was famed for her bright repartee.
   (Holland, *An Explosion of Limericks,* 1967, p. 23)

Allophones and Phonetic Differences

Each phoneme represents a class of sounds, each member of which may sound different from other members. Take, for example, the phoneme /p/. (Phonemes are indicated by slashes around the sound.) If you attend very carefully when you say *pat* and *tap,* you will notice that you pronounce the /p/ differently in initial and final positions (if you have a standard American accent). If you hold your fingers in front of your mouth as you say *pat,* you should feel a burst of air on them as you articulate the /p/. In *tap,* if you pronounce it naturally, you will not separate your lips again at the end of the word, and you will not feel that burst of air. The /p/ in *spat* is like the final /p/—there should be no burst of air. Do you think you can hear the difference? Perhaps it will help you to recognize it if I tell you that it is one of the differences between standard British and American speech—the British *release* their final /p/s and /t/s; they make that burst of air, and Americans do not. We can also demonstrate that the difference is audible by tape-recording *spat* and splicing the "s" off the recording; magically, the resulting syllable sounds like *bat,* not like *pat!* As native speakers, some of our tacit English knowledge includes the obligatory release of /p/ in initial position; if we do not hear the release, we assume a /b/, which, while released in initial position, does not have as prominent a burst of air.

In English, released or *aspirated* [p^h] and unreleased [p'] are different sounds of the same phoneme. (Descriptions of the precise articulation are *phonetic* and are indicated by square brackets.) That is, we cannot make a meaning difference between "tap^h" and "tap'." They are called *allophones* of the phoneme /p/.

Most phonemes have many allophones, and some phonemes share an allophone. For example, in many American dialects, *ladder* and *latter* have the same sound in the middle—the *medial* consonant. Try saying, "The former or the ladder." It should sound perfectly normal. That medial consonant, called a *flap,* is an allophone of both /d/ and /t/. In addition to the medial flap, /t/ has released and unreleased allophones, just as /p/ has. *A phoneme thus is a class of sounds that usually may be interchanged without native speakers noticing the difference.*

It is important to realize that differences that are phonetic in one language may be phonemic in another. As already stated, the difference between aspirated and unaspirated consonants is not used to distinguish meaning in English, although it does distinguish dialects. In Korean, however, the aspiration difference is *phonemic*—different words can be indicated solely by whether or not a consonant is released. In fact, if the consonant is articulated with strong aspiration, it is phonemically distinct from one weakly aspirated *and* from one articulated without aspiration (Lisker & Abramson, 1991).

Phonetic Features

In this discussion and in our initial discussion, we made use of subphonemic units of analysis—place of articulation, release, aspiration—so, clearly, there is a smaller unit of sound structure than the phoneme. We will define *subphonemic features* as those aspects of either articulation or the sound signal itself that distinguish phonemes and/or allophones of phonemes. Different languages of the world have different phonemes, syllables, and words, but all spoken languages share the same set of subphonemic features. Subphonemic features are determined by the structures of the vocal tract and of the auditory system—structures common to all human beings. Although we may argue theoretically about which grammatical structures are universal, the capabilities of the human vocal tract and auditory system, barring physical abnormality, must be universal!

Suprasegmentals

Before discussing subphonemic features in any detail, I note that there is one more level of sound analysis, a level that supersedes syllables, where we began this discussion. Syllables, phonemes, and features are sometimes called *segments,* the individual units we combine to form meaningful sentences. *Suprasegmentals* transcend a single one of these units, applying to several at once. Suprasegmental properties include pitch, pitch changes, overall loudness, loudness changes, speech rate, and linguistic stress (the difference between the verb and the noun form of *contrast*). Note that the statement, "You now understand the difference between segments and suprasegmentals," and the question, "You now understand the difference between segments and suprasegmentals?" use the same segments; the different meaning is conveyed through a change in pitch. The pitch change is marked in one sense on, and in one sense apart from, the segments; each has a pitch and the combination of those pitches, the *pitch contour,* makes the difference between questions and statements. I will return to suprasegmentals below.

ARTICULATORY FEATURES

I begin discussion of subphonemic features with articulation because it is easier to feel intuitively where the articulators are than it is to determine what the characteristics are in the sound. Figure 6.1 shows a model vocal tract to be used for

---

Box 6.1. Levels of Analysis of Language Sounds

— *Syllable:* A unit of sound that consists of no more than one vowel.
— *Phoneme:* The minimal unit of sound that can serve to distinguish words of a language.
— *Allophone:* Sounds that are acoustically and articulatorily different but that native speakers agree represent the same phoneme.
— *Phonetic feature:* An articulatory gesture that produces an audible difference in speech and that serves to distinguish allophones.
— *Suprasegmental:* Intonation, stress, or rate characteristics of speech, which usually are produced over several segments (segment = phonetic feature or phoneme).

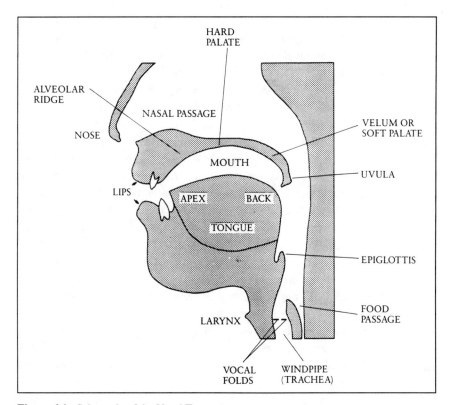

Figure 6.1. Schematic of the Vocal Tract

reference. Sound begins with our forcing air out of our lungs, up through the trachea, and out of the mouth or nose or both. The audible effect of the air may be changed by the path it takes—for example, whether it goes out the mouth, the nose, or both, or by the shape the mouth takes as the air comes out. In the same manner, the sound of a puff of air may be changed by pushing it through a flute, stopping the flute in different places, or humming while playing the flute. The various ways of altering the sound of a puff of air are called *articulatory features* and are arranged hierarchically, as in Table 6.1.

Consonants

The uppermost distinction, consonant-vowel, refers to whether there is constriction anywhere in the vocal tract. When a doctor wants to look at your throat, you say /a/, a vowel. Making an /m/ would allow the doctor a good view of your lips; making an /l/, of the underside of your tongue. These last are consonants, and they block the vocal tract in some way. The consonants may be described by using three articulatory dimensions: manner of articulation, voicing, and place of articulation.

Manner of Articulation

Manner of articulation refers to the nature of the constriction, how much air it allows to pass. *Stop consonants* or *plosives* are consonants articulated so that no air can get through. In English, these are /b/, /d/, /g/, and /p/, /t/, /k/. If you make any of these consonants and attend to what you are doing, you will feel a complete seal; in /b/ or /p/, for instance, the lips are sealed and air gathers behind them. As we articulate, we suddenly break the seal and air "explodes" (= plosive) out. This is called the release. (As we have seen, in American English in final position the stops are unreleased; that is, the seal is not broken, and the built-up air dissipates in the vocal cavity.) If you slowly make a stop and do not release or allow the air to escape through your nose, you feel the air pressure build up—for /b/ and /p/ in your cheeks, for /d/ and /t/ behind your tongue, and for /g/ and /k/ in your throat, as if you were gagging.

Nasal consonants, a second manner of articulation, also have complete closure somewhere in the vocal tract. When you make a nasal, the soft palate or *velum* (see Figure 6.1) is lowered, allowing air to escape through the nose. In stops the velum is fully raised, sealing off the nasal cavity. Nasals of English are /m/, /n/, and /ŋ/. Make an /m/, sustain it, and while you make the sound "mmmmmmmmm," grab your nose. You should feel the pressure build up and either pop your ears or, more safely, force you to open your mouth and articulate a /b/. When we have a cold and the nasal passage is blocked, /m/s turn into /b/s and /n/s to /d/s because the air cannot exit through the nose.

The remaining manners of articulation all involve partial constriction and a smaller pressure buildup. *Fricatives* are consonants produced by constricting almost to the point of closing the vocal tract, causing the air to pass turbulently, with friction, through the constriction. The fricatives used in English are /f/, /v/, /θ/, /ð/, /s/, /z/, /š/, /ž/, and in other languages we also find the guttural sound /x/ (as though you were clearing your throat), and a sound produced by partially closing the lips, /β/. If you pay attention as you make an /s/, you will feel the sides of your tongue sealing off the roof of your mouth, and the tip almost touching it, with the air "whistling" through the hole produced by the near touch of the tongue tip.

Combining a stop and a fricative makes an *affricate;* in English we have /č/ as in *church* and /ǰ/ as in *jump* (or the vernacular "djeatjet" = did you eat yet). In an affricate there is complete closure, but instead of following with complete release as in a stop, the closure releases only partially.

Widening the opening more produces laterals and semivowels. A *lateral* (/l/ in English) has the opening at the side. In /l/, the tongue tip contacts the roof of the mouth, but the tongue's sides do not touch the sides of the mouth, so air can pass without vibration. In English /r/ and /w/, too, there is partial closure: In /r/ the tongue bends back on itself (called *retroflex*) but does not contact the mouth roof; in /w/ the lips begin to close but leave an opening too large to cause vibration (decreasing that opening still further produces the fricative /β/, used in Spanish, among other languages). Because there is constriction, but not contact, these are called *semivowels.*

Finally there is a class of sounds produced by repeated closing and opening, called *trills.* These include the French "r," where the trill is produced in the back of the throat; the Spanish "r," where it is produced by repeatedly tapping the tongue tip on the roof of the mouth; and a lip trill produced by vibrating the lips together while blowing out. A single "tap" of a trill produces a flap, like [ɾ] in *ladder* or *latter.*

Voicing

Voicing refers to when the vocal cords begin to vibrate relative to the release of air: /z/ and /s/ are good instances of the distinction. Place your fingers on your larynx (Adam's apple) as you make the sound z-z-z-z-z-z-z. You should feel a buzz. Now make s-s-s-s-s-s-s without moving your fingers—you should feel nothing. When the vocal folds vibrate simultaneously with the release, as in /z/, the sound is *voiced;* when release occurs first, the sound is *voiceless.* In English, only the distinction between voiced and voiceless is (phonemically) relevant. In other languages this feature can have one other relevant value—the vocal folds may start to vibrate before the release. This is called *prevoicing* and is hard for English speakers to hear or produce deliberately. Try it, using what you know now about articulation: Put your fingers on your larynx, start it vibrating, and then begin the /z/. It should sound something like nz.

All the sounds we have listed for manner may be divided into voiced and voiceless. The voiced stops are /b/, /d/, /g/; the voiced fricatives are /v/, /ð/, /z/, /ž/; the voiced affricate is /ǰ/. The nasals, laterals, and semivowels of English are all voiced. Voiceless stops are /p/t/k/, voiceless fricatives are /f, θ, s, š/, and the voiceless affricate is /č/.

Place of Articulation

The final distinction relevant for English consonants is place of articulation, introduced at the beginning of the chapter. *Place* refers to where in the oral cavity the closure or constriction is. It can be at the lips or *bilabial* (/b/), at the teeth or *dental* (θ), between the lips and teeth or *labiodental* (v), between the teeth or *interdental* (a variant of θ), behind the teeth or *alveolar* (s), back farther or *palatal* (š), and back still farther or *velar* (g). Different parts of the tongue (or lips), as we have seen, can make the constriction—the tip, the sides, the middle, or the back. Sometimes both the parts making the closure are described in labeling articulation. For example, /t/ is a voiceless apical-alveolar stop: This signifies that the tongue tip contacts the alveolar ridge with complete closure and that voicing begins after the release. Again, all the sounds may be classified by place—/b/, /p/, /m/, /w/ are bilabial; /v/ and /f/ are labiodental; /θ/ and /ð/ are dental; /d/, /t/, /s/, /z/, /n/, /r/, /l/ are alveolar; and /g/, /k/, /ŋ/ are velar.

Distinctions Not Used in English

Other languages use places of articulation different from those listed here. One instance is the palatal nasal, as in Slavic, which we transcribe as /ny/. Make an /s/ and then a /y/ and feel the difference in tongue position. Now make an /n/, only instead of using the tip of your tongue, use the middle as you did for the /y/. Another common consonant we do not use phonemically is the glottal stop /ʔ/—farther back than the velar. Cockney uses it in intervocalic positions, for example, in place of the flap [ʃ] in *latter, butter,* or *glottal.* If we suddenly articulate an isolated vowel (like /a/), it will begin with complete closure and sudden release, indicative of a stop but down in the larynx. This is the glottal stop.

Before leaving the discussion of consonant articulation, we should observe that all the consonants we have discussed are produced by pushing air *out* of the vocal tract. We are able to create sounds also by sucking air in, called *implosives* or *ingressives.* Clicking with the tongue, transcribed in literature as "tsk, tsk, tsk," is an alveolar ingressive. Kissing noises are bilabial ingressives, and there are many others. Ingressives are marked with the stop consonant of the appropriate place preceded by an !. In some African languages, implosives can distinguish words. In English, they are not used phonemically.

It is important to realize that the sounds that are not phonemic in English, but phonemic in other languages, are *just as natural* as the sounds we do use to convey meaning differences. We prevoice consonants in *intervocalic* position (between vowels as in *idea*), begin vowel-initial utterances with a glottal stop, and have a palatal value in fricatives but not in nasals. The sounds are not difficult to articulate but are not used to signal meaning differences in English, and so we do not attend to them. Selection of only some of the many possible sounds for productive use is one of the interesting characteristics of language. We return to this later and again in Chapter 12. For now, consider why languages might use some but not all possible sounds.

Vowels

Vowels may also be described by using articulatory features. For vowels, by definition, there is no closure, and therefore manner of articulation is irrelevant.

Place is relevant but is hard to feel because there is no contact of the articulators, only movement in the direction of contact. Vowels are usually described with respect to two principal dimensions. The first is *tongue height,* how close the tongue is to the roof of the mouth. The second is *tongue position,* which part of the tongue is closest to the roof of the mouth. If you pay attention as you articulate /i/ as in *beet,* /ɪ/ as in *bit,* /e/ as in *bait,* and /ɛ/ as in *bet,* you should feel your tongue tip drop progressively. Because it is the tip, the front, of the tongue that is falling, these are called *front vowels*—/i/ is high, and /e/ is medium low. (*High* and *low* do not refer to pitch but to the height of the tongue.) If you now alternate /i/ and /u/, you will feel the distinction between front and back; in /i/ the tip is close to the roof of the mouth; in /u/ the back of the tongue is close.

Contrasting /i/, /u/, and /a/ gives the maximum change: /i/ and /u/ are both high, /a/ is low (the jaw drops maximally, creating the largest opening, and the best throat viewing as your doctor knows), /i/ is front, /u/ back, and /a/ center (the middle of the tongue bulges slightly). Because /i/, /u/, and /a/ represent the vowel extremes, with all other vowels falling in between, as Table 6.1 indicates, they are sometimes called the *point vowels.* Together they enclose the *vowel triangle* or, perhaps more accurately, the vowel quadrilateral.

Other articulatory features differentiate vowels in addition to tongue height and position. Of these, the most *productive,* the feature responsible for differentiating the most minimal pairs, is *tense-lax* or, in the words we were taught in grade school, *long-short.* /i/ is long or tense, /ɪ/ short; they are almost minimally distinct with respect to this feature because they are made in the same place and with about the same tongue height. (They do differ in height, as we observed, but much less than, for example, /i/ and /e/ or /a/.) Similarly, /e/ is tense, /ɛ/ is lax, /u/ is tense, and /U/ is lax. Tense vowels are invariably articulated for a longer time than are lax vowels but are also slightly more extreme in the other dimensions. Lax vowels tend to become *centralized,* or articulated with less movement from the central, *neutral* position (Jakobson, Fant, & Halle, 1951/1969). The most reduced centralized vowel is the *schwa,* /ə/, the sound at the end of *sofa,* representing the very least articulatory effort.

Other Features

The remaining vowel features are not very productive in English: They differentiate one or two vowels but are not responsible for major class distinctions. They are listed here for the sake of completeness and also to underscore that *our language, like others, uses productively only a few of the many possible sounds, and the ones we use are no more natural than the others.* Try to make each of the sounds described. Remember, if it seems unnatural, that you will be trying to use explicit knowledge rather than the tacit knowledge we use for *our* phonemes, and that you are experienced making our sounds but not the others.

Retroflexion refers to curling the tongue back while articulating. We do that to the schwa to make our "r," which is not a true consonant at all. If you make an "r," you will see that there is no constriction in the vocal tract. Retroflexion is indicated with a ˆ on the vowel: Our "r" is phonetically transcribed [ɚ]. It is possible to retroflex other vowels.

Liprounding is a feature we use only for /u/, /ʊ/, and /ɔ/. It refers to a protrusion of the lips accompanying other articulatory gestures. We could lipround any vowel.

A third, minor feature for vowels of English is voicing; all our vowels are voiced except one, /h/, which has a huge number of allophones. While attending to where your tongue is, say *he, who,* and *ha* /hi, hu, ha/. Note that there is no movement of the tongue as you go from the "h" into the vowel. Thus there is no constriction for "h" and it does not differ from other vowels in height or position. Indeed, *phonetically,* our "h" is a voiceless vowel that shares place and height with the vowel that follows it. Distinctions between voiceless vowels could be phonemic, but we class them together as "h." (Voiceless vowels are transcribed with an open circle beneath the vowel [a̦].) ("h" *acts* as a consonant in English, *phonologically;* for example, unlike other vowels, it cannot alone constitute a syllable.)

A fourth vowel feature not used phonemically in English is *nasalization* [~]. The velum can lower so air escapes through both nose and mouth, or raise, so air only goes through the mouth. Spanish and French use nasalization in vowels phonemically.

The final vowel distinction, phonemic in Chinese and some other Asian and African languages, is tone, a change in the pitch, or frequency of vocal fold vibration. Note that when we sing words, we change pitch, holding other articulatory features relatively constant. This does not cause any change in meaning, but in some languages (called *tone languages*) specific pitch changes signal a different phoneme or meaning.

Coarticulation

In the preceding discussion of vowels and consonants, I described idealized target positions for sounds spoken in isolation. *It is important to emphasize that speech does not consist of isolated sounds strung together but of a continuous air flow with continuous movement of the articulators.* Because of movement toward or away from one target position, sometimes the target is never reached, and actual articulation is a modification of what has been just described.

Consider the sounds /gu/ and /gi/, for example, attending to your lips as you make the /g/ portion. For /gu/ the lips may be protruded at the very beginning of the /g/, before the closure, in anticipation of the rounding necessary for the vowel. For /gi/ there is no rounding anywhere during the sound. The same thing may be seen in /di/ and /du/. And we can see this kind of articulatory *smear* across three segments. Consider *bog* (/bag/): As we begin the /b/ the back of the tongue is already assuming the position for /g/, so the /b/ is in fact articulated differently in /bag/ and /bad/, modified by later sounds. (There is long-distance context sensitivity in speech, as in syntax!) The initial consonant will reflect the tongue position for /g/ or liprounding for /u/, making it different depending on what follows, or on what precedes, for the /b/ or /d/ in /gab/ or /ud/. This might suggest that syllables are better units of articulation because they incorporate some of the anticipatory and residual movements. But coarticulation effects exist across syllable boundaries too.

In most cases we are not aware of the modifications produced by coarticulation. One striking example, however, is production of combined vowels, or *diphthongs,* a distinctive characteristic of American English. Nearly all American tensed vowels are not pure but are smoothly coarticulated double vowels (see Lieberman & Blumstein, 1988, for discussion). For example, "ay," which we have been transcribing as /e/, in fact is [e^i]—a pure vowel /e/, as in French, gliding into an /i/ sound. Make one slowly and follow your tongue: You should feel the tip glide from low in your mouth toward the roof. The movement change is indicative of a diphthong, not a pure vowel. The vowel sound in *height* is a diphthong combining [a] and [i]–[a^i]. Our "o" as in *boat* is a diphthong combining [o] and [u]—note the tendency to lipround as you end the sound. This should illustrate a subtlety of coarticulation; when it is done smoothly, a smooth blend results.

It should also illustrate, again, a consequence of phonemic distinctiveness. To American unpracticed ears /e^i/ is the same as /e/: We hear only one vowel. To speakers of other languages, who do not hear the diphthongs as we do, the combination is more obvious. Clearly, our familiarity with the sounds of our own language affects perception of speech sounds generally, an instance of the strong form of the linguistic relativity hypothesis (Hunt & Agnoli, 1991).

Nonsegmentals

The features just described are called segments, and their manipulation differentiates morphemes of the spoken languages of the world. Our speech may be affected also by other aspects of articulation, some of which are, and some of which are not, under our control. These I am treating as a group, nonsegmentals, but they fall into several classes.

Suprasegmentals

The most important nonsegmentals linguistically are the suprasegmentals, introduced earlier. By "linguistic importance," I mean they may also be used to create changes in meaning. As already discussed, suprasegmentals include pitch contour, loudness contour, and duration (speed of production or speech rate and pause length). We change pitch by increasing or decreasing the rate of vocal cord vibration. This changes tone phonemically in tone languages such as Chinese and can signal the difference between a question and a statement in English.

Loudness is affected by the force with which air is expelled and by the size of the mouth opening—in both cases, the greater, the louder. Rate is altered by the speed with which the articulators are moved from one position to another.

In normal speech the suprasegmentals are ever-changing during articulation. Generally loudness and pitch are highest at the beginning of a declarative utterance, an assertion, and then gradually decline, falling off markedly at sentence end. (For pitch, this is known as the *declination effect* and may be a linguistic universal; see Lieberman & Blumstein, 1988, for discussion.) Variations in this typical contour may be introduced for emphasis: A loudness change stresses an internal portion of the sentence, or, as in English, a pitch rise at the end marks the sentence as a question.

Generally, the suprasegmental parameters vary together: Stressing a syllable is likely to make it louder, higher, and longer than its unstressed counterpart (Lieberman & Blumstein, 1988). If you attend to words that are identical in sound except for a difference in stress, minimal pairs for stress such as "de'sert-desert', per'mit-permit', pre'sent-present'," you can observe these changes along with vowel reduction in the unstressed syllable. Note that in English we may change some noun forms to verb forms, or the converse, by changing stress. In the noun-verb pairs just listed, the noun has stress on the first syllable, the verb on the second. This is an instance of a *morpho-phonemic* rule, a rule of sound structure affected by morphological structure. Can you think of other such pairs?

Registers

The larynx has an extremely complex structure, the details of which I will not discuss. It contains the vocal cords and a number of muscles and cartilages. The muscles and cartilages may be manipulated individually to change the tension on the vocal cords or the position of the entire larynx. The opening between the vocal cords is called the *glottis,* and the stream of air passing through it is typically considered in parts: Above the glottis there is the *supraglottal airstream,* which is the part we manipulate by changing our tongue position; there is the *glottal airstream,* which we alter by using the larynx muscles and cartilages; and there is the *subglottal airstream,* which is in our lungs and deep in the throat. In neutral breathing position the vocal cords are open, allowing the air to flow through smoothly. Using the muscles to close them we produce a pressure of air below the glottis, which works to push the vocal cords open again. As the air flows through, if the vocal cords are not very tensed, it may produce a negative pressure (like a vacuum), which aids in closing the vocal cords again. In normal speech the tension on the vocal cords is sufficient to allow the subglottal pressure and negative pressure to cause the vocal cords to vibrate, imparting a particular quality to the sound.

The quality of the voice depends on the quality of the airstream through the glottis. It may be vibrating totally, as in normal speaking, or parts of it may be vibrating differently from other parts. The tension and vibration of the airstream are controlled by tensing or vibrating part or all of the vocal cords. For instance, in *falsetto register* (the way you sing, or mock an effeminate voice), greater tension is placed on the vocal cords than in normal speaking, which prevents the buildup of the negative pressure and changes the quality of the vocal tone (Lieberman & Blumstein, 1988). Note that it is possible to produce the same range of pitches in falsetto as *chest register* (normal voice); the pitch is determined by the regular *rate* of opening and closing of the vocal cords. The quality change is determined by the tension on the vocal cords, which affects airflow.

In normal and falsetto registers the pressure on the airstream (tension on the vocal cords) is even and produces vibration that results in tones. In *whisper register* the tension on the vocal cords is even but not sufficiently great to cause them to open and close and vibrate the airstream. Thus in whispering there is no true pitch, which arises, as I stated above, from the *regularity* of opening and closing of the vocal folds. In other registers the tension may be uneven, producing one kind of tone from one portion of the airstream, combined with another kind from another portion. For example, in *breathy voice* (when you try to sound sexy), there is partial tension on the vocal cords allowing air to escape through them while they are vibrating (Lieberman & Blumstein, 1988). The part with tension produces tones; the other part allows the air through without vibration, which produces a turbulent airflow sound. In *creaky voice,* a mode used, for example, in high-class British speech (called *received pronunciation*), at the end of utterances (it almost sounds as if the speaker is running out of air, teeeerrrrribly bored), there is tension on the whole glottal airstream, but it is uneven and it produces differential vibration of the airstream (Abercrombie, 1967/1982). Try to produce sounds in these different registers; their names are reasonably descriptive of the sound qualities, and we do produce them easily.

As already indicated, in English, register changes can differentiate dialects of English (creaky voice marks received pronunciation) and emotion (breathy voice is used to sound "sexy"). Register changes may be used phonemically (Abercrombie, 1967/1982), although they are not in English.

Languages and dialects may also differ in the register they use as normal or neutral, and in the "meaning" of a register, what sounds upper class, sexy, and so on (Abercrombie, 1967/1982). For example, a Dutch (male) linguist told me, much to my irritation, that American women speak in an "unnaturally" deep register compared with European women. I took this personally and protested that we speak the same register, but, on reflection, I agree—about the vocal difference. However, to me it is the European women who speak with "unnaturally" high voices. What needs to be clear is that both registers *are* natural but sound unnatural to people accustomed to a different mode—an instance of one's own language seeming "the mother tongue of the whole world only the people are too stupid to know it" (recall Dickens from Chapter 1).

Physical Characteristics and Speech

As we have seen, phonetic and suprasegmental differences are achieved by altering the articulators' movements, changing the vocal tract size and shape (as in liprounding, which lengthens the vocal tract), the tension of its muscles, and the quality of the airstream. These changes are voluntary and suggest that any size and shape difference will affect the sound quality. The physical characteristics of the vocal tract differ from individual to individual and often, at different times, within an individual. They give distinct character to each voice.

First, and most obvious, are the effects of size. When we lipround we deliberately increase the size of the vocal tract. Try to talk through protruded lips or through your hands cupped around your mouth and you can hear the effect. The voice seems to get lower. People with naturally larger vocal tracts—men as opposed to women, adults as opposed to children—will naturally have a lower sound, all other things being equal. In addition to affecting the length of the vocal tract, size may also affect the size of the vocal cords; the larger they are, the more force needed to move them, and the more slowly they move if the force is not increased. Slower opening and closing of the vocal cords produces a lower pitch. Thus increased body size produces a lower sound by lengthening the vocal tract and increasing the size of the vocal cords, thereby decreasing their vibration rate.

Second, there are the effects of muscle tension, elasticity, and fluid, which are interrelated. Under conditions of stress the vocal cords are likely to be more tensed, perhaps causing a register shift or perhaps just an increased rate of vibration, producing a higher sound. Emotional stress also may decrease the amount of fluid in the mouth, skin, and vocal cords—in the case of the last, this will make them smaller and allow faster vibration or higher pitch. Lower tension or elasticity affects both the clarity and the pitch of the sound (consider the difference in the sounds produced by plucking a tightly pulled rubber band and plucking one that is loosely pulled). As we age there is a loss in elasticity in the vocal tract generally and a loss in muscle tension specifically, producing a drop in pitch and change in quality. Fluid buildup in the larynx makes the vocal cords harder to move, slowing the rate, dropping the pitch, and preventing compete closure of the glottis: noise leaks—the effect of swelling we recognize as laryngitis (Yanagihara, 1991).

Third, changes in facial expression can affect the shape of the vocal tract and sounds emitting from it (Tartter, 1980; Tartter & Braun, 1994). Smiling retracts the lips and widens the mouth to produce a higher sound, the opposite result of liprounding and curving the mouth down in a frown. Laughing and crying change breathing too, and so produce, along with the changes of the accompanying smile or pout, register and speech rate changes. (I suspect crying or being near tears may alter the fluids in the vocal cavity, although to my knowledge it has not been studied. It does produce swelling of the face, a feeling of a "lump" in the throat, and a general huskiness. The lump and huskiness could be caused by swelling of the vocal cords.)

Finally, of course, there are individual anatomical and physiological differences that can affect sound: Emphysema and asthma affect the subglottal air pressure and nature of the airflow; smoking (or allergies) can also affect swelling in the vocal cords. Laryngectomies, enlarged adenoids, vocal cord polyps, and so on affect the vocal tract and thus sound quality (Rontal, Rontal, & Rolnick, 1991).

Throughout the discussion of articulation I have referred loosely to the effects of articulation on sound. In the next section we consider the structure of sound itself, independent of articulation. At the end I will try to unite articulatory and acoustic characteristics in describing speech structure.

SOURCE-FILTER THEORY

Although speech is normally produced through vocal articulation, it is possible to produce the same sounds through other means—as does a tape recorder, a radio, or a speech synthesizer. That is, we can describe the nature of sound without referring to articulation. Sound results from *pressure variations produced by an energy source and transmitted through some medium.* The quality of the sound may be affected by characteristics of the source or by characteristics of the medium.

Grossly speaking, we can consider a voice a constant source, and the different sound it has when we listen to it in the same room, through a wall or through water, as effects of the medium. Different aspects of the sound get absorbed or passed by different media, which affects what is ultimately heard.

Wave Properties and Their Display

The simplest type of sound consists of a regular pressure change or vibration and is described by a sine wave, like the solid line in Figure 6.2. Each wave has a certain *amplitude,* height from peak to trough, and a certain length, or distance from peak to peak, called *wavelength.* (The dashed line of Figure 6.2 has half the wavelength of the others.) In sound, we do not usually discuss wavelength, but *frequency,* the number of repetitions in a unit of time. (In the figure there are two repetitions of the dashed wave in the amount of time for one repetition of each of the others: The dashed wave has twice the frequency of the others.) Frequency is measured in cycles per second, or *Hertz (Hz).* The longer the wave, the fewer peaks there are per unit time and therefore the smaller the frequency. Thus frequency and wavelength measure the same thing, although they are *negatively* or *inversely related:* frequency = 1/wavelength.

Amplitude and frequency are independent of one another. The dotted line in Figure 6.2 shows a wave with the same frequency as, but greater amplitude than, the solid line, and the dashed line shows a wave with the same amplitude but greater frequency.

Usually, sound consists of more than one frequency at a time. Different sound qualities emerge from the relationship of the component frequencies. If there is no relationship, if frequencies are randomly put together, we hear *noise,* like the sound of /s/. If the component frequencies are all multiples of one frequency, we hear a tonal quality, as in the sound of a musical instrument. This kind of combination is called a *harmonic complex.* The highest frequency shared by the members of the complex is called the *fundamental frequency.* The multiples of the fundamental are known as *harmonics.* For the most part, the fundamental determines what we hear as the pitch of the sound, and the harmonics that are present determine its quality. The complex 200, 300, 400 has the same pitch (100 Hz) as the complex 100, 500, 600, 700 but will have a very different quality. *Timbre,* this quality, is what we hear as the difference in sound between two different kinds of instruments playing the same note.

Most of the sounds we hear (and produce) are noise. Noise can have various qualities depending on how many frequencies are present and what the range of frequencies is; /s/ and /š/ are both noisy but occupy different frequency ranges. How many frequencies are present around a central frequency determines the *bandwidth* of the noise. It can best be illustrated by using a *spectrogram,* as in Figure 6.3, a graphic display of energy present at each frequency (y-axis) with respect to time (x-axis). (A spectrogram is produced by a *spectrograph,* a machine sensitive to

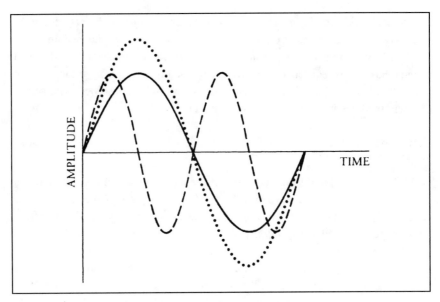

Figure 6.2. Frequency and Amplitude Relations in Sine Waves

NOTE: The solid and dotted lines have the same frequency and different amplitudes. The solid and dashed lines have the same amplitude and different frequencies.

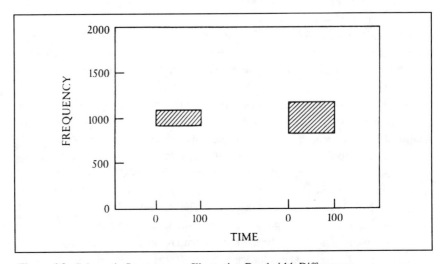

Figure 6.3. Schematic Spectrograms Illustrating Bandwidth Differences

NOTE: Both sounds have the same central frequency, 1,000 Hz. The one on the right has a greater bandwidth.

energies in different frequency ranges.) Figure 6.3 displays schematized spectrograms of two sounds with the same (1,000 Hz) central frequency and different bandwidths—the narrower bandwidth will sound less noisy, closer to a pure tone, than the wider bandwidth.

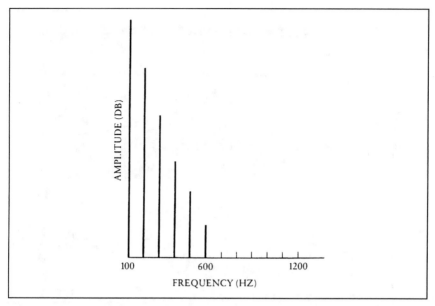

Figure 6.4. Glottal Power Spectrum for the First 600 Hz
NOTE: There is energy up to 3,000 Hz, but it is not displayed.

Our discussion of complex sounds indicates that we need to be able to consider three parameters simultaneously: We need to know how the *frequency* and *amplitude* of each component, or the complex as a whole, change over *time.* A two-dimensional drawing, a graph, allows convenient display of only two dimensions. So, in acoustics, different displays are used, depending on which of the two one wants to focus on. Spectrograms quantitatively show frequency changes over time, but qualitatively display amplitude, in the darkness of the bands. To show how much energy (or amplitude) is present at each frequency, we use a display called a *power spectrum,* in which energy is depicted on the y-axis and frequency on the x-axis; this display ignores time.

Figure 6.4 displays a power spectrum for the glottis, the amount of energy for frequencies passed through a "typical" larynx. The figure indicates that as air passes between the vocal folds, many frequencies are emitted, with decreasing amplitude as frequency increases. *Thus the glottis is a noisy source.*

To round out our discussion of displays of sound, Figure 6.5 shows a waveform, spectrogram, and waterfall display of the sound /ga/. The waveform display emphasizes amplitude changes (y-axis) over time (x-axis), with frequency interpretable as regularity in distance between amplitude peaks. As mentioned, the spectrogram emphasizes frequency changes over time. The waterfall display presents all three parameters at once, through depth perspective. Frequency is displayed on the x-axis, amplitude on the y-axis; both change in time on the z-axis, moving diagonally.

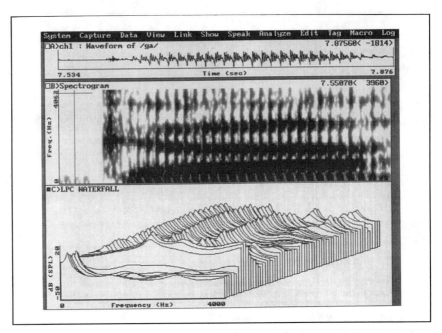

Figure 6.5. Waveform (Top), Spectrogram (Middle), and Waterfall (Bottom) Displays of the Consonant-Vowel Syllable, /ga/

SOURCE: Figure courtesy Kay Elemetrics Corp.

NOTE: A waveform shows amplitude changes (y-axis) with respect to time (x-axis), with frequency changes hard to determine. A spectrogram shows frequency (y-axis) with respect to time (x-axis). A waterfall display, by using a depth dimension, depicts all three parameters: Time is the x-axis; amplitude, the y-axis; and frequency, the z-axis. These were made using Key Elemetrics' CSL.

Resonance

All objects vibrate and vibrate best at a particular frequency, called a *resonance.* Which frequency is the resonance frequency for an object is determined by the object's size and elasticity. If you consider the bars on a xylophone, the resonance concept should be clear: They are made of the same material and are excited by the same source, the blow of a hammer. The blow of the hammer is noisy; it contains many frequencies. Each bar will pick out a frequency from this noise to respond to, its resonance frequency. The larger bars of the xylophone naturally vibrate more slowly than the smaller ones because of their size, their inertia. Although the difference in vibration rate is probably too fast to see, you can hear it: The smaller ones have a higher sound than the larger. The important point is that the vibration rate an object resonates to is determined by the *object's* properties, such as its size.

Some objects can easily be made to vibrate—air vibrates readily to a number of frequencies in response to the use of very little force. Vibration of fluids requires a little more force, and fluids vibrate best at lower frequencies than air. (This is why things sound muffled and deeper when you are under water: The muffling comes from the inability of the low-force sounds to affect your ear through water; the deepening, from the better transmission of lower frequencies.) Vibration of solids is possible but requires still greater force. If a wave contains sufficient force, it can cause any object to vibrate, but a wave of the resonance frequency of the object needs less force to make it vibrate than waves of other frequencies. Virtuoso singers smash glasses by concentrating vocal force into the resonance frequency of the glass. This causes the glass molecules to vibrate, and because glass is rigid, it cannot tolerate the internal vibration and maintain its structure, so it shatters.

Objects are not usually "pure." For instance, a glass of water has several factors contributing to its resonance properties: the density of the glass, the amount of water in it, and the size of the column of air above the water. The vocal tract too is complex: The tissues are soft in some places (the tongue) and rigid in others (the teeth); there are air pockets; and, as we noted, the tissues may be more or less fluid-filled.

The complexity of the object is important when considering sound because several things may happen to a sound when it hits an object: It may cause the object to vibrate, the vibration of the object adding to the power of the wave; it may pass through the object, causing some internal part (like a trapped column of air) to vibrate and thus never escape; or it may bounce off the object and back to us. The first is the property of *resonance,* the second of *absorption,* and the third of *reflection* or *echoes.* As we fill an empty room with objects, more sound gets absorbed, which is why empty, but not furnished, houses echo. These phenomena are important for understanding speech because it is shaped by resonance, absorption, and reflection properties of the vocal tract.

The effect that an object has on sound waves is called its *filter characteristics.* The filter characteristics may be described by a *transfer function,* as in Figure 6.6. This shows for the vocal tract in the shape for the schwa that energies at frequencies of 500 Hz, 1,500 Hz, and 2,500 Hz are passed but that energies at intermediate frequencies are lost through absorption or reflection. The loss is called *damping.*

Resonances of the Vocal Tract

From the preceding we can see that sound quality is determined by two things: the waves emitted by the source and the filter characteristics of the environment. So, if the glottal output (Figure 6.4) is input to the transfer function of Figure 6.6, energies at the frequencies emitted by the glottis and damped by the filter will be weak, and energies at the filter's resonances will be enhanced, illustrated in Figure 6.7.

When we speak we change the filter characteristics of the vocal tract and modify the sounds emitted. In all cases the source is the same—air we exhale from our lungs. Because the source is noisy, as the glottal transfer function indicates, there are many frequencies present for modification by the vocal tract filters. Sometimes we make that air vibrate through our larynx, picking up the resonances of the glottis; sometimes we push it through our nose, picking up a nasal resonance; sometimes we produce a small back cavity and large front cavity in our mouth by closing the mouth off with the back of the tongue; and sometimes we make a large back cavity by closing the mouth at the lips. In the same way we may take a single source—air blowing (in a flute), a finger plucking a string (harp), a hammer hitting a xylophone, or a finger tapping a glass—and change the quality of the sound by changing the

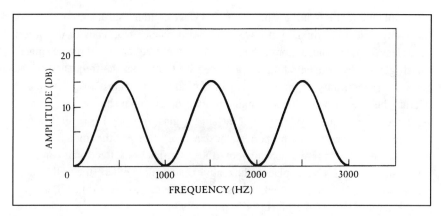

Figure 6.6. Vocal Tract Transfer Function for the Vowel /ə/ (as in "sofa")

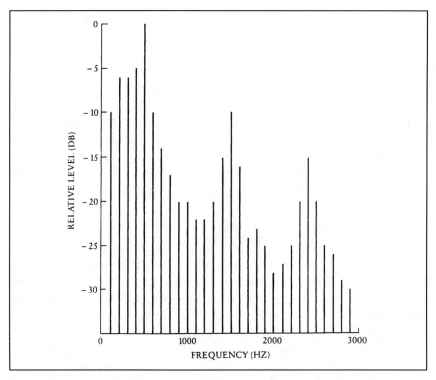

Figure 6.7. Output of the Glottal Source of Figure 6.4 (Including the Higher Frequencies Not Displayed) Passed Through the Transfer Function of Figure 6.6

length of the tube (placing the finger over one hole or another on the flute), the length of the string, the size of the bar, or the amount of water in the glass.

The natural resonant frequencies of the vocal tract are called *formant frequencies*. They arise from changes in the vocal tract and change by changing the length of the vocal tract. We next examine a simplified mathematical derivation of the

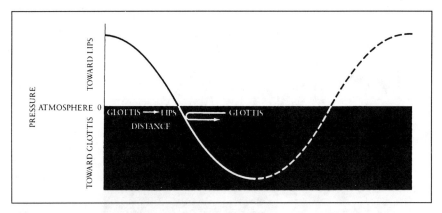

Figure 6.8. Schematic Pressure Wave With a Closed Glottis (Peak Pressure) and Open Lips (Minimum Pressure)

NOTE: The wave moves toward the lips (positive pressure, depicted with white background) and back to the glottis (negative pressure, depicted with black background), together a half wavelength. The dotted line is added just to illustrate a complete cycle.

formant frequencies for a given vocal tract length (Fant, 1956, 1973; Lieberman & Blumstein, 1988; Stevens & House, 1961). (You may skip the next section without losing continuity.)

Deriving Formant Frequencies

The vocal tract can be considered a tube, closed on one end (the lung or larynx end) and opened on the other (the mouth end) for vowels. When we expel air from the lungs into the mouth, we create a pressure, which you can feel on your cheeks and lips if you close your lips and nose and exhale. The air creating the feeling of pressure is moving in two directions, toward the lips and also back toward the larynx. Pressure moving toward the lips we will call positive; a move in the other direction, negative. Atmospheric pressure, the normal air pressure, is zero.

Shortly after expulsion of air, the pressure equalizes at all points in the vocal cavity, until the next perturbation. If perturbations occur slowly, as at low frequencies, there is time to equalize. If there are rapid changes in pressure, as at high frequencies, there is no time to equalize.

If we graph a sound wave's course in the mouth, air pressure (y-axis) versus distance from larynx (x-axis), we get something that looks like a sine wave, as in Figure 6.8 (a sine wave starting later in the cycle than in Figure 6.2; the display indicates a full cycle, back to the wave's starting point). This shows a pressure wave for vowels; the lips are open. There is maximum pressure at the larynx (glottis) if the vocal cords are closed, and zero (atmospheric pressure) at the lips, the point where the line turns from black to white, if they are open. The pressure moves in two directions; the negative represents the wave moving back in the mouth. The "peak" pressure for the back flow is indicated by the lowest *dip*. You can see that the figure resembles a sine wave, with the distance between the larynx and the lips equal to a quarter of the length of the full wave.

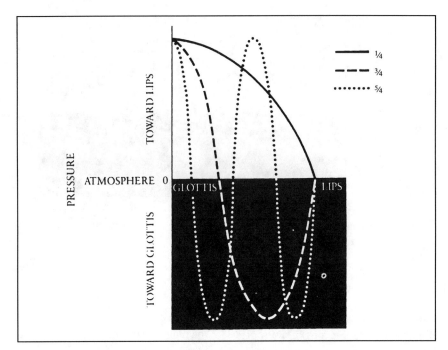

Figure 6.9. A Subset of the Set of Waves Each of Which Has Minimum Pressure at the Lips and Maximum Pressure at the Glottis

NOTE: This illustrates how ¼ of a low-frequency wave, ¾ of a medium-frequency wave, and 1¼ of a high-frequency wave conform to the same constraints.

What is exciting here is that the pressure constraints of the mouth determine the resonance properties. Waves whose characteristics correspond to the pressure points in the mouth will pass untransformed—they are the resonances or formants. Waves whose characteristics do not correspond will get lost in the pressure changes imposed by the vocal tract and will be damped. This applies only to frequencies above about 300 Hz, because lower frequencies permit the pressure changes to equalize between perturbations, so they may pass untransformed.

For frequencies above 300 Hz, as I said, only those that change from peak to zero pressure, that is, go through a quarter cycle, between glottis and lips will pass. This is true for a *class of sine waves*: one that goes through ¼ cycle in the length of the vocal tract, one that goes through ¾ cycle in the length of the vocal tract, one that goes through ⁵⁄₄ cycle in the length of the vocal tract, and so forth, as in Figure 6.9. All we need is a maximum at one end and a zero at the other, regardless of how many ups and downs there are in between. To compute the frequencies of this class of waves, we must know the length of the vocal tract (17 cm for the average adult male). This means that the largest wave that fits will have a wavelength of 4×17 cm (¼ of it fits in 17 cm). We also must know the speed of sound (roughly 34,000 cm/sec). Frequency = 1/wavelength, so the frequency of the first resonance is $34,000/(4 \times 17) = 500$ Hz; of the second, $3 \times 34000/(4 \times 17) = 1,500$; of the third, $5 \times 34000/(4 \times 17) = 2,500$, as we saw for the schwa.

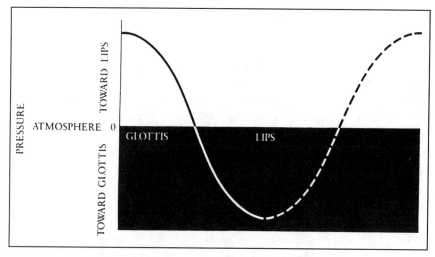

Figure 6.10. Schematic Pressure Wave for Closed Glottis and Closed Lips

NOTE: As in Figure 6.7, the wave travels in both directions, with movement toward the glottis indicated by the negative image. There will be a maximum deviation from zero (a peak or a valley) at lips and glottis (because both are closed). The dotted line, once again, indicates a full cycle; here half of it is in the mouth.

For consonants, the tube is not completely open. If it is closed at the lips as for labials, there is a pressure peak at the glottis and at the lips, as in Figure 6.10, which is half a sine wave. Again, a class of sine waves has this pressure form: one for which a half wave fits in the vocal tract, one for which the whole wave fits, one for which one and a half waves fit, and so on—even multiples of a half. The frequencies corresponding to these wavelengths will be $n \times 34000/(2 \times 17) = 1,000$ Hz, 2000 Hz, 3,000 Hz, for $n = 1, 2, 3$. So if we combine the closed tube (bilabial) and the open tube (vowel) to make a syllable like /bə/, we would expect to see initially a band at 300 Hz (the low frequency emitted by the glottis and not affected by the pressure characteristics in the vocal tract), and one starting at 1,000, 2,000, and 3,000. As we move into the vowel we should maintain the low frequency and add a 500 Hz band, a 1,500 Hz band, and a 2,500 Hz band while losing the 1,000 Hz and 2,000 Hz bands. Because the move from the consonant to the vowel is smooth, we might expect an even transition—the 1,000 Hz band will change into the 1,500 Hz one, and the 2,000 Hz band into the 2,500 Hz one. Examination of the labial-vowel spectrograms in Figures 6.11 and 6.12 in the next section will show that our calculations are roughly accurate. One important difference is that the spectrograms display /a/ and our calculations have assumed neutral position /ə/.

Note that if the vocal tract is shorter because the person is smaller or has retracted his or her lips in a smile, or if it constricts farther back as for /d/ or /g/, the length of the wave described by the two pressure maxima would decrease because the distance between the two maxima decreases. A decrease in wavelength means an increase in frequency, so we should expect a formant frequency rise. You may check the spectrograms in the next section to verify these predictions.

Spectrographic Properties

The sound signal is very complex, containing many frequencies and many modifications of them by the vocal tract. (The preceding discussion of a closed-at-one-end tube or fully open tube represents a substantial simplification. We have not, and will not, consider interactions of frequencies, or the fact that with closure in the middle of the mouth, two chambers are created with pressure characteristics that can interact.) In Chapter 7 we will consider which changes are perceptually relevant, that is, which acoustic information needs to be present to hear a /b/ or an /a/ or whatever. To begin to consider the question it is worth examining spectrograms of real speech.

Stop consonants. Figure 6.11 displays spectrograms of the stop consonants before the vowel /a/ spoken by an adult male speaker. Recall that a spectrogram displays the energy at different frequencies (y-axis) with respect to time (x-axis). Energy amplitude is indicated by the relative darkness; white is no energy, black much energy, and so forth. Notice that each spectrogram is generally gray: Gray indicates energy, and the gray field indicates that there is some energy at most frequencies. Complete white indicates a place where the vocal tract has absorbed the energy, known as *zeros, antiformants,* or *antiresonances.* The darkest bands are places where the energy is maintained or amplified, and these are the resonances or formant frequencies.

Notice that for each syllable there are several formants, the class of waves passed by the particular pressure configurations of the vocal tract, which we computed in the last section. Formants are usually counted from the lowest frequency (= the first) to the highest. The central frequency in the band is usually used as the formant frequency.

Obvious on each of the spectrograms are regular gray striations, running vertically. These represent the energy released when the vocal cords open; the white between them represents the absence of energy while the vocal cords are closed. Notice that they are *periodic*—they appear regularly. You might also notice their absence in the initial portion of the voiceless stops /pa/, /ta/, and /ka/: For the first quarter inch or so of these spectrograms, most obviously on /ta/, there is an even, nonperiodic energy distribution. Recall that for voiceless sounds the vocal cords do not vibrate, so we should not expect to see the gray striations until voicing begins for the vowel.

The next thing you might notice is that the formants are similarly shaped for each place of articulation: For /ba/ and /pa/, /da/ and /ta/, and /ga/ and /ka/, trace the dark bands through the noise portion into the striped portion on the voiceless consonants. For /ba/ and /pa/, there is a large, heavy, straight band crossing the 1,000 Hz line, another band that seems to start at about 2,200 Hz, which then rises to 2,600 Hz, and another straight band at 3,200 Hz. As we computed in the last section, as we shift from consonant to vowel there is a shift in the pressure waves best passed (½-wave class for consonants to ¼-wave class for vowels). The shift is seen in the first half inch of each picture, as a diagonally moving band, known as the *transition.*

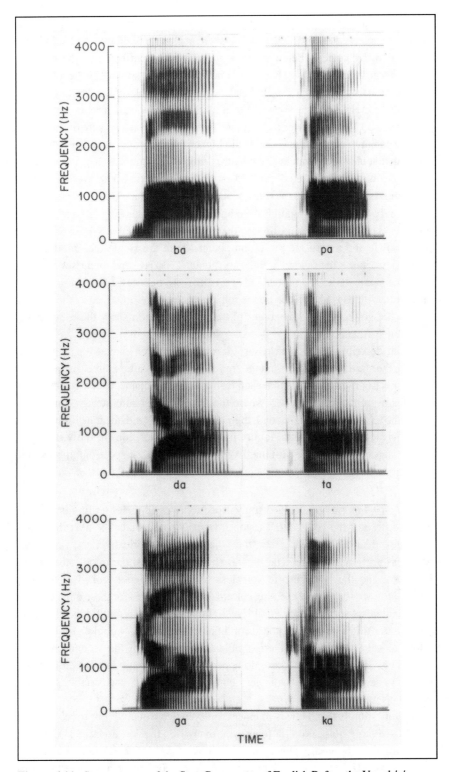

Figure 6.11. Spectrograms of the Stop Consonants of English Before the Vowel /a/

For alveolar and velar consonants, the closure is farther back than the lips, so the distance between the glottis and peak pressure at closure is shorter. As I said in the last section, frequencies below 300 Hz are relatively unaffected by the pressure points because the pressure has had time to equalize, so for all the places of articulation in these spectrograms, the bands below 300 Hz look similar: The lowest band is at about 200 Hz; when the vowel starts, it splits apart, making a transition to 750 Hz.

Above 300 Hz, the shorter the distance between the peak pressure of the glottis and the peak pressure at the closure, the higher the frequency that can be passed. For both alveolar and velar consonants, the second band starts higher (indicative of the shorter distance), centered at 1,700 and falling to about 1,000, overlapping the first band. For /da/ and /ta/, the third, wobbly band also starts higher than the third band for /ba/ and /pa/ but again falls to about the same place. For /ga/ and /ka/, the third formant does not start higher than it did for the labials (the resonance properties of the mouth are more complicated than the single-tube model I described) but meets the second at the start (about 1,700 Hz) and then rises to 2,300 Hz. (The single dark band in /ba/ and /pa/ is likely to be *two* formants, too close to differentiate. This is likely because the same vocal tract has produced all the sounds; all use the vowel /a/; and the other places of articulation show these as clearly separable formants.)

In our description it was necessary to refer to two frequencies for most of the sounds, the starting frequency and the frequency attained after a time. Examination of the spectrograms indicates that each formant has two connected parts, a part that changes in frequency and a part where the frequency remains steady. The first is called the transition, and the second, the *steady state*. As I said, the transition reflects the movement from the initial mouth position to the position for the vowel. The steady states represent the sustained vowel and, for these spectrograms, should occur at roughly the same frequencies, because the vowel is the same.

Other consonants. Figure 6.12 displays spectrograms of the other English consonants in front of the vowel /a/. The top row shows the labials, the next the dental fricatives, then the alveolars, then the voiceless palatal fricative, and finally the voiceless alveolar affricate. The far left shows the nasals, the middle the voiced fricatives, and the far right the voiceless fricatives. Having looked at the stop consonants, we should be expecting certain acoustic features for these other classes. For the labials, the transitions should be slightly rising or straight; for the alveolars, the first transition should rise, the second fall, and the third "wobble"; for the back (close to velar) consonants, there should be a meeting of the second and third transitions. As you can see, these do appear in the spectrograms. We should also expect to see noise for the voiceless consonants initially, and striations for the voiced, as we do.

The question is this: How is manner conveyed acoustically? For fricatives, you should see more noise initially (energy at many frequencies, no stripes) than you do for the stops or nasals. This is most obvious on /ša/ and /ča/, where the noise is below 4,000 Hz, but may also be seen on /va/, /fa/, /θa/, and /sa/ (where the noise is less concentrated and predominantly at higher frequencies, not displayed here).

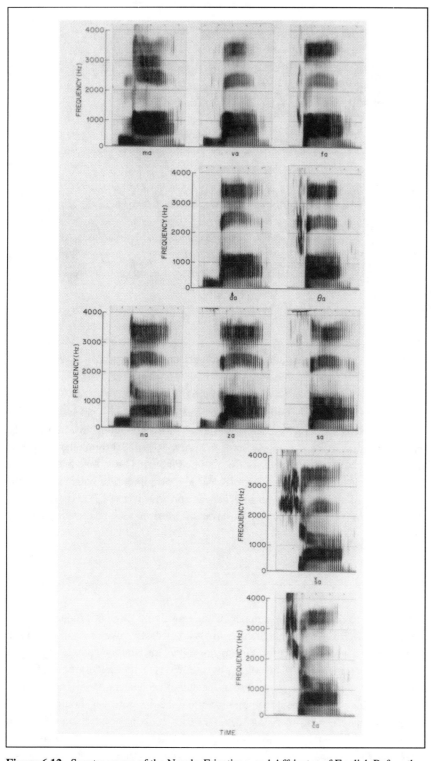

Figure 6.12. Spectrograms of the Nasals, Fricatives, and Affricates of English Before the Vowel /a/

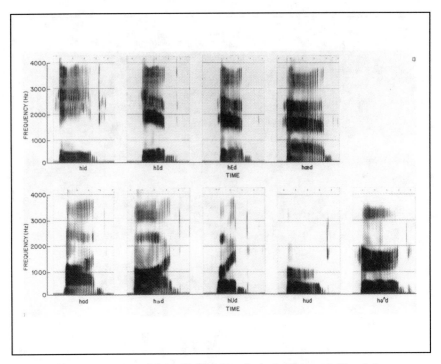

Figure 6.13. Spectrograms of Some English Vowels, in the Context h-Vowel-d

If you contrast the nasals with the voiced fricatives, you see what looks like an earlier and weaker energy at each of the nasal formant frequencies, particularly obvious for /ma/. These are nasal resonances; there is "leak" through the nose after voicing onset but before the release. Reexamine Figure 6.11 and note that this does not happen for the stops; rather, the release is abrupt, sometimes with a short burst of energy (about 1,750 Hz for /ga/ and /ka/ and spread between 1,500 Hz and 3,000 Hz for /ta/). *Bursts* characterize stops; *nasal murmurs,* nasals; and *frication noise,* fricatives.

Vowel

Vowels. Figure 6.13 shows a number of the vowels of English produced in the context h-vowel-d. As you may recall, "h" is a voiceless vowel, so we should see no transitions in initial position but noise-excited formants switching to striped formants at voicing onset. (The noise is most obvious on the spectrograms of /hɛd/ and /hæd/.) We should see transitions at the end of each spectrogram, appropriate to /d/. Because the consonant is in final position, the first formant should fall to its offset frequency instead of rising from its onset frequency, and there should be similar reversals for the other formants. Note the difference in transitions for /d/ in /hid/ and /d/ in /həd/, for example—an instance of context sensitivity of the consonant to the vowel.

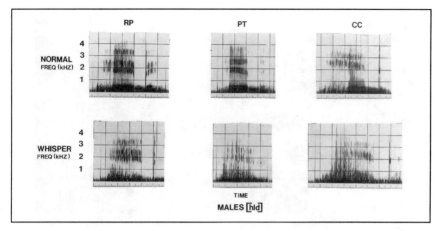

Figure 6.14. Spectrograms of the Syllable /hɪd/ Spoken and Whispered by Three Male Speakers
SOURCE: From Tartter (1991).

Aside from the change in transitions for /d/ across vowels, we can see that the steady state frequencies differ for each vowel. For /i/ the first formant is low, rising some for /ɪ/, /ɛ/, and /æ/. The second and third formants fall from /i/ through /u/. The second formant, for /i/, for instance, seems to be centered just above 2,000 Hz; for /ɪ/, on 2,000 Hz; for /ɛ/, just under it; and for /a/, as we have noted, almost at 1,000 Hz. If you worked through the mathematics, note that the tongue is highest (a sort of constriction and pressure maximum) in the front for /i/, creating a short front cavity (between the constriction and the lips) and a high second formant, while for /u/, with the "constriction" in the back and liprounding, the front cavity is longest, creating the lowest second formant, which, in fact, blends with the first formant in the display.

Nonsegmental differences. The next set of spectrograms shows the effects of vocal tract differences arising independently of phonetic maneuvers. Figure 6.14 displays examples of the word /hɪd/ spoken and whispered by three different adult males. You can see that each speaker has his own speech style; syllable duration, degree of final release, and degree of initial aspiration are maintained across the two registers. You can also see that the *relative* positions of the first three formant frequencies are similar across the three speakers and the two registers, despite the fact that their fundamental frequencies are different in normal register and *absent* in whispering: CC's fundamental is obviously higher if you note the invisibility of the spacing of the striations. (Whispering does cause a slight, but reliable, rise in all formant frequencies; Tartter, 1991.) The striking difference between whispered and normal speech is, for whispered speech, the absence of the striations (arising from periodic pulsing of the vocal folds in normal voiced speech) and the presence throughout of the random gray, noisy energy of the whispered airflow. The similar formant frequency patterns reflect the vocal tract shapes, the filter characteristics, which are relatively constant across register.

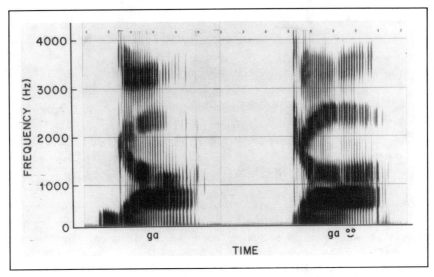

Figure 6.15. Spectrograms of /ga/ Produced by a Male With a Neutral Facial Expression (Left) or While Smiling (Right)

Figure 6.15 shows another effect, shortening the vocal tract, comparing a male's production of /ga/ with a straight face (left) and with a smile (right) (after Tartter, 1980). As our mathematical model suggested, retracting the lips results in a shortening of the vocal tract, which shortens the wavelength that fits between the peak pressure (at the larynx) and zero pressure (out of the vocal tract). Shorter wavelength means higher frequency, which is visible in all three formants. For example, the second formant of the straight-faced /ga/ crosses the 1,000 Hz line, while for the smiled /ga/ it is clearly above it, showing the increase in frequency. The change produced by smiling did not affect the characteristic divergence of the second and third formants. Smiling and /ga/ thus are conveyed simultaneously in the pattern, another instance of context sensitivity, because smiling clearly affects the formant frequency pattern.

Summary

We have looked at some simplified acoustic theory for understanding the sound signal for speech. We noted that there are two contributing and almost independent factors: the source (vocal cord vibration or noise) and the filter (the shape and length of the vocal tract). Manipulations of the source give rise to changes in the periodic pulsing visible on spectrograms either as pitch changes or as changes from voicelessness to voicing, very visible when we contrast whispered and normal speech. Manipulations of the filter by constricting in different places, protruding or retracting the lips (lengthening or shortening the "tube"), or opening or closing the nasal passages affect the position of the vocal resonances or formants. On the spectrograms we see effects of the resonances *at constriction* in the bursts for stops and the frication noise for fricatives. We also see the addition of resonance contributed

---

Box 6.2. Acoustic Measures and Terms

— *Waveform:* Display of amplitude changes over time.
— *Spectrogram:* Display of frequency changes over time, with amplitude qualitatively shown as a grayness change.
— *Power spectrum:* Display of the energy of different frequencies.
— *Waterfall display:* A "3-D" characterization of frequency and energy changes over time.
— *Noise:* Random combination of frequencies.
— *Fundamental frequency:* The highest frequency shared by tones in a complex.
— *Harmonics:* Multiples of the fundamental in a tonal complex.
— *Resonance:* The frequency that an object vibrates to.
— *Formant frequencies:* The resonances of the vocal tract.
— *Source-filter theory:* The airflow provides a stimulating, noisy set of frequencies (the source), which the vocal tract selects according to its resonance characteristics (the filter). Source and filter are relatively independent. We change the resonance characteristics of the vocal tract by moving lips, tongue, jaw, and velum—introducing cavities and changing their size.

---

by the nose in nasals. The place of constriction also affects the frequencies of the formants; so, as the mouth moves from a consonant to a vowel (of a different place), we see frequency changes, the transitions. The pattern on the spectrogram is determined jointly by the consonant constriction and the vowel "constriction," so the spectrogram for the same consonant in different vowel environments will be different: context sensitivity. The pattern on the spectrograms is also determined by the size of the vocal tract, changing with facial expression and between individuals.

DISTINCTIVE FEATURE THEORY

The last two sections have described articulatory and acoustic aspects of speech under the general framework of linguistic distinctive feature theory (Jakobson et al., 1951/1969). I have implicitly employed some assumptions of the theory; here I make them, and where I deviated from them, explicit.

Phonemes may be considered bundles of subphonemic features. /b/ is a voiced bilabial stop consonant, /p/ a voiceless bilabial stop consonant, /t/ a voiceless alveolar stop consonant, and so on. Rather than consider each phoneme as a minimal sound unit, we may consider it a combination of *relatively independent* subphonemic features. Thus the difference between /bæt/ and /pæt/ may be viewed not as a difference in initial phonemes but as a difference in voicing in the initial segment. This implies that /bæt/ and /pæt/ are as different as /væt/ and /fæt/ (also differing in voicing), and more similar than /bæt/ and /tæt/, which differ in two features, voicing and place of articulation.

Box 6.3. Principal Articulatory Features and Their Acoustic Manifestations

— *Consonant-vowel:* Consonants are produced with closure in the vocal tract; vowels, with an open vocal tract. Vowels may be steadily produced and result in steady state formant frequencies. Consonants are characterized by acoustic change, formant transitions, movement in or out of a vowel.

— *Consonant manner of articulation:* How the closure is made.

— *Stop consonants or plosives:* Complete seal of oral and nasal cavities; air builds up behind the seal. The sudden release of air results in a noise burst and aspiration after the release.

— *Nasal consonants:* Oral cavity is completely sealed, but the velum is lowered so that air escapes through the nose. Formants are damped by the closed oral cavity and narrow nasal cavity, and lowered some—the nasal murmur and nasal resonances.

   — (Vowels maximally contrast with stops and nasals: complete opening versus complete closure. Stops greatly contrast with nasals: closed versus open nasal passages.)

— *Fricative consonants:* A narrow opening, through which air and sound travel turbulently. Characterized by a duration of noise during the obstruction, the turbulent airflow.

— *Affricate consonants:* Complete brief closure, moving to partial obstruction (stop + short fricative). Characterized by burst and noise, of shorter duration than for fricatives.

— *Laterals/glides/semivowels:* Greater degree of opening than for the fricatives but not totally open as for the vowels. For /l/, for example, the tongue tip makes contact with the roof of the mouth, but air flows nonturbulently around the sides. Characterized by long formant transitions—no burst or noise.

— *Voicing:* When the vocal folds begin to vibrate periodically relative to the release of air/sound energy. In prevoiced consonants, vibration begins before the closure is produced. In voiced consonants, the vibration and opening of the oral cavity are relatively simultaneous. In voiceless consonants, the oral cavity begins to open before the vocal folds start vibrating. Vocal fold vibration appears as regular gray stripes on spectrograms or as periodicity on a waveform. Voiced sounds have more low-frequency energy than voiceless sounds, a visible fundamental frequency, and less noise. Voicing is measured as voice onset time—the time difference between onset of energy and onset of periodic pulsing.

— *Place of articulation:* The location of the closure or obstruction. Different places of articulation produce different second and third (and higher) formant frequencies.

Vowel Features

— *Tongue height:* While the vocal tract is open, the tongue can create a larger or smaller cavity by changing its position relative to the roof of the mouth. The higher the tongue, the lower the first formant frequency.

(continued)

Box 6.3 Continued

— *Tongue position:* While the vocal tract is open, one part of the tongue may be nearer the roof of the mouth. The further to the front the highest portion of the tongue is (the smaller the front cavity resonance), the higher the second formant frequency.

— *Tense-lax:* In tense vowels, the tongue is more displaced from neutral position, producing less centralized formant frequencies. Tense vowels are longer than lax vowels.

— *Liprounding:* Protruding the lips, lengthening the vocal tract. Lowers formant frequencies.

— *Retroflexion:* Lowers third formant transition; retroflexed phonemes are marked by greater transition excursions.

— *Schwa:* Most centralized vowel.

— *Point vowels:* /i/, /a/, /u/, most extreme vowels.

— *Diphthongs:* Smoothly blended double vowels, like "i," ay.

Nonsegmental Features

— *Suprasegmentals:* Change in vibration rate of the vocal cords over the length of the utterance (= pitch contour); change in energy expended over the length of the utterance (= loudness contour); change in rate of segment production (= speech rate).

— *Register:* Differential tensions on the vocal cords to allow air to pass without vibration, with average or extreme vibration, or with vibration in parts.

— *Facial expression:* Pouting lowers formant frequencies; smiling raises them.

— *Individual differences:* Larger people have longer vocal tracts and weightier larynxes, deeper voices. Swelling of the vocal folds can also deepen the pitch.

Critical to the flexibility of the description of phonemes or syllables as a *bundle of features* is the assumption that at some level the *features are independent* of one another, and, as the preceding discussions indicated, this may be reasonable. Closing the lips or touching the tongue tip to the roof of the mouth does not appear to depend on whether the vocal cords are vibrating or whether the nasal resonance chamber is open. Acoustically, the direction and location of the formant transitions (place information) do not appear dependent on the presence of periodic pulsing or aspiration (voicing), or on the existence of frication noise, a burst or a nasal murmur (manner). Thus each linguistic feature has its own articulatory and acoustic properties, apart from other linguistic features.

Distinctive feature theory bundles the myriad different sounds of languages into universal discrete packages. Each package represents an abstraction from both the acoustic and the articulatory description. For example, we discussed place of articulation with respect to the precise position of closure—bilabial, dental, alveolar, palatal, velar—or, more broadly, front (before the alveolar ridge), middle (between the soft palate and the alveolar ridge), and back (at or behind the soft

Table 6.2 Analysis of Place as Two Binary Features

	± Compact	± Grave
b	−	+
d	−	−
g	+	+

NOTE: The pattern of pluses and minuses is unique for each phoneme. Compact and grave are each the unmarked value (−); the marked, +, values, respectively, are diffuse and acute.

palate). The second description constitutes more of an abstraction, as you can see. Distinctive feature theory is yet more abstract, describing place of articulation, as shown in Table 6.2, in terms of two binary-valued features (recall from Chapter 4 that linguists find binary features simpler to specify in UG and to set parameters for during language acquisition). The features abstract *both* articulatory and acoustic characteristics.

One feature of back consonants is +*compact:* The back place of articulation is tied to a single midfrequency prominent energy, the coming together of the second and third formants we noted in the spectrogram. Front and mid-places of articulation are −compact, or *diffuse:* Energy is spread in the midfrequency region, prominent energ*ies* at separate second and third formants.

Compact-diffuse separates back consonants from mid- and front consonants; *grave-acute* separates mid-consonants from front and back. The acute feature notes the division of the oral cavity into smaller regions, on either side of the constriction, resulting in high-frequency energies above the first formant. Its counterpart, grave, marks an undivided vocal tract with large resonance chamber (and low formant frequency), before (for front consonants) or after the constriction (for back consonants).

The description of articulatory-acoustic characteristics in terms of such features is more abstract than the description we presented earlier because there are many different specific articulatory gestures that could result in a description like "divided vocal cavity." The concept behind distinctive feature theory is that oppositions such as constriction versus no constriction, division versus no division, single prominent energy versus many energies, and so on are basic, universal oppositions that all languages employ in some way. We should note that the precise features best used to describe the articulatory and acoustic aspects of speech have been a matter of some debate among linguists (see Chomsky & Halle, 1991, for one description; Jakobson et al., 1951/1969, for another).

A second notion of distinctive feature theory is *markedness.* For each feature, one of the values, by convention the negative one, is considered more basic or natural than the other. It is called *unmarked.* Relative to the marked value, the unmarked value occurs more frequently across languages and within a language, is less complex acoustically and articulatorily, is more likely to occur with neutralization (in unstressed syllables, for example), and is acquired first. Therefore, consonants are marked relative to vowels: Babies "cry" vowels before they utter consonants; vowels are simpler in that they may be articulated with an open vocal tract and result in steady resonances; the simplest syllable is a single vowel; and vowel variants are more frequent than consonants (do not get confused by the number of each in our only quasi-phonemic alphabet!). It is interesting to note that the characteristics of the unmarked features, the "basic" value, are analogous to the "basic level" in semantics: more frequent, earlier acquired, and simpler to image (perceptual analogue to acoustic property) or pantomime (motor analogue to articulation).

Implicit in the framework is a semihierarchical ordering of features, of unmarked to marked values, and also of features relating to constriction properties (like grave-acute, compact-diffuse, and the various manner of articulation features) subordinate to the consonant-vowel feature, whether there is a constriction at all. Note, however, that these features, while subordinate to the consonant-vowel feature, apply to either member of the category: /i/ with a high-middle tongue tip divides (incompletely) the vocal tract and is acute compared with /u/, a back vowel accompanied by liprounding and resulting in a large, undivided vocal tract. The presumptive hierarchy is therefore only partial because such features can cluster members "separated" by presumptively higher categories.

Distinctive feature theory proposes about 12 features to apply across languages. Each feature polarity characterizes a significant, discrete articulatory property with significant, discrete acoustic consequences. Stevens (1989/1991), an acoustician whose work is grounded in distinctive feature theory, conceptualizes the feature arising from the coincidence of a *quantal* (a sudden jump from one value to another) change in articulation resulting in a quantal acoustic change. That is, there is a range of movement of the articulators, which alters the acoustic signal only slightly and has a small perceptual consequence. Somewhat more extreme movements produce much more extreme acoustic consequences, followed by another area of relative stability with yet more extreme movements.

It is worth considering one more distinctive feature, which cuts across vowel and consonant categories, to illustrate quantal theory. The nasals, semivowels (both consonants), and vowels all group together as *sonorants* (unmarked), characterized by no noise, regardless of whether there is a constriction. Nonsonorants are fricatives, stops, affricates, and voiceless vowels with noisy spectra. According to quantal theory, there is a degree of constriction necessary for turbulent airflow, but *until* that is reached, the airstream will be nonturbulent, regardless of how much movement there is toward that point. It may help to think of this with respect to water dripping: Turning your faucet handle slightly yields a slow drip; more, a faster drip, but still a drip—the drip value of the feature. At some point, turning more turns the drip to a stream, the quantal change, and then stabilizes again because opening the faucet more changes only the quantity (the speed) of the stream, not whether or not it is a stream. Stevens considers that languages have evolved to use such regions of relative stability and quantal change because they allow speakers to be relatively imprecise in articulation within a region and they allow hearers to attend to optimally discriminable changes as relevant to speech.

One criticism we may level at distinctive feature theory, especially from such an evolutionary stand, is its concentration on static articulatory and acoustic configurations, such as an open versus closed vocal tract at a particular point in the

---

Box 6.4. Phonetic Theories

— *Distinctive feature theory:* Each phoneme is represented by a bundle of binary-valued, independent features, abstracting over articulatory and acoustic characteristics. For example, grave = undivided vocal tract, low resonance; acute = divided vocal tract, high resonance. Grave/acute applies to both vowels and consonants (grave = /a/, /b/, /g/; acute = /d/, /i/.

— *Quantal theory:* Existence of distinctive feature change is dictated by acoustic consequences of vocal tract change into a salient perceptual property. Some articulatory changes have small effect; others, immense—the latter are quantal, and yield feature differences, for example, when airflow moves from smooth (sonorant) to turbulent.

— *Markedness:* One of the two values of a feature is more "natural": easier to produce, more common across languages, earlier produced by children. This is unmarked. Vowels are unmarked; consonants marked.

— *Dynamic theories:* Critique feature theory for looking at speech as static. Concentrate on the movement patterns and coarticulation information instead of stable, target configurations.

---

articulation. Speech is dynamic. There are "feature" theories that concentrate on the dynamic relationship of the articulators in determining phonetic segments (Fowler, 1986/1991). Like distinctive feature theory, these emphasize the abstractness of phonetic segments, that what people realize from the sound stream is the vocal-tract configuration producing it. (Thus we can mimic well—see Chapter 8—to synchronize to each other's speech rate and adopt dialectal and stylistic features of the people we affiliate with; we can hear how they make the sound.) However, rather than concentrating on stable properties of the acoustic signal, the regions where there is least evidence of coarticulation, they emphasize the regions where there is most evidence of coarticulation, where the movements of the articulators would be most obvious. In this regard, it is important to note, returning us to the beginning of this section, that one does not produce a distinctive feature in isolation; "grave" does not exist itself but only in the context of consonant or vowel, degree of closure, voicing, and so on. We produce syllables that "are overlapping sets of co-ordinated gestures, where each set of co-ordinated gestures conforms to a phonetic segment" (Fowler, 1986/1991, p. 23).

SOUND STRUCTURE: REVIEW AND OVERVIEW

At this point, we have essentially concluded our discussion of the structure of language, at all levels—semantic, syntactic, and phonetic. You may well be overwhelmed with the complexity of language structure—at the sound level alone. To utter a targeted nonsense word requires a precise coordination of breathing, laryngeal pulsing, and movements of tongue, lip, and velum—each of which has its own individual effect on the sound. To make a syllable or a word sound like standard American English, the King's English, French, or Swahili requires a precise knowledge of the sounds that language employs, the ways they may combine, and the melody or register with which they are spoken. If each morpheme, syllable, or word is learned independently of all others, the memory load is enormous because every language uses a large number of syllables, words, and sentences. If particular elements and rules for combining those elements are learned and then used productively, the task is much reduced.

Let us examine a few examples of this. As I described earlier, the plural morpheme has a number of phonetic realizations in English: [s], [z], [əz] (as well as nothing, as in *deer*). As we observed in Chapter 5, this is true also of the past morpheme—we may mark the past tense by using (among others) the sounds [t], [d], and [əd]. How do we learn which verbs take which past tense and which nouns, which plurals? Examination of the following table may clarify this: In the first column there is a word that may be either a noun or a verb, followed by its plural and past forms, both transcribed. The last four rows contain nonsense words and a native speaker's judgment of their likely plural and past forms. Before looking at them, make the plural and past yourself and see if you agree.

WORD	PLURAL	PAST
dog	dɔgz	dɔgd
tip	tɪps	tɪpt
kiss	kɪsəz	kɪst
cart	caɚts	caɚtəd
wug	wʌgz	wʌgd
wuk	wʌks	wʌkt
wut	wʌts	wʌtəd
wuss	wʌsəz	wʌst

Do you notice a pattern? If you agreed with my intuitions on the nonsense words, you must have absorbed the pattern, at least tacitly, because a random agreement is unlikely. Explicitly, the rule for both plural and past morphemes (this is another morphophonemic rule; our first was changing stress for noun-verb differences) is as follows: (a) Match voicing with the last phoneme in the syllable, and (b) if the last phoneme has the same place and manner of articulation as the sound to be added (alveolar fricative for the plural and alveolar stop for the past), add a schwa and then the voiced phoneme—in this case, voiced because it must match the vowel added, which is voiced. The rule means that we do not have to learn *book-books, plant-plants, seat-seats,* and so forth, separately. The matching rule, as you may recall from the beginning of the chapter, is called assimilation, and languages use assimilation sometimes across more than one phoneme. The addition of the vowel for otherwise identical endings is an instance of the opposite "force," *dissimilation,* which also operates in languages.

Alliteration, the poetic device, selects words so that there is a sound match like assimilation across several phonemes, as does rhyming. A less artificial use of assimilation is in a phenomenon called *vowel harmony,* in which the vowel in the affix is matched to the vowel of the principal morpheme. In an East Sudan language, Moru, we find ma'la'sa (I wash), mɔ' lɔ' s:ɔ' (I served), mi'liite (I wept), and mu'tu'ri (I fear): m + vowel = the prefixed pronoun *I;* which vowel is determined by the verb (Heffner, 1969). (: means lengthen the preceding sound.)

The existence of rules does not mean that all sound combinations are rule-governed. As a language grows and incorporates elements from other languages, exceptions may be introduced or exceptions left as residues. Mao Tse-tung (before we changed how we rendered his name) caused an introduction of a new affricate, /ts/, which does not usually appear in English in initial position. If his name became incorporated into the language, the /ts/ might alter to /č /, a usual English affricate, or /s/, the usual fricative. If many words came in using the /ts/ affricate, we might add that form or replace a form we now use with it. Then it would be productive, that is, used in the generation of new words. The "ed" past is now productive. At one time, past tenses were made by using a vowel change, leaving us the residues *sing-sang-sung, ring-rang-rung, swim-swam-swum.* We no longer do this regularly; it is no longer productive.

It is not my intent to supply an exhaustive list of sound rules but simply to give a hint about how they operate—and a hint at the different levels they may operate on. As I have stated, all languages make use of the same features: These are determined by properties of the vocal tract and auditory system, shared by all human beings. Which features are linguistically distinctive, how they combine, and what level the feature or combination operates on are determined by each language. We do not use /ŋ/ in initial position; consonant clusters like /mb/ initially register changes or tone for phonemic distinctions. There is nothing "natural" about our selection; other languages use these distinctions. Each language selects from the audible group of sounds a set to use to produce words and to convey emotion and syntax.

Selection is constrained in part by production; no language would choose an absolute pitch as phonemic because men, women, or children might not be able to produce that exact note. It is also constrained in part by the desire to be understood: Use of all possible sounds we can produce to convey meaning distinctions would require us to make enormously fine discriminations; classing together some of them allows us to ignore some distinctions. (It has been estimated that all languages use eight or nine distinctive features [Miller, 1956], perhaps indicating the limit of our discrimination capabilities.) Selecting sounds so that there are few words differing only in one feature, so that some features are conveyed redundantly (for example, voicing in both the final phoneme and the plural), enhances the chances of being understood. *Sound selection is a product of two forces: (a) the need to have as few rules or elements as possible to minimize the amount that must be learned (this means that any rule or element introduced is likely to be used over and over again, or be productive), and (b) the desire to maximize discriminability (this means a sufficient number of different elements must be used to be able to tell them apart).*

As we saw in the quantal theory, speech features are constrained by both production and perception.

In this chapter the structure of sound and the utility of that structure for language description were explored. In the next chapter we examine the psychological reality of the sound structure—how we use acoustic features, articulatory features, linguistic distinctive features, phonemes, syllables, and so forth in perceiving and producing language.

REFERENCES

Abercrombie, D. (1982). *Elements of general phonetics.* Chicago: Aldine. (Original work published 1967)

Baken, R. J., & Daniloff, R. G. (1991). *Readings in clinical spectrography of speech.* Joint publication of Singer, San Diego, CA, and Kay Elemetrics, Pine Brook, NJ.

Chomsky, N., & Halle, M. (1991). *The sound pattern of English.* Cambridge: MIT Press.

Eliot, T. S. (1980). *Old Possum's book of practical cats.* London: Faber and Faber. (Original work published 1940)

Fant, C. G. M. (1956). On the predictability of formant levels and spectrum envelopes from formant frequencies. In M. Halle, H. Lunt, & H. MacLean (Eds.), *For Roman Jakobson* (pp. 109-120). The Hague, The Netherlands: Mouton.

Fant, G. (1973). *Speech sounds and features.* Cambridge: MIT Press.

Fowler, C. (1986). An event approach to the study of speech perception from a direct-realist perspective. *Journal of Phonetics, 14,* 3-28. (Reprinted in J. L. Miller, R. D. Kent, & B. S. Atal, Eds., 1991, *Papers in speech communication: Speech perception,* pp. 15-40. Woodbury, NY: Acoustical Society of America)

Heffner, R. S. (1969). *General phonetics.* Madison: University of Wisconsin Press.

Holland, V. (1967). *An explosion of limericks.* New York: Funk & Wagnalls.

Hunt, E., & Agnoli, F. (1991). The Whorfian hypothesis: A cognitive psychology perspective. *Psychological Review, 98,* 377-389.

Jakobson, R., Fant, G., & Halle, M. (1969). *Preliminaries to speech analysis.* Cambridge: MIT Press. (Original work published 1951)

Lieberman, P., & Blumstein, S. E. (1988). *Speech physiology, speech perception, and acoustic phonetics.* New York: Cambridge University Press.

Lisker, L., & Abramson, A. S. (1991). A cross-language study of voicing in initial stops: Acoustical measurements. In R. J. Baken & R. G. Daniloff (Eds.), *Readings in clinical spectrography of speech* (pp. 247-285). Joint publication of Singer, San Diego, CA, and Kay Elemetrics, Pine Brook, NJ.

Miller, G. A. (1956). The magical number seven plus or minus two: Some limits on our capacity for processing information. *Psychological Review, 63,* 81-96.

Rontal, E., Rontal, M., & Rolnick, M. I. (1991). Objective evaluation of vocal pathology using voice spectrography. In R. J. Baken & R. G. Daniloff (Eds.), *Readings in clinical spectrography of speech* (pp. 554-564). Joint publication of Singer, San Diego, CA, and Kay Elemetrics, Pine Brook, NJ.

Stevens, K. N. (1989). On the quantal nature of speech. *Journal of Phonetics, 17,* 3-45. (Reprinted in R. D. Kent, B. S. Atal, & J. L. Miller, Eds., 1991, *Papers in speech communication: Speech production,* pp. 357-400. Woodbury, NY: Acoustical Society of America)

Stevens, K. N., & House, A. S. (1961). An acoustical theory of vowel production and some of its implications. *Journal of Speech and Hearing Research, 4,* 303-320.

Tartter, V. C. (1980). Happy talk: Perceptual and acoustic effects of smiling on speech. *Perception & Psychophysics, 27,* 24-27.

Tartter, V. C. (1991). Identifiability of vowels and speakers from whispered syllables. *Perception & Psychophysics, 49*, 365-372.

Tartter, V. C., & Braun, D. (1994). Hearing smiles and frowns in normal and whisper registers. *Journal of the Acoustical Society of America, 96*, 2102-2107.

Williams, O. (1952). *Immortal poems of the English language.* New York: Washington Square Press.

Yanagihara, N. (1991). Significance of harmonic changes and noise components in hoarseness. In R. J. Baken & R. G. Daniloff (Eds.), *Readings in clinical spectrography of speech* (pp. 534-544). Joint publication of Singer, San Diego, CA, and Kay Elemetrics, Pine Brook, NJ.

STUDY QUESTIONS

---

1. Write your name in phonemic transcription. Then make a schematized spectrogram for the first name (or the first syllable of your first name if your first name is long). (Note that ǰ is a voiced /č/, /w/ is a /b/ with lengthened transitions, and /l/ is a /d/ with lengthened transitions. The other phonemes should appear already in the spectrograms provided.) You should have problems making your spectrogram; discuss the problems and how they relate to context sensitivity. What would the spectrogram look like if your name was spoken by a child?

2. The following is written in phonetic transcription. Translate it back to written English:

a' hæv čozən nat tu 'uz ə pom, wič ma't bi ɚɛkəgna'zd, nɔɚ ɛni wɛlnoʷn pæsəǰ, sɪns ðɛn ɚidʌndɛnsi kʊd hɛlp. si haʷ izi ɪt ɪz tu du "tu bi ɔɚ nat tu bi, ðæt ɪz ðə kwɛsčʌn," fɔɚ ɪnstɪns.

3. Summarize the main tenets of distinctive feature theory: what constitutes a feature; how the feature is an abstraction and a unification of articulatory and acoustic characteristics; what is markedness; how features are quasi hierarchical. Explain how a feature may embody a quantal change or a dynamic speech "event." Why might each language use a small set of features productively?

7

SPEECH PERCEPTION AND PRODUCTION

When next you have the opportunity to talk with a small group of people, pay attention to what is happening during the conversation. How do you understand what each person is saying? Listen as each says, "Hi." They all sound different, which is how you recognize each voice, yet they all obviously say the same thing; you recognize the syllable despite the different voices saying it. What is the same about each articulation?

As the conversation gets beyond the slurred greeting stage, listen to how fast speech is. Average articulation is 900 phonemes per minute (Liberman, Cooper, Shankweiler, & Studdert-Kennedy, 1967/1991). At that rate, individual musical notes would blur (sound like a buzz); they come in too fast for the perceptual system to resolve individual identity. Why doesn't that happen for the phonemes of speech?

You might also think about how the words jump out, clearly set apart from other words. Figure 7.1 shows a spectrogram of a sentence articulated normally. There are spaces on the spectrogram, between acoustic features, such as aspiration and transitions, *within a phoneme* but *not between words*. Where *are* the word boundaries we so clearly hear in the language? The next time you have the chance to eavesdrop on a conversation in a language you do not know, try to figure out where the words are; the boundaries are as hard to locate by ear, when you have no mental dictionary, as they are by eye on the spectrogram. So how do we do it in our own spoken language?

Think too about what you are doing as a participant in the conversation: You have probably contributed your greeting, extracted everyone's phonemes, and glued them together into words, glued the words together into sentences, parsed the sentences to find meaning, looked up the words in the lexicon, started a discourse parse, perhaps contributed your own response—formulating your idea, then finding words and a syntactic form to express the idea, appropriately choreographing your articulators, checking the ongoing conversation for "your turn" to say it without interrupting, and monitoring your audience for their reaction. And at the *same time,* if you have followed my instructions, you have also thought about variation in voices, speech rates, word boundaries, and how you process speech during conversation. How do we do so much so quickly and unconsciously?

And we do it all with very few errors. How often does anyone make a mistake while talking—come out with the wrong word, the wrong phoneme, the wrong intonation, the wrong syntactic frame? When you think about it, you realize that it occurs very seldom actually, although it happens to all of us occasionally. When a slip is made, usually the speaker corrects it, which indicates that in addition to all the things just mentioned, we monitor our own speech (listen to it) to make sure we say what we intended.

In this chapter we will explore the available evidence on how we perform the amazing tasks of perceiving and producing meaningful sound sequences at conversational rates.

LINGUISTIC FEATURES AND PSYCHOLOGICAL REALITY

In Chapter 6, we discussed articulatory and acoustic characteristics of speech features. We saw that they were an abstraction, relating generally to a vocal tract configuration and to broad properties of the sound signal. We also saw that phonetic feature descriptions capture structural properties of the language, say, in accounting for the variants of the plural and the past morpheme as voicing assimilation and place dissimilation. Research into the psychology of speech has focused on the phonetic feature as "primitive," partly because it is the smallest unit and so seems a good starting place, and partly because of its reality in language-structure descriptions. Studies of perception and production of speech also looked to establish the feature as a psychologically meaningful unit.

Features in Speech Perception

There are two principal lines of evidence that features are extracted in speech perception: People rate syllables as more similar the more features they share, and if people mishear a syllable, they tend to get most of its features right, confusing only one, usually place of articulation. Both suggest that people may be hearing syllables feature by feature.

Estimate how different /b/ is from /d/, /m/, /n/, /p/, or /s/. After you make your judgment, you might note that /b/ and /d/ share manner and voicing, /b/ and /p/ share manner and place, /b/ and /n/ share only voicing, and /b/ and /s/ share no

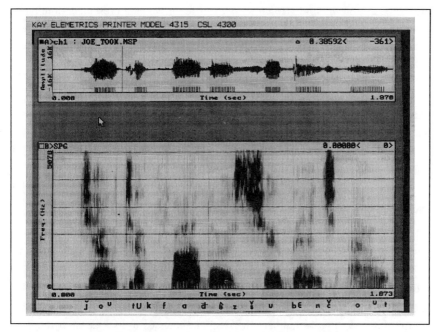

Figure 7.1. Spectrogram of the Sentence "Joe took father's shoe bench out."
NOTE: Note that the pauses, the absence of energy, are not between the words.

features other than consonantal ones. Did your estimate reflect the feature differences such that the more features that distinguished the two sounds, the more different they seemed? According to linguistic feature theory, as presented in the last chapter, if the feature is a speech primitive, double-feature differences should appear more different than single-feature differences, and there should be little difference between different single-feature differences, such as /b/-/d/ and /b/-/m/.

These predictions almost, but not quite, hold. Greenberg and Jenkins (1964) and Mohr and Wang (1968) did find that phonemes distinguished by more feature differences seem more distant psychologically. However, their scaling results (and possibly yours) also suggested that all features are not equal. Manner and voicing distinctions separate consonants more strongly than does place of articulation— consistent perhaps with place being subordinate to manner and voicing. More critically, however, the results support a dependency of one feature on another, inconsistent with the models discussed in the last chapter that suggest feature independence. For example, voiceless stops differing in place of articulation /P/-/t/ seem more different than voiced stops /b/-/d/ differing in the same place feature.

Support for feature extraction and feature dependency has been obtained through examining confusions people make, assuming that the more likely a speech sound is to be confused with another, the closer the two are perceptually. Confusions have been obtained by presenting speech under difficult listening conditions: with noise or filtered to remove high or low frequencies (G. Miller & Nicely, 1955/1991); in divided attention, *dichotic listening,* with different sounds presented simultane-ously to each ear (Studdert-Kennedy & Shankweiler, 1970/1991); and in divided attention tasks where subjects "proofread" meaningful speech, comprehending it while trying to detect deliberate mispronunciations (Cole, 1973).

There are three principal results:

1. If people make a "slip of the ear," they are more likely to report a sound one feature different (/pa/ or /da/ for /ba/) than two (/ta/ or /za/ for /ba/).

2. People are more likely to detect a mispronunciation the more features it has different from the expected word.

3. People are most likely to confuse place of articulation (in stop consonants) and least likely to confuse manner of articulation.

This pattern of results is exemplified in Figure 7.2, a graphic reanalysis by Soli, Arabie, and Carroll (1986) of the confusion patterns obtained by Miller and Nicely (1955/1991). Miller and Nicely asked subjects to identify syllables distorted by noise or filtering. Soli et al. scaled syllable differences given how often the subjects confused them with one another. The scaling allows us to look at the perceptual space (like the semantic differential in Chapter 3 showed conceptual space)—a mental map of the sounds. There are four dimensions accounting for large distances in psychological space, indicated by the axes, and clusters of smaller psychological-space distances, indicated by circles numbered by Roman numerals. The most salient distinctions, in the top panel, separate the nasals (Cluster III), with low-frequency periodic energy from the voiced stops and fricatives (upper clusters) with higher, low-frequency periodic energy, from the high, first formant aperiodic voiceless stops and fricatives. Sounds located close together are sounds frequently confused with one another, so /m/ /n/ are often confused but not often confused with the stops and fricatives. The lower panel shows less important dimensions, which roughly pull apart places of articulation. To the right of the panel are front consonants with rising second formant transitions; to the left are mid- and back consonants with falling second formant transitions. The fourth dimension also separates the high-energy, high-frequency fricatives from spectrally compact stops and nasals and low-energy fricatives. These results suggest that our speech-sound space is organized on feature lines with manner and voicing more salient than place of articulation.

One additional result is worth detailed description because it supports the independent extraction of voicing and place features during perception. In this experiment (Studdert-Kennedy & Shankweiler, 1970/1991), subjects heard only the syllables /ba, da, ga, pa, ta, ka/. Each trial presented two syllables dichotically, one to each ear. As I said, usually subjects made only single-feature errors, and they were less likely to make errors, the more features the dichotic pair shared. The result of interest occurs on those trials in which subjects reported *both* syllables wrong,

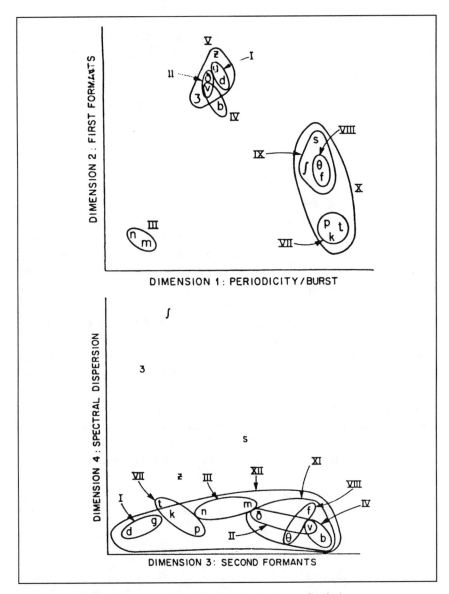

Figure 7.2. A Multidimensional Space Depicting Consonant Confusions
SOURCE: Soli, Arabie, and Carroll (1986, pp. 832-833).
NOTE: Sounds clustered together are easily confused.

a double error. Note that if the stimulus pair is /ba-ta/, there are six possible double errors: /da-pa/, /da-ga/, /da-ka/, /ga-pa/, /ka-pa/, and /ga-ka/. Therefore, if each is equally likely, the chance of reporting any particular one is ⅙, or about 17%. In fact, if subjects made a double error, they reported a particular pair (/da/ /pa/ for /ba/ /ta/) *64% of the time* (Studdert-Kennedy & Shankweiler, 1970/1991)! Note the interesting relation of /d-p/ to /b-t/. Both pairs contain the features alveolar, voiced, bilabial, and voiceless—but in different combinations, as though the sounds were heard in terms of features and the information about which voicing value went with which place value was independently forgotten. These are called *double blend* errors and strongly suggest the feature as a unit of perceptual processing.

Features in Speech Production

On the production side, inadvertent speech errors or slips of the tongue also provide some support for features' psychological reality—as well as for the reality of other units of analysis of the articulatory signal (phoneme, syllable, morpheme). Much of the data on speech errors come from corpuses of spontaneous errors, painstakingly recorded and analyzed but subject to perceptual bias. (As I said, we are more likely to note multiple than single feature errors. We are also more likely to note semantic slips, to be discussed later.) Slips involve errors of units of varying sizes—sound, morpheme, and word (see Dell, 1986, for a review). Errors involving sound alone implicate substitutions of features, phonemes, consonant clusters, or syllable ends. Most frequently slips involve the beginning of the word, the onset, the first consonant or consonant cluster, or the rest as a unit, called the *rime*— "s(tr)ing" = s(tr) + ing. Consider an onset switch: york library → lork yibrary. This could represent a place switch (/l/ is alveolar; /y/, palatal) supporting the feature as a unit. But it could also be a whole-phoneme switch (/y-l/), a greater-than-feature production unit.

Van den Broeke and Goldstein (1980) specifically tested phonetic feature models in cross-language slip-of-the-tongue data. The features of Jakobson, Fant, and Halle (1969/1951) better described the data than any other feature system. As did the l-y substitution above, they found that errors usually maintained voicing and manner class. Thus the speech-error data provide some support for speech production by linguistic features but also suggest larger language units (morphemes and words) and larger speech units (syllables, onsets, and rimes) as production units.

Summary

Much of speech processing research focuses on *how* phonetic features are signaled. This question is relevant only if there is evidence that we do extract features. And there is some: Two feature differences are more detectable than single feature differences and are less likely to constitute a speech error. However, it is also important to note that the evidence is equivocal concerning independence of features: Place differences are scaled differently depending on voicing; morphemes, words, or onsets and rimes are exchanged as units in slips of the tongue. Thus speech is clearly also organized into higher units of analysis. As we examine the perceptual processes underlying linguistic feature identification, it is important to keep in mind that (a) there is evidence that features are indeed identified at some psychological level, but (b) there is also evidence that they are often not the unit of choice.

Box 7.1. The Unit of Speech Perception

There is some evidence that speech is heard and produced by linguistic features:

— Slips of the ear for speech heard in noise or filtered are within phonetic feature classes.
— Mispronunciations are more detectable if the error differs from the target in more than one linguistic feature.
— Sounds presented simultaneously to each ear (dichotic) are reported more accurately the more features they share.
— Errors in reporting dichotic sounds preserve linguistic features but in different combinations.
— The perceived difference between speech sounds is a function of the number of linguistic features distinguishing them.
— Slips of the tongue often distort only one feature.

But there is evidence of perception and production units greater than the feature, and evidence that not all features are equivalent psychologically:

— Slips of the tongue also substitute whole phonemes, morphemes, and words.
— Perceptual feature errors still result in a phoneme, and therefore may be as well described as phoneme substitutions.
— Place of articulation confusions are more common than manner or voicing confusions.

PERCEIVING AND PRODUCING CONSONANT LINGUISTIC FEATURES

The Problem of Pattern Recognition

Most investigations of speech perception have assumed that we perceive speech as bundles of phonetic features, an assumption that we have seen has some support. The question then becomes which aspects of the acoustic signal let us know that a particular feature value is present—a problem of pattern recognition. Generally the goal of pattern recognition is to find some constant in a very variable signal that will always cue the pattern. Think about how you recognize someone, for example: People change their hairstyle, dress, eye color, glasses, and so on. This is variability. The question is this: What stays the same, is unchanging or invariant, that lets us recognize the person?

In speech, variation arises by different speakers and different speech contexts: A consonant is produced differently depending on the vowels or consonants that precede and follow it; sound representing a feature like place is different depending on whether or not there is voicing. As we saw in Chapter 6, the sound is also shaped by the size and sex of the speakers and their emotion, and by suprasegmental linguistic characteristics, such as whether it is stressed or part of a statement or question. With all these sources of variation affecting the sound signal underlying a phonetic feature, what is unchanging? What is consistently present when that feature is heard?

In Chapter 6, I suggested some candidates for acoustic *cues* to distinctive features, portions of the signal that trigger representation of the feature. These include burst and frication noise, which contain information about manner and place of constriction; aspiration and periodic pulsing, which contain information about voicing; direction and location of formant frequencies, which contain information about place of articulation; and steady state frequencies, which contain information about the vowel. This is a simple model of pattern recognition in which there is one aspect of the acoustic signal that we assume is detected, cuing the pattern recognizer for the feature and allowing the feature to be detected.

If this is the way speech is perceived, we would expect, for example, that if we remove the burst of a stop consonant and present it in isolation, we would hear a "pure stop consonant" with no particular vowel. This would indicate that the burst was *sufficient* to cue a stop consonant. What would we expect the remainder of the signal—the transitions plus steady states—to sound like? According to our simple proposal, this should sound like a place of articulation and a vowel, but with the burst gone, not like a stop consonant in particular. If removal of the burst prevents perception of a stop, we can say that the burst is *necessary* to perceive a stop consonant.

One important type of sufficient cue is an *invariant:* a cue that does not change in different contexts. For speech, that means that it should appear regardless of the other features of the phoneme (a burst should not depend on voicing value), regardless of position in the syllable (a burst should signal stop consonants in consonant-vowel [CV] and vowel-consonant [VC] syllables) and regardless of the surrounding vowel (the burst should appear in /ba/ as well as /bi/). Finally, it should not be affected by context beyond the syllable—as in a word with a different vowel earlier in the sentence. If a cue alters as a result of any of these factors, it is not invariant but *context sensitive.* Context sensitivity is a problem for pattern recognition because the pattern recognizer cannot simply search for a single "true" cue but may have to search for several different cues depending on the context. This problem becomes particularly troublesome if the cue is ambiguous, say, if in some environments the cue means /d/ and in others /b/. If we do not also hear the sound as both /b/ and /d/ in alternation, it suggests there must be other information available for pattern recognition.

Methods of Determining
Necessary and Sufficient Cues

Pulling aspects out of the signal for separate presentation is accomplished through digital editing and sound synthesis. Editing allows precision removal of a portion of the signal. The removed portion (or the remainder) may then be presented to subjects for *identification,* for them to say what it sounds like. If removing a

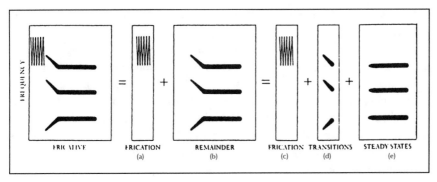

Figure 7.3. Schematic Decomposition of a Spectrogram into Its Various Cue Classes

NOTE: A fricative may be conceptualized as the sum of frication noise, transitions, and steady states.

portion does not change the identification of the rest, we know it was not necessary; if the remaining portion is identified as the whole sound, we know the remaining portion is sufficient. As I mentioned in Chapter 6, removal of the /s/ from *spat* leaves a remainder identified as *bat,* suggesting that the characteristics of /p/ produced after an /s/ are not sufficient to cause perception of an initial voiceless stop.

A sound synthesizer allows the same kind of experimentation but with finer control and with the ability to pull apart frequencies and intensities. There are many kinds of synthesizers, and details of their operation are beyond the scope of this chapter. Suffice it to say that some allow specification of energy values at particular frequencies, in a sense "pronouncing" a spectrogram. Others take real speech input, convert it to an energy specification in time, perhaps approximate some parameters from the input signal, and allow "digital" splicing before playback. Finally, on some personal computers, there are synthesizers that have stored a library of phonemes, syllables, or words that can be accessed by typing and that are then produced in the specified order, in a sense, internally spliced together.

For our purposes, it is the first two types of synthesizers that are of interest because they allow the finest manipulation of the signal. Presentation of synthesized patterns consisting of some but not all of the aspects of real speech to human listeners for identification can indicate which aspects are necessary, sufficient, or invariant cues for speech perception.

The Sound of Isolated Segments of a Syllable

As we have seen, a CV syllable seems to be describable in terms of three sets of cues: one from the constriction (frication noise, nasal resonance, or burst), one from the movement of the articulators from the place of articulation of the consonant to the place of articulation of the vowel (the transitions), and one from the sustained vowel (the steady states). In addition, looking at a spectrogram, we may segment the signal with respect to frequency and consider that it has several separate formants, each of which could be presented in isolation. (Figure 7.3 is a schematic of a spectrogram to help you picture the methods underlying the results described in what follows.)

So, the first question researchers asked was this: If we divide the signal up and present any of these portions in isolation, how is the portion identified and how is the signal identified with the portion missing? Frication noise in isolation (Figure 7.3a) is heard not just as a fricative but as a *specific* fricative, with place of articulation and voicing conveyed simultaneously with manner (Heinz & Stevens, 1961). Examination of the spectrograms in Figure 6.12 should so indicate: The frequency of the frication noise changes from /s/ to /š/ and is periodic for /z/ as opposed to aperiodic for /s/. Frication manner thus has no fixed frequency range, no set periodic quality, and so on; a specific-to-manner cue must be an abstraction. Manner is *smeared* together with place and voicing information across the initial portion of the signal; there is no time at which noise cues frication alone.

With the frication noise removed, the remainder of the syllable (Figure 7.3b) sounds like a stop consonant: Note that it now begins abruptly, although without a burst. This suggests that bursts are not necessary to perceive stops. They are also not sufficient: In isolation they not only do not sound like stops, they do not sound like speech! So the burst is neither necessary nor sufficient to convey a stop.

Continuing our segmenting, we remove the transitions from the remainder of the syllable, as in Figure 7.3d. Given what we have already learned, we might expect them to sound like a place of articulation (our original hypothesis), or like a stop, because the transitions plus steady states sound like a stop and vowel. Isolated transitions, like isolated bursts, do not sound like speech! Indicative of their sound, they are called *chirps*. So we can rule them out as invariants for either stop manner or place of articulation. They too are not sufficient in isolation.

This leaves the steady states as potential cues to the elusive place-of-articulation (and stop) quality. However, a signal such as in Figure 7.3e sounds like a good *vowel only*—the consonant quality has disappeared in our splicing! Therefore, the burst and transitions are not sufficient for the percept of stop consonant and place of articulation but are nevertheless necessary for it. *This should seem like magic: The consonant is nowhere in particular yet there when all pieces are together.*

So far we have tried segmenting the signal with respect to time. We may try segmenting with respect to frequency, presenting isolated formants. This does not solve the problem either. It is possible to hear good stop CV syllables with the first two or three formants only, suggesting the higher ones are not necessary. Presentation of just a single formant again does not sound speechlike; it is descriptively called a *bleat*. A single formant without transitions, however, is in some cases sufficient to cue a vowel (Fry, Abramson, Eimas, & Liberman, 1962).

Thus, although a spectrogram seems to have isolatable acoustic portions, these do not correspond in any straightforward way to phonetic features. It is possible to minimally signal a fricative, using just the noise portion, and a vowel, with one or two steady states: These cue whole phonemes, not particular features. And most phonemes (and features) cannot be so minimally signaled: It takes transitions with steady states at least to hear the stop consonants, for example.

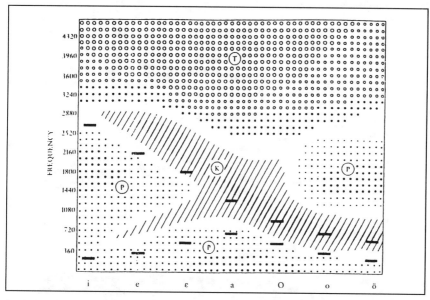

Figure 7.4. Judgments of /p/, /t/, and /k/ From Stimuli Produced by Combining Burst Frequencies Isolated From Each Consonant in Different Vowel Contexts With the Steady States Appropriate to Each Vowel

SOURCE: A. M. Liberman, P. C. Delattre, and F. S. Cooper (1952), "The Role of Selected Stimulus Variables in the Perception of Unvoiced Stop Consonants," in *The American Journal of Psychology, 65.* Copyright © by the Board of Trustees of the University of Illinois. Used with the permission of the University of Illinois Press.

NOTE: There is no burst frequency range that uniquely cues /k/.

Context Sensitivity: Combining Cues From Different Environments

We have just seen that with the exception of frication noise and steady states, portions of the speech signal cannot be presented in isolation and still evoke a speech percept: The steady states are necessary for a burst and transitions to be heard as speech. This suggests that there is a context dependence of the consonant on the vowel. Studies have shown that it is not a simple dependence in which you need a vowel to hear a consonant. Rather, it is a complex interaction: The sound of the consonant (noise and transition portions) changes depending on the steady states it is attached to (Harris, 1958, for frication noise; Liberman, Delattre, & Cooper, 1952, and Schatz, 1954, for stop bursts). And, in naturally synthesized or produced speech, we see dramatic changes in the consonant acoustics depending on the following vowel.

I have reproduced classic figures demonstrating these findings. Figure 7.4 is identification results for bursts isolated from the voiceless stops presented in front of different vowels (from Liberman et al., 1952). The result? No invariance. For example, if you examine the figure you will see that /t/ was heard at burst

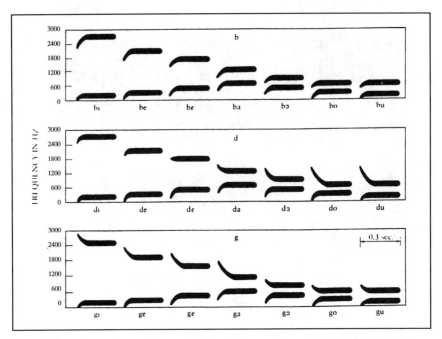

Figure 7.5. Two Formant Patterns Sufficient to Cue /b/, /d/, and /g/ in Different Vowel Contexts

SOURCE: P. C. Delattre, A. M. Liberman, and F. S. Cooper (1955), "Acoustic loci and transitional cues for consonants." *The Journal of the Acoustical Society of America, 27,* p. 770. Copyright © 1970 by the American Institute of Physics. Reprinted by permission.

frequencies above 2,600 Hz regardless of vowel (suggesting that a high burst may be invariant for /t/), but a burst frequency of 1,440 Hz was heard as /p/ before steady states appropriate to /i/, and /k/ before steady states appropriate to /a/. (You can see similar overlap between /p/ and /k/ for other burst frequencies in different vowel environments.) The results indicate that some place information is carried by the burst, but not sufficient information to signal place in all environments.

Figure 7.5 indicates how different transitions for a single place of articulation in voiced stop consonants look depending on the following vowels. The patterns were determined using synthetic speech: which frequencies were needed to produce consistent identification (Delattre, Liberman, & Cooper, 1955). Observe that no particular transition shape determines a place value; /bi/ and /di/, for example, look remarkably alike, as do /gɔ/ and /dɔ/. You can also see that the transitions change across vowel context: For all, they are very separate for /i/ and very close for /u/; for /b/, the second formant transition ranges from 2,400 Hz to 600 Hz at onset; and for /d/, it can either rise or fall depending on the vowel. Indeed, it was the extreme difference between the upward sloping second formant transition for /di/ and the downward sloping transition for /du/, with all other acoustic characteristics the same, that suggested to early investigators that phonetic percepts could not arise directly from invariant acoustic properties.

I have at this point presented aspects of perception of manner and place of articulation in consonants. Before leaving consonant perception, we should consider how voicing is perceived, as this has been one of the most studied features. Lisker and Abramson (1970/1991) defined voice onset time (VOT) as a set of distinctive acoustic properties underlying the distinction of voicing categories across languages. *VOT* in stops is the time difference between the release burst and the onset of periodic pulsing visible on wideband spectrograms. VOT actually entails a complex of acoustic characteristics: A long VOT has a long *temporal* or time interval, a greater degree of aspiration (during that interval), a more pronounced (longer, more intense) burst, and later onset of energy at a higher first formant than at the second formant than does a short VOT.

Lisker and Abramson created a *synthetic speech continuum* for VOT. A continuum is a set of speech stimuli identical except for a single acoustic property, which changes systematically across the continuum. In this case, continuum members shared transition and steady state frequencies, but each stimulus differed from its neighbor by 10 ms of VOT. The greatest voicing lead was 150 ms (this means that periodic pulsing begins 150 ms before the release burst); the greatest voicing *lag* was 150 ms (the release burst preceded the periodic pulsing by 150 ms). The continuum thus consists of voicing leads of 150 ms, 140 ms, 130 ms, . . . 0 ms and then voicing lags of 10 ms, 20 ms, 30 ms . . . 150 ms.

Different continua were created for each place of articulation and then played to speakers of languages with different voicing categories for identification. Speakers of Spanish divided the continuum into two categories: roughly, voicing lead versus simultaneous/lag. Speakers of English divided the continuum also into two categories: voicing lag (voiceless) versus voicing lead/simultaneous. Speakers of Thai heard three categories, corresponding to lead, near-simultaneous, and lag. For all three languages, the synthetic VOT cue (the bundle of acoustic features that constitute VOT) appeared to account for the phonetic categories of the language. However, for all three languages, voicing identification changed with place of articulation: The farther back closure is made, the greater the delay needed for perception to change from prevoiced to simultaneous or from simultaneous to voiceless.

Thus for voicing we may have a *critical* acoustic property. However, it is not an invariant cue because it is affected by other phonetic features.

Summary. Identification experiments indicate that cues to place of articulation are hard to pin down, are context sensitive. The presence of frication noise seems to cue fricative manner, the presence of an abrupt onset seems to cue stop manner, the amount of VOT seems to cue voicing, and sometimes even the presence of a single steady state frequency seems to cue vowel quality. In contrast, place-of-articulation cues are elusive: They are contained in burst, frication noise, or transitions but these do not signal them invariantly; that is, in isolation they do not sound like what they cue, and in different contexts they change. A pattern recognition scheme that attempted to find a particular place of articulation from burst or transitions would have to know which vowel was being presented to identify a 1,440 Hz burst certainly as /p/ or /k/ or falling second and third transitions as /t/ or /k/. This suggests that consonant perception could depend on vowel identification, which, we will see, is incorrect.

Other Proposals for Invariants

Invariants for the feature place of articulation. Instead of looking for a single invariant, such as second formant transition to place of articulation, we might consider the pattern of the second and third formant transitions. Front consonants appear characterized by a rising pattern and the back consonants by the diverging second and third formants (see Stevens, 1975). This still leaves the mid-consonants with variable pattern. And, more important, there is a position dependency: The front consonants rise at the beginning of a syllable but fall at the end (see, e.g., Tartter, Kat, Samuel, & Repp, 1983). So the rising pattern cannot be an invariant.

Some investigators have looked for invariants in dynamic properties of speech. Stevens and Blumstein (1978/1991; Blumstein & Stevens, 1979, 1980) emphasized the set of events put into play at the onset of the consonant, as the articulators move in or out of it. They looked at power spectra (which, as you may recall, average energy over time) for the first 25 ms from the consonant release. For a stop consonant, this includes the burst as well as aspiration at release and some of the transition. Figure 7.6 shows power spectra for stops without and with the burst, and indicates, for the latter, distinctive patterns for each place of articulation, consistent with those proposed in distinctive feature theory by Jakobson et al. (1951/1969). Labial consonants have a falling spectrum; alveolar consonants have a diffuse, flat spectrum (energy across the frequency range); and velar consonants have a rising spectrum with energy compacted in the low-frequency region.

Experiments demonstrate that these properties for the most part hold across manner of articulation. Moreover, Blumstein and Stevens used these patterns to classify successfully (> 70% accuracy) natural speech samples of stop consonants before different vowels pronounced by different speakers. Thus Stevens and Blumstein's onset properties are more nearly sufficient than burst alone, transitions alone, or single formants alone. However, there were still a substantial proportion of consonants that the scheme misclassifies, which the human listener classifies correctly, and listeners were able to identify the vowel as well as the consonant in isolated onsets. This suggests that the onset information does vary with vowel, because the vowel is recognizable. Finally, we have seen that listeners can identify syllables synthesized without bursts, and therefore bursts are not necessary, even if spectra including them are sufficient.

The onset properties are brief, conveying little temporal information, but are spectrally rich, taking into account *energy* at different frequencies. Kewley-Port (1983/1991) developed a set of properties that better classify place of articulation than that of Stevens and Blumstein (classification of place is better than 85%) by

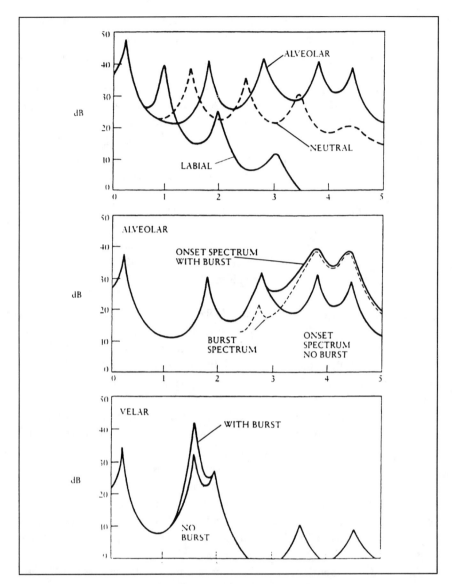

Figure 7.6. Onset Spectra for the First 26 ms of Stop-Vowel Syllables

SOURCE: K. N. Stevens and S. E. Blumstein (1978), "Invariant Cues for Place of Articulation in Stop Consonants," *Journal of the Acoustical Society of America, 64,* p. 1359. Copyright © 1978 by the American Institute of Physics. Reprinted with permission.

NOTE: The top panel displays the patterns for alveolar and labial consonants, compared with the neutral (/ə/) pattern. The lower panels show the spectra for alveolar and velar consonants with and without bursts. Note the accentuation of the difference with the bursts.

including all *three* dimensions relevant to speech: *Energy* and *frequency* change over *time,* derived from the waterfall displays (shown in Chapter 6). Her success emphasizes the *dynamic* nature of speech: If we hear *changes* in the vocal tract configurations, we may not be able to describe either a particular configuration as a static event or the *stream* of speech as a succession of individual "drops," or independent phonetic segments. In the formation of the stream, in the coarticulation of the segments, may lie the information we need to recover the underlying phonetic events (Fowler, 1986/1991).

It is interesting to note that experiments have shown highly accurate consonant identification when *temporal variation,* the *dynamic information, is preserved,* with spectral information reduced to broad frequency bands (< 2,000 Hz and > 2,000 Hz) excited by noise (Shannon, Zeng, Kamath, Wygonski, & Ekelid, 1995). Spectral reduction to a single sine wave at formant center frequency with temporal variation preserved also permits sentence identification (Remez, Rubin, Berns, Pardo, & Lang, 1994).

As a group, therefore, the experiments imply that there is more than one way to achieve a speech percept: tracking of temporal changes with minimal spectral information or recognition of spectral properties in brief temporal intervals. At the level of the feature, there may not be absolute acoustic invariance but, instead, redundant sets of sufficient cues (Lindblom, 1996).

Invariance at a higher level? We have looked for invariant cues to consonant phonetic features in part because this is the smallest reasonable unit of speech and in part because there is some evidence that we may hear speech as bundles of phonetic features. It has proven difficult to find features of the acoustic signal that correspond directly to phonetic features, that signal a feature invariantly, without being affected by other features of the phoneme or the syllable. This might lead us to look at the phoneme or syllable as a potential "unit" of perception, perhaps more immune to contextual effects, with a more invariant relationship to the acoustic signal.

Briefly, this does not work either: Contextual dependencies affect phonemes and syllables as well. For example, Ali, Gallagher, Goldstein, and Daniloff (1971) removed a nasal-consonant-initial syllable from a sentence and presented the remaining sentence to listeners. Listeners could detect that *the nasal had been there,* suggesting that nasal information had to have colored the other syllables of the sentence.

Another demonstration of the context dependence of larger units is provided by J. Miller and A. Liberman (1979/1991). They constructed a /ba-wa/ continuum for which the critical variable is the rate of change of the formant transitions, how quickly they move from the starting frequencies to the steady state frequencies. The rate of change is rapid for /ba/ and slow for /wa/. Miller and Liberman showed that the boundary at which listeners perceive the change from /ba/ to /wa/ depends on how fast they perceive the speaker to be talking. They manipulated perceived speech rate by adding either a short /da/ or a long /da/ to the /ba-wa/ series, changing it to a /bada-wada/ choice. Perception shifted from /bada/ to /wada/ at a faster transition rate when a short syllable was added than it did when a long syllable was added. Thus perception of a consonant or initial syllable is affected by later-occurring syllable information, again an instance of long-distance context sensitivity.

Box 7.2. Pattern Recognition of Consonant Cues

The Problem of Pattern Recognition
— How is a constant percept recovered from a variable signal?
— Which signal aspects—cues—give rise to the percept?

Types of Cues
— *Necessary:* It must be there for the percept to be achieved.
— *Sufficient:* If the cue is there, the percept will be achieved, but other cues may also accomplish this.
— *Invariant:* A cue that is consistently present when the percept is achieved, both necessary and sufficient.

Consonant Cues
— Frication noise in isolation is identifiable as fricative manner.
— Frication noise is identifiable specifically for some fricatives.
— Isolated bursts are unidentifiable.
— Bursts combined with different steady states are perceived variably, depending on the steady state.
— Isolated transitions—chirps—are unidentifiable.
— Transitions differ greatly for the same place of articulation depending on the steady state vowel.
— Isolated formants—bleats—are unidentifiable.
— The property of spectral change at onset, diffuse falling for labials, diffuse rising for alveolars, and compact for velars may be sufficient to cue place of articulation in stop consonants. Vowels are also identifiable within the first 10 ms of onset.
— Preservation of dynamic information with spectral information reduced, by using broad-band noise or single sine waves, allows identification.
— A complex of acoustic characteristics associated with voice onset time (VOT) is sufficient to cue voicing distinctions cross-linguistically. The VOT value distinguishing voicing categories depends on place of articulation.
— Transition duration cues stop-semivowel manner changes but is perceived relative to speech rate.

VOWEL IDENTIFICATION, SPEAKER IDENTIFICATION, AND THE LIKE: SOURCES OF VARIABILITY OR PATTERNS TO BE RECOGNIZED?

Our exploration of the acoustic features underlying consonant perception showed that they are affected concurrently by other consonant properties and by vowel context and perceived speech rate, features occurring within the same phoneme or syllable or in distant ones. When we concentrate on the consonant phonetic features as the "pattern-to-be recognized," these influences seem to be noise—variation that prevents a clear picture of the consonant feature from appearing. We may as easily, however, concentrate on the vowel or the speech rate as the "pattern-to-be-recognized," in which case the variation due to different consonants can be seen as the irrelevant noise.

It is important to recognize that speech *should* communicate many things concurrently: We *need* to have segmental information (consonants and vowels), suprasegmental information (intonation and so on), and speaker information (who is talking, how the speaker feels, and so on). These can all be identified from the same signal: I answer the telephone, hear only "hello," and say, sensitively, "Hi, Mom. What's wrong?" What she said, who she is, and how she felt are available from just *two syllables*! That they are all available suggests that each is a potential source of variation in detecting the other.

In this section we look briefly at vowel perception to show that it is as context dependent as consonant perception. We then turn to evidence that we recognize suprasegmental, speaker, and emotion information from speech.

Perception of Vowels

Since the earliest work on speech perception (Joos, 1948) it was assumed that vowel perception was simpler than consonant perception. The reasons for this are many: First, vowels may be articulated in isolation; second, steady information seems simpler than rapidly changing information; third, as research with consonants revealed vowel-dependent perception, the vowel seemed to be a logical starting point or anchor—if we know the vowel, for instance, we know whether a particular burst frequency signals /p/, /t/, or /k/. Thus we might suggest that speech perception begins with the steady states, uses these to determine the vowel quality, and uses the vowel to judge the transitions and constriction information to recover the consonant. This model, however, fails because vowels are more variable than they seem.

The problems arise as soon as we look at natural fluent speech instead of synthetic speech. Reexamine Figure 7.1—the spectrogram of the fluent sentence. How much steady state is there? As the earliest studies of speech noted, in fluent speech, steady state formant frequencies are rarely attained; instead, they are suggested in the transitions. A natural CVC (consonant-vowel-consonant) syllable looks more like 峯 than it does like 戸, unless the speaker deliberately attempts to sustain the vowel. Because the steady state frequencies are not quite achieved but are, *presumably,* the speaker's target, the actual sounds produced were considered to *undershoot* the target. It was left to some clever perception device to calibrate the undershoot (Joos, 1948), which, for a given speaker, might vary from one production of an utterance to another, *within-speaker variation.*

A second, obvious problem is that steady state frequencies vary enormously from speaker to speaker; therefore, a perceptual routine that searches for particular frequencies and then assigns vowel labels to them will not work across speakers. In a classic study, Peterson and Barney (1952/1991) recorded 76 men, women, and children pronouncing syllables beginning with /h/ and ending with /d/, with 10 different vowels in the middle. The syllables were analyzed acoustically and presented to listeners to identify. Figure 7.7 displays the *vowel space,* the first and second formant frequencies, of the vowels of these speakers. Note the overlap in the figure enclosing the /ɛ/ (the third circle at the top): The same acoustic space applies to some of the /æ/, /ɚ/, and /ɪ/. However, listeners labeled the sounds consistently, as the speakers intended. The speaker variation gets compounded when we consider regular patterns of within-speaker variation as when speakers change speech rate (J. Miller, 1981) or facial expression such as by smiling, which alters the steady state frequencies but not vowel identification (Tartter, unpublished data).

To get around speaker variability, researchers have suggested that we may perceptually "normalize" speaker information, that is, calibrate each speaker's productions with respect to one another, and then adjust them to some mental "normal" vowel values on the basis of the calibration. There is some evidence that listeners do calibrate. Ladefoged and Broadbent (1957/1991) presented a test word /bɪt/ following the sentence, "Please say what this word is." The sentence was synthesized to represent different vocal tracts. Depending on the vocal tract, listeners heard the same sounds as /bɪt/ or as /bɛt/.

To normalize vowels, researchers have suggested that we may use particular vowels as anchor points, vowels that seem to show small effects of speaker variation. One suggestion has been the point vowels /i, a, u/. These are attractive candidates because (a) they occur in all languages and so reasonably could be the start of a basic perceptual routine; (b) there is less acoustic variation between- and within-speaker for these vowels than for the others (Stevens, 1989/1991); and (c) they constitute the extremes of articulation and therefore show vocal tract size, which, as we did in the last chapter, can predict formant frequency values (indeed, an early computerized normalization routine used such a scheme to correctly classify 97% of the Peterson and Barney, 1952/1991, syllables; Gerstman, 1968). However, note that we do not seem to have trouble identifying an unfamiliar speaker's vowels before they say /i a u/ (Peterson and Barney's listeners were not provided /i a u/ before the vowels), nor are we better at it if they do say it (Shankweiler, Strange, & Verbrugge, 1977).

An alternative proposal considers the dynamic properties of speech as providing vowel information along with consonant information, which brings us full circle. Shankweiler et al. showed that identification of isolated vowels spoken by several different speakers is considerably poorer (25% worse) than identification of the same vowels embedded between two /p/s. This suggests that the immediate context, information in the "p's," could provide an anchor. Strange, Jenkins, and Johnson (1983/1991) showed further that natural speech syllables consisting of an initial /b/, a vowel, and a final /b/, were nearly as well identified when the steady state portions of the syllables were *removed,* with a silent interval substituting for them, as they were when they were completely intact. In contrast, accuracy dropped to nearly 50% when the transitions for either the initial or the final consonant were also removed. Thus it appears that for both consonants and vowels, the critical portion of the speech signal may be that which is most coarticulated, which contains information about overlapping articulatory events.

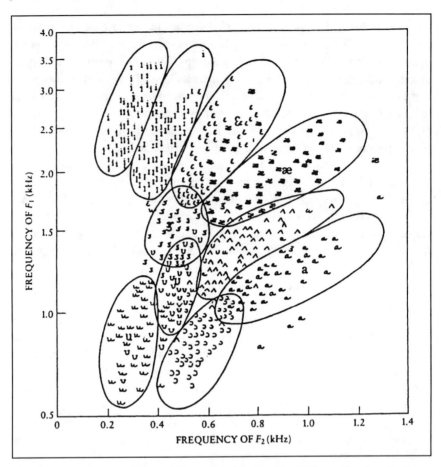

Figure 7.7. The Range of Formant Frequencies Produced by Different Speakers for the Same Vowel

SOURCE: G. E. Peterson and H. L. Barney (1952), "Control Methods in a Study of Vowels," *The Journal of the Acoustical Society of America, 24*, p. 182. Copyright © 1952 by the American Institute of Physics. Adapted by permission.

NOTE: Circles enclose utterances reliably identified by listeners.

Perception of Tone of Voice

Another factor that adds to the variability of acoustic and articulatory specification of segments is differences in "tone of voice." For example, the VOT value differentiating voicing categories depends on the stress of the syllable in which the segment appears, the rate of production of the sentence, and the pause duration. Differences between speakers alter the vowel space, and differences in facial expression alter the formant frequencies of speech. This is only a small list of the effects of tone of voice on segments, and in this section we will not elaborate it further. The purpose of this section is to look at perception and production of "tone of voice" itself rather than its effects on segment perception and production.

As described in Chapter 6, we can break tone of voice into linguistically relevant components of intonation and stress that distinguish segments or grammatical forms, and components that appear because of physical characteristics of the speaker such as size, sex, or emotional state.

Stress, intonation, and duration. As with segmental features, it is difficult to find invariance in the suprasegmentals. Linguistic stress, for example, the feature distinguishing *com'*pact (N) from *compact'* (ADJ), is manifested by an increase in duration, fundamental frequency, and intensity in the stressed syllable; these can offset one another (Fry, 1955; Lieberman, 1960). Pitch value is affected by segmental value (usually there is a higher pitch following voiceless than voiced segments; Lehiste & Peterson, 1961) and, obviously also in English, by grammatical value: In interrogative sentences, pitch rises at the end instead of falling steadily. Recognition of a sentence as a question depends not on *absolute* frequency of the final word but on its being higher than any other frequency in the sentence (Hadding-Koch & Studdert-Kennedy, 1964). Moreover, rising intonation contours conveyed on sentences *interpreted as statements* are judged as falling! The first point suggests that in perceiving or producing questions, listeners or speakers keep track of pitch across many segments; the second suggests that the interpretation of the sentence is used to judge pitch instead of the converse.

Emotion and facial expression. The speech signal has been used to try to diagnose states of the speaker such as personality disorders or mood. The first of these will not be discussed here (see Scherer, 1979, for a review) but will be treated in *Language in Atypical Populations.*

Attempts to measure emotion and facial expression in speech have been motivated by the assumption that these produce a physical change—in breathing rate, muscle tension, or salivation—or a lip retraction or protrusion, which naturally affects speech parameters (Scherer, 1986; see Murray & Arnott, 1993, for a review). Emotional states fall into two broad categories: active and nonactive. Active includes anxiety, lying, fear, or anger, and these increase pitch, loudness, pitch fluctuations, loudness fluctuations, and speaking rate. Nonactive emotions, such as sorrow, grief, or indifference, have the opposite effect on these parameters (see, for stress, Hecker, Stevens, von Bismarck, & Williams, 1968, or Streeter, MacDonald, Apple, Krauss, & Galotti, 1983; for deception, Ekman, Friesen, & Scherer, 1976, or Streeter, Krauss, Geller, Olson, & Apple, 1977; for sorrow and anger, Williams & Stevens, 1972; for contempt, fear, grief, and indifference, Fairbanks & Hoaglin, 1941, or Fairbanks & Pronovost, 1939).

Recall our discussion of the semantic differential in Chapter 3. It universally yields three dimensions of connotative, or emotional, space: activity, evaluative, and potency. Scherer (1986) compellingly discusses physiological changes accompanying the poles of each of these dimensions, together with the vocal effects of the physiological changes. The *activity* dimension I have already discussed. Scherer

(1986) describes the *potency* dimension as affecting breathing and muscle tension. Feeling lack of control increases tension as well as fundamental frequency, amplitude, and their variance. Feeling power deepens breathing and lowers the fundamental frequency. *Evaluative* refers to pleasant versus unpleasant. To Scherer, pleasantness relaxes the vocal tract and expands the *pharyngeal* cavity (the back of the throat, above the larynx). It also results in a smile, or lip retraction. Unpleasantness has the opposite effects. Relaxation of the pharynx produces a *wide voice,* stronger (greater energy) low-frequency resonances, and dampened higher frequencies.

Lip retraction in smiling raises formant frequencies (Tartter, 1980), while the protrusion in pouting lowers them (Tartter & Braun, 1994). And Tartter (1980; Tartter & Braun, 1994) demonstrated that listeners can identify nonsense syllables spoken with a smile or a pout from those spoken neutrally and, without instruction, can label speech produced with those faces appropriately as happier or sadder sounding than neutral speech.

What is interesting to observe is that the various dimensions of emotion affect through one means or another all aspects of the acoustic signal: fundamental frequency, amplitude, the formant frequencies, and the relative power of the different resonances. So this nonsegmental information, within-speaker variation, is carried along with the segmental and suprasegmental information. This adds "variability" to the signal but also enriches the communication value of it, allowing us to perceive other, important patterns from speech.

Speaker Identification

Interest in the physical characteristics of the voice is partly motivated by legal applications: Do people's voices indicate their identities invariantly, as their fingerprints do? The first experiments conducted to measure the reliability of voice identification were prompted by testimony in the Lindbergh kidnapping trial that the kidnapper's voice had been recognized from a telephone conversation held three years earlier. McGehee (1937, 1944) presented listeners with voices from one of five speakers and asked them to select which of the five had been presented. (Note that this is easier than a real life situation in that the subject had only five from which to choose and knew absolutely that the voice was one of those five.) Identification was 80% during the first seven days and fell to 50% after the first month following the presentation (20% is chance).

Subsequent studies have shown better accuracy in speaker identification, probably because of better recording techniques. They have also demonstrated accurate perception of speaker characteristics such as age or sex in the absence of absolute identification. Speaker information is in part carried by pitch, but speakers' normal voices may be matched with their whispered speech (Tartter, 1991), which indicates that speaker information is carried apart from pitch, in the resonances along with consonant and vowel information. Thus speaker information is overlaid on phonetic information, again adding variability to the "speech" signal but enriching its communication potential.

Note that there is communication value in *hearing* speaker characteristics such as size, sex, and age, in being able to tell at a distance whether someone is threatening or not, friend or foe. It is also crucial in normal speaking conditions to be able to track a speaker's voice. Normally, all sounds in the environment mesh into a single complex waveform that perturbs the auditory system (the classic example is the cacophony of voices at a cocktail party). To understand a given speaker's speech we must be able to extract and attend to the contributions that his or her voice makes to this complex waveform, to follow a single source. How we track a source to perform such a separation mentally is beyond the scope of this chapter; interested readers should see Bregman (1990) and Remez et al. (1994).

Summary

Box 7.3 summarizes the acoustic properties we have examined and found informative for both segmental and nonsegmental patterns identifiable from speech. Research has found invariant cues to segments to be elusive, despite the constancy of the phonetic percept—we seem to hear a "b" independent of vowel context, speaker, speaker's facial expression, or the letter's position in the word. The seeming constancy may be the illusion, however: The detectability of all these other patterns from the same signal indicates their perceptual reality; sensitive experiments show that the features are not completely independently perceived.

SPEECH PRODUCTION

As I pointed out earlier, there is evidence from slips of the tongue that phonetic features have a psychological reality in speech production, but, as with speech perception, there is reason to consider the reality of higher order units.

Context Sensitivity of Segments

Note first that no feature can be produced in isolation; we cannot produce a voicing value without also producing a place and manner value for a consonant, and for stop consonants, without also producing a vowel. Aside from this articulatory constraint, there is considerable evidence that we *plan* more than one feature at a time. Slips of the tongue reveal a preponderance of *anticipation errors* (as in *sea sells* instead of *she sells* in the famous tongue twister, anticipating the /s/). Somewhat less common are *perseveration errors* (as in *she shells,* holding the /š/) (van den Broeke & Goldstein, 1980). Both these types of intrusion errors can occur across several syllables, although most are from adjacent syllables (MacKay, 1970). This indicates that in planning and producing a feature, phoneme, or syllable, there is "smear" from the planning and production of other syllables or syllable components; at some level the production program has some large portion of the utterance "in mind," and thus later or earlier productions can influence the current one.

Box 7.3. Acoustic Correlates of Segmental and Nonsegmental Features: Coarticulating Communicative Information

Sufficient Cues

Consonants (Initial Position)
Manner of Articulation

Nasality	Presence of nasal resonance or murmur
Frication	Frication noise
Stops	Sudden onset cued by burst or abrupt transitions
Semivowel	Lengthened transitions relative to stop

Voicing (a group of cues which in initial stops = VOT)

Amount of time between energy release and onset of periodic pulsing
Amount of aspiration noise
Intensity and onset time of higher formants relative to the first formant

For all, more → voiceless

Place of Articulation

Frequency of the burst/frication noise/murmur
Direction, slope, frequency of the second formant transition
Direction, slope, frequency of the third formant transition
Falling, diffuse, or rising spectrum at onset

Vowels

One or two steady state frequencies
First two formant transitions

Linguistic Stress
more → stressed

Fundamental frequency, loudness, or syllable duration

Speaker Characteristics

Fundamental frequency
Formant frequencies
Speech rate
Variance in fundamental/intensity across the utterance

Emotion

Fundamental frequency, speech rate greater for active emotions like anger, stress, or fear than for sorrow
Formant frequencies rise when smiling, fall when frowning
Positive emotions relax, widening pharyngeal cavity. This increases energy at the lower frequencies; negative, the opposite.
Feeling of power deepens breathing and relaxes, lowering the fundamental; powerlessness, the opposite

---

Evidence from slips of the tongue indicates not only a general smear of segments but also a sensitivity to the position of the segment. Slips most frequently involve the initial phoneme or feature in a word, but when other portions are confused, they generally come from the same respective positions within their words (Levelt, 1989). For example, in a lecture on Freud, a colleague made the "Freudian slip" (pun intended) of "sex tez" for "text says," transposing the onsets (and probably anticipating the upcoming discussion of psychosexual stages).

One reason there might be position sensitivity in production is that the associations, the phonological constraints, the transitional probabilities of the segments, are position-dependent. /ŋ/ in English, for example, would never be substituted into initial position because its association to a preceding word boundary would be very weak while its associations to preceding vowels (as in *sing, sang, song*) would be very strong. Therefore a substitution involving it is likely to reflect position dependency. The same sort of strength of association argument may apply, less dramatically, to concatenation of other segments. Thus position sensitivity in production is suggested.

Suprasegmental Plans

We see a direct effect of suprasegmental planning in some slips of the tongue, in which stress or intonation is incorrectly transposed, indicating it is also planned—as a unit. Cutler (1980) reported a substitution of *skyrock'eted* for *sky'rocketed*, perhaps an intrusion of the normal stress for *rocket* when it is not compounded.

We also see effects on suprasegmental production of speech planning generally. Cooper and Paccia-Cooper (1980) reported experiments demonstrating that when reading sentences aloud, subjects begin long sentences at a higher pitch than they do short sentences, presumably to permit "room" for an adequate fundamental frequency decline.

Cooper and Paccia-Cooper also measured pause duration in articulated sentences and found that it increased with the number of constituents terminating at that location. Higher order constituent boundaries were marked therefore with greater pauses, because they and their subordinate constituents simultaneously terminated. This pause effect reflects the mental planning of *future* speech: If there is a level of programming at least partially accessed for a word, a phrase, a clause, and a sentence, termination of any one of these will mean that another program at that level must be accessed. Termination of the higher order sentence program will require accessing of the next sentence program as well as the next clause, phrase, word programs, and so on, and this will take more time. Indeed, Levelt (1989) implicates many levels in speech production planning, beginning with the conceptual structure, through grammatical encoding principles, and word access (he calls the syntactic and conceptual representation the *lemma*), through phonological encoding into inner speech and ultimately into an articulatory plan.

The levels could feed into each other interactively, but there is some evidence that they operate successively, with the conceptual representation, the lemma, derived before phonological and articulatory coding. Van Turennout, Hagoort, and Brown (1997) measured a brain wave called the *lateral readiness potention* (LRP). This reflects preparation of a hand movement. They required different hands to press a button depending on whether a picture was animate (lemma level) and/or its name began or ended with a particular phoneme (phonological level). The LRP emerged based on the semantic decision, even when the phonemes signaled a no-press situation. This result suggests that the picture activates the lemma before it activates the articulatory underpinnings of the pictured object's name.

Speech errors and their corrections can reflect misplans and reformulations at any stage. For example, errors called *blends,* like *stummy* for stomach/tummy or in the sentence "the competition was *stuffer*" for tougher/stiffer (Levelt, 1989) suggest simultaneous equal activation and output of phonetic plans for synonyms (which also are phonetically similar), presumably an error originating in semantic access. As another example of the various levels at which errors occur, Levelt provides "take the freezes out of the *steaker,*" in which two noun stems are transposed with their suffixes maintaining position. He proposes a *unit similarity constraint,* wherein an intruding element is always at the same level, the same type of unit, as the target. So exchanges usually preserve parts of speech; stems interchange with stems, not affixes, and, conversely; onsets exchange with onsets, not rimes, and conversely.

Levels of Production

We have suggested the simultaneous planning of many levels of production. In an influential paper, Lashley (1951) proposed just such an organization for production of any temporally sequenced complex "habit." At the lowest level are complex elements that must be activated (in speech, these may be phonetic features or syllables or onset rimes), and at the highest level is some "determining tendency" or "idea" to organize them. The idea is implemented through the expressive elements hierarchically, in order: order in vocal movements in pronouncing the word, order in the words of the sentence, and order of the sentences in a paragraph. To Lashley, hierarchical organization is a defining property of all higher level brain activity. We see the influence of each level in speech errors, contamination by other units at the same level, and in context sensitivity of the expressive elements that reflect the combined influences of all levels.

Thus, in production as well as in perception, we see *simultaneity and smear:* Each segment simultaneously conveys and reflects influences of other segments through higher levels of organization, and each segment is smeared across other segments by the same means. Lashley pointed out that this is mirrored in perception: After commenting on a typing error producing "wrapid writing," he produced the sentence, "Rapid righting with his uninjured hand saved from loss the contents of the capsized canoe." The initial "error" caused a misinterpretation of "righting," which was not corrected until his audience heard the word "canoe," at least three seconds later. Activation of the appropriate interpretation required the hearer to *maintain* many levels of perceptual structure; the meaning of "canoe" must "smear" backward over the meaning or "righting." Holding several levels simultaneously in perception (our parsing window—recall Chapter 5), or creating several levels simultaneously in production, accounts for the "smear" in both.

Lack of Invariance in Motor Movements

A final similarity between perception and production is the apparent lack of invariance at the lowest level. As we saw in perception, the phonetic feature is abstract, not tied to a particular acoustic configuration. Similarly, production of a feature is abstract: A bilabial stop requires closing the lips with a certain force. That can be achieved with the jaw low and a large lip excursion or with a smaller lip excursion complemented by a jaw closing. A specific gesture is not necessary, allowing us to produce /b/ and /p/ in the context of either low or high vowels. And we can speak with a pipe (or pencil) in our mouths or, in an experimental situation, when forced to clench the teeth on a *biteblock.* These adaptations suggest variability possible in the execution: The target, the movement consequence, is an abstraction (see Levelt, 1989; Lindblom, 1996, for reviews).

Monitoring and Correcting Speech

We have just examined commonalities between perception and production of speech: simultaneous conveyance of several types of information, smear of one aspect across many others, and hierarchical organization. Levelt (1983) examined the process of perception *during* production, relating the mechanism of self-monitoring to perception of others' speech and indicating how speech production is organized. As I observed at the beginning of this chapter, speakers make few errors and often correct those they do make, which indicates that they monitor their productions. The question is this: How? If several levels of constituents are programmed ahead, how can the speaker interpolate the correction?

Levelt examined two theories of *repair* (correction): a production theory, assuming that the speaker could access the output of each of the levels of organization in production before making the utterance, and a perception theory, assuming the speaker to have access only to the final level, the output of all these levels, just before production. In the perception theory, it is assumed that the speaker monitors "inner speech" to check for mispronunciations and deviances from intent.

Examination of the errors, the speaker's detection of errors, and the attempts at repair supported the perception theory. Speaker repairs included changing their minds about what they should be saying (1%), choosing the wrong word (38%), syntactic errors (2%), and pronunciation errors (1%). The repairs only constituted 42% of all errors that were made, suggesting that speakers did not notice most errors, and noticed their lexical errors more often than phonetic errors. Levelt argues that if speakers access each stage of the production process during monitoring, they would correct at that stage. They do not, indicating that they perceive only the final stage, as they would if they were listeners. This supports a perception theory.

Box 7.4. Commonalities Between Speech Production and Speech Perception

— Lack of invariance at lowest level:
　　An articulatory target may be achieved many different ways.
— Simultaneous conveying of many aspects from many levels:
　　Features are coarticulated.
　　Semantic and syntactic plans are activated several segments
　　　　ahead and held for several segments beyond the current one
　　　　and can cause intrusion into the current one.
　　Slips of the tongue can occur across many different levels: onsets
　　　　or rimes transposed, syllables transposed, morphemes trans-
　　　　posed, words transposed; therefore all must be simultane-
　　　　ously active. The unit transposed in a slip is usually preserved:
　　　　unit similarity constraint.
— Smear: The simultaneous plans at many levels leave their mark on each
　　segment so that all the information for a particular pattern is found
　　across several segments.
— Monitoring speech during production and correcting errors show
　　similar influences as perception of others' speech.

Another way that the monitoring data may be examined concerns when the repairs are made on the errors. Levelt (1983, 1989) reports that some repairs are made immediately, interrupting the word, and others are delayed till the end of the word or phrase. Of the ones made immediately, most occur near a phrase boundary, suggesting that the speaker is better able to detect errors in that position. Corrections that were delayed, were delayed until the phrase boundary. (You may recall from Chapter 5 that spurious noise, a click superimposed upon a sentence, is also more likely to be reported as occurring at a major boundary, suggesting the integrity of the phrase as unit.) Speakers' detecting more errors at the phrase boundaries suggests that they did not have access to the output of levels of production early enough to correct before they were integrated into the program for the phrase.

The last use that can be made of the correction data is to look at the manner of repair, how much the speaker changes so as to make the correction. Here, too, Levelt sees analogies to perceiver strategies in production. Speakers do not tend to stop midword unless the word is wrong. Speakers try to incorporate the correction into the syntactic structure of the sentence, backtracking only to the *beginning of the current constituent*. For example, if the error is saying *green* when *blue* is intended, the utterance "to the right is a green" will be corrected with "to the right is a green, a blue node." If the speaker got farther before detecting the error, she or he will still backtrack to the constituent boundary: "to the right is a green node and—to the right is a green node and, uh, a blue node and . . ." Levelt notes that in answering questions, we reflect a similar constituent analysis. If someone asks, "What time?" we will respond, "Noon," but if the question is "At what time?" the response is "at noon." Because the backtracking in correcting resembles that in answering, Levelt concluded that we monitor ourselves the same way we listen to others.

Summary

In the last sections we examined in detail the problems of pattern recognition in speech and related them to production and monitoring of speech. We saw that although there is evidence that phonetic features have a psychological reality in both production and perception, they are affected by surrounding features, making the signal underlying any feature highly variable or context sensitive. The dynamics of speech, the coarticulation patterns, appear to contain critical information for its perception. Perception may be based on a number of different, redundant, sufficient sets of properties, none of which is alone necessary. For production, we hypothesized a multileveled organization, with abstract articulatory features at the lowest level, which are then incorporated into higher level units of production such as words, phrases, sentences, and so on. Like perception, production plans are abstract, specifying a general target that may be achieved by the articulators variably depending on context. We proposed that perception and production may be mediated by similar mechanisms, accounting for similarities in monitoring inner speech and others' speech, and in the similar characteristics of context variability, simultaneity, smear, and hierarchical organization. This suggests that perception of speech may also take place simultaneously on many levels. We turn now to theories and experiments on the various levels at which speech perception might take place.

THEORIES OF SPEECH PROCESSING

Speech is a highly complex, important, and overlearned human skill. Emphasizing one or two of these characteristics of speech has led investigators to radically different models of speech processing: from complex neural networks that emphasize learning and resemble other well-practiced complex human behaviors, to relatively opaque speech processing modules, specially evolved and different from any other kinds of perceptual processing we do. Before looking at these models and the supporting evidence, I emphasize some speech characteristics that we have already noted.

• Speech is for human communication and so normally is used to transmit meaning. Meaning is accessed through knowledge of the sound structure, knowledge of semantics, syntax, and pragmatics. Normal speech perception and production therefore need access to these levels of language knowledge.

• Speech itself appears to involve an abstract, phonetic level of description, which does not bear a one-to-one relation with the underlying acoustic signal or articulatory gestures. Each phonetic unit comprises a specifiable set of acoustic "cues" and articulatory movements that may redundantly or synergistically specify it.

• A particular phonetic segment is produced over time, coarticulated smoothly with other segments. Consequently its acoustic manifestations are smeared together with those of other segments. The apparent linear order of, say, /s/ before /ɛ/ before /g/ in *segment* arises in part from the *relative* influence of each phone in each portion of the signal (there is less /g/ in the beginning and less /s/ effect at the end) and in part from the process of speech perception itself.

These characteristics of speech we refer to as hierarchical organization, smear, and simultaneity.

Connectionist Models: TRACE, Node Structure Theory, and Production Systems

Recall our previous descriptions of connectionist or neural net models, in semantics and syntax. These models incorporate a multilayered structure with connections both within and between layers. Connections can be excitatory, so activation of one unit excites those connected to it, or inhibitory, with activation of one unit preventing connected units from responding. Knowledge is distributed (or smeared) throughout the network in the patterns of connectivity and activation. These patterns are learned in an initial stage in which feedback is given as to the accuracy of the output. If the machine was correct, the connection weights used in that trial are strengthened; if incorrect, they are weakened. This learning stage continues until the weights change little between trials; stability is reached.

One of the earliest successful connectionist models, the TRACE model, identified naturally spoken stop consonants in monosyllables produced by a single talker (McClelland & Elman, 1986/1991). The TRACE model consisted of three levels of units, corresponding to features, phonemes, and words. Each feature was represented by banks of units coding several different sound dimensions over a number of time slices, building in the redundancy and smear that we have seen exists in speech. At the phoneme level, up in the hierarchy, units responded to sets of time slices, with one copy of each phoneme *centered* over three such slices and spanning six such slices, again building in smear and building in the simultaneous conveyance of several phonemes in a particular slice. The word level mapped to the phoneme units as the phoneme units mapped to the feature units.

Spoken input produced a pattern of activation at the feature level that changed over time because of the dynamic nature of speech. As we have seen before in connectionist modeling, particular co-occurrence patterns or rules were not specifically programmed but were learned through the regularities inherent in the input. Thus, after stability is reached, recognition of /i/ as the vowel will empower different acoustic connections for /d/ than would recognition of /u/ as the vowel.

The first version of TRACE successfully recognized 90% of the stop consonants produced by a single speaker. A later version of TRACE regularized the feature input (making it contextually invariant) to concentrate on the potential influences of the lexical level, of knowledge of what words exist, on perception. Here, input consisted of specific feature values along continuous phonetic dimensions, such as consonant-vowel and compact-diffuse, and acoustic dimensions, such as voicing and amplitude of the burst. The values were adjusted to create ambiguity at the phoneme level.

This TRACE successfully modeled perceptual results from an important study by Ganong (1980/1991). Ganong found that labeling of the voiced-voiceless continua was affected by word recognition. He used voicing continua that had as one end point a word and at the other end point a nonword, such as *dash-tash.* At the /d-t/ boundary, where the acoustic information was ambiguous, stimuli were more often heard as the word, here *dash,* than the nonword. The boundary shifted to favor /t/ when /t/ began a word and /d/ did not (as in *dack-tack*). When both end points were nonsense syllables (e.g., *dath-tath*), the boundary was intermediate between those for the two-word/nonword continua. This result was among the first to suggest that speech perception is influenced by lexical status, input from the word level. Other such results we will examine later. Here we note that given excitatory connections from word units to component phoneme and feature units, TRACE also showed a shift to identify words preferentially.

Speech production has also been modeled in connectionist systems, described briefly in the tip-of-the-tongue section of Chapter 3. As with perception, the advantage of connectionism to production is the inclusion of the influences of several levels of processing at each instant of decision. Stemberger (1985) describes an interactive model of language production, as do Dell (1986, Spreading Activation Theory), MacKay (1987, Node Structure Theory), and Levelt (1989). I will not describe these in detail but will use our earlier discussions of connectionist modeling and interactive levels in speech production to motivate the analogy to connectionist models of speech production.

The first step in making the analogy is to realize that input and output must be reversed from the perception case: In production, the input units will be semantic or syntactic slots, which in turn activate particular words or morphemes, which in turn activate phonological components, like syllables, onsets, rimes, or phonemes (which in turn activate an articulatory plan). Obviously, a particular unit at one level may need several units to represent it at a lower level; a morpheme may encompass several syllables, each of which encompasses an onset and a rime. As we saw in Chapter 3 in our discussion of Node Structure Theory, it is necessary to postulate an order to the activation of components so that onsets, for example, are activated before rimes. We must also postulate inhibitory connections among fillers of the same slots (so only one onset is selected) and excitatory connections between a slot and its potential fillers (so that the "call" for an onset is more likely to produce another onset from the speech plan than it is to produce a rime). Dell's model, restricted to morphological and phonological levels, produced errors of different types in comparable proportions to those produced by humans in existing slip-of-the-tongue corpuses, like those I cited earlier (e.g., phoneme substitutions are more frequent than syllable substitutions).

As in all connectionist modeling, we see interconnectivity within levels as well as activation moving in both directions—here not simply from the idea toward the articulatory plan but also from activation of articulatory information to the idea

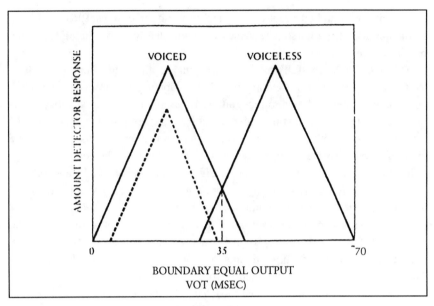

Figure 7.8. Response of Hypothetical Voicing Detectors

NOTE: The detector on the left responds to sound with 0-45 ms VOT with a maximum response at about 20 ms VOT. The detector on the right responds to sounds with about 25-70 ms VOT, with the peak response at about 50 ms VOT. The detectors respond equally at 35 ms VOT, which, then, is the continuum boundary. The dotted line shows diminished detector response after adaptation with a voiced stimulus. Note the resulting boundary shift at the new location for equal response.

level. The simultaneous existence of multiple levels of representation and multiple directions of activation is what accounts for both anticipation and perseveration errors (if there is no activation from a future or past utterance, these could not occur).

Thus connectionist modeling assumes a processing hierarchy, influences from many language levels, and distribution of information across a number of time slices and a number of levels of units. In the stabilized weights after repeated trials, it also models the effects of our considerable practice articulating speech and hearing common co-occurrence patterns. Habit is the origin of our rapid, complex, and context-sensitive processing.

Detector Theory

Connectionist modeling proposes a large number of interconnected units, the *pattern* of activation of which produces a percept or an articulatory plan. *Detector theory* attempted to account for the phonetic nature of speech perception by postulating groups of mutually antagonistic units, with each group representing a phonetic feature and each component unit representing a different value of that feature (Abbs & Sussman, 1971). Figure 7.8 displays the hypothetical output of a pair of detectors responsive to voicing. The solid lines show baseline response gradients for a voiced detector competing with a voiceless detector, as proposed by Eimas and Corbit (1973/1991).

Figure 7.9. A Cartoonist's Depiction of Adaptation in a Place of Articulation Continuum (Courtesy of the artist, Andrew Rothman. Used with permission.)

A detector is a single neuron or a group of neurons working together. According to the theory, a voiced percept would occur when the voiced detector responds more than the voiceless detector. Each detector is sensitive to a range of VOT values, as the figure indicates, and responds with a *graded* output; that is, the magnitude of response differs depending on where in its range it is stimulated. In Figure 7.8, peak response for the voiced detector occurs at a VOT value of about 20 ms. The voicing boundary occurs where the two detectors have equal output; in the figure, at 35 ms.

Detector theory was tested by a technique called adaptation (Eimas & Corbit, 1973/1991). In *adaptation,* a stimulus is presented repeatedly until sensitivity to it decreases. (Semantic satiation, discussed in Chapter 3, is an adaptation effect.) For example, when you first enter a swimming pool, the cold may be shocking; after a while, your sensitivity to the cold diminishes. In speech, adaptation is accomplished by repeatedly presenting one of the continuum end points (e.g., /ba/ repeated 60 times per minute for 3 minutes) followed by identification of a few randomly selected continuum members, followed by another adaptation period, and so on. Compared with unadapted baseline identification, after /ba/ adaptation, subjects hear fewer /ba/s; there is a boundary shift toward /ba/. (Likewise, water that feels cool when you are at room temperature may feel warm to the touch after your finger has gotten used to ice water.) As the dotted line in Figure 7.8 indicates, repeated activation of the /ba/ detector is believed to impair its ability to respond across the continuum. This results in the previously ambiguous stimulus (at 35 ms) now produce a clearly greater activation of the opponent detector, which yields a voiceless percept.

Adaptation effects have been demonstrated for a variety of phonetic features (e.g., Cooper, 1974; Cooper & Blumstein, 1974), as Figure 7.9 humorously suggests for place of articulation. They do not require the identity of the adaptor and test continuum: /da/ will adapt a /ba-pa/ continuum toward /b/, presumably adapting the "voiced" detector; /bi/ will adapt a /ba-pa/ continuum also toward /b/, even though the syllable, and vowel, are not shared. In all cases, if the adaptor and test continuum do not match, the adaptation effect is smaller, evidence of context sensitivity of the detectors.

Adaptation also occurs with a variety of acoustic features: Tartter and Eimas (1975) showed that adaptation with chirps (like the second formant transition) and bleats (like the second formant) shifted the phoneme boundary almost as much as did adaptation with the full-cue stimulus from which they were taken. Adaptation with acoustic components not only shifts the identification boundary but also slows response times for making the identifications; this contrasts with effects of, say, a /da/ adaptor on a /ba-pa/ continuum, which shifts identification but not reaction time (Samuel & Kat, 1996).

The reaction time and identification adaptation effects of the acoustic components and the smaller effect of nonidentical adaptors suggest that adaptation does not affect only a purely *phonetic* feature detector but a lower tier of competing units, sensitive to component acoustic properties (Samuel & Kat, 1996; Sawusch & Jusczyk, 1981; Tartter & Eimas, 1975). There seems also to be a higher "phonetic" level of adaptation reflected by boundary shifts in the absence of reaction time differences (Samuel & Kat, 1996), as when /da/ adapts a /ba-pa/ continuum. This kind of layered model is, of course, consistent with an interactive PDP-type representation.

The Motor Theory

Probably the most influential model of speech perception is "the motor theory" propounded by researchers at Haskins Laboratories over the last few decades (Liberman, Cooper, Shankweiler, & Studdert-Kennedy, 1967/1991; Liberman & Mattingly, 1985/1991). The motor theory was proposed initially to account for the fact that the acoustic signal seemed to have a highly variable, context-sensitive relationship to linguistic features, with articulation assumed to be perhaps more nearly invariant. *Motor theory* proposed that speech is *perceived* as the sequence of articulatory gestures listeners might make to produce such sounds themselves; that articulation is a mediating response between the variable acoustic signal and the phonetic percept. (You may recall our discussion in Chapter 3 of R_ms and muscle mediation of verbs; motor theories constitute a class of models using the perceiver's actions as perceptual anchor.) The articulation reference is necessary mostly for highly *encoded* (i.e., rapid and context-dependent) consonants, particularly stop place of articulation, for which sufficient cues prove elusive, as we have seen.

There is some question as to whether a motor mediator solves the invariance problem. First, our discussion of production indicates that, like perception, articulation is abstract and variable; we achieve the same articulatory configuration and acoustic goal in different ways depending on whether we are clenching something between our teeth as we talk. Therefore, production may not be a safe place to turn to escape the perceptual variation problem! Second, there is a logical difficulty in the idea of an R_m: There must be enough information in the signal to allow an inference about articulation to arrive at the correct R_m; that information *could directly* signal the percept. The articulation step is logically unnecessary (which does not mean that it does not happen). Finally, perception depending on articulation implies that listeners need speaking experience before they can understand, and that people who have articulation difficulties will show comprehension problems, as should preverbal children. Neither of these is true.

Motor theory assumes that speech perception is a special, modular process, distinct from other auditory information processing, dependent on articulation. It has been both controversial and productive in generating data on how speech is perceived. We turn next to the data addressing the assumptions that (a) speech constitutes a special module and (b) the module processes with reference to articulation.

IS SPEECH SPECIAL?

Over the last few decades, different experimental results (see Samuel & Tartter, 1986, for a critical review) have been claimed to support the notion that perception of speech entails a specialized linguistic module, one that perhaps uses articulation patterns to interpret the speech signal. What I am calling here a speech "module" has been referred to as a special "speech mode" (of hearing) or "phonetic perception."

Categorical Perception

We have already discussed the creation of synthetic speech continua for voicing and stop-glide manner. A continuum systematically varies an acoustic property between one identifiable value, such as voiced, to a different identifiable value, such as voiceless. *Systematic* variation means that between adjacent pairs of continuum members, the difference is identical: Stimulus 1 differs from Stimulus 2 in 10-ms VOT; Stimulus 2 differs from Stimulus 3 also in 10-ms VOT; and so on. A synthetic speech continuum can be made between any two sounds (place of articulation, vowel, and so on) provided the acoustic distinction between the two sounds is well defined and systematically manipulated. Likewise, one can be created for nonspeech variants of a speech sound, say, from the /ba/-chirp (second formant transition, as you may recall) to the /da/-chirp. This is indicated in Figure 7.10, which shows the two end points for a two-formant /ba-da/ series (Panel a) and the stimulus intermediate between them (Panel b). Superimposed in Panel c are the five steps of a /ba-da/ continuum between the end points of Panel a, created by varying the slope of the second formant transition. Synthesizing any transition alone in the "fan" of Panel c makes a chirp; the set of transitions in the fan is a nonspeech continuum.

Synthetic continua have been used in identification and discrimination tasks. As we have discussed, in identification, subjects simply label the stimuli, saying what they hear. In *discrimination,* subjects are asked whether they can hear a difference between two stimuli, say, between a stimulus with 0-msec VOT and a stimulus with 10-msec VOT. The discrimination task most frequently employed in speech per-

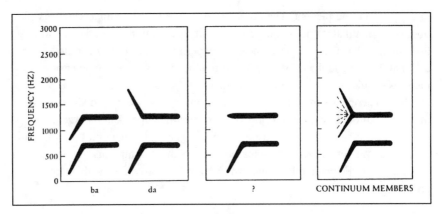

Figure 7.10. Schematized Speech Spectrograms

NOTE: (a) illustrates a /ba/ on the left and a /da/ on the right; (b) shows a sound intermediate between /ba/ and /da/, because the second formant transition is halfway between the second formant transitions of /ba/ and /da/; (c) shows potential continuum members, overlaid on one another. All have the same first formant and second formant steady state. Each stimulus of the continuum has a different second formant transition, indicated either by solid lines (for the end points) or by dotted lines. Note that the lines are equidistant from one another, representing equal acoustic steps.

ception research is the *ABX task:* Two stimuli are presented a short time apart, Stimulus A and then Stimulus B, followed by a third stimulus (X), identical to either A or B. The subject decides whether X matches A or B. If A and B appear identical to the subject, there is no basis for choosing between them, and the subject will guess, with a 50% chance of being correct. If A and B are distinctly different, then it is clear which matches X.

The pattern obtained for identification and discrimination of stop consonants was unexpected. Investigators had anticipated results like those displayed on Panel a of Figure 7.11, *continuous perception:* If Stimulus 1 was a good /b/ and Stimulus 9 a good /d/, Stimulus 2 would be identified most of the time as /b/, Stimulus 3 a little less of the time, and so forth. Discrimination was also expected to be the same throughout the continuum: If people could hear a 10-degree difference in second formant transition slope, they would do so throughout the series, and if they could not, they would not be able to do so throughout. These two hypotheses, one for identification and one for discrimination, constitute continuous perception.

The actual results, obtained for consonant continua, were very different, as Figure 7.11b shows. In identification there appears to be an abrupt shift from b-perception to d-perception; the first four stimuli all seem perfectly good /b/s and the last four perfectly good /d/s, with a sudden change at a boundary stimulus. The boundary stimulus still sounds speechlike but is ambiguous, sounding sometimes like /b/ and sometimes like /d/.

Discrimination also showed a pattern markedly different from what had been expected, as the solid line in panel c of Figure 7.11 indicates. At the end points of the continuum, where subjects labeled all the stimuli as /b/ or all as /d/, they were nearly at chance. These are *within-category discriminations,* judgments between

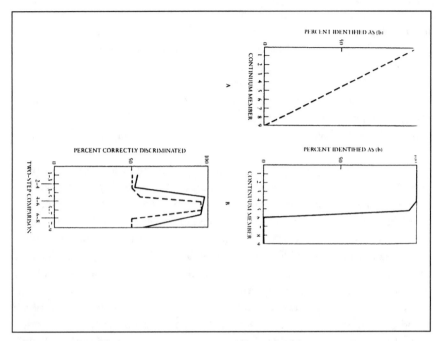

Figure 7.11. The Relation of Identification and Discrimination of Synthetic Speech Continua

SOURCE: Results are from Tartter (1982).

NOTE: (a) shows the idealized continuous perception identification function; (b) shows an actual identification function for a /ba-da/ continuum; (c) shows the predicted discrimination function (dotted line) assuming subjects discriminated no better than they identified the continuum members in (b), along with actual discrimination function (solid line).

two stimuli assigned to the same phonetic category. At the middle of the continuum, where the identification function locates the boundary between the two phonetic features, discrimination was nearly perfect. This means that the same acoustic manipulation, a 10-degree change in transition slope, for example, has a different psychological effect in different places in the series!

The correspondence between the identification boundary and the discrimination peak was so striking that investigators decided that *discrimination was based on identification,* such that sounds labeled the same could not be discriminated, and sounds labeled differently could be perfectly discriminated (Liberman, Harris, Hoffman, & Griffith, 1957). The dotted line in the discrimination panel indicates values for discrimination predicted from identification results alone. *This pattern of results, a sharp division into categories in labeling and an enhanced discrimination* between category *relative to* within category, is called *categorical perception.*

Importantly, nonspeech stimuli derived from consonant continua do not show the peak in discrimination but are relatively consistently and poorly discriminated (Liberman, Harris, Kinney, & Lane, 1961; Mattingly, Liberman, Syrdal, & Halwes, 1971). The differences in sound perception between nonspeech stimuli and speech stimuli in which they are embedded have been attributed to specialized processing for stimuli perceived as speech. Chirps, which are not identified as speech, are not handled by the speech processor and therefore are neither categorized nor categorically discriminated. The special process has been assumed to code the stimuli in terms of articulatory (phonetic) features, stripping away all acoustic information and leaving only the feature labels available to discriminate. (The categorical perception phenomena have generated a huge literature and alternative interpretations beyond the scope of this chapter. Interested readers should see the definitive review by Repp, 1984.)

It is important to note that the nonspeech stimuli used as controls in these experiments could not be produced by a vocal tract or any other natural acoustic source; that is, they are not *categorizable*. To the extent that categorical perception arises from categorization processes—perceiving the causes of sound—we would not expect an artificial sound producible by no possible natural source to allow categorization processes. Indeed, Fowler (1986/1991, 1990, 1996) argues that the categorization process is not special to speech but is the natural mode of any perceptual system—to recover information about the real world object. The auditory system uses sound to recover information about events producing it; for speech sounds, these events are vocal tract movements. Like Fowler, motor theorists attribute categorical perception to perception of the vocal tract movements. Unlike Fowler, they argue that categorization of the underlying event, the dynamic vocal tract configuration, is a special-to-speech process.

Categorical perception and language experience. Could we know *innately* that speech sounds are related to vocal tract events or have we, as English speakers, learned that differences that *mean* /b/ or /d/ are critical, whereas differences signaling "within-category" configurations are not? This second interpretation, that categorical perception arises through language use, would be an example of linguistic relativity: Speakers of different languages would perceive sounds differently; that is, language experience affects thought—here, perception (Hunt & Agnoli, 1991).

Several investigators have specifically attempted to make perception of an initially noncategorical discrimination categorical by training (practicing) within-category or nonspeech-sound discriminations (Lane, 1965; Pisoni, 1977/1991; Samuel, 1977). Practice does alter discriminability by producing sharply categorized identification functions and more categorical-looking discrimination functions, better matching those predicted from identification. This suggests that we may *learn* to categorize salient sound events.

Conversely, investigators have shown that speakers do *not* categorically perceive sounds that are not phonetically distinct in their language, suggesting that they either lost an innate ability to perceive this distinction through lack of practice or never learned to hear it. Miyawaki et al. (1975/1991) compared discriminability of an /r-l/ continuum for American and Japanese speakers. Americans showed typical categorical functions, whereas the Japanese speakers could neither label nor discriminate the stimuli; their functions looked like those for nonspeech stimuli. (Note the support for the Whorfian hypothesis: Language experience affects the percep-tion of auditory distinctions.)

We have described two approaches here: extensive training to heighten distinctiveness and extensive lack of training to lose distinctiveness. These exem-plify two possibilities proposed to account for categorical perception: *acquired distinctiveness,* where overuse or importance emphasizes a difference, such as the boundary between two categories, and *acquired similarity,* where lack of use causes an innate distinction to atrophy. The first suggests that infants innately "hear" all sounds as equivalent and learn to make the phonetic distinctions required by the language. The second suggests that all phonetic distinctions are innate but the ones not used disappear from the infant's repertoire if they are not practiced. Experiments on infant perception support each of these hypotheses, depending on the particular phonetic distinction. We will look at these data in Chapter 9 when we consider language development. In Chapter 8, we will see that even in adults, as dialect features shift, distinctions may be lost or forged.

Categorical perception and auditory sensitivity. We have just entertained, with empirical support, the hypothesis that categorical perception arises because of the extraordinary amount of practice we get differentiating those sounds that are linguistically distinct for us. There is also evidence that the sounds that are linguistically distinct are so not accidentally but are so because our auditory systems are especially sensitive to a particular acoustic difference, which language then comes to exploit. This relates to the quantal theory of speech (Stevens, 1989/1991), presented in the last chapter: Phonetic distinctions arise at articulatory configura-tions that create an acoustic discontinuity, say, between turbulent and nonturbulent airflow, but there is a range of articulation (within category) that produces minor, nondistinctive acoustic changes. The quantal theory relates both articulation and audition (hearing) to the idea of there being natural discontinuities at which phonetic categories may arise.

There is evidence of such auditory discontinuities at some of our phonetic boundaries. For example, in the training studies described (Pisoni, 1977/1991; Samuel, 1977), untrained discriminability peaks arose in places expected from other experiments to have heightened auditory sensitivity. More compellingly, speech identification functions for chinchillas mirror those for humans. Chinchillas, of course, do not articulate, nor do they have meaningful experience with English, but they do have auditory systems physically and psychophysically like ours.

Kuhl (1981; Kuhl & Miller, 1975, 1978/1991) trained chinchillas to cross a barrier to avoid a shock when signaled by a sound at one end of the speech continuum. Presentation of the sound at the other end of the continuum signaled delivery of water (reinforcement) on the side of the barrier where the chinchilla already was located. After training with the continuum end points, the chinchillas were presented with intermediate continuum members to see, for each, whether they crossed the barrier or stayed, thus providing identification data. The chinchillas exhibited the same identification boundaries as English speakers as well as the same feature dependencies: The VOT boundary for both human and chinchilla differs for different places of articulation, with a longer VOT necessary to hear voicelessness the farther back the sound is made. Because chinchillas have no specific linguistic experience, their categorization must take place by general auditory mechanisms, and thus so could ours.

Summary. The results for identification and discrimination of speech reveal that stop consonants are perceived differently from some nonspeech categories. This may be because of special processing for the consonants such as acquired distinctiveness, acquired similarity, relation to an articulatory event, or some other process. Alternatively, it may be that language has evolved to use the auditory and (articulatory) areas that we are most sensitive to—to maximize its perceptual salience and discriminability (see Stevens, 1989/1992). Regardless, it seems that the acoustic distinctions signaling different consonants are more discriminable than many other acoustic distinctions.

Dichotic Listening and Laterality

You may recall dichotic listening from our discussion of consonant confusion data at the beginning of this chapter. Dichotic listening studies have provided strong evidence for a specialized speech processor, located for most people in the left cerebral hemisphere of the brain. Difference in function between the cerebral hemispheres is known as *laterality.*

Different areas of the brain are responsible for different functions: The left hemisphere controls motor movements and sensations of touch on the right side of the body, and the right hemisphere, on the left. Damage to the left hemisphere can cause paralysis and numbing on the right side of the body. Damage to the left hemisphere, for nearly all right-handed individuals and many left-handed individuals, can also cause an impairment in language skills. Thus, as mentioned in Chapter 3, the left hemisphere may be considered the abstract verbal hemisphere.

Hearing does not cleanly divide with the right hemisphere controlling the left ear and the left hemisphere the right ear. However, under special presentation conditions, it appears possible to make the left hemisphere respond preferentially to material from the right ear, and the right hemisphere to material from the left ear. The special condition is dichotic stimulation, which seems to suppress information traveling from the ear to the hemisphere on the same side (Kimura, 1961, 1964, 1967).

Kimura showed that dichotically presented spoken digits are more accurately perceived when presented to the right ear than the left (a *right ear advantage [REA]*), but that excerpted passages of music are better perceived when presented to the left ear than the right. This suggests that the REA does not arise for *any* auditory stimulation but only for linguistic material. Studdert-Kennedy and Shankweiler (1970/1991) showed that to produce an REA, *meaningful* material is *not* necessary: Nonsense syllables differing in consonant only yield an REA. Vowels yield no particular ear advantage (Blumstein, Tartter, Michel, Hirsch, & Leiter, 1977; Studdert-Kennedy & Shankweiler, 1970/1991), unless they are degraded (e.g., presented in noise) to yield enough errors to measure a difference between the ears (Godfrey, 1974). Other aspects of speech have also been tested: Blumstein and Cooper (1974) found a left-ear advantage for dichotic intonation contours, and Tartter (1984) found a slight, nonsignificant left-ear advantage for speaker identification of the same syllables for which a significant REA was obtained when subjects judged consonants.

As a group, the results suggest that segmental speech information may be specially processed by a speech "module" located in the left hemisphere. This module does not appear to process suprasegmental and paralinguistic speech information.

The McGurk Effect

Normally, before this century at least, speech perception has always taken place in person, and so could usually benefit from the redundant visible cues to speech available from lip-reading. McGurk and MacDonald (1976/1991) showed that this visible information is processed together with auditory information to identify speech: Subjects looking at a video image of someone saying "ga" and listening to the sound /ba/, report hearing /da/; /da/, of course, may be considered the "average" of the two signals, being produced midway between them. That the lip movements we see are integrated readily into a speech percept has been taken as evidence of a special speech mode of hearing, one that uses articulatory mediation (Liberman & Mattingly, 1985/1991). Cues to articulation are modality-independent; thus both visual and auditory information can come together.

Note that lip movements and speech sounds inform about the same articulatory event. Fowler (1990) obtained cross-modal interactions for nonspeech when both modalities cued the same event, such as a train looking bigger as its thunder gets louder.

Fowler (1996) demonstrated a McGurk effect when subjects feel the speaker's mouth, integrating that information with degraded speech. She failed to get such integration of written letters with degraded speech. Note that we have no experience feeling someone's mouth and a lot of experience as readers with the sound of a letter. Therefore the McGurk effect does not result from learning a common association of vision and sound but from recognizing the identity of the underlying articulatory event, evidence of articulatory mediation of speech perception.

Trading Relations

Another line of evidence that speech percepts may involve a specialized integration process cuing an articulatory event comes from the fact that there are several sufficient cues for each phonetic feature, which may be "traded" off against one another. That is, as we have seen, a voiced sound differs from a voiceless sound in the time of onset of the voicing relative to the onset of energy, in the amount of aspiration, and in the intensity, frequency, and timing of the first formant. We can produce a voiceless sound either by lengthening the voice onset time per se or by using a shorter voice onset time and raising the first formant frequency (Stevens & Klatt, 1974): These two cues can trade with one another. Best, Morrongiello, and Robson (1981/1991) demonstrated a trade with two other voicing cues and, further, that *subjects could not discriminate between syllables that were synthesized using different acoustic characteristics but that cued the same percept.*

Best et al. also tested the trading relation potential of the cues in a "nonspeech" mode, using *sine-wave speech,* in which, as I mentioned earlier, the temporal properties of speech are preserved, along with minimal formant information. The speech is synthesized as three sine waves at the center frequencies of the first three formants. Sine-wave speech may be heard simultaneously as a set of whistles (nonspeech mode) and, for some listeners instructed to think of it as speech, as speech. Best et al. found that listeners who heard sine-wave speech as speech, when so doing, traded acoustic properties. When the stimuli were perceived as nonspeech, the cues were not similarly integrated and did not trade. The trade is considered to reflect special speech processing and alternative ways of producing the same phonetic target.

We should note that such "trading relations" occur for other natural auditory percepts (and for visual ones): To locate a sound source, we integrate differences in timing and intensity information between our two ears and cannot tell the difference between stimuli cuing the same location differently. One might argue that this is a normal perceptual phenomenon. Indeed, it may be normal for specialized perceptual "modules," which, as you may recall from Chapter 4, are hypothesized to exist for "input systems," which automatically, autonomously, and impenetrably process their innately designated input. Localizing sound information or perceiving speech or any other natural event perception each may entail a specialized modular process.

Duplex Perception

With sine-wave speech we saw that some listeners could choose to perceive an ambiguous signal as speech or as nonspeech. Another such ambiguous signal may be created by splitting the formants and presenting them dichotically. Typically the first formant and second formant steady state are put into one ear and the second formant transition into the other (Mann & Liberman, 1983). Listeners simultaneously hear two percepts: a fused syllable that sounds like it is coming from the middle of the head, and a chirplike sound, which seems to come from the side on which the isolated transition is presented. Listeners can then be asked to attend to either the central locus or the ear locus and to identify or discriminate sounds at those sites.

Given categorical perception tests of such stimuli, listeners show typical categorical functions for the fused, central sound, and typical noncategorical functions (flat identification, generally poor discrimination) for the lateralized (at the ear) chirp. What is critical in this demonstration, though, is the fact that both the speech and the chirp percepts depend only on the second formant transition information: It is perceived categorically when fused into a syllable and perceived as speech, and

---

Box 7.5. Evidence for a Speech Module

— Categorical Perception of Speech:
   Sharply differentiated identification functions
   Excellent discrimination between identified categories; near chance within category
   Occurs for well-practiced speech distinctions and may be trained up for nonspeech
   Does not occur for at least some phonetic distinctions for human subjects who do not speak the language
   Occurs for chinchillas, suggesting the distinction may exploit natural regions of auditory sensitivity
   → A special mode may exist naturally for speech based on our sensitivity, but requiring practice or experience to maintain. Important percepts may acquire a special mode of perception, where "importance" to the organism is determined by degree of practice/experience.
— Dichotic listening suggests a left-hemisphere specialization for phonetic perception.
— Hearing in the speech mode allows the following:
   Trading relations: Redundant cues may offset one another, with the resulting percept indiscriminable from equivalent, but different cue combinations.
   Duplex perception: A chirp in one ear with first formant plus second formant steady state in the other ear is heard as both a chirp and fused syllable simultaneously. The chirp is perceived continuously; the fused syllable it contributes to, categorically.
   The interpretation of sine-wave speech is possible.
— McGurk effect: Visual, auditory, and tactile cues to speech events are integrated in speech perception.

But perception could be "direct," inducing causal events even in nonspeech. Trading and cross-modal integration have been shown for events, such as a train approaching (sound and vision). For speech, the underlying event is the articulation, but that does not make speech special or necessarily modular.

---

is perceived continuously if attended to as a whistle. Moreover, the *fused* speech sound can be created when the chirp intensity is so attenuated (quiet) that it cannot be heard alone but still can contribute to a speech percept (Whalen & Liberman, 1987).

Summary

We have looked at several lines of evidence suggesting that speech may be specially perceived, apart from other auditory signals. The special speech processor appears, from dichotic listening studies, to be located in the left cerebral hemisphere. It appears to integrate different acoustic, tactile, and visual cues to speech into a single percept, which may be differentiated only with difficulty from similarly identified percepts produced by other cue combinations. The integration and differentiation processes appear to rely in part on languages' employment of regions of optimal auditory sensitivity for their important linguistic distinctions (hence, even chinchillas perceive some distinctions as humans do) but also on the extensive experience we have with our language. Thus speechlike perception may be trained for nonspeech sounds, and may not occur for some phonetic distinctions in speakers of languages for which they are not relevant. We seem to see special-to-speech processing when we are encouraged to interpret the acoustic signal as a speech event. We similarly see "special" acoustic processing when we interpret any acoustic information as reflecting a natural sound-producing event (Fowler, 1990, 1996).

SPEECH PROCESSING IN NATURAL LANGUAGE CONTEXT

In discussing Ganong's (1980/1991) experiment, I observed that the *lexical status* of an acoustic signal affects its categorization: We are more apt to identify an ambiguous signal as a word than as a nonword. There have been many dem-onstrations that speech perception is influenced by word recognition, meaning, and syntax. We have already noted that speech production and self-monitoring seem to occur on many language levels simultaneously; we will now see that, likewise, perceiving the speech of others uses any level of language available.

Detecting Mispronunciations On-Line

I mentioned mispronunciation detection experiments at the beginning of this chapter. In these experiments, speech errors are deliberately introduced into text and listeners are asked to detect them. Listeners, as you may remember, are more likely to notice a two-feature error than a one-feature error. In addition, mispronun-ciations are detected faster in the second or third syllable of a multisyllable word than in the first syllable (Cole & Jakimik, 1980). Presumably, in the first syllable, a listener is unsure as to what the word is and so cannot tell if a particular sound sequence is an error or not. Later in the signal the word is recognized, and an error becomes obvious. For instance, if the word *linguistic* is mispronounced as *ringuis-tic,* at the end of the first syllable, there is an acceptable word, *ring.* Sometime in the second or third syllable it would be realized that the initial guess was wrong, and calculation could start again. If it is mispronounced *linguiskic,* when the error appears the word will have been correctly identified and the error will be immedi-ately obvious. Thus the word's identity, the fact that it has a representation in the mental dictionary, affects the way the speech is processed.

Using a variant of the mispronunciation task, Marslen-Wilson (Marslen-Wilson, 1975; Marslen-Wilson & Welsh, 1978) measured the effects of syntax and seman-tics in fluent speech processing. Subjects were asked to *shadow,* that is, to echo speech as they heard it. This is a very complex task—you might want to try it: Repeat as closely in time to the speaker what the speaker is saying (this is also very annoying to the speaker, so make sure you have a patient friend to try it with). In Marslen-Wilson's shadowing task, the speech was altered to contain errors in either the first or the later syllables of a word and of one to three features (/b/ → /d/ or /θ/, for example). It was also distorted so some sentences were scrambled and some semantically anomalous. Thus shadowers would have to listen very carefully while they were talking speedily to reflect the stimulus exactly. Of course, they were not able to do this, resulting in shadowing "errors," correcting speech to real words or real sense. Not surprising, the degree of correction depended in part on the type of sentence; many more corrections were made for normal sentences than anomalous sentences and for anomalous sentences than scrambled sentences. Most important, corrections occurred virtually *simultaneously* with the input, with subjects showing the same correction patterns when ¼ second behind the input or ¾ second behind. They also did not delay after a correction. This suggests that subjects do not hear the error and then correct it, but that, from *the beginning,* they use the syntax and semantics to help "correctly" perceive the speech (as Levelt suggested for production and self-monitoring).

Phonemic Restoration

An exciting auditory illusion demonstrating that lexical status affects speech perception involves obliterating a speech segment (either phoneme or syllable) by removing it, adding an extraneous noise, and then asking subjects to report what they hear. The result is called the *phonemic restoration effect* (Warren, 1970/1991). As the name implies, subjects supply the missing sound, reporting that they hear it. That subjects report hearing intact words suggests that they not only process the signal bottom-up, they use lexical knowledge to fill the gaps.

In an ingenious variant of the restoration task, Samuel (1981, 1996) presented subjects with stimuli that either were whole words, a phoneme of which co-occurred with noise (called "added"), or were words in which the phoneme was missing and the noise replaced it (called "replaced"). Subjects were asked to determine whether a given stimulus was "added" or "replaced." This permitted assessment of whether the restoration effect resulted from guessing or from perceptual fill-in. If the lexical process actually fills in the missing sound, then added versions should be indiscriminable from replaced versions: In the added ones, the sound was on the tape; in the replaced, it would be in the listener's representation. If phonemic restoration is from guessing, the representation of the sound will not be affected, and added and replaced versions should be discriminable.

Samuel found that replaced fricatives and stops were not discriminated well from added ones compared with replaced nasals, vowels, and liquids (like /l/)—because the noise used was acoustically similar to the frication and burst in the former. In addition, he found that subjects were much less able to discriminate added or replaced versions of real words than of nonwords phonologically similar to real words (that is, possible words). This suggests that the lexical status, the fact that they have a mental representation, activates a *perceptual* representation undifferentiatable from auditory stimulus input. The perceptual effect becomes stronger—

that is, it is harder to tell replaced and added stimuli apart—the longer the word is. Indeed, it may be unmeasurable in short words, which allow only a brief window for buildup of lexical activation (Samuel, 1996). Finally, Samuel (1981) found that sentence contexts did not increase discriminability but did increase guessing. As a whole, this suggests that speech *perception* is penetrable by lexical but not syntactic information.

Models of Lexical Access and Word Segmentation

Recall the TRACE model of speech perception, the PDP representation of speech recognition. Samuel's results imply mutual activation or strong weighting among co-occurring phonemes or phonetic features in a word, and also activation from units representing full words. The combination of these activations can raise a given phoneme unit's activation or a given word unit's activation above threshold, so that one cannot tell if it was activated by a stimulus or not. On the other hand, this speech-lexical network appears not to be "penetrable" by activation of a syntactic slot, although the syntactic information may be integrated with the output from the speech-lexical network to effect an informed decision on the likely word.

Now recall the cohort model of Marslen-Wilson and Welsh (1978), introduced in Chapter 3. That model suggested that a word is recognized through a left-to-right activation of phonemes, wherein the first phoneme arouses all possible words beginning with that sound—the cohort—which narrows as incoming sounds rule out members. Word recognition is achieved when there is a unique lexical item remaining in the cohort. We may ask here too whether semantic or syntactic information influences the cohort selection; Samuel's results suggest that semantic information, but not syntactic information, should.

Grosjean (1980) developed a *gating paradigm,* which mimics a cohort activation with spoken sounds in real time. Specifically, a subject is played the initial portion of a word, and asked to guess its identity; then is presented with a bit more of the word and asked again; and so on until the subject has successfully identified the item. Gating results show that cohort activation employs semantic and syntactic information because guesses change if a determiner (*a* or *the*) is presented, increasing the likelihood that the next word will be a noun (McAllister, 1988). There thus is some evidence for the influence of syntactic as well as semantic information in speech perception.

And, in an interesting variant of this task, Tanenhaus, Spivey-Knowlton, Eberhard, and Sedivy (1995) showed that subjects naturally "gate," employing *extralinguistic* information. As we saw in Chapter 5, listening to sentences, subjects naturally move their eyes to fixate mentioned objects and determine sentence structure and meaning. If in front of them are both a candle and a candy, their eye movement time indicates that they wait for the end of the word. If only one object is there, they initiate the eye movement before the end, incorporating the extralinguistic information into their identification of the sounds.

Box 7.6. Influences of Higher Language Levels on Speech

— Mispronunciations are easier to detect in later syllables than in a word's first syllable, presumably because the word's identification affects its on-line perception.

— Listeners shadowing text with mispronunciations automatically correct them with no time delay, suggesting that they "hear" the correct text, influenced by the semantic and syntactic as well as phonological constraints.

— Listeners "restore" missing segments of real words, unable to discriminate stimuli in which the segment is missing from those in which it is masked. Thus lexical information activates units representing the segment. Syntax does not similarly cause sound fill-in but does influence what subjects think they hear.

— Boundary stimuli are more likely to be assigned to the phoneme category that makes a word.

— Speech intrusion errors derive from similar unit levels—features, syllables, onsets, morphemes, or words.

— Gating (how much of a word a subject must hear to identify it) shows that word recognition in running speech is influenced by lexical and syntactic information, and is not complete until well into the following word.

— Eye movement patterns indicate that word recognition is influenced by the likely alternatives given the nonlinguistic setting.

Finally, recall the segmentation problem briefly introduced at the beginning of the chapter as you looked at Figure 7.1: Where are the word boundaries? Evidence suggests that we *must* have interaction of lexical and phonetic information to isolate the words. Many monosyllabic words constitute the first syllable of a multisyllable word: *can* and *Canada, you* and *euphemism*. Using the gating paradigm, Grosjean (1985) found that a word often was not uniquely recognized by subjects until well into the next word, presumably when the multisyllabic members of the cohort could be successfully eliminated.

To some extent, cohort members may be initially selected based on bottom-up information, the incoming segments, together with heuristics for grouping the segments. At some point, though, there must be interaction with information as to possible lexical items and consistency with the syntax and semantics of the input. Cutler and Butterfield (1992) reviewed linguistic evidence on puns and slips of the ear such as *transcend dental medication* for *transcendental meditation* to test segmentation rules. They concluded that English-speaking listeners attempt word boundaries before *strong* syllables, those that receive stress and have full, stressed vowels. Listeners then select the longest word consistent with the input up to the segmentation marker. Note in the example that *transcendental* has primary stress on the third syllable, whereas most English words have it on the first. Locating a word boundary before the "den," making *den* begin its own word, reflects a heuristic consistent with frequency of stress patterns of English. This illustrates again an interactionist approach, combining bottom-up sound information with knowledge of lexical status.

SUMMARY AND CONCLUSIONS

In this chapter we examined the lowest levels of language processing, speech perception and production, and found multiple levels of structure, as we did for the higher levels of language processing, syntax and semantics. At one level, there are acoustic and articulatory properties of the signal, which appear to be extracted or produced in complex combinations to give rise to phonetic features. There is some evidence for a level in which phonetic features are processing units, but little evidence that they are processed strictly independently of one another. At another level, the feature combinations that produce phonemes appear to be the psychologically relevant unit; at another, the syllable; at another, the word. These processing levels interact with one another so that word recognition can influence feature processing, and feature processing, word recognition.

Overlaid on the speech-communication aspects of the signal and motor commands are influences of higher level language functions: We see syntactic and semantic effects apart from word recognition on both pronunciation and perception. Overlaid on the language-communication aspects of the signal are paralinguistic influences that signal emotional overtone and information relevant to person perception. The overwhelming conclusion about organization of information in speech is that the form of any one segment is influenced by values from all levels, producing a lack of invariance on the one hand and, on the other hand, redundancy; vowel information is smeared across "consonant" portions, "vowel" portions, lexical memory, higher level phonological rules, and so on. Hearing the vowel *segment* itself is not necessary; vowel identity is cued elsewhere.

The speech processor, perhaps specially developed for language, or perhaps like other natural perceptual processors interpreting sounds as probable natural events—here, articulations—has the task of parsing and producing the signal into the various levels of features, phonemes, syllables, words, phrases, and sentences. This it seems to accomplish by working on several levels simultaneously, over many segments. By working on several levels simultaneously, the redundancy provided by each level helps narrow the choice of patterns on the perception side and introduces effects of context at different levels on the production side. Having information for any one level smeared across several segments also enhances redundancy, thereby allowing a maximally efficient recognition system.

This ends our discussion of *normative,* adult language processing. In the next chapter we will look at structured patterns of individual differences in language processing: dialectal processes and regular alterations in language processed as a function of social setting, that is, sociolinguistic phenomena. We note that thus far we have attempted to concentrate on the transmission and reception of content in language but have necessarily been "sidetracked" into considering its other communicative functions: connotation as well as denotation, creation or use of common ground with different levels of intimacy among conversants, speaker and emotion characteristics along with phonemes in speech. We shall see in Chapter 8 that "smear" of personal and social functions with the content function is neither a "sidetrack" nor an irrelevant variation but a primary communicative function. Language (and speech) conveys abstract ideas along with personalities or group membership.

REFERENCES

Abbs, J. H., & Sussman, H. M. (1971). Neurophysiological feature detectors and speech perception: A discussion of theoretical implications. *Journal of Speech and Hearing Research, 14,* 23-36.

Ali, L., Gallagher, T., Goldstein, J., & Daniloff, R. (1971). Perception of coarticulated nasality. *Journal of the Acoustical Society of America, 49,* 538-540.

Best, C. T., Morrongiello, B., & Robson, R. (1981). Perceptual equivalence of acoustic cues in speech and nonspeech perception. *Perception & Psychophysics, 29,* 191-211. (Reprinted in J. L. Miller, R. D. Kent, & B. S. Atal, Eds., 1991, *Papers in speech communication: Speech perception,* pp. 313-337. Woodbury, NY: Acoustical Society of America)

Blumstein, S. E., & Cooper, W. E. (1974). Hemispheric processing of intonation contours. *Cortex, 1,* 337-350.

Blumstein, S. E., & Stevens, K. N. (1979). Acoustic invariance in speech production: Evidence from measurement of spectral characteristics of stop consonants. *Journal of the Acoustical Society of America, 66,* 1001-1018.

Blumstein, S. E., & Stevens, K. N. (1980). Perceptual invariance and onset spectra for stop consonants in different vowel environments. *Journal of the Acoustical Society of America, 67,* 648-662.

Blumstein, S. E., Tartter, V. C., Michel, D., Hirsch, B., & Leiter, E. (1977). The role of distinctive features in the perception of vowels. *Brain and Language, 4,* 508-520.

Bregman, A. S. (1990). *Auditory scene analysis.* Cambridge: MIT Press.

Cole, R. (1973). Listening for mispronunciations: A measure of what we hear during speech. *Perception & Psychophysics, 4,* 153-156.

Cole, R. A., & Jakimik, J. (1980). How are syllables used to recognize words? *Journal of the Acoustical Society of America, 67,* 965-970.

Cooper, W. E. (1974). Adaptation of phonetic feature analyzers for place of articulation. *Journal of the Acoustical Society of America, 56,* 617-627.

Cooper, W. E., & Blumstein, S. E. (1974). A labial feature analyzer in speech perception. *Perception & Psychophysics, 15,* 591-600.

Cooper, W. E., & Paccia-Cooper, J. (1980). *Syntax and speech.* Cambridge, MA: Harvard University Press.

Cutler, A. (1980). Errors of stress and intonation. In V. Fromkin (Ed.), *Errors in linguistic performance* (pp. 67-80). New York: Academic Press.

Cutler, A., & Butterfield, S. (1992). Rhythmic cues to speech segmentation: Evidence from juncture misperception. *Journal of Memory and Language, 31,* 218-236.

Delattre, P. C., Liberman, A. M., & Cooper, F. S. (1955). Acoustic loci and transitional cues for consonants. *Journal of the Acoustical Society of America, 27,* 769-773.

Dell, G. S. (1986). A spreading activation theory of retrieval in sentence production. *Psychological Review, 93,* 283-321.

Eimas, P. D., & Corbit, J. D. (1991/1973). Selective adaptation of linguistic feature detectors. *Cognitive Psychology, 4,* 99-109. (Reprinted in J. L. Miller, R. D. Kent, & B. S. Atal, Eds., 1991, *Papers in speech communication: Speech perception,* pp. 3-13. Woodbury, NY: Acoustical Society of America)

Ekman, P., Friesen, W. V., & Scherer, K. R. (1976). Body movement and voice pitch in deceptive interaction. *Semiotica, 16,* 23-27.

Fairbanks, G., & Hoaglin, L. W. (1941). An experimental study of the durational characteristics of the voice during the expression of emotion. *Speech Monographs, 8,* 85-90.

Fairbanks, G., & Pronovost, W. (1939). An experimental study of the pitch characteristics of the voice during expression of emotion. *Speech Monographs, 6,* 89-104.

Fowler, C. A. (1986). An event approach to the study of speech perception from a direct-realist perspective. *Journal of Phonetics, 14,* 3-28. (Reprinted in J. L. Miller, R. D. Kent, & B. S. Atal, Eds., 1991, *Papers in speech communication: Speech perception,* pp. 15-40. Woodbury, NY: Acoustical Society of America)

Fowler, C. A. (1990). Sound-producing sources as objects of perception: Rate normalization and nonspeech perception. *Journal of the Acoustical Society of America, 88,* 1236-1249.

Fowler, C. A. (1996). Listeners do hear sounds, not tongues. *Journal of the Acoustical Society of America, 99,* 1730-1741.

Fromkin, V. A. (1973). *Speech errors as linguistic evidence.* The Hague, The Netherlands: Mouton.

Fromkin, V. A. (1980). *Errors in linguistic performance: Slips of the tongue, ear, pen, and hand.* New York: Academic Press.

Fry, D. B. (1955). Duration and intensity as physical correlates of linguistic stress. *Journal of the Acoustical Society of America, 27,* 765-768.

Fry, D. B., Abramson, A. S., Eimas, P. D., & Liberman, A. M. (1962). The identification of synthetic vowels. *Language and Speech, 5,* 171-189.

Ganong, W. F., III. (1991/1980). Phonetic categorization in auditory word perception. *Journal of Experimental Psychology: Human Perception and Performance, 6,* 110-125. (Reprinted in J. L. Miller, R. D. Kent, & B. S. Atal, Eds., 1991, *Papers in speech communication: Speech perception,* pp. 335-349. Woodbury, NY: Acoustical Society of America)

Gerstman, L. H. (1968). Classification of self-normalized vowels. *IEEE Transactions on Audio- and Electroacoustics, AU-16,* 16-80.

Godfrey, J. J. (1974). Perceptual difficulty and the right-ear advantage for vowels. *Brain and Language, 1,* 323-335.

Greenberg, J. H., & Jenkins, J. J. (1964). Studies in the psychological correlates of the sound system of American English. *Word, 20,* 157-177.

Grosjean, F. (1980). Spoken word recognition processes and the gating paradigm. *Perception & Psychophysics, 28,* 267-283.

Grosjean, F. (1985). The recognition of words after their acoustic offset: Evidence and implications. *Perception & Psychophysics, 38,* 299-310.

Hadding-Koch, K., & Studdert-Kennedy, M. (1964). An experimental study of some intonation contours. *Phonetica, 11,* 175-185.

Harris, K. S. (1958). Cues for the discrimination of American English fricatives in spoken syllables. *Language and Speech, 1,* 1-7.

Hecker, M. H. L., Stevens, K. N., von Bismarck, G., & Williams, C. E. (1968). Manifestations of task-induced stress on the acoustic speech signal. *Journal of the Acoustical Society of America, 44,* 993-1001.

Heinz, J. M., & Stevens, K. N. (1961). On the properties of voiceless fricative consonants. *Journal of the Acoustical Society of America, 33,* 589-596.

Hunt, E., & Agnoli, F. (1991). The Whorfian hypothesis: A cognitive psychology perspective. *Psychological Review, 98,* 377-389.

Jakobson, R., Fant, C. G. M., & Halle, M. (1969). *Preliminaries to speech analysis.* Cambridge: MIT Press. (Original work published 1951)

Joos, M. (1948). Acoustic phonetics. *Language Supplement, 24,* 1-136.

Kewley-Port, D. (1983). Time-varying features as correlates of place of articulation in stop consonants. *Journal of the Acoustical Society of America, 73,* 322-335. (Reprinted in J. L. Miller, R. D. Kent, & B. S. Atal, Eds., 1991, *Papers in speech communication: Speech perception,* pp. 351-364. Woodbury, NY: Acoustical Society of America)

Kimura, D. (1961). Cerebral dominance and the perception of verbal stimuli. *Canadian Journal of Psychology, 15,* 166-171.

Kimura, D. (1964). Left-right differences in the perception of melodies. *Quarterly Journal of Experimental Psychology, 16,* 355-358.

Kimura, D. (1967). Functional asymmetry of the brain in dichotic listening. *Cortex, 3,* 163-178.

Kuhl, P. K. (1981). Discrimination of speech by nonhuman animals: Basic auditory sensitivities conducive to the perception of speech sound categories. *Journal of the Acoustical Society of America, 70,* 340-349.

Kuhl, P. K., & Miller, J. D. (1975). Speech perception by the chinchilla: The voiced-voiceless distinction in alveolar plosive consonants. *Science, 190,* 69-72.

Kuhl, P. K., & Miller, J. D. (1978). Speech perception by the chinchilla: Identification functions for synthetic VOT stimuli. *Journal of the Acoustical Society of America, 63,* 905-917. (Reprinted in J. L. Miller, R. D. Kent, & B. S. Atal, Eds., 1991, *Papers in speech communication: Speech perception,* pp. 365-377. Woodbury, NY: Acoustical Society of America)

Ladefoged, P., & Broadbent, D. E. (1957). Information conveyed by vowels. *Journal of the Acoustical Society of America, 29,* 98-104. (Reprinted in J. L. Miller, R. D. Kent, & B. S. Atal, Eds., 1991, *Papers in speech communication: Speech perception,* pp. 493-499. Woodbury, NY: Acoustical Society of America)

Lane, H. (1965). The motor theory of speech perception: A critical review. *Psychological Review, 72,* 275-309.

Lashley, K. S. (1951). The problem of serial order in behavior. In L. A. Jeffress (Ed.), *Cerebral mechanisms in behavior* (pp. 112-146). New York: John Wiley.

Lehiste, I., & Peterson, G. E. (1961). Some basic considerations in the analysis of intonation. *Journal of the Acoustical Society of America, 33,* 419-425.

Levelt, W. J. M. (1983). Monitoring and self-repair in speech. *Cognition, 14,* 41-104.

Levelt, W. J. M. (1989). *Speaking: From intention to articulation.* Cambridge: Bradford Books of MIT Press.

Liberman, A. M., Cooper, F. S., Shankweiler, D. P., & Studdert-Kennedy, M. (1967). Perception of the speech code. *Psychological Review, 74,* 431-461. (Reprinted in J. L. Miller, R. D. Kent, & B. S. Atal, Eds., 1991, *Papers in speech communication: Speech perception,* pp. 75-105. Woodbury, NY: Acoustical Society of America)

Liberman, A. M., Delattre, P. C., & Cooper, F. S. (1952). The role of selected stimulus variables in the perception of unvoiced stop consonants. *American Journal of Psychology, 65,* 497-516.

Liberman, A. M., Harris, K. S., Hoffman, H. S., & Griffith, B. C. (1957). The discrimination of speech sounds within and across phoneme boundaries. *Journal of Experimental Psychology, 54,* 358-368.

Liberman, A. M., Harris, K. S., Kinney, J. H., & Lane, H. L. (1961). The discrimination of relative onset time of the components of certain speech and nonspeech patterns. *Journal of Experimental Psychology, 61,* 379-388.

Liberman, A. M., & Mattingly, I. G. (1985). The motor theory of speech perception revised. *Cognition, 21,* 1-36. (Reprinted in J. L. Miller, R. D. Kent, & B. S. Atal, Eds., 1991, *Papers in speech communication: Speech perception,* pp. 107-142. Woodbury, NY: Acoustical Society of America)

Lieberman, P. (1960). Some acoustic correlates of word stress in American English. *Journal of the Acoustical Society of America, 32,* 451-454.

Lindblom, B. (1996). Role of articulation in speech perception: Clues from production. *Journal of the Acoustical Society of America, 99,* 1683-1692.

Lisker, L., & Abramson, A. S. (1970). The voicing dimension: Some experiments in comparative phonetics. In *Proceedings of the Sixth International Congress of Phonetic Sciences, Prague, 1967* (pp. 563-567). Prague: Academia. (Reprinted in J. L. Miller, R. D. Kent, & B. S. Atal, Eds., 1991, *Papers in speech communication: Speech perception,* pp. 379-383. Woodbury, NY: Acoustical Society of America)

MacKay, D. G. (1970). Spoonerisms: The structure of errors in the serial order of speech. *Neuropsychologia, 8,* 323-350.

MacKay, D. G. (1987). *The organization of perception and action: A theory of language and other cognitive skills.* New York: Springer-Verlag.

Mann, V. A., & Liberman, A. M. (1983). Some differences between phonetic and auditory modes of perception. *Cognition, 14,* 211-235.

Marslen-Wilson, W. D. (1975). Sentence perception as an interactive parallel process. *Science, 189,* 226-228.

Marslen-Wilson, W. D., & Welsh, A. (1978). Processing interaction and lexical access during word recognition in continuous speech. *Cognitive Psychology, 10,* 29-63.

Mattingly, I. G., Liberman, A. M., Syrdal, A. K., & Halwes, T. (1971). Discrimination in speech and nonspeech modes. *Cognitive Psychology, 2,* 131-157.

McAllister, J. M. (1988). The use of context in auditory word recognition. *Perception & Psychophysics, 44,* 94-97.

McClelland, J. L., & Elman, J. L. (1986). The TRACE model of speech perception. *Cognitive Psychology, 18,* 1-86. (Reprinted in J. L. Miller, R. D. Kent, & B. S. Atal, Eds., 1991, *Papers in speech communication: Speech perception,* pp. 175-260. Woodbury, NY: Acoustical Society of America)

McGehee, F. (1937). The reliability of the identification of the human voice. *Journal of General Psychology, 17,* 249-271.

McGehee, F. (1944). An experimental study of voice recognition. *Journal of General Psychology, 31,* 53-65.

McGurk, H., & MacDonald, J. (1976). Hearing lips and seeing voices. *Nature, 264,* 746-748. (Reprinted in J. L. Miller, R. D. Kent, & B. S. Atal, Eds., 1991, *Papers in speech communication: Speech perception,* pp. 385-386. Woodbury, NY: Acoustical Society of America)

Miller, G. A., & Nicely, P. (1955). An analysis of perceptual confusions among English consonants. *Journal of the Acoustical Society of America, 27,* 338-352. (Reprinted in J. L. Miller, R. D. Kent, & B. S. Atal, Eds., 1991, *Papers in speech communication: Speech perception,* pp. 623-637. Woodbury, NY: Acoustical Society of America)

Miller, J. L. (1981). Effects of speaking rate on segmental distinctions. In P. D. Eimas & J. L Miller (Eds.), *Perspectives on the study of speech* (pp. 39-74). Hillsdale, NJ: Lawrence Erlbaum.

Miller, J. L., Kent, R. D., & Atal, B. S. (Eds.). (1991). *Papers in speech communication: Speech perception.* Woodbury, NY: Acoustical Society of America.

Miller, J. L., & Liberman, A. M. (1979). Some effects of later-occurring information on the perception of stop consonant and semivowel. *Perception & Psychophysics, 25,* 457-465. (Reprinted in J. L. Miller, R. D. Kent, & B. S. Atal, Eds., 1991, *Papers in speech communication: Speech perception,* pp. 395-403. Woodbury, NY: Acoustical Society of America)

Miyawaki, K., Strange, W., Verbrugge, R., Liberman, A. M., Jenkins, J. J., & Fujimura, 0. (1975). An effect of linguistic experience: The discrimination of [r] and [l] by native speakers of Japanese and English. *Perception & Psychophysics, 18,* 331-340. (Reprinted in J. L. Miller, R. D. Kent, & B. S. Atal, Eds., 1991, *Papers in speech communication: Speech perception,* pp. 405-414. Woodbury, NY: Acoustical Society of America)

Mohr, B., & Wang, W. S. (1968). Perceptual distance and the specification of phonological features. *Phonetics, 18,* 31-45.

Murray, I. R., & Arnott, J. L. (1993). Toward the simulation of emotion in synthetic speech: A review of the literature on human vocal emotion. *Journal of the Acoustical Society of America, 93,* 1097-1109.

Peterson, G. E., & Barney, H. L. (1952). Control methods in a study of vowels. *Journal of the Acoustical Society of America, 24,* 175-184. (Reprinted in J. L. Miller, R. D. Kent, & B. S. Atal, Eds., 1991, *Papers in speech communication: Speech perception,* pp. 595-593. Woodbury, NY: Acoustical Society of America)

Pisoni, D. B. (1977). Identification and discrimination of relative onset time of two component tones: Implications for voicing perception in stops. *Journal of the Acoustical Society of America, 61,*

1352-1361. (Reprinted in J. L. Miller, R. D. Kent, & B. S. Atal, Eds., 1991, *Papers in speech communication: Speech perception,* pp. 415-424. Woodbury, NY: Acoustical Society of America)

Remez, R. E., Rubin, P. E., Berns, S. M., Pardo, J. S., & Lang, J. M. (1994). On the perceptual organization of speech. *Psychological Review, 101,* 129-156.

Repp, B. H. (1984). Categorical perception: Issues, methods, findings. In N. J. Lass (Ed.), *Speech and language: Advances in basic research and practice, 10* (pp. 243-335). New York: Academic Press.

Samuel, A. G. (1977). The effect of discrimination training on speech perception: Noncategorical perception. *Perception & Psychophysics, 22,* 321-330.

Samuel, A. G. (1981). Phonemic restoration: Insights from a new methodology. *Journal of Experimental Psychology: General, 110,* 474-494.

Samuel, A. G. (1996). Does lexical information influence the perceptual restoration of phonemes? *Journal of Experimental Psychology: General, 125,* 28-51.

Samuel, A. G., & Kat, D. (1996). Early levels of analysis of speech. *Journal of Experimental Psychology: Human Perception and Performance, 22,* 676-694.

Samuel, A. G., & Tartter, V. C. (1986). Acoustic-phonetic issues in speech perception. *Annual Review of Anthropology, 15,* 247-273.

Sawusch, J. P., & Jusczyk, P. (1981). Adaptation and contrast in the perception of voicing. *Journal of Experimental Psychology: Human Perception and Performance, 7,* 408-421.

Schatz, C. D. (1954). The role of context in the perception of stops. *Language, 30,* 47-56.

Scherer, K. R. (1979). Personality markers in speech. In K. R. Scherer & H. Giles (Eds.), *Social markers in speech* (pp. 147-201). Cambridge: Cambridge University Press.

Scherer, K. R. (1986). Vocal affect expression: A review and a model for future research. *Psychological Bulletin, 99,* 143-165.

Shankweiler, D., Strange, W., & Verbrugge, R. (1977). Speech and the problem of perceptual constancy. In R. Shaw & J. Bransford (Eds.), *Perceiving, acting and knowing: Towards an ecological psychology* (pp. 315-345). Potomac, MD: Lawrence Erlbaum.

Shannon, R. V., Zeng, F.-G., Kamath, V., Wygonski, J., & Ekelid, M. (1995). Speech recognition with primarily temporal cues. *Science, 270,* 303-304.

Soli, S. D., Arabie, P., & Carroll, J. D. (1986). Discrete representations of perceptual structure underlying consonant confusions. *Journal of the Acoustical Society of America, 79,* 826-837.

Stemberger, J. P. (1985). An interactive activation model of language production. In A. W. Ellis (Ed.), *Progress in the psychology of language* (Vol. 1, pp. 143-185). London: Lawrence Erlbaum.

Stevens, K. N. (1975). The potential role of property detectors in the perception of consonants. In G. Fant & M. A. A. Tatham (Eds.), *Auditory analysis and perception of speech* (pp. 303-330). New York: Academic Press.

Stevens, K. N. (1989). On the quantal nature of speech. *Journal of Phonetics, 17,* 3-45. (Reprinted in R. D. Kent, B. S. Atal, & J. L. Miller, Eds., 1991, *Papers in speech communication: Speech production,* pp. 357-400. Woodbury, NY: Acoustical Society of America)

Stevens, K. N., & Blumstein, S. E. (1978). Invariant cues for place of articulation in stop consonants. *Journal of the Acoustical Society of America, 64,* 1358-1368. (Reprinted in J. L. Miller, R. D. Kent, & B. S. Atal, Eds., 1991, *Papers in speech communication: Speech perception,* pp. 281-292. Woodbury, NY: Acoustical Society of America)

Stevens, K. N., & Klatt, D. (1974). Role of formant transitions in the voiced-voiceless distinction in stops. *Journal of the Acoustical Society of America, 55,* 653-659.

Strange, W., Jenkins, J. J., & Johnson, T. L. (1991/1983). Dynamic specification of coarticulated vowels. *Journal of the Acoustical Society of America, 74,* 695-705. (Reprinted in J. L. Miller, R. D. Kent, & B. S. Atal, Eds., 1991, *Papers in speech communication: Speech perception,* pp. 523-533. Woodbury, NY: Acoustical Society of America)

Streeter, L. A., Krauss, R. M., Geller, V. J., Olson, C., & Apple, W. (1977). Pitch changes during attempted deception. *Journal of Personality and Social Psychology, 35,* 345-350.

Streeter, L. A., MacDonald, N. H., Apple, W., Krauss, R. M., & Galotti, K. M. (1983). Acoustical and perceptual indicators of stress. *Journal of the Acoustical Society of America, 73,* 1354-1360.

Studdert-Kennedy, M., & Shankweiler, D. (1991/1970). Hemispheric specialization for speech perception. *Journal of the Acoustical Society of America, 48,* 579-594. (Reprinted in J. L. Miller, R. D. Kent, & B. S. Atal, Eds., 1991, *Papers in speech communication: Speech perception,* pp. 293-308. Woodbury, NY: Acoustical Society of America)

Tanenhaus, M. K., Spivey-Knowlton, M. J., Eberhard, K. M., & Sedivy, J. C. (1995). Integration of visual and linguistic information in spoken language comprehension. *Science, 268,* 1632-1634.

Tartter, V. C. (1980). Happy talk: The perceptual and acoustic effects of smiling on speech. *Perception & Psychophysics, 27,* 24-27.

Tartter, V. C. (1982). Vowel and consonant manipulations and the dual-coding model of auditory storage: A reevaluation. *Journal of Phonetics, 10,* 217-223.

Tartter, V. C. (1984). Laterality differences in speaker and consonant identification in dichotic listening. *Brain and Language, 23,* 74-85.

Tartter, V. C. (1991). Identifiability of vowels and speakers from whispered syllables. *Perception & Psychophysics, 49,* 365-372.

Tartter, V. C., & Braun, D. B. (1994). Hearing smiles and frowns in normal and whisper registers. *Journal of the Acoustical Society of America, 96,* 2101-2107.

Tartter, V. C., & Eimas, P. D. (1975). The role of auditory feature detectors in the perception of speech. *Perception & Psychophysics, 18,* 293-298.

Tartter, V. C., Kat, D., Samuel, A. G., & Repp, B. H. (1983). Perception of intervocalic stop consonants: The contributions of closure durations and formant transitions. *Journal of the Acoustical Society of America, 74,* 715-725.

van den Broeke, M. P. K., & Goldstein, L. (1980). Consonant features in speech errors. In V. A. Fromkin (Ed.), *Errors in linguistic performance: Slips of the tongue, ear, pen, and hand* (pp. 47-65). New York: Academic Press.

van Turennout, M., Hagoort, P., & Brown, C. M. (1997). Electrophysiological evidence on the time course of semantic and phonological processes in speech production. *Journal of Experimental Psychology: Learning, Memory, and Cognition, 23,* 787-806.

Warren, R. M. (1970). Perceptual restoration of missing speech sounds. *Science, 167,* 392-393. (Reprinted in J. L. Miller, R. D. Kent, & B. S. Atal, Eds., 1991, *Papers in speech communication: Speech perception,* pp. 465-466. Woodbury, NY: Acoustical Society of America)

Whalen, D. H., & Liberman, A. M. (1987). Speech perception takes precedence over nonspeech perception. *Science, 237,* 169-171.

Williams, C. E., & Stevens, K. N. (1972). Emotions and speech: Some acoustic correlates. *Journal of the Acoustical Society of America, 52,* 1238-1250.

STUDY QUESTIONS

1. What arguments have been made in support of the notion that speech is special? Critically discuss the evidence both for and against this position.

2. What is the problem of pattern recognition in speech? Is there support for invariant cues to speech features? Critically discuss specific attempts for specific segments.

3. Discuss the evidence supporting the phonetic feature as a "unit" of processing. Assume that the phoneme or syllable is "the unit": What results would you expect to see instead of those obtained in scaling experiments and dichotic listening? Critically consider whether the feature is in fact the best choice of unit.

4. Describe the interactionist approach (combining sound information with lexical or higher level knowledge) to speech perception and production. What

evidence is there that people integrate information from different linguistic levels in speech processing? What evidence is there that speech processing is encapsulated from some of these linguistic levels?

5. Discuss the evidence that speech may be perceived through reference to coarticulation patterns, with speech features exploiting regions of articulatory and acoustic discontinuities. Do you believe that the speech processor is innately developed, or that categorization of certain distinctions is learned through practice.

6. What are simultaneity, smear, and hierarchical organization? Discuss the multitude of percepts that second formant frequency information appears to affect. Discuss "where" in the speech signal consonant place-of-articulation information resides.

7. How do we recognize words? In answering this question, consider segmentation issues, the cohort model, the gating paradigm, the phonemic restoration effect, and the possibility of our understanding a new word, a sound sequence that had no representation in our lexicon.

8. How do we produce words? Discuss the levels of processing that seem to be involved, including self-corrections, and the likely units of articulatory control.

SOCIOLINGUISTICS

What is your favorite music group? Why? Describe their music and its appeal. No, this chapter is not about music; nevertheless, try to flesh out answers to these questions in about a paragraph, whereby with "flesh out" I mean *really* think about what words you would use to answer the questions, how you would string them together in sentences, and how you would pronounce them—the stuff of the previous chapters.

In all likelihood, if you have followed instructions, you will have constructed a reasonably formal essay on the subject—perhaps of a lewd and violent rap group. You may have even decided *not* to select your true favorite group, because it is lewd and violent and you think that would be inappropriate for a formal essay. The context of this book, or perhaps the class it is required for and perhaps the concern that the paragraph may need to be turned in, suggested to you word choice, sentence structure, and (if you switched to a more acceptable group) topic.

Now think about how you would discuss your favorite group with a very attractive person of your own age. Or with a group of "cool," "tough" guys you wanted to impress. Or with your grandmother, whom you hoped would agree to buy their latest CD for you. Again, for each situation, try to flesh out the words, sentences, and even accent you would use. How similar would your discussions sound with the different target audiences you were trying to impress?

Following standard linguistic traditions, this book has thus far explored "unvarying, functional units of language whose occurrence can be predicted by rule" (Labov, 1972b, p. 70) in the abstract, as though we each had a single language competence, with different performance variants emerging in different situations. Labov and others have shown that the effects of social variation on language structure are also predictable by rule and also amenable to serious controlled study. This suggests that our abilities to switch language styles appropriately may be part of our language competence, not only language performance. As our brief foray into popular music suggests, we may have several competencies depending on our audience and goals.

This aspect of linguistic competence, the bending of language to social needs, may underlie language change—the emergence of slang, the creation of dialects or eventually of separate languages. As Table 8.1 satirically illustrates, in science, jargon (specialized vocabulary), idioms (specialized phrases), and the impersonal, seemingly "objective" syntax (passive voice, no first person pronouns) constitute a "dialect" marking insiders, who use this language fluently, and outsiders, to whom it obfuscates rather than clarifies. As you have struggled to master scientific writing in research courses, or struggled to master the vocabulary presented for different disciplines in this book, you have experienced, perhaps consciously, the learning of a new language style.

In this chapter we will examine the rule-governed way in which language varies as we forge (or distance ourselves from) communities through communication style. We will see that it is possible to classify social situations rigorously and to study their effects on speech, the lexicon, and even syntax.

For this purpose we will concentrate on the work of William Labov, for all intents and purposes the father of sociolinguistics, and on the work of Robin Lakoff and Deborah Tannen on language differences between men and women speakers of the same dialect of American English. We will also look at debate on the process of radical historical changes in the formation of pidgin and creole languages.

METHODOLOGICAL ISSUES IN SOCIOLINGUISTICS

The Observer's Paradox and
Obtaining Natural Language Samples

The nature of the issues in sociolinguistics requires that language be studied as it is naturally occurring in different communities, sometimes over a long period of time. Introducing an observer into the community to note language perforce changes the community and thus can change the language sampled: the *observer's paradox* (Labov, 1972a, 1972b, 1994). Labov (1972a), for example, critically reports a dialogue between a young African American child (C) and a large, friendly white examiner (E), who opens the interview with a toy on the table and says:

E. Tell me everything you know about this.
C. [12 seconds of silence]
E. What would you say it looks like?
C. [8 seconds of silence]
　A space ship.
E. Hmmmm.
C. [13 seconds of silence]
　Like a je-et.

Table 8.1 Common Turns of Phrase in the Dialect of Science

Science	Translation
IT HAS LONG BEEN KNOWN THAT . . .	I haven't bothered to look up the original reference.
IT IS BELIEVED THAT . . .	I think.
THESE RESULTS WILL BE REPORTED AT A LATER DATE	I might get around to this sometime.
CORRECT WITHIN AN ORDER OF MAGNITUDE.	Wrong.
IT CAN BE VERIFIED . . .	It won't be verified.
WE OMIT THE DETAILS.	We omit the proof.
TYPICAL RESULTS ARE SHOWN . . .	The best results are shown.
IT IS CLEAR THAT MUCH ADDITIONAL WORK WILL BE REQUIRED BEFORE A COMPLETE UNDERSTANDING . . .	I don't understand it.

> [12 seconds of silence]
> Like a plane.
> [20 seconds of silence]
> E. What color is it?
> C. Orange. [2 seconds] An' whi-ite. [2 seconds] An' green.
>   [6 seconds of silence]
> E. An' what could you use it for?
> C. [8 seconds of silence]
>   A je-et.
>   [6 seconds of silence]
> E. If you had two of them, what would you do with them?
> C. [6 seconds of silence]
>   Give one to some-body.
> E. Hmmm. Who do you think would like to have it?
> C. [10 seconds of silence]
>   Cla-rence.
> E. Mm. Where do you think we could get another one of these?
> C. At the store.
> E. Oh ka-ay! (pp. 205-206)

On the basis of interviews like this, a notion developed that inner-city children had impoverished language, an inability to speak in whole sentences or construct abstract thoughts, and so on. Rather, Labov insists the *pragmatic situation* is one that elicits such language from the child and does not represent the child's true language competence.

Middle-class children, in effect, are raised to accept test situations. So, if I do the seemingly absurd "game" of holding up a very familiar object to Eric (my almost-10-year-old) and ask him if he knows what it is, like the child in the interview, he will know and he will know that I know what it is. Unlike the child in the interview, he will also know that this is a chance to show off his knowledge and he will do so at great length. An example is the following dialogue, also prompted by a toy airplane:

> Eric: Ummm. It's a mini F15 jet. And it's like an airplane, but instead of propellers it has two holes where gasoline, gasoline . . . the explosion from the gasoline shoots out of and then it makes it go fast. Because of the explosion.
>
> Me: Well, what do you do with it?
>
> Eric: This or a real airplane?
>
> Me: This.
>
> Eric: Well. What you do is there's like, well at the front of the plane there is always a wheel and this wheel is extendable so you pull it forward and hold it there and after that you put it on a flat surface and the thing should still be there and you let go of the front wheel and it moves, but it doesn't fly. It just moves along the ground like it's blasting off.
>
> Me: OK. Thank you.
>
> Eric: Hey! I'm not done yet!
>
> Me: So?
>
> Eric: It's about 3 inches, very small, and I'd say it's a piece of junk. (laughs). Umm.
>
> Me: Is that it?
>
> Eric: Yes. But why am I in your book?
>
> Me: I wanted to prove a point, which you have done, very nicely.

Clearly, Eric recognized the pragmatic situation of "a test," conducted by his psycholinguist mother, and took it as a chance to show off (apparently hoping to supply enough dialogue to be listed as coauthor!).

In contrast, a child (or adult) who is not experienced with language exchange in such situations would see the situation as absurd; you can almost hear the child thinking, "He doesn't know what *that* is?!" "Why is he asking me *that*!" "What does he want me to *say*?!" "How do I get out of here and back to something fun?" Indeed, Heath (1983) found questioning children an alien practice in working-class, rural black America:

> Children do not expect adults to ask them questions, for . . . children are not seen as information-givers or question-answerers. This is especially true of questions for which adults already have an answer. Since adults do not consider children appropriate conversational partners to the exclusion of other people who are around, they do not construct questions especially for children, nor do they use questions to give the young an opportunity to show off their knowledge about the world. (p. 103)

Beyond limited exposure to questions, if one's life experience is that saying the wrong thing leads to trouble, the interview, the social situation, may induce silence and one-syllable answers.

It is important to note that this is not a black-white issue. Labov's interviewers of children from the black inner city were African American teenagers from the children's neighborhoods. At first they had the same problem eliciting language as the white examiner had. Using their knowledge of the sociolinguistic and pragmatic factors that control speech, Labov and colleagues "made the following changes in the social situation:

1. Clarence [the interviewer] brought along a supply of potato chips, changing the interview into something more in the nature of a party.
2. He brought along Leon's [the child] best friend, eight-year-old Gregory.
3. We reduced the height imbalance by having Clarence get down on the floor of Leon's room; he dropped from six feet, two inches to three feet, six inches.
4. Clarence introduced taboo words and taboo topics, and proved, to Leon's surprise, that one can say anything into our microphone without any fear of retaliation.
   [. . . the consequence]

Clarence (C): Is there anybody who says *your momma drink pee*?

Leon (L): (rapidly and breathlessly) Yee-ah!

Greg (G): Yup!

L: And *your father eat doo-doo for breakfas'!*

C: Ohhh!! (laughs)

L: And they say your father—*your father eat doo-doo for dinner!*

G: When they sound [a language-insult game also called "playing the dozens"] on me, I say C. B. S. C. B. M.

C: What that mean?

L & G: Congo booger-snatch! (laughs)" (Labor, 1972a, p. 209).

It is vital to note that altering the social situation produces a dramatically different window on the language potentials of the community.

It is also vital to note that we can never entirely avoid the observer's paradox; we can use techniques that indicate the direction, but not the end point, of language in the absence of the observer. In one interview, for example, Labov (1972b) reports a casual conversation between himself and a young African American widow living in New York City. Her speech to him seemed natural:

Their father went back to Santo Domingo when they had the uprising about two years ago that June or July . . . he got killed in the uprising . . . I believe that those that want to go to give up their life for their country, let them go. For my part, his place was here with the children to help raise them and give them a good education . . . that's from my point of view.

Her speech even seemed informal as indicated by the laughter and dialectic speech:

Smart? Well, I mean when you use the word *intelligent* an' *smart* I mean—you use it in the same sense? . . . (Laughs) So some people are pretty witty—I mean—yet they're not so intelligent!

But contrast it with her speech to her child, addressed more naturally, although the interviewer is still present:

> Get out of the refrigerator, Darlene! Tiny or Teena or whatever your name is! . . . Close the refrigerator, Darlene! . . . What pocketbook? I don't have no pocket-book—if he lookin' for money from me, dear heart, I have no money!

This indicates a different style from the one used with the interviewer, more in the direction of her comfortable speech. Later she receives a telephone call, which she takes in another room, and we see further movement toward the end point of her natural conversational dialect:

> Huh? . . . Yeah, go down 'e(r)e to stay. This is. so you know what Carol Ann say? Listen at what Carol Ann say. Carol Ann say, "An' then when papa die, we can come back" [belly laugh] . . . Ain't these chillun sump'm [falsetto]? . . . An' when papa die, can we come back? (pp. 89-90)

Even the laughter changed (from controlled titter to belly laugh) when the audience and perceived stylistic community changed.

There are two methodological points here. One is that to study language as it is used, we must do the best we can to duplicate the situation of language use. We must do this knowing that we can never fully attain that situation. Nevertheless, we can *extrapolate* from the observed changes between formal and less formal language situations to the truly informal, unobserved situation. That requires structuring a comfortable "interview" and being prepared for serendipity—the unplanned interruptions—which, if accurately recorded, can provide a window on natural phenomena. And we must recognize that we can never completely avoid the observer's paradox and so are only looking at a more informal place on the formal-to-natural language continuum.

The other point is that while we recognize that to observe the *vernacular* (everyday language use), we must create informal settings, we also need to recognize that a comfortable setting for one social group may not be such for another: My survey may be your interrogation, and as such elicit very different behaviors and language samples.

Experimental Control of the Samples

We have considered the methodological paradox of structuring a situation to obtain spontaneous language behavior; structure and spontaneity are strange bed-fellows. That does not preclude the study of natural language behavior but does suggest both caution in generalizing the findings and the need to specify the social situation in which they occurred to interpret them accurately. The clever sociolinguist may also plan a study to elicit the desired language behavior under carefully controlled, but still natural, settings. Corroborating findings from structured interviews with anonymously collected data avoids the observer's paradox.

In an ingenious design, Labov (1972b, 1994) probed the New York accent "r-dropping" as a function of both socioeconomic class and attention to speech. What is ingenious in the design is that the two factors were systematically manipulated and yet the language samples were spontaneous and natural. To do this, Labov selected three department stores, each serving different socioeconomic classes: upper, middle, and lower. He hypothesized that sales personnel at each store would reflect the speech of their clientele, being hired in part to serve such clients comfortably. "Interviewers" were then instructed to enter each store and consult the store directory to find departments located on *the fourth floor.* Each interviewer then asked sales personnel for the location of the department, eliciting (and transcribing) many productions of the phrase *fourth floor* (with or without the telltale "r"). In addition, each interviewer was instructed to pretend to have not heard the answer, so the salesperson would have to repeat it, in all likelihood more carefully to ensure accurate transmission this time. Thus each informant presented two natural samples, one of "normal" and one of "careful" speech. For each department store (and presumed socioeconomic class) there were many subjects, as in less natural empirical studies.

The study found less r-dropping, a greater distancing from the local, low-prestige accent, in the higher socioeconomic class store. All sales personnel were also more likely to produce the "r" the second time around, when they were attending to their speech because the questioner had presumably not understood them.

Thus we have two possibilities to obtain natural language samples in normal settings: (a) Structure the laboratory or interview setting to reflect the social setting you wish to study, or (b) select or constrain your social settings and language samples to obtain desired variants of the language.

Collecting and Correlating Social Variables

Thus far we have been concerned with methodological issues in collecting the language samples, that is, how to obtain samples representative of natural language use in a community of users that does not normally contain the observer. To study *socio*linguistics we must also adequately sample social variables, such as socio-economic class in the department store study. The social variables define a *community* independent of *communication.* Interrelating community variables with communication variables specifies the social regularities of language competence.

Aside from socioeconomic class, we may consider social variables of age, sex, profession, ethnicity, and peer group membership, for example. We may also wish to sample attitude toward the community: New Yorkers tend to put down themselves and their city, to consider "a New York accent" undesirable. Upward mobility, a position at a higher class department store, is therefore achieved in part by dissociating from the New York accent. Note that there is nothing inherent in the accent that makes it undesirable; the failure to articulate "r" is a property of high-class British speech as well as the regal speech of the United States—the Boston accent of the Kennedy clan. For the upwardly mobile, r-deletion associated with summers at "the Cape" is desirable; r-deletion associated with summers on

Coney Island is not. To predict and understand the language pattern, we must assess the social context—in my example, where speakers summer and what their social aspirations and identifications are.

Labov (1972b) studied speech patterns in Martha's Vineyard natives, together with historical changes in the island's economics and attitudes of the islanders toward those changes. His study is instructive as to both the power and the importance of joint assessment of social and linguistic variables.

At the time of the study (the early 1960s), there were four ethnic groups among the native islanders: (a) those of English descent (Yankees), (b) those of Portuguese descent, (c) those of Indian descent, and (d) a heterogeneous group of mixed descent, which did not constitute a coherent social force. In addition to the native islanders, in the summer there was an influx of visitors, primarily from Boston, who increasingly were taking up summer residence. The economy of the island was in a state of flux, with one-quarter of the native population living up-island, farming, relatively poor, and relatively isolated from the summer tourists, and three-quarters of the native population living in towns, down-island, mostly serving the tourist trade. The up-islanders, because of their isolation from the tourists, provided a baseline of Vineyard speech. The down-islanders, in contrast, were exposed to language patterns of off-islanders and could show those influences in their speech.

The study used three basic sets of data. The first were tape-recorded, transcribed, and acoustically analyzed interviews, designed to elicit examples of words pronounced or used differently in the Martha's Vineyard and mainland-Massachusetts dialects. Vineyard residents, for example, constitute

> an island of r-pronouncers in a sea of r-lessness. With a 320-year history of continuous settlement, and a long record of resistance to Boston ways and manners, the island has preserved many archaic traits which were probably typical of southeastern New England before 1800. (Labov, 1972b, pp. 6-7)

Tape-recording interviews of subjects describing their lives, Labov could quantify the frequency of occurrence of particular linguistic phenomena, not simply noting the exotic productions. Tape recordings also permitted acoustic analysis.

In addition to the r-pronouncing, islanders also produced different vowel qualities, centralizing /ay/ and /aw/ relative to the mainland speech. They also retained seventeenth-century Englishisms that had been lost to other Yankee American groups, such as the word *belly-gut* for "sled-ride." Thus tracking specific lexical items and phonetic variants through interview and subsequent linguistic analysis identifies a dialect group.

The second source of data is also indicated in the quotation above and peppered across the paragraph: independent historical and geographic data on immigration fluxes, economic patterns, and general demographic characteristics such as age and number of family members in a household. Sources for contemporary statistics include census data or unemployment statistics. Sources for historical data include standard historical records, such as previous census data, town charters, and so on.

Finally, sources for historical word use include written materials from times gone by or compilations such as the *Oxford English Dictionary (OED)*.

The third source of data was the interview content: value judgments, attitudes, and social orientation of the respondents:

> You people who come down here to Martha's Vineyard don't understand the background of the old families of the island . . . strictly a maritime background and tradition . . . and what we're interested in, the rest of America, this part over here across the water that belongs to you and we don't have anything to do with. (p. 29)

or

> I have another son—Richard—is an aeronautical engineer. He really loves the island. And when he decided to be an aeronautical engineer we discussed it—at length—and I told him at that time: you just can't live on Martha's Vineyard. . . . He works at Grumman, but he comes home every chance he gets and stays just as long as he can. (p. 31)

or

> . . . we had an idea that he'd go away to school, but he really didn't want to go away. . . . When he was at Chauncey Hall, they tried to get him to go to M.I.T.; but he said no, he didn't want to go anywhere where he had to learn to do something that couldn't come back to the island. (p. 31)

These quotations reveal an attitude of extreme loyalty and perception of distinction (in both the senses of differentness and betterness) of Martha's Vineyard relative to the mainland. They also suggest a sense of siege: These informants (and their offspring) are loyal and are staying while others are leaving.

The cross-tabulation of the linguistic and the social data yields an exciting and coherent story. Increasingly, economic conditions had worsened and Vineyarders were leaving the Island, selling (out) to summer residents. The phonetic differences were exaggerated among those Yankees who had made the decision to stay; in effect they were clinging to the island and clinging to islander speech. Young Vineyarders who were choosing to better their economic prospects by leaving unconsciously adopted the speech patterns of the tourists. Those, like the student in the third quotation above, who had tried and rejected off-island life, became hyper-island-like, as the parent of one noted: "You know, E. didn't always speak that way . . . it's only been since he came back from college. I guess he wanted to be more like the men on the docks" (p. 31).

Now, this pattern appears to be a relation of attitude and dialect. Relating age and ethnic group to the dialect features also shows an interesting pattern: The strongest vowel centralization, for example, was among the middle-aged Yankees, and the least, among the young Yankees and senior Portuguese and Indians. The middle-aged Yankees constituted those who affiliated with the island despite the

---

Box 8.1. Methodology in Sociolinguistics

— Beware the *observer's paradox:* A situation in which natural language is observed is not a natural situation; the presence of the observer affects the behaviors being observed.
— Try to structure the observation to optimize the likelihood that speakers are natural and relaxed. If possible, structure the situation to produce the speech pattern with the individual unaware of being observed.
— Take advantage of unplanned opportunities— interruptions of the interview, telephone calls, and so on— to avoid the observer's paradox.
— Gather social data along with language data to examine patterns of covariation. Social data include surveys of the speakers and historical records such as census data. Language data include current language patterns and language patterns as suggested in old writings.

---

economic pressure to leave, and so overproduced the differentiating characteristics, relative to their parents. The young Yankees consisted of both those who planned to leave and those who who did not, and so, across the group, showed fewer island-dialect features. The senior Indian and Portuguese group members were people who had not assimilated into the Yankee group; their offspring identified with the island and were seeking full recognition by the high-status "blue bloods." The Indians were second-class citizens and the young and middle-aged Indians displayed ambivalence to the Yankees, both in interviewed attitudes and in degree of dialect change. On the one hand, they felt hostile, rejected, and rejecting of the Yankees; on the other, they recognized the higher status of the Yankees and sought recognition and acceptance from them.

Thus, to understand the system within a dialect or language and the direction of its movement over time, we need adequate data on *social forces.* Our linguistic methods must be accompanied by methods of assessing current and past societal trends; our language samples must be accompanied by demographic data on the age, sex, ethnic group affiliation, and so on of the speaker.

LANGUAGE CHANGE: DRASTIC HAPPENINGS AND GRADUAL EVOLUTION

Our consideration of dialect groups in New York and on Martha's Vineyard indicates that language is not static but changes as a community changes. It is important to recognize that these changes occur independently of a language's ability to transmit meaning (Labov, 1994); both *belly-gut* and *sled-ride* denote the same activity, so the loss of the earlier term, say, from my dialect is not because the activity has disappeared or changed, that is, is not from a change of meaning. Indeed, study of ongoing dialect changes sometimes reveals movement toward greater phonetic distinctiveness and therefore better conveyance of meaning and, sometimes, movement toward merging of sounds, creating new homonyms and greater possibilities of confusion.

Language changes to reflect social pressures. Language serves not only to communicate meanings and transmit information but also to bind group members together. As we saw in our study of speech, we have parallel communication functions in the same signal: phonetic and suprasegmental content, speaker identification, and emotional overtone. Similarly, the phonetic target (centralized vowels versus noncentralized diphthongs), the lexical item (*belly-gut* versus *sled-ride*), and even the syntactic structure ("I don't have no . . ." versus "I don't have any . . .") convey not just meaning information but information about speaker identity (which group he or she belongs to) and emotional overtone.

Normally, language changes slowly, as the community changes slowly. But there are drastic language changes accompanying community upheaval, such as after a war in which one language community is overpowered by another, after colonization of one group by another (either willingly or by force), or in a sudden pooling of "refugees" from different linguistic communities, whether "voluntary" refugees seeking to improve their lives or involuntary "refugees" taken as slaves or prisoners-of-war. We examine first the effects of these radical changes in language.

Creolization and Historical Change

If you needed to create a new language because you were suddenly thrust among people who did not share any language, where would you begin? Prior to this chapter, we have considered creating some new lexical items, borrowing words from other languages, or combining existing morphemes in the language. We also noted that within a language, frequently used words seem to undergo shortening for efficiency. These presuppose an existing language to borrow from, to expand, or to abbreviate. And word names, as we have seen, are a very small part of language: How does one create a syntax, phonology, or semantic structure?

While no one overtly plans to create a new language, it seems as though humankind may have an unconscious common "plan," which is known as the *the bioprogram hypothesis* (Bickerton, 1984). Study of structural features in communities of speakers suddenly bereft of a common language—the human-created equivalent of the Tower of Babel—has shown a remarkable similarity among first-generation, adult speakers (*pidgin language*) and second-generation child speakers (*creole language*).

The social situation is the domination of multitribal, many-languaged cultures by another, with the dominating culture imposing its language on all and forcing their intermingling. (Pidgins also arise, more benignly, when people who do not share a language trade with each other. Used by adults in a specific setting, these may not develop into creoles.) This situation has occurred many times historically. Consider, for instance, English domination of the islands of the South Pacific or Hawaii, or American domination of slaves from many tribes of Africa mixed on a single plantation. In such situations there is no common language because the colonizers have disrupted tribal boundaries and forced different groups to work together.

According to Bickerton (1984), the colonizers interact directly with but a few natives, who transmit the colonizers' orders down some well-established hierarchy. Thus the natives have minimal exposure to fluent use of the now-dominant language, but that may be the only language the natives have in common. The natives sputter the few words they have learned with little syntactic glue. This reduced, mixed language is called a pidgin language.

In many cases, pidgin speakers speak pidgin to their children. The children then are provided with a very impoverished language model because the parents' language is a reduced language. However, often in as little as one generation, a new language develops, an expanded pidgin, with many of the normal features of language. The process of expansion is called *creolization*, and the resulting language, a creole. Bickerton (1984, 1990) believes creoles are created from pidgins without any additional language models. One argument Bickerton (1984) summons for the innateness of creolization is a universal similarity of pidgins and creoles, regardless of the characteristics of the languages of the dominating or dominated cultures.

Most pidgins have disappeared without record through the process of creolization. An exception is Hawaiian pidgins, which Bickerton (1984) has studied extensively, together with their creoles. Note that *pidgins* here is plural: Speakers of different native languages may each make a different pidgin, combining their original language with the now-dominant language. Because communication under such circumstances must be poor, pidgins usually amplify redundancy through repetition and delete subtleties (which would go unnoticed anyway) such as tense or case markings, articles, movement rules, embeddings, and so on (Bickerton, 1984). The syntax and phonology of each pidgin may stay close to the speaker's native language, with words borrowed from the dominating language, a process known as *relexification*. (You may do this yourself when you learn a second language. You still speak English, but with friends from your French class you may suggest that everyone "go to the *bibliothèque*," to be cute. Using the French word here is a trivial instance of relexification.) The reduction in morphological markings results in pidgins' relying on word order to establish grammatical relations. For example, in a Hawaiian pidgin of the early 1900s, Bickerton (1984, p. 174) reports:

1. /mi kape bai, mi chaek meik/
   me coffee buy, me check make:
   I bought coffee, I made out a check.
2. /baimbai wi bai eka yo, 2500 bai, foa eka bai, laend/
   by and by, we buy acre your, 2500 buy, four acres buy, land:
   later we bought four acres of land for $2500.

The speaker was native Japanese, dominated by English in Hawaii. The first quotation shows Japanese subject-object-verb (*SOV*; me = S, coffee = O, buy = V) order, but the second shows the English subject-verb-object (*SVO*) order. Together they suggest both an influence of the native language (Japanese) and, critically, a lack of consistent syntactic marking either through morphology or through word order. Note that as different pidgin speakers speak to each other, each using a different syntactic order in their native language, they would find word order an unreliable indicator of case relations among the speaker group. That, in turn, could lead to inconsistency in using order oneself.

A creole language, unlike a pidgin, has regular syntactic structure and consistent use of lexical items and morphological markers. All creoles tend to maintain the repetitiveness of the pidgins, sometimes repeating whole sentences, sometimes just one word for emphasis. Repetition is also a common way of marking plurals or habitually performed actions. (Repetition of a morpheme for any of these purposes is called *reduplication*.) Unlike pidgins, creoles generally distinguish between definite and indefinite articles, mark tense and *aspect* (a morpheme indicating, among other possibilities, whether an action is one time, habitual, completed, continuous, purposive, and so on), and use relative clauses and other kinds of embeddings. Creoles generally apply some content words regularly also as function words, rarely creating a lexical item for function use exclusively. Examples of these traits are in the following, from Hawaiian Creole (Bickerton, 1982):

1. a ded im ded–he's *really* dead. (Note repetition of "ded" for emphasis.)
2. dei wen go ap dea erli in da mawning go plaen–They went up there early in the morning to plant. (Note "go" for "go" first, and then for "to," a function word, later in the sentence.)
3. so ai go daun Klapu go push–so I went down to Klapu to push (clear land with a bulldozer). ("Go" for both "go" and "to" again.) (p. 23)

Finally, all creoles exhibit features novel to any of the languages in the area. For example, Hawaiian creole distinguishes between *go* (used in the examples above) for successfully completed actions, and a *fo* to be used when an action was attempted but failed. In English we use *to* for both "I managed to escape" and "I failed to escape," so Bickerton argues this distinction cannot be borrowed from the dominating language (but perhaps it is borrowed from one of the indigenous languages).

According to Bickerton (1982, 1984), creolization is performed automatically by pidgin speakers' children, who need a rich, native language and find the pidgin inadequate. (The parents do not have a similar need becuase their native language was rich.) The children apply innate language knowledge to introduce features of grammatical complexity into the language. Because the parents' pidgins do not exhibit the complexities, Bickerton argues that they could not have served as a model. Indeed, Bickerton argues that it is innate language knowledge (LAD or UG) that takes the pidgin input and possibilities of parameter settings or its own core grammar, to produce the creole. LAD is believed to operate only in childhood (analogies to LAD exist in the animal kingdom; these are introduced in Chapter 9 and discussed in *Language in Atypical Populations*), so adult speakers cannot take advantage of the same innate schemes.

Bickerton argues on the basis of informants' reports and his observation of their language to each other and to their children that the children hear no formal language, only the pidgin. I agree that the children's language input may be impoverished, especially under conditions where the two parents come from different language backgrounds and do not share a full language. However, as a parent, I find it highly unlikely that the parents never speak to their children in the language they feel that they think in: I speak fluent English to *noncomprehending infants and pets* and certainly cannot imagine stifling that voice to a sapient child (especially when I am imparting vital instructions, such as how to cross a street or use an oven!). If parents mix their native languages and their common pidgin in talking to their children, the children would be exposed to the power of full language, although inconsistently.

What we may have operating here is a clear example of the observer's paradox. If the parents feel that their native languages are inferior to the dominant language, they are likely to suppress their own languages when they are being watched by educated scientists (like Bickerton) and to deny using it ever, if asked. The opportunity to observe native language use would be at private cultural and social events, from which outside observers would be excluded. Thus we may get a false picture of the degree to which the native languages have disappeared. What the linguists learn from the adults is what the adults think is appropriate to tell them. Like Labov's black informant, adult "pidgin" speakers would present the best formal language they could, leading the linguist to believe that "normal language markers" are absent. They are absent in the speech to the interviewer but perhaps not in speech to compatriots.

A second problem with the bioprogram hypothesis lies in Bickerton's claims of independent creation of the same features in many different creoles. The commentary to his 1984 article points out that in almost all of the creoles that have been studied, the dominating language was one of five Western European languages (English, Dutch, Spanish, French, and Portuguese), the syntactic structures of which are neither dissimilar nor independent. And, likewise, the native languages of the slaves or immigrant plantation workers have been West African or Asian/South Pacific. Therefore, similarities in pidgins and creoles the world over may derive from similarities of the colonizing language, the languages of those colonized, and their interaction.

Regardless of whether the process of creolization is a reflection of an innate bioprogram for language, or a predictable outcome of the mix of the need to communicate and particular features of distinct full-blown languages, there is no question that language dominance of different language groups results in drastic language change. We see this in the development of English too: After the Norman invasion and superposition of the French language, Old English, a Germanic language with originally freer word order and considerable case markings, was relexified (many new words added) and lost case markings and set word order (perhaps the aftermath of creolization). Languages of Western Europe likewise may have evolved from a creolization of Latin, imposed by the Romans of Caesar's time as the language of commerce, power, and culture on the indigenous languages of the regions now called France, Spain, Portugal, and Italy. This produced languages with features in common (the languages are known as the *Romance* languages), but still distinct languages. Likewise, we may see vestiges of West African languages in Ebonics, or African American Vernacular English (AAVE), to be discussed later in this chapter.

Gradual Change and Dialect Drift

As we have just seen, language changes when there are radical changes in the community of speakers. Communities shift less radically also as smaller groups of people migrate voluntarily. This migration introduces both the static community and the migrating community to new speech patterns, which may influence the existing speech patterns of each. We have seen such changes in the Martha's Vineyard study, when the summer residents brought in their dialect, which was deliberately rejected by those Vineyarders who wished to maintain their distinction but accepted by those who wished to emigrate. Similarly, we saw in the Portuguese and Indian subgroups on the island a movement toward the Vineyard dialect, as they tried to assimilate. Changes toward a higher prestige dialect are *changes from above* (Labov, 1972b, 1994). Note that these changes are not legislated by the higher prestige group, as a colonizing language might be mandated for the colony; rather, the lower prestige group adopts the speech pattern as they try to move upward. (Recall from Chapter 7 the view that speech perception entails realization of articulatory configurations. Change from above could take place as "sympathetic" listeners mimic the articulatory configurations they hear rather than the phonetic features or words they perceive from their own language-dialect experience.)

In addition to movements of peoples introducing new language patterns and change from above, there are two other identified factors in language change: internal, phonetically based directions of language movement, and general, social variables predicting who are likely to make such changes. These are *changes from below:* below the level of consciousness and of social awareness of the speakers, and even of trained phoneticians, until the change has run its course and is recognized as a speech marker of that community.

Internal Factors

Labov (1994) identifies a number of types of language change: shifts, chain shifts, mergers, and splits, which together suggest phonological patterns in the language underlying the directions of language change. An example of a *shift* is the movement of a single vowel to a new position: fronted, lowered, rounded, nasalized (or the reverse) relative to its original position. (Consonants may shift also.) A single shift is uninteresting with respect to principles of language change; what is interesting is when shifts occur as a set, that is, a number of vowels undergoing movement *systematically* as a group. This is a *chain shift*. For example, in the

---

Box 8.2. Birth of a Language

Conception

— A number of speakers of different languages are thrown together with no common language. Conditions of their coming together include the desire to trade; economic pressures to move to a land of opportunity; or slavery on a plantation, in a prisoner-of-war camp, and so on. In all but the first case, there is a high-prestige language, the language of the land of opportunity or the language of the conquerors. The immigrants have little exposure to fluent speakers of the dominating language because of their subservient position.

Delivery

— To communicate with one another and the bosses, the immigrants develop a rudimentary languagelike system consisting of an amalgam of words and syntax from the native languages. "Rules" are inconsistent; morphological markings and linguistic subtleties such as tense are omitted. Emphasis is often given by reduplication, that is, repeating a word or phrase. This is a pidgin language. Pidgins also develop as a medium for exchanging goods, that is, trade.

— Relexification is a process of substituting vocabulary from one language into another while maintaining syntax.

First Developmental Milestone: The Creole

— Second-generation immigrants build on the pidgin language to achieve greater linguistic sophistication. (Pidgins, especially those used by adults to trade, do not necessarily evolve into creoles.)

— Creole properties include the following:
    — • systematic use of word order
    — • reduplication for emphasis
    — • use of content words as function words, that is, development of function words
    — • expression of embedded clauses

Maturity

— Creoles are embellished by succeeding generations to become full-blown language.

Good Genes or Vitamin Supplements?

— The bioprogram hypothesis holds that the process of creolization is innately given. Children create the more advanced language forms using innate language knowledge in the absence of exposure to full adult forms. Adult pidgin speakers, who are too old to benefit from UG, never develop the creole from the pidgin.

— This could be a case of observer's paradox, with linguists failing to view use of adult native language in the presence of the children, not of its not being there. Children may be combining pidgin and full-blown language input, in that case, to develop the next stage.

— Similarities among pidgins and creoles may derive from similarities among the dominating language (usually European) and the dominated languages (West African, South Pacific, and so on).

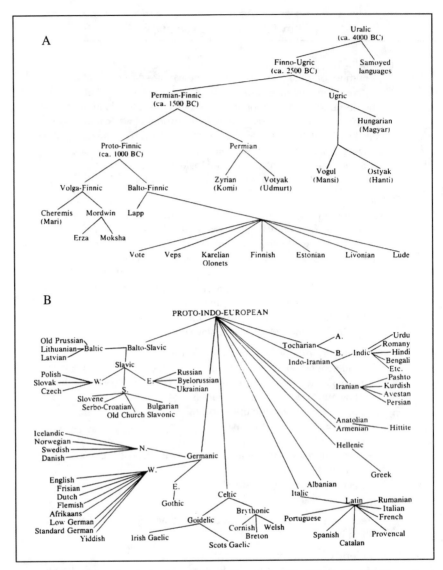

Figure 8.1. A. A Partial Family Tree of Uralic Languages; B. A Partial Family Tree of Indo-European Languages

SOURCE: R. J. Jeffers and I. Lehiste (1979), *Principles and Methods for Historical Linguistics*, p. 28. Cambridge: MIT Press, © The Massachusetts Institute of Technology. Reprinted with permission.

fifteenth century, English underwent what is known as the *Great Vowel Shift* in which the tense or long vowels *all* shifted position, with the high vowels ([i], [u]) lowering and diphthongizing (→ [æⁱ], [aᵘ]) and mid- ([e], [o]) and low ([æ], [ɔ]) vowels rising (→ [i], [u], and [e], [o], respectively; see Pyles, 1993, for discussion). We see vestiges of the old and new forms in our pronunciation of *boot* (preshift [o] reflected in spelling) as [but] (a postshift form), or in "b*ea*ch" (postshift [i]) versus "br*ea*k" (preshift [e]). What is important to note is that the change can be explained parsimoniously as an effect on a *set* of vowels rather than as independent additive single shifts on each. According to Labov, the chain shifts reflect simple principles: Long vowels rise, short vowels/diphthongs fall, and back vowels move forward.

A chain shift in consonants is presumed to have occurred in an ancestral forebear of English. This chain shift is Grimm's law, after Jacob Grimm, one of the brothers of fairy-tale fame, who publicized the systematicity of the change (Pyles, 1993). Figure 8.1 displays two examples of language family trees, constructed from lexical, phonetic, and syntactic similarities in modern languages and among languages for which there is a written record and known historical evolution. Some displayed languages are hypothetical, that is, ancestral links suspected given the languages' apparent family resemblances. In such a hypothetical ancestor, the ancestor to the Germanic and Latin languages (and other languages), *proto-Indo-European,* there was a shift of voiced, aspirated stops to voiced fricatives and then to unaspirated voiced stops, along with a shift of voiced, unaspirated stops to voiceless stops. If you find the idea of a manner or place of articulation change hard to imagine, contrast the Standard American English (SAE) *the* or *with* with the dialect variants [də] or [wɪf]: Like the historical changes, these preserve voicing but slightly change one other feature.

The regularity of the shifts, their co-occurrence, and the systematicity in phonological movement suggest phonological control of the direction of language change.

A merger and a split are opposing processes of language change. In a *merger,* distinct phonemes blend into a single phonetic form while maintaining the same lexical meanings. The Great Vowel Shift, for example, resulted not only in a shift in pronunciation of some words, maintaining their distinctiveness, but in mergers, so we now pronounce *meat* and *meet* and *sea* and *see* identically. Their originally diverse pronunciations are still reflected in their diverse spellings (spelling is more conservative; that is, it changes more slowly than spoken language), but now we can only identify the intended meanings from context. (Recall that language does not change to increase clarity.)

In a *split,* similar phonetic forms (allophones) expressing different meanings are differentiated, creating different words. Labov (1994) suggests that splits are less common than mergers and are tied to them and shifts. For example, one consequence of the language changes occurring during the Great Vowel Shift in Old English had been a backing of [a] to [ɔ], vacating the "spot" for [a]. At the same time, the language had changed so that vowel-final words were reduced, with the final vowel first shortening and centralizing to the schwa and then disappearing altogether (Labov, 1994, p. 332). Thus *made* originally was pronounced as a two-syllable word [madɛ], then reduced to [madə] and finally to [mɔd]. This rendered it confusable with *mad,* once the second syllable had disappeared. The "a" then split into the long and short forms we know today, contrasting *made* and *mad, ban* and *bane,* and so on. The final "e" changing short "a" to long "a" is not a spelling device, as we learn in school, but a vestige of when "e" was pronounced; the "a" was the same with and without the "e," and the word was two syllables. Here we need note that a different allophone of "a" would have been used in the

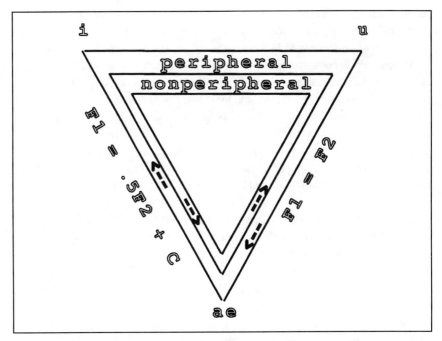

Figure 8.2. The Vowel Triangle Idealized, Displaying Coordinates and Tracking (as Described by Labov, 1994)

NOTE = F_1 maximum implies low vowel height and the minimum implies high; $F_1 = F_2$ implies back vowels, with the complex formula representing front. Peripheral (roughly, tense) vowels, when they change, move in the clockwise direction. Nonperipheral vowels (roughly, lax) move in the counterclockwise direction.

original one- and two-syllable words. As the syllable differences merged, the allophones split into what are now two phoneme classes.

Mergers, splits, and chain shifts all show systematic language change and sound change in small articulatory steps: raising, lowering, fronting, backing, or centralizing the vowel gradually. Like some models of biological evolution, the gradual accumulation of small steps can create a new language "species," a recognizable dialect. Once the dialect is recognizable, people may identify with it and may associate with it the prestige values of its users. This sets the stage for some of the social factors to come into play, discussed in the next section.

Labov (1994) presents a system to account for (and predict) what may seem to be scattered sound changes, some vowels moving one way and some moving another, as shown in Figure 8.2. He suggests that phonologically there are two "tracks": a "peripheral," extreme articulatory track on which we find many of our tense vowels [i, e, o, a, æ, ɔ, u] and a more central, parallel track on which we find many of our lax vowels [ɪ, ɛ, ʌ, ə, ʊ]. (*Tense-lax* as we defined it in Chapter 6 is not strictly synonymous with *peripheral-nonperipheral;* see Labov, 1994, for details.) The articulatory difference between peripheral and nonperipheral is the degree of tongue or jaw movement: [i], for example, is produced like [I] but is more extreme; the tongue tip and jaw are higher, further from the neutral, resting position. Acoustically, peripheral vowels are closer to the boundaries, the periphery, of the "vowel triangle" (see Table 6.1, in Chapter 6), with more extreme F_1 and F_2 values.

Organizing the vowels into groups on these parallel tracks allows "movement" of them in different directions at the same time, as Figure 8.2 shows. Vowels on the peripheral track move clockwise; vowels on the nonperipheral track move counterclockwise. Vowels can "jump" tracks by laxing (from peripheral to nonperipheral) or by tensing or diphthongizing (jump to the peripheral track). The vowel changes of the Great Vowel Shift reflect movement on the peripheral track: /i/ moved back (toward the centralized position of /æ/ on the front-back dimension) and diphthongized; /u/ lowered, fronted, and diphthongized to [aᵘ]; and the mid and low vowels /e/, /æ/, and so on all moved toward /i/, rising.

Labov (1994) claims that, historically, English vowels on the peripheral track have been dynamic and responsible for most sound change in English. Until recently, vowels on the nonperipheral track have been relatively static, their pronunciation changing little over the centuries. Current studies of dialect patterns across the United States and England suggest the dormant nonperipheral track has awakened, with profound sound change taking place there. Of course, in different dialects, different vowels are moving, but his analysis suggests that, with few exceptions, they display the patterns shown in Figure 8.2.

Why languages change is not well understood. That they do change is obvious, from the existence of dialects and from documented changes from one generation to the next within a dialect. Labov's analysis suggests that change is not random but reflects a deep pattern internal to a language's phonology. The fact that this pattern has itself remained stable for centuries suggests that it is perhaps fundamental to English phonology. Indeed, Labov indicates that for languages and language families that distinguish long and short vowels, the principles of movement along the peripheral and nonperipheral tracks apply, although, of course, the vowels that occupy those tracks differ for different languages.

Given our discussion of categorical perception in Chapter 7, it may seem surprising that language *can* change much at all in adult speakers. Supposedly we perceive phonetic feature differences through the dictates of our language experience, barely able to make distinctions that are not linguistically relevant. So when linguistic relevance changes, speaker-listeners should be at a loss. Investigating the perceptibility and producibility of language changes, Labov (1994) concludes the following: (a) All combinations of perception and production can occur (perceive a new distinction well without being able to produce it, produce a new distinction well without perceiving it consistently, perceive and produce a new distinction well, neither perceive nor produce a new distinction well), and (b) there is an asymmetry in communication during a merger. Specifically, speakers of a dialect with two phonetic categories who assimilate with a dialect with one category subsuming their two, suffer more perceptual confusions as to the one-category speakers' intent than conversely. These data suggest that categorical perception is not hardwired but results from experience, which may be reversed, and that it is easier to learn a new distinction than to cease to attend to an old one.

We turn next to the human instigators of language change to see if there are fundamental social patterns predictive of who is responsible for language change and when. In particular, while it is possible for adults to change their language patterns, we will see that young people are more likely to, perhaps because their speech perception and production habits are more flexible.

Social Factors

So far, we have concentrated on how language changes, only briefly considering why language changes, what the motivation for changing a successful meaning-communication system might be. Reviewing these motivators, we have seen

1. the domination of one language group by another with the two melding (e.g., "Spanglish" in many communities in the United States);

2. the merging of linguistic groups with no common language in a work situation, with a basic language created, the pidgin, which may eventually mature into a creole and then a full-blown language across generations;

3. change from above, in which speakers who wish to identify with a high-prestige dialect mimic it;

4. and again change from above, but one in which the community exaggerates its own dialect features to solidify now *against* a perhaps high-prestige, increasingly present social group.

Now, I am not claiming that any of these changes is either legislated or agreed to formally by community members. So how do the changes infiltrate and become operative through a community? To understand this, we need to examine the flow of the change, which community members are likely to be at the cutting edge of change, and how the change then permeates through the group.

During three decades of studying sound change, Labov (1972b, 1994) has observed several different possible effective causes of language change. The most significant effects on language are probably those externally motivated, the drastic changes resulting from war and political and economic domination of one group by another. This will produce more rapid and far-reaching language effects than the change in progress as a language evolves. The next most significant effects come from migrations into a community. For example, Labov observes that the greatest population shift within the United States was the migration of southern blacks to northern cities between 1940 and 1980. Each new wave from the South reintroduced an evolving southern dialect to a somewhat assimilated dialect.

Apart from external factors, Labov identifies four patterns internal to the language. The first is stability, in which one sees little change *longitudinally* in the language of individuals as they mature, or *cross-sectionally*, of different generations of individuals at the same instant of time. The second possibility is *age-grading,* in which individuals change their speech patterns over their lifetimes but there is no apparent change in the community as a whole. An intuitive example of this is the

---

Box 8.3. Gradual Language Change

— Change From Below:
—— Gradual change in sound form, below the level of consciousness
— Change From Above:
—— Gradual change toward the language of the prestige class motivated, perhaps consciously, by a desire to be a part of that group
— Internal Factors:
—— The underlying phonological principles that govern the direction of language change
—— Types of Change:
    shift: small movement in one phonetic value of a single speech sound
    chain shift: movement simultaneously or in close sequence of several speech sounds
    merger: movement of a phoneme to the acoustic position of another phoneme, creating ambiguity
    split: differentiation of allophones of a phoneme to more distinct values, usually in a particular context
—— Principles of Vowel Change Accounting for Chain Shifts:
    "Vowel Triangle": Vowel space can be described as an inverted triangle with coordinates ranging from maximum to minimum F_1 (top to bottom) and from equal F_1 and F_2 to F_2 much greater than F_1 (right to left).
    Tracking System: The vowel triangle can be divided into two tracks, a peripheral and a parallel, more central (nonperipheral) track. Vowels at articulatory extremes (tense) move along the peripheral track, clockwise. Nonperipheral vowels (lax) move counterclockwise along the nonperipheral track. This division accounts for current and historical changes in English and other languages.
—— The Great Vowel Shift:
    Starting in the fifteenth century there was a profound movement of vowels on the peripheral track, with /i/ and /u/ lowering, backing, and diphthongizing, and the mid and low vowels rising. Because spelling is more conservative than speech, we see residues of the original pronunciations in the present homonyms of *meet* and *meat* and split of "a" in *mad* and *made.*
— Motivation for Change:
—— *Not* to increase communication of meaning: Mergers create loss of clarity.
—— Social Factors:
    • Communities seeking to differentiate from other communities will participate less in the language changes of the latter.
    • Lexical items learned from parents will maintain the home dialect.
    • Preadolescents and adolescents are at the forefront of language change.
    • Women show greater language change than men.

(continued)

Box 8.3 Continued

- The more highly educated the community, the less language change.
- Middle-status group shows most extreme style-switching.
- Hypercorrection is the overapplication of a language change-from-above.

---

increase in slang during teenage years relative to childhood, and a decrease again in adulthood, as teens end their "rebellion" and join the establishment, both in fact and in language.

The third pattern is a *generational* change, in which individuals are stable within an age-defined cohort but there are noticeable differences across generations. This pattern is the most common, according to Labov. We have seen generational changes in the Martha's Vineyard study, where the young generation was more likely than their parents to adopt the speech patterns of the summer residents, patterns that they then maintain for life. We also have seen a generational change that is more drastic in the development of a creole from a pidgin.

The final pattern is *communal change,* in which members of the community change their language together. This is a pattern common for lexical changes, in which new words or expressions seem to permeate a group as a whole.

Age. At the cutting edge of language change, as indicated in the foregoing, are preteens and teenagers, which is not terribly surprising if we consider social patterns. Young children are likely to converse primarily with family members because, by and large, the family forms their social group. (Indeed, Labov, 1994, cites one Philadelphia speech-dialect pattern *only* in speakers whose *parents* were born in Philadelphia. This speech pattern is found in words that are among the first lexical items, those learned from one's parents.) On an individual basis, there is a drastic change when children enter school and suddenly spend much of their waking hours with peers who are from different families and different *idiolects* (small, individual difference in language use as opposed to a dialect in which the language differences are shared by a large community). Less drastic than the creation of a pidgin from different languages, but similarly, these idiolects blend, creating a new generation of speech. (Most features of the Philadelphia dialect, Labov notes, are acquired rapidly by children who move to Philadelphia before 9 years of age.) With the peer group staying together through school and work, the generational pattern stabilizes, showing little change in adulthood, as there is little new input.

This explanation of the preadolescent and adolescent propensity for change relies on their greater exposure to different influences. But there appears to be additional, poorly understood, factors that may be responsible. Note that when a family moves, the young members are more likely than the adults to pick up the accent of the new community: Speech patterns seem to stabilize in adulthood and are relatively immune to change. Labov (1994) points out that although the aging process or a new environment causes some variation in the realization of phonetic tokens and in the output of low-level phonetic rules, there is considerable stability in the underlying structure—the distribution of lexical entries in the categories of the system. Many people who travel through different dialect areas are convinced that they change their speech radically with their environment: that they are in effect "chameleons." But close examination of their speech shows that the changes are less extensive and more limited than they thought. The distribution of lexical tokens in phonemic categories is the most stable feature of the dialect and serves to define the dialect origin of a speaker with considerable precision. (pp. 109-110)

So why might incipient adults show more propensity for change than adults? One explanation is a version of "the bioprogram hypothesis," considered in some detail in the next two chapters as well as critically in *Language in Atypical Populations.* It suggests that children genetically may be language "sponges," with their innate capacity for soaking up language details disappearing after puberty in genetically programmed brain development. They are thus biologically more sensitive to language subtleties than adults and are more flexible in adopting new ones.

Another explanation (which may co-occur with a biological one—this need not be either-or) is a social one. Preadolescents and adolescents are very interested in forming peer groups and marking their peer group distinctly from the unbelievably passé (square?) groups of their parents and their (dorky?) brothers and sisters. So, as each generation defines its hairstyles, clothing styles, and music, each creates its own "code," slang, and perhaps a "peculiar" phonetic style.

Group membership. Note that this, like change from above, is a deliberate group marking of language: Those who identify with the group or wish to be identified with the group adopt the style; members of other groups, perhaps coexisting in the same geographically defined community, adopt different speech patterns. Labov (1972b) noted that the most variable language occurred in (lower) "middle"-class speakers, sometimes adopting the speech patterns of the upper class, sometimes *hyper*correcting (overgeneralizing those speech patterns to inappropriate contexts, such as adding an "r" to *law* to not sound r-less) and sometimes speaking their "home" dialect. Upper- and lower-class people, socially less mobile, linguistically show less mobility.

Another example of the importance of group identity in language change is the separate paths of black (AAVE) and white English vernaculars. As I mentioned, there has been a major migration of blacks from the South to northern cities in the latter half of the twentieth century, but AAVE has not participated in the language changes of the urban white dialects (Labov, 1994). It has undergone its own evolution. This is not a racial difference per se but reflects the deep racial division of American society; reasonably, the black community feels apart from the white community, the apart-ness reflected in the language. (In the next section, we will look in detail at AAVE.)

Thus the degree to which one identifies with a community and the degree to which that community is trying to integrate or separate from other communities determines language change.

Sex. At the cutting edge of language change are the women of the community, more so than the men (Labov, 1972b, 1994). There are several possible social factors involved in this sex difference. The first is that, at least in earlier generations, women tended to attain a lesser level of education than men, and Labov has also found that more highly educated individuals display fewer (nonstandard, newer) dialect features. A second factor has to do with the relative size of the social networks of women; until recently, women participated in small, involved communities (they "got out" less) than men, and Labov has isolated small community size together with a dense social network as factors contributing to greater language change. Finally, as we will see in the last section of this chapter, women use language differently from men, to create solidarity within the community as opposed to jockeying for a position in the community hierarchy, the latter being a separation into levels. It may be that the motivation of creating community causes women more than men to synchronize speech and language habits with those seen as compatriots.

Summary. Labov (1994) maps

the trajectory of sound change across the community . . .

1) A linguistic change begins as a local pattern characteristic of a particular social group, located at the interior of the social hierarchy.

2) The change may be accelerated by its use as a symbolic claim to local rights and privileges, defending the original group against claims by new groups entering the community.

3) As the change becomes generalized throughout the group, it becomes associated for others with the social values attributed to that group.

4) The change then gradually spreads to those neighboring populations that take the first group as a reference group for social values, and it is often reinterpreted and accelerated further by groups first gaining entrance to the social structure.

5) As the opposition of the two linguistic forms continues, it may symbolize an overt opposition of social values. This association of linguistic and social values may rise to the level of social consciousness and result in a stereotype, subject to irregular social correction, or it may remain below that level and result in an unconscious marker.

6) Finally, one of the two forms wins out. There follows a long period when the disappearing form is heard as archaic, a symbol of a vanished prestige or stigma, and is used as a form of stereotyped humor until it is extinguished entirely.

7) After the change is completed, the older pronunciation may be preserved in place names or fixed forms and heard as a meaningless irregularity. (pp. 300-301)

We see patterns in the people most likely to contribute to language change in part because of their place in the social hierarchy and their desire to form a cohesive group, apart from other groups. Preteens and teenagers, establishing their own identity as the new wave, are at the cutting edge of change. Women, perhaps in relatively isolated and stable communities compared with men, are in the interior of the network, creating and maintaining their own groups and group language—at the cutting edge of language change. Groups sharing geographic location, mass media, and language inputs may yet diverge linguistically as they define their community as part of or apart from the majority social community of the area.

We now turn to examine the language patterns of a group living among a dominant group yet maintaining its linguistic separateness—the dialect of working-class American blacks.

A DIALECT CASE STUDY:
AFRICAN AMERICAN VERNACULAR ENGLISH

I have chosen AAVE to discuss in detail because I wish to deal head-on with some of the prejudices that surround language differences. As mentioned in Chapter 1, we all have the tendency to feel that our own language is closest to pure reason, and that variants are therefore "inferior." The standard English dialect, the dialect of the educated class in power, of course differs in different English-speaking countries: England, Scotland, Canada, Australia, New Zealand, South Africa, the United States, and so on. Each has its own upper-class variant—which does not prevent speakers of the ruling-class dialect in each country from considering other dialects *sub*standard. Instead, we will call them *non*standard. "Sub" implies an inferiority, one accompanied by prejudicial considerations that a grammatical marking missing compared with the standard dialect is a sign of laziness or incomprehensibility; and a grammatical marking added compared with the standard dialect is a sign of unnecessary redundancy. Each is a false and negative spin on what is simply a language difference.

In the last section we saw internal linguistic change such as mergers occurring in all languages for reasons unrelated to better conveyance of meaning. Phonology, semantics, and syntax are in a constant state of flux—but all languages can express humor and complex philosophy at any point. All languages and dialects change, with different forms at different times identified as high prestige, but none is actually "better" on any objective scale of linguistic complexity.

Because of the divided nature of black and white societies in the United States, and the history of subjugation of African Americans by whites, it is interesting and important to confront differences in the languages of the two communities, and to confront the prejudices against the nonstandard dialect.

Labov (1972a) undertook the study of AAVE (which he termed the *Black English Vernacular* or *BEV*, popularly known as Ebonics) because of significant discrepancies in scholastic performance between inner-city black children and their white suburban counterparts, particularly with regard to reading. This state of affairs in the 1960s (which is not much different today) had promoted racist suggestions about genetic differences in "intelligence" among the races (discussion of the logical errors inherent in such claims is beyond the scope of this book); well-meaning, but wrong, attempts to "dumb down" reading instruction for these children (I discuss how best to teach reading in Chapter 11); and erroneous claims discussed earlier in this chapter, stemming from the observer's paradox, about language structure, language input, and abilities of the black children.

AAVE or BEV is the dialect of the American black working class, originating in the South and moving North as the black population migrated to the northern cities. Many African Americans speak other dialects, or switch between AAVE and standard English as appropriate for their audience. Labov (1972a) studied it in "black youth from 8 to 19 years old who participate fully in the street culture of the inner cities" (p. xiii). There may be significant differences between what I summarize here and current AAVE, given that my review is based on work of more than 30 years ago, and, as we have seen, language changes. However, a conclusion from the work of the 1960s is still apropos: "The major causes of reading failure are political and cultural conflicts in the classroom, and dialect differences are important because they are *symbols* of this conflict" (italics added, p. xiv). As we have seen, dialect differences emerge, and are maintained, in part as groups select and identify with, or apart from, other groups. As we have seen, youth are at the cutting edge of the linguistic group differences, so we focus on them. Identification with a street culture as opposed to a classroom culture shows itself in many ways, notably, for our purposes, including linguistic ways.

AAEV, as described by Labov (1972a), is a dialect of English, not a separate language. AAEV varies in significant ways from standard English: in vocabulary; in syntax; in phonology; and in pragmatics; in, as we have seen, what is considered an appropriate response to a "test" question; and in some language games. However, it shares more with standard English than it deviates from it, and the differences are consistent with differences found in other nonstandard English dialects. AAEV differs from standard English in a coherent and systematic way. Thus, like any language, AAEV is a structured system, and like other dialects, it is a structured subsystem of English.

To study AAEV minimizing the observer's paradox, Labov (1972a) recruited "experimenters" (*participant-observers*) from the inner-city preteen and teen population under study. Study began with individual meetings with leading members of peer groups ("street gangs" named the "Thunderbirds" or the "Jets") and then continued with group outings and group discussions. As indicated earlier, the group meetings were recorded but in a partylike atmosphere conducive to natural interaction and minimizing (but not eliminating) the effect of the observer.

Aspects of AAEV Phonology

The most striking difference between BEV phonology and standard English phonology, particularly when it comes to learning to read, is in the consonants.

Vowels, intonation, and register differ, but these are either not marked by the written word or are highly variable with respect to it: Think of all the different phonemes "a" represents. Therefore, speakers of *any* English dialect, including the standard one, face a decoding problem when they learn letter-to-vowel correspondences.

In addition to some minor differences such as changing place or manner of articulation of the interdental fricatives (/ð/ → /d/, /θ/ → /f/), two "rules" transform standard English phonology to AAEV, eliminating sounds indicated in spelling and thereby potentially causing confusion in learning to read. The first, as with many other English dialects, is r-dropping, which is more extensive in AAEV, effectively eliminating the r altogether. In the New York accent, for example, "r" is not pronounced at the end of a word but is usually pronounced *intervocalically* (between vowels, as in *terrace*) or in a consonant cluster (*truck*). AAEV drops r's consistently in all these positions.

The second, and more serious, difference is reduction or deletion of consonants following a stressed vowel (e.g., word-final consonants), possibly a holdover from languages of West Africa, which, like Spanish and Italian, have vowels at the end of words. (Note that in the historical evolution of English, there was a time when words ended in vowels, and these word-final vowels were reduced and then deleted. Elimination of phonemes is a common language change, not a sign of laziness.) This is more serious because English places most of its grammatical markers in suffixes (word endings); in consonant-final syllables, -ed, -ing, -s (plural, posses-sive, and third person present singular marker on verbs—he walk*s*); -r (possessive in personal pronouns); -'ll (future tense). Inattention to the suffix reduces the contribution of inflectional morphology, the meaning of which must be lost or conveyed otherwise.

A consequence of these consonant deletions or reductions is the creation of a different set of homonyms, words that sound alike but mean different things. Labov (1972a), for example, provides the following homonyms in AAEV:

Paris–pass	(r-dropping)
Carol–Cal	(r-dropping)
terrace–test	(both are [tɛs] *terrace* because of r-dropping; *test* because of final-t deletion)
trial–child	(/tr/ → /tš/; *child* → *chil'* because of d-deletion).

Another consequence is "deviant" plurals: Deleting the final consonant and then applying the usual English morphonemic rules makes the plural of *test, tesses;* without the "t," the word ends in "s" and thus is pluralized by adding the [əz] form.

Now, one argument that AAEV and standard English are dialects of the *same* language is this use of the standard English plural rule, which is clearly productive in AAEV and applies to the same environment as in SAE. The difference is neither in the rule nor in the environment but in a systematic sound change that creates in AAEV the appropriate environment that had not existed in SAE.

A second argument is that both AAEV and SAE show tendencies to reduce final consonants after stressed vowels; AAEV simply reduces them further and more consistently. If you apply the same pressures on AAEV and SAE, they both respond the same way, again suggesting that they are part of the same system. For instance, both AAEV and SAE speakers are more likely to drop the word-final [t] in *past me* than in *passed me* (where it signifies a morpheme) or in *past us* (where it occurs before a vowel).

Thus in phonology we see a regularly occurring phenomenon of final-consonant reduction, a phenomenon that occurs also in other English dialects and is affected similarly by the same linguistic pressures. We might look at this as "simplification," because fewer consonants are pronounced, or as added "complexity," because it requires an additional change of the SAE phonology.

More to the point, though, AAEV's phonology, like that of any "language," is regular, systematic, rule governed, and adequate to differentiate words. AAEV, like SAE, has homonyms, when speech sounds do not differentiate senses, but different homonyms from SAE.

AAEV Morphology and Syntax

We have already implied that AAEV will not mark consistently in overt morphology some things that SAE does mark, that is, those morphemes expressed as consonants in unstressed consonant-final syllables. This means that the third person, present-tense, singular verb is marked overtly in SAE, but not in AAEV, as are the possessive, plural, and past-tense markers. Of course, these distinctions are often clear from context: SAE does not mark the singular and plural differently in many words (like *deer, sheep, fish*) without causing confusion.

AAEV and SAE morphology and syntax also differ significantly in how auxiliaries (*be* and *do*) mark tense and aspect (as we have seen, this tells, for example, whether an action is one-time or habitual, purposive or not), the use of *be* as a *copula* (or link as in "I *am* woman"), and the marking of negatives.

We look at *be* first, both as auxiliary as in "he *is* talking" and as copula as in "he *is* happy." For both, in AAEV the *is* would be deleted in surface structure for "he talkin'" or "he happy." It is important to note that English is unusual in its insistence that every sentence have an overtly expressed verb; many languages declare *rain* rather than expressing an empty "it" that "is" raining. It is also important to examine the phonological forms of *to be:* All are typically unstressed, reduced syllables, and most are simple vowel-consonant structures (*am, is, are*). These are therefore likely to undergo further phonetic simplification as we saw in the last section, and fade from overt expression. *Be, was,* and *were,* on the other hand, beginning with consonants, are not as susceptible to phonetic simplification and are more likely to be overtly expressed.

Labov (1972a) reports, indeed, that the copula (or auxiliary) is dropped in AAEV in the present affirmative, when it would be expressed as *is, am,* or *are.* Syntactically, though, it is still there, but not overtly expressed, as can be seen by its regular use in the negative (*ain't*) and the past (*was*). The copula *concept* is there—the word does not simply carry tense or negativity—because it is as acceptable to say "He not here" as "He ain't here" and both express the negative equally well.

AAEV expresses the copula in *tag questions* (questions of the form "He isn't going, is he?") and at the end of, but not internal to, a clause, as in "There he is." AAEV also uses it in some common contractions such as *wha's* or *tha's,* in the infinitive ("you got to be"), and for emphasis in grave situations as in "Allah is God" or "Is he dead?" (Labov, 1972a, p. 70).

Again, its regular presence in these situations suggests that *it is syntactically present.* This is important for the prejudicial reasons discussed earlier: It has been said that black English *lacks* a copula because of laziness or difficulty understanding the logic. Rather, AAEV contains the syntax of the copula like SAE and, in addition, it has context-sensitive rules that determine whether or not it is overtly expressed. Indeed, Labov (1972a) points out that AAEV deletes the copula in precisely those situations in which SAE contracts it (*it's, he's,* and so on), the same deep rules but a different surface representation.

AAEV marks at least one aspect that SAE does not. "She be married" and "She been married" do not, respectively, mean "She is married" and "She was married." "She married" is the equivalent of "She is married." *Be* is a marker of habitual, durative aspect as in "he be always foolin' aroun'"; this means this is a permanent character trait. *Been* conveys the same aspect, that this is the way it has been for a long time. So "She been married," which suggests to me in my dialect that she was married at one time and is no longer, in fact, in BEV means that she has been married a long time and still is.

This is not the only auxiliary-use difference. *Done* is used in AAEV as a past-tense marker and intensifier as in "I done told you that" or "I done forgot my hat." AAEV has this in common with some southern states' English varieties.

The last difference between AAEV and SAE that we are going to discuss is its formation of negative sentences, a phenomenon called *negative concord,* which refers to the duplication of a negative particle on all indefinite NPs of a negative sentence. Labov's (1972a) most extreme and graphic example follows:

> I ain't gonna sit here in no chair and let no crazy lawyer never tell me no lies about
> no law that no judge told no smart-ass clerk to look up in no book that no smart
> politician wrote or nothin' like that nohow. (p. 147)

Typically, this kind of sentence is looked down upon by speakers of SAE as redundantly proliferating negatives. Note that French and Spanish doubly mark a negative: In French we have "je *ne* sais *pas*" ("I don't know," with the "not" indicated twice) and "je *ne* sais *rien*" (literally "I don't know nothing"). Labov (1972a, p. 131) states that this was the traditional pattern as well in English until it was explicitly proscribed by eighteenth-century grammarians. As a speaker of SAE, you might protest that a double negative is illogical, that the two cancel each other as they do in mathematics, but, as we discussed in Chapter 2, language is not logic (we find meaning, not nullity, in the pairing of opposites, in "colorless green"). AAEV, like all languages, symbolizes the world differently than symbolic logic; real language is richer, more variable, and fuzzier. After the dramatic multiple-negative indictment of the relation of the legal system to reality in the quotation above, my own SAE paraphrase ("I'm not going to sit here and listen to a lawyer . . .") sounds sterile.

Summary

BEV or AAVE differs from standard English in a number of ways: It is r-less, more so than other nonstandard dialects; it reduces or deletes final consonants, simplifying consonant clusters and not expressing suffixes; it does not express the present affirmative copula; it uses *be* and *do* forms to convey aspects not conveyed morphologically in standard English; and it uses multiple negatives, or negative concord. Some of these features are relics of standard English forms of the past or of dialectal forms that are current and may have influenced AAEV in the past (such as a southern English dialect). Their presence in AAEV and not in other dialects indicates the social and linguistic isolation of AAEV speakers from the other speakers, the noninfluence of the linguistic trends across the groups. Some of the features may reflect the original creolization of West African languages with English—relics of the parent, not the dominating, language. In no case, in AAEV or in any other full language, is there evidence of linguistic inferiority: The syntactic patterns, the regularities, and so on are similar. Certainly, the "no crazy lawyer" sentence is syntactically complex: There are eight separate clauses, either conjoined or embedded!

Language Games and Social Variables

As a sociolinguist, Labov (1972a) studied the structure of the language as well as the social structure of its users. As mentioned earlier, his informants were primarily preteen and teen males, members of peer groups. Contrary to the picture that was emerging of impoverished language input in the black community through test situations, Labov determined that creative language use was (and is: Consider rap!) a prized skill in maintaining peer group dominance structures.

There are two points that I want to stress in this regard. The first is that there is a negative correlation between allegiance to the street groups and academic performance: "Gang" members did not do well in school, relative to people on the outskirts of the gang, whom Labov refers to as *lames* (a slang term perhaps no longer in use in Harlem as far as I have been able to learn). Now, at first blush, this might seem effect and cause; people who could not make it in mainstream culture disappear into gangs. But Labov (1972a) is quite convincing that it is cause and effect: People who were rejected from the gang as unable to compete (real fighting *and* verbal fencing) were left with school as the only avenue for success and self-esteem. See for yourself the linguistic/logical cleverness of the street in this passage from Labov (1972a) (JL is the interviewer):

JL: . . . but, just say that there is a God, what color is he? White or black?

Larry: Well, if it is a God . . . I wouldn' know what color, I couldn' say,—couldn' nobody say what color he is or really *would* be.

JL: But now, jus' suppose there was a God—

Larry: Unless'n they say . . .

JL: No, I was jus' sayin' jus' suppose there is a God, would he be white or black?

Larry: . . . He'd be white, man.

JL: Why?

Larry: Why? I'll tell you why. 'Cause the average whitey out here got everything, you dig? And the nigger ain't got shit, y'know? Y'unnerstan'? So—um—for—in order for *that* to happen you know it ain't no black God that's doin' that bullshit. (p. 217)

Contrast this with the cleaner, more standard, but circumlocutory speech of a college-educated black adult (once a lame?):

Well, I even heard my parents say that there is such a thing as something in dreams, some things like that, and sometimes dreams do come true. I have personally never had a dream come true. I've never dreamt that somebody was dying and they actually died, (Mhm) or that I was going to have ten dollars the next day and somehow I got ten dollars in my pocket. (Mhm). I don't particularly believe in that, I don't think it's true. I do feel, though, that there is such a thing as—ah—witchcraft. I do feel that in certain cultures there is such a thing as witchcraft, or some sort of *science* of witchcraft; I don't think that it's just a matter of believing hard enough that there is such a thing as witchcraft. I do believe that there is such a thing that a person can put himself in a state of *mind* (Mhm), or that—er—something could be given them to intoxicate them in a certain—to a certain frame of mind—that—that could actually be considered witchcraft. (p. 218)

All these words express *only* two basic concepts: I have never had a dream come true and I believe in witchcraft. Although the vocabulary reflects education, so does the number of words, which in fact *disguises* the underlying concept. The street passage is linguistically more elegant as well as funny because of the terseness and clarity of the reasoning.

The second point that is worth elaborating is that for those members accepted into peer groups, clever language use marks leaders more than followers. It is quite likely, in fact, that it is skill at verbal parrying that makes a person a leader in this culture—perhaps in all human cultures.

Labov (1972a) studied the phenomenon of "ritual insults," mentioned by one of the informants quoted earlier as "sounding" and in Chapter 1 as "playin' the dozens." (I should note that in studying the language play of teens, we necessarily see "dirty," albeit clever, language. The eloquence of AAVE-speaking ministers and politicians demonstrates the power of the language and its users in a more positive light.) The insults serve several purposes: They are fun (like any pun), they may deflect a confrontation from a potentially dangerous physical fight to the safer verbal game where contestants can still "beat" one another, and they bond players into a group, those who know the rules. Many of the insults are memorized and they rhyme, and the winner of a contest is the one who has committed the most insults to memory. Labov (1972a) reports that one of his informants "remembers long hours spent by his group . . . trying to invent new rhymes, but no one is expected to manufacture them in the heat of the battle" (p. 308). (Indeed, as we will see in the next section, men often parry verbally by telling memorized jokes. The man with the biggest repertoire wins.) Most of the insults are salacious ("dirty") and involve a relative (usually your momma) and/or a body part. To play well, each insult must be parried with an insult of similar syntax and similar content, but elaborated. So,

Your momma drink pee

is ritually answered by

Your father eat shit. (p. 308)

More interesting is

You so fat you could slide down the razor blade without getting cut

answered by

You so thin you can dodge rain drops. (p. 312)

or

Your mother so skinny she could split through a needle's eye

answered by

Your mother's so skinny she can get in a Cheerioat and say, "Hula hoop! hula hoop!"

(If you have trouble seeing that a formula can be creative and funny, consider knock-knock jokes, which, like these, are both.)

The last exchanges to consider are between two members of the same group, Boot, the leader, and Money, an inferior in the group and in sounding (Labov, 1972a):

B. His mother go to work without any draws on so that she c'd get a good breeze.
M. Your mother go, your mother go work without anything on, just go naked. . . .
B. I'd say, "His father got four lips." [thick lips]
M. I'd say, "Your mother got four lips."
B. That ain't nothin'. . . .

[another member] What's the matter, you feelin' all right, or you want some more
  sounding?
M. Uh-uh. (pp. 328-330)

In each case, what makes Boot's sound strong is originality and the connection of
first part to second part—mother wears no clothes (insult) and stays cool. Money
picks up Boot's hypothetical in each case, as he should, but instead of elaborating
a connection, he creates a tautology (mother wears no clothes and so is naked) or
a frank imitation. It is Boot's demonstrated creativity that maintains his leadership
position, as creativity may determine leadership in all human groups.

What is socially interesting here is that the AAEV speakers with the *best* command
of language are those who do *not do well in school* and who do not participate in
the language "games" of the academics, of SAE. This is not because of lack of
ability, because the less able AAEV speakers do better in school. As I said in the
beginning of this section, inner-city youth find mainstream culture alien. If they are
adept enough at creating their own culture—joining, forming, or leading a peer
group—they do so and flaunt their cultural identity and their rejection of alternative
cultures. The flaunting is in new styles of dress (hip-hop), music (rap), and language
(AAEV)—and in nonparticipation in school. That AAEV can have existed side by
side with white dialects, but been relatively uninfluenced by them and the pressures
stimulating the internal changes taking place in them, shows how complete the
separation of the cultures is emotionally, even after legal segregation has ended.

Summary

Our cursory examination of some principal differences between AAVE and SAE
was intended to illustrate some important points made about language change in
this chapter, as well as to consider how different language structures are simply
different, not better or worse. In this regard, we see in AAVE the residue of a drastic
change and creolization: the intermingling of different West African languages with
English (standard and southern English dialects) imposed. The consequence, after
several generations immersed in English, is a nonstandard dialect of English with
some features perhaps of the original languages of the slaves—ending syllables
with vowels, extensive negative concord, aspect marking.

We also see, in comparing AAVE and SAE, what dialects of the same language
system are: They share considerable vocabulary, phonology, and syntax but also
differ in these areas in rule-governed ways. To be a dialect and not a separate
language, the two must be affected similarly by the same pressures: AAVE adds
"es" to pluralize words ending in "s" or "z" as does SAE; it has different words
ending in those sounds because of its slightly different phonology. Similarly, where
SAE contracts the copula, AAEV deletes it—a similar response to the same pressure.

Comparing the dialects, we see there is no objective criterion for inferiority. The
most complex language features—metalanguage in verbal humor, rule-governed
systematicity, context sensitivity, and recursiveness (embedding)—are present in
both dialects. Differences that have been cited as critical are only differences; the

---

Box 8.4. AAVE or BEV (Ebonics) and SAE: Similarities and Differences

— Population that speaks it: working-class African Americans
  — Labov studied it in inner-city youth who identify with the black culture.
— Principal phonological differences between BEV and other English dialects:
  — AAEV drops r's in more positions, especially intervocalically and in clusters.
  — AAEV deletes final consonants or simplifies consonant clusters especially in final word position, after stressed vowels.
  — AAEV also backs the /l/ and changes /θ/ → /f/ and /ð/ → /d/.
— Principal morphological differences:
  — AAEV may not overtly mark those morphemes realized as consonant suffixes—such as the plural, possessive, third person singular, past tense—because of the phonological final consonant deletion.
  — AAEV marks habitual aspect with *be* and *been.*
  — AAEV uses *done* as an auxiliary marker of past tense and intensifier.
— Principal syntactic differences:
  — AAEV variably deletes the copula in present, affirmative, nonhabitual sentences.
  — AAEV variably expresses negative with a negative adverb and a negative marker on all indefinite NPs—negative concord.
— Historical and social influences:
  — AAEV probably derives from a creolization of English and West African (and perhaps West Indian) languages during slave times. Some features may be holdovers from the parent languages (e.g., ending words with a vowel), or stem from the creolization process (reduplication of the negative) or the influence of other nonstandard English dialects of the South.
  — AAEV is a southern states dialect that moved North with the repeated migration of southern blacks to northern urban centers.
  — AAEV has remained separate from the historical changes affecting white urban dialects, first from overt segregation, then from emotional distancing, with BEV speakers wishing to constitute their own group.

---

apparent criticalness, a sign that the language one thinks in *seems* superior to other languages.

Finally, we see the importance of social factors in conditioning language change and in determining which dialect to participate in. Strong speakers of AAEV are youth, at the forefront of language change. The most verbally adept are the group leaders. Alienation from a culture results in alienation from its language patterns, regardless of the physical mingling.

SEX DIFFERENCES IN LANGUAGE

Thus far, this chapter has considered differences in language between cultures—cultures defined either generationally or in socio-politico-economic terms—a geographic group, black or white urban youth, diehard Martha's Vineyarders versus emigrating Martha's Vineyarders, and so on. Within a culture too, we see language differences, which, when explored using sociolinguistic methods, also show a consistent pattern. Specifically, men and women (and boys and girls) use language differently, to different ends.

There are differences between the sexes in every level of language: speech, lexical use, typical syntactic constructions, and pragmatics. The last is the most significant difference so I will briefly summarize the others and then concentrate on it and its effect on communication and impressions between the sexes.

Language Differences Between the Sexes

As we discussed in Chapter 6, men have larger vocal tracts and larynxes than females, with the consequence that their fundamental and formant frequencies are lower. Male speech is typically less variable than female: Male speech is more monotone (less pitch variation) and more uniform in loudness (Lakoff, 1975). Females frequently make assertions with an intonation rise rather than fall, intoning them like questions (Lakoff, 1975). We have already seen that in Western societies, women tend to be on the forefront of phonetic change, another indication of greater variability or, perhaps, flexibility in articulation.

Women also use different vocabularies than men do. Lakoff (1975) has noted a number of differences. Men are less likely to use nonbasic color words, such as *magenta* or *taupe,* for example. Women, more than men, use intense, empty adjectives such as *divine* or *charming,* and intensifier adverbs like *so.* Men, more than women, use coarse language (Haas, 1979). If you are hesitant about the validity of these sex differences, think about whether it would be more likely to hear a woman or man exclaiming, "Ohhhh! That's lovely!"

Lakoff (1975) also notes that women use hedges—*I feel, y'know, kind'a,* or *well*—more than men. Like a questioning tone, the hedge tones down the assertiveness of the assertion.

The principal syntactic difference Lakoff has noted is one that also functions to tone down an assertion for women: the use of tag questions. As you may recall, a tag question is tagged to the end of an assertion, questioning and negating it. "Women use more tag questions then men, *don't they?*" makes the assertion, dilutes its impact with the question, and asks the listener for support. As we will see in the next section, women's speech is designed to elicit cooperation and support from the listener, and the tag question has those effects.

Sex Differences in Discursive Purpose and Effects: Pragmatics

Tannen is a sociolinguist who has extensively studied discourse between American men and women (and members of different ethnic groups). Her method (1994) is to record conversations, identify segments that appear to be creating dissension, play those segments to the participants and other people for their interpretations of what is going on, and then organize the interpretations and precipitating conditions into meaningful patterns. Usually the conversations are live and natural, but she supports her findings with examples taken from literature as well, illustrating the reliability of her observation with the author's similar observations.

Like the constructivists (see Chapter 3), Tannen (1994) argues that a language or discourse feature imparts no meaning alone, independent of context:

1) roles are not given but are created in interaction;

2) context is not given but is constituted by talk and action;

3) nothing that occurs in interaction is the sole doing of one party but rather is a "joint production," the result of the interaction of individuals' ways of speaking; and . . .

4) linguistic features (such as interruption, volume of talk, indirectness, and so on) can never be aligned on a one-to-one basis with interactional intentions or meanings. . . .

No language has meaning except by reference to how it is "framed." (pp. 10-11)

Let's take the example of interruption or simultaneous talking. (It is important to note that the examples and conclusions that follow arise from interactions between modern American men and women. Naturally, what is standard behavior for the sexes will vary in different cultures.) An overlapping talking turn is easy to define operationally—an important criterion for the empirically, but not the ethnographically, oriented researcher (Tannen, 1994, p. 57). Overlap also appears easy to interpret.

Many people consider simultaneous talking to be "rude" and feel that interruptions constitute competition for the floor. Experimentally oriented researchers point out that, in mixed-sex groups, men interrupt women more often than the reverse. This is usually interpreted as a sign of male dominance. But Tannen's research shows that there are at least three kinds of "interruptions" and these occur with different frequencies between the sexes. The first, and least interesting, interruption is, for example, during dinner, when one person asks for some food to be passed or offers some food, during another person's talking turn. This is polite, not a bid for the floor: The business of eating, we agree, takes temporary precedence over the business of talking. The second is an interruption, say, during an argument, where the interrupting party does not want the speaker to finish but wants the floor. This is competitive and dominating, as the experimentalists determine, and is more common among men than women, whether or not there is an argument.

The third type is more common among women, what Tannen labels "cooperative overlap" as in the following (brackets indicate overlapping speech):

Peg:	The part I didn't like was putting everybody's snow pants and boots
	⌐ and
Marge:	└ Oh yeah that was the worst part,
Peg:	⌐ and scarves
Marge:	└ and get them all bundled up in boots
	and everything and they're out for half an
	hour. . . . (p. 70)

What is important to note here is that (a) by a strict definition of interruption as simultaneous speech, this is interruption, but (b) there is no attempt to wrest the floor in the simultaneous speaking turn; it is not competitive and domineering but supportive. We must look at the whole context to see the intent and import of the interruption.

The meaning of simultaneous talk, the meaning of silence between talking turns, the meaning of ostensibly agreeing or disagreeing varies among cultures, including the cultures of malehood and femalehood. (Tannen, 1994, observes that it is a true stereotype that Japanese cannot say "no." They do disagree, but by the relative weakness of their "yes." People who know the culture interpret the weak yes as the intended no.) The male culture, used to interrupting and being interrupted in a friendly competition for the floor, will see such support talk as an interruption for the floor and will view the simultaneously talking females stereotypically as "clucking hens" (Tannen, 1994, p. 72). The female culture, used to support talk, will interpret a man's interruption as support, and will cede the floor thinking it only momentary. Thus, in a mixed-sex dyad, the man comes to dominate the woman, a result of the parts played by both man and woman and by the pragmatic misunderstanding.

Similarly, ethnic groups considered pushy (New Yorkers, for instance) use a lot of simultaneous talk, short pause durations, and driving, personal questions—as a sign of involvement. Interacting with cultures considered to be distant (long silences, little simultaneous talk, spaced, impersonal questions) produces a clash as each style is judged in terms of what it would mean if it had been produced by a person of the listener's own culture.

Studying men and women in conversation, Tannen concludes that they have very different discursive purposes, which begin in early childhood. Men and women learn their conversation styles in sex-separated peer groups as children. The two sexes move in separated worlds, picking up separate cultures.

Women are more likely to discuss personal issues such as friendships, love, disappointments, and other people, and men are more likely to tell jokes and discuss news and sports. In discussing personal issues, "women speak and hear a language of connection and intimacy" (Tannen, 1990, p. 42). In discussing global events, "men speak and hear a language of status and independence" (Tannen, 1990, p. 42). The two overarching, different goals in conversation result in some of the language differences we described, and often in conflict between the sexes.

Girls play in small groups and aim at pairing with a "best friend." Girls' games, like jump rope or hopscotch, are games in which everyone has a chance and there are no winners and losers. Girls do not direct, but suggest, activities: "Let's play . . .," with suggestions usually accepted (Tannen, 1990). As adults, women connect in conversation similarly, inviting support from a listener by "asking assertions." This allows the other to offer an opinion, to reach the factual conclusion as a consensus and not under the direction of the leader. An assertion is asked with a rising intonation or a tag question. Women discuss personal issues, often telling personally embarrassing stories, to invite the other to share vulnerability and to feel comfortable in a humble presence. Women discuss problems similarly, inviting a show of solidarity: "I've been in that situation too; you must be very unhappy—I was." Finally, women create solidarity by grouping together against an absent person (gossip). I would argue that it is this groupiness that contributes to women's being at the forefront of language change: The group shows solidarity by imitating each other's speech patterns and differentiating them maximally from those of other groups.

Men, in contrast, show solidarity through competition. Boys, but not girls, engage in mock fighting and teasing as a prelude to friendship. Consider, for example, Robin Hood's and Little John's fabulous brotherhood, which begins in a fight to cross a bridge. Robin Hood is knocked into the water by his most worthy opponent. Getting up with a laugh, Robin invites Little John to join his band. Tannen describes such mock combat among preschool boys. As adults, the "fight" moves from the physical to the verbal level, with men jockeying for position and respect through their demonstrated knowledge of jokes (the more extensive repertoire wins, as we saw in sounding in AAVE) or of world events. Tannen (1990) contrasts the male and female purposes in conversation as "rapport talk" (female) and "report talk" (male).

When men and women converse with one another, they inappropriately apply the pragmatics of their own sex. When a man raises a problem, he expects either to be offered a solution or to have the problem minimized; when a woman raises a problem, she expects a show of sympathy and solidarity. Each is irritated by the unexpected response given by the other. Take the following dialogue from Tannen (1990) as an example:

> HE: I'm really tired. I didn't sleep well last night.
> SHE: I didn't sleep well either. I never do.
> HE: Why are you trying to belittle me?
> SHE: I'm not! I'm just trying to show that I understand! (p. 51)

From *his* culture, the appropriate response could be "you'll feel better after coffee," minimizing the problem and/or offering advice. From *his* culture, her response could have been seen as an attempt at "winning"—she is *more* tired—or a put-down—he cannot overcome such a problem. She verbalizes the intent from *her* culture: "We are similar."

Recall the constructivist position of Chapter 3, where any simple sentence can have myriad interpretations depending on pragmatics. "Do you have a watch?" most

---

Box 8.5. Male-Female Language Differences

Speech
— Women's voices are higher than men's.
— Women have greater pitch and loudness variability than men.
— Women are more likely to show an intonation rise, rather than pitch declination, on an assertion.

Lexical
— There are words women are more likely to use such as *magenta* or *lovely.*
— Men are more likely to curse and use slang.
— Women are more likely to use intensifiers.

Syntax
— Women are more likely to mark assertions with tag questions.
— Women are more likely to issue a command syntactically as a suggestion, "Let's . . ."

Pragmatics
— Women rapport-talk; men report-talk.
— Women seek solidarity by overlapping speech supportively, sharing similar experiences, placing themselves on an equal footing, and closing ranks against absent persons.
— Men seek respect, acknowledgment of their verbal prowess, command of the news, ability to cope with or solve problems.
— Both indirect and direct requests must be interpreted within the appropriate cultural framework, which is different for the two sexes.

---

often is an indirect request for time but could be an indirect request to hand it over during a robbery. "Today is September 7" can mean "I want a divorce—you forgot our anniversary," "Get up, it's the first day of school," and so on depending on the shared contextual framework. Different cultural backgrounds create different pragmatic frameworks and different ways of using language to communicate intent. The ethnographic approach of the sociolinguist—studying language *and* social attitudes *and* full contextual frame—enables us to appreciate more fully the subtleties of language use, day-to-day misunderstandings, and language change.

SUMMARY AND CONCLUSIONS

This chapter explored language use in social context. We saw that it is possible to study language change systematically as cultures clash, merge, and develop, by studying processes internal to the language and processes reflective of group membership. Human language is a powerful means of symbol manipulation; that is the aspect of language we dwelled on in considering meaning and syntax. But symbol transfer is only one function of human language; another function is communication, the establishment and regulation of communities. Through socio-linguistics we study how language is shaped by, and shapes, such communities.

A theoretical position introduced in this chapter was the bioprogram hypothesis, accounting for language change in successive generations by innate language-inducing capabilities in children. In the next chapter, we look formally at how children *do* acquire language—all aspects of it, phonology, semantics, syntax, and social use. In light of these data we consider the bioprogram hypothesis again. It is also reconsidered in the following chapter, as we compare adult and child second language acquisition.

REFERENCES

Bickerton, D. (1982). Learning without experience the Creole way. In L. Obler & L. Menn (Eds.), *Exceptional language and linguistics* (pp. 15-29). New York: Academic Press.

Bickerton, D. (1984). The language bioprogram hypothesis. *Behavioral and Brain Sciences, 7,* 173-221.

Bickerton, D. (1990). *Language and species.* Chicago: University of Chicago Press.

Haas, A. (1979). Male and female spoken language differences: Stereotypes and evidence. *Psychological Bulletin, 86,* 616-626.

Heath, S. B. (1983). *Ways with words: Language, life, and work in communities and classrooms.* New York: Cambridge University Press.

Jeffers, R. J., & Lehiste, I. (1979). *Principles and methods for historical linguistics.* Cambridge: MIT Press.

Labov, W. (1972a). *Language in the inner city: Studies in the black English vernacular.* Philadelphia: University of Pennsylvania Press.

Labov, W. (1972b). *Sociolinguistic patterns.* Philadelphia: University of Pennsylvania Press.

Labov, W. (1994). *Principles of linguistic change: Vol. 1. Internal factors.* Cambridge, MA: Blackwell.

Lakoff, R. (1975). *Language and woman's place.* New York: Harper & Row.

Pyles, T. (1993). *The origins and development of the English language* (4th ed.). New York: Harcourt Brace Jovanovich.

Tannen, D. (1990). *You just don't understand: Men and women in conversation.* New York: Ballantine.

Tannen, D. (1994). *Gender & discourse.* New York: Oxford University Press.

STUDY QUESTIONS

1. Summarize the internal and external factors effecting language change. To what extent do languages develop to better communicate meaning? Your discussion should touch on conditions for the formation of pidgins and creoles, the bioprogram hypothesis, systematic phonetic drifting (change from below), change from above, and conditions for splitting of dialects.

2. What is the observer's paradox? Discuss how it might have influenced the evidence mustered in support of the bioprogram hypothesis and the idea that inner-city children are verbally disadvantaged. How does Labov minimize the effects of the observer's paradox in his studies? Does he eliminate it entirely? Discuss.

3. Discuss the main linguistic differences between AAEV and SAE. Is there any reason to suppose one dialect communicates better than the other? That either dialect is more sophisticated linguistically? Support your answer with factual details about the dialect, communication, and linguistic complexity.

4. Speakers of the same language can differ systematically in any of the levels of language: phonology, semantics, syntax, discourse, and pragmatics. For each level, cite two or three examples of difference among English speakers from different historical periods, different generations, different cultural identities, different dialects, or different sexes. Try to spread your examples among the different groups discussed in this chapter.

5. The methods of sociolinguistics are quite different from the the data collection methods of psychology and linguistics proper. Consider the differences and elaborate on the methods used to determine social influences on language differences in this chapter.

9

ACQUISITION OF
THE FIRST LANGUAGE

At birth an infant is able to cry and cough but otherwise produces no sounds. At birth an infant "understands" that loud noises are alarming, and that softer noises are interesting, and so responds differently to these noises. As the child gets older, things change. She or he may say, for example,

AGE	UTTERANCE	PRESUMED TARGET
3 months	/ɛ/, /gɛ/	?
5 months	/ba, ba/ /mama/	?
10 months	/bɔ/	There is the ball.
18 months	/der bɔ/	There is the ball.
24 months	I wanna build a high house too.	
36 months	Yes you can open that one but I'm gonna lock it so you can't get in.	

What has happened in three years? And has it finished happening—does the 3-year-old know what the adult knows about language except for vocabulary?

Chapters 2, 4, 6, and 8 discussed the structure of adult language. As we have seen, it is quite complex. There are meaning "elements" and these can have a variety of relationships to their referents. There are a vast number of rules for joining together meaning elements and for interpreting the combination. There are many ways to form the meaning elements, complex articulatory gesture coordination involved in producing them, and a system for combining them, increasing redundancy. There are "rules" governing social interactions that render some forms more appropriate in some contexts to some audiences. Does the "language" of the 3-month-old or 36-month-old or anywhere in between look like an adult's? How does the child learn the mass of elements and rules in three (or more) years? Do the parents actively teach the rules? Are languages designed to contain rules that human infants are born knowing?

Chapters 3, 5, and 7 discussed how native (English) speakers process their language. Does the child process language in the same way or achieve the same ends using a different, "childlike" strategy? Whether the child uses the same or different strategies, are they innate, unfolding, and "tuned" by the language the child hears as the child matures, or does the child *learn* language structures as he or she learns other cognitive skills, with a minimum of structure given by UG, a bioprogram?

These are the questions of child language acquisition. This chapter will attempt to answer these questions, describing the course of language development and the development of processing strategies. Note that if innate linguistic rules or innate processing strategies exist, they must constitute a significant biological constraint on language structure. For, if a system were devised that children could not learn or could not learn easily, the system would not survive: *Language form has been shaped by what the child brings to language learning.* Study of children's language processing is study of the constraints on language form.

INTRODUCTORY ISSUES

Nativism Versus Empiricism in Language Acquisition

Probably the most critical theoretical issue in studies of child development is whether the knowledge the child acquires is innately specified (*native*) or is learned through environmental interaction (*empirical*). As I discussed in Chapter 4, to be innate, knowledge may be explicitly expressed at birth; for example, children do not have to learn to cry, or produce saliva, or startle to loud noises. It may also not unfold until after birth, like teeth development, which happens at fixed times up until about 18 years. Innately specified behavior may also require some input from the environment to be expressed or to develop. For example, a slap or jolt causes a baby to inspire and begin the innate reflex of breathing. And there is considerable research in animal perception and socialization, elaborated in *Language in Atypical Populations,* showing that infant animals are born with a crude "blueprint" of significant stimuli such as their species song or visual patterns. The blueprint is maintained and developed through exposure to such stimuli in the environment. The elaboration, a form of learning, takes place optimally during a *critical period,* a time when the organism is primed to attend to the stimuli and after which the organism is increasingly unable to attend to the relevant stimuli and elaborate the blueprint. Without exposure to the stimulus during the critical period, the organism may permanently lose the ability to respond to such stimuli. Whether such critical periods exist in human learning and perception is under debate, but, if so, they indicate an innate specification of both the blueprint and a time to learn.

One last type of innate specification to consider includes behaviors that themselves are not innately specified but are outgrowths of innately specified physical changes in the body. Consider crying: As we grow older, our vocal tracts change innately and we acquire (innately) the capacity to produce tears, making the sound and appearance of crying change. This does not mean that there is an innately controlled program for crying development per se but innate controls on the body, which affect crying. Analogous indirect effects of genetic control are likely on complex cognitive behaviors like language.

Innate behaviors may thus manifest at any time during life. With physical changes, which were mostly what I used in the previous examples, innateness hypotheses are not controversial. Can cognitive changes also be innate? The table beginning this chapter presented sample utterances tied to different ages in a child's early years. Is the change from crying to syllables to words to simple sentences to complex sentences a manifestation of an unfolding, innate, language acquisition device? Or is the child *learning* language in the first three years, and the changes the result of the infant's exposure to adult models?

To some extent, for each aspect of acquisition, because the data are ambiguous, where you stand on this issue is a matter of choice—and the choice of the dominant thinkers seems to switch from decade to decade. I will briefly review the choices and criteria of some of the dominant psycholinguists of the twentieth century. There are three questions to consider for each position:

1. How much and what is innate in language?
2. How much of what is considered innate is specific for language and how much relates to general cognitive development?
3. What are the criteria for determining innateness and are they reasonable?

Language Acquisition Device (LAD) or Universal Grammar (UG)

The generative linguists, following Chomsky (1965, 1986), hold the most extreme view in favor of innate control of language acquisition. As I presented in Chapters 1 and 4, LAD or UG is believed to equip the child with both innate knowledge about language structures and innate mechanisms for refining that knowledge. The knowledge may be specific—the existence of phonetic features and phrases—or it may be more open, a parameter to be set such as where the head will be in the phrase. Methods the child uses to discover the parameter settings from the input are like those the linguist uses but are tacit.

Thus, innately, UG provides the child parameters, that is, a method for analyzing the input and constraints on permissible generalizations. The environment provides (a) the utterances used to eliminate or select from the innate hypotheses to set the parameters and (b) a prod, the way spanking prods breathing, for the formation of language. UG's guidance is seen as necessary to constrain overgeneralizations, possible because any child hears only a limited set of utterances (Crain, 1991). This is called *poverty of the stimulus.* For example, in Chapter 4, I presented the conditions in which *want to* may be contracted into *wanna,* if and only if the two words are, and have always been, adjacent, with no trace intervening. If by chance a child hears only surface forms where *want* and *to* are adjacent, she or he might incorrectly generalize that *wanna* is allowed even across a trace. UG presumably blocks this hypothesis with an innate filter forbidding contraction across a trace.

Poverty of the stimulus occurs because each child hears too few utterances to generate a complete grammar of a language from scratch. And the utterances constitute only *positive evidence*—how things may be done; they do not rule out how they may *not* be done, as in the *wanna* example above. Nor do parents supply this logically necessary negative evidence (Gordon, 1990; but see Bohannon, MacWhinney, & Snow, 1990, for debate), and so cannot filter the input as the child needs.

Moreover, parents are not consistently correct in their utterances; the input to the child contains performance errors like false starts or incomplete sentences. Using these the child would generate the wrong grammatical model. Parents' language feedback to the child is also unreliable, partly because the parents do not explicitly know the rules they should be teaching, and partly because the language opaquely maps to its referents. We say, "Eat your peas," precisely when a child is *not* doing so; we are unlikely to correct "der ball," but approve it. Why then should a child develop "There is a ball"? Likewise, Chomsky (1986, p. 8) questions how a child could *learn* that "John is too stubborn to talk to" means that someone will not talk to John, while "John is too stubborn to talk to them" means that John will not be talking, given how similar the two sentences are.

Finally, the generative linguists argue that the child acquires language too fast to be only learning. Bates and Ellman (1996) critically point out: "Noam Chomsky, the founder of generative linguistics, has argued for 40 years that language is unlearnable; he and his followers have generalized this belief to other cognitive domains, denying the existence of learning as a meaningful scientific construct" (p. 1849).

Chomsky and his followers have inferred the constraints provided by UG from properties of adult languages, sometimes even only from a single adult language, the grammar of which has been studied in depth to reveal subtleties, presumably beyond the grasp of anything other than an innate guide (Chomsky, 1972). Some researchers sympathetic to Chomsky's position do study child language itself with specific criteria for determining innateness. One method is to search for common developmental milestones cross-culturally and cross-linguistically. Because different languages have different semantic classifications, different structures, and different sounds, the models children are exposed to are vastly different. If they still seem to acquire a class or rule at the same time or at the same time relative to acquisition of other classes or rules, the environment, it is argued, plays a small role.

Another method (Crain, 1991; Lenneberg, 1967) looks for synchrony of language milestones with other physical milestones (such as rapid brain growth or puberty), absent evidence of practice and environmental change. Discovery of physical correlates and no environmental correlates suggests an innate guide.

Unifying these developmental approaches with Chomsky's are the assumptions that aspects of language per se are innately specified, and these are consistent with the G+B (government-and-binding) framework. The difference lies in whether children's performance is directly studied and compared across cultures and biological abnormalities, or whether it is indirectly studied, inferred from the opaqueness of the adult grammar.

Piaget, Vygotsky: Changes in General Cognition

The generative linguists focus on syntax acquisition to conclude that there must be an innate guide. Focusing on semantic development suggests a stronger environmental role: The relationship of words to experience must be secondary to the experience. The problem becomes how children learn the relationships of objects to one another in the environment, how they form classifications, and *then* how they map language onto these forms. Thus language acquisition is seen as secondary to concept acquisition. In Piaget's own words (1983),

> The fundamental difference between Chomsky and us is that we consider all cognitive acquisitions, including language, to be the outcome of a gradual process of construction starting with the evolutionary forms of biological embryogenesis and ending up with modern scientific ideas. We thus reject the concept of preprogramming in any strict sense. What we consider as innate, however, is the general ability to synthesize the successive levels reached by the increasingly complex cognitive organization. (p. 110)

Detailed discussion of concept acquisition or cognitive development is beyond the scope of this book. However, the general approaches of Piaget and Vygotsky will be presented here because they have influenced the language acquisition literature.

The Stage Concept

According to Piaget (see, for summary, Ginsburg & Opper, 1988), particular kinds of thought come into play at different stages of an individual's life. *Stage* refers to a change that affects the child's mental organization and how the child will learn about the world. In Piaget's view, the child changes stages as a function of both maturational (biological) changes and environmental exposure. (Other stage theories emphasize biological changes in particular.) The child responds to the environment by *assimilation* of new information into existing mental structures, and by *accommodation,* or change, of mental structures to fit with new information. The current mental structure, or concept, Piaget called a *scheme,* and schemes are constantly changing through assimilation and accommodation to better represent the world. (*Schema* is sometimes used for *scheme.* Piaget differentiated the terms, with *scheme* referring to a mental concept used for generalization, and *schema,* to a mental image or a map; Piaget, 1981, translator's note, p. 4.)

A stage occurs when schemes radically change through accommodation, producing a new method of thinking. In Piaget's view, development is continuous, with a child gradually acquiring the skills that will cause the thought change. So a child may be at a primitive stage with respect to some schemes and a more advanced one with respect to others. (Other stage theorists see a more abrupt change between stages.)

Cognitive Stages

Piaget described four stages in the development of symbolic thought. The first stage, from about 0 to 2 years, is the period of *sensorimotor thinking.* During this period the child's scheme for the world is totally derived from sensory and motor experience. The child's "representation" of reality is the here and now, what is directly and immediately experienced. During the sensorimotor period the child learns to separate sensory experience from objective reality, ultimately to realize that objects exist outside the self. This is the radical change in thinking that produces a new stage and a new mode of thought, symbolic functioning. Initially children know of an object only when it impinges on their senses; by the end of this period, the child has *object permanence,* the ability to conceptualize an object not in view. This is achieved through the child's active manipulation of the environment (reaching for things, kicking them, and so on), producing schemes for different objects. As the child learns more about objects, the schemes become increasingly elaborate until they are divorced from immediate sense impressions. It is not coincidental that the first words appear at about 1 year of age, when object permanence is established.

Sensorimotor language begins as an accompaniment to perception or action, children describing what they are perceiving or doing. Because language constantly accompanies sensation, the word and the act become confused. In this respect, language takes on a magical quality, in which it seems as though words and actions are one. Piaget (1952) argued that this early experience underlies adult's ritual language, the belief that uttering words in prayers, spells, and curses—"the word being no longer a pure label, but a formidable partaking of the nature of the named object" (p. 3)—affects the objects and events. As the sensorimotor period ends, children use words symbolically, discussing objects or events displaced in time or space.

The next major cognitive change occurs between the ages of 2 and 7, when children begin to organize their ideas, as they had earlier learned to organize their perceptions. This stage Piaget called *preoperational thinking—pre*operational because the thought organization is *un*systematic. During this time, schemes continue to be elaborated, but inconsistently. Children understand that there are categories and that things have names, but, because they do not have a system of rules for manipulating ideas, they do not understand rules of categorization or the general *concept* of naming. In the first case this means that objects are organized into groups, but the principle underlying the organization is idiosyncratic and changes during the grouping (which will be clearer when we discuss Vygotsky). In the second case children respond to the names of objects as intrinsic properties of objects, as color is. So if preoperational children are asked what something is named, they respond correctly, but if asked, for example, why a dog is named "dog," they respond, "Because it is a dog," and if pushed with "Could it be called a cow?" say no, "Because a cow is a cow."

During the course of the preoperational period, as a result of continued experience, children discover "adult" principles of categorization and learn true similarities and equivalents. This produces the knowledge necessary to know what it means that a name names.

The preoperational years also see the beginning of social speech. Initially, Piaget found that language is mostly *egocentric,* consisting of repetitions, monologues, and collective monologues, all characterized by a lack of interest in the response of others and an apparent lack of awareness that others should be responding. In repetition, children just echo what others or they themselves have just said. In a monologue, they give a running description of their activities without taking into account the others' perspectives. In a *collective monologue,* children engage in monologues together, conversationally turn-taking but not responding to each other's content. So, for example, each may be drawing and describing his or her own drawing, ignoring the drawings and commentaries of the other children. At $6\frac{1}{2}$ years old, nearly half of children's conversation can be described as egocentric (Piaget, 1952).

Following the preoperational stage, children develop a system of organization for ideas called *concrete operations* because the system applies to ideas with concrete referents. At this time they learn about group structure, *principles of hierarchical organization.* Early in concrete operations a child will understand that petunias are flowers that are plants but will not understand that this means (a) the class of plants is larger than the class of flowers or (b) petunias have all features of plants but plants do not necessarily have all features of petunias. Learning the principles of group structure occurs between 7 and 11 years of age.

In addition to acquiring a system for dealing with concrete reality, concrete operational children use language socially, not egocentrically; that is, during this period, it seems clear that language is used as communication, cooperatively conveying information, as the child monitors feedback from the audience.

The final stage is *formal operations,* which emerges after age 11. Formal operations are rules for thinking about thinking. Through concrete operations, children develop a systematic approach to concrete reality, the ability to manipulate tangible objects logically and consistently. In formal operations, the logical systematicity is applied to *mental* representations. This permits the understanding of algebra and formal logic. More germane to our discussion, it also permits the complete comprehension of metalanguage (because language is then appreciated as an abstract system) and of figurative language (because a symbol does not only have to apply to a concrete referent), which Piaget (1952) argued was interpreted only concretely at earlier stages.

Vygotsky's Application of Piagetian Theory to Language

Vygotsky (1986/1996) developed a model similar to Piaget's but with greater emphasis on language, instruction, and socialization. Piaget and Vygotsky influenced each other. An important addition to the scheme concept was Vygotsky's notion of *zone of proximal development,* the difference between a child's ability to perform a task alone and cooperatively with an adult. Children's unaided skill indexes their rich, but unsystematic concepts; their skill in cooperation indexes their ability to appropriate adult systematic reasoning. The social instruction facilitates the child's internalization of the systematic scheme.

Children begin using speech correctly before they have use for it or understand what they are doing. Vygotsky sees sensorimotor, egocentric speech as the precursor to *inner speech,* or thought. Egocentric speech, like thought, focuses the child's attention on the current activity. Unlike thought, egocentric speech is perceived by the child as social and changing, say, if the "audience" is deaf or speaks a foreign language. However, it is not *functionally* social until the child fully develops the scheme for speech and communication. With the aid of adult models, the child learns to use speech truly socially.

We see another zone of proximal development with words and syntax in the preoperational stage. The child correctly forms sentences but has not yet conceptualized the rules controlling the structures that are formed.

Sensorimotor thought, the use of speech as redundant to observation, separates from preoperational thought, the use of speech as communication, with the child's sudden interest in learning the names of things and constant requests for names. Development from preoperational speech through to formal operations is observed by dissecting the child's categories.

Vygotsky measured children's categorization schemes using what have come to be known as *Vygotsky blocks,* blocks differing simultaneously on several dimensions such as color, size, or shape. The task is to sort them into some number of piles, with freedom to choose a category "rule"—for example, all red ones in one pile and blue in another, or red triangles, blue triangles, red rectangles, and blue rectangles each in separate piles.

Watching the children as they sort the blocks at different stages of development and getting them to verbalize their reasons for their sorting yield insight into emerging categorization principles, which likely also apply to children's labeling. At the earliest stage, children group on the basis of which blocks are near each other, not on similarity. They may also form a group by taking one block from each existing group, an early hierarchical structuring. Subsequently they group by feature, like picking a blue rectangle and then a blue triangle, verbally emphasizing the blue. However, their attention is distracted, so they may next pick a red triangle sharing the triangle feature. The result is an unorganized heap, but one created through emerging categorizing principles.

The next stages show increasing persistence of focus—blue remains the selected feature—so the piles are organized as an adult would but without the adult's awareness of the organization principle. Here again is a zone of proximal development: Performance exceeds understanding and benefits from practice with and explanation from an adult to produce internalization of the principle.

Of interest, Vygotsky points out that child reasoning is evident in adults encountering new concepts, although we can bring our experience of structured thought to bear on them. If we come across a new word in a sentence and are asked to define it, we usually paraphrase the rest of the sentence as a definition (the word or part = the whole), although we know the "formal operation" that the word must contribute a meaning to the rest. Repeated exposures to the word in new contexts will allow us to add the meanings of the contexts and eventually factor out the common contribution. Likewise the child's principle of organization develops from all the things dumped in the same group as the "meaning" of the category, to the notion of this or that feature in common, to a correct factoring of similarity. Vygotsky also points out that tracing the meaning of a word through a language's history reveals the same kinds of changes as in a child's thinking; metaphorical extensions get applied by an almost haphazard notice of a shared detail between the word's usual meaning and the figurative extension.

Summary

With respect to nativism-empiricism, Piaget and Vygotsky had similar views. They emphasized maturational changes in the child's ability to reason. But these interact markedly with environmental input; they do not just unfold but are a product of the child's active attempts to understand and the child's experience with the world. Experience is not passively imprinted on a child like light on film but gets actively transformed by assimilation with and accommodation of the child's schemes. Moreover, what is innate or maturational, in this view, is not specific to language but to a general program of thinking that serves the language system as well as other thought systems. Finally, their methodology consists of observation of the child's behavior combined with experimental probing of the reasoning underlying the behavior.

Skinner, the Acquisition of Verbal Behavior, and Connectionism

At the other end of the nativism-empiricism continuum are the behaviorists whose model, like Chomsky's, was deduced not from child language but from adult behaviors or (unlike Chomsky) from animals. In this approach, what may be considered innate are the abilities to form associations through classical and operant conditioning, to generalize, and to discriminate. These abilities do not change through life. However, the number and quality of associations formed do change as we gather experience, and, therefore, what can get conditioned has an increasingly greater base of previous associations.

Skinner (1957) saw the beginning of language acquisition as the reinforcing of "relatively unpatterned vocalizations" (p. 31). These spontaneous vocalizations have no obvious "cause"—that is, they may be innate, although Skinner did not use that word. Once they appear, their incidence is increased through reinforcement and then they are shaped toward sounds the verbal community accepts. In Skinner's view, primary reinforcement is always food or the like, and social reinforcement, praise or attention, is secondary (effective because of associations with primary reinforcers. Money is a secondary reinforcer; secondary reinforcers may be as or more powerful than primary reinforcers). The association between social reinforcement and primary reinforcement is one of the first things the child must learn. Whether the parents in fact feed children when they vocalize is dubious, but certainly parents respond to the vocalizations with increased attention and interest. Thus parents encourage increased vocalization.

Many parents also "shape" words, repeating them until the child produces them and then reinforcing the child with praise or hugs. Why children imitate has never been explained; it may be self-reinforcing (innate).

After shaping the production of a word, for example, *milk,* by reinforcing it with milk, the parent extends the concept to situations with milk so the child learns to generalize the name to the class of objects it describes. The parent also begins to reinforce more complete statements of needs so that the child will have to say "I want milk" to get it, or "There is the milk" to get social praise for naming. Correct pronunciations, correct syntax, and so on are specifically shaped: The child hears a model over and over again and imitates it, increasing the strength of that verbal response; the parents reinforce finer and finer discriminations (or generalizations) so that the child's verbal behavior comes to match that of the community.

In Skinner's model the child plays a passive role, and the parent/teacher an active one. Recent connectionist (PDP or neural net) approaches employ association principles together with data from children and simulate the acquisition pattern (Bates & Ellman, 1996; MacWhinney, 1987). In these models there is less emphasis on teaching and more on the learner's inherent abilities to change connection strengths depending on input. Thus the learner "can induce regular patterns [rules] from imperfect, but quasi-regular input, and generalize those patterns to novel instances" (Bates & Ellman, 1996, p. 1849).

Summary and Implications

In the associationist approaches, acquisition of regularities in the language is accomplished through general principles of learning: imitation, reinforcement, and punishment (respectively, increasing and decreasing association weights) and induction of regularity from imperfectly regular stimuli. The child is guided neither by specific innate rule knowledge as in the generative linguistic approach nor by active attempts to learn as in the Piagetian approach; in short, language acquisition happens through general learning principles, not human-specific ones. What may be specifically human (and innate) is the infant's interest in language and imitating adult humans, which forms the input for the induction of the relevant regularities.

The behaviorist approach attributes language acquisition partly to the model the parents provide. Although Skinner has not been credited with initiating such research, many modern students of child language acquisition now study the parents' language to the child as well as the child language back. This allows a search for reinforcement patterns and, more important, a categorization of the language of the adult models, acknowledging that we do not talk to children as we do to other adults.

A final significant contribution of the behaviorist approach is its emphasis on habit strength rather than foreordained structures. In the linguistic outlook, the child knows about distinctive features—words, sentences, deep structures, principles, and parameters—and "learns" only particular settings, that is, which ones are used. The basic structural units are given. For Piagetians the unit is the word, and the child learns what words refer to and how to combine them. Associationists basically propose no unit from which more complex linguistic structures derive: In some cases the child begins with sounds and patterns them into words and phrases; in others the child imitates a whole phrase and later learns to separate it into components that play a role in other sentences. Phonology and syntax are seen as habit strengths. If *Ipledgeallegiance* has greater frequency than *pledge,* children will use that as a unit until they are taught to distinguish the components. If *mama* is experienced in isolation, it will be a unit and the child will have to learn to combine it with others into sentences. In this approach there is no complex system of internalized rules, either innately given or acquired through development, but a system of habit strengths. Again, the behaviorists are not credited with this insight, which, we will see, fits some language acquisition patterns.

Methodology in Language Acquisition Studies

The approaches of interest in the context of this chapter are those that deal with the child's language specifically because we have already discussed characteristics of the adult language and their relative transparency in surface structure. Collecting and interpreting data from children, especially addressing the nature (innate)-nurture (environment) issue introduces special methodological needs.

What to Measure

We are presumably interested in measuring a child's language knowledge. Can we do that by seeing what the children say? Often children seem to understand more than they say, as when they reach for their bottle when asked if they are hungry. Likewise, they may hear their own production of *ball*, /bɔ/, as not quite right but be unable to say /l/ as yet. What would we want to say their speech competence was? And a child may produce something correctly, but for the wrong reason. Should we argue that they have the competence simply because the production was correct?

Box 9.1. Theoretical Positions on Language Development

Chomsky and Followers

— *UG:* There is an innately specified language-specific language development program: universal grammar (UG) or the language acquisition device (LAD). It consists of principles and parameters to be found in all languages (such as binary-branching phrase structures, thematic roles, major syntactic classes) and procedures for perceiving language input (such as a mental version of distributional analysis) to fix parameter settings for a given language. Language input is crucial to specify such settings, such as whether an argument precedes or follows a head.

— *Learnability theory:* We can conclude that UG is innate because the language input the child receives from adults is too inconsistent and incomplete (poverty of the stimulus) to allow for complete specification of the child's language knowledge. That is, UG is unlearnable from the models provided.

— *Positive versus negative evidence:* Part of learnability theory, the assumption that adults do not correct children's language but only provide "positive" examples of what correct language is. This specifies rules of the grammar but also allows forms that are ungrammatical; that is, the models *underspecify* what the child in fact picks up. The child's insight must come from innate restrictions on language hypotheses.

— Methods
  — Study adult language in-depth with an eye toward its learnability.
  — Study structurally different languages and different cultures for common acquisition patterns.
  — Study different people for common acquisition patterns despite, say, general retardation.
  — Look for acquisition milestones that occur before they are of use to the individual or in the absence of environmental change or rehearsal.
  — Look for linguistic milestones co-occurring with sudden physical development.

Piaget and Vygotsky

— Language acquisition co-occurs with concept acquisition and depends heavily on the child's active manipulation of the environment.

— Concepts are represented in mental schemes, which change as new information is assimilated into them, or, if information is too divergent to be assimilated, the scheme radically changes to accommodate it.

— *Zone of proximal development:* When the child can accomplish a task with assistance, but not alone; she or he is on the verge of completing the scheme for it.

— Stages of conceptual reorganization can be identified as schemes get accommodated.

— *Sensorimotor:* When the child's conceptualization co-occurs with sensory experience. This stage ends with object permanence, where the child recognizes objects exist even when not being directly experienced (the beginning of inner speech).

(continued)

Box 9.1 Continued

— *Preoperational:* Some of the principles of object relations are realized but not systematically organized.
— *Concrete operations:* Systematized thought about concrete objects; Vygotsky blocks organized coherently.
— *Formal operations:* Systemized thought about thought, that is, metalanguage.
— Speech develops socially from monologue to collective monologue to social speech.

Skinner and Connectionism
— Correctly imitated language is strengthened through primary (food, for example) or secondary (social acceptance) reinforcement or, in connectionism, positive or negative feedback.
— Imitation is itself reinforcing, possibly innate.
— In behaviorism, parents shape language by successive reinforcement of better approximations to the adult forms.
— In connectionism, teaching is not active; the learner infers regularity from frequently, but not definitely, occurring patterns.
— No particular "unit" is a given: The child may imitate a syllable, word, or phrase and be shaped to combine or analyze the produced units as need be.
— Emphasis on looking at parents' input to children as key to language acquisition.

Production Measures

Two general techniques have been used to study children's productions. One is a cataloguing of the utterances, called *diary studies.* These are made either for all utterances or for specific samples of utterances, say, for all utterances produced during two-hour visits every Friday. (An important set of diary studies, those collected by Brown and his colleagues [Brown, 1973], for example, on "Adam," "Eve," and "Sara," are now on-line, available in the CHILDES database [MacWhinney & Snow, 1985].) Aside from the problem of interpreting what children know given what they produce, diary studies suffer from the possibility that children simply may not elect to talk using everything they know and so the diary may omit a particular kind of utterance.

The second technique attempts to correct for this shortcoming by eliciting utterances from the child. This may be done by (a) asking the child a question, with the answer being the target production; (b) asking the child to describe a picture, or the action of a puppet, with the description expected to contain the target; and (c) prompting the child with several utterances of the desired format and then presenting a new utterance for the child to complete following that format. Note that these elicited productions entail some comprehension—at least of the task "instructions." Thus a failure to complete a sentence or describe a picture could reflect an inability to produce the needed language, a failure to recognize or comprehend the sentence or picture, or a failure to understand what is wanted.

Crain (1991) engineered techniques for eliciting complex syntactic productions from children by ensuring that the situation pragmatics demand, and therefore elicit, the syntax if it is in the child's competence. The child interacts in a scene in which a popular character (X-man, Kermit-the-Frog, or the like) is mediating between other popular characters, and misunderstands them or needs to clarify something for them. The child then either corrects the puppet or vocalizes for the puppet. For example, to see if the child knows when it is permissible to contract *want* and *to* (when there is no intervening trace), the puppet is contrived either to want to eat something or to want another puppet to take a walk. The child is told to have Kermit find out what the puppet wants, eliciting "What do you wanna eat" or "Who do you want [t] to take a walk?" Because children enjoy the pretense and the necessary production has pragmatic validity, Crain has been successful in getting cooperation from the children and demonstrating their syntactic competence.

Comprehension Measures

Use of comprehension as an index of linguistic knowledge is also not straightforward. Techniques for comprehension include measuring children's errors or reaction times in responding to requests to explain or paraphrase utterances, answer questions, select the picture that represents a given utterance, or make a doll act out the utterance. The first two of these implicate language production; a child's failure to answer can be interpreted as an inability to understand the question (comprehension) or to construct the answer (production). For the other methods, comprehension of the task (and the pictures) is necessary in addition to comprehension of the sentence.

Other Measures

Two other indices have been used to assess children's language knowledge: imitation and grammaticality judgments. In *imitation,* the child is instructed to repeat what the experimenter says. Young children often fail to repeat exactly, not understanding the original utterance, not remembering it, or not reproducing what they have encoded. This can indicate the child's language competence, however. Imagine yourself trying to imitate a sentence from a foreign language. Initially you might approximate the sound, reproducing duration, intonation, and a couple of phonemes. Once you recognize words, you will be able to repeat those. Once you understand the sentence and the grammar, the sentence is likely to be reproduced in its entirety. The same is true for the child; the quality of the imitation reflects the similarity between the child's internal structures for the language and the structure of the model.

Grammaticality judgments are designed to probe the child's tacit knowledge of the language, as judgment tasks are designed to probe ours. We can judge, for example, that anomalous sentences are "better" than scrambled sentences, or that a double-embedded sentence is "worse" than a singly embedded one. Can a child make similar judgments? Again, getting the child to understand the task can be tricky. And getting the child to recognize that there may be gradations of nonsense may be trickier. And, finally, with this task, as with all the others, one has the problem of dealing with children's simply being children, exemplified by the following frequently quoted dialogue:

> Interviewer: Adam, which is right, "two shoes" or "two shoe"?
> Adam: Pop goes the weasel. (Brown & Bellugi, 1964, p. 135)

How to Equate Children

All approaches to language acquisition assume some change in language as a result of maturation and therefore some commonalities in language acquisition across children. It is necessary to be able to equate children with respect to maturation to look for similarities in acquisition among different children.

As we saw in Chapter 8, we can look at change longitudinally. Here we would follow the same children through their course of development. This avoids equating different children, but to look at development longitudinally from birth to age 5 takes *five* years. It is more efficient to compare different children (newborns, 1-year-olds, 2-year-olds, and so on) in a short study period and infer the probable course of development from such cross-sectional data. Assuming that the course of development is the same, that the newborn will later look like the 1-year-old, implies that the children are the same except for age.

It would be nice to be able to say all children are the same at a given age. The problem with age is that children develop at different rates because of maturational factors and/or because of different environmental exposures. Physically we note this at puberty, which for some begins before 13 years and others at age 17. Are 13-year-olds equivalent because of age, or are pubescent children equivalent because of stage?

To "stage" language development specifically, Brown (1973) established the *mean length of utterance (MLU)*. The length is counted in morpheme number, so /bɔ/ would be one, *ball* also one, /dɚ-bɔ/ (the ball) two, and so on. MLU calculates the average number of morphemes the child utters in one talking turn. As syntax develops, the child produces more morphemes so MLU increases steadily with increasing linguistic proficiency. To use the MLU as a standard, one compares production, comprehension, and so on in children of the same MLU. For example, do children of MLU = 2 understand the passive? Are there fricatives in the speech of children of MLU = 1? Are abstract nouns used before MLU = 5?

Other researchers have used different language achievements as the equating point of children: children who have uttered their first word or children who have started a *vocabulary spurt,* when the rate of word-acquisition jumps markedly, from one or two per week to several per day. L. Bloom (1993) and her coworkers

---

Box 9.2. Methods of Studying Language Acquisition

— Imitation, comprehension, and production each measure different aspects of competence and performance, and each may entail the other to some extent. A common production measure is a diary study, where children's utterances are recorded as a corpus.

— Children may "fail" at a task because they do not understand the task demands, not because they do not have the skill. They may also "fail" because they are not motivated or become distracted; these are performance errors.

— Teasing apart maturational and environmental factors requires follow-ing children developmentally, either longitudinally, where the same children are followed over the developmental period of interest, or cross-sectionally, where different children are selected to represent different stages of development.

— Equating children implies either matching for age or a cognitive skill of interest. A common language measure is MLU, mean length of utterance, that is, the average number of morphemes the child is producing. Other common measures include the first word and the onset of the vocabulary spurt.

---

compared children's affect, play, and language behaviors, equating them with respect to such early language milestones.

LANGUAGE IN THE INFANT: MLU < 1

Toward the end of their first year, children normally utter their first words. Study of language development usually begins then, when it is possible to elicit language imitation and production. During the first year, however, the infant matures, learns about the world, and produces behaviors, and these factors play a role in subsequent language development. The study of language in infancy has been concerned primarily with sound perception and production because semantics and syntax cannot be studied until there are words.

Physical Changes in the First Year

During the first year of an infant's life, there are profound neural and physical changes. At birth, and perhaps before, there is noticeable asymmetry in the size of particular areas of the left and right cerebral hemispheres associated in later life with language; the left side, subserving language in adults, is larger in most infants than the right side (Witelson & Pallie, 1973). The brain increases in weight by more than 350% from birth to age 2, but only by about 35% from age 2 to the adult weight. Most of this growth derives from proliferating neural connections, not the number of neurons, which is fixed from birth. Some of the additional connections, the additional "brain power," have been hypothesized to underlie the unfolding of an innate language program (e.g., Lenneberg, 1967).

During the first year there are also marked changes in the infant's skeletal development. The vocal tract changes, developing a supralaryngeal, suboral cavity, making the infant less like an ape and more like an adult human (Lieberman, 1987). The infant's mouth changes also, losing fat in the cheeks. Finally, the vocal folds grow much more in the first year than after (Delack, 1976).

Sound Production

The Data

Children's early vocalizations follow a reliable order. At first they only cry, vocalizing only while exhaling, producing no more than eight distinguishable sounds (you may need to review Table 6.1 to "translate" the phonetic symbols)— /ae/ (most frequent), /ɪ/, /ɛ/, /ʌ/, /u/, /h/, /l/, and /ʔ/. Not all neonates produce all these sounds; the front vowels predominate for most infants and /æ/ may be the only sound for some infants. For consonants, back sounds predominate (Irwin, 1949).

Parents sometimes feel that cries differ depending on their child's needs. However, removing the cries from context, presenting them by tape, leaves parents at chance in interpreting the sound (Dale, 1976). It is likely that normally parents use extralinguistic knowledge, such as how long it has been since the last feeding, to interpret that it is a cry of hunger. It may be that this attribution of intent and the parents' monologue to the child ("Oh, are you hungry? I thought so . . .") sows the seeds of communication (*protocommunication*), that sounds transmit feelings and intents.

At the end of the first month, the second "stage" of vocalization occurs. In addition to crying, the infant makes sounds for pleasure, described as *cooing*. These consist mostly of back rounded vowels (/u/) combined with glottal stops.

At about 6 months there begins another change in infant speech production, *babbling*. Babbling likely begins as sound play, for the tactile and auditory enjoyment of vocalization. It includes sounds not heard in the adult language. My son Eric, for example, said /da/ at 4 months, /ga/, /na/, and squeaks at 5 months, adding a bilabial fricative (not in our repertoire!) at 6 months. There followed three months of bilabial sounds—lip-smacking (ingressives), fricatives, /b-m-w/ combined with lax vowels.

Traditionally, this play stage is seen as maturing into a more controlled production of many consonants and vowels, all called babbling. Recently Oller and Eilers (1988) distinguished between the play and controlled babble stages, labeling the first *expansion* and the second, *canonical*. Canonical babbling in many hearing children emerges at 7-10 months and involves deliberate control. Oller and Eilers identified the canonical stage by production of at least one resonant nonnasalized vowel nucleus with one consonant other than a glottal stop, the combination produced with normal syllable duration, breathiness, and intonation. Babbling often involves reduplicated sounds, the *mama* and *papa* of nursery words.

Traditionally, babbling, as a single stage, is described as a coherent change in frequency of the babbled sounds over the second 6 months, with the infant dropping those sounds that are not in the language of the adults and increasing those that are, according to identifiable linguistic principles. First, consonant-vowel production is distinguished, with consonant marked by a front sound /p/, and vowel by a back sound /a/. The next distinction children control is nasal-oral, adding /m/ to the repertoire. Next they acquire labial-dental, adding /t/, along with the low-high distinction in vowels, adding /i/. Subsequently they acquire the back sounds, /u/, /g/, and /k/, and other manner of distinctions such as frication. There are sounds that seem particularly difficult and over which the child may not gain control until after school age: /r/, /l/, and /w/ tend to be confused with one another, and fricatives and affricates, particularly the interdentals, /ð/ and /θ/, tend to be produced as other fricatives or as stops of the same place of articulation (e.g., the dental stop /d/) (Ingram, 1978). Beginning with canonical babbling, sound production appears to reflect a child's active phonological scheme. So a sound may be produced perfectly for a while and then be distorted to the adult ear as the child adds phonological "rules": *Pretty* as /pɚɪti/ simply imitated changes to /piti/ (reducing the consonant cluster), then /bidi/ (voicing the unvoiced consonant), and finally back to /pɚɪti/, for example (data cited in Macken & Ferguson, 1981).

The pattern of difficulty and general order of acquisition of sounds has been hypothesized to be universal (Jakobson, 1968); indeed, most languages have as words naming mother and father sounds that the child produces early, such as our *mama* and *papa*—front nasal or stop consonant combined with back vowel. These universal first syllables adults the world over take as names, incorporating the baby utterance into the language. The universality could indicate the unfolding of an innate speech program or a biological constraint on ease of production. It may be that it is easier to produce full than partial closure (because there is more tactile feedback), for example.

It is important to note that the "traditional" description overlooks considerable individual variation. Neither of my children developed from sound play, the expansion period, into canonical babbling; they abruptly moved from sound play to words. Eric had played with the voiced stops and /a/ at 3 months; his first word was *cat* [gæt'] at 5 months. Alexander vocalized a-da-da-da syllable strings in play at 9 months, followed in three months with his first word, "Eric," pronounced [aʔaʔ]. Neither showed much phonological development but applied their (limited) vocal play directly to words. Both developed normal lexicons and syntax. Dale (1976) notes that a common pattern is babble, silence, and then word acquisition. Sound acquisition patterns may show individual differences because of different language exposure or different innate interests. Individual differences mean there is no universal, purely genetic control.

Infants develop suprasegmental skills along with segmental ones. Throughout babbling the infant uses many intonation contours, the most common being the rise-fall pattern (declination). This is true across languages, and as the infant moves from babbling into real speech, the pattern becomes more frequent relative to other patterns (Delack, 1976). During babbling, infants will often mimic the intonation patterns used by adults talking to them, superimposing the pattern on their own play syllables. Intonation or stress may also be the first "feature" to be used semantically: Dale (1976) cited an instance of a child calling his mother ma'ma and his father mama', later correcting the consonant. Delack (1976) showed that 6- to 12-month-olds use different contours in the presence of their mothers, strangers, objects that they can see, objects that they can hear, and objects that they can touch. This is semantic use of the sound feature they could articulatorily control.

Analysis of Phonological Development in the First Year

The importance of cooing and babbling to the onset of real speech has been much disputed. Regardless of individual differences in babbling, some see it as necessary practice through which children gain control over their vocal tracts. In learning theory formulations, spontaneous babbling provides the base vocabulary for selective reinforcement by the parents.

Arguing against such learning effects more than 20 years ago, Lenneberg (1967) cited a child who was prevented from babbling because of an operation on the mouth who did not evidence delays or different acquisition patterns in producing speech. More recently, Locke and Pearson (1990) studied a child who had a tube in the trachea for surgical reasons from 5 months to 1 year and 8 months of age. They measured her syllable production from three months before the tube was removed to two months after, using the criteria of Oller and Eilers to code canonical syllables. The child produced $\frac{1}{10}$th the syllables of a normal child of her age following removal of the tube, producing fewer canonical syllables than the average 6-month-old child. She also had a slow acquisition of words, although her speech comprehension was normal. By the time she was 4 years of age, both her receptive and productive language appeared to be normal. Thus babbling may help practice articulation and develop the notion that one's own sounds can serve to communicate, but its omission can be compensated for.

As I discussed, traditionally babbling has been considered an innate speech reflex and is observed, with some individual differences, in children of all cultures. It was also traditionally reported that deaf infants who receive no auditory feedback from their productions and no auditory input from their parents go through the crying, cooing, and babbling stages as do normal children, but with vocalizations petering out, not increasing in frequency of occurrence (Fry, 1966). If true, this would be a strong argument for babbling's being an innate reflex.

With their strong criterion for what counts as canonical babbling, Oller and Eilers effectively refute the notion that deaf or hearing-impaired (individuals with some hearing, helped perhaps by hearing aids) infants go through the same sound production stages as normal-hearing infants. Both groups make similar vegetative sounds at similar ages (crying, cooing, and expansion speech play), but only the normal-hearing children canonically babble before their first birthday. The deaf infants studied produced proportionally fewer syllables that met the criteria than did the hearing infants, and those deaf infants who exhibited some canonical babbling did not do so until more than five months after the hearing infants. This suggests that while vocalizing may be innate, vocal control for speech needs experience—either of external speech models or of one's own productions, which can then be shaped through auditory feedback.

Another aspect of sound acquisition in the first year that has been considered innate is the order of acquisition of sounds in real speech (Jakobson, 1968). Jakobson hypothesized that sound acquisition proceeded by successive divisions of sound along distinctive feature lines (see Chapter 6) such that features providing most information are acquired first. Sound acquisition order was presented here following a Jakobsonian framework: Note that the hypothetical (not Eric's) first syllable is *pa* or *ma,* representing both consonant-vowel and front-back differences. Successive acquisitions split the consonant class into manner and place classes and added the other point vowels (/i/ and /u/). Jakobson argued further that the earliest sounds hold a special position in that they are universally found in adult languages, whereas the later sounds may be found only in some.

Generally, studies examining order of acquisition cross-culturally have not supported the description. In part, the order is too rigid; place differentiates in many children before manner so one sees /p/-/d/ rather than /p/-/m/. More important, acquisition of a phonetic feature is context sensitive, so acquisition is not of features but, perhaps, of phonemes or syllables. Thus, if the child has split the consonants into nasal-oral for the bilabials, one would expect to find both /d/ and /n/ entering together, once the bilabial-alveolar distinction enters. Usually only one comes in, and then the child seems to learn the other sound anew without evidence of generalizing the manner change (Ingram, 1978). However, Jakobson's framework does approximate acquisition order, and it has stimulated research, and thus is important, whether ultimately right or wrong.

Sound Perception in the Infant

Measurement of Perception

Although children do not produce speech sounds until the middle to the end of the first year, from very early on infants are responsive to the sounds of their language. Responsiveness is measured by observing a change in the child's activity correlated with the introduction of sounds. The activity change may be gross as in overall body movements such as kicking and pounding the air versus relative quiescence as the child drifts off to sleep. The change may be "fine" as in change in heart rate. A sound new to the infant, which captures its attention, produces an *orienting response,* that is, initial decreased activity and heart rate deceleration followed by increased activity and heart rate acceleration as the infant explores or studies the new stimulus. When she or he loses interest, when it has become familiar, heart rate and activity level generally return to baseline, and if the stimulus continues, the activity level may continue to fall off as the infant becomes bored. This decrease in activity level with increasing familiarity with the stimulus is known as *habituation.* (Note that this pattern persists in adults: We momentarily "freeze" for something surprising and interesting, study it with increasing excitement and activity level, until we get bored, when we may fall asleep if we continue trying to attend to it.)

Using the relative changes in activity level, we may determine whether an infant can discriminate between sounds. First, a sound is presented. If the infant can tell that this is a new sound, there will be an orienting response and increased activity until the infant habituates to it. If the infant cannot discriminate the new sound from the old, habituation should continue after the stimulus change.

Perhaps the most popular method for studying infant speech perception making use of this activity pattern is the *high amplitude sucking (HAS)* paradigm (Eimas, Siqueland, Jusczyk, & Vigorito, 1971/1991). The activity level measured is the amount the infant sucks on an electronically wired pacifier. Each suck causes a sound to be played so that the infants in effect control how much they hear. As they "study" the sound, their sucking rate is great, causing many instances of the sound to be presented; as they habituate, the presentation rate tapers off. (Infants, of course, suck reflexively so there is no difficulty getting the procedure started.) If the sound is heard as different, there is dishabituation, an increase again in sucking back to original levels. Thus HAS tests sound discrimination.

Results: Paralanguage, Body Language, and Suprasegmentals

Studies using such techniques have revealed a prodigious receptive capacity in the infant, both innate and acquired very early. By 3 days, infants respond differentially to their mothers' voices (DeCasper & Fifer, 1980) compared with other women's. One-day-old infants synchronize their body movements (heard turns, kicks, and so on) with phoneme onsets in fluent adult speech but do not exhibit synchrony to isolated words or tapping sounds. Moreover, American infants synchronize as well to Chinese speech as to American English speech (Condon & Sander, 1974). Infants only a few days old discriminate and imitate adult facial expressions (Field, Woodson, Greenberg, & Cohen, 1982) and manual gestures (Meltzoff & Moore, 1977).

By 4 days of age, infants respond preferentially to the sound of their parents' language (Mehler et al., 1988/1991). In this study, French infants sucked more intensely to French than Russian phrases and released from habituation when the language changed. They did not differentiate English and Italian. Four-day-old infants raised in France by parents who did not speak French did not discriminate French from Russian. Filtering the speech leaving only the fundamental frequency did not change this overall pattern of results.

One-month-old infants discriminate rising from falling intonation in single syllables (Morse, 1972) and syllable-initial from syllable-final stress in disyllables (ba'ba versus baba') (Spring & Dale, 1977). At 6 months infants look longer at films in which the soundtrack and lip movements are synchronized than at those in which they are not (Kuhl & Meltzoff, 1982), particularly when they must look right, presumably engaging the language hemisphere (MacKain, Studdert-Kennedy,

Spieker, & Stern, 1983). And Kuhl and Meltzoff noted that their infants babbled and looked preferentially only to synchronized full speech, not to speech filtered leaving only fundamental frequency contours. Initially infants seem to respond to language by the intonation contour, but by 6 months they attend to spectral properties as speech.

Thus, by 6 months, infants recognize their native language, important speakers, suprasegmental characteristics, and the correspondence between lip movements and speech. They imitate communicative facial and hand gestures. While some of these abilities may be innate, unfolding as the baby matures, it is also clear that within the first week of life, infants learn much about their personal language: what their mother sounds like in particular and what their language sounds like in general. These instances of "early emergence" may occur through the focus of an innate language-learning guide, but, clearly, *individual* experience cannot be preset in *universal* grammar.

Results: Perceiving Phonetic Distinctions

Are very young infants similarly able to discriminate segmental information, and do they do this like adults? Recall the issue of acquired distinctiveness versus acquired similarity, raised in Chapter 7. We saw that adults perceived the consonant sounds of their own language categorically, with sharply differentiated identification functions and excellent between-category but poor within-category discrimination functions. Presented with sounds phonemic in other languages, the same adults discriminated only slightly better than chance. Did the excellent between-category discriminations arise from practice in the language (acquired distinctiveness), or are all potential phonemes distinctive initially, with our ability to hear differences atrophying without experience (acquired similarity)?

Eimas et al. (1971/1991) launched several decades of exploration of this question for a number of consonant and vowel distinctions. Generally, like adults whose language uses a given sound, within the first 6 months, infants discriminate most consonant, vowel, and suprasegmental distinctions (see Jusczyk, 1981, for review). This supports an acquired similarity model.

Eimas et al. (1971/1991) tested 1- and 4-month-old American infants' discriminations of the voiced-voiceless distinction in stop consonants. The results, averaged for the 4-month-olds, from the HAS procedure are shown in Figure 9.1. Observe that infants who were habituated to a VOT of 20 msec, a /b/ in the adult language, and then were shifted to a VOT of 40 msec, an adult /p/, markedly increased their sucking; that is, the habituation stopped. If the sound shifted between VOTs of 60 and 80 msec, the same change of VOT but within category, the sucking decrement due to habituation continued. And the same infants were able to discriminate the within-category VOT values if the steady states were removed, as adults are.

These results indicate that (a) infants make the same speech-nonspeech distinctions adults do, and (b) the voiced-voiceless boundary is either innate or learned at an extremely young age. Of course, if the boundary is innate, it may be because the

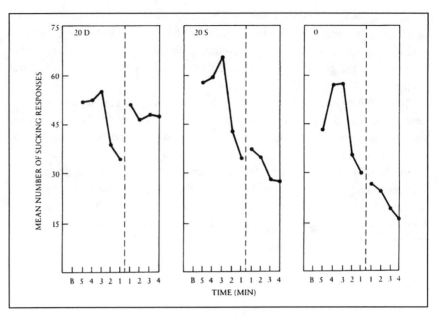

Figure 9.1. The Average Sucking Responses for Stimuli From Different Adult Categories (20 D), the Same Adult Categories (20S), and the Same Stimulus (0)

SOURCE: P. D. Eimas, E. R. Siqueland, P. Jusczyk, and J. Vigorito, 1971, "Speech Perception in Infants," *Science, 171*, pp. 303-306. Copyright ©1971 by the AAAS. Reprinted by permission.

NOTE: The dotted line shows the point at which the stimulus was changed.

Figure 9.2. A Humorous Look at Adapting a /b-d/ Threshold Change in an Infant (Courtesy of the artist, Andrew Rothman.)

linguistic distinction is innate or because auditory discriminability is greatest in this acoustic region and languages have exploited this auditory constraint.

Note that in this study American infants were tested on a distinction phonemic in the language of their parents. Would they perform similarly to adults with sounds with which they had absolutely no experience? One such distinction in English is the prevoiced-voiced distinction. This difference is phonemic in many languages, as you may recall from Chapters 6 and 7, but English speakers categorize prevoiced sounds as voiced. Eimas (1975) found that American infants could discriminate this distinction but only at very large prevoicing values, larger than adults need in languages where the distinction is relevant. Streeter (1976) found that Kenyan infants raised with the Kikuyu language, in which the prevoiced-voiced distinction is phonemic but the voiced-voiceless distinction is not, categorically discriminated both prevoicing from voicing and voicing from voicelessness. Kikuyu adults likewise discriminated the voiced and voiceless categories, although these are not linguistically relevant.

Putting the results together, we conclude the following:

1. Some distinctions are innate, accounting for universal performance with the voiced-voiceless distinction.

2. Some distinctions require no experience to maintain, accounting for the Kikuyu adults' performance.

3. Some distinctions must be acquired, such as prevoicing, accounting for the difference between Kikuyu infants and American infants.

4. Acquisition of such distinctions occurs very early.

This is consistent with a critical period notion in which we have an innate blueprint for speech generally and for some features specifically, but input finely tunes the blueprint to the precise features of the environment, here, the adult language model. I am not necessarily implying that speech itself is innate but that its acoustic underpinnings may be. As languages evolve, they could select distinctive acoustic points for their sounds in the same way that languages may select the sounds *mama* to represent the mother because they are the sounds first produced by most infants.

Innate discriminability appears to be lost for some distinctions in the first year if it is not "practiced," if the blueprint is not stimulated. Werker and Tees (1984/1991) tested 6-month-old infants of an American Indian language, Salish, along with adult speakers of that language and infant and adult speakers of English on a place of articulation dimension found in the Indian language. The infants performed like the adult Salish speakers, with the adult English speakers at chance on the distinction. By 8 to 12 months of age, infants of English speakers did not display the ability (cross-sectional data). Infants who had shown the ability at 6 months lost it at about the same age (longitudinal data). This is strong support for acquired similarity of at least some phonetic categorizations as well as a loss of discriminability very early.

More recently Kuhl, Williams, Lacerda, Stevens, and Lindblom (1992) have shown language-specific changes in the first 6 months of life. Swedish and American infants tested with the same synthetic vowels associated them to different "ideal" stimuli, where the ideal was the best example in the adult language of a phoneme. *The results suggest that around the onset of babbling, infants begin to categorize speech sounds with respect to the phonemic system of the parent language.*

Kuhl (1993) argues that there are innate auditory sensitivities that languages have exploited for some phoneme boundaries, and these account for the 1- to 4-month-old infant's and the chinchilla's categorical perception (Chapter 7). Hearing the adult language over the first 6 months of life provides the infant with phoneme categories, "irrelevant" variations organized around a prototype. By 6 months of life, humans have learned to hear the variants as more similar to the prototype (in their own language) than to variants acoustically as similar. And they do not show this similarity effect for other languages. Nor do animals show the effect at all. This suggests a process in humans only to create and sharpen phoneme categories.

Other studies demonstrate critical developments between infant and adult perception during *early* infancy. Bertoncini, Bijeljac-Babic, Jusczyk, Kennedy, and Mehler (1988), for example, modified the HAS technique so they were not simply testing infants' abilities to tune into a difference between the stimuli before and after habituation. The modification presented a randomization of several stimuli representing a particular dimension, say, consonant, before habituation, such as /bi, ba, bu/. Once the infant habituated, a syllable was added to this set, differing from the members of the set in consonant (/da/), vowel (/bɛ/), both (/dɛ/), or neither (/ba/). Each condition represented a change from the habituated condition, and thus *all* conditions should show dishabituation if the infant is only discriminating change. The question of interest is whether there was a different degree of dishabituation, suggesting that, for example, the infant might recognize that the syllables all began with /b/ and thus that a d-initial syllable was more interesting.

Newborns showed greater response to a new vowel and new syllable (both consonant and vowel change) than to the consonant-only change or the repetition of an item in the set. Two-month-olds showed greater response for *all* stimulus additions, the consonant-only change as well. (One can argue that *as a class,* consonants acquire distinctiveness; *within the class,* most distinctions acquire similarity, pulled toward the prototype, if they are not heard in the adult language.) The results as a whole suggest that newborns are attentive to vowel/syllable properties (which have more energy than the consonant) and begin early to attend to the consonant class, but that segmentation of syllables into smaller units is not available at birth (Jusczyk, 1997). Whether it is the 2 months' language experience that "teaches" the change, or an unfolding of an innate capacity, cannot be answered at this point. The first year develops knowledge of sounds as a *system,* the beginning of phonology over sound play.

The first year also sees important developments in the infant's ability to segment the speech stream into units appropriate to deriving words, clauses, and phrases. Saffran, Aslin, and Newport (1996) tested 8-month-old infants' recognition of "word boundaries." In these experiments the infants always heard sequences of nonsense syllables. A "word" constituted a sequence with high transitional probability between syllables (/da/ always followed /bi/); syllables spanning a word boundary were not as predictable. Note that real words reflect this statistical constraint: The probability of /ti/ is higher following /pɚ/ than /be/ is following /ti/ in *pretty baby*. With 2 minutes' exposure to the "words," the infants oriented more to nonwords. Thus they noted and employed the statistical regularity; they might use differential probabilities normally to analyze the speech stream into language units.

Segmentation into higher level units develops after 6 months of life as well. Jusczyk, Hirsch-Pasek, and colleagues (Hirsch-Pasek et al., 1987; Jusczyk, 1997; Jusczyk et al., 1992) have found that at 9, but not 6, months, infants orient more toward both low-pass filtered and normal speech with elongated pauses placed at major constituent boundaries than they do to speech with the pauses placed within clauses. Adults too judged filtered speech (in which words are unrecognizable) with elongated pauses at constituent boundaries to be more natural than speech with pauses interclausally. The authors suggest that by 9 months, the infants have learned to associate a pitch decline with silence—the cue combination signifying a clause break. Of interest, speech to children is characterized in part by elongation at the boundaries, perhaps facilitating the child's learning of the segmentation necessary for the language.

Summary

By the time children utter their first words, they have considerable knowledge about language and communication. At least in play, speech sounds of many languages are produced, and many speech distinctions are innately perceived (categorically), despite their absence from the adult language. Within their first days, infants learn about *their* language, distinguishing it from a foreign language. Within the first month, infants learn to hear consonants in syllables; by 6 months, they begin to form phoneme categories; by 8 months, they begin to lose discriminations of sounds absent from their language experience. That is, during the first three-quarters of a year the infant's abilities to unitize speech for language develop, moving from segmentation by intonation and stress to recognition of the confluence of frequently experienced segmental and suprasegmental information that characterizes words, clauses, and eventually phrases (Jusczyk, 1997). The infant also develops communication skills, imitating facial expressions, manual gestures, and sounds; synchronizing movements with conversation rhythm; and recognizing the correspondence between facial movements and sounds. Finally, there is some evidence that the 6-month-old infant recognizes that sounds (at least, different intonation contours) may be used to differentiate situations, a beginning semantic awareness. With this base the child sharpens articulatory control, beginning to master word meanings. Segmentation abilities maturing from prosodic cues allow the acquisition of syntax. Reciprocity is likely (Jusczyk, 1997): Segmentation is

---

Box 9.3. Infants' Speech Abilities During the First Year

Production
— At birth, infants can cry.
— At 1 month, infants begin to coo (back vowels and glottal stop) for pleasure.
— At about 6 months, infants are in the expansion stage of babbling, playing vocally for tactile and auditory pleasure, producing sounds of different languages.
— For hearing infants, this develops into "canonical babbling," steadily increasing articulatory control in a definable sequence: front stops or nasals, split of nasal and stop, acquisition of back places of articulation, and fricative and semivowel classes (sometimes not until 7-8 years of age). Vegetative sounds—crying, cooing, and some expansion babbling—may be reflexive, requiring no auditory stimulus to develop. Canonical babbling and phonological control require auditory feedback and perhaps an adult model, and show considerable individual variability.
— Jakobsonian framework has distinctions acquired from maximum distinctiveness to finer distinctions: voiceless-front-stops + voiced-back-vowels → voiced versus voiceless stops or front versus mid stops and front versus back vowels, and so on. This is a reasonable approximation that has motivated research but does not reflect individual differences.

Perception
— Measured by
    — infant's orienting to sound, increasing heart rate, or (for older infants) head-turning, and
    — habituation to the same sound or dishabituation (increased response) to a new sound as in the high-amplitude sucking procedure.
— Within the first days of birth, infants
    — recognize their mothers' voices,
    — discriminate their own language's tone from foreign languages',
    — synchronize body movements to syllable rhythm,
    — discriminate speech sounds, and
    — categorize syllables with the same vowel as the same.
— By the end of the second month, infants
    — respond categorically to most speech sounds, although some need experience to fix the phoneme boundary as do adults;
    — imitate facial expressions; and
    — classify syllables with the same vowel or initial consonant as the same.
— By the first six months, infants
    — prefer and babble to voices synchronized with pictures, especially if presented on the left, and
    — have begun to organize phoneme categories in their language.
— By 9-10 months, infants
    — begin to lose the ability to categorically perceive sounds that are not in their language and have formed phoneme categories for their language, with variants organized around a prototype;
    — use statistical regularity to unitize the speech stream; and
    — recognize the synchrony of pause and pitch decline at clause boundaries.

aided by emerging syntactic and semantic skills, which in turn are enabled by developing a phonological system.

LANGUAGE IN THE CHILD: MLU = 1

Between 10 and 12 months of age on average (there is great individual difference here too), children utter their first words, and then slowly and steadily increase their vocabulary, attaining between 50 and 200 words at 1½ years, and 500-600 words at about the age of 2 (Clark, 1993). The sharp increase between several new words a week and several new words per day is known as the vocabulary spurt, or *naming explosion* (Gleitman & Landau, 1994). It has been interpreted as the child's understanding (a) the scheme of naming and actively seeking to acquire words, (b) that words name concepts that are not identical with things immediately perceived, and (c) that words are systematically related (L. Bloom, 1993). As sound play develops into rudimentary phonology the first year, the vocabulary spurt signifies the development of semantics: the system among words and between words and meanings in the language.

The one-word "stage" is bounded on one side by consistent application of a sound to a situation, separating it from babble. It represents the development of a semantic *system,* as the child realizes that words are related, but not identical, to perceptual events, and that they are related to one another. It is then bounded on the other side by the child's expressing the word relations, combining words. As with development of productive phonology, there are large individual differences in word acquisition patterns: Some children spend months uttering individual words before combining them; others only weeks; and still others almost skip single-word utterances, talking later but with more fully expressed sentences (Clark, 1993).

Bates, Bretherton, and Snyder (1988/1991) examined different motor and cognitive skills along with changes in language production and comprehension longitudinally across many children. They found that naming and word combining follow gesturing for reference and gesture combination, suggesting a single underlying cognitive component. Results also indicated that production and comprehension develop separately up to about 20 months of age.

And they found (as Nelson, 1973, had described earlier) two different language-learning styles. "Expressive" children rely primarily on a social process that lets them imitate holistic, unanalyzed utterances and maintain the flow of speech, presumably for social purposes. Their first words are drawn from many grammatical categories and may include whole phrases (as discussed vis-à-vis the Skinnerian approach to language acquisition). They tend to develop language more slowly. The other process is a referential, analytic, and symbolic one. "Referential" children concentrate initially on count nouns, adding adjectives later, and, overall, develop language faster.

Referential and expressive styles are visible in the acquisition of the first words and also in the later acquisition of function words. *Both* expressive and analytic "strategies" develop all aspects of language. That different strategies allow language development belies the fundamental, strong assumption of UG. The last significant finding of this study is that semantic and syntactic skills are not differentiable; they come in parallel for all children (differently depending on the child's style). We will return to this later.

Phonological Processes

Although words at this point have both regular pronunciation and regular meanings for the child, neither may be the same as the adult uses. With respect to pronunciation, as we have already noted, some feature values do not come into regular use until very late, so naturally they will not be represented in the first words. The child may differ from the adult model in the following general ways (Bloom & Lehey, 1978):

> phoneme deletion: [ɚ:t] for *hurt*]
> syllable deletion: [æᶤnd] for *behind*
> coalescence across syllables: [pæf] for *pacifier*
> assimilation: [gɪk] for *kiss*
>> (The initial and final consonants share both place and manner of articulation in the child's production, unlike in the target.)
> reduplication of a syllable: [tɪtɪ] for "kitty"

This description of the children's productions assumes that they are operating according to phonological rules, but ones different from the adults'. The child's modifications here are mostly simplifications—a deletion of a syllable or a phonetic feature—but this does not have to be. My son Alexander reduplicated *cat* at 14 months, for example, as [kæʔkæʔ], that is, he complicated the production with an extra syllable.

We should also note that none of these variations is peculiar to child language; as Vygotsky noted, child principles pertain through adulthood. Indeed, as we have seen, all are dialect variations or common words in English adult speech: We have phoneme deletion in r-dropping in New York and in AAEV; syllable deletion in *bye* for *goodbye* or in AAEV *pass* for *Paris*; coalescence in *bike* for *bicycle;* assimilation, as in the match of the nasal in place of articulation with the stop in a consonant cluster such as *improbable;* and reduplication in *hoity-toity, pell-mell,* or *itsy-bitsy.* The persistence of these phonological "hypotheses" suggests they are not peculiar to a language *acquisition* device operative only in childhood.

Meaning Processes

The first words acquired are mostly nouns (Clark, 1993) that name people (*dada, mama*), animals (*cat*), food (*juice*), clothing (*shoe*), vehicles (*car*), and household items (*cup*). Early non-noun words describe space and motion (*up* or *open*) and routines *(bye-bye).* Early words usually describe objects or attributes that change (move, make noise, and so on) or actions the child can make or objects the child can act on. Note the consistency with Piaget's sensorimotor theory.

Children's meanings do not match those of adults (e.g., Clark, 1993). In the earliest vocabulary, a word may be restricted to a specific situation, such as a child saying *bye* only when someone leaves the room or *car* only to cars seen from the window. This is an early form of *overrestriction* or *underextension,* where a word applies to a narrower class of objects than in adult use. Children also commonly do the opposite, producing *overextensions,* generalizing a name inappropriately to other objects with some similar perceptual attributes. For example, *daddy* may be used for all men; *doggie,* for all mammals; *ball,* for all round objects. Children develop the lexical meanings of adults through the guidance of some perhaps innate categorizing principles, followed by application of heuristics for restricting those principles.

One important principle is the *taxonomic assumption* (Clark, 1993; Markman, 1994a, 1994b; Markman & Hutchinson, 1984). Recall from Chapter 2 that it is difficult to determine which aspect of a situation a word describes: the object "dog," the color of the dog, the sound the dog is making, and so on. The taxonomic assumption leads language learners to assume that the word applies to the object and, moreover, names not the individual but a *category* of like objects of which the individual is only one representative. While young children frequently group together co-occurring things, like a dog and a bone, Markman has shown that if they are given a label (*dax*) and told to find another dax, they will override their tendency to group by co-occurrence and will choose a category member, another animal. This reflects the assumption that words name categories, which is the taxonomic assumption.

Children's initial category-naming assumptions include that a category will be coherent, that a word names a *whole* object (more likely the person than a body part), and that a word names a class of objects, not an individual (all socks, not just the red one). These principles guide the initial assignments of meaning that we see in the use of the first words and that persist throughout our lives in guessing meanings. Obviously, though, each assumption must be violated for some meanings—such as finger as a part of the hand or "Alexander" as an individual, not a class.

Children's first words usually name basic objects. As you may recall from Chapter 3, the basic level of a category is the level that optimizes shared perceptual features and information content. It was operationally defined, in part, as those category levels that a child first names, so it should not be surprising to find the basic level labeled by the earliest words.

These categorization principles may be general cognitive principles onto which language maps. There are also some language-specific principles proposed by Clark (1993), which concern how words work with respect to one another, and allow for the exceptions to be formed to the aforementioned heuristics for assigning meaning. These too emerge in initial word acquisition and persist through lexical development.

They are conventionality and contrast. *Conventionality* is the child's understanding that for a particular concept, speakers of the community use a preferred, conventional, form—the word name. *Contrast* (related to *mutual exclusivity* [Markman & Wachtel, 1988] and *uniqueness* [Pinker & Prince, 1988]) is the assumption that if two different forms are used, each refers to a different concept. Suppose, for example, that a child has learned the word *Daddy* but applies it to all men, that is, the taxonomic assumption that the word names a type. The child will hear the form *man* from adults in situations where she or he would be planning to apply *Daddy*. The conventionality assumption leads the child to attend to the form the adult uses; the contrast assumption leads to the realization that *Daddy* and *man* *must* refer to different things because they are different forms. Together they will direct the child to the conditions appropriate for the use of each (without the adult providing "negative feedback").

What's in the Word?

Our discussion of the development of the lexicon at MLU = 1 has centered on the child's expressing word names as a reflection of a cognitive category, as though the child's expression reflected only the speech act of naming. Perhaps it means more, even entailing a syntactic competence, immeasurable because of the child's limited production abilities. We can infer greater meaning by augmenting the language produced with contextual information, *rich interpretation* (see, for example, L. Bloom, 1970, 1991). Consider the following arguments critically! Is there evidence that the children are syntactically wiser than they can express, or do we only surmise the syntax because we know they will have it sometime?

Holophrasis

A common description of the one-word stage attributes an entire sentence structure to the word. By *mama* the child could mean "I want mama" or "There is mama" or "It was mama who dropped the bottle," depending on the nonverbal context. Similarly *sock* could reflect a request, a statement of existence, or statement of action ("It was the sock that dropped to the floor"). Expressing a *whole sentence* or *phrase* in a single word is *holophrasis.*

The arguments in favor of holophrasis begin with the fact that during the one-word stage, children seem to understand more than they produce (although so do pets), so perhaps there is a linguistic competence underlying both comprehension and production, which is limited in production by performance deficiencies. Moreover, children's single-word utterances seem marked with different intonations that adults can classify with about 80% accuracy as declarative, interrogative, or imperative (Dore, 1975). Therefore, there seems to be some "syntax" expressed in the single word. The final argument for holophrasis comes from an assumption of innate language combined with rich interpretation of the nonverbal context in which the utterances occur. Children seem to be commenting on the world—using a single word to name an object when it falls, disappears, reappears, or in some other way captures their attention. It seems possible that these comments are in fact predicates.

Alternative Interpretations

A single word's representing the syntax for an underlying sentence is a large inference. Instead, the single word could represent a smaller language unit, a speech act (Dore, 1975), consisting of a force (declarative, interrogative, imperative) plus a rudimentary referring expression. The expression later turns into a proposition with the development of syntax. Others have suggested that the single word represents a predicate alone or a single case relation, such as location. Categorizing the one-word utterances in this way leads to the following acquisition order for cases: object, with self as recipient, as in *bottle* [give me]; possessive as when the child says *Daddy* when looking at Daddy's slipper; patient, as in *shoe* when the shoe falls; and agent as in *Mommy* when the child wishes her to do something.

I find it unreasonable to attribute much underlying competence to the child's single-word utterances (which does not mean that *I* did not overinterpret *my* children's). They may indeed mask a complex syntax or intention, but the data alone, in the absence of knowledge of context or the child's next steps in language development, do not warrant it. Such rich interpretation gives pets "language" and liberally interprets ape language projects as successful, a dubious conclusion as I discuss in *Language in Atypical Populations*.

One-Word "Stage"

Implicit in the last section is the assumption that single-word utterances constitute a "stage" of development. As you may recall, the Piagetian concept of stage refers to a point in development marked by a new cognitive organization. Given this definition it is reasonable to consider the single words a stage (although not one corresponding directly to any of Piaget's stages in particular); they differ from previous utterances in intentionality or planning (L. Bloom, 1993) and seem to reflect for the first time that the child understands something about naming. Assuming that you agree that they reflect little or no syntax—that they are not holophrases—they differ from the next language developments in that they show no syntax or concept of word combination. Thus there does appear to be a critical leap from the notion of words as names to words as units to be combined. Therefore, the one-word period may be considered a stage.

If your concept of stage requires discontinuity, you may not separate the one-word period as a stage. There are points in time when a child may be uttering predominantly single words with one or two two-word utterances and, later, points when the child is producing mostly two-word utterances with some one-word utterances still appearing (Bloom & Lehey, 1978). This suggests that there is no sudden grasp of syntax that would mark an abrupt development. Piaget's concept of stage allows gradual change, a continuity in development from one stage to the next. Thus I am comfortable considering the change from no words to one word and from one word to two words as stages in the development of linguistic thought processes.

About the World
To Craig, One Year
by Pamela Laskin

You talk
enamored of your sounds --
gibberish, with an occasional word
that's comprehensible.

I catch you in these soft
and quiet unnoticed moments,
holding your stuffed dog
up in the air,
telling him all there is to know
about the world.

Figure 9.3. Beginning Language, From a Poet-Mother's View (Courtesy of the poet, Pamela Laskin.)

Summary

Near the end of the first year, children utter their first words. For a period, each word is said alone and then, gradually, words are used in combination. The words usually represent concrete objects, actions, or attributes that the child not only perceives frequently but may actively manipulate, the child's world (see Figure 9.3). It is not clear whether to consider the single words as words or as reduced representations of a larger unit, like a proposition, reduced perhaps because of limited memory. It is also unclear if the one-word period constitutes a stage or a point in the continuum of language acquisition.

LANGUAGE IN THE CHILD: MLU > 1

Once the child puts morphemes together, we may look at language development as acquisition of morphology and syntax, in addition to semantics. Semantic development itself becomes increasingly dependent on the understanding of language as a system; for example, understanding causal words depends on understanding both causal events and how to express them in complex language; understanding of figurative language depends on seeing the relation of sentence topic and vehicle. In this section we look at children's concatenations as indicators of what they understand about units and their combination rules, and as indicators of under-standing of new semantic *relations* expressible only through concatenation. We will return to how the lexicon develops in the linguistically more sophisticated child, after we see how that sophistication is acquired.

MLU = 2

Table 9.1 shows sample utterances produced by children of MLU = 2. Note first that the two-word "stage" differs from the one-word primarily in the fact that words are strung together, not in what is described. Bloom (1991), in fact, points out that in the period before "syntax" is clear, children will express the same concepts in single-word utterances, ignoring word order: "Mommy. Juice." or "Juice. Mommy." Syntax, the concatenation of the words, is indicated when the child attends specifically to word order, expressing the relation. This skill implies that the child has formed rudimentary grammatical categories and has learned (or knows innately) that these must be combined.

Pivot-Open Formulation

Using a distributional analysis of the child's utterances, Braine (1963), for example, noted that two-word utterances comprise words from a small class used frequently (the *pivot class*) together with words from a large class (the *open class*). Pivot words consisted of fundamental relations like *more, allgone,* or *there;* open words consisted of noun categories like *mama* or *papa.* The child's grammar could be written as $S \rightarrow P + O, S \rightarrow O + P, S \rightarrow O + O$. Thus we see "There mama," "Byebye Papa," and could see "Daddy shoe," but never "There allgone." The child assigns words to the pivot class given the order and function in adult sentences. The pivot class grows slowly because it is hard for the child to attend to order. The order-independent open class grows rapidly, as the child develops object categories.

Generative Grammar Formulation

The pivot-open formulation focuses on the surface structure of the child's utterances, suggesting that they result from a relatively primitive rule, but one that is productive and creative because the child's utterances do not mimic the adults'. We might consider the productive rule to emanate from deep structure, with the pivot and open classes perhaps corresponding to SPEC and I′ (subject and predicate) or head and adjunct. If so, children bring to the language-learning situation an idea of deep structure and procedures for isolating constituents from the input language (Bloom, 1970, 1991; McNeill, 1970).

Children may have the competence of deep structure but performance limitations such as insufficient memory prevent their production of a three-term actor-action-object relation. They delete the most redundant term, often the subject, who in a

Table 9.1 Sample Frequent Two-Word Utterances From Three Children

Child							
Child A							
my mommy	see boy	nightnight office	do it	pretty boat	more taxi	allgone shoe	
my daddy	see sock	nightnight boat	push it	pretty fan	more melon	allgone vitamins	
my milk	see hot		close it			allgone egg	
Child B							
all broke	I see	no bed	more car	other bib	airplane bye	byebye ball	boot off
all clean	I shut	no down	more cookie	other bread	siren bye	byebye car	light off
all done	I sit	no fix	more high	other milk		papa byebye	pants off
all dry		no mama	more sing	other piece			
Child C							
want baby	it ball	get ball	see ball	there ball	that box	bunny do	
want car	it boy	get doll	see doll	there book	that dinner	daddy do	
want do	it checker	get Betty	see Steve	there doggie	that doll	momma do	
want get	it daddy			there doll			
want up	it doll			there momma			

SOURCE: Adapted from Braine (1963).

child of this age is egocentrically and obviously him- or herself. "There mama" could be analyzed as "I see mama" with the "I" unstated because, in the child's view, it is redundant. Dropping the subject yields the two-term action-object surface structure of P + O. Dropping the relation or object produces "O + O" or "O + P."

Using rich interpretation, taking into account the context of an utterance and the listener's interpretation as suggested by the response to the child, Bloom (1970, 1991) categorized child utterances with respect to the semantic relations they conveyed to predict which constituents were likely to appear. For example, a sentence expressing ownership needs to express the owner and the owned ("Mommy sock"); the verb is redundant. A sentence expressing a change in location can focus on any pair of constituents: the agent and the patient ("Mommy sock"), the patient and verb ("Sock drop"), or the agent and the verb ("Mommy drop"). (Which term is dropped differs for different situations and different kinds of verbs.) Note that the ownership and agent-patient examples both resulted in the surface form "Mommy sock," different deep structures realized in the same surface structure.

Semantic Relations Expressed

Bloom's (1970) analysis of the underlying grammar of two-word utterances classified the utterances with respect to the new meaning relations they expressed. Exploiting this approach, Brown (1973) reported the following relations occurring in his extensive diary studies of "Adam," "Eve," and "Sarah":

1. Nomination: naming an object either in response to a question or spontaneously
2. Recurrence: comment on or request for repetition
3. Nonexistent expression of negation: comment on the disappearance of something
4. Agent + action: usually animate object with a verb
5. Agent + object: usually animate agent with the object
6. Action + object: verb + object
7. Action + location: verb with the place the action occurred
8. Entity + location: thing or person and place it occupies
9. Possessor + possession: (very frequent)
10. Entity + attribute: specifies attribute of entity that could not be known from the class concept alone
11. Demonstrative + entity: same as nomination, such as "that dog"

This list of two-term relations leaves some still to develop, such as instrumental relations as in "The key opened the door."

"Telegraphic" Speech

Once children have acquired two-term relations, they combine them into three-term relations and more. The utterances have been called "telegraphic" speech, a descriptive term reflecting the absence of inflections (-ing, -ed, -s), the copula (the verb *to be*), auxiliary verbs, and articles—the morphemes you might choose to drop if you had to pay for each morpheme transmitted. In the child's case, "payment" may arise from the heavy cognitive load of remembering the words and syntactic rules to produce what they have heard, or from the perceptual load of attending to the stressed, content words in the input language to learn those meaning carriers. Indeed, the function morphemes that do appear in "telegraphic speech" are perceptually salient: free, not bound, morphemes (like prepositions and pronouns as opposed to suffixes), or regular and frequent changes (in English, the progressive, -ing form, as opposed to the past tense, which has a number of different variants). The following are examples of three-term early sentences (taken from Bloom, 1991):

No want this.
Car go here.
Put this down.
Gia ride bike.

Once again it is important to note that the child does not simply passively imitate adult speech because the adult would never produce these. We do not know if the child's competence is in fact closer to the adult's than these utterances suggest, that telegraphic nature is a performance limitation. However, children do respond better to grammatical adult sentences than to sentences that mimic the structure children produce themselves (Shipley, Smith, & Gleitman, 1969). We also know that focused training of the child to use the adult expression and not the productive child rule is futile, as you may recall from the "other-one-spoon" dialogue cited in Chapter 4.

Syntactic Descriptions

Bloom and Lehey (1978) concentrated on what appears for the first time at MLU > 2: true verbs as opposed to action words such as *allgone*. At MLU = 2 we have *linear syntax,* a simple concatenation of two words, which in the combination does not express a new meaning (such as temporal relationship). True verbs enable real syntax, the construction of a new, higher order meaning unit through the verb's relating the two noun phrases—a critical feature in the power of language.

Bloom and Lehey (see also Bloom, 1991) also analyzed the order of appearance of verbs and concluded that categories of verbs with different argument structures are acquired at different times. First, there are general verbs of simple action, such as *make, get,* and *do,* which may be used with many different subjects and objects; next, verbs of location such as *put, take, go, sit,* and *fall,* which require a destination and perhaps an object; and, finally, verbs of state that have a specific subject relation such as *want, sleep, see,* and *is.* It is fleshing out the arguments that defines the sentence as a higher order structure, not just a linear addition, and it is the creation of the higher order structure that marks the MLU > 2 period as distinctive.

Change in Semantic Relations: MLU > 3

Bloom and Lehey (1978; Bloom, 1991) also described the most significant development beyond MLU = 3, the child's putting more than one proposition in a sentence, usually between ages 2 and 3. The first connective used across languages is *and* and the first multiple-thought sentences reflect simple conjunction, usually of two things occurring at the same time. This is called *coordinate relation,* as in "I put this on the train and this on the train." Subsequently, the child conjoins, creating a new meaning with the conjunction, as in *superordinance,* statements of causality or statements of priorness or simultaneity. Causality is clearly a new relation; the time relations are new also because the conjunction indicates a temporal relation not indicated by the two clauses independently. A third type of conjunction, which also comes in late but adds no new meaning beyond that provided by the clauses alone, is *subordinance,* where a (relative) clause is added descriptively as in "a toilet where you poopoo . . ." Bloom notes that in learning the actual conjunctions and the process of conjoining, children (a) map new forms onto meanings that they already have and (b) show a predictable pattern of mastery, called by Brown (I will return to this below) the *law of cumulative complexity.* The law states that a complex rule must follow acquisition of each of its components. Here, a causal relation involves both an additive relation and a temporal relation and therefore follows the additive and temporal productions. Likewise, syntactically, the formation of a relative clause requires the child to understand pronominalization ("where" is a pronoun standing for "toilet" in the above example), subordination of the clause, and the combination of the meanings. Each of these is simpler than the accumulation and therefore is predicted to be acquired earlier.

Acquisition of Adult Syntax

Universal Acquisition Pattern or Individual Differences: Models

As children develop, in addition to discovering more about the world that can be expressed in new relations like causality and simultaneity and more about the language so that they know how to express these thoughts, they also develop the adult surface syntax. This takes several forms: attention to word order to indicate the important sentential relations (for English); attention to grammatical markers, that is, the inflectional morphemes (in English to mark tense and aspect, and in some other languages to indicate the sentential relations); and attention to other function words such as *not* and *may,* question words, prepositions, determiners, and so on. Depending on your theoretical orientation, you may consider the order of acquisition of these forms to result from (a) the child's freeing attention to the details of the language once the important meaning relations have been mastered, (b) their late unfolding in UG, or (c) the parents finally attending to these details and shaping them.

Inquiry into the acquisition of inflection began from the linguistic-nativist view. A search, initially successful, was conducted to show that the sequence of acquisition of inflections was universal across many languages and that rules were acquired that could be used productively, not just imitated or memorized instances. For instance, it was hypothesized that the progressive tense/aspect (-ing form in English) unfolded earlier than the past. Or that word order, in particular our subject-verb-object (SVO) order, might be the default innate grammar, which children's first sentences reflected, with later sentences reflecting the resettings of parameters to conform to the parent language's structure. More extensive study of individual developmental patterns and of acquisition patterns for languages other than English suggests instead that children universally apply the same set of strategies, or *operating principles (OPs)* (Slobin, 1985). In particular, children acquire early those inflections of the adult language used *frequently,* with relative *consistency* (few changes in form depending on context), *stress,* and *greater meaning,* perhaps following OPs such as the following:

- Attend to utterances that have a readily identifiable meaning.
- Attend to units bounded by silence.
- Attend to beginning, end and stressed portions of a unit.
- Strengthen a frequently occurring unitization.
- Attend to order.

MacWhinney (1987) has proposed a connectionist- (neural net) like model, the *competition model,* which instantiates these operating principles. Children first acquire a "function," an idea that needs to be expressed, whether a simple concept like "dog" or an abstract construct like "sentence subject" or "plural." They then try to map a form, a cue—phonological string, sentence position, morpheme—to the function. There then ensues a period of competition among forms, in which the possible range of forms is narrowed or widened, based on frequency and validity of occurrence. Validity incorporates the concepts of availability (Is the cue there [and salient] when one needs it?) and reliability (Does it lead to correct production or the right interpretation?). As in the neural net models, input is processed in parallel, with all cues in the stimulus activated. The strength of activation varies depending on experience, increasing each time the cue is successful and decreasing each time it fails. The cue with greatest activation wins the competition and specifies the function. The model incorporates the notions that form follows function (the supremacy of meaning and meaning relations), that parameters are not fixed but emerge as a process, and that the outcome of the process is determined by the frequency and regularity of the cues in the input.

I note that every major study of early language acquisition that has followed more than one child has yielded profound differences in learning styles (see, for example, Bates et al., 1988/1991; Bloom, 1991, 1993; Nelson, 1985, 1991), as we noted in differences in babbling → one-word patterns. The OPs and the competition model provide a general framework more than a specific guide, permitting a range of individual differences, particularly if the child is exposed to a range of speech styles, such as differences in the parents' use of language. We might also consider that children may be "programmed" somewhat differently, naturally attending to different aspects of language and its communicative functions (referential or social, for example) and so may have a genetic difference in language acquisition.

Data: Word Order

As you should recall (see Chapter 4), English is largely a noninflected language that uses word order to mark semantic relations. Inflections mark tense (as in -ed, -ing), number (-s), and person (-s is added to verbs for the third person, present tense). Case is marked overtly on pronouns; there are no inflections for noun gender or case, as in many other languages.

We have already noted that English-speaking children attend to word order early, even in the two-word utterances. Braine (1963) suggested that attention to order distinguished pivot from open words; Bloom (1970) and Brown (1973) suggested that order distinguished functional roles in two-word propositions. At the three-word "stage," English children's utterances all follow the subject-verb-object (SVO) word order. Early researchers found this significant, given that the adult language permits many other orders, for example, in questions (VSO) and passives (OVS).

However, in addressing children, English-speaking parents rarely use anything but simple active sentences (Hoff-Ginsberg & Schatz, 1982), so the SVO order is far more frequently input to children. Moreover, the SVO order is more frequent in adult language than the other orders, although other orders do occur. Even rodents are able to temper their response to relative, not absolute, information: They will select an arm of a t-maze in proportion to the frequency of food being found on that arm. Children should be able similarly to match production frequency to the frequency in the language (see Kelly & Martin, 1994, for a thought-provoking review of the probability matching literature and its relevance to language acquisition). Indeed, we have already seen that infants are sensitive to statistical regularity, not invariance, for word segmentation (Saffran et al., 1996); older children could use it to determine higher level language properties, like syntactic structure.

There is also evidence that children do not necessarily use order to interpret sentences if there is overriding information, a stronger, more competitive "cue." At a point when children produce only SVO orders, they understand "irreversible" passives (such as "The plant was watered by the boy") and misinterpret anomalous actives ("The plant watered the boy") (Slobin, 1966b) and actives in which the object is the conversational topic (Strohner & Nelson, 1974), suggesting that the probable meaning takes precedence over a syntactic strategy, innate or otherwise.

Finally, careful cross-linguistic research suggests that children do attend to word order and do structure their early sentences *using the order most frequent in the parent language* (Slobin & Bever, 1982). Even order-free case-marked languages use certain orders less frequently than others, particularly in *child-directed (CD)* speech, and those orders tend to be acquired later. Moreover, children speaking order-free languages show great individual differences in the word orders they produce, although each child tends to produce only one or two orders. And, as English-speaking children take advantage of semantic and pragmatic (topic-focus) cues, children producing only one or two orders in an order-free language (like Turkish) understand commands using any word order, provided the words are correctly inflected. In such languages the object inflection is acquired early, which makes sense because it marks important *semantic* and syntactic function, disambiguating agent and object in a word-order-free language.

The current view, consistent with both Piaget and Skinner, is that children develop schemes for *typical* sentences of their language, where typicality is determined by frequency and salience (together producing differential habit strengths). What are incorporated first into these schemes are the important semantic relationships, with other characteristics either passively imitated or omitted in the child's own production. In English, most sentences spoken to children are in SVO word order—and that order is learned first. The order is also important semantically, accounting for its early productive use. In other languages where order is not semantically salient or not as frequently drilled, it appears to be either passively imitated or ignored, with more linguistically salient markers attended to.

Data: Acquisition of Affixes

Young Turkish children acquire the case marking for object early: It carries important semantic information not otherwise clear from word order. In English, acquisition of affixes appears later than order, perhaps because affixes carry less meaning. Indeed, as we shall see, order of acquisition of affixes in English is predictable from their meaning.

DeVilliers and deVilliers (1973) performed an extensive longitudinal study of the acquisition of 14 grammatical morphemes, first studied by Brown (1973), in 21 English-speaking children. The grammatical morphemes included the progressive (-ing), the third person singular (-s), the past tense, the plural, possessives, articles, auxiliaries, and the copula. Table 9.2 displays the order in which the three children Brown studied acquired the affixes, comparing the acquisition to the age and MLU of the youngest children in the deVilliers and deVilliers study to use them consistently. Note that there is a relatively consistent order of acquisition of the morphemes across children. The first morpheme to come in is the progressive, -ing, which marks verbs describing ongoing actions, a sensorimotor conversation topic. Later, the other tense markers enter, the irregular before the regular past, presumably because the most common verbs are irregular, as we discussed in Chapter 5 with regard to the PDP simulations. The possessive also comes in early, and possessive meanings were clearly conveyed in two-word utterances and possibly in one-word utterances. The last grammatical morphemes that children produce are copula and auxiliary *to be* forms; these are unstressed in speech, irregular, and their semantic function is highly abstract. The course of acquisition does not run smoothly: There is some time between the first occurrence of a form and its perfect use every time, and the interval is marked by regressions.

Table 9.2 The Acquisition Order for Three Children of 14 English Morphemes (*on* and *in* Were Separated)

Rank Order for Brown (1973)	Least MLU > 90% Use	Age (in months)	Mean Percentage Use
Present progressive	1.3	16	87.5
on/in	1.44	21	97.8
Plural	1.3	16	87.6
Past irregular	2.08	26	70
Possessive	3.03	33	50
Uncontractible copula	4.29	36	51.2
Articles *a/the*	2.99	21	60.2
Past regular	4.23	29.5	60.8
Third person regular	4.23	29.5	44.7
Third person irregular	3.16	28.5	67.4
Uncontractible auxiliary	—	—	0
Contractible copula	3.16	28.5	55.7
Contractible auxiliary	—	—	35

SOURCE: Adapted from deVilliers and deVilliers (1973).

NOTE: On the left is the order obtained by Brown (1973) for three children. Testing the same morphemes, deVilliers and deVilliers looked at acquisition order for 21 children. The middle columns show the MLU and age of the youngest child to achieve 90% correct productions of the morpheme. The last column shows the overall accuracy across children for the morpheme. The table indicates consistency in acquisition order.

The morphemes -ing, an early acquisition, and -ed, a later one, do not simply mark tense but also aspect, and it is not clear that when they "come in" they are used appropriately in all situations. For instance, McShane and Whittaker (1988) showed 3- to 5-year old children puppet shows of situations that included ongoing activities with *telic aspect,* a deliberate goal (climb a tree to the bananas) or not (atelic aspect), one time or over a long duration. Note that in English it is preferable to describe a single-time goal-directed action with the simple past (the monkey climbed the tree), while describing an ongoing *durative* activity with no clear-cut end with the progressive form (the monkey was climbing a tree). The children were asked to tell what the show had been about to another puppet, and the relative frequencies of their morphemes were counted for the different aspectual situations. All the children used a large number of simple past forms. The 5-year-olds contrasted with the 3-year-olds in using the progressive in the continuing, no-clear-goal situation. The younger children did not use the progressive for this atelic situation, overgeneralizing the -ed form. Thus, in this context, the -ed form came in earlier, perhaps because the meaning of the atelic situation was not yet clear. That is, morpheme acquisition is tied to both frequency of occurrence and the salient semantic feature of the situation, the function of the form.

Bloom (1991) analyzed the order of acquisition of Brown's morphemes, finding different acquisition patterns depending on the verb a tense marker was attached to or on the general meaning of the sentence. First, she notes that in those languages in which there are separate tense and aspect markers, aspect comes in before tense.

As we have noted in English, aspect is conveyed with tense, so it is hard to separate them. Consider, for example, "I broke the glass." Use of "broke" indicates this happened in the past (tense) and also that it happened once, causing a permanent change of state (aspect). "I was swimming" also happened in the past, but the -ing aspect says that this was a durative (aspect) activity; it went on for some time. Clearly, certain activities are more likely to cause a one-time change of state (spill, break, find, fall) and for these verbs Bloom noted earlier acquisition of the "past" -ed form (i.e., nondurative, completed end state aspect) marker than the -ing form. Other actions—playing, eating, doing, riding—are more likely to be durative, and for these the -ing form comes in earlier. Thus form, the morpheme, follows function, the meaning.

There is no question that children analyze input words into components and construct their own productions, given that, as we noted in the PDP simulation of -ed acquisition in Chapter 5, children overregularize, producing an impossible form like *breaked*. Children initially produce what they see as unmarked, uninflected words. This may, inadvertently, include inflected words like *children* or *walked*. Once the child attends to inflections, they do not just appear in one or two words but in many, along with overregularization.

Experimentally, Berko (1958) showed the productivity of morpheme acquisition in a now famous study. She created nonsense words that she illustrated with a cartoon (see Figure 9.4). Pointing to the picture, she told her subjects, "This a wug. Now there is another one. There are two of them. There are two _ ." Or "This is a man who knows how to niss. He is nissing. He did the same thing yesterday. What did he do yesterday? Yesterday, he _." The children were to fill in the blanks. Because the words were nonsense, subjects' responses could not derive from imitation but had to reflect generative capacities. The children, taken from Boston-area middle-class schools and ranging in age from 4 to 7½, were tested on the plural, progressive, possessive, past, and third person singular. They were also presented with compound words like *blackboard* and asked if they could say why the word named the object, to see if they were conscious of internal morphology.

Recall (end of Chapter 6) that in English, affixing a plural, possessive, or past-tense marker can take a number of phonetic forms depending on the last phoneme of the root. Adults are very uniform in their responses, even with nonsense words, which reflects tacit knowledge of the morphophonemic rules. The children were less consistent than adults but showed more consistency and more adultlike responses in the older age groups tested. For the plural, all children added "s" or "z" where appropriate but had difficulty with the /əz/ form. Berko hypothesized that the children's rule was "plurals have s or z at the end" and therefore they assumed that words that already had an s or z sound (like *niss*) were plural and did not need additional markers.

The same phonological constraints hold for the possessive and third person singular endings, but there the children more often appropriately added all three variants. Thus the difficulty with the /əz/ form can be neither articulatory nor a failure to recognize the requisite context. For the past tense, performance was poorer overall than for the plural, with /əd/ again more difficult than /d/ or /t/,

Figure 9.4. The Drawings of a "Wug" Used to Elicit the Plural From Children
SOURCE: From "A Child's Learning of English Morphology" by J. Berko in *Word*, 1958, p. 154.
By permission.

perhaps for the same reason. As one might expect from Table 9.2, the progressive produced the best performance from the children.

This discussion has focused on English acquisition. As we have mentioned, other languages are much more complex inflectionally. Russian, for example, has three genders and six cases for nouns as well as a complex system of markers for verbs. Slobin has extensively studied acquisition of inflectional morphology in Russian (1966a, and other languages, 1985) and found results parallel to those found for English. First, children begin to apply inflection after the two-word period. Second, the first inflections applied are those that mark the subject and object cases, which English children mark by order. Third, children begin marking a case using one ending and later differentiate this case by gender. This is true for each case individually, suggesting that gender, like the articles in English, is semantically opaque and therefore late to emerge.

Thus, cross-linguistically, for morpheme acquisition and word order, children acquire early the grammatical markings needed to differentiate meaning expressed in units that are frequent in the adult language and perceptually salient. The meaning is there first; form follows meaning. The more abstract the meaning (like the copula or auxiliary), infrequent or irregular the rule (third person markings of verbs), or imperceptible the unit (a bound, unstressed morpheme), the later it is acquired. Essentially, these are the constraints suggested in Slobin's (1985) OPs and MacWhinney's (1987) competition model.

Data: Acquisition of Complex Sentences

So far we have examined acquisition and word markings for concepts express-ible by active affirmative sentences. We have already discussed briefly the devel-opment of conjunction. Other complexities include the development of negation, questions, embeddings, comprehension of verbs that take irregular complements (such as promise), and awareness of traces and their referents. As we saw with inflections and word order, we may consider acquisition of these syntactic categories as syntax acquisition or as concept acquisition.

Looking at negation from a generative syntactic perspective, Bellugi (1967) defined three stages of development into the adult form. In the first stage, the child precedes the core sentence with a negative marker: "No he bite you." As you may recall, this structure resembles the deep structure of a negative sentence in Chomsky's (1965) theory. At the second stage, the negative marker moves in—"He no bite you." In the last stage, the auxiliary is added and the negation applied to that, yielding the adult form, "He won't bite you."

A similar developmental pattern may be seen with questions. The first questions are sentences beginning with a question word and asked in a questioning tone. Next, auxiliaries are introduced. Finally, the main verb and auxiliary are inverted. Again it is interesting to observe that according to early generative theory, the interrogative marker and auxiliary are elements supposed to be present in the base structure, while the inversion is performed by transformation. The linguistic-nativist position predicted the base structure to be innate and therefore early, but that transformations were to be learned, and therefore later.

Brown and Hanlon (1970) provided additional support for a transformational-type theory of syntax acquisition. They analyzed children's complex questions, such as "Ursula's my sister, isn't she?" Such questions employ multiple transformations internal to the question: The first clause is a simple active declarative, while the tag (in this example) is a negative question that substitutes for the subject of the main clause, a pronoun agreeing in gender and number with it, and modifies number and tense of the auxiliary in the tag to agree with the auxiliary of the main clause. Analysis of this type of question alone suggests that we might expect to see the first clause initially produced with just a rising intonation or a tag, "Huh?" at the end. Subsequently, the child may add the tag but incorrectly as in "Ursula's my sister, is she?" Finally, the child will produce the adult form of the question. Seven such predictions for derivational complexity of question forms were confirmed from the productions of the three children studied. From this, Brown and Hanlon derived the law of cumulative complexity I discussed earlier in acquisition of conjunction: If children have a complex grammatical construction such as negative + question, then they must already have the single elements (negative, question).

The next syntactic acquisition we will examine is the complement. Recall that some verbs take clauses, a complement, as objects: "I think Bill should go," "I told Bill what to do," "I asked Bill what to do," "I promised Bill to leave," and so on. As discussed in Chapter 5, usually the subject of the second verb is the noun closest to it, and subjects may parse both sentences using a minimal distance principle, attaching as subject the nearest noun. In the first two example sentences, the subjects of "go" and "do" are "Bill," the noun immediately preceding them; here, the minimal distance principle works. A few verbs have as the subject of the complement their own subject; the "ask" and "promise" examples have "I" as subject, both of *ask/promise* and of the complement, violating the minimal distance principle. When do children learn the deep structure difference, the lexically specified irregularity?

Carol Chomsky (1969) addressed this question experimentally, having 5- to 8-year-olds act out such sentences with Disney puppets. At 5 and 6, most of the children interpreted all sentences by using a minimal distance principle: The NP closest to the verb was interpreted as its subject. So in response to "Mickey told Donald to jump" or "Mickey promised Donald to jump," the child would make Donald jump. As the children matured, they were less likely to make this error. For each child, abilities to differentiate the regular verbs from the irregulars were highly correlated across verbs tested, but the exact age at which the ability developed depended on the individual child.

More recently, Cromer (1994) found similar ages of acquisition in children presented with sentences like "The wolf is happy to bite" and "The wolf is delightful to bite," and asked to enact the sentence with a wolf and a duck puppet. In the first sentence, the subject of "is happy," and the only expressed NP, "the wolf," is also the subject of the infinitive complement "to bite"; that is, the wolf puppet bites the duck puppet. In the second sentence type, "the wolf" is the object of "to bite"—the duck puppet bites the wolf puppet. (Across both sentence types, the wolf and duck will have equal opportunity to be biter, to rule out the possibility that the child chooses a wolf as biter because it is semantically more likely.) The object sentence requires greater movement to connect the NP with its trace, a violation of the minimal distance principle. Cromer found that only 14% of the children tested correctly understood sentences of the object type at 7 and 8 years of age, with a jump to 54% understanding it at 9 years of age. However, they rehearsed one young child on a number of such sentences before a demonstration to British royalty. The experimenters wanted the child to remain *unable* to do it for the demonstration to work. Much to the experimenters' chagrin, the child "spontaneously" improved. She had been given no correction of her performance, and the only plausible explanation was that she had thought about the sentences in the course of the extended exposure, which suggests an advantage of simple experience, absent "negative evidence."

I should note also that there is much individual difference in understanding such sentences. I tried the wolf-duck sentences with puppets on my son Alexander, then $5\frac{1}{2}$, who made no errors (and enjoyed the game).

The last example of complex sentence acquisition is sensitivity to traces in abstract surface structure. As you may recall, Crain (1991) contrived situations in which young children spoke for puppets by asking other puppets what they wanted to have. Adult English speakers will not contract "want" and "to" in sentences like "Who do you want to take a walk?" where the trace of "who" intervenes. Crain found that $2\frac{1}{2}$- to $5\frac{1}{2}$-year-old children produced sentences in accord with this constraint, saying "wanna" only 4% of the time, in contrast to 59% of the time for sentences like "What do you wanna eat?" with no intervening trace. He argues for an innate sensitivity to the possibility of the trace producing the early acquisition.

Functional Interpretation

The above demonstrations of syntax acquisition may be considered from the point of view of *concept* development. Bloom and Lehey (1978; Bloom, 1991) analyzed negation from a functional view. They noted that the negative can be used to describe nonexistence/disappearance/nonoccurrence, an early concept, and rejection and denial, later concepts. We might expect that as they acquire the syntactic negative, they use it first in instances they have already recognized as negative semantically, form following function. In fact, they do—and the other negative concepts are then acquired in the above order. If a child produces the negative after the subject on disappearance sentences (book not here), he or she may still be fronting it on denial sentences (no I break it). This implies that the procedure of moving the negative into the sentence is not learned as a general rule but is learned anew for each functional category.

A similar trend of syntactic recognition following meaning was obtained by Caramazza and Zuriff (1978) for embedded sentences. They tested comprehension with a picture-matching task for reversible (The boy that the girl is chasing is tall), nonreversible (The apple that the boy is eating is red), and improbable (The boy that the dog is patting is fat) sentences. Children under 6 did very poorly on the reversible sentences, although comprehension of the sentences substantially improved between the ages of 3 and 6. It appeared that they learned to interpret the embeddings but on the basis of semantics rather than on the basis of syntax. And we have already seen that such strategies can override syntax, that is, win the cue competition, in determining subject and object of passive and active sentences.

Finally, in commentary to Crain (1991), Slobin suggests a conceptual basis for the *want* + *to* contraction, a kind of conceptual minimal distance principle. Specifically he argues that if the two verbs, *want,* and its complement, *eat/take-a-walk,* have the same subject, they are conceptually closer, which we may express metaphorically by bringing them closer in the sentence, through contraction. If they take different subjects, we express that difference through linguistic distance.

There is no question, as I said in Chapters 4 and 5, that there is a point at which we have inferred syntactic rules and are capable of understanding semantically implausible sentences, like "The plant watered the boy" or "The wolf is delightful [for the duck] to bite." The question is whether initially the child derives syntactic rules using semantic plausibility by mapping sentence structures on reality schemes. This possibility, of using the concepts and semantics, is known as *semantic bootstrapping* (see, e.g., Gleitman & Landau, 1994). There is good evidence for this, but, as we shall see, there is also good evidence that the child is assisted in acquiring concepts and a lexicon by the syntax, or *syntactic bootstrapping.*

Summary of Syntax Acquisition

In the early studies of language development, it was assumed that much of syntax was innate and the innate rules could be used as a guide to vocabulary, other semantic acquisitions, and learning other specifics of the language. In particular, it seemed that the child might have basic relations like nouns, verbs, and sentences and their core relationships in deep structure. Exposure to the adult language would serve to set parameters like position of subject, verb, and object.

Some evidence supports at least aspects of this position. First, children seem to express primitive subject-predicate relations in two-word utterances and structure early sentences like core sentences. Second, across languages, first utterances seem very similar. Third, as language develops, specific grammatical devices are produced, imitated, and understood more frequently as the child is exposed to them in the adult language.

However, the bulk of the evidence refutes a strong syntax-native position. Although the sequence of acquisition of syntax seems to be similar across children exposed to the same language, there are radical individual differences across children. Across languages children show somewhat different developmental sequences, but these can be related to the structure of the language learned and the frequency, regularity, or salience of particular types of utterance, suggesting that they are learned rather than "unfolded." The acquisition data make most sense given a primarily functional rather than syntactic framework: Across languages children talk about the same things, things the concepts for which seem already to have been grasped mentally but nonlinguistically. Thus, for English-speaking children, the present progressive, the tense children would use to describe what they are currently doing, enters early for those actions that are durative; the -ed form enters early for actions producing radical perceptible changes of state. These actions-perceptions are the topics of early communication.

What may be universal therefore is not the notion of subject and predicate or the forms NP and VP but the cognitive tendency to categorize the world in terms of agents and their effects, or nominal categories and their descriptors, and so forth. What may be universal too are general operating principles for categorizing and organizing both objects and language units into patterned structures. Thus, following the Piagetian framework, we see more regularity in syntactic development when we look at the emergence of case, causality, semantic classes of negation, and so on than we see if we look at acquisition of abstract structure: semantic bootstrapping.

That is not to say that children do not use syntax or acquire it; they tend to use the minimal distance principle or SVO strategy in English, they understand syntactically correct sentences from adults better than those that have child surface structures, and like adults they recall more syntactically correct than anomalous or scrambled sentences (McNeill, 1970). They focus early on word function as well as word meaning, perhaps guided by a language module as the syntax-nativists claim. And it seems that acquisition of these rules depends on some combination of frequency of use in the adult language and perceptual or semantic salience, summed up by Brown (1973) as reflecting

> a change in a set of probabilities rather than as the sudden acquisition of quite general rules. If our conception is correct it means that the learning of the intricate network

of rules . . . is more like habit formation and operant conditioning than anyone has supposed. (p. 388).

Thus the evidence for syntax acquisition favors a combination of the theoretical approaches described at the chapter's start, and not one approach in particular.

Maturation of the Semantic System

When we examined children's first words, we discussed first meanings, what children begin to apply labels to, how they see the process of labeling (applying to categories, not individuals and whole objects, not parts), and how a semantic system emerges from general principles of conventionality and contrast, principles that may serve innately as guides. In looking at the development of syntax, we also looked at emerging meaning arising from the combination of morphemes and we saw how meaning can guide parsing strategies, that is, semantic bootstrapping.

It is important to recognize that the lexicon continues to develop—and at a very rapid rate—throughout childhood and most of adulthood. Clark (1993) estimates that from age 2 on, children master on average 10 words per day, resulting in a working lexicon of about 14,000 words at age 6! From age 10, children are exposed to about 10,000 new words per year; between ages 9 and 15, to *100,000* new words in school texts alone. The numbers are astounding and in their sheer size lead one to wonder what magic processes might allow such mastery. We need to consider that the child may have available special, different-from-adult, concepts and learning strategies to accomplish this acquisition. We might also speculate that the burgeoning lexicon will require continual reorganization so that the child can continue to find words and meanings. Both these speculations suggest some discontinuities in meaning processing during development, as a strategy emerges or retreats or as the semantic system is restructured. Alternatively, we can consider the process continuous, with the burgeoning of the lexicon an outgrowth of a recursive (exponential) process: Each word/concept mastered enables some number of words more to piggyback, resulting in the explosive growth.

While there has been some evidence for reorganization and discrete stages of meaning processing historically, careful, subtle studies have generally tended to support a continuous model, with the same strategies applied and reapplied, and concepts piggybacking on other concepts (Locke's abstract ideas piggybacking on concrete ones and then on each other). For example, Bloom (1993) describes lexical development as a consequence of three general principles:

Relevance: the child learns words for concepts already in mind.
Discrepancy: the concepts in mind become increasingly removed from the data of perception.
Elaboration: the contents of the mind become increasingly elaborate.

Initially, the child is forming schemes for his or her own feelings and perceptions, and the child's vocabulary is concrete, the first words describing those feelings and

---

Box 9.4. Acquisition of Syntax

MLU = 2
— *Pivot-open:* Children's two-word combinations seem to reflect selection from two protogrammatical classes: the open class, which grows rapidly and includes words indicating object categories, and the pivot class, which grows slowly and refers to relations among objects. Utterances can consist of only open words or a pivot and an open word, but not two pivot words.
— *Semantic relation:* Children's two-word combinations may instantiate fundamental case relations such as possessor-possession, object-location, and action-patient.

MLU > 2
— *Telegraphic speech:* Early multimorpheme combinations look telegraphic, including only uninflected content words.
— *Inflectional morphology:* Children seem to add inflections in a relatively fixed order determined by frequency and regularity in the input language and perhaps by semantic content. In English, 14 grammatical morphemes have been extensively studied: "ing" enters first, along with the possessive; the *to be* forms enter last.
— *Word order:* English-speaking children structure their early sentences predominantly in SVO order. Children who are learning order-free languages also seem to select a frequently heard order (often also SVO) to reproduce in their own speech, and later acquire different orders and/or the inflections (subject/object cases) that allow order to be freed up.
— *Negation, questions:* Early study of question and negation production suggested that children's speech reflected a transformational model. First children produce core sentences, with a negative or question marker outside. Then children produce the sentence with the marker moved in. Finally, children also invert the auxiliary and subject. More recent study shows individual differences in such production and indicates that a semantic model of negation and questioning may better describe regularities. So, for example, in negation, children learn how to describe the disappearance of something (it is not there) before their rejection of it, before their denial of it.
— *Embedding:* A late-entering syntactic skill.

Models
— *Principles and parameters:* Syntax acquisition is guided by innate principles and preselected binary-valued parameters. The input language sets the parameter to one of the values.
— *Operational principles/competition model:* General cognitive (or linguistic) strategies for extracting patterns from language input.
  — *Conceptual salience:* Children acquire early structures that have a strong referential base. Form follows function.
  — *Frequency:* The most repeated structures are learned first. Each repetition causes a weight to be incremented.
  — *Perceptual salience:* The child's attention is directed to sounds surrounding silence, high-energy sounds, stressed syllables, and so on.

(continued)

Box 9.4 Continued

— *Minimal distance principle:* Children cluster words by proximity, so the subject of the verb in a dependent clause is assumed to be near its trace, making sentences like "He is eager to bite" easier to understand than "He is easy to bite."
— *Semantic bootstrapping:* The learning of syntactic regularities through mapping to likely sense.

---

cued by the immediate perceptible context. As the lexicon develops, the concepts in the child's mind are associations between the words; words are cued by other words, not just outside experience. This has two consequences: (a) A semantic system develops, to organize the word associations, and (b) new lexical items can be acquired to describe the *relationship* between the words. This is a continuous process with ever more abstract-from-perceptual experience concepts being labeled. Her studies of a number of children over a long term in the same "playroom" show ever-decreasing mentions of the familiar objects the children encounter weekly in the playroom. For children, as for adults, there is no need to communicate the expected, common ground.

Apart from analyzing the words that children acquire, there are experimental techniques for probing their semantic memories and their word-learning strategies. We turn to those data next.

Word Associations

One of the first techniques used to look at semantic organization was word association (Brown & Berko, 1960), which initially suggested a discontinuity in development of the lexicon. What is the first word you associate to *mother*? To *dog*? To *run*? To *soft*? Like most adults, you probably gave answers like *father, cat, walk,* and *hard,* respectively. Your association matched the stimulus in part of speech, and was a member of the same hierarchy, differing in a critical feature, perhaps a polar opposite. This form of association is called *paradigmatic association.*

Children's early word associations are not based on word class or on polar features. The most common associations before about age 7 are words that co-occur with the stimulus word, a phrasal chunk: to *soft*, they might say *pillow;* to *run, fast,* and to *dog, bark.* This kind of association is called a *syntagmatic association.* For a long time it was believed that around the age of 7, the lexicon was reorganized to reflect hierarchical, feature-based meanings.

If we consider a child's language experience from the perspective of Bloom's principles, we can see how such a shift might develop. Words cue other words—the beginning of semantics. When one has little language experience there is likely to be a single context in which one uses a word: *Soft* is tied only to *pillow.* With increasing language experience, the word is encountered in many more frames: We hear *soft pillow, soft voice, soft expression, software.* The link between *soft* and a *particular* follower will be diffused as followers are added. At the same time the link between *soft* and a common association of each in the *set* of followers (*hard pillow, hard voice, hard expression, hardware*) will increase. So this relating association will become stronger.

Indeed, recent study of word association suggests a continuum in development from paradigmatic to syntagmatic associations, with the intermediate step being words that are both paradigmatic and co-occur in phrases with the stimulus word (Lucariello, Kyratzis, & Nelson, 1992; Nelson, 1985, 1991). Both the intermediate step and eventually the paradigmatic association arise from the child's organization of experiences into procedural scripts (see Chapter 5), that is, common ritualistic events with plausible substitute scenes (recall the restaurant script and its variants). So a young child might have a "bedtime" script—the set of events (toothbrushing, bathing, story) and objects (toothbrush, bath toys, stuffed animal, blanket) that accompany this nightly and nap-ly occurrence. These become associated in the script along with permissible variants for the same slots. So, for *pillow*, a "*slot-filler*" associate would be *blanket,* both in the same places in the bedtime script. Like *pillow, blanket* is a noun and soft and inanimate and so seems to be paradig-matically related, but like *soft, blanket* will occur with *pillow* in phrases like *pillow and blanket.* Lucariello et al. find "striking continuity in knowledge organization, with slot-fillers salient at all ages [from 4-year olds to adult]" (p. 995). Increasingly abstract associations, true paradigmatic responses, based on abstract features and not co-occurrence in a script or frame, prevail as the child ages.

Inferences of Word Meanings

As part of the wug study, Brown and Berko (1960) asked children to guess the meaning of a nonsense word in a sentence. For example, a sentence might be "The cat wants to niss some fish." A typical adult definition of *niss* would be catch or eat, reflecting the understanding that the word will add a new meaning to the other words and, given the situation, what the new meaning is likely to be. The children, on the other hand, supplied other words in the sentence as "meanings" of the new word: "A niss is a fish—the cat wants a fish." Similarly Piaget (in Vygotsky, 1986/1996) noted that when asked to supply the meaning of "because" in the sentence "The child missed school because he was sick," 7- and 8-year-olds would respond with either clause but not with the relation between the two. Both results demonstrate the inability of the child to separate the part, the new word, from the whole, the rest of the sentence.

Probing a child's language understanding through a comprehension test of a nonsense word placed in a normal sentence is a popular technique, and has shown more similarity than difference between child and adult understanding. One of the earliest studies to use this method was Werner and Kaplan (1950). They presented their subjects with new words in several sentences, each of which added to the meaning. For example:

1. A corplum may be used for support.
2. Corplums may be used to close off an open place.
3. A corplum may be long or short, thick or thin, strong or weak.
4. A wet corplum does not burn.
5. You can make a corplum smooth with sandpaper.
6. The painter used a corplum to mix his paints.

The child heard each sentence and then was asked the meaning of the word. The next sentence was then presented to see how the child modified the answer. Children up to the age of 12 years showed similar patterns of deduction: using the whole sentence as the meaning of the word, and persisting with a guess through the next sentence. For example, given "people like to talk about the borducks of others and don't like to talk about their own," "borduck" was interpreted as people talk about others and not themselves—the whole meaning. Adding "people with borducks are often unhappy" did not change the meaning; rather, the two whole meanings were folded together with "Say this lady hears that another lady is talking about her, so she'll get mad at her and that lady will be very unhappy."

Of course, the "errors" in these studies may occur simply because the children do not have the world knowledge to deduce the relation the word expressed. At what age would you expect a child to know that wood can burn, so that the corplum sentence would provide useful data? A second point to consider is that if, as we discussed earlier, a child is using exclusivity and contrast principles, she or he will resist guessing a known word like *wood* for *corplum,* assuming that this new "word" must denote a new concept. Adults may seem more logical because they understand the demand characteristics, that the experiment is a synonym-guessing game.

More recent studies probing the meaning of nonsense words have created situations in the laboratory that children respond to as natural language learning. Then, even from the age of $2\frac{1}{2}$, they apply quite logical, sophisticated, meaning-assignment strategies. Markman (e.g., 1994a, 1994b) asked children to select an object from among objects either belonging to the same category (e.g., a dog and a cat) or sharing some salient attribute, like color or co-occurrence (e.g., a dog and a bone). If children are told vaguely, "I'm going to show you something. Find another one," they choose objects on the basis of perceptual similarity or co-occurrence, a syntagmatic-type strategy. If the child is placed in a "language-learning set" with "Here is a dax. Find another dax," the child's word-meaning strategies kick in—the taxonomic principle—and the child finds another category member, paradigmatic association. Finally, if given a nonsense word, a picture of an object whose name is known and a picture of an unknown object, both children and adults (Golinkoff, Hirsh-Pasek, Bailey, & Wenger, 1992) select the unknown object as an example of the nonsense word, the principle of exclusivity. If given only the choice of a known object, the children interpret the nonsense word as referring to a part or an attribute of the object (Markman & Wachtel, 1988).

Recall that one reason children may have responded differently from adults in Werner and Kaplan's *corplum* study is that they may not have had enough world knowledge to apply. Gelman and Markman (1986) have shown that, if provided that knowledge in the experiment, young children do indeed use hierarchical, categorical reasoning like adults. In their task, children were shown pictures of similar-looking animals from different zoological classes, such as a shark, a dolphin, and a tropical fish. They were also given information about characteristic features of, for example, the shark and the dolphin, such as "the shark breathes through the water" and "the dolphin surfaces to breathe." The question is whether they can infer how the tropical fish breathes given the categorical information that the shark and tropical fish are fish and the dolphin is a mammal. By the age of 4, they could; they inferred properties based on category membership, not on perceptual similarities.

These studies show that the same taxonomic principles guide the developing lexicon through adulthood, the main difference being that the more mature the language learner, the more knowledge that can be brought to the situation, both extralinguistic knowledge about what can happen and linguistic knowledge about which categories have labels. New items must clearly apply to a part or a superordinate, something that has no preexisting label. It is not surprising that to assign finer meanings to later-acquired words, the language learner uses any linguistic knowledge available. From MLU > 2, that *includes syntactic knowledge, syntactic bootstrapping.*

A number of studies have shown that the sentence frame, as well as the new word and object choices, constrains meaning assignment in children as young as 2½. If the frame suggests a count noun ("show me a dax"), a mass noun ("show me some dax"), or a property ("show me a daxlike doll"), children will select an unknown object, substance, or property, respectively (Waxman, 1994). A transitive sentence frame—"The duck is gorping the rabbit"—causes children to attend to a video of a duck manipulating the rabbit, rather than the duck and rabbit both performing an action, with the converse true of an intransitive frame—"The rabbit and the duck are gorping" (Naigles, 1990).

As we discussed in the last chapters, language has many interacting levels and redundantly specifies the message. This gives children many means to infer convention and intent, exploiting all the redundancy within language and the redundancy of language with extralinguistic context. It allows different acquisition patterns for different children; each can choose from a number of language "anchors" to tie down the meaning and form conventions. They can use syntax to limit meaning possibilities, or meaning to suggest syntactic interpretations— syntactic and semantic bootstrapping. Indeed, you may recall that Bates et al. (1988/1991) found no reason to separate syntactic learning from semantic: They enter hand in hand, following a pattern determined by the particular dominant general cognitive strategy (referential or expressive) for each child.

Metalinguistic Meaning Development

One of Piaget's specific observations about language development is that metalinguistic knowledge emerges fully during formal operations, not until the teen years. This is belied by children's delight at punning and other language jokes, which begins at the earliest stages of language; Horgan (1981/1994) reports consistent joking in a 1⅓-year-old child with a vocabulary of 20 words! It is also hard to explain children's enjoyment of fairy tales and other forms of fantasy if they do not see them both as imaginary and as analogous, that is, metaphorical, to real situations and fears they experience (Gibbs, 1994).

Figurative language. Specific tests of children's metalanguage skills have also shown that this enters early. It is easy to hear metaphors in a child's productions; to an adult, every overextension could be one. Investigators therefore are careful to consider children to be using figurative language only when it is clear that they have a literal alternative in their lexicon or when the child is clearly in "pretend" mode in symbolic play. Using such criteria, 72% of the apparent metaphors (spontaneous renaming or overextensions) were in fact figurative in children between the ages of 3 and 6 (study cited by Gibbs, 1994).

Studies have also shown that young children comprehend the difference between literal and figurative language and will apply them appropriately. For example, Gibbs cites a study in which children were asked to select the best alternative to an "A is like b" sentence or to an "A is the same kind of thing as b" sentence. Both 3- and 4-year-olds responded "figuratively" to the "is-like" frame: "Rain is like tears." Three-year-olds also selected "tears" as the same kind of thing as rain, suggesting that they were only focusing on the shared perceptual attributes of the two. Four-year-olds, however, preferred "snow" to "tears" in the literal condition, with the performance difference suggesting an understanding of the different language demands—figurative and literal—in place by age 4.

However, young children do appear to have difficulty interpreting adult metaphors and proverbs, noted first by Piaget (1952) even for teenagers. Winner, Rosenstiel, and Gardner (1976) tested children between 6 and 14 years old on metaphors that interpreted psychological experience through comparison to a physical event (e.g., "The prison guard was a hard rock") or that represented one physical experience by means of another (e.g., "Her perfume was bright sunshine"). The children were asked either to explain the metaphors or to select the appropriate explanation from among several choices.

Winner et al. categorized responses as magical, metonymic, primitive metaphoric, and genuine metaphoric. In the magical response, the child interprets the metaphor literally and invents a world to account for it; for example, "The king had a magic rock and he turned the guard into another rock." Although these responses were not frequent in any age group, they were most frequent in the 6- to 8-year-old children.

In the metonymic response, an association is formed between the two terms of the metaphor as if they were separate descriptions, for instance, "The guard worked in a prison that had hard rock walls." The primitive metaphor differs from a genuine metaphor in that the meaning of the figurative element is literally rather than figuratively applied, as in "The guard had hard muscles" versus "The guard did not care about the feelings of the prisoners." The 6-, 7-, and 8-year-olds made primarily metonymic and primitive metaphoric responses, but even the 10-year-olds made only 48% genuine metaphoric responses.

Winner et al. did not speculate on the change in strategy with development but pointed out that children produce good metaphors considerably before they appear to understand them. This may be because, to comprehend another's metaphor, one is removed from the immediate sensory experience and must make the relation entirely inside one's head. In Piagetian terms, this relation of thought to thought follows concrete operations, and formal operations usually begin around adolescence.

Language awareness. Aside from metaphor comprehension, metalanguage skills include awareness of the structure of language, that sentences are composed of words, words of syllables, and so on. Scientists have inferred metalinguistic awareness in young children because they backtrack and correct themselves, indicating that they note discrepancies between the structure of their production and their intention. Tunmer and Herriman (1984) cite an example of a child trying to say *shoes*: [š] [šɪ] [šɪš] [šu] [š?] [šuš]—finally rescued by the mother supplying the correct pronunciation.

There have been numerous reports of children practicing language to themselves. Weir (described in McNeill, 1970) recorded "presleep monologues" by hanging a microphone over her child's crib. One instance, when the child was 2½ years old, is "go for grasses—go for them—go to the top—go for pants—go for shoes," an obvious example of play with the "go for" sentence frame. Practice monologues have been noted cross-culturally; for example, Heath (1983) observed, "Walk, walk to de doctor, walk to de sto' [store], git better, walk shoe, walk up . . ." (p. 92) in working-class rural African American children raised with very different conversational expectations from those of middle-class white Americans (see Chapter 8).

The practice and repairs indicate awareness of language form but not necessarily conscious reflection on its structure. As Tunmer and Herriman (1984) pointed out, parrots engage in speech practice, and we would be loath to credit birds with language awareness. A mismatch between an intended and an actual utterance may be recognized without awareness of a structural problem.

Direct tests of children's language awareness have also been conducted. Liberman, Shankweiler, Fischer, and Carter (1974) asked children to tap in rhythm to phonemes, syllables, or words of an utterance. Nursery school children signaled syllables better than phonemes; by first grade, performance was 90% for syllables and 70% for phonemes. This indicates that syllable understanding precedes phoneme awareness, and that sound awareness is generally late in developing (segmenting may be both necessary for, and a product of, literacy—see Chapter 11). Young children (between 4 and 7) are also poor at tapping to words in sentences, sometimes tapping on the basis of syllables, and sometimes to content words only (Tunmer, Pratt, & Herriman, 1984). Moreover, when asked "Does the word *book* have pages?" or to "Name a large word," many young *teens* confuse the concept of a word and the thing it denotes, responding, for example, "yes" to the first question and "house" to the second! (Adults may do this too; they have not been tested.)

Thus it appears that awareness of language as a system and the ability to discuss and appreciate its structure develop through childhood and adolescence. Full metalinguistic awareness appears only in the human adult (and perhaps not even then).

Summary of Semantic Acquisition

Children's meanings for words and the semantic system change as they develop. The changes seem to arise from the acquisition of the lexicon itself: New words allow new relationships to be specified among them recursively. We see a continuity in the process of categorization (syntagmatic → slot-filling → paradigmatic associations; principles of taxonomy, exclusivity, and contrast principles affecting meaning assignment from childhood through adulthood; understanding of language as a means of making analogy from early on) but a change in the categories as more and more world knowledge and language knowledge is assimilated.

Acquisition of Discourse Rules

Piaget's concept of egocentrism notwithstanding, from a very early age children seem to respond to the social demands of the communication situation. In infancy, as we noted, they synchronize to the parent's speech, a kind of feedback, and they also babble contingent on the parent's speech, again providing feedback. Later they respond to commands, indicating that they understand what is expected of them. The first words are usually not demands but observations to share: "Children talk in order to participate, to be human, not in mere imitation but in emulation . . . sociolinguistics begins in the crib" (Menn, 1981, p. 136).

At MLU > 2 we see development of real interaction skills, appropriate monitoring, feedback and turn-taking, and, eventually, tailoring of the conversation to the audience. Children talk in simpler sentences when talking to other children than when talking to adults; they also ask more questions of adults (Bloom & Lehey, 1978). Of more interest, Bloom and Lehey reported that a 2-year-old shifted readily from sign to speech when shifting conversation from a deaf parent to a hearing one, and, as we shall see in the next chapter, children raised with two oral languages, each spoken by a different parent, learn by 2 years of age which language to use with mom and which to use with dad. Children asked to describe something to a blind person tend to provide more details than when asked to describe something to a sighted person. And in my own experience, Eric, at the age of 2, requested me to translate something he wanted to say to his non-English-speaking babysitter. All of this reflects an awareness of the conversational needs of others, that children are not egocentric even in early language use, that they are aware of common ground.

Box 9.5. Acquisition of Semantics

— *Taxonomic principle:* Children's assumption that words name categories of objects.

— *Principle of exclusivity or contrast:* Children's assumption that no two words mean the same thing.

— *Principle of conventionality:* Children's assumption that there is a "correct" way to refer to something, and their attempt to model it from the adult. With exclusivity, this results in their dropping a child-form such as *breaked* when they realize they are using it in the same situation as *broke* is conventionally used.

— *Syntagmatic, paradigmatic, and slot-filler associations:* Children's early word associations (syntagmatic) are of words that co-occur in a phrase (like *soft pillow*). Later they associate words that co-occur in a phrase or in a similar script or frame, filling a slot like for "things that go on a bed" or are needed in the bedtime routine, such as pillow-blanket-sheets. Adult associations primarily consist of "paradigms"—same part-of-speech, many of the same semantic features, including some slot-fillers, but also associations that are unlikely to co-occur in a phrase, such as soft-hard.

— *Syntactic bootstrapping:* The use of syntactic regularities to ascribe meanings to new lexical items.

— *Metaphor development:* Children produce metaphor and wordplay from early on. Even adolescents have demonstrated difficulties in understanding figurative and metalanguage, which is perhaps consistent with the idea that these do not fully develop until formal operations.

— *Discourse development:* Young children are not fully egocentric and adapt their speech to the needs of others. Children's stories are shorter, less detailed, more redundant with the obvious, and less well organized with respect to topic and elaboration the younger they are.

One difference between children's discourse skills and those of adults is in the relation between sentences in conversation; children have not internalized what is cooperative (see Chapter 2) from an adult's point of view. Children's earliest "sentences" echo a part of the adult's previous utterance—too redundant—something that rarely happens in adult discourse (Bloom & Lehey, 1978). Children's utterances also are sometimes irrelevant, unrelated to the adult's previous statement. And, finally, those utterances that fall into neither of these categories tend to expand simply on the adult's utterance (Bloom, Rocissano, & Hood, 1976/1991). Bloom et al. (1976/1991) offer the following examples:

ADULT	CHILD
Noncontingent: Alright. Put the light on.	Cookie.
Imitative: Take your shirt off.	Shirt off.
Contingent: I see two.	I see two bus come here. (pp. 527-528)

The differences are that for adults, 90% of the utterances are contingent on previous sentences as opposed to 70% for children, and in adults the connection is more abstract. Analyzing interviews with politicians, Bloom et al. (1976/1991) reported the following as typical of adult contingencies:

> President Ford: My wife and I watch the Miss America contest all the time. We really enjoy that on TV.
> Miss America: I sure hope you saw it this year. (p. 550)

Note that the topic is the same but that all other parts of the sentence are new. The redundancy may seem greater in children's speech because so much is new to children that they may feel that the contributions they make to the conversation when echoing are as significant as they later do when adding.

Peterson and McCabe (1983) reported developmental changes in children's abilities to describe stories. As you may recall from Chapters 4 and 5, adult stories are usually constructed as elaborations on a theme, with the topic given initially, followed by descriptive details designed to portray the setting, the characters' feelings, the sequence of events, and the causal connections. The oldest children Peterson and McCabe examined (9 years) reflected these constraints on stories to a greater extent than younger children. Four-year-olds, for example, were more likely to omit important events or tell them out of order or to fail to give appropriate orientation, as the following example illustrates (E is the experimenter):

> E. When I go home I have to visit my aunt who's in the hospital. She broke both of her legs . . .
> B. She had to have a cast on.
> E. That's right.
> B. My sister had, she's had. She broke a arm when she fell in those mini-bike.
> E. Tell me what happened.
> B. She broke her arm. She had, she went to the doctor, so I, my Dad gave me a spanking, and I
> E. Your Dad gave you what?
> B. A spanking to me.
> E. A spanking?
> B. Yeah. And she had to go to the doctor to get a cast on. She had to go to get it, get it off, and it didn't break again. (Peterson & McCabe, 1983, p. 44)

Note the lack of explanation for the relation between the spanking, the accident, and the cast as well as the failure to elaborate on the events—the child just jumps from one event to the next.

In addition to providing less detail and omitting necessary relations, younger children are less coherent and tend to provide orienting information, such as setting, at the middle or the end where it is less useful. They also favor descriptive stories, with temporally linked events, over causally connected stories. Finally, younger children tell shorter stories than older ones. Contrast, for example, a 4-year-old's narrative:

E. You went to your grandma's? What happened?

S. I just said "Hiii," and then and then they, Mom said, said, "Say *say* something." And I said, "*Nooo, I wanta go home.*" "Not 'til you say, say, say hello." "I *said* hello, Ma." And then she, and then my Mom goed back to my grandma's and then she said, "Oh, she's just a bad girl," like that. (p. 226)

with this 9-year-old's narrative:

E. What happened the last time you went [to visit your aunt]?

D. Nothing. We went to see our aunt because she, she's getting real old and yet, she's going to die pretty soon, so we went and visited her and, my brother, he found a sh, *rattle* snake and he thought it was one of those *play* snakes, and he, he said, "*Gee, look at this play snake,*" and my Dad goes, "*That ain't no play snake, that's a real snake.*" My mother, "*Drop that durn thing you, and get in here and wash your hands.*" (p. 247)

As Peterson and McCabe conclude, more in language develops than sentence structure: Discourse coherence also develops, and development is not complete at middle childhood.

Practice and the Parent as Teacher

In examining syntactic development, I observed that structures or concepts are acquired earlier the more frequent they are in the adult language to the child (SVO in English, for example). This suggests that there may be language teaching taking place, either passively or actively, as the behaviorist models suggested.

Studies of practice effects in language have taken two forms: study of children's obvious practicing by themselves, as already discussed, and studies of the nature of parent's discourse with the child, or child-directed (CD) speech. I note first that CD speech has been most studied in middle-class, white America, where it is perhaps most extremely different from that of *adult-directed* or *AD* speech. As pointed out in Chapter 8, such parents question their children for information already known to the parent, expecting increasingly elaborate expositions, unlike rural black parents. The latter not only do not ask "obvious" questions but do not direct speech to the infant or child, talking about the baby's doings to other adults in the baby's presence: "'Dis young 'un wet his britches more'n any young 'un I know" (Heath, 1983, p. 75). Nevertheless, Fernold (1994) finds that features of adult speech in the presence of a child across cultures differ from AD speech, adults' language to adults, in similar ways but to different degrees.

CD speech shows a more marked intonation contour, with a wider excursion ending and a rising tone to get attention or a long, smooth falling contour to soothe (Fernold, 1994). This captures infants' gaze more than AD intonation. Compared with adults, children are addressed with shorter, simpler, more redundant utterances, with fewer inflections, syntactic complexities, or performance errors. Mothers have longer MLUs when talking to older than younger children (Seitz & Stewart, 1975). This may be because parents are actively trying to teach their children, or the children may simply be imitating the parents.

In middle-class America, adults talk to children about what the child is currently doing; children respond in kind (in rural black America, the topic is still the baby's activity; what is different is whether the baby is directly addressed or being discussed while present with another adult). To children, adults use more gestures and talk more in basic category levels. When the child's understanding has increased, gesturing decreases, and finer or grosser category distinctions are made (Hoff-Ginsberg & Schatz, 1982). Thus children's language may reflect features like basic level because this is what is being modeled to them.

Children's acquisition, as we have observed, also seems to reflect salient features of adult speech. Hoff-Ginsberg and Schatz (1982) suggested that word categories could be learned by noting the similarity of inflections used; thus verbs could be classed together as those things that take -ed. And many words, especially nouns (which enter early), are spoken by the parents in isolation. This can aid recognition. Other syntactic categories can be learned from semantic regularities, although these are not usually sufficient to differentiate all abstract, arbitrary syntactic forms. However, they can provide an initial prod (Hoff-Ginsberg & Schatz, 1982).

As a final point in favor of the child's modeling language from adult speech, researchers note that children's speech develops differently given different parent talking styles and that parents do "correct" aspects of child language. Children's vocabulary develops more quickly when the parents provide labels for objects or situations the child is focusing on than they do if the parent is directive (e.g., Bates et al., 1988/1991). While caretakers do not specifically correct grammar, they do respond appropriately only to what they understand, which reinforces those communications. And they modify children's speech by expanding it: If the child says, "There shoe," the parent may rejoin, "That's right. There are your shoes." Indeed, studies indicate more rapid syntax development when there is much expansion relative to other types of verbal input (Hoff-Ginsberg & Schatz, 1982). Children are also much more likely to imitate the recasts than a repetition of what they said (Bohannon et al., 1990), as though they were practicing the "correction." We should note that these feedback patterns from adult to child do not occur cross-culturally, and so while they may aid language learning, they are not necessary (Gordon, 1990; Heath, 1983).

On the negative side, there are the studies that show language learning without parent direction, as just mentioned. And there are studies that indicate that the parents do not respond differentially to poorly formed and well-formed utterances, and so are not consistently effective teachers (Brown & Hanlon, 1970). There is also the argument that the high correlation between the parents' utterances and the children's comes from the parents' matching the children rather than the other way around. Indeed, it is not clear that most parents are conscious enough of syntactic

---

Box 9.6. Child-Directed (CD) Speech

— Adults talk differently to children than to other adults, with more exaggerated intonation and simpler sentences.
— CD speech is more attractive to children than is adult-directed speech.
— CD speech deals with the here and now, but less so, the older the child is who is being addressed.
— Children's speech develops more rapidly if parents provide names for what the child is attending to, and if the parents expand on the child's own utterances, gently modeling correct production.
— But CD speech is not a universal phenomenon (in all cultures), and it is not clear that it is necessary for language learning. Often direct teaching fails.

---

levels to know how to scale down their speech to be effective language teachers. Finally, there are wonderful counterexamples cited to show how ineffective teaching is. Recall the "other-one-spoon" dialogue of Chapter 4, or consider the following (from McNeill, 1970):

Child: Nobody don't like me.
Mother: No, say "nobody likes me."
Child: Nobody don't like me.
(eight repetitions of this dialogue)
Mother: No, now listen carefully; say *"nobody likes me."*
Child: Oh! Nobody don't likes me. (p. 1103)

So, parents may not play an active, obvious teaching role, but in supplying language models, they provide the child with the experience necessary to develop schemes for the language.

Summary

In this section, we examined development of syntactic, morphological, semantic, and discourse concepts in children at MLU > 2. Not a surprise, we found that there is a steady increase in language sophistication with age, and that the acquisition process is by no means over when children enter school. Generative-grammar accounts to the contrary, it appears that language acquisition occurs through children's attention to semantically and phonologically (stressed) salient features of the language, from which syntactic structure is learned, although once syntactic regularities are noted, they help semantic acquisition. Moreover, it appears that in interacting with children, parents do provide a model and some do try to teach, with beneficial effects on the speed of language learning.

SUMMARY AND CONCLUSIONS

Our examination of the acquisition of the first language indicates similarity across children at a general cognitive level. All children cry, coo, babble, then produce words; perceive certain phonetic distinctions categorically, regardless of experience, and other distinctions noncategorically, until they have experience; use the same phonological processes of reduplication, assimilation, and reduction. In syntax we see a steady progression from one word to two and more, production of the same cases initially across languages, and reproduction of the most frequent forms of the adult language first, increasing attention to rarer constructions. In semantics similar strategies are used to infer meanings and assign words to concepts through adulthood, changing as a function of the existing language knowledge and developing understanding of the world.

The similarities in sequence across children can be explained by an innate language mechanism but are at least as well explained as general cognitive changes coordinated with similar real world environments. Children learn a sentence construction, past tense, negation, or causality only when they understand the underlying real world situation.

In any event, if there is something innate about language, it does not seem to be specific syntactic structures but more general cognitive and perceptual strategies that allow for the deduction of syntax. On the language innateness side, however, is the urge to communicate using language, the attention paid to these particular environmental noises, and the fact that syntax is acquired or used in language at all. As newborns and pets are usually well cared for, it is clear their needs for food, water, or social contact are effectively communicated without language.

Another aspect of language that we considered possibly innate is the time of acquisition. In this chapter we discussed language acquisition given normal input from 2 years to adolescence. Innateness was defined not only as reflex responding, which we investigated by looking for similarities across children in production, but also as a tuning of the individual to critical features in the environment at a particular time. If there is an LAD, it may require input to become activated. We saw that parents communicate with their children early in a manner (unconsciously) designed to attract their attention, provide a comfortable social environment to allow expression of sociolinguistic needs, provide model utterances, and shape the children's outputs. These do not indicate that language develops exclusively from experience; experience can interact with an unfolding bioprogram or blueprint to allow language development.

Child language acquisition may be accomplished through a seamless coordination of the child's initially primitive and innate sensory, social, and communicative skills, with adults' innate caregiving responses, both gradually developing in tune with the child's developing cognitive skills and increasingly complex social and communication needs. *All* cultures must have lullabies, with similar soft, pitch-declining, repetitive structures, because all adults need sleep and need to get their babies to sleep to get to sleep themselves, and all infants will find the same sounds soothing. Likewise, even if cultures differ in the degree to which they play with or talk to babies, for all, smiles are rewarding, and similar sounds will make babies smile.

Infants initially need to socialize to have their basic needs met; they vocalize about hunger, fatigue, and so forth. As adults meet these needs, the infant learns the controlling effect of the vocalization and the importance of the parent as caregiver, apart from the care being given.

The developing social interest coincides with an increasing interest in the outside world. The child's developing attention to categories of interesting experiences (Mommy, Daddy, ball, sock, shoe) provides the optimal stimulation for acquisition of the basic vocabulary. This sets the stage for increasing social skills and cognitive development, which in turn provide the breeding ground for complex discourse and syntax skills.

It is likely that at no other time in human development is there such a match of social and cognitive needs with language skills. Older children or adults understand more about the world and so must "regress" their thinking to focus on basic nouns and adjectives. Second language learners, as we will see in the next chapter, can easily be frustrated with beginning discourse skills that relegate them to the here and now, not necessarily polite rejoinders and simple, active uninflected sentences.

Our discussion of normal language acquisition necessarily confounds the similar nature and nurturing of normal children by normal parents. "Universals" may not be uniquely attributed to any of the shared potential causes. In *Language in Atypical Populations,* "experiments of nature" that decouple these causes are explored: the rehabilitation of children denied language and socialization through abuse or neglect, the communications of children who are socialized but do not hear language and are not taught a visual language and children with language learning disabilities, perhaps indicating genetic problems in the "bioprogram," if it exists, for language acquisition.

We turn next to study a normal, sometimes primary and sometimes secondary, language process, one common to most peoples of the world—acquisition and processing of more than one language.

REFERENCES

Bates, E., Bretherton, I., & Snyder, L. (1991). *From first words to grammar: Individual differences and dissociable methods.* New York: Cambridge University Press. (Original work published 1988)

Bates, E., & Ellman, J. (1996). Learning rediscovered. *Sciences, 274,* 1849-1850.

Bellugi, U. (1967). *The acquisition of negation.* Unpublished doctoral dissertation, Harvard University.

Berko, J. (1958). The child's learning of English morphology. *Word, 14,* 150-177.

Bertoncini, J., Bijeljac-Babic, R., Jusczyk, P. W., Kennedy, L. J., & Mehler, J. (1988). An investigation of young infants' perceptual representations of speech sounds. *Journal of Experimental Psychology: General, 117,* 21-33.

Bloom, L. (1970). *Language development: Form and function in emerging grammars.* Cambridge: MIT Press.

Bloom, L. (1991). *Language development: From two to three.* New York: Cambridge University Press.

Bloom, L. (1993). *The transition from infancy to language: Acquiring the power of expression.* New York: Cambridge University Press.

Bloom, L., & Lehey, M. (1978). *Language development and language disorders.* New York: John Wiley.

Bloom, L., Rocissano, C., & Hood, L. (1976). Adult-child discourse: Developmental interaction between information processing and linguistic knowledge. *Cognitive Psychology, 8,* 521-552. (Reprinted in L. Bloom, 1991, *Language development: From two to three.* New York: Cambridge University Press)

Bloom, P. (Ed.). (1994). *Language acquisition: Core readings.* Cambridge: Bradford Books of MIT Press.

Bohannon, J. N., III, MacWhinney, B., & Snow, C. (1990). No negative evidence revisited: Beyond learnability or who has to prove what to whom. *Developmental Psychology, 26,* 221-226.

Braine, M. (1963). The ontogeny of English phrase structure: The first phase. *Language, 39,* 1-13.

Brown, R. (1973). *A first language.* Cambridge, MA: Harvard University Press.

Brown, R., & Bellugi, U. (1964). Three processes in the acquisition of syntax. *Harvard Educational Review, 34,* 133-151.

Brown, R., & Berko, J. (1960). Word association and the acquisition of grammar. *Child Development, 31,* 1-14.

Brown, R., & Hanlon, C. (1970). Derivational complexity and the order of acquisition in child speech. In J. R. Hayes (Ed.), *Cognition and the development of language* (pp. 11-53). New York: John Wiley.

Caramazza, A., & Zuriff, E. B. (1978). Comprehension of complex sentences in children and aphasics: A test of the regression hypothesis. In A. Caramazza & E. B. Zuriff (Eds.), *Language acquisition and language breakdown* (pp. 145-161). Baltimore: Johns Hopkins University Press.

Chomsky, C. (1969). *The acquisition of syntax in children from 5 to 10.* Cambridge: MIT Press.

Chomsky, N. (1965). *Aspects of the theory of syntax.* Cambridge: MIT Press.

Chomsky, N. (1972). *Language and mind.* New York: Harcourt Brace Jovanovich.

Chomsky, N. (1986). *Knowledge of language: Its nature, origin, and use.* Westport, CT: Praeger.

Clark, E. V. (1993). *The lexicon in acquisition.* New York: Cambridge University Press.

Condon, W. S., & Sander, L. W. (1974). Neonate movement is synchronized with adult speech: Interactional participation in language acquisition. *Science, 183,* 99-101.

Crain, S. (1991). Language acquisition in the absence of experience. *Behavioral and Brain Sciences, 14,* 597-650.

Cromer, R. F. (1994). Language growth with experience without feedback. In P. Bloom (Ed.), *Language acquisition: Core readings* (pp. 411-419). Cambridge: Bradford Books of MIT Press.

Dale, P. S. (1976). *Language development.* New York: Holt, Rinehart & Winston.

DeCasper, A. J., & Fifer, W. P. (1980). Of human bonding: Newborns prefer their mothers' voices. *Science, 208,* 1174-1176.

Delack, J. B. (1976). Aspects of infant speech development in the first year of life. *Canadian Journal of Linguistics, 21,* 17-37.

deVilliers, J. G., & deVilliers, P. A. (1973). A cross-sectional study of the acquisition of grammatical morphemes in child speech. *Journal of Psycholinguistic Research, 2,* 267-278.

Dore, J. (1975). Holophrases, speech acts, and language universals. *Journal of Child Language, 2,* 21-40.

Eimas, P. D. (1975). Speech perception in early infancy. In L. P. Cohen & P. Salapatek (Eds.), *Infant perception* (Vol. 2, pp. 193-231). New York: Academic Press.

Eimas, P. D., Siqueland, E. R., Jusczyk, P., & Vigorito, J. (1971). Speech perception in infants. *Science, 171,* 303-306. (Reprinted in J. L. Miller, R. D. Kent, & B. S. Atal, Eds., 1991, *Papers in speech communication: Speech perception,* pp. 681-684. Woodbury, NY: Acoustical Society of America)

Fernold, A. (1994). Human maternal vocalizations to infants as biologically relevant signals. In P. Bloom (Ed.), *Language acquisition: Core readings* (pp. 51-94). Cambridge: Bradford Books of MIT Press.

Field, T. M., Woodson, R., Greenberg, R., & Cohen, D. (1982). Discrimination and imitation of facial expression by neonates. *Science, 218,* 179-181.

Fry, D. B. (1966). The development of the phonological system in the normal and the deaf child. In F. Smith & G. A. Miller (Eds.), *The genesis of language* (pp. 187-206). Cambridge: MIT Press.

Gelman, S. A., & Markman, E. M. (1986). Categories and induction in young children. *Cognition, 23,* 183-209.

Gibbs, R. W., Jr. (1994). *The poetics of mind: Figurative thought, language, and understanding.* New York: Cambridge University Press.

Ginsburg, H., & Opper, S. (1988). *Piaget's theory of intellectual development* (3rd ed.). Englewood Cliffs, NJ: Prentice Hall.

Gleitman, L., & Landau, B. (1994). *The acquisition of the lexicon.* Cambridge: MIT Press.

Golinkoff, R. M., Hirsh-Pasek, K., Bailey, L. M., & Wenger, N. T. (1992). Young children and adults use lexical principles to learn new nouns. *Developmental Psychology, 28,* 99-108.

Gordon, P. (1990). Learnability and feedback. *Developmental Psychology, 26,* 217-220.

Heath, S. B. (1983). *Ways with words: Language, life and work in communities and classrooms.* New York: Cambridge University Press.

Hirsh-Pasek, K., Kemler Nelson, D. G., Jusczyk, P. W., Cassidy, K. W., Druss, B., & Kennedy, L. (1987). Clauses are perceptual units for young infants. *Cognition, 26,* 269-286.

Hoff-Ginsberg, E., & Schatz, M. (1982). Linguistic input and the child's acquisition of language. *Psychological Bulletin, 92,* 3-26.

Horgan, D. (1981). Learning to tell jokes: A case study of metalinguistic abilities. *Journal of Child Language, 8,* 217-224. (Reprinted in R. P. Honeck, Ed., 1994, *Introductory readings for cognitive psychology,* 2nd ed., pp. 214-219. Guilford, CT: Dushkin)

Ingram, D. (1978). The production of word-initial fricatives and affricates by normal and linguistically deviant children. In A. Caramazza & E. B. Zuriff (Eds.), *Language acquisition and language breakdown* (pp. 63-85). Baltimore: Johns Hopkins University Press.

Irwin, O. C. (1949, September). Infant speech. *Scientific American, 181,* 22-24.

Jakobson, R. (1968). *Child language, aphasia, and phonological universals* (H. Keiler, Trans.). The Hague, The Netherlands: Mouton.

Jusczyk, P. W. (1981). Infant speech perception: A critical reappraisal. In P. D. Eimas & J. L. Miller (Eds.), *Perspectives on the study of speech* (pp. 113-164). Hillsdale, NJ: Lawrence Erlbaum.

Jusczyk, P. W. (1997). *The discovery of spoken language.* Cambridge: MIT Press.

Jusczyk, P. W., Hirsh-Pasek, K., Kemler Nelson, D. G., Kennedy, L. J., Woodward, A., & Piwoz, J. (1992). Perception of acoustic correlates of major phrasal units by young infants. *Cognitive Psychology, 24,* 252-293.

Kelly, M. H., & Martin, S. (1994). Domain-general abilities applied to domain-specific tasks: Sensitivity to probabilities in perception, cognition, and language. In L. Gleitman & B. Landau (Eds.), *The acquisition of the lexicon* (pp. 105-140). Cambridge: MIT Press.

Kuhl, P. K. (1993). Early linguistic experience and phonetic perception: Implications for theories of development of speech perception. *Journal of Phonetics, 21,* 125-139.

Kuhl, P. K., & Meltzoff, A. N. (1982). The bimodal perception of speech in infancy. *Science, 218,* 1138-1141.

Kuhl, P. K., Williams, K. A., Lacerda, F., Stevens, K. N., & Lindblom, B. (1992). Linguistic experience alters phonetic perception in infants by 6 months of age. *Science, 255,* 606-608.

Lenneberg, E. (1967). *Biological foundations of language.* New York: John Wiley.

Liberman, I. Y., Shankweiler, D., Fischer, F. W., & Carter, B. (1974). Explicit syllable and phoneme segmentation in the young child. *Journal of Experimental Child Psychology, 18,* 201-212.

Lieberman, P. (1987). *The biology and evolution of language.* Cambridge, MA: Harvard University Press.

Locke, J. L., & Pearson, D. M. (1990). Linguistic significance of babbling: Evidence from a tracheostomized infant. *Journal of Child Language, 17,* 1-16.

Lucariello, J., Kyratzis, A., & Nelson, K. (1992). Taxonomic knowledge: What kind and when. *Child Development, 63,* 978-998.

MacKain, K., Studdert-Kennedy, M., Spieker, S., & Stern, D. (1983). Infant intermodal speech perception is a left hemisphere function. *Science, 219,* 1347-1349.

Macken, M. A., & Ferguson, C. A. (1981). Phonological universals in language acquisition. In H. Winitz (Ed.), *Native language and foreign language acquisition* (Annals of the New York Academy of Sciences, 379, pp. 110-129). New York: New York Academy of Sciences.

MacWhinney, B. (1987). The competition model. In B. MacWhinney (Ed.), *Mechanisms of language acquisition* (pp. 249-308). Hillsdale, NJ: Lawrence Erlbaum.

MacWhinney, B., & Snow, C. (1985). The child language data exchange system. *Journal of Child Language, 12,* 271-296.

Markman, E. M. (1994a). Constraints children place on word meanings. In P. Bloom (Ed.), *Language acquisition: Core readings* (pp. 154-173). Cambridge: Bradford Books of MIT Press.

Markman, E. M. (1994b). Constraints on word meaning in early language acquisition. In L. Gleitman & B. Landau (Eds.), *The acquisition of the lexicon* (pp. 199-227). Cambridge: MIT Press.

Markman, E. M., & Hutchinson, J. E. (1984). Children's sensitivity to constraints on word meaning: Taxonomic vs thematic relations. *Cognitive Psychology, 16,* 1-27.

Markman, E. M., & Wachtel, G. F. (1988). Children's use of mutual exclusivity to constrain the meanings of words. *Cognitive Psychology, 20,* 121-157.

McNeill, D. (1970). The development of language. In P. H. Mussen (Ed.), *Carmichael's manual of child psychology* (pp. 1061-1161). New York: John Wiley.

McShane, J., & Whittaker, S. (1988). The encoding of tense and aspect by three- and five-year old children. *Journal of Experimental Child Psychology, 45,* 52-70.

Mehler, J., Jusczyk, P., Lambertz, G., Halsted, N., Bertonicini, J., & Amiel-Tison, C. (1988). A precursor of language acquisition in young infants. *Cognition, 29,* 143-178. (Reprinted in J. L. Miller, R. D. Kent, & B. S. Atal, Eds., 1991, *Papers in speech communication: Speech perception,* pp. 697-732. Woodbury, NY: Acoustical Society of America)

Meltzoff, A. N., & Moore, K. (1977). Imitation of facial and manual gestures by human neonates. *Science, 198,* 75-77.

Menn, L. (1981). Studies of phonological development. In H. Winitz (Ed.), *Native language and foreign language acquisition* (Annals of the New York Academy of Sciences, pp. 130-137). New York: New York Academy of Sciences.

Morse, P. A. (1972). The discrimination of speech and nonspeech stimuli in early infancy. *Journal of Experimental Child Psychology, 14,* 477-492.

Naigles, L. (1990). Children use syntax to learn verb meanings. *Journal of Child Language, 17,* 357-374.

Nelson, K. (1973). Structure and strategy in learning to talk. *Monographs of the Society for Research in Child Development, 38*(149), 1-137.

Nelson, K. (1985). *Making sense: The act of shared meaning.* New York: Academic Press.

Nelson, K. (1991). Event knowledge and the development of language functions. In J. F. Miller (Ed.), *Research on child language disorders: A decade of progress* (pp. 125-141). Austin, TX: Pro-Ed.

Oller, D. K., & Eilers, R. E. (1988). The role of audition in infant babbling. *Child Development, 59,* 441-449.

Peterson, C., & McCabe, A. (1983). *Developmental psycholinguistics: Three ways of looking at a child's narrative.* New York: Plenum.

Piaget, J. (1952). *The language and thought of the child.* New York: Humanities Press.

Piaget, J. (1981). *Intelligence and affectivity: Their relationship during child development* (T. A. Brown & C. E. Kaegi, Eds. and Trans.). Palo Alto, CA: Annual Reviews.

Piaget, J. (1983). Views on the psychology of language and thought. In R. W. Rieber & G. Voyar (Eds.), *Dialogues on the psychology of language and thought* (pp. 107-120). New York: Plenum.

Pinker, S., & Prince, A. (1988). On language and connectionism: Analysis of a parallel distributed processing model of language. *Cognition, 28,* 73-193.

Saffran, J. R., Aslin, R. N., & Newport, E. L. (1996). Statistical learning by 8-month-old infants. *Science, 274,* 1926-1928.

Seitz, S., & Stewart, C. (1975). Imitations and expansions: Some developmental aspects of mother-child communications. *Developmental Psychology, 11,* 763-768.

Shipley, E. F., Smith, C. S., & Gleitman, L. R. (1969). A study in the acquisition of language: The responses to commands. *Language, 45,* 322-342.

Skinner, B. F. (1957). *Verbal behavior.* New York: Appleton-Century-Crofts.

Slobin, D. I. (1966a). The acquisition of Russian as a native language. In F. Smith & G. A. Miller (Eds.), *The genesis of language* (pp. 129-148). Cambridge: MIT Press.

Slobin, D. I. (1966b). Grammatical transformations and sentence comprehension in childhood and adulthood. *Journal of Verbal Learning and Verbal Behavior, 5,* 219-227.

Slobin, D. I. (1985). Cross-linguistic evidence for the language-making capacity. In D. I. Slobin (Ed.), *The cross-linguistic study of language acquisition: Vol. 2. Theoretical issues* (pp. 1157-1256). Hillsdale, NJ: Lawrence Erlbaum.

Slobin, D. I., & Bever, T. G. (1982). Children use canonical sentence schemas: A cross-linguistic study of word order and inflections. *Cognition, 12,* 229-265.

Spring, D. R., & Dale, P. S. (1977). Discrimination of linguistic stress in early infancy. *Journal of Speech and Hearing Research, 20,* 224-232.

Streeter, L. A. (1976). Language perception of two-month-old infants shows effects of both innate mechanisms and experience. *Nature, 259,* 39-41.

Strohner, H., & Nelson, K. E. (1974). The young child's development of sentence comprehension: Influence of event probability, nonverbal context, syntactic form and strategies. *Child Development, 65,* 567-576.

Tunmer, W. E., & Herriman, M. L. (1984). The development of metalinguistic awareness: A conceptual overview. In W. E. Tunmer, C. Pratt, & M. L. Herriman (Eds.), *Metalinguistic awareness in children: Theory, research and implications* (pp. 12-35). New York: Springer-Verlag.

Tunmer, W. E., Pratt, C., & Herriman, M. L. (Eds.). (1984). *Metalinguistic awareness in children: Theory, research and implications.* New York: Springer-Verlag.

Vygotsky, L. (1996). *Thought and language* (A. Kozulin, Trans. and Ed.). Cambridge: MIT Press. (Original work published 1986)

Waxman, S. R. (1994). The development of an appreciation of specific linkages between linguistic and conceptual organization. In L. Gleitman & B. Landau (Eds.), *The acquisition of the lexicon* (pp. 229-257). Cambridge: MIT Press.

Werker, J. F., & Tees, R. C. (1984). Cross-language speech perception: Evidence for perceptual reorganization during the first year of life. *Infant Behavior and Development, 7,* 41-63. (Reprinted in J. L. Miller, R. D. Kent, & B. S. Atal, Eds., 1991, *Papers in speech communication: Speech perception,* pp. 733-747. Woodbury, NY: Acoustical Society of America)

Werner, H., & Kaplan, E. (1950). Development of word meaning through verbal context: An experimental study. *Journal of Psychology, 29,* 251-257.

Winner, E., Rosenstiel, A. K., & Gardner, H. (1976). The development of metaphoric understanding. *Developmental Psychology, 12,* 289-297.

Witelson, S. F., & Pallie, W. (1973). Left hemisphere specialization for language in the newborn: Neuroanatomical evidence of asymmetry. *Brain, 96,* 641-646.

STUDY QUESTIONS

1. Critically compare and contrast the generative, Piagetian, and behaviorist approaches to language acquisition. What is the major philosophical position of each with respect to the roles of innate structures and learning? In your view, which position best represents the language acquisition data presented in this chapter? Why? Pick a few (not all!) examples.

2. Prepare a chart for language development. Try to assemble, with respect to rough age groups, the phonological, semantic, morphological, syntactic, metalinguistic, and discourse skills discussed.

3. Critically discuss the child language acquisition data presented from the points of view of "stage" theory, a "language module" theory, and a neural net/cognitive operating principles theory. Is there evidence for discontinuities in language processing? Is there evidence for language developing independently of other cognitive functions, or does language seem linked to general cognitive, emotional, and social development?

MULTILINGUALISM AND FOREIGN LANGUAGE ACQUISITION

D o you, or does someone you know well, speak more than one language? Do you (or they) *think* in both languages? Do you (or they) use them interchangeably, or is each reserved for a particular situation or particular sets of people? If you or someone you know does think in more than one language, are these languages that were learned from infancy, or was one learned after puberty, when a putative "critical period" might have ended? In your opinion, does knowing more than one language confuse a person or broaden his or her horizons? To what extent does knowledge of more than one language entail a single language competence and single storage in the brain, or separate competencies and conceptualizations?

Living in the United States, I have grown up with a prejudice shared by many U.S. citizens that *most* people speak one language, an "official" language tied to their nation. I have also grown up assuming that foreign-language acquisition requires "talent" and "youth," assumptions based on the idea that there is a critical period for genetically specified language acquisition. However, I do know that more peoples speak two or more languages than speak only one and that there are few nations whose boundaries encompass one language. One nation-one language is the exception, not the rule (Grosjean, 1982).

Intranational multilingualism arises because political boundaries are drawn without regard to linguistic divisions. Great Britain encompasses Wales, Cornwall,

Scotland, and Ireland, each with its own Celtic language as well as English; Celtic peoples also live across the English Channel in Brittany in France. India comprises 14 national languages plus English and Hindi (Grosjean, 1982). A political border divides the Somali people of Kenya and Somalia.

Multilingualism also arises within a nation when people immigrate and establish their own enclaves. Multilingualism arises between nations, as we discussed in Chapter 8, when one nation conquers another. It arises benignly at national borders as two language communities trade and in other mutually beneficial ways interact.

As I write this, the U.S. Congress is trying to enact a law establishing English as the official language of the United States, exempting, for example, our currency, so that *E Pluribus Unum* can remain on our money, and exempting place names so that "Los Angeles" could still be so known ("A Law," 1996, p. 14). Clearly, the necessity of these particular exemptions declares the United States to be multi-cultural and multilingual in its symbols, from its inception. Why is the law then proposed? Its proponents argue that it will "prevent the Government [from] catering too heavily to a growing number of immigrants who do not speak English well" ("A Law," 1996, p. 14). Its passage will ensure that non-English speakers will be more disenfranchised and stigmatized than they are now. As I have said in previous chapters and will expound here, discriminatory attitudes toward languages can affect both language structure and its cognitive processing.

In this chapter we explore the nature of language when a speaker naturally uses more than one, investigating how the use of each language changes because of the speaker's competence in the other. We also look at language processing in the multilingual, investigating the independence and interaction of vocabularies, parsing heuristics, and so on in comprehension and production. We will need to consider the pragmatic situations underlying the use of each language: Does a speaker use the languages with different people, for different topics? Are the people in conversation monolinguals or also multilingual (in the same languages)? What is the speaker's attitude toward each language and culture? And we will look at the effects of the age at acquisition and number of years of experience on the language competencies of the multilingual to see to what extent a critical-period-advantage-of-youth bias is valid. Finally, we will briefly discuss methods of foreign-language instruction.

BILINGUALISM IN SOCIETY

Born in a Two-Language Family

Psycholinguists have favored study of the *balanced bilingual* (Grosjean, 1982), a person raised with two languages interchangeably from birth, equally fluent in both. A person who has acquired two languages before the age of 3 years is considered to have acquired them *simultaneously;* if one of the languages is learned after the age of 3, this is considered *successive* acquisitions (Grosjean, 1982). Apart from simultaneous acquisition, "balance" demands equivalent use, that the person be equally comfortable with both languages. Fluency may be assessed experimentally by *reaction time* to respond in both languages, *equal,* say, in responding to commands in each language (Lambert, 1955), listing associated words in each language (Peal & Lambert, 1962), or in translating from each language to the other (Mohanty & Babu, 1983). This puts perhaps an unwarranted premium on speed. Timed tests may also be accompanied by other measures (see Grosjean, 1982): questionnaires (self-)assessing the individual's language history, attitudes toward the languages, and degrees of comfort in each language in speaking, listening, reading, and writing; or experimental techniques, like picture naming and word association in each language, comparing the results with monolingual norms; or dominance tests, in which an item that is a word in both languages is presented for the subject to pronounce and one sees which language is selected.

Balanced bilingualism may occur when parents are fluent in different languages and have decided to speak to their child in their different languages, so that the child becomes bilingual. To the psycholinguist, this situation presents some ideally controlled conditions: Age of acquisition is the same for the two languages, both languages are used in the home, both languages are acquired as concepts are acquired, and the child has a positive attitude toward both languages. Each of these constants between the two languages is obviously missing, say, when children acquire a second language because their parents emigrate, or when they enter school and learn the language of instruction, different from their home language.

Balanced bilinguals are rare, so the very considerations that make them appear ideal controls make them unrepresentative of multilinguals in general. And the "balance" *is* only apparent: Children interact differently with their parents: discussing (to be stereotypical) clothing with mom and sports with dad. So the use of both at home does not imply that the child is learning the same concept names or the same scripts in both languages; clothing terms may be more available in one language and sports terms in the other. What the balanced bilingual is likely to have is a positive attitude toward both languages, allowing study of multilingualism to be uncontaminated by low self-esteem.

One Language at Home, One in School

In the United States (and in many truly multilingual societies), the more typical situation is that one language is used by both parents in the home, and that language is the child's "native language." Another language (English in the United States) may be the language of instruction, which children hear and need to learn when they start school. The push to learn the language of school may come with strings attached: The children's native language may be considered inferior, the children "handicapped" by not already knowing the language of instruction. There may be real pressure on the children to assimilate, submerging their native culture, their roots. In the United States such an attitude is common, exemplified by a quotation from the congressional debate about institutionalizing English:

> There is also a trend in this country for American citizens not knowing English, which inhibits their ability to improve themselves and prepare themselves for the 21st century. . . . If you want to keep your people in a barrio, if you want to keep them restricted in little tight communities so only you can communicate with them, and we can't in English, then be my guest. ("A Law," 1996, p. 14, quoting Representative Randy [Duke] Cunningham, of California)

The pressure to assimilate may come not only from those who speak the language of power but also from within the minority community, from parents who want their children to be competitive in the dominant culture, who see that occurring only with fluency in the dominant language (Hakuta, 1986).

Learning the language of instruction need not be a negative experience and need not be accompanied by submersion of the children's native languages. Cultures throughout history have promoted their children's learning other languages, as we still do today. Wealthy Romans sent their children to Greece to assimilate the language and culture of that conquered, but highly respected, nation; aristocratic Russians learned French in Paris and spoke it in czarist Russia as the language of privilege; many college students enter foreign exchange programs to improve their fluency, maintaining their own language while adding in-depth knowledge of another. In nations where multilingualism is the norm, say, for example, Tanzania, children speak their tribal languages at home until school starts, and then join the majority of children in learning as second languages the official languages of instruction, English and Swahili. Under these circumstances, learning additional languages is like learning to read: All the children enter similarly ignorant, and language learning is not an obstacle to be overcome but a matter of course.

I am stressing the possible differences in attitude because, as we shall see, negative attitudes toward both the dominating language or one's parents' language depress learning. It is not surprising that a child who feels inferior will not approach school or the demanding task of learning a new language with a "can-do" attitude. On the other hand, a positive attitude toward oneself and one's culture, along with the acquisition of a new language, yields cognitive advantages beyond knowing more than one language (discussed later in this chapter; see, too, e.g., Bialystok, 1988; Grosjean, 1982; Hakuta, 1986; Lambert & Tucker, 1972).

To produce such a positive attitude, Grosjean (1982) advises,

> A nation that wishes to openly support and preserve its linguistic minorities can recognize minority languages in the national constitution and give them some official status in the regions where they are used. The government can also allow children of the minority group to be educated in that language . . . and defend the minority culture and promote its literature, its music, its press, and its theatre. (p. 25)

In the United States, *without* an English-only law,

> more than half the foreign-born immigrants shift over to English as their usual language within a short period of time, retaining their mother tongue essentially as

a second language. . . . Even among hispanic Americans of Texas the anglicization rate of new Spanish immigrants is ten times higher than that of the French in Quebec. (p. 57)

Do we need a "law" institutionalizing English as the language of the United States if it happens anyway?

Bilingual Education

In the United States, bilingual education programs take many forms (see Grosjean, 1982, for a detailed presentation), most of them *transitional,* easing children into English as the primary means of instruction. In contrast, *submersion* programs require children to use the new language full-time, often punishing them for resorting to the language they know. Ideally a school *should* be "a place where the child is made welcome and made to feel secure, where learning can be a constructive experience, and where teachers are supportive and expect the child to succeed" (Grosjean, 1982, p. 208). Submersion programs, by their very nature, are *not* such welcoming environments.

Submersion may be accompanied by formal instruction in English as a second language (ESL). Although the formal training can be helpful, it may also be isolating. If children are selectively removed from the classroom for the special instruction, the differentiation of them from their peers may be stigmatizing.

The transitional approaches provide instruction in both the child's own language and English, shifting the proportion of each gradually toward submersion over some number of years. For example, in the first year, 90% of instruction may be in the native language; the second year, 50%; and by the fourth year, the child may be *mainstreamed,* taking all instruction in the majority language in a regular class comprising majority children. This situation may be less isolating for the children because (a) they will understand much of what is going on in school from the first, and (b) they are with other children, in the same circumstances, with whom they can talk comfortably. On the other hand, if this is a single bilingual class in a predominantly mainstream school, the class as a whole may be stigmatized.

Another approach emphasizes the importance of the children's native culture and language. *Maintenance* programs teach children about their own culture and language while they teach the new language. These are particularly effective when the teacher belongs to the culture of the children he or she is trying to teach. *Immersion* programs reintroduce the child's native language after a period of submersion so that both languages are maintained (I will discuss some of these further at the end of this chapter). Typically these approaches are used when the child's native language is the language of power, considered the high form by the society, as English is in French-speaking Canada. While English-speaking children must learn French in school, there is a recognized premium for them to maintain their ethnic and linguistic identity. This type of situation is what happens in a naturally multilingual society such as Tanzania's: It maintains the children's sense of self during foreign-language learning; it also creates a community as all the children are sharing the language-learning experience; and to the extent that *all* children are exposed to all languages and cultures, it increases everyone's multi-cultural awareness. It also is the attitude that prevails in "foreign"-language instruction; when we learn a second language in school there is no suggestion that we suppress our first language even if we are immersing in the new language.

Indeed, *bi*lingualism—maintenance and use of both languages—flourishes when both cultural (ethnolinguistic) groups have vitality in the society at large. *Vitality,* or life, includes such factors as a substantial community of users, institutional and cultural support, and status and prestige within the community (Clement & Bourhis, 1996).

In the ideal immigration situation, as the immigrant child is learning the language of instruction in school, the family is learning it also, so both languages are used both at school and at home. (Adults too can opt for foreign-language instruction programs: Some are short-term immersion programs; some are transitional instruction in the new language; and, of course, there is the at least "part-time" submersion of immigrants in the new culture, part-time because they usually associate with other immigrants with whom they can speak.) Often, though, the parents either do not learn the new language or choose not to use it at home, so that the child identifies one language with friends and education, and the other with family. In this circumstance children sometimes "reject" their parents' language, refusing to speak it back, dissociating themselves from what they see as perhaps an inferior and less vital culture, certainly one different from that of their peers. (This can happen too when one parent uses one language to the child and the other parent communicates in the language used by the child's friends and the school.) This can lead to a child's fluent comprehension but inability to speak a language, or even a formerly fluent child losing both comprehension and production abilities in the native language (e.g., Burling, 1978). For adults, the perception of lesser vitality of their group produces a similar tendency to eschew their language when they can—in talking with other bilingual speakers, especially those more clearly identified with the more vital group (Clement & Bourhis, 1996).

As the current debate rages on a law mandating English as the official language of the United States, in fact, many who identify with the Spanish-speaking community are finding it difficult to maintain their children's interest in the Spanish language and culture (Navarro, 1996):

> Parents send their children to foreign countries for summer vacation, hire bilingual nannies and read bedtime stories in a cacophony of tongues, all in an effort to pass on the family's language, give the children a linguistic advantage for the future or simply enrich them culturally. Still, the languages, parents say, often lose out to television, schools and peer pressure.
>
> Even in Miami, one of the country's most Hispanic areas, parents say it is hard to get their children to learn Spanish. The challenge to raise a child to be bilingual can be even greater for families speaking less-prevalent languages like German, Swedish or Japanese, parents say. (p. 7)

The Bilingual in Conversation

As we have discussed in previous chapters for presumably monolingual speakers, the situation and the people being addressed in conversation dictate appropriate word choice: We use slang for body parts with our "cool" friends but scientific jargon equivalents in the classroom. For speakers of a nonstandard dialect, such pragmatic considerations influence pronunciation and syntax as well as word choice—whether, for example, to use AAEV or standard English in a particular context. For a bilingual, the choice is between full languages, or even the mix of them. This is called *code-switching.*

In the case of balanced bilinguals who speak a different language with their mothers and fathers, the "choice" of language is determined by which parent they are addressing. It is likely, though, that both parents know both languages. After all, the parents probably do talk to one another. Therefore, the children could interchange or intersperse the languages when addressing either parent and expect to be understood. If two people bilingual in the same languages are talking, they may freely code-switch, mixing the languages, sometimes because they access a word in the other language more readily, and sometimes deliberately to create a mood, attract attention, or emphasize a point. The mixing of the languages has led outside observers to assume (incorrectly) that bilinguals fail to master either language, resorting to the other language when stuck for a word or structure beyond their grasp (Grosjean, 1982). In fact, studies of code-switching show that it is a highly regulated and well-structured phenomenon, dictated by the internalized constraints of both languages as well as the pragmatics of the conversation (Grosjean, 1982; Grosjean & Soares, 1986).

In effect, a fluent bilingual has three linguistic competencies: one for each of the two languages when speaking with a person monolingual in those languages, and a bilingual competence—the "rules" for interweaving the languages when speaking with someone who likewise is bilingual. Grosjean and Soares (1986) advise:

> Bilinguals should be studied as such and not always in comparison with monolinguals. Instead of being the sum of two monolinguals, bilinguals are competent "native speaker-hearers" of a different type; their knowledge of two languages makes up an integrated whole that cannot be easily decomposed into two separate parts. (p. 179)

Summary

Most people speak more than one language, with varying degrees of fluency. The languages are never completely interchangeable; each language is used with specific people and therefore in different situations. The language used in school will be the language in which science, history, and math terms are most available; the language of the family, the one in which terms describing caretaking and mother's and father's work are most available.

Box 10.1. Bilingualism in Society

— *Balanced bilingualism:* Equal fluency in both languages, which usually have been acquired simultaneously. Equal fluency is often measured by equal reaction time in the two languages.
— *Simultaneous acquisition:* both languages acquired before the age of 3.
— Bilingualism is the norm, not the exception, internationally. It is cognitively advantageous, provided the individual has a positive attitude toward both languages and cultures.
— Language instruction to a minority or immigrant population is often transitional, easing the learner into relying on the dominant language. It can submerge the learner's native language and culture, or promote it, in immersion programs.
— Bilinguals choose which language to use based on situation pragmatics: which language they are most used to dealing with a particular topic in, and which language the people they are addressing know.
— When speaking with other people bilingual in the same languages, bilinguals will code-switch in a rule-governed way, exploiting the common knowledge of both languages and their strengths in each.
— True bilingualism, free use of both languages, is favored when both ethnolinguistic communities are, and are seen as, vital within the society at large. Vitality includes a prominent speaking community, prestige, and institutional and cultural support.

People may acquire a second language in many ways, ranging from "mother's knee" to formal instruction in school. Instruction situations can promote bilingualism and a positive attitude toward all languages, if the students' native language(s) and culture(s) are recognized as valuable and acceptable, and if the student is among other (multilingual) language learners. This is the attitude underlying most "foreign" language instruction; it must be accompanied by sufficient motivation, as in immersion situations, for the learners to try to use the new language.

ACQUIRING TWO LANGUAGES

As in monolingual language acquisition, studies of the acquisition of two languages include diaries, often kept by the parents; scheduled observations in school, day care, or in the home; and experimental studies in which the child's comprehension, production, and imitation skills are tested. Most of the data on simultaneous acquisition derive from diaries kept by parents who each spoke a different language to the child (Grosjean, 1982). The experimental studies usually focus on areas where the two languages are different, as when one signals sentence relations through word order and the other, through morphology. There has been specific interest in comparing the acquisition process for the same language at different ages: Does an older child acquiring English as a second language in an immersion setting progress through the same stages as does an infant? Is the older child faster, helped by existing language knowledge, or slower, with UG no longer modifiable? There is also interest in the case of simultaneous acquisition of two languages, in how and when the child separates them into two systems. Finally, there is interest in the little studied phenomenon of language loss: Natural observation has shown that people forget language when they do not use it, and may relearn it, as they use their other language less (Grosjean, 1982).

Case Studies of Simultaneous Acquisition

Perhaps the most famous study by a parent of a child's language acquisition is the four-volume work of Leopold, on his daughter Hildegard, summarized in Leopold (1978). From the time she was born, Hildegard's mother, her primary caretaker, spoke English with her, while her father addressed her only in German. She lived in the United States for her first five years, but then traveled to Germany to visit her father's family, where she stayed for six months before returning to the United States. Leopold's record of her acquisition of the two languages is extremely detailed and has provided data for many child language researchers. He also proposed fruitful areas of study in child language acquisition generally and of bilinguals in particular.

Hildegard did not learn bilingually at first but acquired words and phonology from each language into one doubled system. Leopold points out that if the two languages are structurally similar, it is difficult to record their separate contributions given that a word like *mother* ([mʌðɚ] in English and [mutɚ] in German) rendered through the child's own phonological system into, say [mama], may not betray an origin clearly unique to one language. Moreover, German and English differ phonologically only in sounds that typically come in late in acquisition (e.g., the consonants [θ, ð, v, X]) so observation of separate phoneme acquisition in the first two years is unlikely, and did not happen with Hildegard. Leopold also noted a problem in attributing causes to a particular phonological occurrence: Hildegard devoiced final voiced consonants in English (*dog* would be pronounced [dɔk]), which could have been a manifestation of a German phonological constraint. However, many children (who are not simultaneously acquiring German) naturally devoice final consonants in early acquisition. Thus Hildegard's deviations in English are not clearly attributable to interference from German or to the normal monolingual phonology acquisition pattern.

Before the age of 2, Hildegard acquired words of both German and English, combining them into one "system" to address all speakers. At 2, she seemed aware that they were in fact two languages, to be used with different people, commenting to her father, "I say . . . " but "you say . . ." and asking for synonyms in the other language. She also attempted to get her father to speak English with her, asking him, "How does Mama say . . .?" And once she asked her father if *all* fathers spoke German.

I find this last query particularly interesting because it illustrates to me that children are actively trying to construct order from their world by generating rules. And this particular hypothesis is one that most children would have no use for (aside from being wrong) and so is unlikely to have originated in a bioprogram, UG! It seems therefore that a hypothesis like "add '-ed' to all verbs to make a past tense" could also be actively constructed from the observed pattern, not requiring guidance from a UG.

By her third year, Hildegard had pretty much mastered the phonologies, and her English clearly outstripped her German. She also had made great gains in English morphology and syntax, showing all complexities. Her German, which she heard less often, remained at the simplest level.

This reversed when she visited Germany at age 5: Her English receded and her German developed, although the influence of English was clear because she maintained English word order and rendered English idioms in German. Suddenly, after three months in Germany, she mastered German sentence construction, appropriately placing the verb at the end.

There was again a reversal when she returned to the United States. For a few days she would not use English with her friends; after one month she used German and English interchangeably, as appropriate for different speakers; after six months, while both languages were fluent, vocabulary was more available in English, but she sometimes spoke English in German word order, as in "I was earlier there" or "Where my tooth out is, that's where I bite" (p. 31).

The general pattern Leopold noted for Hildegard is as follows:

— A single system combining the two languages at first
— Conscious division of them into separate systems at about the age of 2, with some interference between them
— Dominance and faster acquisition of the most-heard language
— Dominance of one language leading to regression of the other, perhaps ultimately leading to loss of the unused language

Other parents of simultaneous bilinguals have confirmed and extended these general findings (Hatch, 1978b; Vihman, 1985). Celce-Murcia (1978) described a child learning English from her mother and French from her father. English developed faster presumably because she heard English more because her mother was the primary caretaker. She appeared aware of her own competence using French over English words when they were phonologically simpler, favoring, for example, *couteau* [kuto] over *knife.* She also created her own word seemingly to avoid an "f": *pied-ball* for *football,* using the French word for *foot.*

Burling's (1978) son Stephen showed dominance of Garo (a language of India) over English, although he had heard and begun to use English words before he moved to the Garo Hills, when he was more than a year old. In the Garo Hills, his English continued to develop while he added Garo words. Garo came to dominate when his mother, the main English speaker in his life, became ill and was hospitalized for several months, leaving him in the care of a Garo nanny until he was 2½. Until well into his third year, Stephen spoke primarily Garo with some English words inserted, and pronounced English vowels with the nearest Garo vowel equivalent. Thus his was a clear case of English regression. When his mother returned from the hospital, his English "exploded" (apparently it was gone but not forgotten), and he seemed to realize that the two languages constituted separate systems to be used with different people. For example, he had learned color terms in each language but applied them to their referents within each language randomly. When he acquired the concept of color, it affected both languages simultaneously; he applied the terms correctly in each. Apparently he had the equivalences already for both languages and needed the core concept to connect the words to.

Stephen's English had regressed when his mother went into the hospital, and Garo came to dominate. Shortly after his mother returned, the family left the Garo Hills and most of the people to whom Stephen spoke Garo. English predominated, but his father noted that Garo was still his "first language" because it was the tongue he used when he talked in his sleep. However, he consciously avoided English, even when talking to his Garo-speaking father. On the plane returning to the United States, his father reported that Stephen (mis)identified a man as a Garo native, and "a torrent of Garo tumbled forth as if all the pent-up speech of those [last] weeks had been suddenly let loose. [However] I was never again able to persuade him to use more than a sentence or two [of Garo] at a time" (p. 70). In addition, very shortly he began not to comprehend Garo, or at least to pretend that he did not understand it. As I suggested in the previous section, children may reject a language that they do not identify with—apparently even if they use it in their sleep.

Studies of Successive Acquisition

Case Studies of Young English-as-Second-Language Learners

Hatch (1978b) includes a number of studies of young, temporary immigrants to the United States (the parents were visiting faculty or research associates) observed as they integrated into the school environments. These children arrived relatively fluent in their native language, which continued to be used in the home, but they needed English to interact with the other children and their teachers. The children who were studied approached this task with different degrees of enthusiasm and assertiveness: One child withdrew into a shell for three months, refusing to play with the other children, respond to the teachers' English, or even to stop the other children from destroying his sand castles and block constructions (Itoh & Hatch, 1978); another child immediately imitated unanalyzed phrases, such as "get out of here," and within one month produced his own constructions, such as "this kite" (Huang & Hatch, 1978).

There is little evidence across the case studies to support the idea that children naturally "soak up" a new language; as it is for adults, the task is daunting, and frequently frustrating (Hatch, 1978b). Feeling different and unable to communicate is intimidating, although for some children (and adults), it is also challenging. As we saw for first language acquisition, there are individual differences in second language learning style and rate of acquisition (Hatch, 1978b).

The studies also confirm patterns observed in simultaneous acquisition studies in the family: The most frequently heard constructions are learned first and forgotten last; language skills regress when they are not used; and children actively construct regularities, sometimes incorrectly and only sometimes influenced by the way their first language does things.

For example, Ravem (1978) studied two Norwegian-speaking siblings' (age 3¾ and 6½) acquisition of English. The children's utterances were analyzed against two competing hypotheses: one predicting interference from the first language on the second wherever the two differ (the *contrastive analysis* hypothesis), and the other predicting the same learning sequence in second language (L2) acquisition as is seen in acquisition of it as a first language (L1)—the L1 = L2 hypothesis. Ravem looked at the acquisition of negatives and questions because these are different in Norwegian and English. Some of the children's utterances reflected Norwegian structure ("Like you school?"). Some conformed to neither the contrastive analysis nor the L1 = L2 learning hypotheses: The children created constructions, as in "Does him eat my finger?" However, most of the utterances showed the same pattern as is found in L1 English acquisition: omission of the auxiliary (I not build the house) and use of a question word (What Jane give him?) or rising intonation in the earliest interrogative and negative utterances, then insertion of the auxiliary (What he's doing?) and finally inversion of the auxiliary (What did you do yesterday?).

Second Language Learning at Different Ages

It is interesting to note that the same acquisition order for English negatives and questions has been found in native Spanish speakers learning English whether in childhood, adolescence, or adulthood (Cancino, Rosansky, & Schumann, 1978). That learners of different ages proficient in different languages acquire the constructions roughly in the same manner as children learning English as L1 suggests that the acquisition pattern derives from the salience of a structure in English, the semantic importance of the question words or negative element, the more usual placement of the auxiliary, and so on. Although guidance of UG is not ruled out, studies of recovery of language following brain damage or neglect (see *Language in Atypical Populations*) indicate that the "bioprogram" ceases to assist after puberty, if not before. Thus UG should not underlie the similarity in acquisition patterns for a given language at different ages. Likewise, with similar acquisition orders regardless of what L1 is, it appears unlikely that the pattern results from influence of L1's structure.

Most investigators of L2 acquisition at any age, like Ravem, find striking similarities in acquisition order and errors to acquisition of that language as L1, suggesting that order is determined by frequency and regularity of occurrence particularly (Larsen-Freeman, 1978) and/or semantic and phonological salience of the structures of the language, more than influence of heuristics from the L2 learner's first language. Ervin-Tripp (1978) found, for example, that English-speaking children at a French school in Geneva, adept at non-SVO (subject-verb-object) structures in English, first tried SVO order in French (where it is SOV when the object is a pronoun). And, as their English regressed, they lost first the non-SVO constructions.

Several studies have looked at the order of acquisition of the 14 morphemes studied by Roger Brown (1973; see Chapter 9). Regardless of the language background and age of the subjects, as for English L1 learners, the progressive -ing form enters early, before the past tenses; the simple plural and past forms come in before the [-əd] or [-əz] forms, and the third person singular -s marker on present verbs enters latest (Bailey, Madden, & Krashen, 1978; Dulay & Bart, 1978). Teaching at a university where easily half the students have learned English as a second language, I note a "random" -s placement in essays: "s" and null suffixes are applied almost haphazardly to verbs, as though the students are aware that "s" *should* be there sometimes but haven't a clue as to when in this "silly" language. Note that -s *is* a rare occurrence: English only marks the third person singular verb, and then only in the present tense when the sentence is not in the subjunctive mood!

MacWhinney (1987) reviewed some more recent studies of second language acquisition to conclude that there are different patterns of L2 learning deriving from "cue competition" and depending on the learner's use of language in the community. In his cue competition model (discussed in the last chapter for monolingual child language acquisition), alternative indications of an intent—syntactic, morphological, and semantic—are available and compete for attention in understanding or producing the intent. The competition is won by the cue(s) with sufficient strength or weight, which, as in neural net conceptualizations, increases each time it has been successful.

MacWhinney describes four general patterns of learning the second language's system: (a) abandonment of L1 for L2, (b) merger of L1 and L2 to create a single system used for both (although perhaps totally appropriate for neither), (c) partial construction of separate systems for the two languages, and (d) transfer of L1 onto L2 (L1 = L2). Which emerges depends on social history, which affects the weight of cues from each language. If L1 is no longer used, its processing heuristics, cues, will lose strength (a). A bilingual community that engages in much code-switching will merge frequently experienced and therefore highly weighted cues from each system (b). If the two languages are used under different circumstances, separate systems strongly weighted to their eliciting situations will develop (c). And, finally, the L1 = L2 (d) strategy will prevail in older L2 learners who are willing to tolerate a (syntactic) accent to be able to communicate their complex topics and engage in adult discourse and so on. For this group, as long as they communicate successfully, there is little pressure to correct their speech, that is, to modify the weights, and the inappropriate transfer "fossilizes."

Operating Principles for L2 Learning

How does a language learner internalize the rules and lexicon of a second language or of two languages simultaneously? As we look at the acquisition pattern at different ages, it seems consistent with the general "stages" and principles that we saw in monolingual L1 acquisition. In both monolingual and bilingual environments, children say their first word at roughly the same time, on average, at just under 1 year. They acquire vocabulary in the two languages at the same rate; bilingual children are not slowed by hearing a second language. (Vihman, 1985, studied a simultaneously raised bilingual who had a total vocabulary of 500 words at just under 2 years, which, as she points out, is certainly not delayed!) They find the same sounds difficult or easy to produce, they overextend and overrestrict meanings in the same way, and they attempt simpler constructions before more complex ones (Grosjean, 1982).

As I discussed in the last chapter, words are acquired by principles of taxonomy, conventionality, exclusivity, and contrast. That is, the language learner expects that (a) words will name coherent, basic categories, not objects, features, or parts of an object; (b) for a particular concept, there will be a unique preferred form, the conventional word name; and (c) if two different forms are used, each refers to a different concept.

Now apply these assumptions to a child exposed to two languages from the start, like Hildegard or Stephen. Until the children recognize (a) that there are two systems, or (b) more likely in the one parent-one language situation, that different "conventions" apply with different parents, they will add forms naming different concepts from each language into one lexicon. Indeed, Clark (1993) finds that the youngest bilinguals begin by producing a label for a particular category from *only one* of their languages. And we have already seen that the early lexicon contains words from both languages, and that early word combinations employ both languages (see also Vihman, 1985). Once the child realizes that there are *two* sets of conventions, at about the age of 2, she or he applies contrast within each, not between them, and starts acquiring forms for the same concept in both languages. At around 2 years of age, children raised with two languages have, for more than half their vocabulary, *doublets,* a word in each language (Clark, 1993).

It is interesting that bilingually raised children begin to view the inputs as separate systems at the same time as they and monolingually raised children start to combine words; the combination, how words go together—emerging syntax— also suggests a realization of the input language(s) as a system(s) in that the child is learning to express *relations between words,* not objects. Two years may be a critical age in cognitive development, or it may constitute a critical amount of communication experience.

For a child acquiring a second language after the first, the principles are the same, but we can expect that the process of having learned and systematized one language will affect acquisition, even if specific constructions of that language do not. That is, a child or adult who has words for whole objects, attributes of those objects, and pieces of those objects in one language need not begin in L2 with the idea that words will name only basic categories but can assume that there are attribute names, part names, and so on. Children raised with two languages do ask for word equivalents (How would Mommy say . . . ?), as do L2 learners, indicating that they are anticipating that some things will work the same. And children in the successive situation may insert an L1 word, if they do not have an equivalent, into the L2 structure, thereby requesting its equivalent. Of course, the expectation that words will name the same categories can lead to an overgeneralization or underrestriction reflective of L1. But the child will also apply contrast and conventionality within the new language system, making some errors inconsistent with the contrastive analysis hypothesis.

Is L1 and Maturity Advantageous or Harmful to L2 Acquisition?

Ervin-Tripp (1978) finds that successive language learners have an advantage for L2 over L1 learners: They can use rules that they have already discovered (e.g., words can name attributes), they have better motor coordination and therefore better phonetic skills, they have better semantic skills and better memory. She argues also that languages are more alike than different, so what children have learned about language in general from L1 is more likely to assist than confound them in making hypotheses about L2. Thus, while one sees many of the same stages traversed in L2 acquisition as in L1, governed by the difficulty, frequency, and regularity of the structures of the language, the L2 learner traverses them faster.

For example, Ramirez and Politzer (1978) found that Spanish-speaking junior high and high school students in a two-year English immersion program had reached the level of mastery of third graders in immersion programs from kindergarten. Now this result can be considered in two ways: Uncharitably, we can say that the adolescents were performing at the level of 8-year-olds, or, more reasonably, we can argue that the adolescents learned in two years what a young child learns in four years!

Snow and Hoefnagel (1978) performed a long-term study of native English speakers living in Holland, acquiring Dutch at various ages from 3 years old to adulthood. At three- to four-month intervals, study participants were given a battery of tests of Dutch language skills: auditory discrimination, pronunciation, productive knowledge of morphology (a Dutch "wug" test—see Chapter 9), picture-naming vocabulary, repetition of increasingly complex sentences, and translation. There was no difference among the age groups in auditory discrimination but a decided advantage for the younger learners in pronunciation; none of the adults acquired a nativelike accent. However, all other results showed significantly faster acquisition as age increased, up through adolescence, with adults performing only slightly worse than the adolescents. The authors conclude that

> older learners seemed to have an advantage over younger learners in acquiring the rule-governed aspects of a second language—morphology and syntax. This advantage of age was, however, limited, as the teenagers did better than the adults, and reflected simply rate of acquisition, not an upper limit on ability, since age differences on these tests diminished and disappeared with longer residence in Holland. It also seemed to be possible to attain native levels of performance on these tests within a couple of years of exposure to the second language. (p. 342)

However, recent work by Newport (1990, 1994; Johnson & Newport, 1989) suggests that many older learners may *never* achieve nativelike competence in subtleties of morphology and syntax; they reach an asymptote short of native performance that younger learners surpass. Reviewing the literature on L2 acquisition, Johnson and Newport (1989) point out that studies (such as those just presented) that compare rate of learning of L2 acquirers of different ages focus on *early* stages of acquisition, one to four years, say, from the onset of language learning. Although these, as we reviewed, find that adults learn most aspects of language faster and/or better, even they concede that there is probably an advantage to early learning for pronunciation, that is, the accent (see Snow, 1987, for example). More important, Johnson and Newport stress that there is an advantage in syntax and morphology acquisition to learning early if one studies *ultimate linguistic attainment,* what people who have been using the language for many years do with it.

Johnson and Newport (1989; Newport, 1994) tested speakers of Asian languages who had arrived in the United States between ages 3 and 39, had not been immersed in English prior to arrival, and had lived here continuously since. Subjects were asked to judge the grammaticality of recorded English sentences constructed from a phonologically simple, high-frequency vocabulary. The sentences tested perception of correct or incorrect morphology (e.g., tense markers or determiners) or syntax (e.g., question formation or how a verb subcategorizes its arguments). They found that performance on this test correlated strongly with age of arrival: almost 100% correct, nativelike performance for those arriving before age 7, and a steady decline thereafter, to about 77% correct for those arriving after puberty. For the subjects who arrived in early childhood, performance was relatively consistent, while for late arrivals there was great variability, ranging from nearly 60% to nearly 100% correct. There was no age effect in acquisition of word order of the language or the progressive -ing form: Everyone performed like a native on these but not on the more subtle morphological and syntactic structures.

Johnson and Newport also surveyed their subjects on their attitude toward the English language and American culture, and on how important they felt it was to speak correctly. Both attitude and motivation correlated significantly with performance on the English judgment task. However, the age at which the subject had begun acquiring English still correlated significantly when the attitude and motivational factors were parceled out.

Johnson and Newport argue that their results strongly support a maturational component to language acquisition, such that different mechanisms operate before and after the age of 7. One way that maturation could affect language learning is the UG/critical period/bioprogram hypothesis, specifically, that there is a genetically specified cognitive ability for language learning that becomes inactive, or less active, during childhood. Johnson and Newport offer an intriguing alternative, expanded by Newport (1990), in which maturing cognitive skills paradoxically impede the nature of language learning: the "less is more" hypothesis.

Such skills include increased memory. While child learners must store salient *components* of language because they cannot retain a large chunk of language, the adult learner can and so does not need to reduce (analyze) language units to their smallest components to reproduce the whole complex. Children are more likely to see productive patterns because the right units and their productive parts get repeated. Adults looking at greater chunks of language can find more potential analyses, which work up to a point on the input language but result in more inconsistent and less componential forms. This renders the productive nature of morphology less useful to the late learner, who in the early stages communicates well without it but then never acquires the morphological nuances of a native speaker.

Newport (1990), in fact, notes that late learners' errors include "frozen" structures (stock phrases or frequent forms) and highly variable and inconsistently inflected constructions. This, she argues, suggests that they are unable to analyze the complex structures of the language consistently. In contrast, early learners' errors are reductions, forms stripped of their inflections or affixes, reflecting the beginnings of analysis into units, some of which will be productive in the language.

Late learners have also reached formal operations. This interferes with tacit learning, causing a conscious search for rules and systematicity.

The less-is-more hypothesis is, of course, consistent with Ervin-Tripp's (1978) and Snow and Hoefnagel's (1978) observations that late learners have an advantage over, and learn differently from, early learners. Unlike Ervin-Tripp and Snow and Hoefnagel, Newport concludes that in the long run, as a result, they may not learn the subtleties of the language as well.

Both the less-is-more and critical period hypotheses explain the differences in language learning abilities and ultimate attainment between early and late learners seen in the correlational data between performance and age of learning. Birdsong (1992) collected such data for French learners, all of whom had been in France for at least three years. Like Johnson and Newport, he found significant correlations of performance with age of arrival, but *all the subjects he tested had arrived after puberty!* He observes that while age at learning is important, its effect cannot be readily accounted for by *any* maturational hypothesis, given that both the critical period and memory/formal operation changes should be completed before puberty. Age at arrival encompasses not just maturation but number of years experience with L1 (and perhaps therefore the degree of dependence on contrastive analysis), and social variables, like the number of friends one has speaking each language and the motivation to be identified as a member of the L2 community.

I should also note that late learners receive input different from that received by early learners: A child talks to adults and to other child peers, while an older learner talks mostly to older peers. Child learners likely only have social contact with speakers of the new language, while adults will retain contact with speakers of their first language. Talking to adult rather than child speakers of the new language, the adult learner receives a wider range of topics, with less redundancy and less relation to the immediate environment. Thus the adult's first task is to determine the topic, which may not be evident from what is going on. The older learner needs to acquire content vocabulary rapidly to be able to guess at the topic and use top-down language processes. The child is freer to acquire productive chunks of language along with vocabulary (Hatch, 1978a).

Finally, young children conversing are able to guess less well than older ones at what the other speakers intend, and are less able to accommodate their language to what listeners can understand. The pragmatic situations that young learners find themselves in therefore demand different language-learning characteristics than those of older learners, who are more likely to be conversing with people who are working harder at trying to make the older learners understand and to understand them (Peck, 1978).

Our examination of L2 learning at different ages suggests that there are differences in acquisition heuristics and ultimate attainment, differences based on experience with L1, experience with language generally, age of acquisition, and the pragmatics of whom one talks to and how they talk. It is important to note that *it is possible for late learners to achieve native competence.* And as Birdsong (1992) observes, even one such counterexample should be enough to disprove a hypothesis of maturational changes or limitations. Recall that Johnson and Newport had late learners who achieved near 100% scores (the precipitous decline was only to 77% correct!), the nativelike accuracy they find consistently in their early learners. And Snow (1987) points out that there are adult learners who shed their accent and are taken to be natives by native speakers. Indeed, other investigators have found strong effects of acculturation, that is, desire to assimilate, in late learners successful at acquiring nativelike pronunciation (Hansen, 1995). It may be that maturation changes the way we learn, but it does not dictate the ultimate outcome.

The world has great authors who wrote in their second or third, late-acquired language, some of them Nobel laureates in literature, achieving (better than) native language competence. Joseph Brodsky emigrated to the United States from the Soviet Union at the age of 32, was poet laureate of the United States and Nobel laureate (Kenner, 1996). Joseph Conrad, a native Polish speaker, decided against Polish and between French and English (in favor of English, his third language) for his novels to increase his potential readership (Kenner, 1996). Samuel Beckett won the Nobel prize in literature for works published in English *and* in French, which he learned in school (Grosjean, 1982). While such writers were highly motivated and seriously interested in language, they were certainly able to overcome the putative maturational limitations to language learning.

Schumann (1978) stresses that language attainment depends on the degree to which the learner wishes to be perceived as a full member of the group speaking the language. (Note that it is more likely for a child than an adult to so desire because adults usually already have a social group and social identity that they are comfortable with, while children need to integrate into a peer group.) If the speakers see themselves as different and distant from the other speakers of the language, they will restrict themselves to learning what they need to get by, the essentials of communication, not the subtleties needed to be perceived as a member of the group. However, recall that Johnson and Newport did look at attitude and found that although it significantly correlated with attainment, age of acquisition still accounted for attainment over and above it. Apparently, both attitude and age of learning affect ultimate attainment, but a strong motivation may be able to prevail.

Summary and Conclusions

Examination of the acquisition of two languages or of a second language shows similarities with, and differences from, monolingual language acquisition. A child reared with two languages, like one reared with one, begins concept and vocabulary acquisition using the full range of input, acquiring the most frequent conventional forms (of either language) as names for the emerging concepts. This results in a combined early lexicon for bilingually reared children. At about the age of 2, children see language as a system and start combining words; bilingual children also realize that they are dealing with two systems, and begin to separate them, forming hypotheses about the nature of the two languages and their usage patterns, and requesting synonyms. Order of acquisition and retention of structures and vocabulary is determined, for all language learners, by the frequency and regularity of their use in the input, and (perhaps less so) by their semantic and phonological salience. For bilingually raised children, this means that they may forget the language they are not regularly using.

L2 learning is affected by knowledge of L1 and by other cognitive experiences. Children, as well as adults, may be intimidated by suddenly not being able to communicate and may only slowly affiliate with the new language community and speaking situation. L1 knowledge implies that language learners need not start from scratch; they can expect, for example, to find content and function elements, attribute, superordinate and subordinate names, as well as basic level names and so on. The similarities among languages, together with the older language learner's superior memory, attention, and cognitive skills, seem to speed L2 relative to L1 acquisition. Nevertheless, we see similar structures acquired in similar order in L2 learning as in learning that language as L1, regardless of the particular language background of the learner and regardless of the age of acquisition (Snow, 1987). This suggests that the order of acquisition of the language is determined by the perceptibility of patterns within the language, of the input environment.

There is some controversy as to the degree to which a person beginning language learning late, after 7 years of age or later, fully attains the fluency of a native. Although there are clearly exceptional people who do, late language learners as a group rarely attain nativelike pronunciation and they vary in attainment of morphological and syntactic subtleties. A strong motivation to learn the language and affiliate with the culture assists in the learner's acquiring nativelike skills but may not always be sufficient to compensate for the late start.

Late language learners may be beyond a critical period for language acquisition; UG may no longer be adaptable. Alternatively, they may be disadvantaged by their superior cognitive skills: Better memory precludes the need to analyze the input into small, manageable components; formal operations allows the testing of complex, explicit hypotheses as opposed to implicit language learning. Finally, they are in a different discourse situation, perhaps more pressured to learn content words to recognize more varying and abstract-from-immediate-context topics in conversation. They can also be less accurate because their audience typically is more accommodating.

As Snow (1987) concludes:

> The popularly accepted view . . . [is] that children learn second languages quickly, automatically, effortlessly, and to a level indistinguishable from that of native speakers, whereas adults even with the help of specially designed materials and trained teachers learn slowly, with great effort, and imperfectly. . . . Second language learning appears, upon more careful examination, to be slow, effortful, and often less than perfectly acquired for younger as well as older learners. In fact, speed of second language acquisition seems in general to be positively correlated with age. For most domains of acquisition studied, older learners acquire more in the same amount of time than younger learners. . . . Of course, it is not the case that age is the only factor of influence in speed of second language learning. It is well documented that such factors as amount of exposure, quality of language exposure, motivation to learn, desire to identify with the second language group, tolerance for the psychological stress associated with functioning in two cultural settings, and language aptitude play important roles as well. . . . . All [these] . . . factors would, in fact, work in favor of the younger learners, who nonetheless end up learning more slowly. (pp. 192-193)

COGNITIVE AND NEUROPSYCHOLOGICAL PROCESSES IN BILINGUALISM

We have examined the social conditions under which a person may come to know more than one language and, in more detail, the acquisition processes that are involved. We turn next to look at how knowing two (or more) languages affects language processing. To what extent are the systems independent, and to what extent and under which circumstances do they interact? Are representations of the languages in the brain shared or independent? And how does knowledge of more than one language affect cognitive processing generally—does it help or does it hurt?

Bilingual Language Processing

Speech Processing in Two Languages

With some notable exceptions perhaps resulting from a strong desire to assimilate into the new culture, people acquiring a second language after childhood rarely achieve nativelike pronunciation, as we have just seen. We also noted in the last chapter some compelling results of Werker and Tees (1984/1991), that between 6 months and 1 year, infants appear to lose the ability to discriminate speech sounds that are not in the language that they are hearing. Both these observations suggest that speech patterns acquired early may be relatively fixed, that a person bilingual from infancy might perceive and produce each language like a monolingual speaker

Box 10.2. Acquiring More Than One Language

Simultaneous Bilingual Acquisition Stages
— Simultaneous bilingual acquisition proceeds along roughly the same developmental path as monolingual acquisition.
— The first word comes in at under 1 year for both.
— The first combination comes in at about 2 years for both.
— Stage 1: Both languages provide vocabulary items for a single, integrated lexicon, with conventionality, contrast, and exclusivity applying to it.
— Stage 2: Around age 2, the child realizes that the two languages constitute two systems and starts testing hypotheses like "Daddies speak German" (as well as viable ones) and requesting vocabulary words in the other language. Many doublets, synonyms in the two languages, enter the lexicon.
— Stage 3: One language usually predominates and the other may be avoided or forgotten if it is not needed in certain or most social situations.
— The two languages are never completely equivalent: Some things may be easier to say or construct in one, some topics may arise more often in one, with the community of speakers the child has for that language. Bilinguals may code-switch to take advantage of these differences in experience.

Successive Acquisition
— There are individual differences in style: Some children are enthusiastic and actively try from the first to speak the language; others are intimidated and are quiet for a period, taking it in, before they try.
— Acquisition of structures depends on their frequency and regularity and, perhaps secondarily, on their semantic and phonological salience. Generally the order of acquisition and errors of L2 are similar to those made when acquiring it as L1, supporting a competition model where weights of associations increase with frequency of occurrence and success.
— Contrastive analysis—applying devices from the first language (sometimes incorrectly) to the second—accounts for some of the second language learner's errors and hypotheses, but not many.

Age
— Learning L2 in late childhood or adulthood is somewhat different from learning it in early childhood.
— At least initially, older learners progress through language learning faster than younger ones.
— Late learners may never attain the same degree of control over syntactic and morphological subtleties as early learners.
— Most older learners never achieve nativelike pronunciation.
— But some older learners do master the language.
— Attitude toward the culture and motivation to master the language affect ultimate attainment, but age of acquisition may have an effect nevertheless.

(continued)

Box 10.2 Continued

— *Less-is-more hypothesis:* The superior memory and formal operation skills of older learners may actually impede their language learning by allowing them to store and manipulate large language units, entertain more (wrong and conscious) hypotheses about rules, and preclude analysis into small, fundamental, productive units.
— Discourse processes are different in older learners.
   — They must struggle to determine the topic because there are a wider range of topics less connected to the immediate environment.
   — Older fluent conversants will work harder than younger ones to understand and make themselves understood, demanding less. This affects older learners more than younger because the older learner is rarely challenged by conversation with children.

---

of that language, but a late acquirer would have a single system, more fitting L1 than L2. Of course, distinctions could be reacquired, and, in fact, we observed in Chapter 8 vis-à-vis dialect shifts, that adults can learn to perceive distinctions that they do not produce, produce distinctions that they do not perceive, fail to learn either to produce or to perceive distinctions, or learn to do both (Labov, 1994). We turn now to consider studies on whether and how adult (French-English) bilinguals separate their phonologies.

Cutler, Mehler, Norris, and Segui (1992) investigated bilinguals who were considered by native monolingual speakers of each language to be fluent and unaccented. They were particularly interested in comparing segmentation strategies for the two languages because other research has shown that French and English have different rhythmic structures, which in turn are used differently in finding syllable and word boundaries. In particular, as you may recall from Chapter 7, Cutler has proposed that English is a language that alternates strong (stressed) and weak syllables (*stress-timed*), with listeners locating word boundaries before the strong syllable. In French, on the other hand, the rhythm or regularity is determined by all syllables (*syllable-timed*), not just the stressed syllable. Time intervals dictate syllable and word boundaries.

Research has shown that monolingual French speakers, naturally segmenting syllable by syllable, more easily detected an entire syllable in a string than a prominent component: They are faster at targeting "bal" than "ba" in *balcon*, but "ba" than "bal" in *balance*. In contrast, monolingual English speakers do not differ in detecting a part versus a whole syllable, because English speakers probably do not segment by syllable.

The questions are, What do bilingual English-French speakers do? Do they switch segmentation strategies as they listen to each language? Or do they segment using the language with which they more strongly affiliate? Does it matter which is their better language? Cutler et al. tested only subjects rated by outside observers as balanced bilinguals, the majority of whom in fact had been raised through the one parent-one language strategy. Each subject was forced to name a preferred language and on this basis divided into French- or English-preferred speakers. Across several experiments, the French-preferred subjects segmented French and English as the monolingual French speakers did (only one study showed French-dominant speakers processing English like English speakers), and the English-preferred subjects processed both languages as monolingual English subjects process English. Cutler et al. concluded that each person can use only one segmentation strategy and will use it for both, or all, languages learned. Indeed, foreign-language learners report their greatest pronunciation difficulty is getting the rhythm of L2.

Grosjean and Soares (1986) acoustically analyzed productions of bilingual speakers (not necessarily balanced) as they incorporated words from one language into a sentence in another, as they code-switched. The question is, "When in planning the bilingual utterance does the articulation program change to accommodate the new language?" Bilingual speakers were asked to pronounce a sentence containing a nonsense word, "I saw the dack," in English and its French translation, "J'ai vu le daque," along with sentences in which the French and English nonsense words, *dack* and *le daque,* occurred in the other language frame ("I saw le daque"). Spectrograms of the code-switched and monolingual versions showed features in between the two languages in the code-switched versions. For example, as you may recall from Chapters 6 and 7, a stop-consonant-initial word in English usually begins with a burst. This occurred for "I saw the *d*ack" but not "J'ai vu the dack." The beginnings and ends of the code-switched unit generally reflected *assimilation to the language of the carrier frame.* And sentences with code-switched words maintained the suprasegmental, rhythmic characteristics of the carrier language through the code-switched segment.

As a whole, these results suggest that French-English bilinguals use two independent phonologies for segment production and mesh them fluently during code-switching to produce a hybrid. Cutler et al.'s results suggest that some suprasegmental features, basic timing and its effect on segmentation, may be fixed by the first or preferred language and then applied to both languages. Of course, if the two languages employ the same timing (unlike French and English), there will be ready transfer of segmentation heuristics.

Grosjean and Soares also conducted some perceptual experiments with bilinguals. They created a French "r" to English "r" continuum, and asked French-English bilinguals to identify and discriminate continuum members. The language decision was sharply categorical; as you may recall from Chapter 7, this means discrimination is no better than identification. In this case, discrimination of the continuum members was no better than the listener's accuracy at determining which language was being spoken. Grosjean and Soares suggest that a quick all-or-none decision may be adaptive for people who are frequently listening to discourse incorporating both languages, and thus who must know quickly which lexicon to search.

The few studies of speech processing in bilingualism indicate that the bilingual must have two articulatory and perceptual codes, one for each language, and also the facility to interweave them rapidly and fluently. This is a necessity because, as I said at the beginning of the chapter, a bilingual often does not operate in monolingual mode but combines the languages in talking to other bilinguals or to select *le mot juste* (an expression English has borrowed from French, meaning "the precise word") while in a monolingual mode.

Grosjean (1982) frequently observes that a bilingual is *not* the sum of two monolinguals. We can see in speech processing that knowledge of the two languages gives rise to something more, the ability to interweave them fluently in perception and production, a cross-language context dependency.

One Semantic Memory or Two?

By far, the area of the bilingual's language processing most studied has been semantics, to determine the interconnections of the two lexicons. In fluent bilinguals one can imagine a single semantic system with words from both languages, or two separate systems linked to a common conceptual core. In less fluent bilinguals one may imagine that L1 is directly linked to the conceptual system, with L2 linked to it only through L1, requiring a translation through L1 from L2 to "thought." And, of course, given the Whorfian hypothesis and differences among languages in underlying conceptual metaphors (e.g., "love as a journey"—see Chapters 2 and 3 for review), there is also the possibility that often no common conceptual core may be possible.

The first three possibilities—a single system, two parallel systems, and one system as intermediary—have been historically labeled, respectively, compound, coordinate, and subordinate (Grosjean, 1982). This differentiation is not fully accurate because all bilinguals show some degree of independence and direct connections of their lexicons to a common conceptual core as well as some degree of overlap and interconnection among them. The interesting question is where one sees which.

Evidence for separate representations. When giving word associations, most bilinguals block associates by language; that is, they might give all French associates and then all English associates, suggesting that the two lexicons are divided and independent (Grosjean, 1982). Bilinguals are also likely to remember the language a word was presented in, although other "surface" features, such as typeface, are not remembered well (Kirsner, 1986). And there is no cross-language priming in *lexical* decision tasks in bilinguals (i.e., presenting a semantic associate such as *docteur* [doctor in French] does not speed recognition of *nurse* as a word). Finally, presenting letters that form a word in only one language does not slow the lexical decision "nonword" in the other language (e.g., *docteur* is a nonword in English; Scarborough, Gerard, & Cortese, 1984).

These results all suggest that the languages are separate for low-level lexical access: Words in one language seem to be connected to one another, apart from those of the other language. And, of course, such independent connections are necessary for the bilingual to converse fluently in monolingual mode.

Evidence for at least partly combined representations. In deeper semantic process-ing tasks, the two languages each appear to access a common conceptual repre-sentation as well as, at least for some items, separate representations. Access of the common representation may be differentially facile (quick and easy) in one lan-guage depending on the speaker's fluency or language-learning history, as sug-gested, albeit too strongly, by the compound-coordinate framework.

In the semantic differential task (discussed in Chapter 3), words of one language and their translation equivalents in the other are rated similarly by fluent bilinguals who have learned the two languages together and use them interchangeably. However, different semantic differential ratings are given by fluent bilinguals who have learned the languages in different settings, such as home and school (Grosjean, 1982).

In word-association tasks, translation equivalents produce equivalent associa-tions in the two languages about 25% of the time, but also very different associations 25% of the time—too many for either fully overlapping or fully independent connections (Grosjean, 1982). This implicates some common, but also some independent, representation.

The existence of both common and separate representations suggests that a bilingual's semantic memory and concept organization must differ from those of people monolingual in either language. Word associations suggest both common and independent representations, different from monolinguals, to the same words. Associating to *child, sickness,* and *doctor,* monolingual French speakers, respec-tively, provided *baby, hospital,* and *sickness,* while monolingual English speakers provided *mother, health,* and *nurse.* Bilinguals responded *baby, bed,* and *sickness* in French and *mother, bed,* and *sick* in English (Agar, 1991). Clearly, the bilinguals associated differently in the two languages but their experience of another language also clearly influenced each set of associations.

Differences in association patterns make sense when we consider that even if words in two different languages are good translations of each other, that means only that they *denote* reality similarly in the two languages; they are unlikely to carry the same connotations (Hummel, 1986) or the same syntagmatic relations in both languages. For example, in English, a common expression is *ice cream,* so *cream* might be a reasonable associate of *ice.* In French, both *ice* and *ice cream* are translated as *la glace,* and *cream* is translated as *crème,* but *glace* and *crème* do not frequently co-occur. So, different associations for this concept would naturally arise in the two languages, even with a common conceptual store.

A common conceptual store accessed perhaps somewhat differently by both languages for fluent bilinguals is implicated in a number of semantic processing studies, requiring *understanding* of words' meanings, unlike lexical decision, which simply requires, more shallowly, recognition that something is or is not a word. As you may recall, in a semantic decision task a category name is followed by an instance, and the subject must say whether it is an instance of the category, that is, must identify its hierarchical relations in semantic memory. Subjects are as fast at making such semantic decisions when the category name and instance are in different languages as when they are in the same language, suggesting that the hierarchical relations are represented in semantic memory in a common code.

Fluent bilinguals also report semantic satiation (the experience of loss of meaning after repeated presentation of a word) across languages (repeat the word in one language and its meaning fades from both). At the same time, nonexhaustive presentation of an item primes its translation equivalent (Grosjean, 1982; Kirsner, 1986), a cross-language repetition effect (see Chapter 3). Both effects presumably arise from activation of the common conceptual underpinning of the words, either slightly (priming) or to the exhaustion point (satiation).

Fluent bilinguals can also read as quickly passages with both languages mixed as passages in one language (Grosjean, 1982), perhaps facilitated by their natural intermingling of the languages in code-switching. This suggests that the read representations are processed in a common conceptual store and produce a common frame for the narrative.

Connections between the two languages are not direct but are mediated by the common store. Giving bilingual subjects a word in one language does not quickly facilitate its translation equivalent's retrieval in the other language (Hernandez, Bates, & Avila, 1996; Potter, So, Eckhardt, & Feldman, 1984). A quick facilitation would be expected with a direct connection. If the priming word is presented a long interval before the translation equivalent is needed, there is priming by translation (Hernandez et al., 1996). The long interval presumably allows traversing the indirect route between languages, through the common conceptual store. Moreover, translating between the two languages is no faster than picture-naming in either language (Potter et al., 1984). The picture is presumably a language-independent representation of the concept. We would expect translating to be faster if the route from the conceptual store (the picture representation) to one language was through the other language; in that case, translating would directly employ this shorter route. Rather than one language mediating between the other and a common conceptual store, the common store appears to mediate between the two languages.

Differential access to the common representation. Conclusions of equal access and a common conceptual core for both languages hold only after a certain point in L2 acquisition. For less fluent bilinguals there is an asymmetry: faster translation from L2 to L1 and greater priming in semantic categorization by L1 of L2 words than conversely. These asymmetries diminish as proficiency in L2 increases (Dufour & Kroll, 1995). While Dufour and Kroll (1995) found cross-language priming in semantic categorization, for the less fluent bilinguals they found more priming if both word and category name were in the same language, *whether it was L1 or L2.* The results underscore that there are strong within-language connections with both languages directly connected to a common conceptual store. However, for less fluent speakers, the connections of L2 to the common store are weaker and slower than those of L1.

Likewise, Sholl, Sankaranarayanan, and Kroll (1995) found asymmetries in less fluent bilinguals in the degree to which translation between the languages was facilitated by prior picture-naming. Picture-naming presumably first activates the concept (the picture) and, from it, the words. Picture-naming did facilitate translation from L1 to L2, especially when the naming was in L2. This supports a direct link that can be primed between the common conceptual representation and L1. Naming in either language did not facilitate translation from L2 to L1, which suggests that the common conceptual store is not as strongly linked to L2. As fluency increases, the associative weights between L2 words and the common conceptual store may increase to the strength of those of L1.

In the case of second language learners, what appear to develop first are strong links between the surface forms of the word and other surface forms in *that* second language, a within-language associative net. These intralanguage associations may dominate in lexical decision, word association, blocking, and so on—the effects we saw earlier that showed language independence. They appear to form early and underlie production of words in response to surface prompts, like letters, that is, when the subject is asked to list words beginning with "a." This is as fast and as productive in recent adult immigrants in both their native and their new language (Snodgrass & Tsivkin, 1995). Strong connections of L2 to the common conceptual core develop more slowly, resulting in the asymmetries I have described, and also asymmetries in production to deeper conceptual prompts, as when the subject is asked to name fruits: Here, adult immigrants are faster and produce more instances in their native language than in the new one (Snodgrass & Tsivkin, 1995).

In the early stages of second language learning, the adult learner, attending to word recognition and production, develops the strong weightings of surface features to the word names. Only in later stages of fluency, when there has been much greater exposure to the language in context, do the strong weights develop between L2 and the common conceptual store. And, of course, if L1 is abandoned, it is likely that the weights between it and the conceptual store will weaken over time.

Common Conceptual Store in Bilingual Metaphor Processing?

Our discussion of lexical and semantic effects in bilinguals suggests that there is separation of at least the surface features—word-name, pronunciation-type features—in the two languages, for all bilinguals. Associations among these surface features may be as strong in L2 as in L1 even in nonfluent bilinguals. The evidence suggests further that for at least the most fluent bilinguals, for many items there is a single conceptual store, accessed through relatively strong associations from the name features in both languages, although there is evidence in some cases as well for language-independent conceptual stores. For less fluent bilinguals, there still seems to be a single conceptual store, with associations to it stronger for L1 than L2. The evidence is that subjects do not access the conceptual base from L2 through L1. The conceptual store for the bilingual develops from knowledge of both languages and will not necessarily match the conceptual store of monolingual speakers.

If two languages have different worldviews and underlying conceptual metaphors, from a Whorfian perspective, their sharing a common conceptual store would be unlikely, and there may be interference in understanding one language from the other. In particular, bilinguals are often (but not always; Johnson & Rosano, 1993) reported to have trouble interpreting metaphors in their second language.

Radencich and Baldwin (1985) postulated three potential causes for difficulty in metaphor interpretation: less familiarity generally with the vocabulary of the second language, less familiarity with the nuances of the vocabulary, and less familiarity with the culture in general. The last two possibilities reflect the need in metaphor understanding to relate a salient aspect of the vehicle (the predicate term) to the topic (the subject term), as you may recall from Chapter 3. If a subject does not know all the attributes of a word, or if the word has different salient attributes in the two languages or cultures, there will be a mismatch. For example, given the sentence, "The teenager's face was like a coral reef," North American English speakers usually transfer *bumpy* to "face" to conclude that the teenager had acne. Caribbean Islanders transfer the features *happy, colorful, beautiful* from "coral reef" and come to a radically different interpretation. Clearly, any individual who knows what a coral reef is can understand both interpretations and appreciate their geography-specific origins, so cross-cultural communication is possible; equally clearly, the two natural interpretations are radically different.

Radencich and Baldwin surveyed subjects with respect to their language fluencies and then gave them tests of vocabulary, attribute knowledge (a checklist on, say, which features apply to "coral reef"), and a metaphor interpretation test. It is not surprising that more fluent students did better on all tests. Regardless, metaphor interpretation ability correlated most strongly with performance on the attribute checklist. Thus it is the nuance of meaning, which features are salient in a particular language, that accounts for the difficulties in interpretation.

Of course, most studies of bilingualism have looked at two languages or two cultures that are related: French and English Canadians, for example, share a "First World," northern hemisphere way of life, and the countries in which the two languages originated, France and England, also frequently intermingled. Recall the "love" metaphors in Chapters 2 and 3, dependent on the understanding that a relationship is like a journey and so can have ups and downs, be smooth sailing, and so on. Both French and English speakers will share the cultural predispositions, for example, for lifelong monogamous marriage, transportation in similar vehicles, and so on. Thus the underlying cognitive metaphor of marriage as a journey together and so on can prevail, and could organize a common conceptual store.

Could a common conceptual store underlie metaphor interpretation between radically different cultures and languages? Gibbs (1994), for example, describes the location system of a Mexican Indian group in which spatial positions are related to a metaphorical projection of the body. Roughly, to say, "The stone is under the table," they say, "The stone is at the table's belly." This conceptual system would challenge me to describe locations correctly, but, more relevantly, I think it would cause its natural users to misinterpret English metaphors using body parts as location metaphors. Their conception would work for the dead metaphor "foot of the mountain" but would cause confusion for metaphors such as "ruled by one's belly" or "led by one's nose." As I said in Chapters 2 and 3, we can translate "God" from language to language, but it takes on radically different connotations if the culture's conception of the Creator is a nurturing mother or disciplining father.

Indeed, projective tests of bilinguals in their different languages yield very different results. In a *projective* test the subject is shown an ambiguous stimulus, like an inkblot (the *Rorschach* test) or a photograph of, say, two people looking at each other meaningfully (the *Thematic Apperception Test,* or *TAT*). The subject must say what he or she sees (Rorshach) or elaborate a story describing the stimulus (TAT). Generally, people's interpretations depend on their own experiences; they "project" something of themselves into their response.

What is interesting is that a bilingual will project different things into a TAT description depending on the language of description (Agar, 1991; M. Engel, personal communication; Ervin, 1964; Grosjean, 1982). And some bilinguals report that when they change languages, they feel their attitudes shift, presenting slightly different political views in the two languages and sometimes even feeling different (more tense or aggressive in one) in them (Grosjean, 1982).

We also see evidence of separate conceptual processes in their two languages attested to by bilinguals who have conversed with each other only in English, who then switch to a mutual and fluent language with more rigorous rules of address, such as a polite and a familiar *you.* They experience embarrassment, not knowing which form to choose (Hunt & Agnoli, 1991). English does not require a thoughtful decision in this regard, and apparently it is not a necessary "common conceptual core." When they switch languages, they are confronted for the first time with this "need" and it is awkard, because the relationship is "old," and this point already should have been fixed.

Some have argued that bilinguals undergo a personality split in their two languages, with which Grosjean strongly disagrees. Rather, he says that using the different languages with different people in different settings about different topics necessarily means that different associations are aroused by each. I am suggesting, in addition, that the fact that different associations are aroused itself implicates a different set of thought patterns or conceptual relationships. Moreover, and more directly, the languages may have different underlying cognitive "metaphors," thereby necessitating different conceptual organizations. In the fluent bilingual, these result in different projections and different feelings, and in the less fluent bilingual, perhaps, in confusion when the appropriate cognitive metaphor does not exist or is inaccessible. Agar (1991) makes a similar suggestion, arguing the two languages of the bilingual differ in the organization of concepts and attributes at the frame/script level, a high level of cognitive organization.

Syntactic Processes and Code-Switching

In discussing the acquisition of two languages, we have seen that a child will pick up frequent regularities in either language and perhaps apply the "easier" "rule" to the other language. Learning a second language produces some syntactic "interference" by L1 when the learner creates structures based on the previous model (as Hunt & Agnoli, 1991, point out, this is a case of language experience affecting thought, or our ability to perceive patterns in the new language). And we have seen that even fluent bilinguals, who acquired L2 "late," may not fully master its syntactic and morphological subtleties.

Wulfreck, Juarez, Bates, and Kilborn (1986) describe a set of studies (see also MacWhinney, 1987) aimed at examining syntactic processes of multilinguals in their two languages by setting up a cue competition in comprehension. For example, a sentence like "The pencils is biting the dog" suggests by word order that "pencils" is the subject, but by subject-verb agreement and semantic likelihood, that "dog" is the subject. The question is, "Will the different cues be differentially weighed depending on the person's language experience?" If the person hearing the sentence primarily uses English, the word-order cue should override the others; if Spanish or Italian, with freer word order, the semantic and inflectional cues should prevail.

As a group, bilinguals interpreted such sentences more variably than monolinguals. The majority applied the dominant syntactic process of their first language to sentences in *both* languages. A significant proportion used an amalgamation— attending to the salient cues of each language—but, again, applied this single process to *both* languages, a common sentence processing "core." Bilinguals seem to create a single sentence processing heuristic, which, like segmentation in speech processing, may work less efficiently for one language.

How does the bilingual amalgamate the languages when both are being used at once, during code-switching? First, it must be reemphasized that, while to the monolingual, sentences mingling the two languages appear to reflect incomplete competence in either, in fact, code-switching is rule governed and requires more, not less, language competence (Grosjean, 1982). One has to understand both languages *and* how they may be interwoven without causing confusion. Relative to less fluent speakers, more fluent speakers of both languages code-switch more (Grosjean, 1982; Nishimura, 1986), and more often do it on only a single word. A point of contention is whether code-switching involves specific rules to generate an interlingual sentence, or derives from a single phrase structure (X-bar level; see Chapter 4) for each sentence into which language-specific surface structures are plugged at possible switch points (Grosjean, 1982).

In any event, most code-switches involve single words, usually a content word; in fact, 74% occur on nouns. Sentences are verified faster and seem more natural if code-switching occurs at constituent boundaries, again suggesting grammatical awareness, not incompetence, in code-switching (Grosjean, 1982).

Investigators (see Grosjean, 1982; Nishimura, 1986, for review and discussion) have proposed different sets of constraints on code-switching, which seem to apply much, but not all, of the time. The *asymmetry constraint* holds that for a given speaker, one language dominates and into it are inserted items from the other language; that is, switching takes place in only one direction. The *equivalence constraint* holds that word order immediately before and after a switch point must be the same in the two languages. So, one could say, "j'ai acheté an American car" ("I bought . . ."), switching the entire object NP, because the SVO word order holds in both languages. French postposes adjectives, so a code-switch of "j'ai acheté an American voiture [car]" or "j'ai acheté une voiture American" would be prohibited.

However, Nishimura (1986) found code-switching in Japanese-English bilinguals of nonequivalent constituents. He suggests that there is a "guest-host" relationship between the languages. The *host* is the basic language of each sentence, and its constituent order is maintained, into which constituents of the "*guest* language" are inserted, regardless of a constituent-order match in the two languages. Nishimura's production data did not support the asymmetry constraint either: Across the corpus, the host sentence alternated between Japanese and English.

There appears to be a constraint against switching a bound morpheme, an inflection. Generally, only open-class free morphemes are switched and then integrated phonologically with the affixes of the carrier language (the *free morpheme constraint*). And bilingual subjects make many errors and take a long time initiating sentences in which prepositions (or postpositions) constitute the switched item (Azuma & Meier, 1997). Finally in this regard, subject pronouns act as closed-class, "bound" items; the subject pronoun, informationally redundant and phonetically unstressed, is integrated with the predicate and spoken in the language of the predicate (Grosjean, 1982).

We should also note the pragmatics of code-switching. Bilinguals addressing people bilingual in the same languages are expected to code-switch, thereby declaring themselves to belong to the bilingual community. If they choose not to, they are perceived as trying to show off (if they are exclusively using the language with greater prestige) or as trying to distance themselves from the bilingual community in general, or the community of speakers of the eschewed language (Grosjean, 1982).

Summary

Our discussion of language processing in bilinguals makes it very clear that the bilingual has more, not fewer, linguistic processes to draw upon. It is also clear that to draw conclusions about the relationship between the processing of the two languages and the cognitive system in general, it is important to understand each individual's language-learning history.

With respect to speech processing, we have seen nativelike accents in both languages when they are acquired early, but also in late acquisition for some speakers, especially if there is considerable motivation to align with the new language community (and/or shed the old one). There is some evidence that speech timing principles are only acquired once, and then transferred, perhaps inefficiently, to the new language, but this shows up as a nonnative processing difference only with subtle tests. The fluent bilingual appears to know more, not less, than the monolingual about pronunciation; is able to perceive and produce both languages; and is able to fluently mesh the two, producing interlingual segments during code-switching.

Semantic processing tests support a common conceptual core underlying most words in both languages, even in a late-learned language that is not quite fluently accessed. The more poorly learned language usually has weaker ties to the conceptual core than the better learned language, while both have strong within-language connections to sound-alikes and so on. While a common conceptual core underlies much of both lexicons, enabling between-language translations and priming effects, there is also evidence for language-independent concepts: Word associations often differ in the two languages, speakers project different feelings and make different semantic differential ratings in the two languages, and word connotations and word attributes (and their relative salience) differ in the two languages.

Thus knowledge of two languages gives the bilingual different slants on reality, from the independent conceptual systems along with the general view provided by the shared store. The degree to which cores develop independently depends on fluency and how the two languages were learned: L2 processing may depend on L1 (subordinative) or interact less with it (coordinate) if the languages are learned separately than if they are learned together (compound).

Finally, syntactic processing studies show that while some bilinguals may be "stuck" with inappropriate L1 heuristics in processing L2, most do acquire substantial syntactic knowledge of both languages. Like monolinguals, bilinguals may use a single set of syntactic processes to understand sentences, but their processing approach is drawn from their experience with both languages. They are able to competently mesh their languages in fluent discourse with other bilinguals. This requires fluid interweaving of lexical, phonological, and syntactic information in both languages, as most code-switches are smooth transitions between the two languages and take place at syntactic boundaries appropriate to both languages. Both languages must be available to the language planner and perceiver, as frequent changes between languages are normal.

The Bilingual Brain

I have mentioned in earlier chapters that there is an asymmetry in the brain's processing of language such that the left half of the brain or left *hemisphere* is responsible for abstract, verbal processes, while the right hemisphere processes holistic images. This conclusion derives from studies of people's cognitive losses following brain damage as well as from studies of normal brain waves (evoked potentials) and techniques for measuring laterality, such as dichotic listening, discussed in earlier chapters. Similar research has been conducted on bilinguals' language processing to specify the degree to which (a) their brain organization may differ from monolinguals' and (b) their languages employ the same brain regions.

Lateralization of Function in Bilingualism

There has been a persistent suggestion that more often than in monolinguals, the right hemisphere is involved in bilingual language processing (e.g., Chary, 1986; Grosjean, 1982; Schneiderman, 1986; Vaid & Hall, 1991; Zatorre, 1989). These

Box 10.3. Bilingual Language Processes

— Most people learning a second language retain an accent, although this is not necessary. Older learners can learn new perceptions, new productions, both, or neither.

— A bilingual may have a single rhythmic heuristic, the first one learned, for segmenting syllables in both languages.

— In code-switching, bilinguals smoothly blend segments at language boundaries, producing intermediate segments.

— Studies of semantic processing in bilinguals suggest a common conceptual core accessed by words in both languages.

— One language may have stronger ties to that core, which results in faster primed productions.

— There is marginal evidence for three broad types of bilinguals:
   1. *Compound:* The two languages are acquired interchangeably.
   2. *Coordinate:* The two languages are acquired in separate settings and used differently.
   3. *Subordinate:* L2 is learned dependently on L1.
   Roughly, differences in dependence on a common conceptual core and in word association patterns, and asymmetries in priming or semantic satiation tasks in the two languages, are predictable from the L2 and L1 learning conditions.

— Links between words and surface features (like pronunciation) in L2 develop before they do to the conceptual core.

— L2 is not understood through L1, although L1 may be more strongly tied to the common conceptual core.

— Often there are problems in metaphor interpretation in the second language. Word denotations are usually clear, but the relative ranking of attributes or the general knowledge of characteristic features of the words is not fully fluent.

— Although a common conceptual core is implicated in the ability to translate, commonalities in word association, the ability to code-switch, cross-language priming studies, and so on, many bilinguals use their two languages differently, projecting different stories and feelings in them. Many languages and cultures are likely to have at least some unshared cognitive metaphors, so there may exist a within-language cognitive core as well as the common one.

— Bilinguals seem to use a common syntactic process, either influenced predominantly by their first language or consisting of an amalgamation of "cues" from both languages but applied in the same way to both languages.

— Code-switching in bilinguals most often, but not exclusively, occurs on single words—free morphemes with content.

— Code-switching increases with bilingual fluency.

— Code-switching most often, but not exclusively, occurs at constituent boundaries, with constituents that are structured similarly in the two languages.

— Most often there is a "host" language, in which the "guest" constituent is inserted and affixed to the host. The host is not necessarily L1.

— Code-switching is considered polite in a bilingual audience; reliance on only one language is seen as avoidance of the other and denial of that culture.

reports have surfaced either as case studies of language deficits in one or both languages after right-hemisphere damage, as evoked potential studies favoring the right hemisphere in late versus early language learners, or as smaller laterality effects in dichotic listening studies in bilinguals than in monolinguals.

Zatorre (1989), among others, however, finds these reports suspect. First, there is always a bias to publish the unusual result; "Man Bites Dog" is news, but "Dog Bites Man" is not. In the case of *aphasia* (brain damage resulting in language problems), language deficits from left-hemisphere damage are not newsworthy, leaving perhaps a biased overrepresentation in the literature of published cases of *crossed aphasia,* aphasia from right-hemisphere damage. Second, Zatorre cites his own observations of many patients undergoing a *Wada* test, anesthetization of one hemisphere by injection prior to surgery. These have shown no greater incidence of crossed aphasia in bilinguals than in monolinguals. Finally, Zatorre notes that the psychological tests, like dichotic listening, are good only for diagnosing group trends, not individual differences in laterality: These tests are insensitive and unreliable with individuals (but not groups), switching ear advantage for a given set of stimuli on successive tests (e.g., Blumstein, Goodglass, & Tartter, 1975).

Grosjean (1982) also criticized the right-hemisphere claims. He found that the evoked potential studies supporting them failed to take into account confounding factors like sex and handedness on lateralization. No difference in representation was found in studies that undertook the appropriate controls.

Finally, Vaid and Hall (1991) performed a meta-analysis of all laterality studies (dichotic listening, evoked potentials, and so on) of bilinguals. A *meta-analysis* looks across studies for consistent trends. They found *no* basis for greater right-hemisphere involvement relative to any aspect of second language acquisition: change in L1 processing after learning L2, degree of proficiency in L1 and L2, age of acquisition of L2, type of learning (formal versus informal) of the second language, and so on.

The conservative conclusion is that language in a multilingual is primarily represented in the left hemisphere, as is true for monolinguals. It is worth flagging the possibility of more right-hemisphere involvement in at least some multilinguals. Chary (1986), for example, studied 100 patients in India, all of whom were multilingual naturally, and found a predominance of aphasia following left-brain damage but a greater incidence of crossed aphasia than is found with monolinguals.

Representation of Languages in the Brain

Assuming that a multilingual's languages are left-lateralized, as is a monolingual's language, does not necessarily entail that the languages are represented in similar ways in the brain. Direct measures of brain activity and recovery of language skills after brain damage suggest (a) there are areas of common representation and areas of difference, and (b) there is vast individual difference among bilinguals, at least partially derived from language learning history.

Ojemann (1983) investigated the naming of simple objects by bilinguals during *electrical brain stimulation (EBS)*. In EBS, an electrical current is applied to specific regions of the brain's surface or *cortex,* while the subject (a person undergoing brain surgery for medical reasons) is awake and performing some cognitive task. The electrical stimulation neither hurts nor causes any permanent damage but, while on, disrupts performance of those tasks on which the region presumably works. Ojemann tested three bilinguals and found large areas of their cortexes responsive to both languages; that is, a single stimulation site inhibited performance in *both* languages. However, he also found some locations that affected naming in only one language. Most intriguingly, he found that the area, the amount of the brain, devoted to the *less* competent language was *larger* than that devoted to the more competent language in each of the subjects. He concluded that with increased competence there is a greater efficiency of storage. In turn, this suggests that the brain's representation of language flexibly restructures as fluency increases, even in adulthood.

Studies of the recovery of language function in the multilingual after brain damage also predominantly suggest a single representation for both languages. *Most commonly* the languages recover in parallel (Grosjean, 1982; Zatorre, 1989), although there are intriguing instances of other recovery patterns. In *successive restitution,* one language recovers before recovery begins in the other. The language that recovers first is the one most frequently used (the rule of *habit strength*), the one that is first learned (*primacy* rule; Grosjean, 1982), or the one that was most frequently used at the time of brain injury (Obler, Albert, & Lozowick, 1986). Of course, these are often one and the same. Grosjean cites a review by Albert and Obler, which reported half of successive recoveries to follow habit strength and the other half, primacy. More recently, Obler et al. concluded that for patients who suffer brain injury under the age of 65, the language that first recovers is more likely to be the language most recently used. Chary (1986) found a similar result in her 100 patients: The language that recovered first and/or best was the language the patient reported using routinely for thinking and calculating, not necessarily the mother tongue.

In addition to parallel and successive restitution, there are reports of *antagonistic* recovery patterns, with one language regressing as the other recovers. An intriguing case often cited, for example, is of a French-Arabic bilingual aphasic who on a daily basis alternated the language she could speak, never able to translate between them (Grosjean, 1982)! More common is *mixed* recovery, where the bilingual aphasic has some function in both languages, mixing them unacceptably.

While the cases of nonparallel recovery are intriguing, remember that parallel recovery is most common. Recovery from brain damage occurs initially when inflammation following the injury recedes; in effect, swollen brain tissue that was not functioning because of the swelling resumes its normal function. Secondarily, possibly following rehabilitative therapy, regions of the brain that did not perform that (language) function prior to brain damage may assume responsibility for it. In either case, what parallel recovery suggests is that the region performing the

---

Box 10.4. Brain and Languages

— There are occasional reports of greater right-hemisphere involvement in bilinguals, but these likely result from reporting bias and/or failure to control for confounding factors, such as handedness, in the subjects.

— Electrical brain stimulation studies show that the same brain regions underlie both languages most of the time, but there are regions that respond to only one language.

— Stimulation studies indicate that the language in which a person is more fluent takes up less brain "space," suggesting a consolidation, even in adulthood, with fluency.

— The most common language loss and recovery pattern after brain damage is of both languages in parallel, suggesting common brain storage and processes.

— Nonparallel damage or recovery is likely to result in the most practiced language best spared, but it may also preserve the most recently used language or the first language preferentially (when these are different).

---

language function in one language is also performing it in the other: a common "store" model.

It is also worth noting that the most common cases of nonparallel recovery are consistent with the findings that we have presented in non-brain-damaged multilingual processing: There is a greater weighting or salience for the language patterns of the language most practiced and/or for the language first learned or most recently used. We can conceptualize multiple language processes as a competition among heuristics or associations in each of the different languages for access to the common conceptual store, with increments to the strength of access determined by the amount and nature of the individual's experience. The greater the preinjury strength, the more likely the language is to recover. Indeed, Chary (1986) found the best prognosis for recovery in any language to be among those patients who were highly literate—and we can take high literacy as an indicator of intense language experience.

Summary

By and large, studies of neural processing in bilinguals show more commonalities than differences with monolinguals. For most, both (or all) languages are left-hemisphere-based, with the same regions of the brain responding to words or functions in both languages. There is a suggestion that the right hemisphere may be more implicated in bilingual language processing than in monolingual, which cannot be dismissed out of hand but is likely to reflect a reporting bias for the unusual. There are also regions of the brain that appear to respond to only one language, surrounding the larger, "bilingual" regions. Finally, aphasia usually strikes and shows similar recoveries in both languages together; when it does not, the language most used, most recently used, or earliest learned seems to be better spared, perhaps reflecting a more solid representation. It is interesting in this regard to consider the finding that less brain area seems to be needed for the more fluent language; the less that is needed, the less likely it is to be damaged.

Effects of Bilingualism on Cognition: Advantage or Disadvantage

I began this chapter revealing my incorrect, but common U.S. bias that second language learning is rare, and very difficult or impossible to accomplish, unless the learner is gifted and/or young. I hope that at this point in this chapter, the restatement of these preconceptions, which you may have shared, produces head-shaking disbelief: Second (and more) language learning is common, requires work, but is attainable by all, probably in similar ways whether young or old.

I have restated the preconceptions because we are about to consider another prejudice commonly held by monolinguals in the United States about bilinguals, that their knowing *more* somehow puts them at a *dis*advantage, at least compared with monolinguals processing their single, non-interfered-with native language. I am proud to say that this was a preconception that *I* never held: As an educator, it is clear to me (and in my best interest) that knowing more can only be an advantage and, as a psycholinguist, that knowing more about the way words and other units can work can only add to flexibility in language use and thought.

We will see in this section as we examine the evidence that, while *my* prejudice is closer to the truth, it is not an absolute truth: There are tests in which bilinguals are slower than monolinguals and tests in which bilinguals outperform monolinguals; there are cultural attitudes that advantage bilinguals and those that hurt them; there are ways of construing evidence to favor or disfavor bilinguals if the evidence collector has a particular agenda.

The earliest studies comparing monolingual and bilingual cognitive performance generally showed more favorable results for the monolinguals (Peal & Lambert, 1962; Reynolds, 1991) but also generally failed to equate the groups for socioeconomic status and degree of bilingualism (Peal & Lambert, 1962). Typically too, they only compared the two groups in *one* language. While this might seem reasonable, consider that, for example, a bilingual may know 50 different kinds of fruit, 25 each in "coordinated" languages (I am hypothesizing for the sake of argument that this person knows no fruit doublets, the names in both languages), while the comparison monolingual knows 40 fruit names in one language. Who knows more? Well, if we only test in their common language, the monolingual knows more (40 > 25), whereas, in fact, the bilingual has a greater fruit knowledge generally (50 > 40). So we need to frame the question carefully; a particular framing can lead to a preferred solution.

When Monolinguals Outperform Bilinguals

Magiste (1979) tested German immigrants living in Sweden, for one to seventeen years, on their speed at picture- and number-naming in both languages. As experience with Swedish increased, speed at naming items in Swedish improved (took less time) but never reached the speed of naming items in German. At the same time, as speed improved in Swedish, it slowed in German, so the performance of the bilinguals, in either language, was never as fast as when they were monolingual; indeed, compared with monolinguals, the bilinguals as a group were slower.

We may consider the "advantage" in speed of naming to result from knowing fewer words, those of only one language. There is a smaller lexicon to search, from which it is therefore faster to select the correct item. There is also an absence of competition: If the picture activates associations to both lexicons, which compete with one another for output, there is a stronger output message for the monolingual who has no such competition.

Indeed, Bialystok (1988) found better performance by monolinguals than non-fluent bilinguals, who were in turn better performers than fluent bilinguals, on the *Peabody Picture Vocabulary Test,* a standard naming test. And Ransdell and Fischler (1987) found a speed advantage for English monolinguals over English-dominant bilinguals in recognizing which English words had been previously presented and in performing English lexical decision tasks, but no difference in accuracy of performance or in total recall of the words presented. In all cases, a particular word seems to be more accessible when there are fewer competing words to search, but apart from this added facility, there is no performance deficit.

When Do Bilinguals Outperform Monolinguals?

Bilinguals have an advantage over monolinguals when higher levels of cognition are measured rather than speed of word access or implicit recognition in the following areas: in "cognitive flexibility," with respect to language itself, and in nonverbal skills (Peal & Lambert, 1962). The nonverbal advantages of bilinguals emerge on tests that require symbol manipulation (Reynolds, 1991).

In a now-classic study, Lambert and Tucker (1972) followed English Canadian kindergartners through fifth grade during immersion in the (minority) French language. It is important to note that English is the majority and dominant language in Canada and that, at the time the participating English families requested bilingual education, there was a movement, ultimately successful, to require French and make it the "official" language of Quebec. The families therefore wanted their children to have the advantage of French knowledge but were in no way rejecting their English or the dominance of English in the country.

The participating children *never* performed worse than the monolingual controls on any intelligence measure. By second grade, two years into the program, the bilingual children were outperforming the monolinguals on arithmetic and computation subtests. By third grade, the bilingual class was also outperforming the monolingual classes on a subtest of the Lorge-Thorndike intelligence test, requiring students to derive novel uses for everyday objects, presumably a flexibility measure.

Lambert's studies carefully compared only majority-language speakers, equated on socioeconomic status, either bilingual in the minority language or not. Without such controls the bilingual group may be at a disadvantage, with "minority" or "immigrant" status affecting performance. Conversely, selecting balanced bilinguals may bias conclusions in their favor because they may be more motivated or talented than typical language learners, and it is this, not the experience of the two languages, that accounts for the advantage (Reynolds, 1991). In Lambert's studies, typically the comparison groups were equated on academic performance and intelligence tests before the language teaching. Degree of change due to language learning per se can then be measured. Still, families who selected the program differed in attitude from those who did not, perhaps influencing the results.

Other studies have shown that bilingual children appear to have metalinguistic abilities earlier than, and beyond those of, monolingual children. With the appropriate controls established, bilinguals appear to more readily understand the arbitrariness of language, that any word name could be applied to a particular concept (e.g., the sun could as easily be called *moon;* see, for example, Mohanty & Babu, 1983).

Bialystok (1988) distinguished between high and low levels of language knowledge: Low levels suffice for everyday use but high levels allow writing, understanding of language differences, and awareness of language structure. Language measures designed to capture this difference include picture-naming (the Peabody Picture Vocabulary Test, mentioned earlier), conception of what a word is (finding words in a list, then spelling and defining them), arbitrariness of language (Could an object have another name?), correcting sentences with grammatical errors, and metalinguistic knowledge. Monolinguals and nonfluent bilinguals did better on the Peabody test, as we noted, but were outperformed by fluent bilinguals on *all other* language measures. More recently, Bialystok (1997) demonstrated that bilingual preschool children have better pre-reading skills than monolinguals: They rely less on pictures as backup in reading and are less likely to see word length as reflective of the referents' size.

Apart from differences in general cognitive ability, bilinguals and monolinguals have been compared for language proficiency. If social conditions are equated, bilinguals have been shown to have an advantage in *both* languages. Lambert (see, for example, Reynolds, 1991) distinguished between additive and subtractive bilingualism, based both on method of language acquisition and attitude toward the languages, cultures, and oneself. In *additive bilingualism,* L1 is viewed as prestigious, so L2 is added without threatening it as an additional skill. In *subtractive bilingualism,* the dominant L1 is overshadowed by the more prestigious L2, so L1 use ceases; it is partly forgotten; and the loss of skill in it is only partly replaced by increased skill in L2, which may be incompletely mastered.

Poorer performance on intelligence tests and language measures in subtractive bilingualism than in monolingualism has been documented from the earliest days of bilingualism research and may underlie the early findings showing better performance by monolinguals. Appropriate controls are difficult again because we cannot separate the effects of self-confidence, immigration, and subjugation status from the effect of "subtractive bilingualism," losing a language itself, on performance.

On the other hand, it is clear in the additive situation that not only are there improvements in general intelligence scores but also in language scores, even in L1, once L2 is introduced. Lambert and Tucker (1972), for example, found that children who were learning French, and taught to read in French only, transferred that knowledge, without training, to read English. More recently, Swain and Lapkin (1991) found that children in additive immersion programs, by their third year in the program, scored higher in L1 than children not in the program (although in the first two years, they scored somewhat more poorly). Note, though, that ultimate attainment in L2 in such immersion programs reflects syntactic irregularities (Eckman, Highland, Lee, Mileham, & Rutkowski Weber, 1995), as we discussed earlier with Newport's studies—I will return to this in considering ideal methods of second language instruction.

In subtractive bilingual situations, Swain and Lapkin have found that minority language students do better when they are literate in their first language. The advantage of literacy may stem from three causes: (a) L1 is more likely to be practiced and retained if the individual is able to read and write in it as well as speak it; (b) L1 and L2 are more likely to be used in similar situations, rather than L1 being reserved for informal use and L2 for educational settings; and (c) the individual is likely to have greater self-esteem and respect for L1, seeing it as an educated, literate language. Indeed, Swain and Lapkin found that literacy in L1 was predictive of skill at learning a *third* language: Immigrants to Canada from a non-English- or non-French-speaking country, who were literate in their first language, were better at acquiring both the majority language of English and, thereafter, the minority language of French.

Since Lambert's seminal work (Lambert & Tucker, 1972), many researchers have explained the advantage bilinguals have in higher language processing following predictions made by Vygotsky, who felt that the more conscious learning of a second language allowed the learner explicit comparisons with the first language and more opportunity "to see his language as one particular system among many" (Reynolds, 1991, p. 145). At the same time, as we have seen, the more conscious learning allows faster acquisition, but different kinds of processing, which perhaps results in less-than-native ultimate attainment. Nevertheless, apart from language-specific ultimate attainment, the experience of more than one language leaves the bilingual "with a mental flexibility, a superiority in concept formation, and a more diversified set of mental abilities. . . . There is no question about the fact that [the bilingual] is superior intellectually" (Peal & Lambert, 1962, p. 20).

Summary

For the most part, learning a second language fluently is an advantage to the learners: They have acquired a new language, appear to have some positive transfer in the original language, and have some added benefits in cognitive flexibility, measured both verbally and nonverbally. These conclusions depend on the language-learning environment. A bilingual who is confident in the language and culture of L1, and "adds" L2 while L1 is supported, is likely to experience the advantages, particularly if both languages are practiced both orally and in reading and writing. A learner who is pressured into acquiring L2 and feels that L1 knowledge is a handicap (often because L1 is seen as the language of a lower social class) may learn L2 while losing L1, not learn L2 perfectly, and not be advantaged cognitively.

Even under the best circumstances, though, the bilingual may be slower at shallow language tasks, such as lexical decision or picture-naming in either language than monolinguals, who have smaller lexicons to search and/or more strongly weighted connections between word names and the conceptual core. The bilingual, with broader connections from the conceptual core, may be slower than the monolingual (although just as accurate) but can use the breadth of knowledge for added cognitive flexibility. Lambert and Tucker (1972) quote Vygotsky quoting Goethe, "He who knows no foreign language does not truly know his own" (p. 210).

SECOND LANGUAGE TEACHING

Consider Chapter 9: Learning a first language takes four years of total immersion (with continued fine-tuned syntax acquisition over another five years and vocabulary acquisition over the life span). Yet most people would like to find some magic technique that allows them to acquire a second language in three or four hours per week of classes during a single year. I think we are all disappointed when we do not become fluent users of "high school French" (or whatever) although we do not practice it during the summer and, during the school year, limit its use to a single academic class, in that language itself.

It is also frustrating and disappointing how quickly all the mind-bending work fades from memory when the classes end. Here again, though, we must realistically appraise the likelihood of our retaining the language without practice, given, for example, Hildegard's or Steven's demonstrated forgetting of their mother tongues after three months of disuse. Language is complex, and fluency, speedy retrieval of words, and knowledge of how to combine them fade with disuse. So, to achieve fluency, one must work hard, and to maintain it, one must constantly practice.

Methods for teaching foreign language vary with respect to the degree of immersion, the degree to which they use L1 as a tool for teaching L2, and the degree to which they ground the practice pragmatically in topic, content, and communication the learners are invested in. Immersion programs, such as that described by Lambert and Tucker (1972), present academic content through the "foreign" language so that the learner must invest in the language to learn mathematics, history, and so on. These, as we discussed, are successful in providing fluency in L2 and have benefits in improved skill in L1, even when not specifically taught, and in general cognitive flexibility.

However, research has also shown that immersion programs alone do not necessarily result in full acquisition of the fine points of morphology and syntax (Eckman et al., 1995; Larsen-Freeman, 1995). And detailed observation of the children's behavior in immersion settings indicates why: Alone with their classmates, the children use L2 only when discussing classroom topics (the subject matter that had been presented in L2); with the L2 teachers, they are careful to speak L2 (again the pragmatic situation in which L2 is normally expected of them). They use L1 when talking with other children socially on nonacademic topics and when academic topics become too difficult (Parker, Heitzman, Fjerstad, Babbs, & Cohen, 1995). In other words the two languages are presented in different contexts and remain segregated to those contexts. Moreover, the children themselves report fear of naturally conversing in L2 on the playground, for example, when they could be overheard by native speakers who would be aware of their errors.

Other methods of second language teaching focus the students on the finer points of syntax. In *translation,* the students are provided with the rules of the new language, and exercises in translating between L1 and L2 are required of them. The *direct* method focuses less on reading and writing and more on oral drills in the foreign language; like the translation method, this does not create a situation in which the learner practices natural communication. (The Berlitz school and others like it emphasize oral skills, with students conversing with a fluent tutor in the language-to-be-acquired, a small-scale immersion.) Finally, the *audiolingual* method drills all language skills—speaking and listening before reading and writing—and contrasts the two languages overtly to teach the rules of the new language.

The advantage of structure-focused methods is that they may be more efficient, capitalizing on the adult learner's knowledge of L1, symbolic reasoning capacity, larger memory, and so on to teach specific ways of processing the new language in relation to the old. The disadvantage of such methods is that, instead of forcing the development of links between the new language and the common conceptual core, and between the new language and social situations, they foster links between L1 and L2 (which we have seen is not how bilinguals process L2), and fluency is in practiced drills, not with natural communication needs.

Based on the accumulated lore presented in this chapter, we can advocate, following Lambert and Tucker (1972),

> If A is the more prestigious language, then native speakers of A would start their schooling in language B, and after functional bilingualism is attained, continue their schooling in both languages. . . . Rather than teaching language A and B as

---

Box 10.5. Cognitive Consequences of Multilingualism

— *Additive bilingualism:* When the second language is acquired without loss or subjugation of the first. Usually occurs when the dominant language group learns a minority language.

— *Subtractive bilingualism:* When the second, higher prestige language is learned to replace the first language, usually seen as inferior baggage to be carried.

— Additive bilinguals are more cognitively flexible and better at symbol manipulation and arithmetic than are monolinguals.

— In additive situations, L2 often positively transfers to L1, with bilinguals scoring better in both languages than monolinguals.

— At first bilinguals may trail monolinguals in, say, vocabulary acquisition. They catch up and overtake them in other areas.

— Subtractive bilingualism hurts: L1 is lost, L2 is never mastered, and there are cognitive disadvantages. This may be from low self-esteem; greater separation of the languages' topic and settings, which precludes their comparison; and/or poorer teaching.

— Immersion programs maintaining L1, and teaching L2 as a medium for conveying content, are most likely to be successful. This is the right pragmatic context to motivate the learner to master the language and to draw comparisons between the two languages.

— Immersion programs provide communicative fluency but alone usually do not result in nativelike mastery of morphology and syntax. For this, specific teaching and drills targeted to the student's mastery level and errors are needed to augment immersion.

---

languages, emphasis would be shifted from a linguistic focus to one where languages are thought of primarily as vehicles for developing competence in academic subject matters, including various forms of creative work. (p. 216)

I also suggest the recommendations of Hatch (1978a), that foreign-language teaching take advantage of the topics of interest to the foreign-language learner and build lessons around discourse on those topics. Clearly, topics would differ for the different-aged learners. As in much of education, student-centered learning is likely to be preferable to a teacher-designed curriculum: If the class selects a topic or vocabulary on a need-to-know basis and the teacher, presumably fluent in the language, provides vocabulary and content material around those topics, the motivation will be greater on the part of the students, as will the likelihood that the new material will be used outside the classroom.

And we may follow suggestions from other researchers who have attempted to apply to the language-teaching situation knowledge of linguistics and psycholinguistics. Foreign-language learners in immersion settings do communicate, relating language to meaning and function. To correct the fine points of morphology and syntax, teachers must recognize the errors and drill them specifically, with a flood of either positive evidence (Bardovi-Harlig, 1995) or negative evidence (White, 1995).

Positive evidence constitutes examples of the structure as a native speaker would correctly use it. Bardovi-Harlig speculates that it is most beneficial if the learner has already mastered the simpler and more common structures underlying the targeted structure and has also established the semantic and pragmatic environments where needed. Then, as in early L1 acquisition, the language learner is primed to take advantage of the pattern presented in the positive evidence.

Negative evidence specifies which structures are wrong; generative linguists believe it is absent in L1 acquisition. Following the UG framework of Chomsky's principles and parameters theory (see Chapter 4), White suggests that negative evidence may be necessary in parameter *re*setting for L2 acquisition, even if unnecessary in the original parameter setting in L1.

Finally, it is important to stress that a language teacher be fluent in the language of instruction and respectful of the native languages and cultures of the learners. An instructor who uses, unaware, a language different from that of the students can neither instruct in the language nor communicate content material. In the education of linguistic minorities (e.g., American Indians or the deaf), especially in the past, too often the children's natural communication system was actively suppressed in the school and the children punished if caught using it. These are instances par excellence of subtractive bilingualism, which, as I have emphasized, are conducive neither to second language learning, the explicit goal, nor to general cognitive development.

SUMMARY AND CONCLUSIONS

In this chapter we looked at both natural and contrived situations in which people learn more than one language. We have seen that knowing more than one language is more common than is the monolingual state prevalent in the United States. When that language knowledge is respected, the individual benefits with respect to performance in both languages and in general cognitive tasks. Where one language is suppressed or submerged, learning of the second language may be less complete, and there is no overall cognitive benefit; in fact, there is likely a loss.

As Grosjean (1982) points out repeatedly, a bilingual is not the sum of two monolinguals. Language processes are similar in both bilinguals and monolinguals, with common areas of the brain devoted to both languages, perhaps representing their fusion. The bilingual expresses different attitudes in each language like, but not identical to, those of monolinguals in each language.

At the same time, the bilingual has brain regions devoted exclusively to each language. Bilinguals adeptly switch between their languages, reflecting mastery of each but also of a new set of processes needed to effect such fluent code-switching. Bilinguals are also aware of their different personas, in both languages, and so, unlike monolinguals, have a broader, personal view of the possibilities of ethnic outlook. Aware of the different ways their languages code the world and the arbitrary nature of each, bilinguals develop greater cognitive and linguistic flexibility than monolinguals. Finally, in amalgamating a unified conceptual core and a single language processing scheme perhaps from features and concepts of each language, the bilingual may process each language fluently but not in the same way as does a monolingual.

This chapter also examined how languages are acquired and lost, during childhood and by adults. We see more similarities in second language learning and first language learning than we do differences, whether the two languages are acquired simultaneously or successively. Whether they are mastering one or two languages, children acquire the concept of naming, vocabulary, and the concept of semantics as a system at about the same ages. If they are mastering two languages, at the age when they begin to recognize language as a system, joining words, they also recognize that they are dealing with two systems, requesting synonyms in their other language and actively trying to discern a pattern of use of each of the languages.

Language acquisition and language loss follow principles of frequency (habit strength), regularity, and perceptual and semantic salience, so that generally the structures that appear earliest and easiest in acquisition are the same whether the language is L1 or L2. On the other hand, even with young children, if a language is not practiced—that is, has low habit strength—it is forgotten, perhaps actively if the speaker also has reason to detach from that linguistic community.

And, in loss of language following brain damage, we also see evidence that frequency of use, and practice with language generally, most often predicts recovery: Usually either the languages recover together in the same order, reflective of shared brain areas and processes, or the most recently used and most frequently used language recovers first. In either case, the language(s) of the literate, the language well practiced in another modality, recover(s) better.

Finally, we discussed the effect of age of learning on second language acquisition. There is considerable evidence that young children struggle, experience frustration, test hypotheses, and so on—that is, do not simply soak up language— and that their overall language learning rate is slower than that of adults, perhaps counter to intuition and to a bioprogram/UG/critical period hypothesis. And there is no doubt that adult learners attain considerable fluency, in every feature of language except perhaps accent. On occasion, the adult learner may even acquire exceptional, Nobel prize-winning, language skills. Nevertheless, ultimate attainment of the "little" idiosyncrasies of a language, the niceties of its morphology and syntax, seems to be poorer the later a language is learned, even beyond puberty. This perhaps reflects differing communities in language use for older and younger learners.

Our discussion of bilingualism intersected repeatedly with political and social attitudes toward either L1 or L2, or toward multilingualism in general. As Lambert (1991) observed, in the United States, a fiercely and protectively monolingual society, most of the research into bilingualism has been inspired by the desire to prove that it is a disadvantageous state of affairs, and, indeed, so the early studies found. This justifies inertia on the part of the dominant monolingual English speaking majority: "I" do not have to invest in the effort to learn a second language and can feel smug in not having achieved fluency in or having forgotten the language that was half-heartedly taught in school. It has also justified linguistic subjugation of linguistic minorities. Whether they are immigrant, deaf, or native American, the onus is on *them* to submerge their language and culture and assimilate to English. The subjugation has adverse cognitive and language-learning consequences but has produced an impressive rate of Anglicization—whether that is desirable is moot.

The chapter also broadly presented alternative ways of teaching languages, attempting to use research from this and earlier chapters to suggest optimal ways of achieving second language learning along with its cognitive advantages. In the next chapter we will look at reading and writing, other arenas of natural language use usually acquired through mediation by a teacher. We will again consider how our understanding of language processes could produce better teaching techniques.

REFERENCES

Agar, M. (1991). The biculture in bilingual. *Language in Society, 20,* 167-181.

Azuma, S., & Meier, R. P. (1997). Open-class and closed-class: Sentence imitation experiments on intrasentential code-switching. *Applied Psycholinguistics.*

Bailey, N., Madden, C., & Krashen, S. D. (1978). Is there a "natural sequence" in adult second language learning? In E. Hatch (Ed.), *Second language acquisition: A book of readings* (pp. 362-370). Rowley, MA: Newbury House.

Bardovi-Harlig, K. (1995). The interaction of pedagogy and natural sequences in the acquisition of tense and aspect. In F. R. Eckman, D. Highland, P. W. Lee, J. Mileham, & R. Rutkowski Weber (Eds.), *Second language acquisition theory and pedagogy* (pp. 151-168). Mahwah, NJ: Lawrence Erlbaum.

Bialystok, E. (1988). Levels of bilingualism and levels of linguistic awareness. *Developmental Psychology, 24,* 560-567.

Bialystok, E. (1997). Effects of bilingualism and biliteracy on children's emerging concepts of print. *Developmental Psychology, 33,* 429-440.

Birdsong, D. (1992). Ultimate attainment in second language acquisition. *Language, 68,* 706-755.

Blumstein, S., Goodglass, H., & Tartter, V. C. (1975). The reliability of the right-ear advantage in dichotic listening. *Brain and Language, 2,* 226-236.

Brown, R. (1973). *A first language.* Cambridge, MA: Harvard University Press.

Burling, R. (1978). Language development of a Garo and English-speaking child. In E. Hatch (Ed.), *Second language acquisition: A book of readings* (pp. 54-75). Rowley, MA: Newbury House.

Cancino, H., Rosansky, E. J., & Schumann, J. H. (1978). The acquisition of English negatives and interrogatives by native Spanish speakers. In E. Hatch (Ed.), *Second language acquisition: A book of readings* (pp. 207-230). Rowley, MA: Newbury House.

Celce-Murcia, M. (1978). The simultaneous acquisition of English and French in a two-year old child. In E. Hatch (Ed.), *Second language acquisition: A book of readings* (pp. 38-53). Rowley, MA: Newbury House.

Chary, P. (1986). Aphasia in a multilingual society: A preliminary study. In J. Vaid (Ed.), *Language processing in bilinguals: Psycholinguistic and neuropsychological perspectives* (pp. 183-197). Hillsdale, NJ: Lawrence Erlbaum.

Clark, E. V. (1993). *The lexicon in acquisition.* New York: Cambridge University Press.

Clement, R., & Bourhis, R. Y. (1996). Studies and research: Bilingualism and intergroup communication. *International Journal of Psycholinguistics, 12,* 1-21.

Cutler, A., Mehler, J., Norris, D., & Segui, J. (1992). The monolingual nature of speech segmentation by bilinguals. *Cognitive Psychology, 24,* 381-410.

Dufour, R., & Kroll, J. F. (1995). Matching words to concepts in two languages: A test of the concept mediation model of bilingual representation. *Memory and Cognition, 23,* 166-180.

Dulay, H. C., & Bart, M. K. (1978). Natural sequences in child language acquisition. In E. Hatch (Ed.), *Second language acquisition: A book of readings* (pp. 347-361). Rowley, MA: Newbury House.

Eckman, F. R., Highland, D., Lee, P. W., Mileham, J., & Rutkowski Weber, R. (Eds.). (1995). *Second language acquisition theory and pedagogy.* Mahwah, NJ: Lawrence Erlbaum.

Ervin, S. M. (1964). Language and TAT content in bilinguals. *Journal of Abnormal and Social Psychology, 68,* 500-507.

Ervin-Tripp, S. M. (1978). Is second language learning like the first? In E. Hatch (Ed.), *Second language acquisition: A book of readings* (pp. 190-206). Rowley, MA: Newbury House.

Gibbs, R. W., Jr. (1994). *The poetics of mind: Figurative thought, language, and understanding.* New York: Cambridge University Press.

Grosjean, F. (1982). *Life with two languages: An introduction to bilingualism.* Cambridge, MA: Harvard University Press.

Grosjean, F., & Soares, C. (1986). Processing mixed language: Some preliminary findings. In J. Vaid (Ed.), *Language processing in bilinguals: Psycholinguistic and neuropsychological perspectives* (pp. 145-179). Hillsdale, NJ: Lawrence Erlbaum.

Hakuta, K. (1986). *Mirror of language: The debate on bilingualism.* New York: Basic Books.

Hansen, D. (1995). A study of the effect of the acculturation model on second language acquisition. In F. R. Eckman, D. Highland, P. W. Lee, J. Mileman, & R. R. Weber (Eds.), *Second language acquisition theory and pedagogy* (pp. 305-316). Hillsdale, NJ: Lawrence Erlbaum.

Hatch, E. (1978a). Discourse analysis and second language acquisition. In E. Hatch (Ed.), *Second language acquisition: A book of readings* (pp. 401-435). Rowley, MA: Newbury House.

Hatch, E. (Ed.). (1978b). *Second language acquisition: A book of readings.* Rowley, MA: Newbury House.

Hernandez, A. E., Bates, E. A., & Avila, L. X. (1996). Processing across the language boundary: A cross-modal priming study of Spanish-English bilinguals. *Journal of Experimental Psychology: Learning, Memory, and Cognition, 22,* 846-863.

Huang, J., & Hatch, E. (1978). A Chinese child's acquisition of English. In E. Hatch (Ed.), *Second language acquisition: A book of readings* (pp. 118-131). Rowley, MA: Newbury House.

Hummel, K. M. (1986). Memory for bilingual prose. In J. Vaid (Ed.), *Language processing in bilinguals: Psycholinguistic and neuropsychological perspectives* (pp. 47-64). Hillsdale, NJ: Lawrence Erlbaum.

Hunt, E., & Agnoli, F. (1991). The Whorfian hypothesis: A cognitive psychology perspective. *Psychological Review, 98,* 377-389.

Itoh, H., & Hatch, E. (1978). Second language acquisition: A case study. In E. Hatch (Ed.), *Second language acquisition: A book of readings* (pp. 76-88). Rowley, MA: Newbury House.

Johnson, J. S., & Newport, E. L. (1989). Critical period effects in second language learning: The influence of maturational state on the acquisition of English as a second language. *Cognitive Psychology, 21,* 60-99.

Johnson, J., & Rosano, T. (1993). Relation of cognitive style to metaphor interpretation and second language proficiency. *Applied Psycholinguistics, 14,* 159-175.

Kenner, H. (1996, April 14). On grief and reason [Review of *Essays* by Joseph Brodsky]. *New York Times Book Review,* p. 14.

Kirsner, K. (1986). Lexical function: Is a bilingual account necessary? In J. Vaid (Ed.), *Language processing in bilinguals: Psycholinguistic and neuropsychological perspectives* (pp. 21-45). Hillsdale, NJ: Lawrence Erlbaum.

Labov, W. (1994). *Principles of linguistic change: Vol. 1. Internal factors.* Cambridge, MA: Blackwell.

Lambert, W. E. (1955). Measurement of the linguistic dominance of bilinguals. *Journal of Abnormal and Social Psychology, 51,* 197-200.

Lambert, W. E. (1991). "And then add your two-cents worth." In A. G. Reynolds (Ed.), *Bilingualism, multiculturalism, and second language learning: The McGill Conference in Honour of Wallace E. Lambert* (pp. 217-249). Hillsdale, NJ: Lawrence Erlbaum.

Lambert, W. E., & Tucker, G. R. (1972). *Bilingual education of children: The St. Lambert Experiment.* Rowley, MA: Newbury House.

Larsen-Freeman, D. E. (1978). An explanation of the morpheme accuracy order of learners of English as a second language. In E. Hatch (Ed.), *Second language acquisition: A book of readings* (pp. 371-379). Rowley, MA: Newbury House.

Larsen-Freeman, D. (1995). On the teaching and learning of grammar: Challenging the myths. In F. R. Eckman, D. Highland, P. W. Lee, J. Mileham, & R. Rutkowski Weber (Eds.), *Second language acquisition theory and pedagogy* (pp. 131-150). Mahwah, NJ: Lawrence Erlbaum.

A law to learn 'em a thing or two about the American language. (1996, July 28). *New York Times,* "The News of the Week in Review," p. 14.

Leopold, W. F. (1978). A child's learning of two languages. In E. Hatch (Ed.), *Second language acquisition: A book of readings* (pp. 24-32). Rowley, MA: Newbury House.

MacWhinney, B. (1987). Applying the competition model to bilingualism. *Applied Psycholinguistics, 8,* 315-327.

Magiste, E. (1979). The competing language systems of the multilingual: A developmental study of decoding and encoding processes. *Journal of Verbal Learning and Verbal Behavior, 18,* 79-89.

Mohanty, A. K., & Babu, N. (1983). Bilingualism and metalinguistic ability among Kond tribals in Orissa, India. *Journal of Social Psychology, 121,* 15-22.

Navarro, M. (1996, August 31). Immigrant parents dismayed by English's pull on children. *New York Times,* pp. 1, 7.

Newport, E. L. (1990). Maturational constraints on language learning. *Cognitive Science, 14,* 11-28.

Newport, E. L. (1994). Maturational constraints in second language learning. In P. Bloom (Ed.), *Language acquisition: Core readings* (pp. 543-560). Cambridge: Bradford Books of MIT Press.

Nishimura, W. (1986). Intrasentential code-switching: The case of language assignment. In J. Vaid (Ed.), *Language processing in bilinguals: Psycholinguistic and neuropsychological perspectives* (pp. 123-143). Hillsdale, NJ: Lawrence Erlbaum.

Obler, L., Albert, M., & Lozowick, S. (1986). The aging bilingual. In J. Vaid (Ed.), *Language processing in bilinguals: Psycholinguistic and neuropsychological perspectives* (pp. 221-231). Hillsdale, NJ: Lawrence Erlbaum.

Ojemann, G. A. (1983). Brain organization for language from the perspective of electrical stimulation mapping. *Behavioral and Brain Sciences, 6,* 189-230.

Parker, J. E., Heitzman, S. M., Fjerstad, A. M., Babbs, L. M., & Cohen, A. D. (1995). Exploring the role of foreign language in immersion education. In F. R. Eckman, D. Highland, P. W. Lee, J. Mileham, & R. Rutkowski Weber (Eds.), *Second language acquisition theory and pedagogy* (pp. 235-253). Mahwah, NJ: Lawrence Erlbaum.

Peal, E., & Lambert, W. E. (1962). The relation of bilingualism to intelligence. *Psychological Monographs: General and Applied, 76,* 1-23.

Peck, S. (1978). Child-child discourse in second language acquisition. In E. Hatch (Ed.), *Second language acquisition: A book of readings* (pp. 383-400). Rowley, MA: Newbury House.

Potter, M. C., So, K-F., Von Eckhardt, B., & Feldman, L. B. (1984). Lexical and conceptual representation in beginning and proficient bilinguals. *Journal of Verbal Learning and Verbal Behavior, 23,* 23-38.

Radencich, M. C., & Baldwin, R. S. (1985). Cultural and linguistic factors in metaphor interpretation. *Bilingual Review, 12,* 43-53.

Ramirez, A. G., & Politzer, R. L. (1978). Comprehension and production in English as a second language by elementary school students and adolescents. In E. Hatch (Ed.), *Second language acquisition: A book of readings* (pp. 313-332). Rowley, MA: Newbury House.

Ransdell, S. E., & Fischler, I. (1987). Memory in a bilingual mode: When are bilinguals at a disadvantage? *Journal of Memory and Language, 26,* 392-405.

Ravem, R. (1978). Two Norwegian children's acquisition of English syntax. In E. Hatch (Ed.), *Second language acquisition: A book of readings* (pp. 148-154). Rowley, MA: Newbury House.

Reynolds, A. G. (1991). *Bilingualism, multiculturalism, and second language learning: The McGill Conference in Honour of Wallace E. Lambert.* Hillsdale, NJ: Lawrence Erlbaum.

Scarborough, D. L., Gerard, L., & Cortese, C. (1984). Independence of lexical access in bilingual word recognition. *Journal of Verbal Learning and Verbal Behavior, 23,* 84-89.

Schneiderman, E. I. (1986). Leaning to the right: Some thoughts on hemisphere involvement in language acquisition. In J. Vaid (Ed.), *Language processing in bilinguals: Psycholinguistic and neuropsychological perspectives* (pp. 233-251). Hillsdale, NJ: Lawrence Erlbaum.

Schumann, J. H. (1978). Second language acquisition: The pidginization hypothesis. In E. Hatch (Ed.), *Second language acquisition: A book of readings* (pp. 256-271). Rowley, MA: Newbury House.

Sholl, A., Sankaranarayanan, A., & Kroll, J. F. (1995). Transfer between picture naming and translation: A test of asymmetries of bilingual memory. *Psychological Science, 6,* 45-49.

Snodgrass, J. G., & Tsivkin, S. (1995). Organization of the bilingual lexicon: Categorical versus alphabetic cuing in Russian-English bilinguals. *Journal of Psycholinguistic Research, 24,* 145-163.

Snow, C. (1987). Relevance of the notion of critical period to language acquisition. In M. H. Bornstein (Ed.), *Sensitive periods in development: Interdisciplinary perspectives* (pp. 183-209). Hillsdale, NJ: Lawrence Erlbaum.

Snow, C. E., & Hoefnagel, M. (1978). Age differences in second language acquisition. In E. Hatch (Ed.), *Second language acquisition: A book of readings* (pp. 333-344). Rowley, MA: Newbury House.

Swain, M., & Lapkin, S. (1991). Additive bilingualism and French immersion education: The roles of language proficiency and literacy. In A. G. Reynolds (Ed.), *Bilingualism, multiculturalism, and second language learning: The McGill Conference in Honour of Wallace E. Lambert* (pp. 203-216). Hillsdale, NJ: Lawrence Erlbaum.

Vaid, J., & Hall, D. G. (1991). Neuropsychological perspectives on bilingualism: Right, left, and center. In A. G. Reynolds (Ed.), *Bilingualism, multiculturalism, and second language learning: The McGill Conference in Honour of Wallace E. Lambert* (pp. 81-112). Hillsdale, NJ: Lawrence Erlbaum.

Vihman, M. M. (1985). Language differentiation by the bilingual infant. *Journal of Child Language, 13,* 297-324.

Werker, J. F., & Tees, R. C. (1984). Cross-language speech perception: Evidence for perceptual reorganization during the first year of life. *Infant Behavior and Development, 7,* 41-63. (Reprinted in J. L. Miller, R. D. Kent, & B. S. Atal, Eds., 1991, *Papers in speech communication: Speech perception,* pp. 733-747. Woodbury, NY: Acoustical Society of America)

White, L. (1995). Input, triggers and second language acquisition. In F. R. Eckman, D. Highland, P. W. Lee, J. Mileham, & R. Rutkowski Weber (Eds.), *Second language acquisition theory and pedagogy* (pp. 63-78). Mahwah, NJ: Lawrence Erlbaum.

Wulfreck, B. B., Juarez, L., Bates, E. A., & Kilborn, K. (1986). Sentence interpretation strategies in healthy and aphasic bilingual adults. In J. Vaid (Ed.), *Language processing in bilinguals: Psycholinguistic and neuropsychological perspectives* (pp. 199-219). Hillsdale, NJ: Lawrence Erlbaum.

Zatorre, R. J. (1989). On the representation of multiple languages in the brain: Old problems and new directions. *Brain and Language, 36,* 127-147.

STUDY QUESTIONS

1. Evaluate the pros and cons of second language learning on L1 skills and general cognitive development.

2. The critical period hypothesis holds that there are special language-learning heuristics (perhaps universal parameters) guiding language acquisition during early childhood, definitely ending by puberty. Evaluate second language learning with respect to the critical period hypothesis. Consider both simultaneous language learning from infancy and successive language learning.

3. How does a bilingual differ from two monolingual individuals? Critically consider the following:

the evidence bearing on common and different conceptual cores,

the evidence suggesting different personalities,

the phenomenon of code-switching, and

the difference in pragmatic situations for the use of each language for the bilingual, relative to the monolingual.

4. This chapter presented considerable evidence for the importance of habit strength and frequency of occurrence of linguistic structures for acquisition and loss order. Critically review this evidence.

5. In your opinion, what is the most effective way to teach or learn a foreign language? Support your views with data.

11

PROCESSING PRINT: THE PSYCHOLOGY OF READING AND WRITING

In what color is the word *blue* printed? To answer this question, you must force yourself to look before the meaning of the word, to an earlier stage when you simply saw lines, arcs and ink, and note the color of the ink. As a fluent reader, you should find this very difficult: The meaning of the word jumps out at you, seemingly before you note the letters. But if you look at a script that you are not fluent in—Hebrew, Greek, or Chinese—it is clear that letters are only abstract, hard-to-discriminate designs in which we have learned powerfully to see meaning. And, although it is hard to focus on the ink color before you in the word *blue,* it is easy to "hear" its sound pattern and quickly generate rhymes—zoo, you, two, few, queue, do, voodoo—none of which uses the same letter pattern, or *orthography,* in the rhyme.

How does "our" print acquire such power to bridge the sound and the meaning, signifying something?

Now consider two common reading experiences. The first I call "the highlighter phenomenon." There I am, reading normally, highlighter in hand, marking the important points. Aroused from a reverie, minutes later I discover that I have yellowed in *all* of the previous 10 pages, with no recollection of a word on any of them. Yet I am sure that anyone watching me would think I am reading normally; I am sure I move my eyes scanning the pages and rhythmically turn them—but none of their message gets in.

The counterpoint experience is losing oneself in a text. There was a day I started a novel, expecting a visitor in half an hour. Six hours later, with legs too cramped to stand up, I reentered *my* world to realize the visitor was a no-show! How can a story become so all-absorbing that we lose all sense of time and daily functions? How can we *re*read a suspense story, holding our breath as we did the first time—when we know the outcome?

Clearly, reading encompasses at least two very different processes. One is shallow and automatic, and allows us to daydream while exercising the habitual motions of reading. And one is deep and involved, causing us to create, inhabit, and care about imaginary worlds, induced into them by the printed letters.

In this chapter we explore both the shallow and the deep processes in reading—at the shallow level, recognizing letters, scanning pages, accessing words and word meanings from letter patterns; then, at the deep level, developing coherent text representations, filling in necessary inferences, creating narrative worlds, and enjoying traveling to and from them.

We will also look at the presumably related process of writing, bypassing the issue of how letters are formed motorically, to consider how written language is different from spoken language. Why, for instance, can many children write before they can read? Or why, after years of speaking in grammatical sentences, is it so hard to learn explicitly what a sentence is so as to punctuate it correctly?

We will begin by looking at print processes in the fluent adult reader/writer because we cannot assume for print the same language structure or processes we have explored so far. Reading and writing are clearly *secondary* to primary language: They are learned later, presumably mapped explicitly to primary language as well as inculcating their own processes. Print does not disappear as you process it the way speech does; it is not *rapidly fading,* so it makes smaller memory demands. It also is not interactive communication: There is no feedback from reader to writer; reader and writer do not exchange roles as do a speaker and hearer in conversation; there is no dynamic social situation between reader and writer. The implications of the different cognitive (memory) and social constraints of reading/writing and conversing on the language structure and processing need to be considered first.

We will then turn to how literacy is acquired—how children (and adults) learn to read. We touch briefly on reading and writing failures in *dyslexia,* either as a developmental learning disability or as one acquired from brain damage. (Dyslexia is treated in more detail in *Language in Atypical Populations.*) As in the last chapter, we will also look at how this language skill is taught and, given what we understand as psycholinguists, evaluate the teaching methods.

WRITING SYSTEMS AND THEIR HISTORY

As we discussed in Chapter 6, our alphabet is roughly phonemic; each letter roughly corresponds to a phoneme. The one-to-one correspondence fails for sounds like /s/, written as "c" or "s," or, more confusingly, for a letter like "a," which represents many sounds, such as /æ/, /a/, /e/, /ɔ/, and the schwa.

The capriciousness of the sound-letter "correspondence" is often deplored by English learners and reading instructors but is more than made up for by a less noted feature of our writing system: Spelling captures morpheme regularities as well as sound regularities. So, although at the sound level "ea" is sometimes /i/ and sometimes /ε/, which is confusing, the spelling pattern, or orthographic similarity of *meant* and *mean,* facilitates the reader's relating the meaning of the two words. As another example, note that the different sounds of the regular past and plural in different environments (/d, t, əd/; /s, z, əz/) *look* the same (d; s) and so they may be more easily identified as variants of the same morpheme in writing than in speech.

The main task for the reader is to retrieve the meaning of the word, not its pronunciation. Our writing system clues meaning both through the sound code, which tells us how we would say the word, and thus allows us to employ the lexical access route we use normally when we hear a word, and through the spelling pattern, which tells us, often more directly, how words are related to one another and how they interact in the meaning system.

History of Writing

"Pictographs"

Not all writing systems code spoken language as we do; in fact, the first writing systems likely did not code spoken language at all (Olson, 1994; Pyles, 1993). Writing systems evolved to record important events or resources in a permanent form. As such, the code was between graphic and object, not between graphic and word. The earliest transcriptions we have are baked clay shapes from Mesopotamia 4 millennia ago, indicating ownership through geometric signs (as do modern brands on cattle; Olson, 1994) and counting quantities (Schmandt-Besserat, 1978). Later, the clay was imprinted with the thing being tallied, a graphic symbol of the content (Olson, 1994; Schmandt-Besserat, 1978). This, Olson postulates, may have led to recognition of the possibility of symbolizing things with imprints and, still later, to the connection of graphic symbol with phonic symbol, of picture with word. Figure 11.1 depicts the clay shapes and their relation to imprinted symbols.

Early humans, as do their modern descendants, recorded the rituals and history of their culture in rock paintings, sand paintings, wampum belts, and so on. These early records ranged from arbitrary to iconic. The picture stories, although iconic, could only be "read" or divined by seers, who, like modern seers and text interpreters, did not always agree on the meanings. Indeed, the meanings of these depictions are *not* obvious: Modern humans, although certain that a painting might represent, say, a bull and a hunter, remain puzzled as to the intent of the artist or the significance (meaning) of the painting.

What the etched-in-stone record certainly provided for the artist and the viewer was a memory aid, a backup for the rapidly fading primary language system. The utility of an aid for unmemorable, but important, information was probably recog-

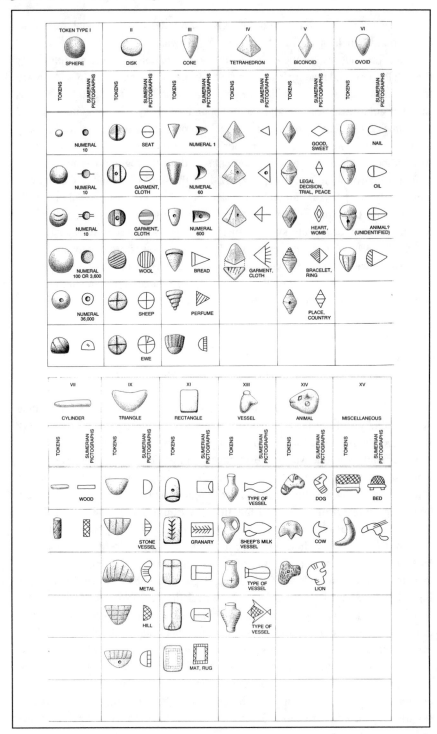

Figure 11.1. Schematics of the Clay Tokens and the Ideographs Depicting Them From Ancient Mesopotamia of About 5,000 Years Ago

SOURCE: From D. Schmandt-Besserat (1978), "The Earliest Precursor of Writing," *Scientific American, 238*, pp. 56-57. Copyright © 1978 Scientific American, Inc. All rights reserved. Used by permission.

"OH, HOW I HATE THE RE-WRITING!"

Figure 11.2. A Humorous Look at the Advantages of Paper and Pen on the Development of the Writing Process. (© 1997 by Sydney Harris.)

nized immediately, expanded to other important information "for the record," and copied by other cultures. The writing systems created were shaped by what was to be recorded, not at first by a desire to represent language. (And as Figure 11.2 depicts, once writing comes to tell stories, it develops its own requirements.)

Initially, "writing" was at least partly iconic (i.e., looking like its referent, as you may recall): The number of pieces of clay stood nonarbitrarily for the number of cattle; icons or stylized pictures of people, animals, and geographic and astronomical features recorded culturally significant historical or sacred events. These are picture symbols, or *pictographs*.

"Logographs"

In cuneiform in the third millennium, the writing systems evolved syntax, again inspired by the need for record keeping, not by recognition of corresponding syntax in the language. A symbol for quantity was combined with another symbol for what was quantified. It is important to recognize that although we relate the written to the spoken word, that is not necessary: Is /// a depiction of threeness, or a way of writing "three"? In our culture, is the waving of an American flag a visual *expression of a statement* such as "I am patriotic" (or "I am waving a flag"), or does it in itself denote what the word *flag-waving* denotes?

Writing historians (Olson, 1994; Pyles, 1993) argue that the pictographs initially directly denoted quantity and object, later inspiring the insight that words similarly denote objects, and thus that graphic symbols could be words. The insight that writing could be *logographic,* that graphic signs could stand for words, in turn, promoted the development of more such logographs.

"Syllabaries"

As a writing system develops complexity, describing more and more things or words, logographs become impractical: One needs a symbol for each thing to be symbolized, a heavy memory load. Alternatively, one can depict smaller aspects of meaning or language, combining the smaller units productively, resulting in fewer graphemes but adding combination rules. Sumerian cuneiform employed three types of graphic symbols to these ends: *iconic* symbols, like a circle for the sun, which is easy to remember because of the similar appearance; *phonographic* symbols, like applying the circle to *son* because it sounds like *sun,* and will therefore connect in memory through sound; and *determinatives,* unverbalized characters that assist the reader in determining the role of the other characters in the script.

These basic principles apply to all writing systems to this day, even to our "phonemic" system. Our letters represent sound, are phonographic. They likely originated as icons, although the iconography blurs with conventionalization. For example, "A" derives from the Semitic *aleph,* a word meaning ox. It was drawn on its side ⊁, perhaps a stylized, conventionalized ox head. "A" was originally a pictograph of ox, then a logograph for ox, and finally a letter representing a sound (Pyles, 1993).

And determinatives exist in our writing of capital versus small letters, spaces, or punctuation. We recognize "A" and "a" as the same and verbalize them the same way; the difference between them is therefore unverbalized. We use the difference to mark the beginning of a sentence or signify a proper name; that graphic difference is a determinative. Punctuation and spaces also are unverbalized; their function is to group letters to find meaning—and, as I pointed out in Chapter 7, words are *not* delineated by spaces in the speech stream. Spacing is a convention developed for writing and is not modeled on speech.

Now, consider what must happen if a new ethnolinguistic group borrows the writing system developed for a different language. The iconic symbols, like circle for sun, can transfer readily and be easily learned, but the phonographic symbols cannot: *Sun* and *son* sound alike in English, so we could mnemonically employ the same circle symbol; in French, we have *le soleil* and *le fils,* which have no direct relation. The adopters have three choices: invent a new symbol for one of the words, modify the original symbol to indicate the different pronunciation (as in adding a tilde [Spanish] or umlaut [German]), or abandon the iconographic principle and use the symbol to represent the syllable /sʌn/ regardless of meaning.

The difficulties encountered in transferring the symbols between languages, Olson speculates, led to heightened awareness of the symbol-to-sound potentials so that the newer Babylonian and Canaanite cuneiforms expanded the phonographic potentials. A symbol like ⳩ in one language came to be recognized not as an icon for "man" but, rebuslike, as a representation of the syllable /mæn/ in the next. In short, the developing writing systems gave rise to finer-tuned analysis of the spoken language—first words as units in the sound stream, then syllables as isolatable components in words, and finally phonemes as isolatable components of syllables. Olson (1994) concludes that "the syllable is as much a product of the graphic system as a prerequisite for it. . . . The old script is fitted to the new language as a model is to the data; the data are then seen in terms of the model" (p. 81).

Writing Systems as Language Models

As writing systems were extended into new domains, they caused their adapters to recognize patterns in the language explicitly, to create language models, recognizing perhaps for the first time the structure of their language, analyzing discourse into sentences, words, syllables, and eventually phonemes (Olson, 1994). None of these is self-evident in talking: Speakers are aware of the *ideas* to be communicated, and not until they try to note the ideas are their potential verbal components considered; then the writing becomes a model for the language. Olson argues that learning to read entails more than mastery of letter/sound and letter-pattern/meaning correspondences but also a mastery of an explicit model of their language. Literate individuals therefore not only read and write but analyze language and have different metalinguistic awareness than preliterate people.

It is important to note, in this regard, that the model that writing provides does not fit speech perfectly. There are speech features that writing fails to transmit explicitly, such as the suprasegmental cues to irony. In writing, it is either implied by context, or "lexicalized"—metalanguage like *ironically* is added to the sentence. This we need not do in speech. Writing therefore calls for a different vocabulary and/or set of conventions for expressing these features.

There are also speech features that writing transmits more explicitly than speech, such as sentence boundaries and clausal dependencies. The greater explicitness calls for an often unfamiliar awareness, which makes writing difficult. Consider: Why do we see so many sentence fragments and run-on sentences in the writing of fluent speakers? Why do I (and possibly you) struggle so to decide whether to use a period, colon, or semicolon to separate interconnected propositions? These are issues we do not have to confront explicitly when talking.

Finally, there are arenas in which writing models speech incorrectly, as when we represent the single sound /š/ with two letters, s and h, or when we follow proscriptive rules—for example, do not begin a sentence with *and, but,* or *or.*

Once we are fluent readers and writers, our literacy affects our speech (I believe I talk with semicolons and parentheses now—I certainly lecture using words like *parenthetically*) and our understanding of our language. In teaching phonetics, for example, I have encountered resistance to the idea that /š/ is not articulated as s + h but is a single phoneme—students have accepted their writing system's, here incorrect, model.

"Inventing" Writing

Despite the apparently different writing systems in use worldwide, the idea of writing may have originated only twice in human history: once in Mesopotamia, as we have been discussing, and once in Mexican Indians, around 500 B.C. (Diamond, 1995). All other systems—and as we shall see, they are diverse—arose either from copying and modifying a model to fit the new language or by diffusion of the general idea of writing.

As an example of diffusion of the general idea, Diamond (1995) describes the known development of the Cherokee writing system. The Cherokee, Sequoyah, observed Anglos' use of black marks on paper during speech-giving. With no ability to speak or read English and therefore to interpret the print, he designed a marking system for Cherokee. First he tried pictures, then separate signs for each word, and, finally, separate signs for simplified syllables—the best compromise of sign number (85 versus hundreds) and language structure. Note that his attempts as an individual mirror the sequence we have discussed for our writing system's ancestry and—as Olson argues—suggest that in the conscious attempt to depict language on paper, one becomes increasingly aware of its structure.

Diamond points out that mankind was illiterate for millennia, and then, within a few centuries, there were writing systems throughout Eurasia. He argues that after millennia of illiteracy, it is unlikely that all were spontaneously and independently invented. More likely, writing spread along trade routes, changing through diffusion and/or copying and extending.

Our alphabet emerged from the Greeks' copying and extending a derivative of the Sumerian cuneiform, the Semitic writing system (*aleph,* discussed above, becomes *alpha* in Greek). In Greek, like English, consonants and vowels differentiate words. In contrast, in spoken Semitic languages (such as modern Hebrew and Arabic), word identity is given by the consonants, with different interspersed vowels marking subject, tense, and aspect: *ktv* signifies "write"; *katav,* "he wrote"; *kotev,* "writing"; and *katuv,* "being written."

The normal Semitic script does not usually represent vowels, although it can, using a system called *pointing*. Pointing is used as an aid to train the reading of Hebrew, a *matres lectiones* (Latin for "mothers of reading"; Pyles, 1993). In unpointed script, each of the inflected variants of *write* is transcribed the same, as *ktv*. While making the relationship to spoken sounds less transparent, omission of pointing heightens the morphological relations as does our similar orthography for *mean* and *meant*.

Because Greek does not use vowels in the same way as the Semitic languages, the Semitic script was a poor model for Greek. The Greek adapters were likely struck by the Semitic abstraction of identity (k) across what Greeks certainly would have heard as different syllables (ka, ko, ku). Expanding on what seemed to be a principle of phoneme components for the syllable, they used Semitic (consonant) graphemes with no phonetic equivalent in Greek for Greek vowels. Thus the Semitic "he," an aspirated consonant, the Greeks called "e-simple"—in Greek, "e-psilon" or epsilon (Pyles, 1993). So emerged the phonemic alphabet.

Modern Writing Systems

As I have said, our writing system consists of a roughly phonemic code, which compromises its sound depiction with the depiction of morphological relationships and includes conventions for interpreting text itself, determinatives, like spacing and capitalization. (It also includes logographs such as $ and &.) The advantage of a sound-based system is that it yields a very small number of designs to recognize: 26 letters or graphemes (52 if we count both capital and small), along with the small number of punctuation points. (A *grapheme* is the smallest productive unit of writing—for us, a letter or letter cluster like "ch" [č] or "tion" [šʌn].) This is kind to memory. However, the grapheme-to-phoneme correspondence (GPC) is rough, so we must memorize how to pronounce a number of different letter patterns— *common* spelling-to-sound correspondences render *ghoti* as *fish,* as I pointed out in Chapter 6.

Other modern writing systems, such as Serbo-Croatian, more consistently represent their phonologies. That is, like the phonetic alphabet, there is a reliable (near one-to-one) match between speech sound and grapheme, a more *shallow* orthography (Frost, 1994). This leads more immediately to a phonological representation but does not as readily capture morphological regularities; that is, there is a trade-off. And, as we have discussed, there are languages with deep orthographies: Unpointed Hebrew does not represent vowels, which makes it phonologically deeper than English and certainly deeper than pointed Hebrew.

Do you think there might be differences in how readers process pointed and unpointed Hebrew? As we will see, comparing reading processes in languages with shallow and deep orthographies is informative as to how necessary a transparent sound representation is for deriving the meaning of the text.

Modern writing systems are not necessarily phonemic at either a shallow or a deep level. Chinese graphemes represent morpheme syllables; they spawned a similarly morphemic system in Japanese, *Kanji.* The Japanese have a second system, *Kana,* a truer syllabary in that the character represents the sound, not the meaning, of the syllable (Tzeng & Wang, 1983). Both systems contain a large number of forms to memorize; Kanji is said to have 50,000 differentiable characters (compared with our 26 or so). In Kanji, we see all the historic writing developments in a single character: Each character consists of a morpheme marker (originally iconic), a phonographic marker, and a determinative (Olson, 1994). Compensating for the greater number of characters is a more direct relation between the form and the meaning. And it may be easier to learn to analyze a language into syllables than into phonemes, speeding learning to read.

Box 11.1. History and Principles of Writing Systems

— Writing did not arise to model language or speech but to record important information. The language model was an insight gained as the system extended from its original purpose. Modern systems do not perfectly match writing and speech.

Grapheme Types
— *Pictographs:* Iconic representations, such as :) for happy
— *Logographs:* A stylized graphic representation of words
— *Syllabaries:* Graphemes that represent single syllables, word components
— *Phonemic alphabet:* Graphemes that represent syllable components

Common Grapheme Characteristics
— A stylized, conventionalized core symbol of meaning or pronunciation, such as "n" or "sh" or "tion"
— A stylized, conventionalized phonetic symbol, or pronunciation guide, such as "ñ"
— *Determinative:* An unverbalized interpretation guide, such as the distinction between capital and small letters

Modern Writing Systems
— "Phonemic" alphabet, which also captures morphemic regularities, violating strict grapheme-phoneme regularity: such as *mean* and *meant*
— Orthographically shallower systems, such as Serbo-Croatian, which are more phonemically regular
— Orthographically deeper systems, such as unpointed Hebrew, which represents only consonants
— *Pointing:* A way of representing vowels in Hebrew, to assist learning to read
— *Syllabaries,* like Japanese Kanji, that employ more basic symbols, each representing a syllable- or morphemelike unit, perhaps combined with a phonographic or determinative symbol as well

---

FLUENT READING PROCESSES

Lexical Access From Print

In discussing speech perception, we began with the smallest unit of articulation, the phonetic feature, and examined its extraction from the available information in the acoustic signal, and its integration with other features, for phoneme, syllable, and, ultimately, word perception. The smallest unit that we will examine in the visual signal is the single letter, although, clearly, letters are composed of lines and arcs, which we (learn to) perceive as a unit (LaBerge & Samuels, 1974). Most studies of reading begin with perception of the letter or higher units—grapheme, syllable, and word perception—considering them either in isolation or in sentence or narrative context.

We have seen that our writing system permits consideration of two ways of relating letter patterns to words: (a) indirectly, through the phonological code, or grapheme-to-phoneme correspondence (GPC), and (b) through the letter pattern or orthography itself, a "direct" route. This is true also of individual letters. Each names itself phonologically ("bee," "dee," and so on) and depicts a distinct pattern. Thus "b," "d," and "p" are phonologically confusable because they rhyme, and orthographically confusable because they are composed of a vertical and a circle. "Q" is only confusable orthographically with "b," "d," and "p"; its name "cue" does not sound like theirs.

In addition to the orthographic and phonological properties of individual letters, the fluent reader is aided by knowledge of letter frequency patterns as well as patterns of letter co-occurrence. So "q" is a letter that is rarely used (it earns more points in Scrabble), and therefore might be unexpected and take long to recognize. "Q" also rarely occurs by itself, without "u." In fact, you might expect to recognize the picture "qu" at least as quickly as "q" because you have seen "qu" so much more often.

Likewise, the fluent reader may recognize many common letter combinations (co, ca, ch, cl, and so on) rapidly, perhaps more rapidly, than their component letters. Compare, for example, your own ease of recognition of

brave   vbrae   baver

respectively, a word, the same letters in an impossible sequence, and the same letters as a *pseudoword,* a graphemically possible and pronounceable nonword. *Vbrae* has some unusual two-letter combinations, or *digrams*—vb and ae—that may make it harder to see than *baver,* all digrams that are common in English orthography and therefore quickly recognizable.

Finally, the fluent reader, like a fluent speaker, is aided by context, by how the meaning of the text up to the word being read constrains the likely choices of words. Thus retrieval of a lexical item from print may come from activations of the following:

- The sound of the word
- The individual letters
- A common cohort of letters in a spelling pattern
- The meaning suggested by the text

Words and Letters

One might suppose that reading proceeds bottom-up: that one sees letters, combines the letters, and then sees words. That would suggest that letter recognition would be faster and/or more accurate than word recognition because word recognition depends on it. There are a number of different demonstrations that this is certainly not the whole story.

The *word superiority effect* demonstrates our greater facility at identifying letters in briefly displayed words than in equally long letter strings that do not constitute words. We are better able also to detect letters in common than in uncommon words, the *word frequency effect.* Both effects are related to the *word-letter effect:* We are quicker and more accurate at detecting letters in words containing them than when they are presented in isolation. Paradoxically, precise instructions on where to look within the word for the letter makes it harder to find. Viewing

cat

or

a

you would better report seeing the "a" in *cat* than alone, and you would be better off looking at the whole word, *cat,* than focusing on the second letter position (e.g., Johnston, 1978, 1981; Johnston & McClelland, 1974, 1980; Matthei, 1983; Samuel, van Santen, & Johnston, 1982, 1983).

Several explanations have been offered for the word-letter effect: a special perceptual level that implicates words as such (see Figure 11.3), a special perceptual level that implicates several co-occurring letters (the second "digram" [hidden] layer, shown in Figure 11.3), and a more analytic process for meaningful, open-class words. Each of these has some empirical support to indicate that word and letter identification is a complex of processes, involving letter features, letters themselves, digram features, words, and possibly word meanings.

Adams (1979) presented words to detect letters in mixed upper- and lowercase letters and different fonts like

Ca*T.*

Because words are rarely written like this, we should not have developed digram units for them. Nevertheless, it was easier to recognize letters in such mixed-font words: The word advantage does not arise only from the familiarity of its visual pattern.

The word-letter effect is also no stronger in contexts appropriate for only one or two letters (like _nob—s or k), a highly weighted digram set, than in contexts permitting many alternatives (like _ill—b, d, f, g, h . . .) where activation would be spread among many digram possibilities (e.g., Johnston, 1981). This too suggests only a weak influence of a visual digram or greater unit. But letter detection is better in pseudowords than in isolation, and better in longer than shorter words (Samuel et al., 1982, 1983). So common letter patterns, whether or not they are a word, facilitate recognition of the components.

Studies of the word superiority (Adams, 1979) and word frequency (Johnston, 1978) effects demonstrate that it is faster to detect a letter in a common word than in an uncommon word or pseudoword in a masking task where the stimulus is

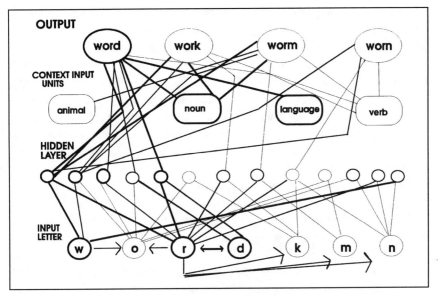

Figure 11.3. A Reproduction of Figure 3.4 Showing the Possible Interconnections of Letters, Digrams (Hidden Units), and Meanings Underlying Word Recognition
NOTE: A possible phonological route is also available but is not depicted in the diagram.

briefly flashed in isolation and then quickly replaced with another stimulus, a *mask.* The mask obliterates the memory image of the stimulus, preventing the subject from "reading" the letter *postperceptually* from memory after seeing it. Thus there is a perceptual advantage to a letter string's being in the lexicon.

Letters and Words in Context

Paradoxically, opposite effects, a *dis*advantage to detecting letters in familiar words, are obtained in more natural, on-line reading tasks. In letter-monitoring tasks, subjects search for a particular target letter as they read running text. In the previous sentence, if you were monitoring for a "k," you would have found it only in "tasks." Now, suppose that I mistype: "In letker-monitoring . . .," you could detect the "k" unexpectedly in the nonword. Under these conditions, it is easier to detect the letter in a *non*word than in a word—easier to notice the "k" in "letker" than in "tasks." This is the *missing letter effect,* also known, facetiously, as "the word inferiority effect" (Healy & Drewnowski, 1983; Healy, Oliver, & McNamara, 1987). A particular letter is also harder to detect in a common word than in a rare one, a "word frequency disadvantage."

Note that the missing letter effect and the word frequency disadvantage are paradoxical in that components are harder to detect in the very stimuli that are easier to perceive as a whole. Healy argues that it is in fact the rapid perception of the word as a unit that interferes with perceiving the components: As soon as the word is recognized, we stop identifying letters. This is *the unitization hypothesis.*

Unitization is supported by experiments that show that enhancing the identifiability of the word containing the target increases the missing letter effect, that is, reduces the chances of detecting the letter. To understand this, it is helpful to review the logogen and cohort models described in Chapters 3 and 7. In these, word candidates are activated by incoming stimulus letters (or sounds) and by sense from context. A particular activation level is needed for a word to become conscious, a lower level for more frequent words. As one reads or hears a word, component by component, a cohort of candidates consistent with the information thus far is activated. Recognition is complete and unambiguous when the cohort is narrowed to only one item over threshold.

Healy's unitization hypothesis is a version of these models. Real, common words have lower thresholds than less common words or than a never-seen-before pseudoword and so are recognized using less stimulus information, automatically ending processing of the stimulus, and reducing the chance of processing a component.

Healy et al. (1987) have shown that context increases the missing letter effect: It occurs only when several words from the sentence are simultaneously visible, not when words are presented one at a time. Unitization may result from the way we scan words when reading, fixating words we are not sure of in our accurate, central, foveal vision, and "skimming" familiar words, letting their image fall in the less central and less accurate *parafovea,* the area around the fovea. Spacing words so that the eye is forced to fixate each in the fovea, or presenting the words from right to left, contrary to our eye-movement habits, diminishes the missing letter effect (Hadley & Healy, 1991).

I should note that most of Healy's research has centered on the word *the,* the most frequent word in the English language. *The,* however, has other, perhaps confounding, properties: It is a function (closed-class) word, which contributes little meaning. Koriat and Greenberg (1991; Greenberg & Koriat, 1991) examined the missing letter effect with respect to whether the items were closed or open class—in Hebrew. Hebrew's closed-class items are rarely short, single words; usually the function is prefixed on content words. Despite the fact that there is no greater frequency for Hebrew function than content words, they found a "missing letter effect" in function words: poorer detection of a target letter in a function item than in a content one. In cases where a prefix was ambiguous, with one meaning a content item and the other a function item, the missing letter effect occurred only when the context biased the interpretation to the function reading. And they (and later Moravcsik & Healy, 1995) found that using function words for content in English—as in "the proposal—are you *for* or against" or "*the* is a definite article" or "*in* group"—enhanced the detection of letters within them, relative to their normal use. Finally, they showed that a nonword in function word position, such as "I'm doing this fom your own good," is as hard to detect a letter in as a real word is. They argue that it is not frequency, familiarity, or the like but role in the sentence that produces the missing letter effect.

Thus it is not simply recognition of a familiar letter pattern that underlies unitization but recognition of an expected letter pattern in a particular context. In fact, Koriat and Greenberg argue that we read function words purposefully to establish sentence structure and relegate them quickly to the background thereafter: We are not aware of *the* as an item but as an indicator of a noun phrase; once the NP is structured, we focus on the noun. It is this backgrounding, Koriat and Greenberg believe, that underlies the missing letter effect.

Summary

So, what is the role of letters in fluent reading? Clearly, letters provide bottom-up information as to word and sentence identity. But recognition of higher units also plays a role, lowering the threshold for usual components (→ word superiority in masking), but making the component stand out less as an individual (→ word inferiority in on-line reading). Commonly seen words may be recognized quickly as a unit (they have lower thresholds for activation than less commonly seen items). Meaning activates word units top-down, speeding recognition apart from thorough analysis of individual component letters. And the meaning and structural roles of the word in the sentence can determine how much attention is focused on it.

This is not surprising, perhaps. This is what makes us such poor proofreaders, particularly on function words. We mentally see the *correct* letter and, despite the input, recognize the whole word. And this is quite analogous to what we learned about speech perception, in the phonemic restoration effect, for example: We are geared to perceive meaningful units, not their meaningless building blocks.

Eye Movements in Reading

In discussing the word-letter and missing letter effects, I referred to points of focus, the fovea and the parafovea. Our central vision is our most acute, the best able to see details, such as whether a vertical has a crosshatch through it, changing it from an "l" to a "t." You can see for yourself how inaccurate your peripheral vision is by focusing on the X in the center of the demonstration line below and attempting to read the surrounding letters (DO NOT MOVE YOUR EYES—THAT'S CHEATING!):

btkrn   para **X** fovea   ljmfh.

The X that you stared at, if you followed instructions, is at the center of the fovea. Three or four spaces to either side of the X is the parafovea, which should still be legible, and then there is the illegible periphery. As we read a line of text, our eye moves across the line placing the letters and words in the fovea.

We have looked at eye movement patterns in previous chapters as indicators of attention and processing time. In Chapter 5, for example, in sentence processing, we saw that fixation time, the length of time that the eye stopped at a word, was related to the structural complexity and ambiguities of the sentence. We saw that subjects make *regressive eye movements,* backtracking, after traveling a garden

---

Box 11.2. Perceiving Text

— *Word superiority effect:* It is easier (faster, has greater accuracy) to recognize a letter in a word than in a pronounceable nonword than in a random string of letters.
— *Word frequency advantage:* Common words are more perceptible than less frequent words.
— *Word-letter effect:* It is easier to recognize a letter in a word (or pronounceable nonword) than in isolation.
— *Word-length effect:* It is easier to recognize a letter in a longer than a shorter word.
— *Content-function word effect:* It is easier to target a letter in a content than in a function word.
— *Missing letter effect:* In running text, it is easier to target a letter in a nonword (i.e., a typo) than in a real word. Ease of detection of a given letter is greater in rare than common words, and in content than function words.

---

path, creating a structure that turns out to be incorrect as additional words are read. (For example, "Put the apple on the napkin on the plate" is typically first processed with "on the napkin" as the destination; when the next prepositional phrase proves this impossible, it is reviewed as the modifier of "apple.")

Thus *eye gaze is not simply for seeing* but is also for fixing attention. I just stared out the window, unseeingly, as I tried to come up with an example of when we fixate purposefully, but unseeingly; I am sure you have experienced similar such fixations during exams or temporary writing blocks. As we look at the pattern of eye movements in reading, we are observing a process determined simultaneously by the need to see the letters, identify the word, establish the role of the word in the ongoing sentence, and understand the text.

Eye movements in reading consist of a series of *saccades,* controlled jumps from one fixation point to the next. In skilled readers (of English and other left-to-right writing systems):

- Each fixation lasts about a quarter second during which new information is extracted from the text.
- Each jump spans seven to nine characters.
- Each saccade brings a new area of text into the fovea.
- The *perceptual span,* the region of useful information during a fixation, is from three characters to the left, to 15 characters to the right, of fixation (Rayner, 1986).

At the fixation point, all details of individual letters are available. Parafoveally, at the limits of the perceptual span, skilled readers initiate the identification process: Parafoveal preview of a word reduces fixation time on that word, especially if it is a common word, a savings that nonskilled readers do not also experience (Kennison & Clifton, 1995).

Briihl and Inhoff (1995) found that skilled readers benefit from parafoveal preview of the full word or the initial or final letters but not of the *word body*—the rime (see Chapter 7, the sounds following the first phoneme or consonant cluster) for monosyllabic words, and the letters between the first and second vowels for multisyllabic words. Skilled readers may automatically access word units on the basis of gross word shape at the parafoveal limit. Between fixation and this outer parafoveal limit, they may use the boundary letters as well to delimit or narrow a cohort. Thus, for a skilled reader, within a saccade, many aspects of visual information from detailed to gross are likely extracted automatically in parallel.

As I said, during a fixation, new information seems to be extracted from the text and integrated into the mental representation. Fixation durations—not a surprise—depend on how difficult extracting new information is. Fixations are longer for beginning readers, unpracticed at extracting information from text, than they are for skilled readers (Rayner, 1986).

Skilled readers' fixation times are longer depending on ambiguity. Balanced homonyms (such as *mean:* "nasty" versus "intend"), the meanings of which are equally likely in the language, are fixated longer than unambiguous words or unbalanced homonyms signifying their most frequent meaning. When the less common meaning of an unbalanced homonym (*mean* as average) is primed by context, the unbalanced homonym also gets a lengthy fixation—the reader must resolve a conflict between the activation of the more usual sense and the sense suggested by context (Folk & Morris, 1995). In all these cases, longer fixations indicate more complex processing to access the correct meaning.

Fixations are also longer for infrequent than frequent words (Hyona & Olson, 1995). We are not as practiced at recognizing these and so they may require more supportive detail to reach a recognition threshold, as described in the cohort or logogen models reviewed above. Long words also require longer fixations than short words. This effect may be related to the frequency effect; if you recall Zipf's Law (Chapter 3), frequency has a reliable, inverse relationship with word length (more frequent words are less long). The length effect may also have a physical cause: Longer words extend beyond the fovea and thus require more than one fixation to view fully (Hyona & Olson, 1995).

Infrequent or unfamiliar words are not only fixated longer initially but often stimulate a lookahead presumably for help in interpretation, followed by a regressive eye movement to the difficult word (Hyona & Olson, 1995). Skilled readers thus use a large window of text, and many cues to word identity from gross word shape to letter patterns to meaning from context, to effect word identification and/or its meaning's retrieval.

The Phonological Route

Thus far we have explored the word identification processes in reading that could be entirely dependent on visual information—the features that make up the letters (briefly), the letters that compose words, digram patterns, whole-word patterns, and

---

Box 11.3. Eye Gaze Patterns in Reading

— Fixation time indexes processing difficulty in seeing the word, in recognizing the word, in determining the structure of the sentence, in incorporating the information into the constructed script of the narrative.
— A fluent reader engages in many reading processes in parallel.
— Fixating puts information in the fovea, which sees detail.
— The eye moves in saccades—jumps—changing fixation points.
    — Each fixation lasts about a quarter second.
    — Each saccade spans seven to nine characters.
    — Each saccade brings a new area of text into the fovea.
    — The *perceptual span*, the region from which useful information is extracted during a fixation, is from 3 characters to the left of fixation to 15 characters to the right of fixation.
— Parafoveal view permits gross information extraction, like word shape, and is used to advantage by skilled readers, especially for common words, shortening the time they need to fixate the item.
— Fixation times are longer for ambiguous words, infrequent words, and less common meanings of homonyms—reflecting longer time to access meaning.
— Fixation times are longer for longer words.
— Fluent readers look ahead of a difficult word, and then backtrack, fixating it, presumably using the lookahead for contextual cues to identifying its meaning.

---

boundary-letter/word-body patterns. Another possible route to word meaning is indirect, through observation of the spelling-to-sound correspondence. The evidence strongly supports our hearing the words mentally as we read; the question is when relative to word recognition we do so. If the sound leads to word recognition, it is *prelexical;* if it is activated after we have accessed the word from the direct visual route, it is *postlexical.*

Many of the studies that have investigated the role of a phonological route in identifying read words use homographic and heterographic homophones (or heterophones). *Hetero* means different and *homo* means the same; *graphic* refers to appearance, and *phone* to sound. *Bank* in the senses of "river" and "place to store money" are homographic homophones; *sail* and *sale,* pronounced the same with different meanings and different spellings, are heterographic homophones, and the present and past tense of *read* are homographic heterophones.

Priming and Confusion Evidence

As you may recall from Chapter 5, an ambiguous word activates all its meanings for about 200 ms after it is presented. This is measured by presenting a sentence containing a word like *bank,* and then looking at the lexical or semantic decision times for words related to each of *bank*'s meanings, like "river" or "place to store money." People more quickly decide about words that have been "primed" through activation of associated meanings, so if their decision times are better for associates of *both* meanings even though context suggests only one reading, we know that both meanings were activated. If meanings are aroused from phonological coding, we should also expect priming by *flower* of *rows* through /roz/, the phonological code in common with *rose*. This turns out to be the case (van Orden, Pennington, & Stone, 1990).

By the same token, if a word activates the meaning of a heterographic homophone (*rows* and *rose*) through the common phonology, it should be harder (slower, with more errors) to reject the heterograph as belonging to the same semantic category as its homophone, to say, for example, that *tulip* and *rows* do not belong together. This too seems to be true (Luo, 1996).

Finally, if a word is briefly presented and then immediately another word is presented in the same place, the second, the mask, interferes with processing of the first word, the target. If the "mask" is a phonological associate of the target (*hear* and *here*), people identify the target better than if it is an orthographic associate (like *head*). Because these effects occur with presentation times of less than 100 ms, the phonological route is immediately in play (van Orden et al., 1990; Luo, 1996).

It is important to note that the apparent effects of phonology in lexical and semantic decisions have also been obtained for Japanese and Chinese scripts, which, as you may recall, are not as phonologically based (Perfetti & Zhang, 1995; Tan, Hoosain, & Siok, 1996; Wydell, Patterson, & Humphreys, 1993). For these logographic scripts too, phonological priming or interference effects seem to materialize early, along with visual-graphic effects, before meaning associates are activated. That is, the phonological process is prelexical (Perfetti & Zhang, 1995; Tan et al., 1996).

The Frequency Effect

However, the effects of phonology on word recognition are, interestingly, limited to low-frequency words in English and, as we shall see, in Chinese. Note that high-frequency, common words constitute the majority of tokens in our working vocabulary. They tend to be named very quickly whether or not they are "regular," that is, use the "normal" grapheme-to-phoneme correspondence (GPC) rules. For example, *have* is an irregular high-frequency word ("e" should make "a" say its name, in the parlance of my sons' first-grade teachers) and *make* is a regular one. Both are named very quickly by skilled readers. In contrast, low-frequency words are slower to name, especially by poor readers and when they are spelled irregularly (Seidenberg, 1985).

Seidenberg suggests that *all* readers recognize high-frequency words quickly from a direct visual route. Fast readers, he presumes, are also very familiar with low-frequency orthographic patterns and so can employ this route for them. Slower readers, on the other hand, take longer to recognize low-frequency words, and this longer time course allows for phonological information to build up from sublexical units. (Phonological information is also activated for fluent readers for high-frequency words like *the,* but the words are recognized and understood before the information has an opportunity to influence.)

Indeed, Jared and Seidenberg (1991) find homonym priming (*flower* to *rows*) *only* when the homonym is low frequency. They also find that a contradictory homophonic meaning, such as *meat* being a noun and *meet* a verb, does not impair categorizing a high-frequency word (here as noun or verb). This supports the view that high-frequency words access meaning directly and rapidly via a visual route, before phonology is aroused.

As I said earlier, Chinese and Japanese, like English, show rapid priming and interference consistent with their accessing a phonological code, despite their logographic nature. In Chinese the phonological route is also frequency dependent: low-frequency Chinese characters are slowed by phonographic irregularity, while high-frequency characters, which, as in English, constitute the bulk of text, are more quickly recognized and not delayed by irregularity (Seidenberg, 1985). Seidenberg argues that for both languages, phonological effects in irregular words arise from sublexical associations of the component characters.

The similarity between processes in the different kinds of scripts is striking. We have seen a phonological process implicated in a nonphonological script. We have seen the bulk of the tokens in both scripts coming from a subset of high-frequency words. And we have seen implications of a direct visual process for high-frequency words in both scripts. The commonalities strongly suggest that the mental association of script with spoken words, regardless of how the script is designed, is a perhaps-necessary process in the fluent reader, one who has internalized the script as a model of the spoken language.

Orthographic Depth

The *orthographic depth hypothesis* holds that we should see regular differences in naming (i.e., pronouncing a read word) versus lexical decision or semantic priming tasks between languages that have regular GPCs and those that do not. Regular GPC is orthographic shallowness (such as Serbo-Croatian); orthographically deep languages include English and Hebrew, especially unpointed Hebrew. The idea is that in the shallow languages, one can pronounce quickly, without recognizing the word, but in the deeper languages, pronunciation depends on recognizing the word and therefore is postlexical and can be influenced by anything that speeds lexical access, such as semantic priming.

For shallow languages (Serbo-Croatian) as compared with a deeper language (English) and a deep language (Hebrew), in fact, a smaller frequency effect is observed: (a) There is not such a large difference between naming times of high- and low-frequency words; (b) irregular low-frequency words are not differentially slowed; and (c) nonwords are no slower to pronounce than real words. In addition, there is a smaller effect of semantic priming on naming times the more orthographically shallow the language—Hebrew > pointed Hebrew > English > Serbo-Croatian

(Frost, 1994; Frost, Katz, & Bentin, 1987). All systems give fluent readers access to pronunciation—some immediately, and some rapidly but in parallel with access to the meaning.

Inability to Suppress Phonological Associations

Phonological interference is demonstrable in other tasks. For example, when frequency, sense, and so on are controlled, in English it is hard to read (silently) sentences composed of words with the same first letter, such as "Peter Piper picked a peck of pickled peppers . . ."—appropriately called the *tongue-twister effect.* Zhang and Perfetti (1993) found such an effect also in Chinese. This is interesting for two reasons. The first is that in English we cannot be sure whether the effect arises because of the repetition of the grapheme "p" or the phoneme /p/ it stands for; in Chinese, words with the same initial sounds do not look alike, and so the effect cannot arise from a visual route—as Figure 11.4 illustrates. The second is that here we see an automatic, unstoppable phonological process in silent reading, a phonological process not directly indicated by the writing system and not required by the task, as it is in, say, naming.

We also see an automatic phonological interference in a variant of the Stroop effect (Tzelgov, Henik, Sneg, & Baruch, 1996). In the Stroop effect, a subject is asked to name the color of the ink a color word is printed in; that is, to say "black" when the word *blue* (in black ink) is printed. Unable to suppress reading for meaning, the subject is slowed or inaccurate relative to color-neutral words. The Stroop effect is obtained in all languages and with all writing systems, perhaps more strongly for logographic scripts (like Chinese) than for syllabic or alphabetic ones (see Tzeng & Wang, 1983, and correspondence).

Tzelgov et al. transliterated English and Hebrew color words and presented them to Hebrew-English bilingual readers. Now note that even balanced bilinguals would have no experience seeing *blue* in Hebrew letters—in Hebrew the transliteration is a nonsense word—and so *could not* arouse the interfering meaning directly from the orthography. For interference to occur, readers had to use the script to reconstruct the sound, recognize the sound from the other language, and access the meaning. In the Stroop task there is no need to read the word or access its meaning; the task in fact demands that the subject attend to surface features of the print and suppress reading-for-meaning. Nevertheless, a Stroop interference effect was obtained. Thus the letters automatically activated the sound, and the sound pattern activated the meaning in the other language, slowing a competing meaning-name access in the language of response.

Auditory/Articulatory Interference Evidence

Another method for showing that we read using phonology is to interfere with the reader's ability to "hear" the word: asking the reader to articulate a rote utterance while reading. This is known as *articulatory suppression.* Research has dem-

Alveolar Stop Story

deng dan dan bu dan dai tu ding de ding duan zhang de du duan du xing ta jue
邓　单　丹　不　担　待　秃　顶　的　丁　段　长　的　独　断　独　行，她　决

ding diao dong dao di di de tai deng chang zuo dian du gong dong tian dian
定　调　动　到　弟　弟　的　台　灯　厂　做　电　镀　工。冬　天，电

du gong de dan diao te dian shi de ta tong ding si ding jue xin da dan tou
镀　工　的　单　调　特　点　使　得　她　痛　定　思　定，决　定　大　胆　投

kao da ti qin yue dui deng tai da ding yin gu wei yue dui ding diao ta da
考　大　提　琴　乐　队，登　台　打　定　音　鼓　为　乐　队　定　调。她　打

dian de du dao te dian shi ta duo de le yue dui tao tai sai de te deng jiang
点　的　独　到　特　点　使　她　夺　得　了　乐　队　淘　汰　赛　的　特　等　奖。

Alveolar Stop Control Story

zhang xiao ying bu zai ren nai guang tou wu ke zhang de yi yi gu xing
张　晓　迎　不　再　忍　耐　光　头　吴　科　长　的　一　意　孤　行，

ta jue xin yao dao shu shu de deng ju chang zuo dian du gong mei tian dian
她　决　心　要　到　权　权　的　灯　具　厂　做　电　镀　工。每　天　电

du gong de ku zao sheng huo shi de ta xin fan yi luan jue xin nu li bao kao
镀　工　的　枯　燥　生　活　使　得　她　心　烦　意　乱，决　心　努　力　报　考

jiao xiang yue dui zuo ge da ji yue shou wei yue dui pei yue ta ji gu de
交　响　乐　队　做　个　打　击　乐　手　为　乐　队　配　乐。她　击　鼓　的

te you zhuan chang shi ta ying de le yue dui biao yan sai de yi deng jiang
特　有　专　长　使　她　赢　得　了　乐　队　表　演　赛　的　一　等　奖。

Figure 11.4. Tongue-Twisters in Chinese

SOURCE: From S. Zhang and C. A. Perfetti (1993, p. 1085). Copyright © 1993 by the American Psychological Association. Reprinted with permission.

NOTE: The Chinese script does not visually code initial sounds in the same fashion, so that the tongue-twister reflects a repetition at the phonological level only, unlike English.

onstrated that many judgments about the sounds of items, as in whether two words rhyme (Kleiman, 1975) or whether a word and alternate spelling (*ocean, oshun*) sound the same, are impaired by suppression (see Besner, 1987, for review). And suppression makes it much harder to spell words, a task that also may require a conscious, active employment of a phonological code.

A more critical question, though, is whether lexical access is impaired during suppression: Is it harder to identify the word to retrieve its meaning? Here, some studies say it is, a dam*m*ing of the phonological route, while many say it is not, perhaps a dam*n*ing of it. Besner resolves the conflict between studies with the suggestion that there are several levels of phonological processing, not all of which suppression affects.

I will briefly consider two suppression studies with conflicting implications for a phonological route. The first is the seminal and frequently quoted experiment of Kleiman (1975). Using articulatory suppression, he compared rhyme judgments (definitely implicating phonology), visual similarity judgments (presumably not implicating phonology), and synonym judgments (the experimental condition asking whether phonology is necessary to access meaning from a printed word). Rhyming judgments were affected during suppression, but synonym judgments were no more affected than were judgments about the visual similarity of items. From this he (and others citing him) have argued that the phonological route is not employed in retrieving words' meanings.

Clearly, suppression affects phonological processes in determining rhyming. Besner notes, though, that there is better memory for pseudohomophones like *oshun* than for other pronounceable nonwords, an effect that is explicable, like rhyming judgments, only through phonological processes—here, in short-term memory. This effect does not disappear under suppression; that is, suppression does not interfere with the phonological process that enables access to the lexicon and meaning. Therefore we cannot rule out a phonological process in reading normal words simply because we do not see impairment during suppression. In fact, in a final experiment, Kleiman found a suppression effect, critical perhaps when subjects needed to remember read words to decide if a sentence hung together, if the sentence was anomalous. Of course, *natural* reading always involves memory of early items to integrate into narrative structure, as we will explore in detail in the next section, so access to phonology may be a must in reading.

More recently, V. Coltheart, Avons, and Trollope (1990) measured suppression's effects on detecting sentence anomaly created by erroneous heterographic homonyms, such as "The none said her prayers," or by visually similar control words as in "The nine said her prayers." As others have shown, it is harder (slower and less accurate; e.g., van Orden et al. 1990) to reject homophones than nonhomophones in silent reading; that is, the subject is more than twice as likely to accept the sentence, a high *false positive* rate. Coltheart et al. replicated this and also found many more errors generally in the suppression experiment—which is not surprising because subjects must talk and read at the same time.

However, importantly, the homophones were *no more often* accepted than the controls—that is, their homo*phon*y was not noticed during suppression. This suggests that the phonological route to lexical access is blocked in a phonology-demanding task such as articulatory suppression. This implies that normally, without such suppression, a phonological route may be traveled toward lexical access. While the task, like Kleiman's, involves memory to note an anomaly, it implicates the phonological route not only in the memory code but also normally in lexical access, when the homophones activate their heterographs.

Given the conflicting results, we can conclude only that the phonological routes suppression affects are used by some readers for some tasks at some times, but probably are not necessary.

Eye Movement Evidence

Folk and Morris (1995) review the evidence for phonological mediation and conclude that much of it derives from unnatural tasks, such as interrupting the text for a lexical decision, or shadowing or articulating nonsense while reading for comprehension. Instead, they used eye movements during self-paced reading to indicate the role of a phonological code. As we have seen, homographs are fixated longer than unambiguous words if both meanings are common and when the preceding context is neutral. If the *following* context suggests the less common meaning, it is read more slowly, but readers do not regress and refixate it (Folk & Morris, 1995). Critically, too, we are not slowed in reading correct heterographs (*sail* or *sale*); the correct meaning is aroused before the phonological ambiguity interferes. However, homophonic *errors* (*sale* for *sail*) are read faster than nonhomophonic errors (*sale* for *salt*): The common phonology assists (Daneman, Reingold, & Davidson, 1995).

Folk and Morris (1995) also implicated phonological mediation in reading heterophonic homographs. Consider the word *tear.* Its spelling pattern is ambiguous: It could represent either /tir/ or /ter/, and we normally know which one only from context. (And sometimes we don't know even with context: The source of the Hudson River is a lake high in the Catskill Mountains, the name of which I frequently read aloud in a favorite children's book. It is Lake Tear-in-the-Clouds, and I have no idea whether the namers intended to evoke an image of a rift or a drop of water in the clouds.) The heterophonic words slowed reading time and produced regressive fixations compared with phonologically unambiguous words. So if you derive the wrong *sound,* you must backtrack (heterophones); if you derive the wrong meaning and right sound (homophones), you merely slow down. This suggests that the phonological representation obligatorily mediates between word and meaning, even if words are identified from orthography.

Thus, for fluent readers it appears that a direct visual route may be faster for lexical access than an indirect phonological route, but the route to the word's sound is aroused in any event, perhaps postlexically and automatically, to access meaning or when the direct route does not provide sufficient information. There appears to be some need for phonological activation for a memory representation, which in turn is needed for constructing sense. When the correct phonological representation emerges from a heterographic homonym, it can be used to reconstruct the appropriate meaning; if it has not been aroused, for a heterophone, the visual representation, more ephemeral perhaps, is not available and the word must be reexamined.

Heterography and Regularity:
How Useful Is the Phonological Route Anyway?

As I have been pointing out throughout this chapter, and you were probably aware anyway, the path from writing to phoneme is not straightforward in English. It is possible that we assemble the sound of the word by adding GPCs, but that would make for serious difficulties in words such as *enough* or even *have.* For these words, as perhaps for the logographic scripts of Chinese or Japanese Kanji, it may be that the "sound" derives from something like the whole-word pattern, *addressed phonology,* as opposed to being put together letter by letter, *assembled phonology.* For all languages, we may recognize a word through either addressed or assembled phonology, whichever reaches a solution for a particular word first (Frost, 1994).

When we read aloud or name, we *must* convert the print to an articulation pattern; the task requires retrieval not just of meaning but of the pronunciation. The dual-route model (M. Coltheart, Curtis, Atkins, & Haller, 1993) holds that a regular word is recognized in one of three ways: indirectly, the letters are processed through GPCs to assemble the phonology; directly, the letters address phonology; and directly, the letters arouse a semantic representation, which in turn also addresses phonology.

The dual-route model was developed after observing different patterns of reading disturbance following brain damage: *acquired dyslexia* (M. Coltheart, 1996; M. Coltheart, Patterson, & Marshall, 1980; Patterson, Marshall, & Coltheart, 1985). These will be discussed in detail in *Language in Atypical Populations.* Here I note that so-called *deep dyslexia* and *phonological dyslexia* disrupt phonological assembly, while *surface dyslexia* preserves the assembly route, eliminating direct addressing. Deep dyslexia also disrupts phonological addressing, which is spared in phonological dyslexia, a more mild disorder. Each of these patient types has difficulty reading different types of English words, making a characteristic error pattern, as we see next.

Consider different kinds of letter strings: *scythe, baver,* and *fire.* Both deep and phonological dyslexics are impaired on the nonword *baver*—this must be assembled. In contrast, it is accessible to the surface dyslexic's intact assembly route because *baver* may be read using regular GPCs. *Fire,* a high-frequency regular word, causes difficulty primarily for deep dyslexics, for whom regularity holds no advantage. Attempting its visual address, the deep dyslexic may access by mistake a semantic neighbor, *mis*reading it therefore as, say, *burn. Scythe,* an irregular word, can be correctly read *only* on the direct address route, possibly spared for deep and phonological dyslexics. It will be regularized (read as /skayð/) by surface dyslexics.

Normal subjects show parallel results using speed rather than accuracy as a measure. Known irregular words, like *scythe,* and nonwords, like *baver,* they name more slowly than regular, familiar words. Traditionally it is argued that even with all routes intact, pseudowords take time to assemble and uncommon and irregular words can be neither assembled nor quickly addressed. Known regular words quickly access their names via all routes.

In a seminal set of experiments, Glushko (1979) presented alternatives to this explanation. Glushko created pseudowords that modeled irregular spelling patterns to some degree. For example, *heaf* could be pronounced /hif/ following *leaf* or *sheaf,* or it could be pronounced /hɛf/, following the pattern for *deaf.* In contrast, *hean* has an unambiguous model in *mean, bean,* and *lean.* Overall, the "rules" for English support the regularity of the /i/ reading for "ea," with /ɛ/ an exception to the normal pattern. Glushko reasoned that if readers read pseudowords assembling GPCs, there

---

Box 11.4. Phonological Mediation in Reading?

— Heterographic homonyms *(sail/sale)* prime both meanings.
— Words with regular grapheme-to-phoneme correspondences are quicker to name and recognize in lexical decision.
— Frequency effect: High-frequency words are quicker to name and recognize regardless of the regularity of their GPC in all languages (whether or not there is a strong phonological code), and low-frequency words are slower, particularly if they are irregular.
— *Orthographic depth hypothesis:* Different writing systems reflect phonology more (shallow) or less (deep) transparently. Readers employ phonological processing strategies to the degree their writing systems permit. Deeper languages show stronger frequency effects; for shallow languages, even nonwords are quickly named and recognized. For shallow languages, there is only a small facilitation by semantic priming.
— But even for deep languages there is a "tongue-twister effect"—slower reading when the same sounds repeat in a sentence even though the words do not resemble one another.
— And for Hebrew-English bilinguals, transliterated English color names produce Stroop interference when subjects name the color in Hebrew. The interference can only arise from the homonymy to the English word, and Hebrew is a deep language.
— *Articulatory suppression:* Speaking nonsense while reading retards recognition of homonymy, which prevents access to a normal phonological route. It also retards recognition of rhymes but not of synonymy.
— Eye movements suggest that readers misinterpreting homographic or heterographic homonyms (same or different spelling, same pronunciation) slow down in reading but correct their structures without reexamining the word.
— Readers misinterpreting heterophonic homographs (same spelling, different pronunciation, such as *tear*) return to the word.
— Results as a whole are consistent with a phonological level in reading that mediates memory of the words, which is necessary in meaning construction but not necessary in identifying the word.
— *Addressed phonology:* Whole word activates its pronunciation, which is presumed necessary for reading irregular words.
— *Assembled phonology:* Readers put together the word's pronunciation from grapheme-to-phoneme correspondences, which is presumed to be at least necessary for reading nonwords.
— *Direct visual route:* Orthographic pattern arouses the semantic representation and name.
— Different brain damage patterns support differential impairments on these routes.
    — Deep dyslexia disrupts both direct and assembled phonology, which leaves patients reading using the direct visual route. Patients cannot read nonwords and make semantic substitutions even on regular, high-frequency words.

(continued)

Box 11.4 Continued

— Phonological dyslexia disrupts the assembled phonological route. Patients cannot read nonwords but make few errors on real words, recognizing them through both direct routes.
— Surface dyslexia impairs direct routes but leaves assembly intact. Patients regularize the pronunciation of even common irregular words (*have* → /hev/) but can read regular nonwords.
— *Neighborhood effect:* Readers are slower at naming irregular words that have many "neighbors" with regular pronunciation, such as *have*, in the context of *cave, wave, . . .*" They are also slower at reading nonwords, such as *mave*, which have a common alternative pronunciation in the lexicon.

---

should be no difference naming *heaf* and *hean*. However, if they pronounce *by analogy* to known words (implying that each letter string activates at least one entry in a lexicon), they should be relatively slowed for *heaf* because there are competing analogies for pronunciation.

Glushko found that not only did it take longer to read aloud pseudowords with irregular models, it also took longer to read aloud *regular words* like *leaf* with irregular *neighbors* like *deaf* than it did to read regular words like *mean* with only regular neighbors. This suggests that phonology is not simply addressed, nor is reading (aloud) determined strictly by rule. Rather, the orthography arouses pronunciation *by analogy.* The stronger the analogy, the fewer alternative models there are, and the faster a pronunciation is determined.

Interactive Models

The competition model presented in the last two chapters may come to mind. In this case, what we are competing for is control of the articulation, the winning pronunciation scheme. The letter patterns and past experience form a "cue," the strength of which is determined by frequency of exposure. For a word with consistent neighbors, there is no direct competition, and the unique pronunciation is decided quickly; there is only one "cue" and it wins by default. For a word with inconsistent neighbors or "cues," there is a competition, resulting in less activation weight to the most frequent alternative and thus a slowing. Glushko, in fact, found reading errors indicative of a winning of the competition by the wrong alternative: /hev/ for *have*, particularly if *wave* or *cave* had been recently read.

However, the disadvantage of unlike neighbors, or the *neighborhood effect* on *common* words holds *only* if the inconsistent neighbors have been recently presented or blocked—*cave, save,* /hev/. Normally, high-frequency words are quickly and correctly recognized despite their irregularity or neighborhoods (van Orden et al., 1990). This suggests that the weighting of high-frequency words to their pronunciations is very strong and relatively stable in the normal language environment.

It is important to recognize that the analogy model arose from a task that specifically required subjects to access a word's pronunciation. We may ask "What kinds of competitions or cues are there to *meaning* access, the goal of reading?" Clearly, one possibility is that the understanding of narratives read aloud and to oneself both employ (a) the same weights between spelling pattern and pronunciation; (b) weights determined by frequency of exposure and regularity, that is, a "mechanism" for deriving analogy; (c) a name "layer" weighted to meaning associates (as we saw in Chapter 3); and (d) meaning associates stimulating sound associates, which in turn stimulate spelling patterns.

Alternatively, as we have been suggesting, the pronunciation routes may be critical *only* in reading *aloud,* with silent reading allowing interpretation from the visual letter patterns themselves, especially when highly familiar as in frequently encountered words. Regardless, neither a visual nor a phonological route nor their combination necessarily entails the incorporation of explicit correspondence "rules," like "w" = /w/ or *word* = WORD (I am using the capitals to indicate the visual representation)—as in the original dual-route model. Rather, encountered associations can be represented in proportion to the frequency of encounter. So, as in Figure 11.3, "w" slightly activates both /w/ and WO (and the reverse), and WORD is realized by the strong and stable activation pattern of a set of associated units. If we assume that both routes are traveled in parallel with "cross-talk," or interactive activation, we have a class of parallel distributed models of lexical arousal, which account for many of the results that we have examined.

Finally, for normal reading, that is, reading in context, we need to add contributions to this stable activation pattern of units responding to co-occurring words and meaning associations. These would not only contribute to the pattern of activity that constitutes a word but would also prime orthographic and phonological associates.

Such interactive neural net-type models include the covariant learning model, proposed by van Orden et al. (1990), a resonance model proposed by Grossberg and Stone (1986), and a distributed developmental model proposed by Seidenberg and McClelland (1989). The simulations differ in some mathematical assumptions, which are beyond the scope of this book, and some psycholinguistic assumptions, which we will consider.

The covariant learning model stresses the role of "subphonemic phonology," the speech features that print is supposed to activate, as central to the reading process, not simply as an alternative to a direct visual route. Like the neural net models we have examined in other chapters, this model trains itself by comparing input and output and readjusting, or *covariant learning.* Beginning readers, and the model, rely on associations between orthographic and linguistic subsymbols, not on programmed rule-governed processes. The product of this learning yields a *subsymbolic phonology,* that is, context-dependent letter patterns (like "gh" in final position = /f/), which take into account the frequency patterns in the language. Thus the program learns more than one pattern for "ave" because of its association to both *have* and *wave;* its performance is affected by the statistical regularity of input-output correspondences.

Van Orden et al. claim that the advantage of the subsymbolic phonology as mediator is that it is more reliable than the visual route: There is a greater degree of correspondence between morphemes and sound than between orthography and morphemes. This is questionable because, as I said earlier, our writing system is "deep," in part because it captures morphemic correspondences sometimes in lieu of phonological ones. However, van Orden et al. note that our writing also includes many pseudomorphemic possibilities, like *relish* (which is not "to lish again"). They find these more transparent if phonologically mediated.

Now, in fact, studies have shown an influence of the grapheme-to-morpheme correspondence. Words like *relish* are harder to name and make lexical decisions about than are true-prefixed words. This could be because the "re" is associated both with /rɛ/ and /ri/-, and therefore the reaction time for lexical decisions is slowed by the competition between them. We also see an effect of morphological structures on judgments of homonymy: It is harder to recognize the pronunciation similarity between *fined* and *find,* which have different morphological structures, than between pairs like *healed* and *heeled,* which are consistent on both morphological and phonological levels. Van Orden et al. acknowledge that these demonstrations indicate a grapheme-to-morpheme route, but they point out that the demonstrations have not controlled for orthographic-phonological covariance patterns, and so could also arise from a phonological-to-morphological mediation. This distributed model takes orthographic-phonological regularities (neither learned by rule nor representing graphemes and phonemes per se) as the pattern of activation that instantiates lexical items.

Grossberg and Stone's (1986) resonance model stresses the interaction of the input pattern, either visual in reading or auditory in speech, with meaning, that is, with existing representations in long-term memory. A representation, here, as in other neural net models, is not a stored item in a fixed lexicon but an activity pattern distributed over a number of units. Recognition is achieved when the activity pattern stimulated by the input (bottom-up) "resonates" with activity patterns generated from memory (top-down) to achieve a dominating pattern, the experience of which is the word or meaning. The model accounts for the faster recognition of high-frequency words by their stronger top-down activity pattern, which is more likely to "select" (produce resonance with) incomplete input until bottom-up information is strong enough to override it.

An important construct in this model is that of *masking field,* a "subsymbolic" level, in which common serially ordered "chunks," like "tion" or "ough," yield a stronger activity pattern than is predicted by the sum of individual activities. These fields compete with one another, and the cooperative (within-a-field)-competitive (between-fields) interactions result in the word-length effect that we saw in the word-letter tasks: faster detection of a given letter in a longer string than a shorter string, independent of whether the letter is itself a word (like *a* or *I*). The model permits resonance with any size or quality of input, even a single letter, but resonance with a masking field increases the activity pattern common to the components synergistically, which speeds recognition.

Van Orden et al.'s model emphasized the phonological route; the resonance model emphasized the visual route. Both rely on distributed representations and cue competition leading to a dominating activity pattern that is the word or meaning. Seidenberg and McClelland implemented an interactive visual and phonological route model along the lines I have described for the PDP group in previous chapters and consistent with Seidenberg's work in this chapter. Input simultaneously stimulates visual and phonological associations in parallel and will, in a yet-to-be-implemented version, integrate the activation patterns with semantic activations arising either from experience or from context. (This model has come to be called "the triangle model"—Coltheart, 1996—because of the three-way activations by phonological, visual, and semantic sources.) A key feature of this model is parallel activation, so that phonological effects are visible primarily for low-frequency words for which strongly weighted visual connections have not emerged through experience.

The simulation regularized pronunciation of irregular words, particularly after a block of inconsistent words (*wave, cave, save* → /hev/ for *have*), and showed priming by rhymes with consistent orthography (*rough-tough*) and hindrance by inconsistency (*cough,* for this pair). These effects occur as weights to the hidden units are modified after training: Most hidden units respond to consistent orthographic rhymes, fewer to orthographic nonrhymes, and the fewest, to unrelated words.

The other key features of the model lie in what is not programmed. There are no word units per se, but context is provided by coding grapheme triples, as was done in the past-tense model reviewed in Chapter 5. GPC rules and morphemes also are not explicitly programmed. All arise implicitly as weights are modified given the co-occurrence patterns in the training set and the feedback comparing output attempts to input structure. Indeed, Besner, Twilley, McCann, and Seergobin (1990) critique the model as effective primarily for words it was trained on, and Coltheart et al. (1993), implementing a similar model but with GPC rules, produced stronger performance, a better simulation of human behavior. Programming rules allows one to avoid perhaps arbitrary segmentation features such as grapheme-triples and their phonology match.

As a group the interactive models simulate an impressive array of results, notably without programming GPC rules or words themselves. All of the models employ a "subsymbolic" level, either explicitly (van Orden et al., 1990) or implicitly in masking fields (Grossberg & Stone, 1986) or hidden units (Seidenberg & McClelland, 1989). The subsymbolic level encodes common patterns of orthographic associations not corresponding to graphemes, digrams, or morphemes. If these in fact model human orthography processing, the subsymbolic level is the encoder of analogies or neighborhoods. They are not hardwired but emerge through experience, what van Orden et al. term *covariant learning.*

Box 11.5. Interactionist Models

— *Dual-route model:* There is both a visual (direct) route and a phonologically mediated (indirect) route to a word stored in a lexicon. Items in the lexicon are activated visually and through addressed phonology. Nonwords are assembled, so there are different mechanisms for words and nonwords. They use both a visual and a phonological route.

— *Analogy model:* We arrive at a pronunciation through recognition of the input's visual and auditory similarities to known words, and pronounce the word by analogy to them.

— *Subsymbolic phonology:* Orthographic components map to sound components, which mediate interactively between orthography and the lexicon.

— *Resonance model:* Mutual and reciprocal arousal of components of sound and orthography, which produce a wave of activation that resonates with activation patterns from memory. Cooperation between frequently activated components, a masking field, increases their arousal potential relative to components acting alone. Competitive interaction among masking fields together with the cooperation within them yield word-length effects, that is, better recognition of a component among frequently co-occurring units than alone.

— *Distributed developmental (triangle) model:* Units coding grapheme triples serve as input and communicate through hidden units to phonological units and orthographic units. The output pattern is mapped to the input pattern and weights of the associations producing the output pattern increased or decreased depending on the degree of match. Hidden units come to reflect activation patterns corresponding to commonly experienced grapheme associations. Words arise as lexical activation, not lexical access; there is explicit programming of neither words nor grapheme-to-phoneme rules. Ultimately the model will allow mutual interaction between orthographic and phonological units and, between each of these, hidden units, and meaning-representing units.

Uncovering and Establishing Coherence in Text

Our discussion of reading to this point makes it dull: Why would anyone *like* reading if what it entails is merely the discovery of words from letter patterns or, worse, of letters from within words? While we have focused on these building blocks, we must recognize that words and letters are only tools to the true purpose, the experience of a story. To some extent, reading a narrative is like hearing a story "out of someone's head" (quoting a child I told stories to). And to that extent, reading should use the discourse processes of speech as well as, perhaps, its phonological route.

Writing has different conventions from speech, though, and makes different demands: It is divorced from the immediate context and must establish its own coherence, building characters, settings, and feelings verbally; it does not disappear as it is uttered (is not rapidly fading), but provides its own hard memory form; there is no opportunity for writer and reader to interact to establish common ground, as there is for participants in conversation. And, in the case of fiction, the reader knows and willingly enters into a "contract" of deception and pretense, at first blush, unlike the presumptions of truth, informativeness, and brevity that participants bring to conversation.

In this section we examine studies showing how readers construct representations for written discourse and how they employ and/or modify spoken language processes to do so.

Constructivist Versus Minimalist Positions

As I discussed in detail in Chapter 5 on discourse processing, work on sentence processing in the 1970s showed that subjects do not retain verbatim text for long. They encode from it key propositions or simple relationships, which are then connected through overlapping arguments into a microstructure. The propositions represent semantic relations like agent-verb, independent of the surface structure from which the relation was derived (e.g., passive versus active). Consequently, subjects are more likely to think they read sentences consistent with meaning than those that better match the input words and structure.

In Kintsch and van Dijk's (1978) model (see Chapter 5 for review), macrostructure is derived cyclically from microstructure through a process of systematic editing: removing propositions that are not causes or consequences of subsequent propositions, replacing propositions with their generalizations, and constructing factual inferences to replace propositions that tap into general knowledge. These operations eventually produce the gist of the story: first, the topic, and then ever-more-detailed developments of it. The macrostructure determines coherence of, and, importantly, memory for, the narrative. In research on reading, for example, Lorch (1993) showed that, following a distraction, readers benefit more from a reminder of the topic than from the development that had been interrupted.

In producing a mental construction of the narrative's structure, the reader does not rely only on the words in the text. The reader makes *inferences,* defined by McKoon and Ratcliff (1992) as "any piece of information that is not explicitly stated in a text" (p. 440). Inferences may be logically trivial, like those licensed by syntax such as gap-filling (e.g., Who is it difficult to argue with in "the stern judge was difficult for the defense to argue with [t] about the pending appeal"?—an example from Chapter 5) or connecting a pronoun (or generalization like "vehicle") to an antecedent (or specific instance like sports car). They may also be logically trivial deductions based on a combination of the text and extralinguistic knowledge, for example, if the tree is to the left of the house, then the house is to the right of the tree (Bransford, Barclay, & Franks, 1972). Or they may be complex deductions, as in an example from Chapter 5, where the text includes only that a building collapsed and *earthquake* is primed.

According to constructivist hypotheses (see Graesser, Singer, & Trabasso, 1994), readers may approach a text from different motivations: a desire to be entertained (and therefore drawn in to the text), a desire to understand and learn (as with an expository text like this one), or a desire to proofread, not actually reading for meaning. The goal determines the depth of the processing and the kind of structure the reader actively attempts. As in speech, the reader confronts the text from a Gricean perspective (see Chapter 2), that the author is being cooperative; that is, the narrative will be coherent and each sentence will be informative with respect to the author's goals. Readers who are reading for meaning attempt not only to establish coherence but also to relate each proposition to communication goals, either those of the author or, in reading for entertainment, of the characters.

As we read *on-line,* Graesser et al. argue, we make three types of inferences: superordinate goals (e.g., the hero is seeking revenge), earlier events that have caused current ones, and global thematic inferences that integrate the major components of the text. In contrast, we do not infer the next twist in the plot or alternate twists it might have taken; that kind of active speculation that we do also engage in is not automatic, as the text is flowing, but occurs during deliberate breaks.

The importance of goals and causes has been deduced by analyses of readers' descriptions of their comprehension attempts: Readers claim to focus on "*why* episodes in the text occur and *why* the author explicitly mentions particular information in the message" (Graesser et al., 1994, p. 379). In addition, subjects rating the relatedness of sentences derived from text consider causally connected sentences to be psychologically closer, and consider those causally connected through fewer inferences to be the most connected (Trabasso, van den Broek, & Suh, 1989). Of course, these results do not mean that readers necessarily search for these causes while reading; they may do so only when making explicit the organization of the text. Thus Graesser et al. advocate synthesizing discourse coherence analyses with readers' descriptions of how they comprehend and with semantic priming studies that intercept reading on-line but create an unnatural reading task. When these converge on the same finding, each offsets the others' shortcomings.

A significant issue in the cognitive psychology of reading is the extent to which the reader creates and maintains different types of inferences in working memory to assist with the on-line establishment of a mental structure for the narrative. This has typically been addressed in a priming-type recognition memory paradigm (see McKoon & Ratcliff, 1980, 1992; Ratcliff & McKoon, 1978, 1981; Chapter 5). In this task, a text is presented, consisting, for example, of several sentences, such as these from McKoon and Ratcliff (1992):

Introduction
The crowd's cheers alerted the onlookers to the president's arrival. The assassin wanted to kill the president. He reached for his high-powered rifle. He lifted the gun to his shoulder to peer through its scope.

Control continuation
The assassin hit the president with the first shot he fired from his rifle. Then he started to run toward the west. The searing sun blinded his eyes. (p. 447)

At the end of the passage, the subject decides whether "kill" appeared in the passage. Decision time is expected to be rapid and correct if the word is in working memory and slower or incorrect if it is not. Working memory, of course, is not the only memory we have; "kill" would be in semantic memory whether or not it was in the story and it may exist in a comprehensive memory for the story itself. Working memory contains some select, small amount of information immediately active for the task at hand, in this case the understanding of the text.

According to the constructivist hypothesis, working memory should contain key macrostructure elements, such as overall topic and goal, for as long as they are relevant. So, in the assassin example given above, the goal of "kill" should be active until the second sentence of the continuation, when the assassination was accomplished. Then it is replaced by the goal of escaping. In either of the following continuations, the goal is not accomplished and so constructivists hold that it should remain actively available (McKoon & Ratcliff, 1992):

Try again continuation
The scope fell off as he lifted the rifle. He lay prone to draw a sight without the scope. The searing sun blinded his eyes.
Substitution continuation
The scope fell off as he lifted the rifle. So he reached for his hand grenades. The searing sun blinded his eyes. (p. 447)

In contrast, McKoon and Ratcliff's (1992) *minimalist* approach holds that while such goal/topic information or any other inferences may be retrieved if needed, they are not present in working memory unless the reader needs them to create *local* coherence; unless the text makes sense only with them. Indeed, McKoon and Ratcliff found that goals were not maintained unless needed for local coherence. Thus, as we saw in Chapter 5, the building collapse → earthquake inference is not immediate but develops over time as it is needed (Till, Mross, & Kintsch, 1988). On the other hand, referents of an anaphor are immediately available in working memory because, without them, the text locally makes no sense.

Likewise, some global, causal inferences may remain active, but only if needed to interconnect the incoming text (Albrecht & Myers, 1995). Consider, for example, the serenade from street level of a woman on a high floor, accomplished by launching speakers via helium balloons (Chapter 5): Each sentence fits with the rest only with respect to the context, so we might expect contextual information (high floor, balloons, serenade, and so on) to be constantly available so that each sentence may be construed.

Many studies have examined when inferential information is available in working memory. As I said, anaphors usually activate their referents. In fact, in coherent discourse, the context activates in working memory relevant character information for a pronoun before it actually appears (McKoon, Gerrig, & Greene, 1996). Of course, grammatical use of a pronoun (or empty category) requires predictability—the binding conditions. Psychologically, predictability means that the referents' characteristics are aroused without explicit reference.

Inferences that narrow word meanings to fit context also seem to be automatic. They include, as we have seen, which meaning of a homonym is needed (Chapter 5; Till et al., 1988). They also include greater leaps of logic: If the word *container* appears, and some sentences later it materializes that the *container* is for apples, *basket* is automatically primed more than, say, *bottle* (McKoon & Ratcliff, 1992). And it includes still greater leaps, that is, bridging inferences, provided they are needed for local coherence (Lea, 1995).

Bridging inferences are deductions connecting propositions through an unstated, but temporally and causally intermediate event. For example, "In a fit of anger, he threw the vase against the wall. The replacement was expensive" entails the anaphora that "the replacement" was a "vase," as well as the bridge that throwing the vase caused it to break, so it needed replacing. If the second sentence focused on the anger rather than the vase replacement, as in "He began seeing a therapist," the vase breaking is still logical but is not necessary for coherence. As predicted by McKoon and Ratcliff (1992), in a lexical decision task Lea (1995) found priming for bridge words like *break* only when they established local coherence, not when they were probable but not immediately relevant as in the therapist case.

While bridging inferences and meaning-narrowing inferences are automatically available, there are ready inferences that are not made unless required specifically by the text. Instruments are usually not inferred: "She stirred her coffee" does not activate *spoon* (McKoon & Ratcliff, 1992). Counter to constructivism, causal or resulting inferences may not be automatically made—like the breaking of the vase after it hit the wall, or "death" after a character is described as falling from a high floor (McKoon & Ratcliff, 1992).

However, these inferences can become activated on a need-to-know basis, if they are not already in working memory, regardless of local coherence. Klin and Myers (1993) showed that causal information is reactivated if it is necessary for understanding the text (as "death" would be if the passage continued to talk about a funeral). Hurtema, Dopkins, Klin, and Myers (1993) found a reactivation of the goal information in a McKoon and Ratcliff -like task, provided the new action was sufficiently discrepant from the original goal. And Albrecht and O'Brien (1993) found that actions uncharacteristic of a described character, despite their local coherence, took longer to read than characteristic actions, suggesting that the reader was reactivating the character description and noting the global inconsistency.

Readers seem, perhaps after the fact, to construct greater representations of the story than are needed for local coherence. For example, there is evidence that the characters' feelings are activated given only a description of the situation the characters find themselves in. Gernsbacher, Goldsmith, and Robertson (1992) found that subjects read sentences describing a character's emotion more quickly the more likely it was given the story, and named emotions more quickly that described the activated emotion. For example, in one of their stories a character robs a store at which a friend works, to learn later that the friend loses his job as a result. Although *guilt* was never mentioned, subsequent sentences mentioning guilt were more quickly read than those mentioning pride or shyness, and subjects were faster at reading the word *guilty* out loud.

Not only do readers infer and assume the emotional point of view of the protagonist, but they may also take the protagonist's physical point of view, slowing their reading if that perspective changes. For example, it is slower to read "Carmen went into a museum. She approached the pigeons quietly" than it is to read either "Carmen went into a museum. She approached the mummies quietly" or "Carmen went out of the museum. She approached the pigeons quietly" (de Vega, 1995). To produce such physical perspective taking, the conflicting sentences must be next to one another—locally incoherent—or special instructions must be given to the reader (O'Brien & Albrecht, 1992). Thus setting information is probably not maintained normally in working memory but recedes into the background. It is not as clear for the emotion information, which may remain in working memory.

Graesser et al. propose 13 classes of inferences, roughly half of which are constructed during reading, either automatically or strategically. Consistent with McKoon and Ratcliff's minimalist view, they propose automatic construction of reference, case structure, and bridging causal inferences to maintain local coherence. Constructivists and minimalists also both accept that readers think about text and actively make other inferences "off-line," not as the words are being taken in. Inferences that Graesser et al. list as generated off-line are causal consequences (what will happen next rather than what precipitated the current action or state), possible subcategories of a generalization presented (like "bacon and eggs" from "breakfast"), subordinate goals (how the assassin actually held the gun), general character traits, the emotion the reader feels during a passage, and the author's intent: If you think about your own reading, you often break and look away to absorb the implications and your own feeling; after the off-line break, you return to the text. (Or the text may end, and you walk around "in it," for some time after, making these inferences.)

Graesser et al.'s constructivism differs from the minimalist view in supposing that readers automatically and necessarily infer *on-line* the agents' superordinate goals, the main point or moral of the text, and the characters' emotional reactions.

As a mystery reader, I subscribe to the minimalist view; I believe that a good writer like Agatha Christie exploits my tendency to *not* construe the main goals and antecedent events. In a well-constructed mystery, all the clues have been presented; thus the perpetrator should be self-evident. However, when the detective assembles the suspects to review the crime, I am surprised at the conclusion, even though I have recognized each clue and have had as goal, from the moment I selected the book, the outsmarting of the author and detection of the murderer. Clearly, if I were constructing all possible inferences to maintain global coherence, the denouement would be a foregone conclusion. It is a surprise because the skilled writer has led me down many garden paths to local coherence, which caused me to lose global coherence, or lose the forest for the trees.

The Narrative Experience

Speech acts and reading. I just suggested that in reading a mystery I am trying to outsmart an author, who in turn is trying to outsmart me. I also suggested earlier that in reading a narrative, readers bring to it "Gricean assumptions"—that the author will be cooperative; the text, coherent and informative; and so on. In other words, although the author and the reader will never meet (indeed, the author may be a recluse and never meet *any* readers), the expectations of face-to-face communication transfer to the narrative experience.

Authors write for an imagined general reader and design the text around the assumed expectations and knowledge of that reader (Gerrig, 1993). Readers also have a set of expectations that they bring to their experience of the narrative. Both sets of expectations derive from normal face-to-face interaction and also from conventions of the literary genres.

Discussions and analyses of face-to-face interactions, such as speech act analysis (see Chapter 2), typically consider a single speaker and a single hearer, and focus on the speaker's intent with respect to that hearer. This puts a reader in a funny position, because the author does not intend the speaker in a dialogue, for instance, to influence the reader in the same way as the hearer of the dialogue.

Gerrig (1993) points out that the single-speaker-hearer situation is neither typical of face-to-face discourse nor the right model for a speech act analysis of reading. Many speech situations involve multiple hearers, all of whom the speaker takes into account to some extent. Take a lecture situation, for example. When a student asks a question in a class, I attempt to answer it, but differently than if we were alone: If the student is more knowledgeable than the rest of the class, I may be "redundant," to maintain common ground with the class; I will also be less likely to refer to personal knowledge I have of the student, such as how she or he is doing in the course, than if there were not an extended audience. In this case, the other students in the class are *participant observers*. They are not directly addressed, but their presence affects the discourse and they are expected to overhear and respond. This role, participant-observer, is the one readers assume, and is the role that an author projects for them.

The author expects a set of common knowledge from "typical" participant-observers, different from the character in the work, just as I do from my class in general, different from the particular student addressed. Authors, like lecturers, can choose to consider knowledge only known to the addressee (the character), leaving the participant-observers (readers) temporarily in the dark, or they can consider the common knowledge of the readers. Authors can expect readers to supply general script knowledge to flesh out a setting not explicitly described, such as what will happen in a fine restaurant (see Chapter 5). Authors can also place into text well-known characters from real life—the Beatles, Michael Jordan, or Hitler—and expect the reader to apply common knowledge about them to the narrative. Authors, like speakers, can create common ground in the discourse or can rely on "common ground" given likely characteristics of the projected audience.

As an interesting example, Gerrig (1993, p. 114) cites a novel that uses the metaphors "an Eddie Haskell," "Nancy Drew of the psyche," and "I'm turning into Morticia Adams." He points out that the references themselves limit the audience that shares common ground. *This creates intimacy* between the author and the reader; readers know that they are part of an "in-group" that had the needed understanding. If the novel becomes a classic and extends its readership beyond that audience, Gerrig points out, it will require scholarly annotation to bring the new audience into the fold, albeit more distantly than the original audience.

Inferences from narrative worlds. Authors count on our use of real world information to understand their narratives. A striking question is not how real world knowledge helps us interpret text but the extent to which creation of a macrostructure for text in turn affects our real world knowledge. Do we set up a special structure for fiction that compartmentalizes it from "fact"?

Certainly we learn truths in reading works of fiction. As a mystery reader, I know that a poison (arsenic) can be synthesized from the "nut" inside peach pits; it makes the characteristic bitter taste. Probably for most of us, our "historical" knowledge of Richard III or Julius Caesar is a product of Shakespeare and at least in part fictional. And we all have learned about human character from the great characters of fiction, such as Scrooge, Lady Macbeth, Huckleberry Finn, or Sydney Carton.

Now imagine a narrative about George Washington. Immediately, you bring to bear upon the narrative your knowledge that he led the American colonies to victory over the British in 1776, that he became the first president of the United States, perhaps that he owned slaves, had wooden teeth, and wore a powdered wig, and that his picture is on the dollar bill. Suppose that the imagined narrative is a historical fiction, exploiting some facts about the real George Washington but changing the story so that, after the war, he declines the presidency and retires to his farm (Gerrig, 1989). Do you reject the story because you know it is counterfactual? Or do you play along and segregate the story macrostructure from the rest of your memory because you know you are reading fiction? If so, when do you allow a fictional presentation to supply you with facts that enter your "real" memory, like the peach pit poison?

Gerrig (1989; Gerrig & Prentice, 1991) presents strong, though perhaps surprising, evidence that in fact we incorporate fictional possibilities into our world knowledge so that for at least a moment George Washington and the first president are a less weighted association than before the narrative raised the doubt. Subjects are slower to verify truths like "George Washington was the first president" after reading passages that leave it in doubt (he declined the offer but may reconsider). They still are slower if the real outcome is stated explicitly at the start of the passage and the verification task delayed so they have time to consider the passage in light of their real world knowledge.

The penetrability of outcome knowledge by the story line is akin to *anomalous suspense* when we reread a book but fear and hope for a different outcome at the same points as on the first reading. Specific hopes or fears ("Don't go to the theater Abe [Lincoln]!") are *participatory responses*. Participatory responses intensify the imagined narrative world and become incorporated into our representation of it; when the reader's response contradicts the story, verification of the story outcome is slower (Allbritton & Gerrig, 1991). Thus the narrative world is compartmentalized from neither the real world nor our emotional world: We use real world knowledge and conventions to relate to the narrative, and it, in turn, informs our real world knowledge and emotion base—not necessarily factually.

Gerrig and Prentice (1991) explored when fictional information intrudes into our real world knowledge. Details provided about the setting, like where the story took place or who the president was at the time, whether true or false, did not affect the reaction time to verify the real president or the reader's real location. These were stored with a representation of the story per se. Assertions not overtly tied to the story as setting information, like my arsenic-peach example, whether true or false, presented during the course of a narrative significantly affected the readers' verification times, which suggests that they are, at least partly, incorporated into the knowledge base.

However, assertions made in a story are associated more strongly with elements of the story than other general knowledge. Potts, St. John, and Kirson (1989) introduced a concept, *takahe* (a type of bird), in a story and then measured lexical decisions to it. These were primed by other words from the story but not from likely associates in memory such as, here, *feathers*. Gerrig and Prentice found similar results for other, not definitional, story-presented facts.

So while context-free assertions presented within a story do become part of the knowledge base, they are still segregated from it, attached specifically to the story representation, within the general knowledge structure. And, indeed, I know (and wrote here) where I got the poison-in-the-peach-pit information, from works of fiction, and therefore that while I believe it to be factual, I need to acknowledge (and worry about) its source.

Note that Gerrig and Prentice found that story-presented facts stay separate from real world knowledge, while Gerrig (1989) found they were incorporated at least temporarily into it. I see the difference resulting from whether the "facts" are given to the reader who can passively absorb them, or whether the reader is actively trying to create or interpret them, making an inference or worrying about the outcome because of (anomalous) suspense. When readers are induced to make a participatory response or inference, the "fiction" has a measurable effect on memory. Thus we see that the feeling of being lost "in" the fictional world has a psychological reality: The fictional world is in fact less segregated from our real world knowledge.

Transport to and from the narrative world. Gerrig (1993) suggests that even when good fiction is recognized as fiction, it is not dismissed as untrue because it arouses memories of similar experiences, equivalent situations, analogous fears, and so on—the conditions that provoke participatory responses. These memories remain active after the fiction is recognized as such, and so still influence our behavior. Thus, after seeing the movie *Jaws*, many people were afraid to go in the water, despite knowing it was only a movie.

It might seem reasonable to assume that we engage special processes for reading, especially fiction—processes that are influenced by the goal of entertainment and the a priori knowledge that we are entering the realm of the imagination, not the real. However, as we have seen, and Gerrig cogently argues, comprehension and enjoyment of fiction relies on normal processes—normal speech acts as side participants, normal construction of memory representations, normal inferences and attribution. It even entails the normal assumption that what we are reading is true, by analogy to similar experiences we have had.

What Gerrig argues is unique in reading fiction is the *process* that encapsulates the story as untrue. We do not suspend disbelief to interpret the story, but we construct a schema of disbelief afterward to place it in (Gerrig, 1993, p. 220). This occurs when we exit the narrative world—in a good story, at the end; in a poor one, at a point of inconsistency or bad writing, when we are jarred out of the fictional world.

Reading in Other Cultures

Thus far we have examined literacy in middle-class Western cultures, where the presumption is that people are literate and that literature is used for knowledge acquisition (newspapers, texts, nonfiction) as well as for out-of-this-world experiences, in fiction. In an important study, Scribner and Cole (1981; Rogoff, 1982; Scribner, 1984) examined literacy and cognition in a preliterate society, in Vai speakers of Liberia. The Vai culture has its own script, used to log business arrangements and exchange information in letters, which is known to some but not many adults. Some Vai adults also read Arabic for religious study, particularly to commit the Koran to memory. Schooling and government are conducted in English, so the "educated" are English-literate. However, many adults remain nonliterate but also nonstigmatized, as they would be in our culture.

Scribner and Cole examined the effects of literacy acquisition and experience of different scripts on cognition. They tested their adult subjects on a variety of cognitive tasks related to literacy, typical Western verbal tasks and writing instructions to a popular game in letter form or recalling orally presented words. English literates were at least as good as Vai literates on the Western tasks, which Scribner and Cole attribute to practice with such tasks per se in school. Cognitive advantages to knowledge of the other scripts arose for tasks they were normally used for. For example, Vai script users better transmitted instructions in letter format than users of Arabic. And Arabic script users could better recall strings of words, a memory task like that for which they used the Arabic script.

I raise this here because we must keep in mind that our ability to move in and out of narrative worlds, establish macrostructures, make inferences, and acquire factual information from text does not derive inherently from print but from our specific experience with it. As we will see, children need such experience to become what we think of as good readers.

Scribner and Cole also showed cultural differences in low-level aspects of reading—segmentation and memory—depending on the script type, which supports the notion that literacy acquisition is in part acquisition of a particular model, not necessarily the unique "correct" model, of the primary language. The Vai script is a syllabary with the syllabic characters written as a continuous stream (no spaces). Vai literates had no concept of "word," and when asked to segment their writing, marked off phrasal units. However, they could analyze and recall both syllables and words better than illiterates. Relative to those literate in English, Vai speakers literate in Vai were better at comprehending spoken Vai presented slowly, syllable by syllable. They were no better than English literates at analyzing or remembering Vai presented word by word. Presumably the different relative skills resulted from the different models provided by no script, by syllabary script, and by English script.

It is interesting to note that we can find such different uses of script within a single community in the United States. Heath (1983) studied the language patterns of middle-class and working-class blacks and whites in a mill town in the Piedmont region of the South. We are familiar with the language and literacy patterns of the middle class; they are primarily what we have focused on in this book. The working-class black and white families spoke differently with their children (as mentioned in Chapters 8 and 9) and also modeled different uses of narrative and print. Black children expected stories to be fantasies (tall tales) and were judged on how well they could produce such creations. They were neither drilled on facts known to adults, nor did they expect to learn facts explicitly from "lecture" or print; they learned by doing. They learned to read, but for specific functions like following a shopping list. Thus their literacy experience was very different from both the narrative structure and the spoken performance expectations of a middle-class American classroom, with consequent difficulties.

The working-class white children's experience was more consistent with what is encountered in the first years at school but is also deviant from the middle-class literate traditions. For the working-class whites, stories were either factual accounts of a set of events told to illustrate a moral value, or they were a recount of a parable or story from the Bible. Children were deliberately introduced to print to learn to read but were expected to listen passively, answer factual, "what" questions, but not participate: "Listen and learn and repeat" (p. 226). The words of the story were taught as absolutes, not to be questioned, not as vehicles for seeking other interpretations, but to arrive at the true moral. Thus these children were ready for "basal" reading and the school routine but had trouble with the analysis of print required for middle-class literature in later years in school, unprepared for the inferences, ambiguities, or identifications of our narrative worlds.

So, reading and writing enhance both a particular cognitive/discourse framework and particular language analysis, or low-level language modeling skills. These are neither a *general* result of literacy nor a prerequisite for it; they are a specific set of skills dependent on the writing model and the use to which it is typically put.

Summary

In this section we examined a number of different processes readers use to interpret text in their society. Adult readers have sophisticated knowledge of the conversational discourse practices of their culture, such as in ours: what speakers (characters, narrators, and authors) are likely to do, what the role of participant-observer entails, and how discourse is structured on both the macro and the micro

---

Box 11.6. Constructing Narrative Representations

— Narrative representations use proposition-isolating and organizing principles to construct a topic- and cause-centered representation of the narrative, from macro- to microstructure.

— Representations use facts from the text, augmented by real-world knowledge and inferences bridging text propositions where necessary.

— Representation depth depends on the goal of reading, from proofreading (little meaning construction) to entertainment (continued conscious processing after reading).

— Inferences made on-line include antecedent-pronoun, narrowing of word meaning, gap-filling and case assignments, bridging inferences for coherence.

— The minimalist position holds that only the inferences necessary for establishing local coherence will be made on-line and remain available in working memory.

— The constructivist position holds that, in addition to those necessary for local coherence, readers will infer causes and goals preceding the action; consequences of the current state and reader reaction to the text are considered later.

— Readers may infer characters' perspectives on-line.

— Readers assume cooperative principles from the view of a side participant, such as that of audience members, but not the addressee in the conversation.

— Even reading fiction generates "truths" that readers integrate into their memory representations, partially compartmentalized for the narrative itself and partly affecting general memory.

— Participatory responses—such as urging characters not to take a path to doom—demonstrate commitment to the text, increase the effect it has on memory generally, and indicate that the reader is making inferences (perhaps later) as to probable outcomes and alternatives.

— Anomalous suspense: Feelings of worry and hope even though the reader knows the outcome because the story has been read before or is historical.

— Narrative representation and narrative models depend on narrative experience. Cross-cultural work shows that literacy acquired for memorization enhances memory, while middle-class literacy in English, for example, enhances fact extraction, inference-making, and constructing narrative worlds, the uses to which our text is put.

— Literacy increases awareness of those units the writing identifies. Syllabaries make syllables more accessible; we presumably are more aware of phonemes.

---

levels. Readers also have sophisticated knowledge about language, cause and effect, categories, and script structures. All of this general language and world knowledge we bring to narrative interpretation to create a detailed representation, supplying unverbalized common ground and making necessary inferences.

The creative process is itself entertaining: It engenders feelings of intimacy with the author, and arouses emotions and memories of real experiences that stimulate, as do the real experiences and emotions themselves. These processes depend in part on our expectation that text can transport us, that reading is to enter narrative worlds and acquire information. Literate peoples who employ reading and writing to different ends do so with different cognitive consequences.

Apart from the language and real world knowledge necessary to create the meaning representation of the text, the adult reader brings to reading a familiarity with how to read and how our writing reflects our spoken language. This includes knowledge of how writing represents meaning units of language, whether they are alphabetic, syllabic, or logographic. It includes extensive experience with the visual representation of language, particularly for frequently encountered items. It includes the automatic, habitual eye movements needed to preprocess, take in, or revisit text. And it includes the readily available association of visual pattern to spoken pattern, whether this is the route taken automatically between written word and meaning.

Finally, literate adults have a specific, sophisticated language model, which develops in greater detail the more we read and write. We are aware of the segmentation of the speech stream because we segment it to write it; we become more aware of propositions, interconnections of phrases, and clauses as we learn punctuation; and we become consciously aware of the overtones of speech—irony, sarcasm, ecstasy, despair—when we lexicalize them because we cannot otherwise transcribe inflection.

Thus, for the literate adult, reading is easy because it calls on highly practiced and specific knowledge sets. Reading is challenging and entertaining because the application of these knowledge sets is a nontrivial and involving language game. We turn next to consider how the skills needed to read and write are acquired and/or specifically taught.

LEARNING TO READ AND WRITE

Reading Readiness

We have just examined the prodigious set of skills literate adults bring to understanding a light novel, let alone a heavy text like this one. It is clear, and worthy of repeated emphasis, that to become a facile reader, to feel like you are reading effortlessly, you must read a lot. Practice allows the low-level skills—the eye movements, the letter-to-meaning transformations, and the minimalist inferences—to occur automatically, "on-line." It is these low-level skills that are usually stressed in teaching reading and as differentiators between "good" and "poor" readers.

But apart from low-level skills, practiced readers have a great familiarity with the language in general and with text processing conventions in particular. This experience with narrative is also crucial to position the reader, either while reading or after, to construct the right causal connections, the characters' perspectives, participatory responses, and so on, that is, to integrate the text into a meaningful whole and a meaningful experience. Thus individuals may be "readied" for reading through immersion in language and narrative—in the rich language used in the home among family members and shared stories, both those "out of the heads" of adults and those read aloud from books.

Over some years I worked with disadvantaged children, most of whom readily acquire low-level reading skills at roughly the same ages as advantaged children but who then fall farther and farther behind, never achieving full literacy. I am discussing two distinct groups of children: deaf or hard-of-hearing children who either do not sign or whose families do not, and poor children, handicapped only by poverty. Both groups are significantly, but in different ways, language-deprived.

Many deaf children do not experience full language until they reach school (see *Language in Atypical Populations* for further exposition). Their interactions with their parents are often very controlled the parent quizzing and teaching rather than richly communicating with the child (Schlesinger, 1992). Looking at deaf readers of differing achievement levels, Schlesinger (1992) finds that "advantaged" parents "talk responsively with rather than at or to their children. They tend to be responsive to the children's communications, their actions, desires and initiatives . . . [they] ask genuine questions of their children and . . . drill their children less in colors and numbers" (p. 52). All this gives the child power through language, producing high reading achievement.

Disadvantaged children, on the other hand, (a) rarely have been the addressee, let alone a fully informed side participant, in a real conversation; (b) have limited experience with how complex propositions are constructed or with things being declared, questioned, emphasized, or said ironically, all of which they will need to "decode" the lexical items and punctuation peculiar to writing; and (c) have not "heard" stories that require fact abstraction, bridging inferences, and causes and consequences in the company of someone who can help them make these connections. So, even when such children are taught the GPCs, a direct visual code or a logograph (the whole word) to sign correspondence, they have less infrastructure on which to construct the narrative.

As Schlesinger points out, socially disadvantaged children experience many of the same conversation patterns with their parents as do deaf children: The parent often is controlling and didactic rather than empowering and communicative, sharing stories. Note that parents do not need to be literate to foster storytelling: Narrative does not mean print! My favorite stories—fairy tales, folklore, mythology, Bible stories, the Iliad and Odyssey—were all originally oral stories ("twice-*told* tales"), written down long after they were part of the culture.

In a sense, in our culture, *literacy inhibits us* from creating or memorizing stories and telling them out of our heads. The complete reliability of written stories seems a shameful counterpoint for the vagaries of our memory, vagaries that result in no two oral tellings being the same but, perhaps, therefore, each being more vibrant and tuned to the particular narrator and addressees. There is a children's book by

Figure 11.5. The Ideal Protoliterate World (Artwork rendered by James J. Kempster; used by permission.)

Raymond Briggs, *The Snowman,* that tells a wonderful story, frame by frame, *in pictures.* Every literate adult I have ever seen pick up that book (myself included) with a young child "freaks" on discovering that there are no words, even though the story is all laid out and the telling is quite easy. In achieving mass literacy, our culture has lost spontaneity in storytelling! This is something we must try to recapture so that we orally share with our children events of the day or the family's history together with cultural lore, enveloping them in rich language and relevant narrative, accompanied by print or not.

As we teach reading, it is also important to recall that the storytelling traditions of different cultures serve different purposes, and so children may come to class with different expectations of narrative. Heath's (1983) working-class white families learned (Bible) stories to recite *as told* and to demonstrate a moral value. Her black families heard and created fantasy stories for entertainment and were unaccustomed to factual narrative accounts. Both sets of children had little experience with realistic fiction: To appreciate middle-class Western narrative, children must experience such stories, whether orally or through print, and thus become aware of narrative structure and its inferential demands. To appreciate print as relevant, children should write (dictate) their own stories and hear stories from their culture's perspective as well as those from a middle-class perspective. *Whole-language* programs of reading instruction (e.g., Goodman & Goodman, 1990) emphasize these higher level narrative experiences in teaching reading, sometimes, unfortunately, to the exclusion of instruction on the lower level processes (Adams, 1990).

It is important to recognize what *one-on-one* reading (or story) time with a young child develops. As I have been saying, it familiarizes the child with the flow of the language and the stories of the child's culture. It also connects stories with a *primarily social experience:* It is a "cuddle time" when an adult and child are sitting close and embracing a single purpose (see Figure 11.5). Given that language, especially in the beginning, is social, reading together marries print to the primary function of real communication. And, in a one-on-one situation, an adult can help with bridges, causal inferences, and extralinguistic knowledge, modeling for the child both the interest in narrative and how to process it. It is easy to get hooked on stories in such a setting, and then easy to transfer the interest to more distant story experiences, such as *Reading Rainbow* (televised reading), books on tape, or group reading in a library.

It is also important to note that, once hooked and even fluently literate, we still enjoy sharing stories aloud. In a seminar for college students involved in reading mentorship at an inner-city elementary school, we often shared books that we had discovered for the schoolchildren. When read-alouds began, a hush fell over the (college!) class, and, until the story ended, there was never a rustling paper, a watch check, or a movement to leave. This is not a unique experience; Trelease (1989) observes that we never outgrow picture books:

> I read a picture book (*Ira Sleeps Over*) to every adult group I address and no one ever objects; in fact, it may be the best part of my entire presentation. A good story is a good story. Beautiful and stirring pictures can move fifteen-year-olds as well as five-year-olds. A picture book should be on the reading list of every class in every grade through twelve years of school. (p. 60)

One final observation in this regard: From time to time the press questions "why Johnny can't read." At least part of the answer to this is, "Johnny doesn't have books!" In the inner-city elementary school we were working in (which had an excellent and dedicated administration and many fine teachers), schoolbooks could not go home (because there were no funds to replace them if they got lost or damaged). The school itself had had no lending library in living memory; the room named "Library" still existed but funds to maintain it had long ago disappeared in budget cuts. Most of the families could not afford the basics and so certainly did not buy books for their children. And many of them were legitimately suspicious of authorities so they did not want to register for a library card, even if they had happened to know that libraries do circulate books.

The consequence of this, particularly in the inner cities, is that "Johnny" has no time to read—at best, 20 minutes per day if the class setting encourages "sustained silent reading"! And often teachers are so focused on bringing basic skills up to snuff that this relaxed, practice time is forgone, even in preschool years (see, e.g.,

McNamee, 1990). How could Johnny ever, under such circumstances, recognize high-frequency words? No word will have ever been frequently encountered!

Indeed, Trelease (1989) continues,

> I might also add that most U.S. high school students were not read to regularly in primary grades and have done little or no reading on their own. In spite of this shallow foundation, we insist on rushing them into the classics during high school . . . let's *also* let them hear what they missed in primary years. . . . The fact is that many of our students are at the doorstep of parenthood. . . . If they and their friends are ignorant of childhood's stories, how can they share them with their children? (p.60)

Learning to Decode

I have stressed the necessity for two sets of skills, and their convergence, to produce a fluent reader. Techniques to teach reading that concentrate on both sets of skills are the most effective (Adams, 1990). The first set of skills is low level, *decoding* or translating the squiggles into recognizable language: in the English script, recognition of the letters, letter combinations in whole words, recognition that letters are roughly phonemic (the *alphabetic principle*), and recognition of the sounds of recurring letter patterns (like "ing" or "tion"). The second, higher level set includes experience of print as telling a culturally significant story, and familiarity with story structures from print and oral language. I will return to the higher level and now focus on the low-level decoding skills.

Protoliteracy

Before beginning to read, children are usually familiar with books and print and know that they relate to language; these are elements of *protoliteracy*. Protoliteracy also includes knowledge of the alphabet, what the letters look like and their names, which, of course, do relate to their sounds. Protoliterate children have rudimentary word-analysis skills, developed through songs, nursery rhymes, and other language games. These focus their attention on segmenting the speech stream into sound components: speech rhythm and syllables, onsets and rimes as subsyllables (Adams, 1990; Adams & Bruck, 1995; Barron, 1991). Adams estimates that a middle-class American child *enters* school with *several thousand hours* of prior exposure to print and its sound.

Learning Orthography in Reading and Writing

Learning to read is typically seen as encompassing several overlapping stages (Frith, 1985; Goswami, 1993). The first "stage" is *logographic*. Here, the beginning reader recognizes some small number of whole words, a memorized "sight" vocabulary, based on length, first letter, and shape. The second, more analytic "stage" is *alphabetic,* where letter-to-phoneme correspondences are learned, often through explicit tutoring in common letter co-occurrence patterns and their sounds, such as consonant clusters, prefixes and suffixes, and regular "irregularities" like "tion." This familiarization leads to the third and final "stage," the *orthographic,* in which the child readily recognizes larger spelling sequences as well as the morphemic basis of most, and the most frequent, words of the language.

The orthographic stage, like the logographic stage, is direct from print to meaning but differs from it in being systematically analytical. Unlike the alphabetic stage, the orthographic stage operates on larger letter groups and is nonphonological (Frith, 1985).

Reading and writing often develop independently for a time, and advancing each skill helps the other. Frith (1985) suggests that logographic, whole-word recognition is the first strategy for reading, and that segmentation and alphabetic correspondences are the first strategies for writing. It is easier to learn the alphabetic correspondences with respect to writing because the alphabet was *designed* to facilitate writing, not reading.

We see the independence of the two when young children successfully write a word but cannot read back what they have written. Reading their own writing involves learning the assembly process (Henderson, 1985): Children at first do not recognize their writing; then may pronounce the words so that they are recognizable to adults but still not be able to recognize them themselves; finally, they can assemble their codes and connect the assembly to their lexicon. The attempts at reading what they have written connect reading and writing and develop full orthographic strategies.

Although children may develop enormous sight vocabulary, if they are exclusively dependent on it and do not learn to analyze letter patterns into relevant units, they will have severe reading difficulties. Adams and Bruck (1995) stress that reading proficiency requires awareness of spelling-sound links. Spelling and sounds of words can be learned independently, but programs that teach the link specifically are most effective.

Dialect differences. In this regard, we must also consider the effect of a nonstandard dialect, like AAEV (see Chapter 8), on learning to read standard English text. If the phonology is sufficiently different from standard English, the writing will be "orthographically deeper." This does not mean that it is impossible to learn: Children learn to read and write in deep orthographies around the world. It does suggest that English teachers pointing out spelling-to-sound correspondences should be aware of the sounds of the children's actual spoken language so they are not *mis*guiding the children in decoding (Labov, 1972). However, non-standard-English-speaking beginning readers do not appear to be handicapped by the correspondence differences; they are as able as standard English speakers to match printed with spoken words with or without the final consonant articulated (it is not pronounced in AAEV; Hart, Guthrie, & Winfield, 1980). The AAEV speakers in this study read at an earlier level than the white comparison group (equated for poverty); however, the difference did not appear to be a result of the dialect but of teaching and reading practice in the different schools. (And there are likely motivational differences, as you may recall from Chapter 8, with minority children disaffected from the majority institutions.)

Good versus poor readers. Throughout the learning-to-read period, children are absorbing print through analogy to spoken language. Reading proficiency changes their model of language, and vice versa. Consequently, as we look at differences between early and developed readers or between "good" and "poor" readers at the same age, we see different levels of language awareness but we cannot tell which is the cause and which the effect. An undeveloped language model will arrest development of reading proficiency; a child's primitive understanding of print will slow development of a fine-tuned language model.

One difference between beginning and older American readers is their ability to isolate the units of language. As we saw in Chapter 9, younger readers more readily recognize syllables as units (tapping in rhythm with them) than they do phonemes. Phoneme knowledge seems to be acquired as a consequence, not a cause, of reading (Liberman, Shankweiler, Fischer, & Carter, 1974) and is not acquired by literate users of syllabic alphabets unless they also learn a phonemic one (Barron, 1991).

Another difference between beginning and mature English readers is in recognition of units in different positions in the word. Goswami (1993) examined children's abilities to read words analogous to those they already knew. The youngest children (5 years), taught the word *bug,* could only readily transfer to rhyming words like *rug;* children a year older could transfer both the rime and the initial consonant-vowel (*bug* to either *rug* or *bud*). He proposed that the protoliterate phonological knowledge of the syllable onset and rime bootstraps reading; reading in turn feeds back, developing a phonemic model analyzing the rime.

Practice reading not only develops a language model but also develops familiarity and automaticity so that larger and larger chunks of text may be recognized, perhaps on a direct route. Rayner (1986) measured eye movements in good and poor readers with varying degrees of experience. Beginning readers had greater difficulty holding a fixation and they made longer ones, along with more frequent saccades and more regressions. Rayner used a moving window, under the subject's control, which varied in size and controlled the number of clearly presented letters, to see what the optimal presentation rate was. Fluent sixth-grade readers' perceptual span, the number of letters they optimally took in, was not much different from the span of the beginning reader, 29 versus 23 letters, respectively. However, for the sixth graders, one look within this window sufficed to identify the word, probably because they were efficiently able to use the partial, degraded information outside the window for "preprocessing." Beginning readers were less able to use peripheral-to-fixation information, requiring repeated fixations on a word to identify it. So practice develops use of partial information as part of an automatic, parallel process.

Practice also develops familiarity with larger spelling patterns. Backman, Bruck, Hebert, and Seidenberg (1984) looked at first- through third-grade "good" and "poor" readers' errors and reaction times to naming words differing in frequency, regularity, and consistency of "neighbors." Unlike younger and "poor" third-grade readers, "good" third graders quickly and accurately pronounced high-frequency exception words such as *have* and *said,* which indicates automatic recognition. And if they mispronounced a word, they were more likely than the poorer and younger readers to regularize their pronunciation, reflecting better and more automatic knowledge of spelling-sound correspondences. Backman et al. argue that what a good, experienced reader has acquired is both better analytic knowledge to apply to assemble a word as well as a more automatized process that precludes the necessity for assembly. In this regard, they see no difference between a poor reader in third grade and a younger, less experienced reader.

Zinna, Liberman, and Shankweiler (1986) also looked at the sensitivity of developing readers to frequency, consistency, and regularity of the spelling-to-sound relationship in words. *All* their readers, from first through fifth grade, were faster at reading high- than low-frequency words, with accuracy for the high-frequency words increasing with age and practice. In addition, *all* their readers were faster at reading words with no inconsistent neighbors, words with invariant pronunciations. However, more than younger children, the older children were better at reading high-frequency words with inconsistent neighbors than such low-frequency words, and the older children were also differentially better able to read consistent low-frequency words than younger children.

The authors suggest that the beginning readers' performance for high-frequency words may reflect a whole-word recognition scheme. With age, consistency makes a difference, as the reader learns to recognize spelling-to-sound patterns in smaller-than-word units. The recognition of consistency of the smaller pattern assists in low-frequency word pronunciation, and hurts in pronouncing words with inconsistent neighbors. This model also accounts for a finding reported by Henderson (1985) that younger readers are much faster at reading real than pseudowords, while mature readers show little advantage for real words. The younger reader may "automatically" recognize whole words; the mature reader as automatically recognizes and assembles subword orthographic patterns, relevant for both pseudo- and real words.

It is clear that reading experience correlates with phonological knowledge and automatic access. More experienced, better readers name letters, words, digits, and common objects faster than less experienced or poorer readers (Wolf, 1991; Wolf, Bally, & Morris, 1986). Good (English) readers are also better able to generate rhymes or add, delete, or reverse phonemes within a word (Barron, 1991). As I have suggested, these observations do not tell whether the language model, the phonological ability, is enabling the reading skill, or the reading ability is generating the phonological skill: We have seen that Vai—syllabary—readers better segment Vai into syllables as a consequence of their reading/writing experience, not as a precursor to it.

Importance of phonology in acquiring English literacy. While literacy may develop a specific language model, training in the model also develops reading skills. In an important study, Bradley and Bryant (1983) measured sound categorization and skills in children, from the age of 4 years, when they were prereaders, over 4 years, when they should know how to read. They could thus at any time correlate reading ability and sound-categorization ability; they could also correlate early sound-categorization ability and ultimate reading skill. In addition, they trained a subset of their nearly 400 children to recognize the similarity in sound of words sharing a beginning (*hen-hat*), middle (*hen-pet*), or end (*hen-man*) phoneme. They could then compare the reading development of the "experimental" (trained) group with the "control" (untrained) group.

The results showed a clear causal effect of sound experience on reading skill several years later. Children who, at the age of 4, were best able to repeat three or four similar-sounding words, recognize that all but one of them shared a common phoneme, and then name the "odd" word, performed the best on standardized reading tests three years later. The better performance came from the sound-analysis aspect of the test because it emerged for children independently equated for memory and other cognitive abilities. More important, training alphabet analysis changed outcomes: The trained group outperformed the controls on standard reading tests, and more so if, in addition to sound analysis, they were taught the letters labeling the sound distinctions.

Thus, while learning to read appears to develop an explicit model of the language, it also requires such a model. Explicit training in sound analysis and in the relationship of the sound units to the script can facilitate learning to read.

Reading Recovery

We have just seen that explicit training on decoding, the low-level skills of literacy, facilitates learning to read, and that practice with reading continues to develop low-level automaticity—in recognition of larger spelling patterns, regular "inconsistencies," and use of partial and degraded information to narrow word identification.

Good readers also seem to better use contextual cues. They have a greater semantic priming effect (although this result is not consistently obtained; e.g., Merrill, Sperber, & McCauley, 1980). And their "errors," called *miscues* (Goodman & Goodman, 1990), are more likely to reflect substitution of a contextually appropriate word than a graphemically close word: to read, for example, "they ran from the burning *house*" as "they ran from the burning *building*" rather than "they ran from the burning *horse*." The good reader reads for meaning, using the letter pattern as only one of many cues to the content. Poor readers may be overly focused on GPCs and fail to extract and use the content cues.

Explicit training on the higher levels of reading analysis, on whole-word recognition, script construction, and developing inferences, like explicit GPC training, facilitates reading development. I should note before continuing that many children seem to learn to read "naturally," without any specific training, but, of course, with plenty of "natural" exposure to print and language. And most children, given such exposure as well as explicit guidance in school, learn to read. Some children, however, fail to learn given this guidance, perhaps because of a learning disability (*developmental dyslexia*), which will be discussed in *Language in Atypi-*

cal Populations, or perhaps because of impoverished protoliterate skills. Here I present approaches to developing the higher language skills explicitly.

Reading Recovery is a program developed by Marie Clay (e.g., Clay & Cazden, 1990) to provide "low-progress" readers with the rich set of "cues," both high- and low-level, that "good" readers use to infer meaning from their text. The daily lesson in Reading Recovery consists of several reading activities, including the children's rereading already familiar books, the teacher's introducing and reading a new book aloud, independent reading by the children of the teacher-read book from the day before, the children's writing and analyzing a story, and low-level activities like letter identification.

There are three points to stress. The first is the emphasis on *re*reading, both of familiar stories and the story recently introduced. This gives the child confidence as well as practice at absorbing print into a mental structure without having to create it from scratch. Indeed, Trelease (1989) notes that children love being read aloud the same story: Familiarity is soothing and repetition permits absorption of larger units of print each time.

The second point relates to the first: The teacher does not simply read a book out loud but builds a scaffold for its comprehension. Introducing a story sets the story's topic, title, and major characters. The teacher also introduces new or important vocabulary in context from the story and sketches the plot. While reading the story, the teacher also interactively makes it more accessible, elaborating vocabulary or unusual syntax, which prompts the children to search for links and build inferences.

The third point is that while all reading teaching is done in context, and not with vocabulary lists isolated from the story, there is still teaching within this context of low-level skills. There is some work with letters and sounds, work with vocabulary from the story, and work with "units of writing." Exercises include cutting up the stories the children write up, and having the children individually reassemble the story, in a way teaching constituent and discourse structures.

Mechanical skills connected with the story are critical; Adams (1990) estimates that a child has a 5%-20% chance of learning a word (what it means and how it is used) with only one presentation in a story. The probability of learning new words is clearly enhanced if they are studied in context and reviewed in rereading. Similar increases in understanding phonology and syntax can also be expected with story-related work on mechanics.

Reading Recovery had remarkable success in New Zealand, where it was developed, and has been imported to the United States. Only children who were among the poorest readers after one year in school were eligible for the program, and none of these were screened out; 90% of the participants were brought to average reading level for their age within 12-15 weeks!

The Reading Recovery program is similar in some ways to whole language, which has been in vogue in the United States (Goodman & Goodman, 1990). Whole language arose as a movement against phonics approaches in which children spent reading time in school on drills, worksheets, and study of primers that had no story and no interesting language but repeated the sounds and letters to be learned. Reacting against the dullness of this approach, whole language stressed the need for "authentic" language experience. An authentic experience is meaningful, inducing readers to build inferences and create the intimacy. Whole language also stresses the need for the learner to be in control of the learning, for learning to involve active construction and not passive filling out of forms.

Nothing in these laudable goals specifically precludes teaching phonics within a meaningful context, as the child actively develops the need for understanding the GPCs. In fact, this is what Reading Recovery does: It provides "temporary instructional detours [from the main story line] in which the child's attention is called to particular cues [to the language and meaning] available in speech or print" (Clay & Cazden, 1990, p. 217). But in practice, many whole language advocates do not teach phonics (see Murray, 1995). And, as we have seen, it is important to help the child develop the low-level language model as well as narrative interpretation skills.

Reading to Learn

Books in the early years of school are designed to enhance the child's acquisition of reading: The child learns to read. In an ideal program, children hear stories at their *thinking* level; interactively practice reading books with limited, repetitive vocabulary that focuses their attention on GPCs; and also read books silently (free voluntary reading [FVR], sustained-silent-reading [SSR], or drop-everything-and-read [DEAR] programs) at, or just slightly above, their reading levels. Such programs simultaneously develop low- and higher-level reading skills while inculcating the reading habit (Krashen, 1995).

Starting in fourth or fifth grade, schoolbooks shift focus. They are no longer teaching the child to read but are presenting critical information through text. That is, the child is not *learning to read, but reading to learn.* If children are not facile, automatic readers at this time, they cannot read to learn: A hard text requires active attention; if the reader must attend to the mechanics of reading, there is no attention left for understanding (Adams, 1990). It is at this level that we often see a break for disadvantaged children, whether they are deaf or impoverished (Schlesinger, 1992). Their lack of reading experience means that their perhaps adequate decoding skills are less than automatic, and they cannot turn their attention to the new ideas and new words in their books. And each year they fall further and further behind.

Recall that the emphasis on literacy, and on using books to transmit new information, is a peculiarity of our culture. While increasing transmitted knowledge, reliance on the written word may handicap abilities to memorize, tell stories spontaneously, and be creative in this regard. And, as we have seen cross-culturally, scripts used for letter writing enhance letter-writing skills, and those for memory enhance memorization. Thus our script should enhance information acquisition *only if acquired in that context.* In promoting literacy in Western culture, it is thus imperative that we develop the reading-to-learn aspect from the first.

Box 11.7. Learning to Read

— Reading readiness encompasses considerable exposure to narrative, best accomplished through oral storytelling and one-on-one read-alouds, associating social aspects of communication with reading, and assisting in constructing inferences and supplying real world knowledge.
— Protoliteracy includes reading readiness, familiarity with the medium of print, some logographic recognition, knowledge of the alphabet in both appearance and sound, and basic sound-analysis skills such as decomposition of words into syllables, onsets, and rimes.
— A popular model of early reading suggests that there are three stages:
  — Stage 1—Logographic: Whole-word recognition based on word length and first letter
  — Stage 2—Alphabetic: Learning of grapheme-to-phoneme correspondences; some learning of sound of larger common letter groups
  — Stage 3—Orthographic: Recognition of common letter sequences
— Reading instruction is most effective if it explicitly teaches the spelling-sound link.
— Teachers of children of nonstandard dialects need to be aware of differences in spelling-to-sound correspondences, although there is no clear evidence that these differences especially handicap the children.
— As children practice reading, their oral language model develops; the finer the model, the faster reading develops.
— Practice develops automaticity in use of spelling patterns, more rapid recognition of common words regardless of consistency and regularity, use of partial information in the parafovea, and better ability to narrow cohort from context.
— Specific training on GPCs advances reading (of English).
— Specific training of language-in-context, whole language, or reading recovery, which assists construction of a narrative macrostructure, advances reading.
— At 8 to 9 years of age, schooling switches from learning-to-read to reading-to-learn. At this point, reading must be automatic and children must be familiar with the idea of using text to acquire knowledge and build structures; the initial decoding skills are not sufficient, and disadvantaged children can fall further and further behind.
— Oral and written narratives serve different purposes in different cultures. Children's experience with narrative traditions may not conform to "standard" expectation: reading for facts, truthful and/or fanciful recounts, consideration of alternatives. Teachers should recognize these differences and encourage reading within the child's own tradition as she or he develops awareness and skills in the standard tradition.

This is in a sense a tenet of the whole-language approach to reading teaching. Children must be acquainted not simply with the decoding process but with the purpose of stories and print, the way we use it and want them to use it. Stories as analogies, morals, and learning tools must be experienced from a child's earliest days as a central tool of the culture, shared among adults and respected transmissions from children to adults, and the reverse as well (McNamee, 1990).

And, finally, perhaps more important than the phonology difference between a nonstandard and standard dialect, we must teach middle-class Western literacy taking into account the oral and written traditions of different groups of learners. Encouraging children and adults of a community to tell their own stories, writing these stories down, and familiarizing the learners with print in the rhetorical traditions of their own culture will enable them to appreciate literature from their own developed narrative traditions, to see print as relevant, and to use print to create a model for language. If teachers can take into account the different discourse traditions and places of print in communities, they can create a student-centered, optimal environment for literacy in the children's own and the standard literate traditions (Heath, 1983).

Summary

Acquiring literacy requires the simultaneous development of two sets of skills: low-level decoding skills that explicitly teach the writing's model of units of language, and high-level discourse/narrative skills, which explicitly model how writing will be used pragmatically in the culture. Both sets of skills ideally are present from the first, so that children entering school have good knowledge of stories and the importance of print as well as of the graphemes and some of the print-to-sound correspondences. Teaching programs that explicitly instruct at both levels are the most effective, provided they also give children adequate opportunity to practice so that the print-to-language conversion becomes automatic. "Good" and "poor" readers appear to differ in automaticity: Poor older readers look like early readers. As literacy develops, a finer and finer language model develops; conversely, the finer language model promotes rapid literacy acquisition.

SUMMARY AND CONCLUSIONS

This, our final content chapter on typical, normal language processes, has examined a secondary language process, reading and writing. Reading and writing are secondary to primary language processing in at least three ways: They are always acquired after a primary language if they are acquired at all; for the most part they "code" primary language rather than independently coding thought; and they create an explicit model for primary language, a model that depends on intuitive knowledge of the primary language.

We began by discussing the historical development of print, noting that it did not begin as a code for primary language but evolved to be one. At the same time, because of the difference in medium between print and primary language and because of cultural differences in the function of print, we see different "conventions" emerging in print from those in speech. In print we must lexicalize context and feeling and explicitly mark constituents with punctuation because nonverbal communication is impossible. Because print is not rapidly fading, we lengthen sentences and distance between references and complicate sentence structure; we eliminate rhythm and rhyme, not needing those as aids as we do in oral histories. Because our culture "reads to learn," we mentally make inferences, search for causes and connections, and record details into a narrative structure as we read.

We next examined the psychological processes required in reading and saw that they fell into two broad categories, each of which benefitted from repeated practice: low-level processes including eye movements, grapheme recognition, and phonological decoding, and high-level processes involving extraction of the structure of the narrative, complete with unstated inferences and our own emotional reactions to it. The fluent reader appears automatically to chunk or unitize print into relatively large meaningful units: We recognize letters in words faster than in isolation, but unitize words in running text; we use parafoveal information to constrain letter and word possibilities at fixation; we have a larger span of letters that we can absorb in a fixation; we quickly background function words to create sentence structure and concentrate on content words for meaning; we use both GPC rules and direct access of words and morphemes from letter strings; we create on-line bridging inferences and some causal and character inferences; we resurrect on-line reference; and rapidly, but not on-line, we detect and resolve discrepancies.

The need for both low-level and high-level processing in fluent reading underscores the need for extensive narrative experience in the protoliterate child. To discover the model of language that print provides, children must have considerable exposure to rich oral language, to that which must be modeled. At the same time, children need to be presented explicitly with the language model, to be taught letters and their sounds (for English), as well as how to chunk them to become "orthographic" readers. We examined how both normal and disadvantaged children learn to read, and how reading is most effectively taught—by building both low-level and high-level skills simultaneously, and often explicitly.

Remember: Print is a secondary process; primary language may be more concrete and not need to be taught. Necessarily, it is grounded in the here and now, often in terms of topic, but always with respect to social demands. Moreover, primary language can, and perhaps must, be learned tacitly. Print, or at least the way print models spoken language, must be learned explicitly, involving the addition both of the mapping of print to spoken language and knowledge of the way the writing system models structures in the spoken language. As it is easy to walk, but hard to describe how you do it, it may be easier to talk than characterize the talking process in a writing model.

We have now completed our review of normal and abnormal language processes. In the concluding chapter we revisit some initial questions in light of our explorations into language and its processing: What is language? Is it unique? How does it relate to thought? And how is it shaped by biological, social, and cognitive constraints?

REFERENCES

Adams, M. J. (1979). Models of word recognition. *Cognitive Psychology, 11,* 133-176.

Adams, M. J. (1990). *Beginning to read: Thinking and learning about print.* Cambridge: MIT Press.

Adams, M. J., & Bruck, M. (1995). Resolving the "great debate." *American Educator, 19,* 7-20.

Albrecht, J. E., & Myers, J. L. (1995). Role of context in accessing distant information during reading. *Journal of Experimental Psychology: Learning, Memory, and Cognition, 21,* 1459-1468.

Albrecht, J. E., & O'Brien, E. J. (1993). Updating a mental model: Maintaining both local and global coherence. *Journal of Experimental Psychology: Learning, Memory, and Cognition, 19,* 1061-1070.

Allbritton, D. W., & Gerrig, R. J. (1991). Participatory responses in text understanding. *Journal of Memory and Language, 30,* 603-626.

Backman, J., Bruck, M., Hebert, M., & Seidenberg, M. S. (1984). Acquisition and use of spelling-sound correspondences in reading. *Journal of Experimental Child Psychology, 38,* 114-133.

Barron, R. W. (1991). Proto-literacy, literacy and the acquisition of phonological awareness. *Learning and Individual Differences, 3,* 243-255.

Besner, D. (1987). Phonology, lexical access in reading, and articulatory suppression: A critical review. *Quarterly Journal of Experimental Psychology, 39A,* 467-478.

Besner, D., Twilley, L., McCann, R. S., & Seergobin, K. (1990). On the association between connectionism and data: Are a few words necessary? *Psychological Review, 97,* 432-466.

Bradley, L., & Bryant, P. E. (1983). Categorizing sounds and learning to read—a causal connection. *Nature, 301,* 419-421.

Bransford, J. D., Barclay, J. R., & Franks, J. J. (1972). Sentence memory: A constructive versus interpretive approach. *Cognitive Psychology, 3,* 193-209.

Briihl, D., & Inhoff, A. W. (1995). Integrating information across fixations during reading: The use of orthographic bodies and of exterior letters. *Journal of Experimental Psychology: Learning, Memory, and Cognition, 21,* 55-67.

Clay, M. M., & Cazden, C. B. (1990). A Vygotskian interpretation of Reading Recovery. In L. C. Moll (Ed.), *Vygotsky and education: Instructional implications and applications of sociohistorical psychology* (pp. 206-222). New York: Cambridge University Press.

Coltheart, M. (1996). Phonological dyslexia: Past and future issues. *Cognitive Neuropsychology, 13,* 749-762.

Coltheart, M., Curtis, B., Atkins, P., & Haller, M. (1993). Models of reading aloud: Dual-route and parallel-distributed processing approaches. *Psychological Review, 100,* 589-608.

Coltheart, M., Patterson, K., & Marshall, J. C. (Eds.). (1980). *Deep dyslexia.* London: Routledge & Kegan Paul.

Coltheart, V., Avons, S. E., & Trollope, J. (1990). Articulatory suppression and phonological codes in reading for meaning. *Quarterly Journal of Experimental Psychology, 42A,* 375-399.

Daneman, M., Reingold, E. M., & Davidson, M. (1995). Time course of phonological activation during reading: Evidence from eye fixations. *Journal of Experimental Psychology: Learning, Memory, and Cognition, 21,* 884-898.

de Vega, M. (1995). Backward updating of mental models during continuous reading. *Journal of Experimental Psychology: Learning, Memory, and Cognition, 21,* 373-385.

Diamond, J. (1995). Blueprints, bloody ships, and borrowed letters. *Natural History, 3/95,* 16-21.

Folk, J. R., & Morris, R. K. (1995). Multiple lexical decisions in reading: Evidence from eye movements, naming time, and oral reading. *Journal of Experimental Psychology: Learning, Memory, and Cognition, 21,* 1412-1430.

Frith, U. (1985). Beneath the surface of developmental dyslexia. In K. E. Patterson, J. C. Marshall, & M. Coltheart (Eds.), *Surface dyslexia: Neuropsychological and cognitive studies of phonological reading* (pp. 301-330). Hillsdale, NJ: Lawrence Erlbaum.

Frost, R. (1994). Prelexical and postlexical strategies in reading: Evidence from a deep and shallow orthography. *Journal of Experimental Psychology: Learning, Memory, and Cognition, 20,* 116-129.

Frost, R., Katz, L., & Bentin, S. (1987). Strategies for visual word recognition and orthographic depth: A multilingual comparison. *Journal of Experimental Psychology: Human Perception and Performance, 13,* 104-115.

Gernsbacher, M. A., Goldsmith, H. H., & Robertson, R. R. (1992). Do readers mentally represent character's emotion states? *Cognition and Emotion, 6,* 89-112.

Gerrig, R. J. (1989). Suspense in the absence of uncertainty. *Journal of Memory and Language, 28,* 633-648.

Gerrig, R. J. (1993). *Experiencing narrative worlds: On the psychological activities of reading.* New Haven, CT: Yale University Press.

Gerrig, R. J., & Prentice, D. A. (1991). The representation of fictional information. *Psychological Science, 2,* 336-340.

Glushko, R. J. (1979). The organization and activation of orthographic knowledge in reading aloud. *Journal of Experimental Psychology: Human Perception and Performance, 5,* 674-691.

Goodman, Y. M., & Goodman, K. S. (1990). Vygotsky in a whole-language perspective. In L. C. Moll (Ed.), *Vygotsky and education: Instructional implications and applications of sociohistorical psychology* (pp. 223-250). New York: Cambridge University Press.

Goswami, U. (1993). Phonological skills and learning to read. In P. Tallal, A. M. Galaburda, R. R. Llinas, & C. von Euler (Eds.), *Temporal information processing in the nervous system* (Annals of the New York Academy of Sciences, 682, pp. 296-311). New York: New York Academy of Sciences.

Graesser, A. C., Singer, M., & Trabasso, T. (1994). Constructing inferences during narrative text comprehension. *Psychological Review, 101,* 371-395.

Greenberg, S. N., & Koriat, A. (1991). The missing letter effect for common function words depends on their linguistic function in the phrase. *Journal of Experimental Psychology: Learning, Memory, and Cognition, 17,* 1051-1061.

Grossberg, S., & Stone, G. (1986). Neural dynamics of word recognition and recall: Attentional priming, learning, and resonance. *Psychological Review, 93,* 46-74.

Hadley, J. A., & Healy, A. F. (1991). When are reading units larger than the letters? Refinement of the unitization reading model. *Journal of Experimental Psychology: Learning, Memory, and Cognition, 17,* 1062-1073.

Hart, J. T., Guthrie, J. T., & Winfield, L. (1980). Black English phonology and learning to read. *Journal of Educational Psychology, 72,* 636-646.

Healy, A. F., & Drewnowski, A. (1983). Investigating the boundaries of reading units: Letter detection in misspelled words. *Journal of Experimental Psychology: Human Perception and Performance, 9,* 413-426.

Healy, A. F., Oliver, W. L., & McNamara, T. P. (1987). Detecting letters in continuous text: Effects of display size. *Journal of Experimental Psychology: Human Perception and Performance, 13,* 279-290.

Heath, S. B. (1983). *Ways with words: Language, life, and work in communities and classrooms.* New York: Cambridge University Press.

Henderson, L. (1985). Issues in the modelling of pronunciation assembly in normal reading. In K. E. Patterson, J. C. Marshall, & M. Coltheart (Eds.), *Surface dyslexia: Neuropsychological and cognitive studies of phonological reading* (pp. 459-508). Hillsdale, NJ: Lawrence Erlbaum.

Hurtema, J. S., Dopkins, S., Klin, C. M., & Myers, J. L. (1993). Connecting goals and actions during reading. *Journal of Experimental Psychology: Learning, Memory, and Cognition, 19,* 1053-1060.

Hyona, J., & Olson, R. K. (1995). Eye fixation patterns among dyslexic and normal readers: Effects of word length and word frequency. *Journal of Experimental Psychology: Learning, Memory, and Cognition, 21,* 1430-1440.

Jared, D., & Seidenberg, M. S. (1991). Does word identification proceed from spelling to sound to meaning. *Journal of Experimental Psychology: General, 120,* 358-394.

Johnston, J. C. (1978). A test of the sophisticated guessing theory of word perception. *Cognitive Psychology, 10,* 123-153.

Johnston, J. C. (1981). Effects of advance precuing of alternatives in the perception of letters alone and in words. *Journal of Experimental Psychology: Human Perception and Performance, 7,* 560-572.

Johnston, J. C., & McClelland, J. L. (1974). Perception of letters in words: Seek not and ye shall find. *Science, 184,* 1192-1194.

Johnston, J. C., & McClelland, J. L. (1980). Experimental tests of a hierarchical model of word identification. *Journal of Verbal Learning and Verbal Behavior, 19,* 503-524.

Kennison, S. M., & Clifton, C., Jr. (1995). Determinants of parafoveal preview benefit in high and low working memory capacity readers: Implications for eye movement control. *Journal of Experimental Psychology: Learning, Memory, and Cognition, 21,* 68-81.

Kintsch, W., & van Dijk, T. A. (1978). Toward a model of text comprehension and production. *Psychological Review, 85,* 363-394.

Kleiman, G. M. (1975). Speech recoding in reading. *Journal of Verbal Learning and Verbal Behavior, 14,* 323-329.

Klin, C. M., & Myers, J. L. (1993). Reinstatement of causal information during reading. *Journal of Experimental Psychology: Learning, Memory, and Cognition, 19,* 554-566.

Koriat, A., & Greenberg, S. N. (1991). Syntactic control of letter detection: Evidence from English and Hebrew nonwords. *Journal of Experimental Psychology: Learning, Memory, and Cognition, 17,* 1035-1050.

Krashen, S. D. (1995). Free voluntary reading: Linguistic and affective arguments and some new applications. In F. R. Eckman, D. Highland, P. W. Lee, J. Milsham, & R. Rutowski Weber (Eds.), *Second language acquisition: Theory and pedagogy* (pp. 187-202). Mahwah, NJ: Lawrence Erlbaum.

LaBerge, D., & Samuels, S. J. (1974). Toward a theory of automatic information processing in reading. *Cognitive Psychology, 6,* 293-323.

Labov, W. (1972). *Language in the inner city: Studies in the black English vernacular.* Philadelphia: University of Pennsylvania Press.

Lea, R. B. (1995). On-line evidence for elaborative logical inferences in text. *Journal of Experimental Psychology: Learning, Memory, and Cognition, 21,* 1469-1482.

Liberman, I. Y., Shankweiler, D., Fischer, F. W., & Carter, B. (1974). Explicit syllable and phoneme segmentation in the young child. *Journal of Experimental Child Psychology, 18,* 201-212.

Lorch, R. F. (1993). Integration of topic and subordinate information during reading. *Journal of Experimental Psychology: Learning, Memory, and Cognition, 19,* 1071-1081.

Luo, C. R. (1996). How is word meaning accessed in reading? Evidence from the phonologically mediated interference effect. *Journal of Experimental Psychology: Learning, Memory, and Cognition, 22,* 883-894.

Matthei, E. H. (1983). Length effects in word perception: Comment on Samuel, van Santen, and Johnston. *Journal of Experimental Psychology: Human Perception and Performance, 9,* 318-320.

McKoon, G., Gerrig, R. J., & Greene, S. B. (1996). Pronoun resolution without pronouns: Some consequences of memory-based text processing. *Journal of Experimental Psychology: Learning, Memory, and Cognition, 22,* 919-932.

McKoon, G., & Ratcliff, R. (1980). The comprehension processes and memory structures involved in anaphoric reference. *Journal of Verbal Learning and Verbal Behavior, 19,* 668-682.

McKoon, G., & Ratcliff, R. (1992). Inference during reading. *Psychological Review, 99,* 440-466.

McNamee, G. D. (1990). Learning to read and write in an inner-city setting: A longitudinal study of community change. In L. C. Moll (Ed.), *Vygotsky and education: Instructional implications and applications of sociohistorical psychology* (pp. 287-303). New York: Cambridge University Press.

Merrill, E. C., Sperber, R. D., & McCauley, C. (1980). The effects of context on word identification in good and poor readers. *Journal of Psychology, 106,* 179-192.

Moravcsik, J. E., & Healy, A. F. (1995). Effect of meaning on letter detection. *Journal of Experimental Psychology: Learning, Memory, and Cognition, 21,* 82-95.

Murray, B. (1995, April). Merits of reading techniques debated. *APA Monitor,* p. 44.

O'Brien, E. J., & Albrecht, J. E. (1992). Comprehension strategies in the development of a mental model. *Journal of Experimental Psychology: Learning, Memory, and Cognition, 18,* 777-784.

Olson, D. R. (1994). *The world on paper.* New York: Cambridge University Press.

Patterson, K. E., Marshall, J. C., & Coltheart, M. (Eds.). (1985). *Surface dyslexia: Neuropsychological and cognitive studies of phonological reading.* Hillsdale, NJ: Lawrence Erlbaum.

Perfetti, C. A., & Zhang, S. (1995). Very early phonological activation in Chinese reading. *Journal of Experimental Psychology: Learning, Memory, and Cognition, 21,* 24-33.

Potts, G. R., St. John, M. F., & Kirson, D. (1989). Incorporating new information into existing world knowledge. *Cognitive Psychology, 21,* 303-333.

Pyles, T. (1993). *The origins and development of the English language* (4th ed.). New York: Harcourt Brace Jovanovich.

Ratcliff, R., & McKoon, G. (1978). Priming in recognition: Evidence for the propositional structure of sentences. *Journal of Verbal Learning and Verbal Behavior, 17,* 403-417.

Ratcliff, R., & McKoon, G. (1981). Does activation really spread? *Psychological Review, 88,* 454-462.

Rayner, K. (1986). Eye movements and perceptual span in beginning and skilled readers. *Journal of Experimental Child Psychology, 41,* 211-236.

Rogoff, B. (1982). Literacy, schooling and cognitive skills [Review of *The psychology of literacy* by S. Scribner and M. Cole]. *Science, 215,* 1494-1495.

Samuel, A. G., van Santen, J. P. H., & Johnston, J. C. (1982). Length effects in word perception: We is better than I but worse than you or them. *Journal of Experimental Psychology: Human Perception and Performance, 8,* 91-105.

Samuel, A. G., van Santen, J. P. H., & Johnston, J. C. (1983). Reply to Matthei: We really is worse than you or them, and so are ma and pa. *Journal of Experimental Psychology: Human Perception and Performance, 9,* 321-322.

Schlesinger, H. S. (1992). The elusive X factor: Parental contributions to illiteracy. In M. Walworth, D. F. Moores, & T. J. O'Rourke (Eds.), *A free hand* (pp. 37-64). Silver Spring, MD: T. J. Publishers.

Schmandt-Besserat, A. D. (1978). The earliest precursor of writing. *Scientific American, 238,* 50-59.

Scribner, S. (1984). The practice of literacy: Where mind and society meet. In S. J. White & V. Teller (Eds.), *Discourses in reading and linguistics* (Annals of the New York Academy of Sciences, 433, pp. 5-19). New York: New York Academy of Sciences.

Scribner, S., & Cole, M. (1981). *The psychology of literacy.* Cambridge, MA: Harvard University Press.

Seidenberg, M. S. (1985). The time course of phonological code activation in two writing systems. *Cognition, 19,* 1-30.

Seidenberg, M. S., & McClelland, J. L. (1989). A distributed, developmental model of word recognition and naming. *Psychological Review, 96,* 523-568.

Tan, L. H., Hoosain, R., & Siok, W. W. T. (1996). Activation of phonological codes before access to character meaning in written Chinese. *Journal of Experimental Psychology: Learning, Memory, and Cognition, 22,* 865-882.

Till, R., Mross, E. F., & Kintsch, W. (1988). Time course of priming for associate and inference words in a discourse context. *Memory and Cognition, 16,* 283-298.

Trabasso, T., van den Broek, P., & Suh, S. Y. (1989). Logical necessity and transitivity of causal relations in stories. *Discourse Processes, 12,* 1-26.

Trelease, S. (1989). *The new read-aloud handbook.* New York: Penguin.

Tzelgov, J., Henik, A., Sneg, R., & Baruch, O. (1996). Unintentional word reading via the phonological route: The Stroop effect with cross-script homophones. *Journal of Experimental Psychology: Learning, Memory, and Cognition, 22,* 322-345.

Tzeng, O. J. L., & Wang, W. S.-Y. (1983). The first two R's. *American Scientist, 71,* 238-243 [The following letters to the editor and replies on correspondence pages: D. Besner, pp. 452-456, and N. A. Hall, pp. 566-570].

van Orden, G. C., Pennington, B. F., & Stone, G. O. (1990). Word identification in reading and the promise of a subsymbolic psycholinguistics. *Psychological Review, 97,* 488-522.

Wolf, M. (1991). Naming speed and reading: The contribution of the cognitive neurosciences. *Reading Research Quarterly, xxvi,* 123-140.

Wolf, M., Bally, H., & Morris, R. (1986). Automaticity, retrieval processes, and reading: A longitudinal study in average and impaired readers. *Child Development, 57,* 988-1000.

Wydell, T. N., Patterson, K. E., & Humphreys, G. W. (1993). Phonologically mediated access to meaning for Kanji: Is a *rows* still a *rose* in Japanese Kanji? *Journal of Experimental Psychology: Learning, Memory, and Cognition, 19,* 491-514.

Zhang, S., & Perfetti, C. A. (1993). The tongue-twister effect in reading Chinese. *Journal of Experimental Psychology: Learning, Memory, and Cognition, 19,* 1082-1093.

Zinna, D. R., Liberman, I. Y., & Shankweiler, D. (1986). Children's sensitivity to factors influencing vowel reading. *Reading Research Quarterly, xxi,* 465-480.

STUDY QUESTIONS

1. Does reading entail more than recognizing and combining individual letters? Your answer should consider the evidence both from eye movements and accuracy/reaction time for other-than-letter-size orthographic units. Your answer should also consider sound/meaning associations to letters and letter clusters, and how we use the narrative's structure to activate meanings and likely word candidates.

2. Contrast the dual-route and single-route models, carefully attending to the difference between addressed and assembled phonology and pre- and postlexical access of phonology. Critically discuss the evidence for the dual-route position.

3. The chapter emphasizes that print models language. Discuss this concept with respect to different writing systems, both as they evolved through time and as they exist currently in different cultures. Consider also how writing conventions and skills may differ depending on the way a culture uses writing. Finally, consider how children learning the English alphabet appear to acquire more and more accurate language models.

4. Critically consider the inferences and responses that we make when we enter a narrative world. Which seem to happen automatically, on-line? Which happen perhaps later? (How) Are these integrated with knowledge from our real world?

12

RETROSPECTIVES ON NORMAL LANGUAGE

T his book began by observing how language has been considered the fire Prometheus stole from the heavens to give us civilization. We noted that human interest in language is age-old because of the intimate relationship of language to thought and because of its potential to separate us from animals. People also long have wondered whether language is intrinsic to the human makeup, whether we "do" language differently from other mental activities—in modern terms, whether there is a language "module." We have now explored in detail knowledge of language structure and processes acquired in the last few decades that begins to answer these ancient questions. We also touched on the biological foundations— neurophysiological, auditory perceptual, and genetic—of the language faculty. This should pique curiosity as to whether animals can or do have language, and whether the same capabilities exist in *all* people, regardless of cognitive or social impairment. Indeed, study of "exceptional" populations has provided data that separate nature and nurture, and allow determination of the specifications of the putative language bioprogram.

In this book we focused on normal, typical language processing in people and as modeled by machines. The data we have examined have been made possible by particular advances in science this century, which we also explored, such as the following:

1. Behaviorism and connectionism suggest methods of learning and teaching common to all animals, including humans (Chapters 3, 5, and 11).

2. The tools of cognitive psychology enable scientific study of mental processes not accessible by introspection (Chapters 3, 5, 7, 10, and 11, in particular).

3. Computer science tests and models structural and processing descriptions of language (Chapters 3 and 5 particularly, as well as PDP models throughout).

4. New methods and findings of linguistics and anthropology generate and compare descriptions of languages and how they are used (Chapters 2, 4, 6, 8, 9, and 10).

5. Increased knowledge of, and access to, neural mechanisms, studied here to a limited extent, allow studies of normal brain laterality, electrical brain stimulation, evoked potentials, and language after brain damage (Chapters 3, 5, 7, 9, 10, and 11).

However, another important advance in science that has had great impact on consideration of language remains to be explored, the theory of evolution. This suggests that our language capacity did not arise de novo, and thus should have analogues in the animal kingdom and in other human cognitive and communicative functions. I urge readers to continue exploring language and its processing by examining language and communication in atypical populations, some human and some animal, in the companion volume, *Language in Atypical Populations*. I also more fully treat there the consequences of the advances in neurobiology, genetics, and evolution on our understanding of language processing.

SUMMARY OF OUR EXPLORATIONS

Chapter 1 analyzed language into three principal levels—phonetic (and cherological, for sign), semantic, and syntactic—and differentiated them from social/pragmatic aspects of communication. The book has followed this breakdown but showed that the levels are very interdependent, and very dependent on social/pragmatic factors.

Thus we find for speech (Chapters 6 and 7) that a reasonable descriptive system of structure includes salient acoustic features like bursts and transitions. These map directly to features like voicing and place of articulation, which combine to form phonemes, which in turn form syllables, and they form multisyllabic words.

However, the mapping and combination are not straightforward. There is context and speaker sensitivity in both articulation and perception, so one cannot study the lowest level mapping, that is, acoustic to phonetic features, without considering influences of higher language levels and of social use. Both production and perception of language, from a very young age, are guided by syntactic and semantic knowledge, which segments the acoustic stream into constituents and substitutes, in slips of the ear or tongue, meaning- or morphologically related units for the actual target. And both production and perception of language, again from a young age, signal, simultaneously, linguistic segments, speakers' physical and social group characteristics, and the speakers' current emotions.

For meaning and meaning processing (Chapters 2, 3, and 11) we also observed an interdependence of levels. We began discussing linguistic meaning, analyzing it into units such as morphemes, words, and phrases, but found that interpretation of these individual units is affected profoundly by their combination. Attempting to analyze meaning into characteristic and defining features underscored the fuzzy, arbitrary nature of our mental categories and their relation to extralinguistic features. So we turned to describing the mental representation of meaning as a massive, parallel-interactive associative network of features. The pattern of activated associations gives rise to spoken and written word names at one level, connotative and denotative semantic representations at another level, and perceptual features of the environment at a third level. Word representations, whether they are distributed patterns of activation or specifically activated nodes, arouse other word representations. A "simple" concept like "dog" is defined mentally through many other "simple" concepts, like "bark" and "setter," each of which is circularly defined in terms of "dog."

Our explorations also emphasized the dependence of linguistic meaning on other language and communication levels. We saw that words are not strictly arbitrary with respect to meaning but may be iconic (in writing or sign) or sound-symbolic or onomatopoetic (speech). And they also often carry meaning from formational associations to similar words; for example, a homonym arouses all its meanings temporarily through the sound association; "-gate" productively takes on the meaning of scandal from its connection to Watergate. And word meaning changes with linguistic context as we see dramatically in figurative language, when new meanings are mapped onto existing words. Meaning also radically changes with social context: Words take on connotations related to their users, identifying and solidifying peer groups; conversational interaction directs meaning, again dramatically, in cases like irony and sarcasm, or in the normal interpretation of seemingly literal sentences like "Do you have a watch?" or "Today is September 7" against different contexts and common grounds. We comprehend language constructively, making bridging inferences in spoken and written discourse, bringing the appropriate common ground to bear in any situation.

In syntax and syntactic processing (Chapters 4 and 5) we found the need to hypothesize at least two levels of structure: (a) a deep structure or proposition level, which specifies the relationships of the constituents of the sentence to one another, and (b) a surface structure level that implements the deep structure through the conventions of the language. We discussed various ways of relating deep and surface structure, including argument specification by key lexical items, transformations, universal phrase-structure rules, and perceptual and semantic heuristics—form following function. We found for syntax, as for the other levels of language, good reason to hypothesize top-down processes, or at least processes that worked simultaneously on several linguistic units.

And throughout this book we have found the need to temper all discussions of language-in-the-abstract with the social conditions giving rise to it. Formally, in

Chapter 8 we considered social constraints on language change, how dialects are formed or maintained, and how language, in serving different social needs for the different sexes in our culture, reflects sex differences. We also saw social effects in language acquisition, with (a) language optimally coinciding with increasing socialization in the child (Chapter 9) and (b) second language and literacy being better acquired when they serve a desired social purpose (Chapters 10 and 11).

Now that we have summed up the major findings, it is time to return to some of the initial questions, as follows:

1. How does language relate to thought?
2. Are language skills unique or do they employ general cognitive functions of perceiving, learning, reasoning, and remembering?
3. How does language forge and/or divide communities?
4. To what extent is language the unfolding of a genetic program?
5. What is language and how is it shaped by human social, sensory, and cognitive mechanisms?

LANGUAGE AND THOUGHT

Evidence for Thought Without Language

Data from normal language processes point to a form of thought that is not specifically linguistic. In normal adults, we saw evidence of imaging and of dual-coding into imagery and propositional representations. This suggests that there is a form of thought that is nonverbal. In addition, in normal child language acquisition we saw that, usually, "form follows function"—that both words and complex syntactic structures (negation, causality, questions) map to existing and emerging conceptual categories. Therefore the conceptual categories exist prior to language; nonlinguistic thought precedes and shapes linguistic thought. And we found, in examining bilingual language processes, a common conceptual core, presumably language-independent, underlying the language-specific semantic memories.

Finally, we saw little support for the strongest form of the Whorf-Sapir hypothesis, that language affects *the way* we think. We do see language-affected differences in linguistic and cognitive *structural* categories, such as whether arrows fly straight and straight is desirable; which acoustic values constitute a phoneme category; which concepts associate most immediately with one another; and which language units are delineated by writing. But cross-culturally, the same basic cognitive *processes* are manifested: categorizing; forming prototypes; associating by category, contiguity, script, and form; and responding to frequency and regularity to acquire syntax. These basic cognitive processes are thoughts without language, that is, nonlinguistic thought that enables language.

The Influence of Language on Thought

That is not to argue that language or language structure plays no role in shaping conceptual structures. We have seen that we often make associations by language sounds (homonym meanings, rhymes, first letters) rather than conceptual meanings. Our conclusion that linguistic meaning was defined in terms of other linguistic meanings, that semantic memory is organized in terms of semantic relatedness, part of speech, or overarching conceptual metaphors like "language is a conduit," suggests that it is its own form of thought, not isomorphic with extralinguistic thought. And we have many examples of associations, metaphor interpretations, responses on projective tests, and categorizations suggesting that thinking is affected by common salient associations within a language, and thus differs between speakers of different languages. Finally, we saw that knowing a language influences internalization and acquisition of new knowledge, as we saw in Chapter 10, with bilinguals thinking and feeling differently in their two languages, and second language learning informed by first language knowledge.

The ability to "think through language," apart from nonverbal thought, accounts for much that is philosophically wonderful and troublesome about meaning. It allows us to say that lions and tigers are both similar in ferociousness although we may never have seen either beast awake or outside a zoo. It also allows us to create unicorns and say that they are like horses, although we have certainly never experienced a horned horse. Thus through linguistic thought we can create conceptual categories without having had relevant nonlinguistic experience.

There is also evidence that linguistic experience can influence development and organization of nonlinguistic thought. Concepts that are more codable in language are more memorable and produce quicker reactions than concepts that are not easily coded in language. Phonetic features that have been strengthened through categorical relevance in the language are perceived differently from those not so reinforced. We see evidence in adult concept organization that the first words map to specific concepts from which a linguistic structure is deduced, but that, subsequently, similar concepts are acquired with respect to this structure, producing partial cognitive economy. And we see in bilingual adults, in addition to the common conceptual core on which both lexicons rely, separate language-internal conceptualizations, or thought specific to a language. In these cases it looks as if thought can both precede and follow language.

Thought for Language

There is, of course, also a part of the conceptual structure devoted specifically to language, the part responsible for our knowledge of language structure and our metalinguistic knowledge. Our at least tacit awareness of linguistic aspects of conceptual structure shapes our behavior in the creation of language games, creation of words, or extension of existing words' meanings and in attempts to legislate a language form for sociopolitical purposes. It also permits the devising of "rules" for grammar instruction or proscription as well as explicit language-teaching techniques. Finally, we saw that in acquiring the language skills needed for literacy, we create a linguistic model using new, often explicit, insights as to language units and some of the conventions of speech to represent primary language in text. This necessitates developing language expressing heretofore tacit thoughts.

Conclusions

Thus, with respect to the question of thought's relationship to language, we may consider that in humans thought precedes language with language mapping onto it; thus complex thoughts are possible without language. The nonlanguage thought base could be something we share with animals, onto which linguistic thought piggybacks. Once we have acquired language, linguistic thinking may be a dominant mode of thought, or at least of thought by one cerebral hemisphere, shaping additional knowledge acquisition.

Whether animals are capable of languagelike thought also is at this point an open question. But data do exist: from comparative psychology, looking at natural communication and cognitive skills in animal societies, and from experimental psychology, examining whether humanlike language may be taught to animals. We consider these data and their implications for the language and thought question in the companion volume, *Language in Atypical Populations*.

IS LANGUAGE PROCESSING A COGNITIVE "MODULE"?

Evidence for Special-to-Language Processes

At each level of language we have seen suggestions that there is a unique-to-language mode of processing. In speech, we found that most linguistic features are discriminated, even by infants, differently from stimuli constructed of inarticulatable acoustic components of speech. Moreover, stimuli derived from speech, like sine-wave analogues or noise-stimulated time waves, are perceived differently when people hear them "as language" rather than merely as sounds. Special-for-language perception appears to be based in the left hemisphere of the brain, unlike, for example, melody perception. And it appears to incorporate multimodal cues to articulatory events: their acoustic consequence and visible lip movements (even for infants) and the tactile feel of the producer's articulators.

Special-to-language processes for meaning are more questionable but are indicated in an abstract verbal code, again, located in the left cerebral hemisphere, distinct from an imagelike code, which is right hemisphere based. The verbal code is needed for abstract symbols, which possibly have no cognitive representation outside of language, certainly then a special-to-language meaning process. The verbal code is also involved in understanding concrete concepts, along with a second, nonverbal code. We might suggest that the added verbal code for concrete concepts is language module-specific; the imagistic code, "general cognitive."

In discussing meaning and semantics, we see possibilities of special-to-language abstractions. Language meaning is decontextualized, arbitrary, and symbolic, so once a thing is named, regardless of how concrete the connection between the name and the thing, the name takes on a conceptual life of its own, divorced from its origins. Consider, for example, lexical innovation: A favorite example of Gerrig's (personal communication) is a waitress referring to a customer by his order, "The hamburger now wants a Coke." I used this example of lexical innovation to a stellar graduate student, Hilary. Later in the conversation I told her that another colleague and I wished all graduate students were "Hilarys." That I followed comprehensibly (!) with, "See, Hilary is 'a hamburger.' " Thus *hamburger* leapt in meaning from the dish, to the customer, to lexical innovation itself. The recursive abstraction of meaning, the possibility of metalanguage itself, may be a special-to-language cognitive process. If so, it may be one that enables language, or one that language enables.

We also saw suggestions of possibly innate language-learning heuristics, such as the taxonomic principle, conventionality, and contrast. Children behave as though they understand that words name categories of basic-level objects, that different words name different things, and that they should attend to the form of the utterance. These could be specific innate cognitions to enable *language* learning, not general cognitive strategies.

Considerations of syntactic processes initiated the language module concept. We saw that language structure is too complex to be accounted for by an associative chain; at the very least it needs that and a good, long, short-term memory to keep track of the long-distance context dependencies and partially completed structures. We also discussed poverty-of-the-stimulus: Language data are too variable and incomplete and contain no negative evidence, so the necessary rules cannot be induced, that is, determined by inductive reasoning. And we found that second-generation learners of impoverished languages, pidgins, induce a more languagelike structure into creoles, perhaps with no guidance but that of their innate syntax modules. Finally, in keeping with the module position, we found that human parsing is performed very rapidly, fades quickly from conscious memory, and is at least partly encapsulated from considerations of sense: We fill gaps at least momentarily based on structure considerations alone, as in "the businessman knew which article the secretary called [t] this morning." The potential of the proposition relationship—the simple interaction between basic phrases and the logical consequences of connecting them hierarchically and recursively—may be peculiar to a language "module."

Evidence for General Cognitive Underpinnings to Language

At the same time, there is considerable evidence that language processing depends on general cognitive mechanisms. In speech, we noted that chinchillas perceive many speech distinctions categorically, as do humans, while it is unlikely that they share with us a predisposition for our language. Rather, it may be that distinctions that were critical to human survival, our communication elements, mapped onto acoustic regions to which our ears (and those of the chinchilla) are most sensitive. Constrained by the universal need to be able to articulate easily and hear distinctively, features of speech fall in the same broad categories in all languages—not a language-specific development but a perceptual/cognitive one.

From among these broad feature regions, a group selects a subset constrained by memory, the number of distinct bits we can keep track of. Groups are also socially motivated to have a distinct identity (change from above), shown nonlinguistically in distinct ethnic dress and architectural styles. Humans are constrained by memory and our auditory system, vocal tract, and the particular language's internal rules (change from below). Together these result in dialect and language groups using different features and combinations of them to form phonemes.

Learning phoneme categories in the first year of life appears to be a product of generalization, a general learning mechanism: The language-unique aspect is the infant's attention to speech; animals, unlike infants, do not automatically develop the similarity groupings given speech exposure.

Much of language learning is not language-specific but uses general cognitive mechanisms. We looked at classical and operant conditioning, generalization, and probability matching as accounts of some language phenomena. Classical and operant conditioning both rely on repetition of two events to create an association, with the strength of the association dependent on the frequency of exposure to the contiguous events—habit strength or connection weights. We have seen that in many instances what is induced about language structure is redundant and/or conflicting cues, different events that often, but not always, occur with that structure. Thus "agent" is usually animate, occurs first in a sentence, and may have a characteristic morphological marker. The cue most strongly associated with any structure is the one that most frequently and reliably occurs with it. This accounts for the similarity in acquisition patterns of a given language whether acquired as L1 or L2; the language most resistant to errors normally; the fact that a "native" language *can be forgotten,* if its vocabulary and syntax are not practiced, that is, fail to occur frequently; and the overriding winner of the cue competition in experimentally induced conflicts, such as "us is biting the dog" (here, sense, the singular verb, and the object-pronoun indicate that the dog is the agent, but order is such a common indicator of case in English that it overrides all other cues).

Generalization is a general learning phenomenon in which a class of stimuli are automatically related to an associate in proportion to the similarity between each and the stimulus actually experienced with the associate. We saw that a word denotes a class of objects linked by "family relationships." The word is most strongly tied to the prototype, decreasingly linked to peripheral stimuli in proportion to their deviance from the prototype. We saw that a prototype can come to represent a category even if never experienced itself, through the frequent occurrence of each of its features across the class. Thus, through the repeated pairing of the name and subsets of features of the referent, conditioning and generalization generate the prototype-periphery organization.

Finally, we saw that infants respond to and learn readily from statistical regularity, not perfectly predictable association. Infants use the difference in probability of phoneme associates to segment syllables (frequently co-occurring segments) from word boundaries (more random co-occurrence). Computer simulations show acquisition of rule-like behavior (e.g., add -ed for the past tense) given the regularity and frequency of this construction, even though most of the most common verbs form the past differently (*is-were, ran-run,* and so on). Animals likewise match their responding to the probability of getting reinforced, indicating that this is a general cognitive phenomenon. Responsiveness to regularity and not perfection diminishes the force of the poverty-of-the-stimulus argument: The model need not be consistent—simply more often do things one way than any single other.

The operating principles we suggested for language acquisition constitute a general cognitive counterpoint to the language-specific parameter-setting of the language module, UG. These suggested that the infant's attention is focused on the acoustically salient: speech and regions therein of prominent acoustic change such as the sound-silence boundary or the stressed intonation. The child then induces "rules" given the frequency and regularity of structures. And the child ties elements to the nearest potential filler—the minimal distance principal. Respectively, these are perceptual, learning, and memory "heuristics"—general ones, not necessarily tied to language function. We also saw that it is quite possible that the child's general "primitive" cognition enables language learning: If smaller memory prevents rote learning of large chunks, and perception selects the stressed small chunks, the child may have an innate aid to language acquisition. This is not a bioprogram or UG, but less is more—the cognitive difference between adult and child results in children being ideal language learners.

General Cognitive–Language-Specific Interactions

While it appears that much that is mysterious about language learning—the ability to induce rules from inconsistent input; the speed of vocabulary acquisition; indeed, the speed of language acquisition generally; and the complexity of language structures—may be accounted for by general cognitive mechanisms, it is also clear that language gives us a cognitive tool that enriches and alters perception, attention, learning, and memory, that is, the very same cognitive functions. We saw, for example, that learning a second language increases children's symbolic flexibility; that acquiring literacy increases memory for language, ability to learn another language, and ability to sustain function after brain damage; and that different languages focus attention on different aspects of events, whether they are color categories, separation or fusion of action and object, characteristics of the acoustic signal, or the nuances of tense, or aspect, or categoricalness imposed by sharing linguistic gender.

There is also no doubt that knowing a language allows us to learn new concepts; it is how knowledge is transmitted, and we have seen that it can be used to devise teaching techniques for learning literacy and other languages per se. *Mnemonic devices,* techniques for enhancing memory, often employ verbal strategies such as creating an acronym from the first letters of the to-be-remembered objects' names, rehearsing (saying over again to oneself), or creating a new unit by verbally *chunking* two independent units (1, 2, → 12). Verbalizing and systematically applying grouping rules develop hierarchies that supersede perception, as in the scientific classification of animals or the periodic table of the elements (which in turn restructure semantic memory). It is likely that the practice that we have of creating hierarchical structures, solving recursive language "equations," and using metalanguage to understand ever-more-abstract concepts generalizes not just to additional language skill but to similar symbolisms in the nonlinguistic domain: in art, music, mathematics, dance, and so on.

Conclusions

The best way to tease the potential interactions of general cognition and language-specific cognitions is to examine the rare individual or family in which they appear separated naturally: people who are severely retarded, but for whom language is preserved, or, conversely, people who have language-learning difficulties in the absence of other cognitive deficits. We consider their skills in *Language in Atypical Populations.* As we will see, there is evidence for at least partial encapsulation of language and cognition, for a special language module. As we have seen, this certainly piggybacks, depends on, and fosters general cognitive skills.

LANGUAGE AS A COMMUNITY FORCE

In the first chapter I defined language as the way people communicate, and communication as the active transfer of information from one to another. As we studied it in this book, we subtly introduced refinements in this definition. Language as a speech act has components of perlocutionary and illocutionary force—effects apart from content on both the speaker and the hearer as a consequence simply of there being an utterance. To be "good," an utterance takes into account the hearer's likely knowledge, imparting no more and no less than necessary to transmit the information. To understand an utterance, a hearer deliberately and actively brings to bear the necessary common ground, *constructing* meaning, not simply being passively stimulated. And this "dance" the speaker and hearer engage in may be by design a close one, with more active participation invited from the hearer by the speaker's using language creatively, in a way that limits common ground with other hearers. We saw that this dance begins early, with infants less than a week of age synchronizing to their caregivers' speech rhythms, differentially responsive to their mothers' voices and the sound pattern of their own language, and for some seeming to acquire language from a social (let's talk) over an analytic (differentiating objects verbally) perspective. And we saw that literacy is best acquired if experienced early within the appropriate social context, in this culture, the sharing of stories as a "cuddle time."

Language is essentially a social phenomenon, used to establish links to others in one's community. At the same time the language used defines the community, those who understand and share the common ground. And as language perceivers, we are well able to use the language signal not just to deduce content but as a marker for the physical, emotional, and social group characteristics of the speaker. Indeed, information as to speaker identity, facial expression, and emotion is smeared with the segments in the speech signal, perhaps extracted in parallel. As listeners, we can focus attention on either linguistic (content) or social characteristics (paralanguage) in the same acoustic regions of the same syllables.

The synchrony that begins with a baby's copying rhythm from its caretaker develops into imitation of the speech style of someone he or she affiliates with, allowing speech even as an adult to migrate toward the dialect or language of a group he or she wished to join. And we saw that degree of affiliation determines movement toward or away from a particular dialect: On Martha's Vineyard the residents joining the newcomers adopted their dialect; those resisting the newcomers strengthened their "native" characteristics and the distance from the newcomers' dialects; AAEV has been relatively unaffected by changes in white American speech, developing in its own way.

Note that by *speech* here I am referring to, say, vowels and register as well as lexical items (the new slang or jargon), and sometimes grammatical features like negative concord or code-switching (using both languages with other bilinguals) and general style, such as what one chooses to talk about, how to joke, whether to talk simultaneously, and so on. A group bonds in part by showing its identity through language.

And, of course, human beings have used the social implications of language for both good and cruel social ends: to legislate the use of a particular language or prohibit one so as to keep a group subjugated, to commingle people of different tribes and languages to prevent their communicating, to create new terms (*black* for *Negro*), or to teach a language (resurrecting and establishing Hebrew as the language of the new land of Israel) to unite a disparate people.

The study of social effects on normal language can be augmented by studying people deprived of normal social experience. This happens, unfortunately, to some abused and neglected children, who may also deliberately be language-deprived, only experiencing rich language and a nurturing social environment after their condition has been recognized by authorities. It also happens endogenously, in psychological diseases like autism (childhood schizophrenia) or after language has been acquired, in the social deviance caused by adult-onset psychosis. We examine the effects of lack of normal social motivations and experience on language in *Language in Atypical Populations.*

IS LANGUAGE LEARNING INNATELY DRIVEN?

In Chapter 9 we considered whether human beings learn language using innate language "blueprints" (of which UG could be one) and how these interact with the language environment to develop language. We noted uniformity of language learning across children: In the first year they are tuned to speech, have rudimentary phonetic categories, and are ready to develop categorization principles. Children also seem to use similar heuristics to develop language: principles of exclusivity, contrast, and conventionality; analysis of language into productive units; attention to order and regularity. These could derive either from language blueprints or from common exposure (parents talk similarly to infants cross-culturally) and from the operation of general cognitive (such as probability learning) and perceptual (attend to beginning and end segments) strategies.

Whether there is an innate language blueprint and a critical period for its stimulation is best determined from data from atypical populations: Can children deprived of language learn it at a later age? Do deaf children who acquire language visually show similar acquisition patterns (belying the necessity of speech and hearing for language)? Can apes or dolphins, who presumably have no language bioprogram, acquire languagelike behavior similarly to us? These will be examined in the companion volume. Here, we can cautiously infer a rudimentary bioprogram from the existence of universal acquisition patterns and universal language features.

Cautions for Interpretation

We must be conservative in attributing power to a bioprogram on the evidence of universals because what might seem to be a universal feature may, in fact, reflect common environmental features or contamination from exposure to other languages, or chance, rather than an innate endowment. The possibility of common environmental features producing common language structures was discussed with respect to the notion of basic objects (prototypes), natural categories, and some conceptual metaphors: All people look up to the warm, light-giving sun through similar visual systems; the world's languages could therefore all have a word for sun, a positive connotation to light and up, and similar color-naming schemes. In the same vein, recognition of basic category features such as human versus nonhuman, animate versus inanimate, and so on might be expected to prevail not because those concepts are innate as such but because those categories are perceptually distinct and cognitively salient.

Environmental commonality, not universal biological determinism, may account for the similarity of children's language acquisition around the world: All babies are exposed to mothers and milk and are fascinated by objects appearing and disappearing from sight (allgone, bye-bye, peek-a-boo); all parents need to sleep and therefore to get their babies to sleep, lulling them with universal rhythmic movements and soothing sounds in lullabies. Infants worldwide experience similar environments, which are different, perhaps critically, from those provided older language learners.

The second possibility, of contamination by other languages, we saw in the spread of scripts worldwide (Chapter 11) and perhaps in the commonality of pidgins and creoles derived from a basic set of nonindependent conquering and conquered languages (Chapter 8). Moreover, scientists are biased to search for features from their own language, asking, for instance: How is tense expressed? How is causality expressed? How is actor-action-object expressed? Their own language structure directs discovery of tense, causality, and actor-action-object expressed somehow in another language, even if these would not be structures that linguists raised in that language would themselves delineate. Some of this natural bias and its correction are reflected in the changing views on the universality of word order in child language acquisition, for example.

Communication and Articulatory Structure Universals

Be that as it may, we might *cautiously* suggest some features that seem universal and therefore perhaps innate. The first is the urge to communicate. The second is the use of the vocal-auditory system, if available, for communication. Again, all cultures—except deaf cultures—seem to prefer oral language for communication, although sign systems have been developed secondarily among speaking peoples. Within the oral language systems the world over, we find the same speech features, innately determined by the characteristics of the auditory system and the possibilities for articulation. Thus they look superficially alike in all cultures.

Higher Level Language Universals

At more interesting linguistic levels we find units corresponding to words, phrases, and sentences in all languages, perhaps indicating an innate tendency to categorize and construct propositionlike representations, and to construct them hierarchically from smaller constituents. We also see, universally, the *symbolic* use of words rather than a signaling use. No culture uses words rigidly to refer to single concrete objects in a stereotyped fashion. All cultures use figurative language, play language games, and have a mythology, which demonstrate symbolic use of words.

Another general feature of language (and perhaps of all human information processing) that may be universal and innate is hierarchical organization. We see this at all levels of English structure and processing. There exists hierarchical organization of motor commands in speech production, hierarchical organization of speech perception reflected in part through the interaction of top-down and bottom-up processing, hierarchical organization of categories in conceptualization, and hierarchical organization of words into phrases, phrases into sentences, sentences into (embedded) clauses, and recursively back into sentences, sentences into coherent discourse, and so on. Psychologically we represent, separately and interactively, words in semantic memory, semantic relations within propositions, mental propositions, and connections between propositions through inference, anaphoric or filler-gap reference and related meanings.

Other Universals?

Many investigators have suggested more features of language as innate. For example, it has been suggested that there are innate ideas such as time and motion, innate syntactic structures such as that of phrases with heads and arguments (to their left or right), innate constraints on government and binding, and innately perceived phonetic feature distinctions. (There are also investigators who think very little is innate, with only the basic abilities to form associations predetermined.)

It is, of course, possible that some or all of these language characteristics are innate and specific for language, but to me the evidence does not compellingly point only in this direction. Consider, for example, observations that *initially* suggested innateness only to be disconfirmed later, such as the following: that SVO word order is understood earlier than other orders used in the language, or that under strained communication conditions (those good for producing pidgins and creoles), inflections disappear and word order is used to express semantic relations. But it turns out that SVO order is only preferentially understood if it is more frequently used than other orders in the language; what is universal is neither attention to order nor the particular parameter-setting but, instead, the fastest acquisition of frequent, regular, and functional (meaningful) structures. Likewise, inflections that are neither phonologically nor meaningfully salient go unattended and so are acquired late in full or partial (pidgin and creole) second language acquisition. The argument that the inconstancy of language input makes it unlearnable is belied by finding that infants respond to statistical regularity; they do not need perfect constancy (Chapter 9).

Therefore, the evidence for "universal" language features like SVO order and inflection loss in pidgins can be explained, respectively, by reference to regions of general auditory hypersensitivity that languages have mapped onto, frequency, regularity (not constancy), relevance of experience (form follows function), and constraints imposed by general attention and memory. A similar appeal to perceptual and cognitive processing constraints combined with commonality of outside experience could explain the relative universality of time and motion or government and binding principles.

Conclusions

So, for now, at least until evidence suggests more strongly otherwise, we suggest that innate determinants of language include

1. the urge to communicate and establish social bonds,
2. use of the vocal-auditory system if possible for communication,

3. some general idea of what language looks like (words and so on),

4. the tendency to make *symbolic* associations,

5. a general blueprint for neural organization of language,

6. some general psychophysical processing constraints imposed by articulatory and perceptual abilities as well as cognitive abilities (attention, memory, and information processing preferences as in hierarchical organization).

As they evolve, languages will move toward optimizing these determinants. Thus they share features we can attribute to the common restrictions imposed by the human mind and body and the common experiences provided by the environment and our nurturing.

WHAT IS LANGUAGE?

Our explorations of language and language processing in this book suggest some salient characteristics of language, defining it more specifically than as the way humans communicate. These characteristics underlie its power as a social and a cognitive force. They include the following:

- *Rapidly fading:* Speech is ephemeral, as are many of the structural language characteristics.
- *Redundant:* Information comes from several channels *simultaneously* conveyed and *smeared* together: Thus we get segmental and paralinguistic information in the same portion of the signal, and information concerning a single percept (like voicing) smeared across several portions of the signal.
- *Hierarchically organized:* A segment participates in nested constituents at both speech and syntax levels.
- *Arbitrary:* A segment's form is not the primary indicator of its referent.
- *Dually patterned:* A segment can be attended to as a meaning conveyer or as a form in itself (as in rhyme), and repetitive use of form or order can ultimately come to convey meaning.
- *Symbolic:* Words, morphemes, and constituents represent a fuzzy class of things with connotative as well as denotative characteristics.
- *Productive:* Language is used not as a rote string but in continually creative combinations, from the combination of segments to form words, to the combination of words and morphemes to form new meanings.
- *Recursive:* A powerful form of productivity allows a unit to be created by incorporating itself, as in sentence embedding or metalanguage.
- *Interactive* (actively, constructively): Hearers and speakers can switch roles and both participate in communication by constructing common ground and providing and searching for feedback that indicates the success of the interaction.

This list of features is motivated by our discussions of language structure, processing, and conversation; it is also informed by influential papers by Hockett (1960; Hockett & Altmann, 1968). In *Language in Atypical Populations* we return to these (and other proposed defining language and communication features) and critically consider whether they apply to other communication systems found in nature, to the ape's successes at acquiring human language, and, indeed, to other human communication systems. You might want to consider now, for example, if these features define language, at what age do children "have language," that is, meet these criteria? Are pidgins language by these criteria?

CONCLUDING REMARKS

Remaining Questions

At this point it may seem as though we have answered all questions, but realize that in this chapter I addressed only the ones I began with. Along the way other questions have been raised, and it is important to keep in mind in summarizing that we know more about the way language is not structured and not processed than we do about the way it is. At the basic level we do not know how speech is perceived, where or how it takes place in the brain, whether there are invariants, whether we compensate for variability or employ it in simultaneously recognizing several regular but not invariant patterns. At higher language levels we do not know if meanings are constructed or more passively activated; if connotation is processed differently from denotation, figurative language from literal language, concrete words from abstract words, and so on. Although we have discussed an underlying conceptual structure to which linguistic units map, whether the units are directly represented (nodes) or emerge as activation patterns or what the units are (meaning features, morphemes, words, propositions, nonverbal forms) have not been specified. And while the evidence seems to favor semantic "bootstrapping" of syntactic processing in acquisition and brain damage and cue competition, we do not know how syntactic processing is normally performed and how it interacts with semantic processing.

This is just a brief and necessarily incomplete summary of questions left to answer. Every chapter has raised many more.

Applications of Available Answers

In closing, we should consider the use to which discoveries about language have been put, that is, mention areas of application of psycholinguistic research.

One important consequence of linguistic and psycholinguistic research has been the recognition that *there are no inferior languages in terms of structure or processing,* and therefore that it is not imperative that all children be made to conform to a specific language or dialect. As we will see in the companion volume, this has been particularly poignant with respect to sign language, which only in the last 30 or so years has been recognized as a fully expressive language, given study of its structure and processing. Likewise, comparison of standard English to the African American English Vernacular, as we saw in Chapter 8, has shown that

AAEV is a *nonstandard dialect, not a substandard language:* It shares many words, structures, and internal processes with standard English but is different in pronunciation, morphology, and, to a lesser extent, syntax. This has permitted understanding of why AAEV speakers may have problems learning to read: They are taught spelling-to-sound correspondences for sounds they do not hear; they are taught morphemes that do not correspond to their use of tense and aspect. The solution to this problem is far from settled given that there are social stigmas attached to being taught a nonstandard dialect in schools; however, presumably, making teachers aware of the differences and the possibilities of "code-switching" will help.

By this time, recognition of the validity of all languages in expressing complex thoughts in structurally complex ways has led to development of *additive* immersion programs. Study of their success and benefit I hope will lead to their proliferation.

Aside from modifying attitudes toward language, research in language has been applied to techniques of teaching or reteaching language and in testing linguistic competence. There have been changes in foreign language instruction from rote memorization of vocabulary items and overt grammatical rules to concentration on language *as used* with emphasis on acquisition of tacit knowledge of structure. Language rehabilitation programs for language-learning-delayed, dyslexic, or autistic children and people suffering brain damage have been developed using psycholinguistic findings, as we will discuss briefly in the next volume. These try to recruit languagelike skills through other routes, such as emphasizing concrete, image processes to compensate for a damaged abstract verbal route, teaching phonological coding, or conditioning language and social interaction explicitly.

We have seen that language processing is multifaceted. Recognition of this has changed intelligence tests (see Sternberg, 1983, for example) to emphasize a *variety of processes* in verbal reasoning (as needed for metaphor comprehension, creation, and appreciation or in giving a spontaneous talk, for example) rather than "verbal knowledge" measured typically in paper-and-pencil tests. Moreover, the processes used to solve the verbal problems are studied specifically, rather than just the answers, by formulating each problem with respect to component processes and testing for each of these separately.

Increased understanding of language processing has led to improved diagnostics for language-disordered patients, as we will discuss in *Language in Atypical Populations.* But the techniques and data we explored are being applied as well to "normal" people and situations. For example, Streeter (personal communication) debunked a hand-held (expensive) "lie detecting machine" as a simple pitch-change detector; as you may recall from Chapter 7, typically under stress (including deception), our pitch rises and becomes more variable. And Oestricher (1996), with the help of a Lenape Indian informant, proved that a document detailing (in a hieroglyphic script) the settling of the Americas by Indians crossing the Bering Strait was a hoax. The text contained, for example, impossible-in-Lenape translated-English idioms, such as a reference to the chief as *Talegawil,* or *head.*

But in Lenape, unlike English, *head* refers only to the body part. Therefore the author of the document knew English better than Lenape.

As a result of our increased knowledge of language and language processing (combined with technological advances), and despite the great gaps in knowledge, there are now adequate reading machines for the blind (they take text and convert it to speech), computer programs that correct or teach spelling and grammar, and automated knowledge bases that can be accessed for information about virtually anything. Although humans may have to modify their language somewhat to interact with these systems, the systems are increasingly "user-friendly," requiring less adaptation on the part of the human users.

Conclusions

Study of normal language processes has provided a wealth of information this century on how we perform one of our most basic, and most complex, cognitive activities, and in turn, how it changes our perception and cognition of our world. Although we have reviewed a vast reserve of data, we must realize that there are exciting data still to consider. This century has seen controversial, perhaps success-ful, attempts at teaching animals (apes, dolphins, and a parrot) language; deep and broad studies of animal communication that contextualize our system in nature; extensive study of the sign language of the deaf and its processing, which dem-onstrate the degree to which languagelike skills are independent of speech and hearing; study of language and its processing after brain damage, in psychosis, and with developmental abnormalities; and study of language and communication in people reared without language because of abuse or neglect. These data are fascinating with respect to the individual histories, the resilience of different language processes in the face of abnormality, and their implications for the biological foundations of language. I hope you are inspired to continue your inquiry with *Language in Atypical Populations*.

REFERENCES

Hockett, C. F. (1960). The origin of speech. *Scientific American, 203,* 88-96.
Hockett, C. F., & Altmann, S. A. (1968). A note on design features. In T. A. Sebeok (Ed.), *Animal communication* (pp. 61-72). Bloomington: Indiana University Press.
Oestricher, D. M. (1996). Unravelling the *Walam Olum. Natural History, 10/96,* 14-21.
Sternberg, R. J. (1983). Components of human intelligence. *Cognition, 15,* 1-48.

Index

ABOUT THE AUTHOR

Vivien C. Tartter is Professor of Psychology at City College and member of the doctoral faculty of psychology and speech and hearing sciences at the Graduate and University Center of CUNY. She received her doctorate in psychology from Brown University and completed an undergraduate "cognitive sciences" major there, before such majors formally existed. Her research focuses on speech perception in normal and hearing-impaired adults and children but includes excursions into language in aphasia, sign language perception, and literacy acquisition. Her research has been funded by NSF, the National Institute of Deafness and Communication Disorders, the Deafness Research Foundation, and the U.S. Department of Education. In 1987 she was a Fogarty Senior International Fellow. She is a committed teacher at both graduate and undergraduate levels, and strives to involve all students in the excitement of research. From her own educational experience through to her research, she strongly advocates interdisciplinary study. She is married and has two children who have taught her much about language and literacy acquisition.